SAP HANA® 2.0 Certification Guide: Technolog

MW01053145

SAP PRESS is a joint initiative of SAP and Rheinwerk Publishing. The know-how offered by SAP specialists combined with the expertise of Rheinwerk Publishing offers the reader expert books in the field. SAP PRESS features first-hand information and expert advice, and provides useful skills for professional decision-making.

SAP PRESS offers a variety of books on technical and business-related topics for the SAP user. For further information, please visit our website: *www.sap-press.com*.

Denys van Kempen

SAP HANA® 2.0 Certification Guide: Technology Associate Exam

Rheinwerk Publishing

Editor Megan Fuerst
Acquisitions Editor Hareem Shafi
Copyeditor Julie McNamee
Cover Design Graham Geary
Photo Credit Shutterstock.com/1238271697/© CARACOLLA
Layout Design Vera Brauner
Production Kelly O'Callaghan
Typesetting SatzPro, Krefeld (Germany)
Printed and bound in the United States of America, on paper from sustainable sources

ISBN 978-1-4932-1967-4
© 2021 by Rheinwerk Publishing, Inc., Boston (MA)
1st edition 2021

Library of Congress Cataloging-in-Publication Data
Names: Van Kempen, Denys, author.
Title: SAP HANA 2.0 certification guide : technology associate exam / Denys
   van Kempen.
Description: 1st edition. | Bonn ; Boston : Rheinwerk Publishing, 2020. |
   Includes index.
Identifiers: LCCN 2020023826 (print) | LCCN 2020023827 (ebook) | ISBN
   9781493219674 (paperback) | ISBN 9781493219681 (ebook)
Subjects: LCSH: Relational databases--Examinations--Study guides. |
   Business enterprises--Computer networks--Examinations--Study guides. |
   SAP HANA (Electronic resource)--Examinations--Study guides. | Computer
   programmers--Certification.
Classification: LCC QA76.9.D32 V345 2020 (print) | LCC QA76.9.D32 (ebook)
   | DDC 005.75/6--dc23
LC record available at https://lccn.loc.gov/2020023826
LC ebook record available at https://lccn.loc.gov/2020023827

Contents at a Glance

Dear Reader,

To ace a test, you need a good teacher.

In my experience, the best teachers have several key qualities: a deep knowledge of the content, the patience to repeat information to better instill learning, and a keen enthusiasm for the subject matter. Good teachers don't just tell you what's on the test—they impart the knowledge you need to explain the subject, and take your exam, with confidence.

Denys van Kempen possesses these qualities in spades. In additional to his experience authoring multiple books on SAP HANA 2.0, teaching has been an integral part of Denys' career with SAP for more than a decade. From creating hundreds of tutorials for SAP HANA Academy on YouTube to contributing numerous posts to SAP Community, Denys is at the heart of the SAP HANA education community. In this book, you'll find not only his SAP HANA 2.0 certification expertise; you'll also discover his test tips, subject matter insights, and passion for teaching SAP HANA topics. I certainly learned a lot while editing this certification guide, and I'm confident that you'll come away from this book well-prepared for your exam day.

What did you think about *SAP HANA 2.0 Certification Guide: Technology Associate Exam*? Your comments and suggestions are the most useful tools to help us make our books the best they can be. Please feel free to contact me and share any praise or criticism you may have.

Thank you for purchasing a book from SAP PRESS!

Megan Fuerst
Editor, SAP PRESS

meganf@rheinwerk-publishing.com
www.sap-press.com
Rheinwerk Publishing · Boston, MA

Contents

2   System Architecture   47

3   Installation Preparation   85

6   SAP HANA Cockpit

7   Database Administration Tasks

12 Contents

Contents

13   Troubleshooting and Performance Analysis   487

14   Database Migration   547

Preface

The SAP PRESS certification guide series is designed to provide you with the review, insight, and practice you need to pass your SAP-certified exam. The series is written in practical, easy-to-follow language that provides targeted content focused on what you need to know to successfully take your exam.

In this book, we explain the topics you need to know for the SAP Certified Technology Associate – SAP HANA 2.0 exam and the type of questions you can expect. We cover the key concepts for the different topic areas and point you to resources where you can find more information for additional study. With the practice questions included for each chapter topic, you can test your understanding of the topics. We also provide explanations for further clarification. This book is closely aligned with the course syllabus and the exam structure, so all the information provided is relevant and applicable to what you need to know to prepare. You'll also find useful diagrams to clarify concepts and screenshots that depict key SAP products and features, so you can prepare for the exam and improve your skills in your day-to-day work as an SAP HANA technology consultant.

Who This Book Is For

This book is written for those preparing to take the SAP Certified Technology Associate – SAP HANA 2.0 exam. The book has been targeted for the current C_HANATEC_16 release (as of the time of writing, summer 2020), but is up to date for SPS 05 and is equally valid for earlier editions. The exam tests you in the areas of installation, system administration, performance analysis, and migration. The focus is on SAP HANA, and not on any of the business applications running on the SAP HANA platform (for example, SAP S/4HANA or SAP BW/4HANA). The SAP Certified Technology Associate – SAP HANA 2.0 exam can be taken by anyone who signs up. There are no prerequisites.

How This Book Is Organized

Each chapter begins with a clear list of the techniques you'll master after reading the chapter. After a short introduction, we then cover the topic area(s) and objectives. Then, the majority of the chapter is dedicated to a refresher of the key concepts, where we highlight the most important information that you need to know for the exam. Pay special attention to the illustrations, commands, and bulleted lists as these make for great exam questions.

Each chapter also contains a section of important terminology you should remember.

We then proceed to a number of practice questions, which will help you evaluate your understanding of the topics covered in the chapter. Most questions are similar in nature to those found on the certification examination. Although none of these questions will be found on the exam itself, they will allow you to review your knowledge of the subject. Select the correct answers, and then check the completeness of your answers in the "Practice Question Answers and Explanations" section.

Each chapter concludes with a takeaway that reviews the areas you should now understand, followed by a summary of the chapter.

Throughout the book, we've also provided several boxes with additional information to support your endeavor.

Real-World Scenario

Real-World Scenario boxes explain how the topic area relates to a real-world scenario. It will help you understand why the topic is a relevant part of the exam.

Note
Notes provide relevant information about the topic area.

Learn More
Learn More boxes indicate where to find more information about a specific topic. Although typically beyond the scope of the exam, the information might be highly relevant for the job role.

Exam Tip
Exam tips aim to keep you on track. There is always a lot of information and typically not quite so much time to prepare. With this box, we aim to keep you out of rabbit holes, away from cul-de-sacs, and focused on the exam objectives.

SAP HANA 2.0 SPS 05: What's New?
The SAP HANA 2.0 SPS 05: What's New? boxes highlight new features of this release, which are likely candidates for exam questions.

Let's review briefly what is covered in each chapter of this book:

- **Chapter 1: SAP Certification for SAP HANA**
  We'll begin with an introduction to the certifications for SAP HANA provided by SAP. You'll learn how to prepare for your exam with resources in addition to this book, as well as the various exam levels and editions that are available to you. We'll also explain how the exam is structured, including key topic areas

and sample questions. We'll end with some sample practice questions to illustrate how questions are formulated with some tips how to increase your changes of responding correctly.

- **Chapter 2: System Architecture**
  We start the exam preparation with the system architecture of SAP HANA, including in-memory computing concepts, use cases, deployment types, and more. We'll also touch on the available editions, options, software components, and add-on products. We'll end with practice questions and answer explanations to test and then solidify your understanding.

- **Chapter 3: Installation Preparation**
  Next, we proceed with the installation topic divided over two chapters. In this chapter we'll cover installation preparation steps, including requirements for sizing and hardware. We'll discuss how to use tools like the Quick Sizer, Product Availability Matrix (PAM), and the SAP HANA hardware directory. Configuration for the network, persistence, and recommended file system will also be covered. We'll end with practice questions and answer explanations to test and then solidify your understanding.

- **Chapter 4: Installation and Updates**
  Next, we'll move on to the activities to install and update your SAP HANA system. These include application lifecycle management (ALM) and platform lifecycle management (PLM). We'll use the SAP HANA database lifecycle manager (HDBLCM) tool to perform installation, updating, and post-installation tasks. We'll end with practice questions and answer explanations to test and then solidify your understanding.

- **Chapter 5: Database Administration Tools**
  In this chapter, we'll discuss the key database administration tools you'll need to know for the exam. This includes the SAP HANA cockpit, the SAP HANA database explorer, the SQL Analyzer, and more. We'll also explore a few other SAP tools for administration, like SAP Solution Manager. We'll end with practice questions and answer explanations to test and then solidify your understanding.

- **Chapter 6: SAP HANA Cockpit**
  We'll dive deeper into the SAP HANA cockpit in this chapter. We'll explore deployment options, architecture, installation, updating, provisioning, and more, so that you have a complete understanding of this critical tool. We'll end with practice questions and answer explanations to test and then solidify your understanding.

- **Chapter 7: Database Administration Tasks**
  In this chapter, we'll walk through the most important database administration tasks that you must know for the exam. We'll explain how to start and stop the system, how to navigate the SAP HANA cockpit applications to perform key tasks, how to configure database administration in your system, and how to

manage tables. We'll end with practice questions and answer explanations to test and then solidify your understanding.

- **Chapter 8: Working with Tenant Databases**
  We'll dial in on tenant database systems in this chapter, from the architecture to key management steps in the SAP HANA cockpit. We'll also explain how to create, monitor, and move tenant databases, in addition to key functionality like fallback snapshots. We'll end with practice questions and answer explanations to test and then solidify your understanding.

- **Chapter 9: Scale-Out Systems**
  Next, we move on to multiple-host or scale-out systems. We'll explain key exam concepts like host auto-failover, system architecture, installation, configuration, and data distribution. We'll end with practice questions and answer explanations to test and then solidify your understanding.

- **Chapter 10: Security**
  In this chapter, we'll focus on SAP HANA security topics. We'll cover key SAP HANA cockpit applications for security and user management, and dig deeper into role management, authentication, and encryption. Another key security topic, auditing, will also be discussed. We'll end with practice questions and answer explanations to test and then solidify your understanding.

- **Chapter 11: Backup and Recovery**
  Backup and recovery will be covered in this chapter, including the architecture that underlies memory and storage, as well as backup types, destinations, encryption, and the backup catalog. We'll also walk through configuration steps, key features such as data snapshots, fallback snapshots, scheduling, and both recovering and copying your database. We'll end with practice questions and answer explanations to test and then solidify your understanding.

- **Chapter 12: System Replication**
  In this chapter, we'll explore high availability and system replication concepts that you need to know for the exam. These include storage replication, log replication and operation modes, and enabling, disabling, monitoring, and configuration steps. We'll also discuss takeover processes, secondary time travel, active/active (read-enabled) system replication, and more. We'll end with practice questions and answer explanations to test and then solidify your understanding.

- **Chapter 13: Troubleshooting and Performance Analysis**
  Next, we'll walk through how to troubleshoot errors and monitor your system performance. We'll explore exam topics like alerts, workload management, and admission control, as well as monitoring memory, CPU usage, and more. We'll end with practice questions and answer explanations to test and then solidify your understanding.

- **Chapter 14: Database Migration**
  We'll conclude with a final chapter on migrating to SAP HANA with the Software Update Manager (SUM) and the Database Migration Option (DMO). We'll discuss topics like how to prepare for your migration, perform and monitor a DMO run, and reduce downtime with benchmarking. We'll end with practice questions and answer explanations to test and then solidify your understanding.

Acknowledgments

It has been a privilege to work together again with SAP PRESS to write this certification guide. I would like to thank my editor, Megan Fuerst, in particular, for accompanying me on this journey. Your contributions have greatly improved the clarity and usability of this book.

Thank you to Rudi de Louw, author of the SAP PRESS certification guide for the SAP HANA 2.0 Application Associate exam. I appreciate our conversations, your advice, and your inspiration to start this endeavor.

Thanks to my colleagues at SAP who have produced the software, documentation, support notes, articles, training material, white papers, and other material which served as input for this book.

Thanks to my partner Karin and family for your support.

Last but not least, thank you, dear student, for picking up this volume! What's a book without a reader, after all? I trust this guide will help you achieve the goal of passing this SAP Certified Technology Associate exam.

Wishing you success with the exam and advancing your career.

Denys van Kempen

Chapter 1
SAP Certification for SAP HANA

Techniques You'll Master

- Understand why you should get certified
- Learn how to prepare for your SAP certification exam
- Discover what exam levels and editions are available
- Understand what topic areas are on the exam
- Explore the structure of exam questions

Interested in getting certified as technology consultant for SAP's flagship product? Whether you're new to the technology or want to update your certification to the latest SAP HANA 2.0 release, you've come to the right place. In this exam guide, we cover all you need to know to get certified in SAP HANA 2.0 administration!

SAP is the world's largest provider of enterprise application software, and SAP HANA is the leading in-memory platform for both on-premise and cloud deployments. SAP HANA started as a university research project under the wings of one of SAP's founders, Dr. Hasso Plattner, as attested by the origins of the name: Hasso's New Architecture. It was released to the market in 2010 and quickly evolved into the database engine for the SAP Business Suite and SAP Business Warehouse (SAP BW) applications. First "powered by SAP HANA," soon "/4HANA" products were specifically developed, such as SAP S/4HANA for business applications and SAP BW/4HANA for the enterprise data warehouse. The SAP HANA in-memory database is also available as a service in cloud-hosted environments such as SAP HANA Cloud where it acts as a single gateway to all your data.

Given SAP's presence in the global enterprise application software industry, its growth ambitions, and the central role that the SAP HANA in-memory platform plays, it's clear that investing time and effort into SAP HANA certifications is an excellent choice. But which certification should you choose?

In this chapter, we'll describe the target audience of this book so you can quickly check if this matches your profile and interests. Next, we provide an overview of the different SAP HANA certifications available, again, to help you make the right choice. We proceed with describing in detail the subject of our book, the SAP Certified Technology Associate – SAP HANA 2.0 exam, and explain the exam objectives, structure, and process.

Target Audience

In this section, you'll learn why certification is a good investment and how digital badges enable you to showcase your achievements.

Why Should You Get Certified?

This book will help you get certified as a technology associate for the profile SAP HANA technology consultant, as it's officially stated. Before we cover the different profiles and certification levels, let's first briefly address why you might want to get certified in the first place. It's a topic of heated debate at times, not restricted to SAP certifications, but common to the software industry. Usually, we find the following two characteristics of a professional opposed: experience and knowledge. Those not in favor of certification typically will argue that hands-on project experience is what matters and not the theoretics of certification. And they are right, of course, on the first part of the argument. Experience is important, and most certifications will include a recommendation of several months to two- or three-years' experience before taking the exam. Although it's hard to test experience in an exam, to answer some of the questions successfully, intimate knowledge of the software will be required. This is easily obtained when working closely with the product over a longer period of time but will be much harder to acquire through intensive study alone. However, knowledge and experience aren't opposed but strengthen each other. Studying the product, in particular the latest features of a new release, ensures your knowledge is up to date. This provides both the 10,000 feet overview and the opportunity to tinker with some functionality in a test environment, hands-on, under the hood.

Certifications help validate the expertise and experience of SAP consultants and, in many situations, are even required for the job. When hiring an SAP professional, what would you use to triage the candidates? What about number of years of experience on the job in combination with certifications acquired? When selecting a partner for your next implementation project out of a long list of potential candidates, how do you compare? Reference projects and number of certified consultants would be a good place to start. Most software implementation partners have specific programs to assist consultants to achieve and maintain their certification status because it helps to differentiate their business from the competition, which is equally true for the consultants themselves.

SAP certifications and SAP training are tightly coupled, much more than you might have experienced with other software vendors. All the questions and answers for the exam are taken directly from the associated SAP training course manuals. The fact that there is only a single manual to study is an advantage to those who have attended the course and a disadvantage to those who have not. This is also a challenge for those who attempt to pass the exam with hands-on experience alone. You need to study the material in detail and be familiar with all the exam topics. However, attending the official SAP training courses for the certification isn't a requirement or prerequisite. The SAP Global Certification program is accessible to everybody. Whether you're working on an SAP implementation project, studying at university, or considering a career change, anyone can register for an SAP exam. According to the SAP Global Certification FAQ, more than 60,000 professionals get certified every year. This benefits organizations with a motivated and productive workforce and individuals with the opportunity to keep their skills current with the latest SAP technologies, progress in their careers, and get professional recognition.

Learn More

For an overview of the SAP Global Certification program, we recommend the following resources:

- Infosheet: *http://s-prs.co/v507800*
- FAQ: *http://s-prs.co/v507801*

Digital Badges

In 2018, the SAP Global Certification program joined the Open Badges initiative developed by Acclaim, part of the Pearson VUE company that proctors the exam. These digital badges can be used online to promote your proficiency in SAP subject areas and can be shared on social media platforms such as LinkedIn, Twitter, Facebook, and Xing; by mail; or embedded on your professional blog post channel. The badges themselves are also certified and can be verified directly online by the receiver.

Figure 1.1 shows the badge for the SAP Certified Technology Associate – SAP HANA 2.0 (SPS 04) certification.

Figure 1.1 Digital Badge on Acclaim

Learn More

For more information on this topic, see the SAP Global Certification digital badges FAQ at *http://s-prs.co/v507802*.

How to Prepare

In this section, you'll learn about the tools SAP provides to get certified: learning journeys, training courses, and SAP Learning Hub.

Learning Journeys

To help you prepare for your certification, SAP Training has mapped out learning journeys. They are made available on the documentation site SAP Help Portal which means they publicly accessible. Learning journeys are visual guides that show the recommend sequence of courses to take for a particular SAP solution. The journeys are subdivided into the following sections:

- **Overview**
  Introduces the solution.
- **Become Competent**
  Lists the courses related to certification.
- **Stay Current**
  Lists the courses to take to maintain certified status.
- **Expand Your Skills**
  Provides suggestions for additional training.

What exactly is listed in each section depends on the learning journey; most will be official SAP courses with the available formats (e-learning, classroom, e-book), but you also might find links to free openSAP courses included in the journey (most often in the **Expand Your Skills** section).

At the time of this book's publication, more than 200 learning journeys are available for the consultant, developer, architect, administrator, business user, or data analyst roles.

For SAP HANA, the following journeys are listed:

- SAP HANA Administration (administrator)
- SAP HANA Modeling (consultant)
- SAP HANA Application Development (developer)
- SAP HANA ABAP Programming (developer)

The SAP HANA learning journey supports the certifications for SAP Certified Technology Associate, SAP Certified Development Associate, and SAP Certified Application Associate. We explain the exam codes and exam levels in the next section.

Figure 1.2 shows the recommended courses for the SAP Certified Technology Associate certification and how to stay current and expand your skills with openSAP courses.

Figure 1.2 SAP HANA Administration Learning Journey

> **Learn More**
>
> To access the learning journeys, visit the SAP Help Portal at *https://help.sap.com/learn-ingjourney*. You can search for "SAP HANA" or choose **Explore all Learning Journeys** under the search box, and select **Product Categories · Databases & Data Management · SAP HANA and Databases**.

SAP Learning Hub

To prepare for the exam, SAP recommends taking either a classroom course or joining a learning room on the SAP Learning Hub. These learning rooms are like virtual classrooms. For the SAP Certified Technology Associate – SAP HANA 2.0 certification, the learning room called SAP HANA Installation and Operations.

With the SAP Learning Hub, as advertised, you can learn how and when you want. There are different editions available specifically for students, professionals, SAP partners, and those signed up to SAP Enterprise Support. If you want to take the platform for a test-drive first, a free trial is available.

The SAP Learning Hub is of particular interest when you're nowhere near an SAP office or prefer online training over the classroom format. You can ask questions, and a learning room moderator is available to support you on your journey. They also host live sessions, as shown in Figure 1.3.

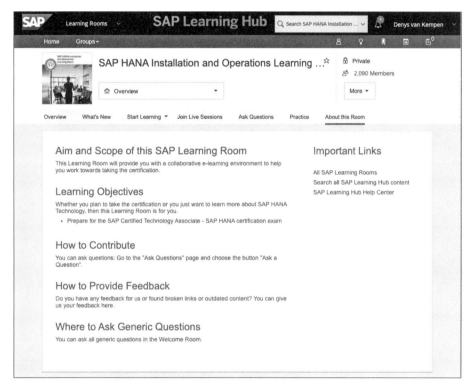

Figure 1.3 SAP HANA Installation and Operations Learning Room

---

Learn More

For more information about the different SAP Learning Hub editions and pricing, go to *http://training.sap.com/learninghub*.

SAP Training and SAP PRESS Certification Guides

SAP learning journeys, SAP Learning Hub, learning rooms, or the more traditional classroom format for the SAP Training courses are very helpful of course when preparing for an SAP certification. However, these training options come at a cost, and attending all recommended classes might not be within budget for everyone. The course manuals are written to support the classroom training with slides and text, and you may find this format less suitable for study. For this reason, SAP PRESS exam guides like this one provide an excellent additional or alternative study resource. In a single book, we cover the material you need to know to pass the exam successfully. The format is designed to match the exam experience and contains an extensive list of questions. In the answer section, we not only tell you what's wrong and what's right but also explain why to enable you to learn from your mistakes and keep track of your progress. Study the guide attentively, and you can be confident that when you book the exam, you have the required knowledge to pass.

Additional Resources

In this section, you'll learn about additional resources you can use to prepare for the exam. Most of the information is freely accessible, such as product documentation or video tutorials on YouTube. The openSAP courses and SAP Community require you to sign up for an account, but this comes at no charge. Only the SAP product support page on the SAP ONE Support portal requires a support account (S-user) available only to licensed customers. We'll reference these resources in the rest of the book as places you can turn to in order to learn more about a particular topic.

SAP Help Portal

The official documentation set for the SAP HANA platform is publicly available on the SAP Help Portal (see Figure 1.4). Tabs organize the different guides under the **Discover**, **Implement**, **Use**, **Operate**, and **Develop** sections. Under **Learn and Get Certified**, you'll find the learning journeys mentioned previously. For the topic areas of the SAP HANA technology exam, the most relevant guides are as follows:

- SAP HANA Administration Guide
- SAP HANA Master Guide
- SAP HANA Server Installation and Update Guide
- SAP HANA Troubleshooting and Performance Analysis Guide
- SAP HANA Security Guide

The master guide and installation guide are most relevant for the installation topic areas, and you'll want to keep the administration guide handy for all other topics, complemented with the performance and security guides.

The SAP HANA training courses cover the same material, often verbatim, but there is also a lot of material in these guides beyond the scope of the exam. The SAP HANA Administration Guide alone is well over 2,000 pages, and reading the guides from cover to cover may not be the best use of your time. In their defense, as reference guides, they have been written for a different purpose. However, should you want some more information about a particular topic, it's always a good idea to look it up in the documentation. The excellent search functionality of the SAP Help Portal makes it easy to find the information.

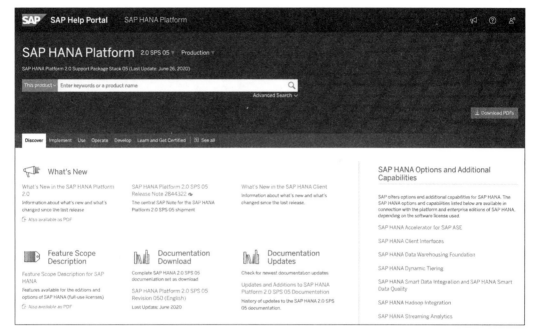

Figure 1.4 SAP HANA Platform Documentation on SAP Help Portal

> **Learn More**
>
> To access the SAP HANA platform documentation set, go to *http://help.sap.com/hana*. In the header you can filter on the version, e.g. 2.0 SPS 05.

openSAP Courses

Over the years, the openSAP massive open online courses (MOOC) platform has published a number of courses about the SAP HANA platform:

- Introduction to SAP HANA Administration
- Introduction to SAP HANA Dynamic Tiering
- Analyzing Connected Data with SAP HANA Graph
- Software Development on SAP HANA (several editions)

These courses are offered at no charge and provide a great way to learn about new topics. However, as the SAP Certified Technology Associate exam specifically targets the latest SAP HANA 2.0 releases, you should be aware that most of these openSAP courses are based on older SAP HANA versions. If you have some extra time, you could consider watching parts of the Introduction to SAP HANA Administration course. For a small fee, you can reactivate the course for a record of achievement but just watching is free.

Learn More

To access the openSAP courses, go to *http://open.sap.com*, and search for the name of the course or simply the topic "HANA".

SAP Developer Center

Although this book is about the SAP Certified Technology Associate exam and not the developer exam, we still recommend a visit to the SAP Developer Center where you can find all the information you need to get started with the free SAP HANA, express edition. This edition is a mini-version of the platform edition with everything included except a few enterprise features requiring more complex system landscapes. It's a great way to explore the SAP HANA cockpit; for example, you can practice with backup and restore without the risk of breaking anything, and you can monitor the effect of changing system parameters. If you have a very powerful computer, you can run the express edition locally: it requires 8 GB for the database and another 16 GB for the application server with applications. Otherwise, using the cloud offerings from Google Cloud Platform, Microsoft Azure, or Amazon Web Services (AWS) might be a better alternative. These cloud providers also offer free trials for the platform so if you shop around a bit, this could be a low- or no-charge option. SAP HANA, express edition, is free of charge with a developer license for configurations up to 32 GB of RAM.

The SAP Developer Center is also a great place to learn about SAP HANA with tutorials that help you get started with administration basics, spatial, machine learning, dynamic tiering, and many other topics, as illustrated in Figure 1.5. In addition, the SAP Developer Center also provides links to documentation and blogs on SAP Community.

Learn More

To access the SAP HANA area on SAP Developer Center, go to *http://developer.sap.com/hana*.

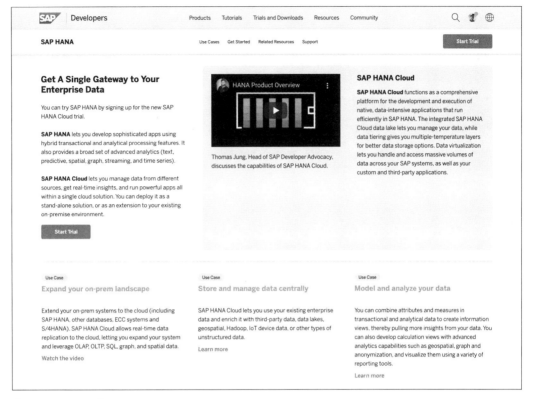

Figure 1.5 SAP Developers Center

SAP Community

Another good web page to bookmark is the **SAP HANA In-Memory Computing** topic area on the SAP Community. In the **Resources** section, you'll find references again to the Help Portal, openSAP courses, SAP Developer Center, and learning journeys, as well as the latest news and updates, information about upcoming webinars, and the latest blogs and forum Q&A tagged with SAP HANA (see Figure 1.6). You need to sign up to contribute, but otherwise the SAP Community is freely accessible and provides a great opportunity to learn and engage with fellow professionals.

Learn More

To access the **SAP HANA In-Memory Computing** topic area on SAP Community, go to *http://community.sap.com/topics/hana*.

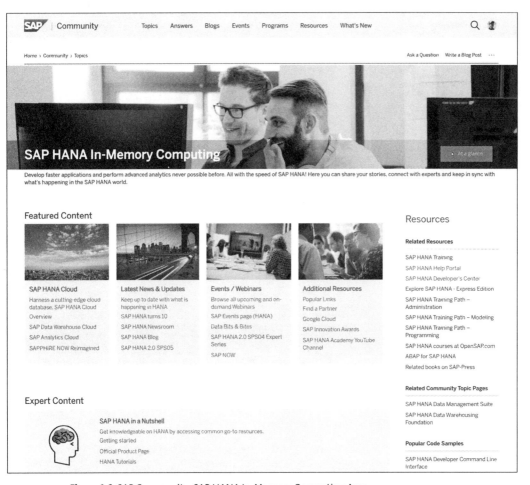

Figure 1.6 SAP Community: SAP HANA In-Memory Computing Area

SAP HANA Academy on YouTube

SAP HANA Academy provides technical enablement, implementation, and adoption support for customers and partners with thousands of free tutorial videos about SAP HANA, SAP Cloud Platform, and other SAP technologies. It's on YouTube, freely accessible, and easy to use. As illustrated in Figure 1.7, the tutorial videos are bundled in dedicated playlists such as **Installation and Update**, **Administration**, **Security**, **SAP HANA Cockpit**, to name a few, in the **Database Management (Database Administrator)** section, which is the focus of the Technology Associate exam.

Learn More

To access SAP HANA Academy on YouTube, go to *http://youtube.com/saphanaacademy*.

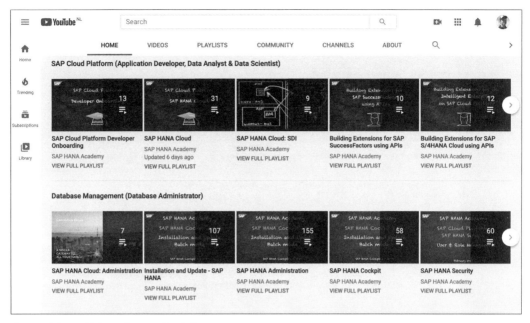

Figure 1.7 SAP HANA Academy on YouTube

SAP Product Support

Another recommended resource is the SAP HANA product support page on the SAP ONE Support Launchpad. Unlike most of the resources mentioned so far, the launchpad isn't publicly accessible and requires an SAP support or S-user account for licensed customers. Both the documentation and the training manuals reference knowledge base articles (KBAs) and SAP Notes for additional information, and, in this guide, we'll also list the most relevant material. However, as with the documentation set, using the support knowledge base to study for the exam may not be the best use of your time as the number of FAQ and how-to documents is overwhelming and typically much more detailed than required for the exam. Each note also references other notes for additional information, so beware that you can easily spend hours just trying to map the material.

As illustrated in Figure 1.8, the launchpad page lists recommended KBAs, relevant links to tools, video tutorials, documentation, and software downloads. If not for the exam, familiarize yourself with the SAP HANA product support page for the job as it's often the easiest way to get the latest information about all related and relevant topics.

Learn More

To access the product support page for SAP HANA, platform edition 2.0, go to *http://s-prs.co/v507803*.

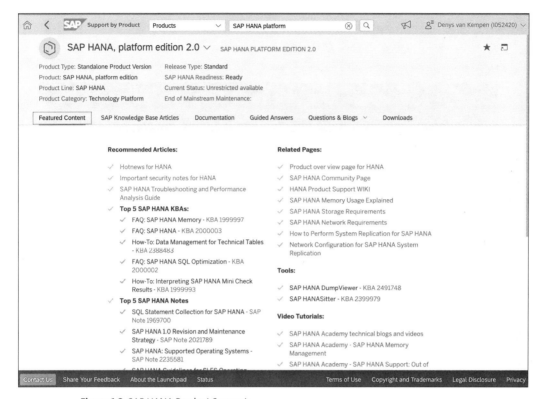

Figure 1.8 SAP HANA Product Support

Exam Levels and Editions

In this section, you'll learn about the different exam levels and editions.

Associates, Professionals, and Experts

According to the list maintained on the SAP Training portal, there are more than 150 certifications available in multiple languages. For SAP HANA, three associate level certifications are listed:

- SAP Certified Technology Associate (C_HANATEC)
- SAP Certified Application Associate (C_HANAIMP)
- SAP Certified Development Associate (C_HANADEV)

> **Learn More**
>
> For the complete list of valid SAP certifications, visit *http://training.sap.com/certification/validity*. At the bottom of this page, you'll also find the **Soon to expire Certifications** link, which you might want to check occasionally to find out whether you need to study again.

What exactly is understood with technology and application associate differs per product, but, for SAP HANA, the technology associate is concerned with installation and updates, system architecture, and system administration, including performance monitoring, backup and recovery, security, and high availability (HA). The application associate, on the other hand, covers information modeling and building calculation views, and modeling functions (including SQLScript), with more advanced topics such as text analytics, predictive analytics, spatial, graph, and series data. This profile is closer to that of the development associate where the focus is on native platform development with OData services, SAPUI5 for the user interface, SQLScript for the business logic, and multitarget application (MTA) programming models.

The primary tool for the technology associate is the SAP HANA cockpit, a topic that will be tested extensively on the exam. Conversely, the application and development associates are more likely to work with development tools such as SAP Web IDE. In the past, these certifications matched the three different perspectives of the SAP HANA studio tool (administration, modeling, development), but as this tool has been deprecated with the SAP HANA 2.0 SPS 02 release (2018), it's no longer part of the exam.

The associate level is one of three certification types available, next to specialist and professional, and it's by far the most common. As of the time of writing (summer 2020), there are only five professional-level certifications available (of which one is exclusive to SAP employees) and nine at the specialist level. Professional-level certifications include real-life scenarios and require several years of practical on-the-job experience; however, this type of certification isn't available for SAP HANA (exam codes starting with "P_"). Specialists exams require an associated exam as prerequisite, but again, there are none for SAP HANA. The SAP HANA-related specialist certifications concern ABAP development and SAP BW (exam codes starting with "E_"). The rest of the certifications (over 90%) are associate level types (exam codes starting with "C_").

The technology associate exams have the code C_HANATEC_*nn* with *nn* matching a particular SAP HANA release. For the application associate, the code is C_HANAIMP_*nn*, with the IMP from implementation; for the development associate, the code is C_HANADEV_*nn*.

Learn More

If you're interested in the SAP Certified Application Associate (C_HANAIMP) exam, you've got the wrong book! Instead, get *SAP HANA 2.0 Certification Guide: Application Associate Exam* by Rudi de Louw (SAP PRESS, 2019; *http://sap-press.com/4876*).

Certified Installations with Tailored Data Center Integration

With the introduction of the tailored data center integration (TDI) program in 2013, SAP Training acquired the responsibility to certify technology consultants for SAP HANA installations. Initially, SAP HANA was only available as an appliance (predefined hardware module with preconfigured software) provided exclusively by SAP hardware partners. With TDI, customers could now install SAP HANA on their own data center on the condition that both the hardware and consultant were SAP certified. Initially, this concerned a specialist certification SAP Certified Technology Specialist: SAP HANA Installation (E_HANAINS), but since 2016 and SAP HANA 1.0 SPS 12, this is now part of the technology associate certification.

Exam Editions

In the past, the exam code version number was mapped to the relevant SAP HANA release, so you would instantly know that the C_HANATEC_12 exam was for SAP HANA SPS 12. Since the release of SAP HANA 2.0, the software counter was reset to SPS 00, whereas the exam counter continued, resulting in SAP HANA 2.0 SPS 01 mapping to C_HANATEC_13, making the mapping a more challenging mental exercise. Table 1.1 shows the exam codes, their corresponding SAP HANA version, and their validity status.

Exam Code	Exam	Valid Until*
C_HANATEC_17	SAP HANA 2.0 SPS 05	June 2025
C_HANATEC_16	SAP HANA 2.0 SPS 04	June 2021
C_HANATEC_15	SAP HANA 2.0 SPS 03	Expired
C_HANATEC_14	SAP HANA 2.0 SPS 02	Expired
C_HANATEC_13	SAP HANA 2.0 SPS 01	Expired
C_HANATEC_12	SAP HANA 1.0 SPS 12	June 2021
* As with most rules, there are exceptions. For the final word on the topic, see the list with available and valid certifications on the SAP Training portal at *https://training.sap.com/ certification/validity*.		

Table 1.1 Certification Status

As a rule, the certification is valid as long as the release is in mainstream maintenance which is why the C_HANATEC_12 certification for SAP HANA 1.0 SPS 12 from 2016 has a five-year validity while the first four SAP HANA 2.0 certifications were only valid for two years.

Mainstream maintenance for SAP HANA 2.0 SPS 05 is also extended to five years, which makes this an excellent and highly recommended certification candidate. The learning efforts will be the same, but the certification will be valid for five instead of two years!

How to Book the Exam

In this section, we'll describe how to book the exam and the rules of the game.

Exam Product

To book the exam, go to the SAP Training portal, and adjust the country/language of the portal to where you want to take the exam. Next, search for "C_HANATEC" for the list of available certifications. As illustrated in Figure 1.9, you can book the exam directly from the page either through the Certification Hub (see the next section) or by selecting country, location, and **Class times**. The price of the exam and available dates are listed. Select **Add to basket** and check out.

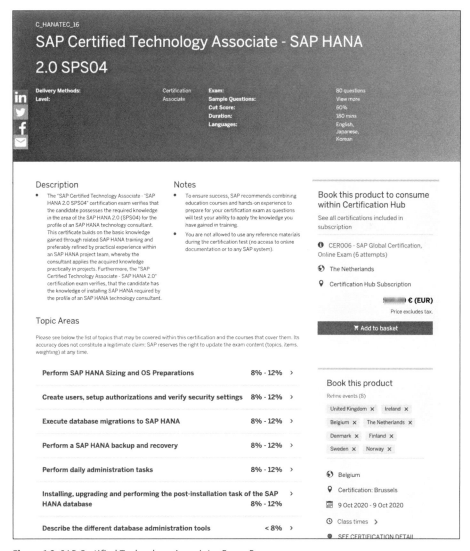

Figure 1.9 SAP Certified Technology Associate: Exam Page

SAP Certification Hub

As with the SAP Learning Hub, if you're nowhere near an SAP office or you prefer to take the exam online, you can subscribe to a Certification in the Cloud subscription on the Certification Hub. There are different subscription types available, but the most common one—CER006—gives you access to the Certification Hub for a year, during which you can schedule up to six exams. The exams are remotely proctored using the webcam of your computer, and—good news for night owls—you can schedule your exam any day, any time. The same rules apply as with the classroom exams (see the next section), and after successfully passing the exam, you'll get your SAP Global Certification digital badge just the same.

Figure 1.10 shows the exam dashboard where you can schedule your exam.

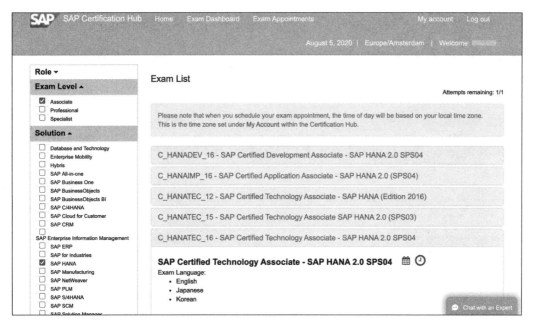

Figure 1.10 SAP Certification Hub

Learn More

To book your subscription, go to **CER006 – SAP Certification, Online Exam (6 attempts)** at *http://s-prs.co/v507804* or **CERS01 – SAP Certification in the Cloud for Students (1 attempt)** at *http://s-prs.co/v507805* if you're a student and are confident to pass the exam in one go. Prices are listed for your country or region. For more information and other available offers, go to the SAP Training portal at *http://training.sap.com*.

Certification Test Security Guidelines

SAP certifications are an important investment, and SAP makes considerable effort to protect this with some strict rules and regulations. This is a good thing because you wouldn't want your serious study efforts undermined by cheaters with a bunch of exam dumps. Here are the rules:

- You need to present two forms of valid identification, one of which must be a nonexpired government-issued photo ID (passport, driver's license). A debit card or credit card with full name and signature can be used as a secondary form of ID.

- You're not allowed to use any reference materials during the certification test, and you'll have no access to online documentation or to any SAP system. Cell phones, bags, notepads, or any other personal items must be stored away and aren't allowed into the testing room. You can use scratch paper, but this must be returned at the end of the exam.

- You'll get your score immediately after finishing your exam. If you pass the exam, you'll receive an SAP Global Certification digital badge through mail.

- You can take each exam up to three times, after which, you'll have to wait for the next edition.

Learn More

For the details, see the following resources:

- SAP Global Certification Program – Exam Process FAQ: *http://s-prs.co/v507806*
- SAP Global Certification Program – Post-Exam Process FAQ: *http://s-prs.co/v507807*
- Exam Security Guidelines: *http://s-prs.co/v507808*

Topic Areas

In this section, we'll describe what courses support the certification journey and what is listed for the different topic areas.

Topic Areas

The exam product information page shown in Figure 1.9 lists the different topics that are part of the exam. There have been slight changes to the topic areas over the years, and because SAP reserves the right to update the content of the exam—topics, items, and weighting—at any time (as stated on the exam guide), we'll only provide a more generic description to avoid any misleading information. What hasn't changed is that the questions on the exam are extracted from the content of the training course manuals, which in turn are based on the documentation, papers, and SAP Support KBAs.

The relative weight provides an indication of the number of questions you can expect for each of the topics. In total, there are 80 questions, so > 12% corresponds to 10 questions or more; 8%–12% corresponds to 6–10 questions; and < 8% corresponds to fewer than 6 questions. In other words, in theory, a minor topic may have up to 5 questions while a major topic only has 6, making the distinction not all that relevant. In practice, however, you can expect 8 questions for major topics and 4 for minor ones, although, again, your mileage may vary.

System architecture has been on the topic area list since the very first edition of the exam and rightly so (although this topic has lost some weight for the SPS 04 edition). Understanding the benefits of in-memory architecture, deployment models, system types, editions, components, services, operating system processes, and memory management, to name but a few topics, is essential to tackle more advanced topics such as scale-out, HA, and troubleshooting. For this reason, we'll start the certification journey with a discussion of architecture in Chapter 2.

As mentioned in the "Certified Installations with Tailored Data Center Integration" section, the former expert certification required for SAP HANA installations has been merged with the SAP HANA technology associate certification for the SAP HANA 1.0 SPS 12 release. It should come as no surprise that installation and update is a major topic area and includes both preparation and post-installation activities. With the SAP HANA 2.0 SPS 04 exam, the topic area has been split into one section about operating system preparation and sizing, and another about the installation and upgrade itself, resulting in an overall heavier weight for this topic area. For this book, we've followed this separation (see Chapter 3 and Chapter 4, respectively), although these topics may be merged again in the future for the exam.

Security for SAP HANA covers data access management with user authentication and authorization, encryption of data at rest and in flight, effectively protecting unauthorized access, plus auditing for compliance and to detect security breaches and potential security vulnerabilities. For some exam editions, data access management and data access control were separated as topics. With the SAP HANA 2.0 SPS 04 exam, the dedicated training course on SAP HANA security was moved to the SAP Certified Technology Professional – System Security Architect (P_TSEC10_75) certification. If you're interested in this topic area and you're familiar with SAP NetWeaver, SAP Business Suite, and SAP S/4HANA, this certification might be of interest. We cover all security-related topics in Chapter 10.

Database migration is another major topic on most editions of the technology associate exam and addresses very specifically how to use the Database Migration Option (DMO) of the Software Update Manager (SUM) tool to migrate SAP applications running on third-party database management systems to SAP HANA. For students with a more generic database administration background and not familiar with SAP NetWeaver and Basis technology, this part of the exam might be the most challenging also because the topic isn't covered in the SAP HANA documentation. As a topic area, it's more closely related to the material for the SAP Certified Technology Associate for SAP NetWeaver exams. We end the book with a dedicated chapter about SUM DMO (see Chapter 14).

The remainder of the exam topics are all related to system administration and address typical database administration tasks such as monitoring, backup and

recovery, performance analysis, and troubleshooting. For this book, we've separated the topics into chapters about the database administration tools and the SAP
HANA cockpit (Chapter 5 and Chapter 6, respectively), database administration
tasks (Chapter 7), working with tenant databases (Chapter 8), scale-out systems
(Chapter 9), backup and recovery (Chapter 11), system replication (Chapter 12), and
troubleshooting and performance (Chapter 13).

Some topics get some extra attention and weight. One example is SAP HANA cockpit 2.0 introduced with SAP HANA 2.0. This web-based tool replaces the popular
SAP HANA studio, now deprecated for this release. As both the architecture and
the UI are very different, spending some extra time on this topic is a good investment (see Chapter 6). The same applies to tenant databases or multitenant database container (MDC) systems, to use an older term. Although it's the default
operation mode for SAP HANA 2.0, it significantly changed many operation activities compared with older SAP HANA releases; for this reason, we cover the topic in
a separate chapter (Chapter 8). The more advanced system administration topics
about scalability and HA with multiple-host systems and system replication also
get a separate chapter (Chapter 9) to make sure concepts and operations are well
understood.

> **Learn More**
>
> For the latest information about topic areas and weight, always check the exam page for
> the SAP Certified Technology Associate exam on the SAP Training portal. Although
> changes are rare, it's better to be safe than sorry.

SAP Training Courses

The certification exam web page lists the SAP Training courses that cover the certification topics. For most of the topics, the HA200 course is listed with the SAP
HANA Administration and Installation learning room on the SAP Learning Hub as
alternative. The following courses are listed:

- HA200: SAP HANA 2.0 – Installation and Administration (5 days)
- HA201: SAP HANA 2.0 – High Availability and Disaster Tolerance Administra-
  tion (3 days)
- HA215: SAP HANA 2.0 – Using Monitoring and Performance Tools (2 days)
- HA250: SAP HANA 2.0 – Database Migration Using DMO (2 days)

Earlier versions of the exam also included course HA240: SAP HANA 2.0 – Authorizations, Scenarios, & Security Requirements (3 days).

> **Learn More**
>
> For more information about the courses, see the course information page on the SAP
> Training portal. You can access (download) the course index with the objectives listed for

each lesson. Although some courses list other courses as prerequisites, the certification exam doesn't have course attendance as a requirement. Anyone can book an exam and attempt to pass on experience and study of exam guides like these.

Sample Questions

To pass the exam, you need to answer 60% of the questions correctly, that is, 48 out of a total of 80 questions. You don't get any points if you answer a question partly correct in case of multiple-choice questions nor do you lose any points when answering a question incorrectly. When in doubt, guess! Never leave a question unanswered.

To give you a realistic idea of what kind of questions you might expect, the exam product page includes a link to a sample exam, as shown in Figure 1.11. The simulator is a web application hosted by the Questionmark online assessment platform.

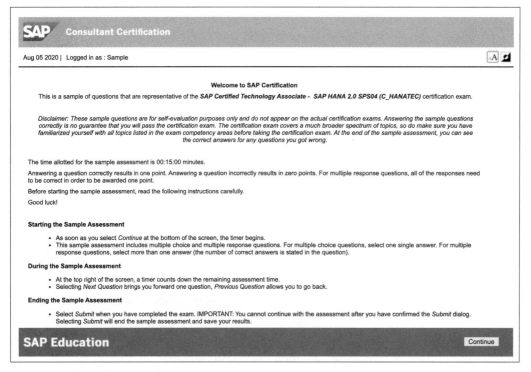

Figure 1.11 Sample Questions

There's no point in learning the questions and answers by heart as they don't appear on the actual certification exam, of course. The sample questions are purely for self-evaluation purposes and to familiarize yourself with the format. You can try the mock exam as often as you like.

There are 10 questions for which you get 15 minutes, a little less time compared to the actual exam (180 minutes for 80 questions). The Assessment Navigator helps you keep track of the questions answered, and you can mark questions you're not sure about (or do the opposite: mark those that you know for sure; it's up to you). When you're done with all questions, click **Submit**.

Some questions require a single choice (radio button) from a selection of three or four. Other questions are in the format of multiple-choice checkboxes with two or three correct answers.

Let's look at an example of the single-choice, radio button format:

1. Where does SAP HANA process data?

☐ **A.** In memory

☐ **B.** On disk

☐ **C.** On paper

Next, let's consider an example of the multiple-choice format:

1. An SAP HANA system provides different services. Each service is hosted by a different operating system process. Which are valid names for these processes? (There are 3 correct answers.)

☐ **A.** `hdbserver`

☐ **B.** `hdbnameserver`

☐ **C.** `hdbindexserver`

☐ **D.** `hdbcompileserver`

☐ **E.** `hdbwebserver`

Note the format of the questions: short statement, short question, short answers. This is typical for the exam questions. You won't be tested for your command of the English language. The questions are phrased as simply as possible.

If only a single answer is correct, you can only provide a single answer. The format of the questions and answers isn't intended to trick you.

Although the real exam questions won't be as easy as the ones provided here, you might be able to arrive at the correct answer by elimination alone. The output of the HDB info command, for example, illustrated in Figure 1.12, lists the name of the operating system processes. SAP HANA system administrators frequently run this command and may be expected to be familiar with the output.

```
hdbadm@hana-vml:/usr/sap/HDB/HDB00> HDB info
USER          PID    PPID  %CPU         VSZ          RSS  COMMAND
hdbadm       3486    3485   0.3       14260         4108  -sh
hdbadm       3546    3486   0.0       13392         3404  \_ /bin/sh /usr/sap/HDB/HDB00/HDB inf
hdbadm       3577    3546   0.0       34852         3164     \_ ps fx -U hdbadm -o user:8,pid:
hdbadm       2401       1   0.0      710080        50700  hdbrsutil  --start --port 30003 --volu
hdbadm       2021       1   0.0      710080        50936  hdbrsutil  --start --port 30001 --volu
hdbadm       1848       1   0.0       22700         2992  sapstart pf=/usr/sap/HDB/SYS/profile/H
hdbadm       1855    1848   0.0      454436        69176  \_ /usr/sap/HDB/HDB00/hana-vml/trace/
hdbadm       1875    1855   9.4     6309392      3199976     \_ hdbnameserver
hdbadm       2082    1855   0.4     1478760       137724     \_ hdbcompileserver
hdbadm       2085    1855   0.5     1746168       169140     \_ hdbpreprocessor
hdbadm       2131    1855  15.6     6901440      3847072     \_ hdbindexserver -port 30003
hdbadm       2134    1855   2.3     4461876      1369268     \_ hdbxsengine -port 30007
hdbadm       2541    1855   1.0     3451436       446156     \_ hdbwebdispatcher
hdbadm       1675       1   0.0      435668        30052  /usr/sap/HDB/HDB00/exe/sapstartsrv pf=
hdbadm       1598       1   0.0       41380         4876  /usr/lib/systemd/systemd --user
hdbadm       1599    1598   0.0       86584         1812  \_ (sd-pam)
hdbadm@hana-vml:/usr/sap/HDB/HDB00> █
```

Figure 1.12 HDB Info

> **Learn More**
>
> To access the sample questions, go to the exam product page, and click the **Sample Questions** link in the header (refer to Figure 1.9). The exam simulator opens in a new browser window.

Summary

In this chapter, you learned about the SAP Global Certification program, the different certification levels, exam rules, and how to prepare and book your exam, as well as suggestions regarding where you can turn for additional information. After a more general discussion, we then zoomed in to the topic areas specific to this exam guide. We provided two sample questions for the exam and pointed out how questions are phrased and what strategies you can use to optimize the chances of getting it right. In the remainder of this book, we'll cover the topic areas in dedicated chapters with objectives, key concepts refreshers, important terminology, and lots and lots of questions. We'll begin with the system architecture and your SAP HANA deployment options in the next chapter.

Chapter 2
System Architecture

Techniques You'll Master

- Explaining in-memory computing
- Understanding use cases (scenarios)
- Describing system types, deployment types, editions, and options
- Explaining the overall system architecture
- Describing the startup process
- Explaining the delta merge process

In this chapter, we both explain the SAP HANA architecture from a high level and go "under the hood" to describe specific parts. In the exam, you'll be tested on your knowledge of monitoring and troubleshooting, working with tenant databases, performing backup and recovery, and managing scale-out systems. To perform any of these tasks successfully, you'll need a solid understanding of the overall architecture.

Real-World Scenario

You're in a meeting and are asked to explain the SAP HANA system architecture and deployment options. The CFO wants to know his options to reduce costs. How can you optimize resource usage? The CIO wants to know about high availability (HA) and infrastructure requirements. He started his career as an Oracle database administrator and wants you to explain the SAP HANA terminology of systems, instances, and databases. What exactly does it mean? Each vendor uses these terms differently. The discussion gets technical, and you need to explain the delta merge process. Are you up to the task?

People expect SAP certified consultants to be intimately familiar with the topic. Of course, nobody knows the answers to all questions but in your role as SAP HANA technology consultant, you should have a firm grip on system architecture topics. Just as important, when you don't know the answer to a particular question, you should know where to look it up. Familiarize yourself with the documentation and other important resources, such as the KBAs on the SAP ONE Support Launchpad. These are critical skills for a technology consultant.

Topic and Objectives

In this chapter, we cover the SAP HANA system architecture topic area. This is partly a general introduction/high-level overview and partly a more technical discussion of how certain parts of the SAP HANA database work, such as memory management and system startup. For the exam, you're expected to have a good understanding of the following topics:

- Benefits of SAP HANA as in-memory platform
- Common use cases (scenarios)
- SAP HANA system types and deployment options: on premise versus cloud on a high level but also technically, which concerns tenant databases, virtualization, and co-hosting with multiple systems or databases on a single server
- SAP HANA editions and options

- The different parts (components) that together make up the SAP HANA platform: database, client, application server runtimes, application function libraries, and advanced analytics technologies, such as graph, spatial, and text
- SAP HANA system architecture with the different services (also called components) and operating system processes
- Startup sequence of the system and of the database
- The different components of the index server process, memory usage, and memory management in the column store

---

Note

This topic area was listed with medium weight (8%–12%) for most editions of the exam but lost some weight for the SPS 04 version (< 8%). With 80 questions in total, you can expect about 4 questions on this topic, although the exam guide clearly states that this can change at any time. Regardless of the weight, as most other topics areas build on the foundations of this chapter, we highly recommend that you familiarize yourself with the concepts.

Learn More

For the high-level overview, we suggest browsing the SAP HANA Master Guide. This guide is the entry point for planning SAP HANA installations, and you should be familiar with how it's structured and what type of information it documents. For the under-the-hood technical parts, consult the SAP HANA Administration Guide to find the system architecture documented in more detail, along with topics such as memory management and data persistence as an introduction to the different hands-on activities in the "System Administration" section of the guide.

- SAP HANA Master Guide (2.0 SPS 05) (*http://s-prs.co/v507809*)
- SAP HANA Administration Guide (2.0 SPS 05) (*http://s-prs.co/v507810*)

Key Concepts Refresher

In this section, we'll highlight the most important concepts for SAP HANA architecture. We'll also walk through the deployment options that you'll need to know.

In-Memory Computing

In the previously mentioned SAP HANA Master Guide, SAP HANA is defined as a modern, in-memory database and platform, deployable on premise or in the cloud. This definition includes three key characteristics:

- Modern
- Both a database and a platform
- Available for customer data center and public/private cloud deployments

What makes SAP HANA a "modern" database? Here you find the in-memory architecture opposed to the more traditional, disk-based architecture of relational database management systems (RDBMS). When the first commercial databases came on the market over half a century ago, computing power was extremely expensive while storage, comparatively, was relatively cheap. Databases were mainly used to support online transactional processing (OLTP) and were architected to read a row from disk; process the data in memory with create, read, update, delete (CRUD) operations; and then write it back to storage again.

To speed up the read time for often-queried columns, indexes were added. In simple terms, this creates a copy of a column, but this time, with the data sorted. Indexes duplicate data and add maintenance overhead—update the table, and you also need to update the index.

To speed up calculations for often-queried columns, aggregates were added. These aggregates persisted the results of calculations such as SUM, COUNT, MAX, and AVG, as values on disk. Given the limited resources, it would simply take too long to calculate an aggregate each and every time. Initially, these aggregates were typically calculated as batch processes overnight when there was no order entry activity. To report on the data and get the results of last month or last year, batch processes would run all weekend. Although aggregates more often than not would return stale values or approximations, it was good enough at the time.

As hardware costs came down in the 1980s and 1990s, "online" reporting and analytics became feasible, although not with batch processes on transactional systems, but by creating a dedicated system for online analytical processing (OLAP). This required, once again, a data copy, this time to a data warehouse system bringing together enterprise data from multiple systems of record. With the help of an enterprise data warehouse (EDW), decision support systems (DSS) were created to enable business intelligence (BI). To massage the data in the right format for analysis, extract, transform, and load (ETL) processes and tools made their appearance on the market. To optimize analytics, the OLAP database was architected based on columns and not on rows as with OLTP. Columnar storage facilitates the calculation of aggregates: total number of widgets sold per year and per region. Aggregates are also called key figures or facts. Time and geography are common dimensions or "characteristics."

> **Note**
>
> The "big five" RDBMS database vendors—IBM, Informix, Oracle, Sybase, and Microsoft—all go back to the 1970s and 1980s. Today, the market has consolidated with the acquisitions of Informix by IBM and Sybase by SAP. Microsoft SQL Server originated as the Windows version of the Sybase UNIX database. Cognos, Hyperion, BusinessObjects, and other well-known OLAP, EDW, and ETL technology vendors were founded a decade later and in turn for the most part acquired by larger companies such as SAP, IBM, and Oracle.

In the first decade of the 21st century, Moore's law—the observation that the number of transistors on a microchip doubled every two years—started to slow down, and processor manufacturers started to put multiple processor cores on a CPU, making parallel processing much easier and cheaper. In addition, the capacity of RAM was no longer expressed in kilobytes or megabytes but gigabytes and terabytes at a fraction of the cost. Disk access times, that is, input/output (I/O), remained a bottleneck for the traditional database architecture, although with cheap memory, data caching was common. Caches are employed at the database, file system, hardware, application server, and other layers with prefetching algorithms further speeding up access. At the storage layer, the introduction of memory-based flash storage as found on USB drives and smart phones also improved access time, in particular the solid-state drive (SSD) type for enterprise databases. Traditional spinning disks with magnetic heads continue to be used in cheap redundant arrays of independent (or inexpensive) disks (RAID) devices. Figure 2.1 illustrates current and past performance bottlenecks: from disk to memory for the traditional database and from memory to CPU for in-memory databases.

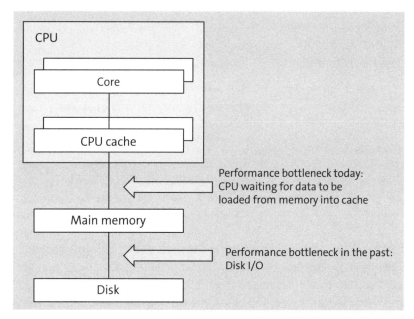

Figure 2.1 Hardware Architecture: Current and Past Performance Bottlenecks

With half-century of experience building enterprise applications, system architects at SAP had an intimate understanding of enterprise workloads. More often than not, these combine OLTP and OLAP characteristics and don't neatly fit either category. Over time, advances in hardware technology made massive parallel processing (MPP) possible not only for supercomputers but also on commodity hardware, and large memory configurations made it feasible to store a complete enterprise data set into memory. Technology evolutions together with software innovations inspired SAP to develop SAP HANA as an in-memory database containing both column and row store engines. With all data stored in memory, all the aggregates and indexes created to speed up read access times were no longer needed. This significantly reduced the size of the database. In addition, with most of the data located in columnar storage, considerable compression rates could be achieved, making the actual size of the database to load into memory even smaller. At the high end, you find systems that support up to 32 processors with 28 cores each and up to 24 TB of addressable memory. However, to get started, you can launch an instance of SAP HANA, express edition, with as little as 8 GB and a couple of (virtual) CPU cores.

To summarize, SAP HANA leverages the latest developments in hardware technology—a recent example is the support for persistent memory—combined with software innovations such as these:

- Combined column and row store
- Sophisticated compression algorithms
- Partitioning
- Removal of aggregate tables and other common database structures that once served to optimize data access
- Insert-only on the delta store

SAP wasn't the only vendor working on a database that combines OLTP and OLAP technology. In the industry, this is referred to as hybrid transactional/analytical processing (HTAP).

Exam Tip

For the exam, you're not expected to be familiar with database history, but it may help to understand some of the architecture decisions made. The preceding history is distilled to the essentials with many nuances and related topics left uncovered.

Indexes, aggregates, OLAP, and data warehouses are all examples of solutions proposed over time to address the disk I/O performance bottleneck, and they all come with data duplication. To this, you can add the three-tier application server architecture with the web client on top responsible for rendering the user interface, the app server in the middle processing the business logic, and the database below to provide data persistence. To improve response times, caching was important. In its extreme, developers would simply code a SELECT * and pump all the data from the database to the middle tier, reducing the often highly sophisticated database to a data dump or bit bucket.

For the SAP HANA platform, this approach is the reverse. The paradigm, as we like to say, is code-to-data, also known as code push-down. Where and whenever possible, processing should be done by the database. For native applications, a lightweight application server sufficed called SAP HANA extended application services

(SAP HANA XS). By *native applications*, we mean applications specifically developed for the SAP HANA platform and not generic Java applications, for example.

Apart from an application development and runtime platform, there are also many other use cases that benefit from having all enterprise data stored together in memory. Text analytics, spatial, graph, series data, and predictive analysis are some examples of what is called advanced analytics with SAP HANA. They all have in common that data is processed inside the database and not first extracted to a separate tier, as shown in Figure 2.2 with database services, application services, integration services, and several advanced analytics processing technologies all around a single data copy.

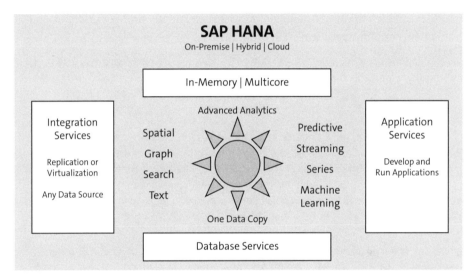

Figure 2.2 Characteristics of SAP HANA

SAP HANA is data source-agnostic, which means that it doesn't matter where the data is coming from. This could be structured data as found in relational databases used by SAP or third-party applications but also as stored in NoSQL databases with a more flexible data model. In addition, SAP HANA also integrates data from social networks, geospatial sources, machine data, or big data environments such as Hadoop. There are different technologies available to manage data replication, event streaming, and ETL. In some cases, this concerns separate products such as SAP Data Services or SAP Replication Server. But there are also built-in or add-on technologies such as SAP HANA smart data access (SDA), SAP HANA smart data integration (SDI), SAP HANA smart data quality (SDQ), and SAP HANA streaming analytics. These technologies are out of scope for the exam, although you may find the occasional reference in a question.

> **Learn More**
>
> For a more complete coverage of this topic, see *SAP HANA 2.0: An Introduction* (SAP PRESS, 2019; *http://sap-press.com/4884*), which describes the technologies and the different personas (administrator, developer, security officer, data integration architect) working with SAP HANA in more detail.

You can run SAP HANA on dedicated hardware inside a corporate data center or consume the database-as-a-service (DBaaS) in the cloud. On premise, you have two choices:

- As an appliance, which means preconfigured software on predefined hardware provided by SAP hardware partners
- On SAP-certified hardware installed by an SAP-certified engineer under the tailored data center integration (TDI) program

The certified and supported SAP HANA hardware directory lists all currently certified configurations.

> **Learn More**
>
> Initially, SAP HANA was only available as an appliance, and the HANA acronym stood for High-Performance Analytical Appliance, echoing the High-Performance Analytics tag of an earlier product delivered as an appliance: SAP Business Warehouse Accelerator (SAP BW Accelerator). After the TDI program was launched for custom data center installation, the term High-Performance Analytical Appliance was no longer used in SAP promotional material or documentation, but you may still find it in use by SAP hardware partners that deliver SAP HANA as an appliance.
>
> Appliances originally came in T-shirt sizes (XS, S, M, L), and the "tailored" TDI program responded to customer requests of a more made-to-measure solution. TDI requires both certified hardware and certified technical consultants. This is the origin of the SAP Certified Technology Associate exam.

There are several cloud offerings for SAP HANA as well:

- Public cloud providers infrastructure-as-a service (IaaS)
- SAP HANA Enterprise Cloud, an SAP-managed private cloud
- SAP HANA Cloud on SAP Cloud Platform (DBaaS)

SAP HANA can be hosted on the public cloud infrastructure provided by SAP partners such as Microsoft Azure, Amazon Web Services (AWS), Google Cloud Platform, or Alibaba Cloud. This is a bring-your-own-license (BYOL) model.

Alternatively, you could opt to have SAP HANA hosted and managed by SAP. This comes with the license and additional management services, an offering called SAP HANA Enterprise Cloud.

On-premise and cloud deployments are illustrated in Figure 2.3.

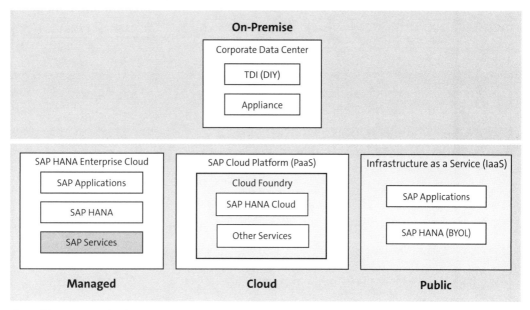

Figure 2.3 SAP HANA Deployments

Use Cases

As described, the SAP HANA platform combines OLTP with OLAP for database services and includes application services, integration services, and advanced analytics processing. Over time, different use cases and scenarios have been architected for the in-memory platform, which we'll discuss in this section.

Application Server

After SAP HANA was released, SAP development started to update the most relevant business applications to support the new in-memory platform. Although optimized for the platform, the products were in essence still the same as the editions for the other support databases, such as Oracle, IBM Db2, and Microsoft SQL Server—commonly called Any Database (AnyDB). This concerns SAP BW powered by SAP HANA and SAP Business Suite powered by SAP HANA. The application server is SAP NetWeaver Application Server for ABAP (SAP NetWeaver AS for ABAP) and could be deployed on a separate system or, with enough resources, on the same host.

In the next round, SAP started to re-architect its business applications to integrate the in-memory technology. These versions run exclusively on SAP HANA as reflected in the name: SAP S/4HANA for enterprise resource planning (ERP) and SAP BW/4HANA for the data warehouse solution.

Figure 2.4 shows the application server architecture of SAP HANA in comparison with the sidecar (data mart) scenario and the SAP HANA XS scenario, which we'll discuss next.

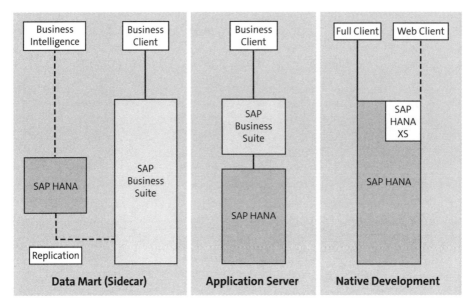

Figure 2.4 SAP HANA Scenarios

Data Mart

After the platform was released, besides "primary persistence for SAP NetWeaver-based applications," as the documentation labels the first scenario, other use cases also were considered and implemented. A common one in the early days was SAP HANA as data mart. In the industry, data mart refers to a small repository of an operational data source, and this still reflects the old paradigm of OLTP data pumped into an OLAP environment. Data marts, however, are typically lightweight and simple to implement when compared to a full data warehouse with ETL processing. To load operational data into SAP HANA, the following different replication technologies were proposed:

- **SAP Data Services**
  SAP Data Services includes data integration and data quality technology and is categorized as an ETL tool.

- **SAP Replication Server**
  SAP Replication Server performs log-based replication and works at a low level on the database side, on any database, and can be used, like SAP Data Services, to replicate data from both SAP and other third-party applications.

- **SAP Landscape Transformation Replication Server**
  The curiously named SAP Landscape Transformation Replication Server performs trigger-based replication, and this technology is integrated with the ABAP stack, understands the semantics, and is only used to replicate SAP applications. Originally, the technology was used to carve out or merge business applications in an SAP landscape, hence the name.

The main objective of the sidecar scenario was to improve the performance of reporting and analytics, also known as BI. The production systems with accompanying business applications could continue to run untouched, and adding SAP HANA as a sidecar was relatively easy to implement and a great way to start discovering its benefits. To facilitate reporting, information views had to be created, which initially was all do-it-yourself but later arrived as licensed software bundled for specific SAP applications, called SAP HANA Live or SAP HANA & Analytics.

Similarly, you can use the Direct Extractor Connection (DXC) in SAP HANA for this purpose. This leverages a technology originally conceived for data modeling and data acquisition for SAP BW using SAP Business Suite data source extractors. Its batch-driven, so unlike the previously mentioned replication technologies, it's not real real-time, but with a 15-minute interval close enough compared to latency usually seen with data warehouses.

Accelerators

In the early days, for some SAP Business Suite applications, SAP also developed accelerators, such as the CO-PA accelerator for the Profitability Analysis module or the CO-PC accelerator for Product Cost Controlling. This required the setup of a secondary database connections via a database shared library (DBSL).

A specific implementation of the sidecar scenario is the SAP HANA accelerator for SAP ASE, first released in 2014 and currently with different versions for SAP HANA 1.0 and 2.0. Commercially, it's available as an option and adds business analytics capabilities to the relational SAP Adaptive Server Enterprise (SAP ASE) database.

Native Development with SAP HANA Extended Application Services

The third use case concerns SAP HANA as a native development platform. This scenario takes the code-to-data paradigm to the max with the application server completely integrated with the in-memory platform. There are two different application server architectures for SAP HANA, both called SAP HANA extended application services (SAP HANA XS). The first release is based on the Mozilla SpiderMonkey JavaScript engine for server-side JavaScript. The second is based on Cloud Foundry and is similar to the SAP Cloud Platform environment, making it easy to develop applications first on premises and then deploy them at scale to a cloud-hosted environment. Called SAP HANA extended application services, advanced model (SAP HANA XSA), it was released with SAP HANA 1.0 SPS 11. The older architecture was labeled SAP HANA XS, classic model and later deprecated together with the related SAP HANA repository and SAP HANA studio development tool with SAP HANA 2.0 SPS 02 with removal announced for the next major release of SAP HANA (effectively SAP HANA Cloud).

> **Exam Tip**
> Although we'll touch on both architectures of SAP HANA XS in this book, the application server is mostly out of scope for the exam.

System Types

You can run an SAP HANA system on a single host (computer) or on multiple hosts. In the documentation, these are referenced as the two system types with the multiple-host system also called a distributed or scale-out system. Whereas scale-out systems are usually technically complex, creating a multiple-host system for SAP HANA is remarkably easy. In fact, a single-host system is already prepared for distribution as the recommended configuration places both the software (binaries or program files) and the database (data and redo log volumes) on shared storage. We explain how this all works in the Chapter 3 and Chapter 4 on installation and Chapter 9 on scaling in more detail, but, in short, all you need to do to create a multiple-host system is to add a second host to your single-host system. Only data that is relevant to the instance on the local host, such as trace files, are stored on a local file system. All other data is stored in a shared location. As a consequence, adding a host doesn't involve much installation: the SAP HANA binaries are already stored in the shared storage location. However, after you have some data, adding and removing hosts quickly becomes more complex and time consuming because you need to balance and distribute the tables and partitions across all hosts.

The main driver for multiple-host systems is the requirement to support larger memory configurations and table sizes. Scale-out systems can handle a larger number of concurrent connections and host bigger databases. Ideally, multiple-host systems provide better performance, although there are many reasons why performance could suffer as well. To avoid the complexity inherent with multiple-host systems, SAP recommends to scale up (upgrade hardware) before scaling out. In addition, not every SAP application is supported in scale-out scenarios.

When configured correctly, multiple-host systems can also provide HA because the failure of a single host doesn't cause the entire system to become unavailable. For HA, you need to add one or more standby hosts to the multiple-host environment. However, multiple-host systems aren't the only approach or even the best approach to obtain HA with SAP HANA. In most cases, SAP HANA system replication or storage replication provided by SAP-certified hardware partners is a better choice, and this can be implemented for both single-host and scale-out systems. Scale-out is covered in more detail in Chapter 9.

Deployment Types

Irrespective of whether you're working with a single-host system or a multiple-host system, there are also different technical deployment types as illustrated in Figure 2.5.

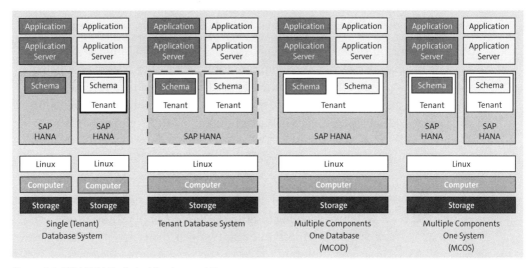

Figure 2.5 SAP HANA Technical Deployment Types

The following deployment types are used:

- Single (tenant) database system
- Tenant database system
- Virtualization
- Multiple components, one database (MCOD) and multiple components, one system (MCOS)

In the most basic configuration, a single host (operating system) is dedicated to a single SAP HANA system, containing a single tenant, with a single database schema connected to a single application server to host a single application. This is shown on the left side of Figure 2.5 with a single database system; the first configuration is the original design of SAP HANA and only available on the 1.0 release.

Using tenant databases, or multitenant database container (MDC) systems, as they were called at the time of introduction, is the default deployment type for SAP HANA 2.0 systems although this mode is also available on the later releases of SAP HANA 1.0. Here, each application is hosted inside a dedicated tenant database and database schema. A single SAP HANA instance host all databases, which are completely isolated from each other. We cover this deployment type in detail in Chapter 8.

Virtualization is an alternative approach to optimizing hardware resources. This isn't illustrated as each of the configurations can be virtualized, including multiple-host systems.

We'll take a closer look at MCOD and MCOS deployments in the following sections.

Multiple Component, One Database and Multiple Components, One System

Prior to the introduction of tenant databases, hosting multiple applications inside a single database (system) or installing multiple SAP HANA systems on a single host (operating system) were common approaches to optimize resource usage. These scenarios are called MCOD and MCOS, respectively, as illustrated previously on the right side of Figure 2.5. As the S from system in MCOS references the underlying hardware system and not the S of an SAP HANA system ID (SID), this term can be confusing. For this reason, this deployment is also called multi-SID.

Installing multiple SAP HANA systems on a single host provides application isolation and independence at the cost of more overhead as you need maintain two or more SAP HANA systems. Installing multiple SAP HANA applications inside a single database removes the overhead but also removes the isolation. Tenant databases provided an elegant solution to both issues as it reduces the overhead yet adds isolation. For this reason, since the introduction of tenant databases, MCOS and MCOD deployments became less common.

One of the issues with an MCOS deployment is that it's difficult to configure in terms of resource management. You need to adjust the system parameter `global_allocation_limit`, for example, to account for multiple systems. After installation, this parameter defaults to 90% of the first 64 GB of available physical memory plus 97% of each additional gigabyte, but the installer doesn't consider the presence of any other SAP HANA system. Both MCOS and MCOD scenarios are supported for production and nonproduction use cases on single-host and scale-out systems.

Multiple Components, One System Scale-Out

Initially, support for MCOS in multiple-host systems was restricted to nonproduction use cases only. When this was extended to production as well, this triggered a renewed interest in the deployment type. Although it remains complex to configure, using MCOS in a scale-out environment enables you to optimize load distribution and maximize the resource utilization. In particular, you can leverage the host acting as standby server for tenant database DB1 to take up the role as master or worker for database DB2 and DB3, as illustrated in Figure 2.6.

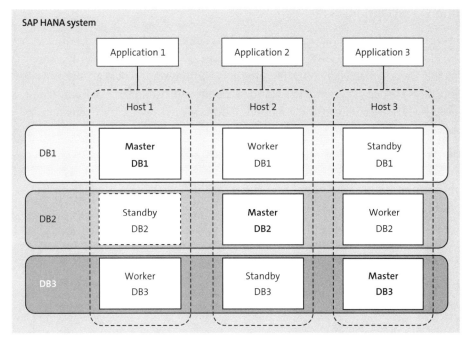

Figure 2.6 MCOS Scale-Out Scenario

As with MCOS on a single host, the global allocation limit for each SID needs to be configured carefully as this system parameter can be set at both the global system and the individual host level. In addition, you need to consider processor affinity to benefit from non-uniform memory access (NUMA). Using workload classes is recommended as this enables SAP HANA to dynamically manage resource consumption at the session level and even the statement level.

Exam Tip

You aren't expected to be intimately familiar with the MCOD deployment type and the list of supported (whitelisted) applications, but you should understand the architecture and the considerations for deployment.

MCOS (multi-SID) scenarios are still relevant as they provide application isolation and version independence, for example, to host different SAP HANA releases for different applications.

Take some time to consider the MCOS (multi-SID) deployment with tenant databases and how this works in a multiple-host architecture.

Learn More

The topic is documented in the SAP HANA Master Guide where you'll also find references to the relevant SAP support KBAs that document the conditions for these deployment types.

Editions and Options

The Product Availability Matrix (PAM) only lists single editions of the product with the official name of SAP HANA, platform edition 2.0. This is also the only version available for download (although the previous edition, 1.0, is still available as well). PAM doesn't list any reference to a standard or enterprise edition, nor does it mention SAP HANA, express edition, as these editions are created for licensing purposes.

To know what is and what isn't included in each of the editions, consult the Feature Scope Description document, which is part of the SAP HANA, platform edition, documentation set. The guide includes an illustration of the scopes similar to Figure 2.7.

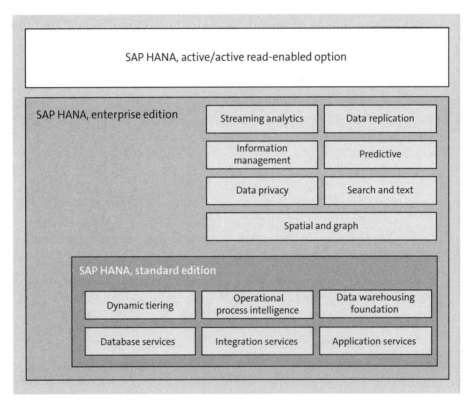

Figure 2.7 SAP HANA Feature Scope

There are slight changes with each release. For the SAP HANA 2.0 SPS 05 release, only the SAP HANA active/active read-enabled system replication feature is listed as a licensed option. The standard edition includes the core database, integration, and application services, each with its own feature list, such as *store and access data in-memory and column-based*, for example, for the database service. Dynamic tiering, operational process intelligence, and data warehousing foundation are optional components that require installation yet are included in the standard edition. Data privacy and spatial and graph, on the other hand, are included with every platform database installation and require no special configuration yet are licensed separately.

Technically, however, there is only a single license for the SAP HANA platform. This license doesn't enforce or enable commercial license editions or options and only specifies the amount of memory licensed; however, unless configured otherwise, this isn't enforced.

SAP HANA, express edition, is a special streamlined version of the platform edition designed to run on laptops and cloud-hosted virtual machines. It's a free edition for both development and productive use cases for up to 32 GB of RAM. You can expand SAP HANA, express edition, to 64-, 96-, and 128 GB with the purchase of an additional license from SAP Store. The express edition comes with a developer license and community support.

SAP HANA, runtime edition, refers to a special license to use SAP HANA as the database for SAP applications. This is documented in the SAP Licensing Guide.

Exam Tip

Unless you aim for a career in sales, you're not expected to be familiar with the licensing options of SAP HANA. However, you should be aware that, technically, there is only the platform edition of which the express edition is a special streamlined version.

Learn More

For more information on this topic, see the following references:

- Feature Scope Description for SAP HANA at *http://s-prs.co/v507811*
- SAP HANA, express edition (SAP Developer Center), at *https://developers.sap.com/hana*
- SAP Licensing Guide at *http://s-prs.co/v507812*

Software Components

In SAP terminology, software components are independently installable units. SAP HANA, platform edition, includes many components, as illustrated by Figure 2.8, which lists the components of the platform edition available for installation.

The mapping isn't always obvious. SAP HANA runtime tools, for example, refers to the SAP HANA database explorer. XS Runtime refers to the Java, Node.js, and Python buildpacks, whereas SAP HANA XS refers to the core SAP HANA XSA web applications provided by SAP.

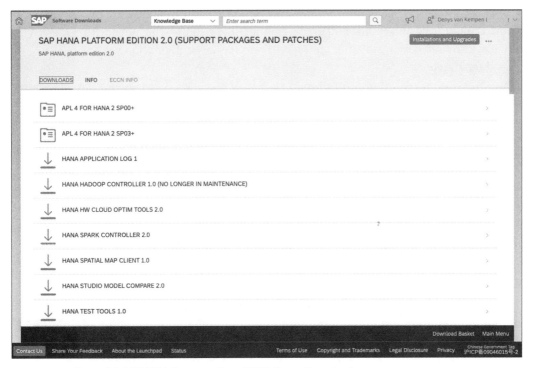

Figure 2.8 SAP HANA Components on SAP Software Downloads

The list of components differs per release. The following are the most common:

- SAP HANA Application Function Library (AFL) 2.0
- SAP HANA Client 2.0
- SAP HANA Cockpit 2.0
- SAP HANA Database 2.0
- SAP HANA demo model (SAP HANA Interactive Education [SHINE])
- SAP HANA studio (deprecated)
- XS Runtime, which includes the following applications:
  - SAP Web IDE
  - SAP HANA runtime tools
  - SAP HANA XS

There are component dependencies. The SAP HANA AFL plug-in needs to correspond to a specific SAP HANA database version. For the SAP HANA client, this is less strict. As of SAP HANA 2.0 SPS 04, only a single public release version is maintained, and SAP recommends that you adopt a recent SAP HANA client.

To complete the picture, we should also mention SAP liveCache used in SAP Supply Chain Management (SAP SCM) and SAP S/4HANA production planning and detailed scheduling (PP-DS). SAP liveCache is an in-memory object store technology, which, together with the row and column store, has been included with the platform from day one. The technology was originally developed for SAP Advanced Planning and Optimization (SAP APO) for SAP MaxDB.

> **Learn More**
>
> For more information about SAP liveCache, see KBA 2593571 – FAQ: SAP HANA Integrated liveCache. This technology isn't in scope for the exam.

Add-On Products

Not included on the list of SAP HANA components for the platform edition are related and dependent add-on products such as the following:

- SAP HANA accelerator for SAP ASE
- SAP HANA data warehousing foundation
- SAP HANA dynamic tiering
- SAP HANA smart data integration
- SAP HANA streaming analytics

Add-on products typically have their own documentation set on the SAP Help Portal, are shipped as a separate download set, and might require additional licenses. For the full list, check the PAM.

> **Exam Tip**
>
> The SAP HANA add-on products are out of scope for the exam.

System Architecture Overview

When you install the SAP HANA platform server (database) component, an SAP HANA system is created with a unique system identifier (SID) and instance number, as specified for the installation. If you add additional hosts and create a scale-out system, each host will share this SID and instance number. A default installation contains two databases: the system database and a tenant database. Additional tenant database can be added after the system is up and running.

As mentioned, there are two different environments to develop and deploy native applications for the SAP HANA platform. The SAP HANA XS, classic model is completely integrated and always installed with the server (although this functionality can be disabled). SAP HANA XSA, on the other hand, is a separate component that requires installation and supports dedicated hosts for the application server runtimes.

Figure 2.9 shows the **Database Directory** of SAP HANA cockpit with two databases listed: the system database with label **SYSTEMDB@HDB** and a tenant database with label **HDB@HDB** using the default name format. HDB is the SID. The initial tenant database, unless specified otherwise, uses the SID as the database name.

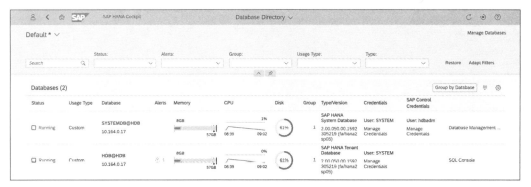

Figure 2.9 SAP HANA Cockpit: Database Directory

Now, let's dig deeper into the key components of the SAP HANA architecture.

Operating System Processes

Conceptually, the SAP HANA platform contains database, application, and integration services. Technically, these services are provided by a number of operating system processes. Some of these processes are essential and always up and running. Other processes are related to either shared services or optional components.

The Manage Services app in the SAP HANA cockpit displays the status of the different services of each database. Each service corresponds to an operating system process. Figure 2.10 and Figure 2.11 show a sample output for the system and tenant database, respectively. The exact services displayed will depend on the configuration and components installed.

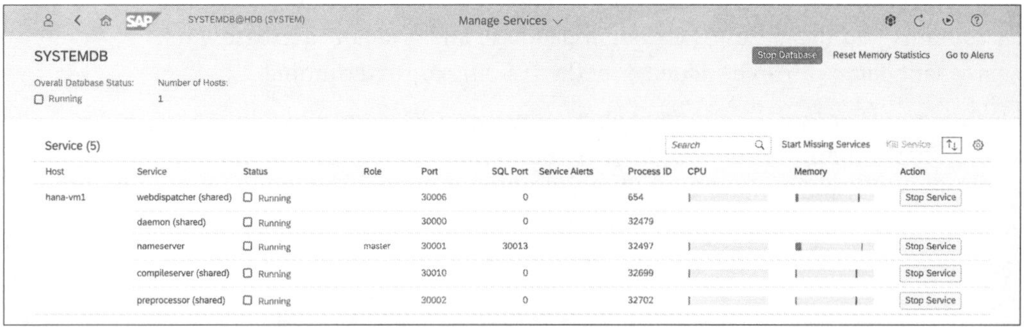

Figure 2.10 Manage Services: System Database

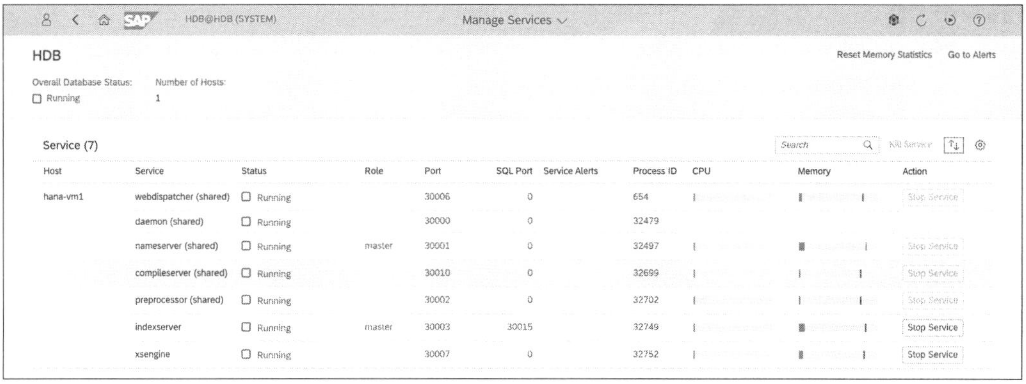

Figure 2.11 Manage Services: Tenant Database

The name server service hosts the system database. The corresponding operating system process is called hdbnameserver. You manage the SAP HANA system and each of the tenant databases from the system database. The name server owns the system topology, which means that it keeps track of the services running on the platform and their current role: worker or standby and master or slave. This is of particular relevance for multiple-host systems as you'll see in Chapter 9, when we cover scaling SAP HANA. The name server also manages system replication, a topic addressed in Chapter 12.

> **Note**
>
> In the documentation, the server component is written with spaces while the service name and operating system process are written without: hdbnameserver. HDB comes from one of the internal code names used for SAP HANA (NewDB is another one) and stands for hybrid database, referencing the combination of row, column, and object stores.

The index server service runs as the hdbindexserver operating system process and hosts the tenant database. There is an index server process for each database. The index server hosts both the row and column store engines.

The compile server and preprocessor service run as shared system processes for tenant databases with the respective operating system process names hdbcompileserver and hdbpreprocessor. The compile server compiles procedures and SQLScript programs, while the preprocessor supports text search and text extraction.

The SAP HANA XS engine service (hdbxsengine) hosts SAP HANA XS, classic model applications. You see this process typically together with web dispatcher (hdbwebdispatcher), which acts as a HTTP/S server. This process is similar to the SAP Web Dispatcher found on SAP NetWeaver systems. You can also configure the SAP HANA XS engine service to run embedded with the name and/or index server processes; in this case, it would not be listed. The same is true for the statistics server service (hdbstatisticsserver), which may be found listed on older SAP HANA systems but now typically runs embedded.

When the XS advanced runtime component is installed, the processes hdbcontroller, hdbxsuaaserver, and hdbxsexecagent will be added. Although technically independent, with SAP HANA XSA also comes the SAP HANA deployment infrastructure (HDI). The service is called the diserver (hdbdiserver).

To execute the AFL, the script server (hdbscriptserver) needs to be enabled. This is another shared service, but it's disabled by default and not displayed in Figure 2.10.

SAP HANA add-on products also come with their own services such as the extended store server (hdbesserver) for SAP HANA dynamic tiering and the data provisioning server (hdbdpserver) for SAP HANA smart data integration.

Each service has its own TCP port for internal communication. The name server, for example, always listens to 3xx01 where xx stands for the instance number. As the name server also performs database services, it also listens to a SQL port: 3xx13. This is the port used to make connections with database clients. Figure 2.10 shows both the SQL and internal port of the name server process.

The index server for the initial tenant database listens to SQL port 3xx15, but for all other tenants, the port range 3xx40–99 is reserved. Apart from a SQL port, each tenant also reserves a port for internal communication and one for HTTP—in all, three TCP ports per tenant. With a range of 60 ports available (40–99), this results in a limit of 20 database tenants. If this doesn't suffice, the range can be extended.

Learn More

Server components, ports, and connections are documented in the SAP HANA Administration Guide. For more detailed information, see KBA 2477204 – FAQ: SAP HANA Services and Ports.

System Startup Process

With the HDB info command, you can look at the SAP HANA processes from an operating system point of view, as shown in Figure 2.12. The output shows HDB info with process identifier (PID) 3504 as the parent process identifier (PPID) of the ps command (PID 3535). In other words, the HDB info command runs the ps with the fx flag and a number of additional parameters.

Similarly, you can see the process tree for the SAP HANA system HDB. The root process with PID 1 has started sapstart (PID 32472), and this, in turn, has started PID 32479, which is listed as the parent of all the hdb processes.

PID 32479 is the daemon process also shown in the Manage Services app in the SAP HANA cockpit. The operating system process isn't instantly recognizable as it's started in a special way, but, as shown in Figure 2.12, using the ls command shows that this does concern the hdbdaemon process.

```
hdbadm@hana-vm1:/usr/sap/HDB/HDB00> HDB info
USER         PID    PPID  %CPU        VSZ      RSS  COMMAND
hdbadm      3105    3104   0.0      14260     4208  -sh
hdbadm      3504    3105   0.0      13392     3456  \_ /bin/sh /usr/sap/HDB/HDB00/HDB info
hdbadm      3535    3504   0.0      34852     2868     \_ ps fx -U hdbadm -o user:8,pid:8,ppid:8,pcpu:5,vsz:10,rss:10,args
hdbadm     32472       1   0.0      22700     3004  sapstart pf=/hana/shared/HDB/profile/HDB_HDB00_hana-vm1
hdbadm     32479   32472   0.0     454628    70140  \_ /usr/sap/HDB/HDB00/hana-vm1/trace/hdb.sapHDB_HDB00 -d -nw -f /usr/sap/HDB/HDB00/h
hdbadm     32497   32479   4.2    6319912  3262312     \_ hdbnameserver
hdbadm     32699   32479   0.3    1482800   147720     \_ hdbcompileserver
hdbadm     32702   32479   0.3    1749048   172204     \_ hdbpreprocessor
hdbadm     32749   32479   5.9    6765096  3776948     \_ hdbindexserver -port 30003
hdbadm     32752   32479   1.0    4850200  1339532     \_ hdbxsengine -port 30007
hdbadm       654   32479   0.5    3453604   448720     \_ hdbwebdispatcher
hdbadm     12260       1   0.0    1822632    36012  /usr/sap/HDB/HDB00/exe/sapstartsrv pf=/hana/shared/HDB/profile/HDB_HDB00_hana-vm1 -D
hdbadm      2416       1   0.0     710080    50728  hdbrsutil --start --port 30003 --volume 3 --volumesuffix mnt00001/hdb00003.00003 --i
hdbadm      2028       1   0.0     710080    50880  hdbrsutil --start --port 30001 --volume 1 --volumesuffix mnt00001/hdb00001 --identif
hdbadm      1597       1   0.0      41380     4912  /usr/lib/systemd/systemd --user
hdbadm      1598    1597   0.0      86552     1760  \_ (sd-pam)
hdbadm@hana-vm1:/usr/sap/HDB/HDB00> ls -l /usr/sap/HDB/HDB00/hana-vm1/trace/hdb.sapHDB_HDB00
lrwxrwxrwx 1 hdbadm sapsys 32 Aug  6 11:55 /usr/sap/HDB/HDB00/hana-vm1/trace/hdb.sapHDB_HDB00 -> /usr/sap/HDB/HDB00/exe/hdbdaemon
hdbadm@hana-vm1:/usr/sap/HDB/HDB00> ▮
```

Figure 2.12 HDB Information

On UNIX and Linux operating systems, the daemon process runs as a background process and not as an interactive user process (similar to a service on the Windows operating system). For SAP HANA, the daemon process acts a "watchdog" and has the responsibility to restart any of the hdb* processes, which is why all the hdb* processes run as child processes.

Figure 2.13 shows the different components involved with the SAP HANA startup sequence.

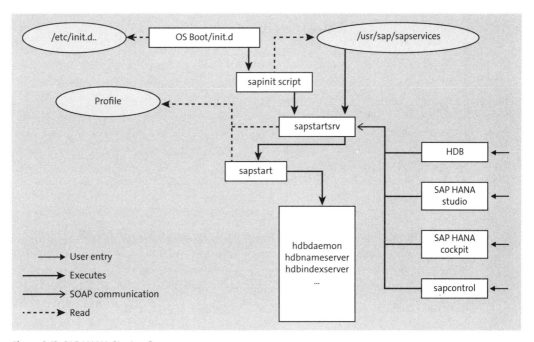

Figure 2.13 SAP HANA Startup Process

The sequence starts with the operating system calling the sapinit script, which parses the sapservices file. This file contains an entry pointing to the sapstartsrv executable and the system profile with flags -D -u hdbadm to indicate that the process needs to run as a daemon for the hdbadm user.

```
/usr/sap/HDB/HDB00/exe/sapstartsrv pf=/usr/sap/HDB/SYS/profile/
HDB_HDB00_hana-vm1 -D -u hdbadm
```

The profile format is <SID>_HDB<instance_number>_<host>; here, HDB_HDB00_ hana-vm1 indicates that the SID is HDB, the instance number 00, and the host name hana-vm1. The instance number is always prefixed with HDB, but this isn't a reserved word. You also see the SID and HDB<instance number> reflected in the path /usr/sap/HDB/HDB00/exe.

Figure 2.14 illustrates the contents of the profile file. First, a number of operating system environment variables are defined, such as SAP_RETRIEVAL_PATH, followed by the export (SETENV). You can see the SID, instance number, and host name defined and also whether the instance should start with the service with parameter AUTOSTART=1. This parameter is set during the installation. The profile also points to the personal security environment (PSE) for the server, which is a topic we'll return to in Chapter 10.

```
hdbadm@hana-vm1:/usr/sap/HDB/HDB00> cat /usr/sap/HDB/SYS/profile/HDB_HDB00_hana-vm1
SAP_RETRIEVAL_PATH = $(DIR_INSTANCE)/$(SAPLOCALHOST)
DIR_HOME = $(SAP_RETRIEVAL_PATH)/trace
DIR_PERF = $(SAP_RETRIEVAL_PATH)/trace
DIR_LOGGING = $(SAP_RETRIEVAL_PATH)/log
SECUDIR = $(SAP_RETRIEVAL_PATH)/sec
Autostart=1
SETENV_00 = PATH=$(DIR_INSTANCE)/exe:%(PATH)
SETENV_01 = SAP_RETRIEVAL_PATH=$(SAP_RETRIEVAL_PATH)
SETENV_02 = PYTHONPATH=$(SAP_RETRIEVAL_PATH):$(DIR_EXECUTABLE):$(DIR_INSTALL)/global/hd
SAPSYSTEMNAME = HDB
SAPLOCALHOST = hana-vm1
SAPSYSTEM = 00
INSTANCE_NAME = HDB00
DIR_CT_RUN = $(DIR_EXE_ROOT)/linuxx86_64/hdb
DIR_EXECUTABLE = $(DIR_INSTANCE)/exe
DIR_PROFILE = $(DIR_INSTALL)/profile
ccms/enable_agent = 0
service/status_procs = hdbdaemon
service/protectedwebmethods = SDEFAULT
service/init_system_pki = ON
ssl/server_pse = $(SECUDIR)/SAPSSLS.pse
ssl/client_pse = $(SECUDIR)/SAPSSLC.pse
```

Figure 2.14 SAP HANA Profile

The sapstartsrv service executes the sapstart process with the profile, which in turns starts the instance with hdbdaemon (assuming auto start is enabled). Once up and running, this daemon operating system process provides no services other than a watchdog service. The daemon monitors and controls the SAP HANA instance state and automatically restarts any stopped process.

Learn More

Basis administrators will have recognized the startup process as it's common to SAP Net-Weaver systems. The SAP HANA startup process isn't documented in the SAP HANA documentation. For a step-by-step explanation, see the following SAP Community blog posts:

- SAP HANA Under The Hood: SAPInit and SAPStartSrv at *http://s-prs.co/v507813*
- SAP HANA Under The Hood: HDB at *http://s-prs.co/v507814*

Index Server

The index server service is the main database service. The architecture diagram in Figure 2.15 shows the different components, which is a word used in multiple contexts in the SAP HANA terminology. There is a component responsible for connection and session management, authentication, authorization, and metadata management. There are different engines, runtimes, and relational stores.

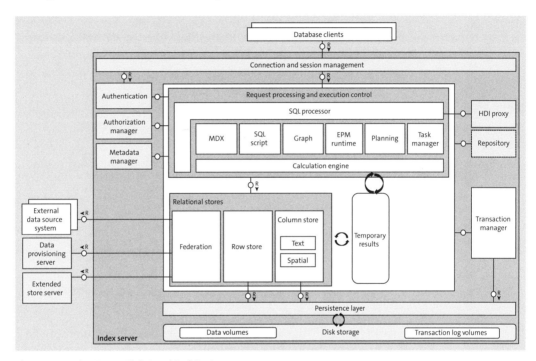

Figure 2.15 Index Server High-Level Architecture

The persistence layer is responsible for making sure that should there be a power loss, this never results in a data loss, with different volumes for data and the transaction log. Whenever a transaction commits, this is persisted in a log file. At intervals, data changes are also written to the data volume at events called savepoints. A *savepoint* is a consistent image of the database on storage and can be used as a snapshot. We return to this topic in Chapter 11.

Database Startup Sequence

We already looked at how the SAP HANA system starts from an operating system point of view, but how does this work after control has passed to the database? The following steps are executed in sequence:

1. Open data and log volumes.
2. Initialize persistence (storage).
3. Load row store tables into memory.

4. Replay logs to redo all changes performed since the last savepoint. Roll back uncommitted changes.

5. Synchronize all services to ensure transactional consistency, and execute a savepoint.

6. Open the SQL port for remote access. The database is now "started."

7. Load column-store tables into memory column by column only upon use ("lazy loading"), except for the columns (or tables) marked for preload.

Recent SAP HANA releases have added enhancements to the database startup sequence. For example, to reduce the load time of the main store of column tables, persistent memory was introduced with SAP HANA SPS 03. It's also possible to configure SAP HANA to keep the row store in memory during restarts.

Learn More

You're not expected to be intimately familiar with the startup process but if you're curious and want to learn more, see KBA 222217 – How-To: Troubleshooting SAP HANA Startup Times.

Memory

As no surprise, memory is a key resource for an in-memory database. The SAP HANA memory manager manages the memory pools, which Linux operating system tools (e.g., top) may not report accurately; therefore, always rely on SAP HANA regarding memory usage statistics.

Total used memory is literally the amount of memory in use. This counter can be queried using SQL and is displayed in tools such as SAP HANA cockpit, as illustrated Figure 2.16. A small portion of this is for the program code and stack. The rest is for the row and column store, computations, and database management.

SAP HANA periodically saves a copy of used memory to the statistics system table so you can monitor resource usage over time. This includes peak used memory, which will be a relevant counter for your SAP HANA license because it's memory-based. We return to the topic of memory usage in Chapter 13.

Most of the memory used by SAP HANA is for column store tables. Column store tables are characteristic for OLAP-type databases and optimized for read operations through compression and sorting. Single row updates are very expensive operations on column store tables as you need to decompress, modify, sort, and compress the data. For this reason, a delta structure was added to handle modifications in SAP HANA, as depicted in Figure 2.17.

Changes are written to the delta on insert only. During asynchronous (background) delta-merge operations, main and delta are combined into a new main, while writes are written to a newly created delta for that table, as shown in Figure 2.18.

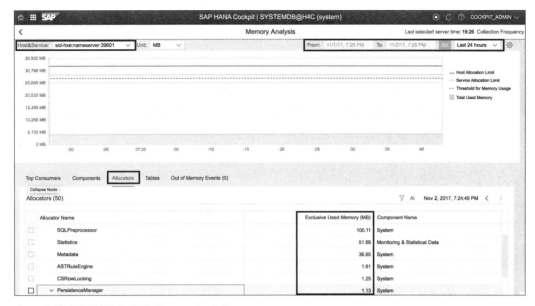

Figure 2.16 SAP HANA Cockpit: Memory Analysis

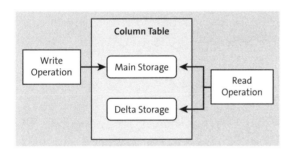

Figure 2.17 Main Storage and Delta Storage

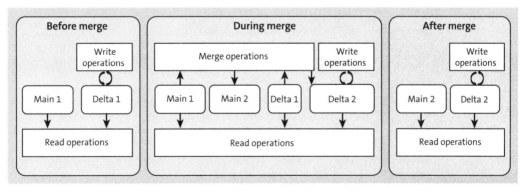

Figure 2.18 Delta Merge Operations

Delta merges require a significant amount of memory as main, delta, and the merged result (plus some overhead) need to be stored in memory. If there are columns partially unloaded, they will need to be loaded into memory as well. When the delta merge operation is finished, it's persisted (written to storage). Besides requiring a significant amount of memory, delta merges may involve considerable read and write operations to storage, which makes this a performance-sensitive operation. Delta merges are executed at the partition level, which is a topic we'll return to when we discuss SAP HANA scale-out systems in Chapter 9.

The different merge motivations are as follows:

- Auto merge controlled by parameter `auto_merge_on`
- Smart merge controlled by parameter `smart_merged_enabled`
- Hard merge with `MERGE DELTA OF <table_name>` when sufficient resources available
- Forced merge with `MERGE DELTA OF <table_name> WITH PARAMETERS ('FORCED_MERGE' = 'ON')`
- Critical merge if auto merge is disabled and the size of the delta grows to large

Manual activation of the merge process doesn't trigger any compression optimization of the new main storage area of the table.

Learn More

Memory usage is documented in the SAP HANA Administration Guide. For more detailed discussion, see the paper on the topic and FAQ articles:

- "SAP HANA Memory Usage Explained" at *http://s-prs.co/v507815*
- KBA 1999997 – FAQ: SAP HANA Memory
- KBA 2057046 – FAQ: SAP HANA Delta Merges

Important Terminology

For this exam objective, you're expected to understand the following terms:

- **Accelerators**
  Accelerator may refer to the sidecar use case of SAP HANA where the in-memory platform is used to accelerate reporting and analysis for production systems as well as to specific applications such as the CO-PA accelerator for SAP HANA or products such as the SAP HANA accelerator for SAP ASE.

- **Advanced analytics**
  Data modeling with "regular" analytics is a core feature of the database combining online transactional processing (OLTP) and online analytical processing (OLAP). Under advanced analytics, SAP HANA bundles spatial, graph, series data, document store, search and text analysis, predictive analytics, machine learning, and business functions. With SAP HANA, this type of data processing doesn't require data replication and duplication with a separate tier (server) because all processing is performed on the same platform with all enterprise data stored in memory for best performance.

- **Appliance**
  SAP HANA was originally only available as an appliance with predefined hardware and preconfigured software provided by SAP hardware partners. At the time, SAP HANA was marketed as the High Performance Analytical Appliance reminiscent of the High Performance Analytics tagline used for one of SAP HANA precursors, SAP BW Accelerator. The appliance came in T-shirt sizes but because requested a more custom solution, the tailored data center integration (TDI) program was launched. In time, SAP HANA was also made available for cloud deployments and as database-as-a-service (DBaaS) with SAP HANA Cloud.

- **Column store tables**
  Column store tables are characteristic for OLAP-type databases and optimized for read operations through compression and sorting. Single row updates are very expensive operations on column store tables as you need to decompress, modify, sort, and compress the data. SAP HANA adds a row store like a delta storage area, which is regularly merged with the main column store to take away this limitation.

- **Components**
  Component is a term that may describe different concepts depending on the context. From the SAP NetWeaver terminology, we inherit component as a synonym for application, as in multiple components, one database (MCOD). In the context of installation, components refer to independently installable units such as the SAP HANA client or Application Function Library (AFL). Components may also refer to architecture concepts, for example, when we describe the persistence layer component of the index server, which is itself one of the core components of an SAP HANA system.

- **Deployment types**
  Deployment types can reference appliance, on-premises, cloud, or "technical" deployments with tenant databases, MCOD, MCOS, and virtualization.

- **Hybrid database (HDB)**
  SAP HANA is a HDB combining row store, column store, and object store (SAP liveCache). HDB is also a script with command-line administration commands (HDB start).

- **Hybrid transactional/analytical processing (HTAP)**
  HTAP combines OLTP and OLAP workloads. SAP research indicated that typical enterprise workloads are neither pure OLTP nor OLAP, but a combination. This discovery was one of the motivations behind the development of SAP HANA.

- **Index server**
  The index server component provides the indexserver service and runs the hdbindexserver operating process. This component contains both the row and column store processing engine as its persistence (storage). In a tenant database system, each tenant database is hosted by a separate index server process. In a multiple-host system, each host may run one or more index server processes. A tenant database may span multiple hosts. In other words, multiple index server

processes may support a single tenant database. The name goes back to the text retrieval and information extraction (TREX) search engine component of the SAP NetWeaver platform, one of the original building blocks of the SAP HANA in-memory database.

- **In-memory technology**
  SAP HANA leverages the advancements made in hardware technology, such as multicore processors enabling massive parallel processing (MPP) and systems supporting very large memory configurations, and combines this with several software innovations such as a combined column and row store, sophisticated compression algorithms, partitioning, insert-only on the delta store, and the removal of aggregate tables and other common database structures that once served to optimize data access to create a modern in-memory database platform.

- **Multiple components, one database (MCOD)**
  MCOD is a deployment that supports installing two or more applications (components) in a single SAP HANA database. This deployment predates tenant databases and addresses the issue of system overhead, but it doesn't provide database isolation.

- **Multiple components, one system (MCOS)**
  MCOS is a deployment that supports installing two or more applications (components) on a single (operating) system. This deployment predates tenant databases and addresses the issue of application isolation but not system overhead on single-host systems. On multiple-host systems, MCOS deployments can help to reduce system overhead on the standby hosts.

- **Multitenant database container (MDC)**
  An MDC system is an older term used for what is now called tenant databases in the documentation. You still may find references to MDC in KBAs and blog posts. Tenant databases were introduced with SAP HANA 1.0 SPS 10 and support running multiple isolated databases inside a single SAP HANA system. Each database has its own catalog, security, and persistence.

- **Online analytical processing (OLAP)**
  OLAP is one of two standard database workloads. A typical OLAP workload is characterized by a limited number of users processing large amounts of data for analysis and reporting mainly through read operations. OLAP is column oriented.

- **Online transactional processing (OLTP)**
  OLTP is one of two standard database workloads. Typically, this workload involves a large number of users reading and modifying a limited amount of data as transactions. OLTP is row oriented. The alternative to online processing is offline batch processing.

- **SAP HANA extended application services, advanced model (SAP HANA XSA)**
  SAP HANA XSA is a second implementation of the SAP HANA XS concept using a distribution compatible with the Cloud Foundry environment hosted on SAP

Cloud Platform. The initial SAP HANA XS implementation (once referred to as SAP HANA XS, classic model) is deprecated for the current SAP HANA 2.0 release.

- **SAP HANA extended application services (SAP HANA XS)**
  SAP HANA XS provides native (built-in) application server functionality to the database. This serves as an alternative to the common three-tier architecture separating presentation, business logic, and storage. With the application server tightly integrated with the database, you no longer have to move data between tiers, losing precious time, but can execute the processing where the data resides. This is also referred to as code pushdown.

- **System identifier (SID)**
  Each SAP HANA system has a unique SID using three alphanumerical characters, for example, HDB, A01, or DB2. The first character needs to be a letter, and some combinations are restricted (e.g., SAP or IBM). Each SAP HANA system also has a two-digit instance number [00–99]. Multiple-host systems share the SID and instance number.

- **System types**
  SAP HANA supports two system types: single-host and multiple-host. A multiple-host system is also known as a scale-out environment or a distributed system. These terms are used synonymously.

- **Tailored data center integration (TDI)**
  The TDI program was initiated by customer demand to support customized (tailored) SAP HANA installations to complement or supplement SAP HANA as an appliance, which came with fixed T-shirt sizes. The SAP HANA hardware directory and the SAP Certified Technology Associate certification are cornerstones of the TDI program.

- **Three-tier architecture**
  Traditional architecture for web applications succeeding the older two-tier client/server architecture. The responsibilities of the three tiers are as follows: client for the UI rendering, application server for business logic processing, and database for data persistence. With a built-in application server and an in-memory architecture, SAP HANA enables you to process the data where it resides and avoids wasting precious time by pumping data from the persistence layer to the mid-tier for processing.

Practice Questions

These practice questions will help you evaluate your understanding of the topics covered in this chapter. The questions shown are similar in nature to those found on the certification examination. Although none of these questions will be found on the exam itself, they will allow you to review your knowledge of the subject. Select the correct answers, and then check the completeness of your answers in the "Practice Question Answers and Explanations" section. Remember that on the exam, you must select all correct answers and only correct answers to receive credit for the question.

1. What are examples of software innovations leveraged by the SAP HANA in-memory database? (There are three correct answers.)

☐ **A.** NoSQL

☐ **B.** Hybrid database combining both row and column store

☐ **C.** Separation of computing and storage

☐ **D.** Partitioning and parallel processing

☐ **E.** Compression

2. What are the advantages of columnar tables? (There are three correct answers.)

☐ **A.** Don't require compression

☐ **B.** Eliminate need of additional indexes

☐ **C.** Eliminate need of materialized aggregates

☐ **D.** Simplify parallel execution

☐ **E.** Enable in-memory storage (row tables require persistence)

3. What is the significance of multicore processors?

☐ **A.** Provides support for multitenancy

☐ **B.** Provides MPP support for column store tables

☐ **C.** Provides high availability by removing a single point of failure (SPOF)

4. Which SAP HANA capabilities support code pushdown? (There are two correct answers.)

☐ **A.** Advanced analytical processing features such as spatial, graph, text analysis, and predictive analytics

☐ **B.** SAP HANA extended application services (SAP HANA XS)

☐ **C.** SAP HANA used as primary persistence for SAP NetWeaver-based applications

☐ **D.** SAP HANA accelerator for SAP ASE

5. Which deployment types are made obsolete by tenant databases? (There are two correct answers.)

☐ **A.** Single container systems

☐ **B.** MDC systems

☐ **C.** MCOD

☐ **D.** MCOS

6. Which license is required to activate SAP HANA system replication active/ active read-enabled?

☐ **A.** Standard edition license with the SAP HANA system replication option.

☐ **B.** Enterprise edition license with the SAP HANA system replication option.

☐ **C.** Platform edition license.

☐ **D.** Capabilities aren't activated with a license.

7. Which component has a strict release dependency on the SAP HANA server (database) release?

☐ **A.** XS Runtime 1

☐ **B.** SAP HANA Client 2.0

☐ **C.** SAP HANA Cockpit 2.0

☐ **D.** SAP HANA AFL 2.0

8. Which services are shared? (There are two correct answers.)

☐ **A.** `compileserver`

☐ **B.** `nameserver`

☐ **C.** `preprocessor`

☐ **D.** `xsengine`

9. What is the default SQL port of the name server?

☐ **A.** 5xx13

☐ **B.** 3xx01

☐ **C.** 3xx15

☐ **D.** 3xx13

10. What makes delta merge operations sensitive to overall system performance?

☐ **A.** Delta merge operations cause an increase in memory usage as data needs to be loaded and the main and delta storage areas copied.

☐ **B.** Delta merge operations cause an increase in I/O operations for persistence and the redo log.

☐ **C.** Both A and B.

☐ **D.** As tables are locked during delta merge operations, this causes lock waits and transaction time-outs.

Practice Question Answers and Explanations

1. Correct answers: **B, D, E**

   SAP HANA combined recent hardware innovations with five software innovations: row and column store, no aggregate tables, insert only on the delta store, compression, and partitioning.

   Answer A is incorrect because, although a document store was added to the architecture with SAP HANA 2.0 SPS 01 in 2017, a NoSQL database wasn't part of the original implementation of SAP HANA. Answer C is incorrect because the separation of computing and storage is a characteristic of cloud computing. Although SAP HANA is available in the cloud, it was originally designed as an appliance for on-premise implementations.

2. Correct answers: **B, C, D**

   Columnar storage provides much better performance for search and aggregate operations as the data is stored contiguously and compressed. This eliminates the need for additional indexes in many cases as a column store table is similar to an index structure. Column store tables also make it possible to calculate aggregates on the fly (in real-time) without the use of precalculated materialized aggregates. Because the data is already sorted (by time dimension, geography, or other), column store data can easily be partitioned for parallel processing.

   Answer A is incorrect because column tables provide much higher compression rates compared with row store tables. Depending on the data it contains, different compression methods can be used. To be able to store the data efficiently and take advantage of parallel processing and better performance, data needs to be compressed. Answer E is incorrect because both row and column store tables can be stored in memory, and both table types require persistence to guarantee no data loss in case of power loss.

3. Correct answer: **B**

   When it was no longer possible to improve CPU clock speed due to physical limits, processor manufacturers (e.g., Intel) introduced the first dual-core and later multicore processors with as many as 64 or 72 cores. Column store tables and table partitions are very suitable candidates for parallel processing as each core can process separate parts (e.g., huge fact-type tables with sales data partitioned by date, region, product, etc.).

   Answer A is incorrect because SAP HANA doesn't uses multicore processors to implement tenant databases. Answer C is incorrect because HA isn't a characteristic of multicore processors. To limit the CPU as SPOF, you would use multiple CPUs, not multicore processors.

4. Correct answers: **A, B**

   Code pushdown refers to pushing data processing down to where the data resides, that is, the database, instead of moving the data to a processing middle tier, such as an application server or special-purpose processing engine (e.g., spatial or graph).

   Answer C is incorrect because using SAP HANA as the primary persistence for SAP NetWeaver-based applications references a traditional three-tier architecture. Note that this doesn't apply to more recent products such as SAP S/4HANA, SAP BW/4HANA, and other SAP business applications specifically re-architected for SAP HANA, as these products implement the code pushdown paradigm. Answer D is incorrect as data is replicated with this product.

5. Correct answers: **A, C**

   As of SAP HANA 2.0, the original single container system architecture is no longer available, although the database mode is still supported for SAP HANA 1.0.

   Compared to MCOD, tenant databases not only reduce system overhead but also provide strong database isolation. This makes MCOD use cases exceedingly rare.

   Answer B is incorrect because multitenant database container (MDC) system is only an older term for tenant databases and refers to the same technology or deployment type. Answer D is incorrect because MCOS, also known as multi-SID deployments, are still relevant in particular for multiple-host systems.

6. Correct answer: **D**

   Technically, there is only a single license: SAP HANA, platform edition. This license contains the hardware key of the system with SID and can't be transferred. The license also references the licensed amount of memory although by default this limit isn't enforced.

   Answers A, B, and C are incorrect because you can't activate features with a license.

7. Correct answer: **D**

   Most components have a dependency on the release of the SAP HANA server (database), and this includes the AFL component, which enables the execution of C++ functions inside the database.

   Answer A is incorrect because the component XS Runtime 1, as listed on SAP Software Downloads, references the SAP HANA XSA runtime, which doesn't have a strict release dependency on the server, and you can update the SAP HANA XSA runtime without updating the server. Answer B is incorrect because the SAP HANA client doesn't have a strict release dependency on the server. SAP recommends to always use the latest SAP HANA client regardless of the server version used. Answer C is incorrect because the SAP HANA cockpit runs on a separate system (although installing the product inside the database is also supported).

> **Exam Tip**
>
> Tough question? You're not expected to be familiar with all the component names and their functionality as listed on the SAP Software Downloads on the SAP ONE Support portal. However, you should be aware that component dependencies exist. You should also understand why a component tightly integrated with the server, such as AFL, has dependencies, while a loosely coupled component, such as the SAP HANA client, doesn't. We'll cover this topic in more detail in the next chapter.

8. Correct answers: **A, C**

   The services of the compile server and preprocessor are shared by all database tenants on a system. Refer to Figure 2.10 and Figure 2.11.

   Answer B is incorrect because `nameserver` hosts the system database and owns the system topology. Answer D is incorrect because the `XSengine` hosts the SAP HANA XS, classic model application server runtime for a single tenant database. This service can also be configured to run embedded with the index server.

9. Correct answer: **D**

   The default SQL port of the name server is 3*xx*13.

   Answer A is the HTTP port of the SAP start service. Answer B is the internal communication port of the name server. Answer C is the SQL port of the initial tenant database (index server). Subsequent databases use a port in the range 3*xx*40–99.

10. Correct answer: **C**

    Delta merges cause an increase in both memory consumption and I/O operations, making the operation sensitive to overall system performance.

    Answer D is incorrect because the table is only briefly locked during the delta merge operation, and this doesn't affect overall system performance.

Takeaway

After reading this chapter, you should be familiar with the benefits of SAP HANA as in-memory platform and understand the common use cases or scenarios. The pros and cons of the different technical deployment types, such as tenant databases and MCOS for scale-out systems, should be clear, as well as how this works with editions and options. We covered the different components of the platform, the idea behind code pushdown, and the different parts of the system architecture with all of its services and processes. The startup sequence of an SAP HANA system and the database was briefly described, and we also introduced the components of the index server and how memory is used.

Summary

In this first exam topic chapter, we covered the essentials of the system architecture and refreshed the key concepts. On several occasions, we stated that would return to the topic in a subsequent chapter for a more detailed coverage. Although you only may get a few questions about this material on the exam, the overall concepts are important to understand, not only for the remainder of this book but also for any SAP HANA technical consultant-related job roles.

In the next two chapters, we describe the SAP HANA installation process. As explained, the TDI program requires both certified hardware and certified technology consultants to perform the installation, and this kicked off the program for SAP HANA certification. It's no surprise then that installation is still a major topic area for the exam. First, we describe the prerequisites, preparations, and sizing. The other chapter covers the installation and update itself.

Chapter 3
Installation Preparation

Techniques You'll Master

- Understanding SAP HANA sizing and how to use the Quick Sizer tool

- Explaining hardware and software requirements and how to use the hardware configuration check tool

- Using the Product Availability Matrix (PAM) and the SAP HANA hardware directory

- Describing network and persistence configuration

- Understanding the recommended file system configuration

In this chapter and the next, we'll cover the SAP HANA installation topic. To keep the size of the chapters balanced and digestible, we've separated the material of this topic area into two chapters: one for the preparation and one for the actual installation. For those already familiar with the SAP HANA documentation, this roughly corresponds to the SAP HANA Master Guide for this chapter and the SAP HANA Installation and Update Guide for the next.

Real-World Scenario

Performing an SAP HANA installation isn't rocket science. Even installing a multiple-host system with standby hosts for high availability (HA) isn't difficult and requires little time if the environment is properly prepared. Before rolling up your sleeves and getting your hands dirty, a little reflection and preparation is necessary. How should you size your system such that you get the expected performance boost from running your applications on SAP HANA not only right from the start but also in the future? What hardware should you select? How should you configure and harden the operating system, and which SAP hardware and software partners can assist you with this task?

Preparing an SAP HANA installation needs to be understood from a business perspective. This is addressed with sizing and making sure that the system performs and continues to perform as expected. But you also need to consider the installation preparation from a technical point of view, and this covers the actual hardware and software configuration.

Exam Tip

For most of this topic area, we stay at the overview level as this exam is about SAP HANA technology and not about Linux system administration. This means that for the exam, you're not expected to know how to turn off kernel samepage merging (KSM), but you might be expected to know where such a requirement might be documented.

Topic and Objectives

Sizing is a challenging topic as it isn't extensively documented in the SAP HANA guides but instead in a large selection of SAP Notes, blogs, and other resources, which are not all publicly accessible or up to date. The same is true for the operating system preparations, mostly documented in SAP Notes and in the relevant guides from SUSE, Red Hat, IBM, Cisco, Dell, and many others. With so much information at our disposal, it's easy to get lost. You can use this chapter as a guide to stay on track. We'll refresh you on most important concepts and cover what you need to know for the exam. This includes the following topics:

- SAP HANA sizing, including greenfield and brownfield sizing, appliances, tailored data center integration (TDI), Quick Sizer, and expert sizing, with a special focus on memory sizing
- Hardware and software, including IBM Power Systems, Linux, Product Availability Matrix (PAM), the SAP HANA hardware directory, and the hardware configuration check tool
- Network and storage configuration
- Recommended file system layout

Note

This topic area was listed with medium weight (8%–12%) for most editions of the exam but gained some weight since the SPS 04 version due to the split into a topic area on installation preparations and on the actual installation. With 80 questions in total, you can expect about 8 questions each. As mentioned before, keep in mind that the exam guide states this can change at any time, so always check online for any updates.

Learn More

We already recommended that you browse the SAP HANA Master Guide (2.0 SPS 05) (*http://s-prs.co/v507816*) in the first chapter. This guide is also the best supplementary resource to prepare an SAP HANA installation and you should be familiar with how it's structured and what type of information it documents. Of particular relevance is the "Important SAP Notes" section because these notes contain essential information.

The list of notes is long and includes release notes for the platform and the database, information about the maintenance strategy, supported operating systems, operating system guidelines, and much more. Anticipate that it will take some time to digest this material as each note typically points to other notes with additional information. As we describe the key topics in this chapter, we'll also point to the most relevant notes for you to study.

Key Concepts Refresher

In this section, we'll highlight the most important concepts for preparation of an SAP HANA installation, starting with the deployment model as this has the biggest impact on sizing and other "hot" topics for this part of the exam.

SAP HANA 2.0 SPS 05: What's New?

Although each support package stack (SPS) release comes with a technical update, on a more conceptual level, the installation process and preparation requirements are identical for all SAP HANA 2.0 releases. If you have some experience with installing an earlier SAP HANA version, the learning curve for this and the next chapter will be small.

Delivery Models

In Chapter 2, we already mentioned that for the first three years, SAP HANA was only available as an appliance: predefined hardware with preconfigured software provided by certified SAP hardware partners. In the appliance delivery model, the initial setup is performed by the hardware partner while the customer takes ownership for maintenance and operations. Appliances are standardized and optimized but may require changing IT operation processes and introducing limitations regarding hardware flexibility (single-purpose use case).

The tailored data center integration (TDI) program responded to customer requests for more flexibility. TDI enables customers to integrate SAP HANA into the data center using custom assembled hardware and offers more choice regarding the operating system and processor architecture. TDI also supports virtualization. There have been different phases in the TDI program, but you're not expected to be familiar with its history and all the ramifications of the program.

In the early days, appliance sizing was done with T-shirt sizes (small, medium, large), and hence the "tailored" alternative provided by TDI reflects a more custom, made-to-measure approach that enables SAP HANA customers to reuse existing hardware or repurpose hardware after upgrades, to use preferred storage solutions, or to implement alternative processor architectures such as IBM Power instead of Intel.

Learn More

For more information about TDI, see the following:

- SAP HANA Tailored Data Center Integration (2017) at *http://s-prs.co/v507817*
- SAP HANA Tailored Data Center Integration FAQ (2018) at *http://s-prs.co/v507818*

Exam Tip

For the exam, you need to understand the differences between an appliance and the TDI approach and understand the consequences for sizing, but you don't need to memorize the specifics (different phases, technical details).

Sizing

Cloud computing provides elasticity that enables you to scale up and down according to demand. For the systems where you host in your own data centers on premise, you need to invest time and resources into sizing. The best time to start is the early stages of a project. SAP landscapes typically require a significant hardware investment, and SAP HANA is no exception with configurations for production systems requiring multicore high-end processor architectures into the terabytes of memory. Allocate too much, and your capital is locked up in hardware that as an asset has a quick write-off. Allocate too little, and the end users might get frustrated with slow performance, jobs taking forever to run, and with the service hotline under stress.

The objective of sizing is to translate business requirements into hardware requirements and determine the right configuration for a given workload. This is an iterative process, "rinse and repeat," and results in specifications for CPU, memory, storage space, and throughput for both storage and network, also referred to as the input/output (I/O) capacity.

We'll explore sizing for different implementations, as well as the Quick Sizer tool and memory sizing, in the following sections.

Greenfield, Brownfield, and Expert Sizing

Sizing for new implementations is called greenfield, and sizing for existing landscapes that require a system upgrade or migration is known as brownfield. For regular greenfield and brownfield sizing, standard tools such as the Quick Sizer and sizing guidelines can be used. For nonstandard situations of more complicated scenarios, you may need to involve an expert sizing service from SAP or one of its implementation partners as this requires significant expertise and experience.

For new SAP software implementations, you first need to distinguish whether to size for an SAP HANA appliance or for an installation under the TDI program. For appliances, you only need to consider the amount of RAM (memory). For TDI, you also have to consider processor, network, and storage.

Exam Tip

Check the SAP HANA In-Memory Database Sizing Guideline (PDF) document attached to SAP Note 1514966 – Sizing SAP In-Memory Database. The latest version is from August 2013 and describes generic sizing considerations, for example, for the SAP HANA as data mart use case with SAP ERP data replication. The note also provides a formula for disk space, but for this, also see the SAP HANA Storage Requirements paper (*http://s-prs.co/v507819*) for TDI.

The memory sizing formula stipulates the following:

$$\text{RAM} = ((\text{source data footprint} + \text{dynamic objects}) / 7) * 2$$

Here, 7 is the assumed compression factor of the SAP HANA database, and 2 is the assumed compression factor of the source database.

For disk, the formula proposes the following:

- Size data volume = (1.2 * net data size on disk)
- Size log volume = (0.5 * RAM) | max 512GB
- Size shared volume (binaries) = (1 * RAM) | max 1024GB
- Size shared volume (distributed) = (1 * RAM) per 4 hosts
- Size backup = (size data + size log) * backup cycle

For brownfield sizing, dedicated SAP Notes document exactly what you need to know for each of the applications (which falls beyond the scope of this exam).

There are notes for SAP Business Suite, SAP S/4HANA, and SAP BW/4HANA, as well as for non-SAP NetWeaver-based applications. These notes typically have one or more SQL scripts attached that report the sizing recommendations. Additional information can be found in the sizing guides listed on the SAP Help Portal under **SAP In-Memory Computing Sizing Guidelines**.

Brownfield sizing is also required when you need to migrate existing systems running SAP applications from any database (AnyDB) to SAP HANA. Although not an official term, AnyDB is often used to refer to the other supported databases. Sometimes this only concerns non-SAP databases such as Oracle, Microsoft SQL Server, or IBM DB2, to name the most common ones. However, AnyDB also includes SAP Adaptive Server Enterprise (SAP ASE) and SAP MaxDB. We return to this topic in Chapter 14.

The use cases described in Chapter 2 also impact the sizing exercise. SAP HANA as data mart has different resource requirements compared to SAP HANA as database (primary persistence) for SAP NetWeaver-based applications. SAP HANA options such as dynamic tiering or integration with SAP HANA streaming analytics require additional considerations and expertise not covered by standard tooling. This also applies to more complex business requirements such as system consolidation or system carve-out, when you need to remove a company, or more complex technical objectives not yet fully incorporated into the sizers, for example, the usage of persistent memory (PMEM).

> **Learn More**
>
> The SAP HANA Master Guide lists the SAP Notes to consider for migration sizing of the different SAP applications. For more general information about this topic, see *http://sap.com/sizing*. Most of the material will be beyond the scope of the exam, but we can recommend the technical articles and the SAP HANA sizing decision tree at *http://s-prs.co/v507821*.
>
> Another important source of information is the SAP In-Memory Computing Sizing Guidelines document (*http://s-prs.co/v507820*) listing sizing recommendations for specific SAP applications powered by SAP HANA. See, for example, the "Sizing Approaches for SAP HANA" best practice document.

Quick Sizer

There are different versions of the Quick Sizer tool. For the exam, we're only concerned with the version for SAP HANA. Although you can use the Quick Sizer for SAP HANA for both the appliance and TDI scenarios, they aren't the same. For appliances, you only need to perform a memory sizing, whereas for TDI, you need to consider the following as well:

- Memory (RAM), for both static and dynamic data
- Disk sizing for persistent storage
- CPU sizing (in SAP Application Performance Standard (SAPS): 300 SAPS/active user)

The essence of sizing is to map business requirements to hardware. As SAP HANA appliances are standardized offerings, there is no such mapping, nor does an appliance allow for an iterative approach. Although the appliance is preconfigured, sizing is needed to select the right appliance for the workload. The different configurations of hardware vendors are listed in the SAP-certified SAP HANA hardware directory.

For new implementation projects of SAP applications on SAP HANA, SAP recommends using the Quick Sizer tool. As shown in Figure 3.1, the tool provides sizing information about the CPU, memory, and disk I/O.

Quick Sizer uses SAPS as a unit, which is a hardware-independent CPU performance unit conceived to measure the throughput power of a server, as CPU measurements are highly configuration dependent and otherwise difficult to compare. With SAPS, you can compare apples with apples even though the underlying hardware may be completely different. For example, 100 SAPS equals 2,000 fully business-processed order line items per hour.

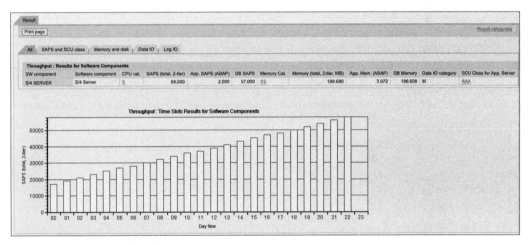

Figure 3.1 SAP Quick Sizer (Detail)

Figure 3.1 shows the SAP Quick Sizer for SAP S/4HANA scenarios. This is one of the configurations or presets. There are also presets for SAP Business Suite, SAP BW/4HANA, standalone SAP HANA, and industry-specific solutions.

Exam Tip

For this topic area, you're not expected to be intimately familiar with Quick Sizer, but you should have a general understanding of what you can do with the tool and when to use it. For a demonstration of the Quick Sizer tool, watch the video tutorial on the SAP HANA Academy at *http://youtu.be/9zWuNlwQGM4*.

Memory Sizing

It should come as no surprise that for an in-memory database, memory sizing is key. In the context of SAP HANA, memory sizing is understood as estimating the amount of memory required to run a certain workload. How does the size of a database loaded into memory compare to the size on disk? As explained in Chapter 2, aggregates and performance-motivated indexes are no longer required. We also pointed out that the column format of a table is very suitable for compression. SAP HANA uses a number of compression algorithms on column store tables. The compression ratio obtained depends on the data types, presence of repeated values, and other factors.

Apart from the expected compression ratio, to properly size the memory requirement, you also need to factor in the anticipated growth of the tables. Then, you also need to estimate the extra amount of memory for temporary computations. Working memory is required when performing joins but also for analytical queries, which each need their own workspace. Apart from future table growth, you also need to come up with a number for expected workload and concurrent access.

The default compression applied to all columns is dictionary compression. Instead of storing the full country name in each column, you only store a number as a dictionary pointer. Other "advanced" compression types are as follows:

- Sparse
- Prefixed
- Clustered
- Indirect
- Run length encoding (RLE)

The compression is automatically calculated and optimized as part of the delta merge operation, when the delta store in row format is merged with the main store in column format. This is configurable with system parameter `index-server.ini/[optimize_compression]/active=yes`.

You can view the compression rate of a column on the **Runtime Information** tab of the SAP HANA database explorer, as shown in Figure 3.2. This view also shows the size of the main store in memory, the delta store, the record count, number of distinct records, and whether the column is loaded into memory. The equivalent SQL statement queries the `M_CS_COLUMNS` system monitoring view (CS = column store). The column `COMPRESSION_TYPE` lists the compression type used.

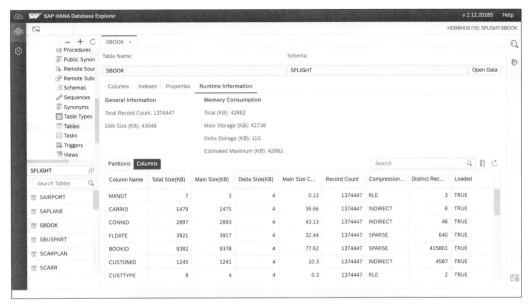

Figure 3.2 SAP HANA Database Explorer: Runtime Information

Learn More

Memory sizing, memory management, data compression, and the delta merge operation are documented in the SAP HANA Administration Guide. For more detailed information about RLE or clustered compression, beyond the scope of the exam, see KBA 2112604 – FAQ: SAP HANA Compression.

Product Availability Matrix

The PAM lists information about SAP software releases: support information, planned availability, upgrade paths, and so on. There are two entries in the PAM for SAP HANA, platform edition, for version 1.0 and 2.0. Add-ons such as SAP HANA dynamic tiering and SAP HANA data warehousing have their own entry in the PAM but not components such as SAP HANA cockpit or SAP HANA studio.

The PAM for SAP HANA lists release information, related product versions, SPS information with links to the release notes and links to software downloads on the SAP ONE Support Launchpad. The PAM entry for SAP HANA, platform edition 2.0, is illustrated in Figure 3.3.

Learn More

For general information about the PAM, see the SAP Support Portal at *http://support.sap.com/en/release-upgrade-maintenance.html*. The PAM requires an SAP Support (S-user) account. The details of the PAM entry for SAP HANA are beyond the scope of the exam.

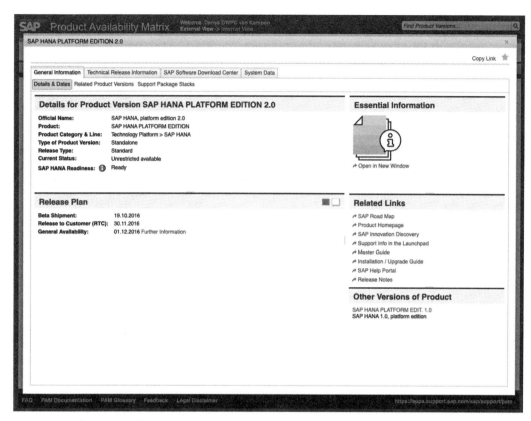

Figure 3.3 Product Availability Matrix

SAP HANA Hardware Directory

The SAP HANA hardware directory lists hardware that has been certified or is supported within the SAP HANA certification program. As illustrated in Figure 3.4, the directory lists different vendors, CPU architectures, and configurations for both the appliance and the TDI program.

The directory also lists supported IBM Power Systems, certified enterprise storage solutions for network attached storage (NAS) and storage area network (SAN) configuration, and certified cloud providers (infrastructure-as-a-service [IaaS] platforms). The abbreviations used aren't official product names and refer to the "powered by HANA" releases of SAP Business Suite and SAP Business Warehouse (SAP BW) and the "/4HANA" releases. DM is short for data mart in the hardware directory. Scale-out refers to multiple-host configuration (distributed systems), and scale-up refers to single-host configurations.

PMEM is listed under the TDI program as Intel Optane DC persistent memory modules (DCPMM).

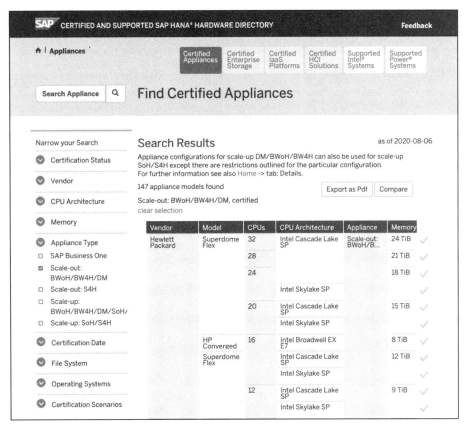

Figure 3.4 SAP HANA Hardware Directory

Linux

SAP HANA only runs on Linux. The server, that is, the client, supports a larger number of operating systems, including several flavors of UNIX, Linux, macOS, and Microsoft Windows. On the appliance, SUSE Linux Enterprise Server (SLES) is installed. Under the TDI program, both SLES and Red Hat Enterprise Linux (RHEL) are supported. SUSE and Red Hat (IBM) are SAP software partners and provide a special distribution for SAP software—SLES for SAP applications and RHEL for SAP solutions, respectively—which is recommended by SAP due to their features and extended support cycles.

The SAP HANA Server Installation and Update Guide only provides general information about the hardware and software requirements for SAP HANA. For the details, you need to consult the relevant SAP Notes for the platform and operating system. More recently, these notes have been consolidated in a central note about supported operating systems with the specifics in separate notes for each release. In addition, there are also configuration guides published (again, attached to notes) that provide an end-to-end sample installation description of Linux and SAP HANA.

The Linux operating system is highly configurable. For those not familiar with Linux system administration, all the different settings and configuration parameters might be a bit overwhelming. This includes recommended operating system settings such as the following:

- Turn off automatic non-uniform memory access (NUMA) balancing.
- Turn off kernel samepage merging (KSM).
- Disable `transparent_hugepage`.
- Configure C-states for low latency.

Exam Tip

You're not expected to be familiar with all the different Linux kernel parameters, but you should know where and how this is documented.

Learn More

For general information from the Linux software partners for SAP solutions, visit *http:// suse.com/sap* and *http://redhat.com/sap*. The number of SAP Notes listed on the **Hardware and Software Requirements** page is extensive. As mentioned, the specifics are beyond the scope of this exam but as introduction, we recommend browsing the following SAP Notes, which go from all supported operating systems, to SUSE Linux as operating system, and ending with the recommendations for a specific SLES release:

- SAP Note 2235581 – SAP HANA: Supported Operating Systems
- SAP Note 1944799 – SAP HANA Guidelines for SLES Operating System Installation (configuration guides attached)
- SAP Note 2684254 – SAP HANA DB: Recommended OS Settings for SLES 15/SLES for SAP Applications 15

IBM Power Systems

As part of the TDI program, support for IBM Power Systems was introduced with release SAP HANA 1.0 SPS 10 in 2015. IBM Power Systems use a different processor architecture than the x64 produced by Intel, among others, and well known out-side the technical world through the "Intel Inside" branding campaign. IBM Power Systems are typically used for enterprise computing, but, like x64 (and x86), the technology has been around for decades. The R in Power stands for the Reduced Instruction Set Computer (RISC) processor architecture, also found in Advanced RISC Machine (ARM) processors powering our smartphones.

Exam Tip

You're not expected to be familiar with the support restrictions and configuration requirements for IBM Power Systems, but like the operating system information, you should know where and how this is documented. Remember that SAP HANA 2.0 only sup-ports the little-endian (LE) mode of the processor architecture.

Learn More

For general information from IBM for SAP services, visit *http://ibm.com/sap*. IBM pub-lishes Redbooks, which contain technical information about products, platforms, and solutions that explore integration, implementation, and operating of client scenarios, including those for SAP. These guides are highly recommended (see *http://ibm.com/red-books* and search for "SAP HANA"), as well as the following resources:

- For IBM documentation specific to SAP HANA, see **SAP HANA on IBM Power Systems and IBM System Storage – Guides** at *http://s-prs.co/v507823*. This contains detailed information about how to configure IBM hardware and software for SAP HANA, includ-ing topics such as PMEM, IBM Power Systems, and SAN storage.

- Also make sure to include the SAP point of view by consulting SAP Note 2055470 – HANA on POWER Planning and Installation Specifics - Central Note.

The contents of these notes and technical documentation are beyond the scope of the exam.

Network

For optimum security and best performance, SAP HANA requires different net-work zones:

- Internal
  For both intra-node (single host) and inter-node (host to host) process commu-nication; also used for system replication.

- Storage
  Connects the SAP HANA host to an enterprise storage system for persistence and backup.

- Client
  Connects the SAP HANA system to SAP HANA clients using Java Database Con-nectivity (JDBC)/Open Database Connectivity (ODBC), Python, .NET, and other client libraries, or using HTTP/S for web clients such as SAP HANA cockpit or the SAP Web IDE browser-based development environment. Some clients may

make both types of connections as is the case with SAP NetWeaver-based applications or those running on the ABAP platform such as SAP S/4HANA. Client connections also include external data sources, including those made for event streams (SAP HANA streaming analytics), replication (SAP Replication Server), extract, transform, and load (ETL; SAP Data Services), etc.

Appliances come with internal and storage networks preconfigured. For TDI projects, the zones need to be set up appropriately.

Apart from the network zones, you also need to consider host name resolution, both internal and for SQL client communication. The host name is configured in the SAP profile, which you encountered when we described the SAP system startup process in Chapter 2. All internal communication between services (e.g., the name and index server) uses the host name.

For a single-host system, the listen interface (network) is set to `local` and points to the loopback adapter with IP address 127.0.0.1, which simulates a network interface. For multiple-host systems, you need to modify this to either the `internal` or `global` value in system parameter file `global.ini/[communication]/listeninterface` by adding the virtual hostname and virtual IP addresses. The SAP HANA installation tool, SAP HANA database lifecycle manager (HDBLCM), which we'll address in more detail in Chapter 4, can be used to modify the listen interface. SAP HANA also supports IPv6 in dual stack, that is, with both v4 using the well-known 172.16.254.1 format and v6 as 2001:db8::ff00:42:8329.

Learn More

Network administration is documented in the SAP HANA Administration Guide, where you'll find information about the ports and connections used, with hands-on information about how to configure host name resolution and IPv6. The concepts are repeated in the SAP HANA Master Guide and the SAP HANA Security Guide, here with focus on how to secure data communications, a topic we'll return to in Chapter 10. The original source of all this information is a technical paper published for the TDI program titled "SAP HANA Network Requirements" (*http://s-prs.co/v507824*). When you have time, we recommend at least reading/browsing this paper.

For those with a bit more study time at hand, take a look at the following KBAs:

- KBA 2382421 – Optimizing the Network Configuration on HANA- and OS-Level
- KBA 2222200 – FAQ: SAP HANA Network

Persistence

Elegantly formulated, persistence is the continuance of an effect after the removal of its cause. In computer science, this means that data or state outlives the process that created it. If you forget the tape stage, which only the most senior IT professionals will remember, storage usually means disk or more precisely, hard disk drive (HDD), the ubiquitous electro-mechanical data storage device connected to the computer using Small Computer System Interface (SCSI), or Serial Advanced

Technology Attachment (SATA). More recently, you can also obtain persistence with flash memory as used in smartphones. For enterprise storage, flash storage comes as solid-state drives (SSD), which are connected using non-volatile memory express (NVMe). Technically, this is still categorized as storage. The last innovation in this domain is called persistent memory (PMEM), also referred to as non-volatile RAM (NVRAM), which for SAP HANA refers to the 3D XPoint technology developed by Intel and commercialized as Optane.

Because of all these very different technologies, the SAP HANA documentation typically uses the generic term *persistence* over *disk* or *storage*, although you'll also find these terms used as synonyms or in combinations (persistent data storage).

SAP HANA uses storage for data, redo log, software, and backups. SAP recommends to store each of the different storage types on separate devices, as reflected in the recommended file system layout (which we'll discuss later in this chapter). Except for training and development environments, such as SAP HANA, express edition, storage typically doesn't reside on a built-in HDD or SSD, known as direct-attached storage (DAS), but is rather provided by an externally attached storage subsystem device either using a Network File System (NFS) with NAS or block-based storage on a SAN. External storage provides the flexibility of dynamic mount points, the performance of different storage type devices for the required throughput (I/O), and security against data corruption or damages for the required HA. We return to this topic in more detail in Chapter 9.

Figure 3.5 shows the hierarchy of persistent data storage with storage partitions (mnt00001) and data volumes for the system database and tenant database for each of the services with persistence: name, index server, and SAP HANA XS engine.

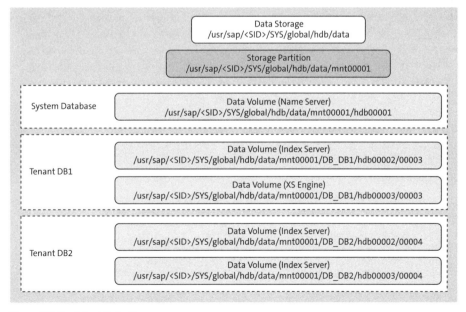

Figure 3.5 Persistent Data Storage

Figure 3.6 shows the output for volume I/O statistics for one of the volumes in the **Disk Volume Monitor** of the SAP HANA cockpit. This app displays read and write types for each of the volumes with more detailed volume page statistics. Another view shows the disk volume configuration; from here, you can navigate to the related trace files.

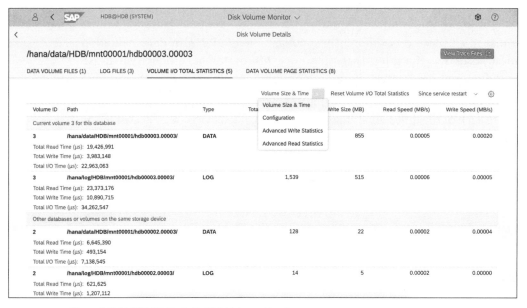

Figure 3.6 SAP HANA Cockpit: Disk Volume Monitor

Learn More

Persistent data storage is documented in the SAP HANA Administration Guide. As for the network, the source of most material comes from a TDI paper on the topic titled "SAP HANA Storage Requirements" (*http://s-prs.co/v507825*), which we can recommend as additional study material.

We're also lucky to have an FAQ KBA on this topic (KBA 2400005 – FAQ: SAP HANA Persistence), which is also recommended reading although, as with the paper, most of the content will be beyond the scope of the exam.

Persistent Memory

Most of the memory used by SAP HANA is allocated for the column store table's main storage area. As described, this data structure is compressed and provides fast access because it's read only and only gets updated during delta merge operations. As of SAP HANA 2.0 SPS 03, the column store main area can be placed in PMEM, which stores data permanently in memory. The column store delta area, row store, caches, and temporary compute zones remain in dynamic RAM (DRAM).

Besides PMEM, other abbreviations used are NVRAM and NVM (both mentioned earlier), or storage class memory (SCM); however, don't confuse PMEM with SSDs, another type of flash storage and marketed by Intel also under the Optane brand as NVMe.

PMEM combines the access speeds (latency) of memory with the persistence of storage to provide two advantages:

- Significant reduction of startup times as most of the data is already loaded into memory when the system starts (from hours to minutes)
- Lower total cost of ownership (TCO) and increased memory capacity, along with lower prices than DRAM

The SAP HANA cockpit includes a **Persistent Memory Monitor**, as shown in Figure 3.7. With this app, PMEM can be configured (enabled), and you monitor the size of the tables stored in PMEM.

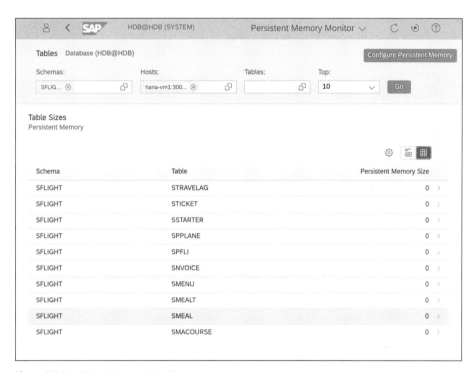

Figure 3.7 Persistent Memory Monitor

PMEM is configured at the database or object level. PMEM can be enabled during installation or at a later stage by configuring the following system parameters:

```
global.ini/[persistence]/basepath_persistent_memory_volumes
indexserver.ini/[persistent_memory]/table_default
```

When not enabled at the database level, you can make changes to the PMEM settings with the CREATE or ALTER TABLE statement and PERSISTENT MEMORY ON|OFF clause for the table, partition, or column involved.

Learn More

How to configure PMEM is documented in the SAP HANA Administration Guide. For more general information about the topic, see *http://sap.com/persistent-memory*.

There are two KBAs that document how to perform database sizing with the technology:

- KBA 2700084 – FAQ: SAP HANA Persistent Memory
- KBA 2786237 – Sizing SAP HANA with Persistent Memory

As elsewhere, these KBAs are beyond the scope of the exam.

File System Recommendations

SAP recommends using XFS as the file system for SAP HANA, but other supported Linux file systems are ext3, IBM Spectrum Scale (GPFS), NFS, and Oracle Cluster File System (OCFS2). File system specifications, however, usually come from the hardware and software partners. SAP does provide clear instructions on the recommended file system layout, as depicted in Figure 3.8.

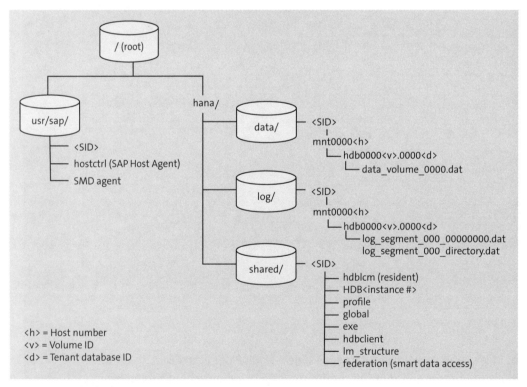

Figure 3.8 Recommended File System

This configuration makes it very easy to scale out from a single-host system to multiple-host, distributed systems. The layout defines a local mount point (/usr/sap) and a shared one (/hana). From the shared location, you go down one level to the location of the data volume, log volume, and program files, under /data, /log, and /shared, respectively. These directories will be mount points that link to separate storage devices. The next level for all four location is the SID, which makes it possible to install multiple SAP HANA systems on a single operating system host. On the local /usr/sap location, you only find the files relevant to the local system instance, such as log files. The program files or binaries are symbolic links that point to the shared locations, as shown in Figure 3.9.

```
hdbadm@hana-vm1:/usr/sap/HDB> ls -l
total 12
lrwxrwxrwx 1 hdbadm sapsys   22 Jun 26 15:19 HDB00 -> /hana/shared/HDB/HDB00
drwxr-x--- 3 hdbadm sapsys 4096 Jun 26 15:23 hdblcm_uploads
drwxr-xr-x 8 hdbadm sapsys 4096 Aug  6 09:04 home
drwxr-x--- 3 hdbadm sapsys 4096 Jun 26 15:16 SYS
hdbadm@hana-vm1:/usr/sap/HDB> ls -l SYS
total 4
drwxr-x--- 2 hdbadm sapsys 4096 Jun 26 15:16 exe
lrwxrwxrwx 1 hdbadm sapsys   23 Jun 26 15:16 global -> /hana/shared/HDB/global
lrwxrwxrwx 1 hdbadm sapsys   24 Jun 26 15:16 profile -> /hana/shared/HDB/profile
hdbadm@hana-vm1:/usr/sap/HDB> ls -l SYS/exe
total 0
lrwxrwxrwx 1 hdbadm sapsys 36 Jun 26 15:16 hdb -> /hana/shared/HDB/exe/linuxx86_64/hdb
hdbadm@hana-vm1:/usr/sap/HDB> █
```

Figure 3.9 Local File System

Local files also include an installation of the SAP Host Agent and Solution Manager Diagnostics (SMD) agent when used.

> **Learn More**
>
> The recommended file system is documented in the SAP HANA Server Installation and Update Guide on the SAP Help Portal.

Hardware Configuration Check

As an appliance, the SAP hardware partner is responsible for making sure that the SAP HANA software is correctly installed and configured. Under the TDI program, this responsibility is owned by the customer—the SAP-certified engineer in particular. To support the engineer with this activity, SAP provides the hardware configuration check tool and, more recently, the SAP HANA hardware and cloud measurement tool.

SAP Support provides the SAP GoingLive Check as a service, which includes the usage of the hardware configuration check tools.

We'll discuss the available tools in the following sections.

> **Learn More**
>
> For more information about the SAP GoingLive Check, see **SAP GoingLive Check** on the SAP Support Portal at *http://s-prs.co/v507826*.

SAP HANA Hardware Configuration Check Tool

The SAP HANA hardware configuration check tool has been developed to perform an extensive list of checks and verifications. The tool is available for download from the SAP Software Download Center as a component for the SAP HANA platform from the same location where you also find the server, client, and so on, as described in the previous chapter.

The hardware configuration check tool isn't so much a single tool but more of a framework that provides tests and reports. You can use it for both appliances and TDI installations, including single- and multiple-host systems to determine if the hardware you intend to use meets the minimum performance criteria required to run SAP HANA in production. The tool is mentioned in the documentation, but for the documentation, you need to consult a note with the guide attached. The note also contains the configuration files in JavaScript Object Notation (JSON) format for landscape, file system, and network tests. There are different versions, so make sure to select the one corresponding to your SAP HANA version.

With the hardware configuration check tool, you can check both hardware and software settings, including the following:

- Core/memory ratio (dual in-line memory modules [DIMM] population rules)
- Linux kernel settings such as the transparent huge pages configuration
- Data throughput rates and latency times between hosts and external storage
- Minimum bandwidth for an intra-node network
- Logical partitioning (LPAR) settings on IBM Power System servers

SAP HANA Hardware and Cloud Measurement Tool

The latest incarnation of the hardware check tool is called SAP HANA hardware and cloud measurement tool, which shares objectives and configuration (JSON) with its predecessor but includes an analysis service, as illustrated in Figure 3.10, making it easier to interpret the results. The SAP HANA hardware and cloud measurement tool includes a quick check, a network server and network client test, execution plan test, and more.

> **Exam Tip**
> You're not expected to be familiar with the internals of the hardware configuration check tool but you should be familiar with what the tool does and how it works. At the time of writing, summer 2020, the SAP HANA hardware and cloud measurement tool was just released and not yet part of the exam, but it may be included in future versions.

Figure 3.10 SAP HANA Hardware and Cloud Measurement Analysis

Learn More

The latest SAP HANA hardware and cloud measurement tool is documented on the SAP Help Portal at *http://s-prs.co/v507827*. For the hardware configuration check tool predecessor, see the central note as there are a number of different versions.

- SAP Note 1943937 – Hardware Configuration Check Tool - Central Note
- SAP Note 1652078 – SAP HANA Database: Hardware Check

Important Terminology

For this exam objective, you're expected to understand the following terms:

- **Appliance**
  An appliance is predefined hardware with preconfigured software. During the first three years, SAP HANA was only available as an appliance, marketed as the **H**igh performance **AN**alytic **A**ppliance. Available appliance configurations are listed in the SAP HANA hardware directory.

- **Hardware configuration check tool and SAP HANA hardware and cloud measurement tool**
  The hardware configuration check tool and its successor, the SAP HANA hardware and cloud measurement tool, help validate hardware and software requirements.

- **Host**
  A host is a computer that provides CPU, memory, network, and optionally storage.

- **Instance**
  An SAP HANA instance is the set of SAP HANA system components installed on a host. A single-host system typically hosts a single instance, while a multiple-host system contains as many instances as hosts, which all share the same SID and instance number. SAP supports installing multiple systems on a single host, although this is usually reserved for testing, training, and demo environments and not for production. Instance numbers are in the range of 00–99.

- **Persistence**
  Persistence is a generic term for storage and disks as opposed to volatile memory, which loses its state at power-off. Services such as the `nameserver` and the `indexserver` have persistence and require backup in case the data volume becomes unavailable.

- **Persistent memory (PMEM)**
  This special type of memory persists in its state at power-off. PMEM is sometimes also described as non-volatile RAM (NVRAM) but not to be confused with other types of memory storage such as the flash memory found inside smartphones, USB drives, or SSD.

- **Quick Sizer**
  The Quick Sizer tool facilitates greenfield sizing projects for new SAP implementations.

- **SAP Application Performance Standard (SAPS)**
  SAPS is a hardware-independent CPU performance unit conceived to measure the throughput power of a server, as CPU measurements are highly configuration dependent and otherwise difficult to compare. For example, 100 SAPS equals 2,000 fully business-processed order line items per hour.

- **SAP HANA sizing decision tree**
  The SAP HANA sizing decision tree helps you to decide whether to perform greenfield, brownfield, or expert sizing, as well as which tools to use or SAP Notes to consider.

- **System**
  An SAP HANA system is a single operating environment defined by a system identifier (SID) and an instance number. A system contains a system database and one or more isolated tenant databases and can be installed on a single host (system) or multiple hosts.

- **Tailored data center integration (TDI)**
  The TDI program was introduced to support made-to-measure installations on existing corporate hardware. Certified TDI configurations are listed in the SAP HANA hardware directory. Besides certified hardware and software, TDI also requires the installation to be performed by a certified SAP engineer holding the C_HANATEC certification.

Practice Questions

These practice questions will help you evaluate your understanding of the topics covered in this chapter. The questions shown are similar in nature to those found on the certification examination. Although none of these questions will be found on the exam itself, they will allow you to review your knowledge of the subject. Select the correct answers, and then check the completeness of your answers in the "Practice Question Answers and Explanations" section.

1. For which SAP HANA scenarios is sizing from an SAP sizing expert required? (There are three correct answers.)

   ☐ **A.** When consolidating multiple source systems into a single system

   ☐ **B.** When carving out functionality from the source system

   ☐ **C.** When migrating a high-volume legacy system

   ☐ **D.** When migrating SAP BW and SAP Business Suite

   ☐ **E.** When migrating SAP NetWeaver-based systems from AnyDB to SAP BW/4HANA and SAP S/4HANA

2. Where can you find certified and supported SAP HANA hardware appliances centrally listed?

   ☐ **A.** On the SAP-certified SAP HANA hardware directory

   ☐ **B.** On the PAM

   ☐ **C.** On the SAP ONE Support Launchpad

   ☐ **D.** On the websites of SAP-certified hardware partners

3. Which templates are available in the Quick Sizer tool for SAP HANA? (There are two correct answers.)

   ☐ **A.** SAP S/4HANA Cloud

   ☐ **B.** SAP NetWeaver

   ☐ **C.** SAP BW/4HANA

   ☐ **D.** Standalone SAP HANA

4. What's the difference between sizing for an SAP HANA appliance and TDI?

☐ A. SAP HANA appliance sizing is performed by the hardware partner.

☐ B. You don't need to consider CPU and storage sizing for an appliance.

☐ C. The SAP HANA appliance is preconfigured and doesn't require sizing.

☐ D. The Quick Sizer tool can only be used in TDI sizing projects.

5. How do you size brownfield implementations? (There are two correct answers.)

☐ A. Use the Quick Sizer tool for SAP HANA.

☐ B. Use the latest sizing report for the application attached to an SAP Note.

☐ C. Brownfield implementations always require expert sizing.

☐ D. Consult the SAP in-memory computing sizing guidelines.

☐ E. Use the SAP HANA sizing decision tree.

6. How do you perform SAP HANA in-memory sizing for generic migration scenarios?

☐ A. Use a formula that considers the source data footprint (tables only), adds the requirements for dynamic objects, divides by an assumed compression ratio, and multiplies by the source database-specific compression factor (if applicable).

☐ B. Use the latest sizing report for the application attached to an SAP Note.

☐ C. Use the Quick Sizer tool for AnyDB.

7. How do you calculate disk space requirements for generic migration scenarios?

☐ A. Use a formula that considers the net data size on disk plus 20% additional space for delta merge operations; plus anticipated growth for the data volume and 0.5 * RAM with a maximum of 512 GB for the log volume; plus 1 * RAM for the software installation with a maximum of 1TB.

☐ B. Calculate the required inputs/outputs per second (IOPS).

☐ C. Use the rule of thumb of three times RAM.

8. Which technology directly impacts SAP HANA memory sizing?

☐ A. SAP HANA smart data access

☐ B. SAP HANA dynamic tiering

☐ C. SAP HANA persistent memory

☐ D. SAP HANA extension nodes

9. Which is the recommended approach to perform a comprehensive hardware configuration check for custom SAP HANA installations?

☐ **A.** The hardware configuration check is performed automatically by the SAP HANA installer prior to server software installation.

☐ **B.** Implement the recommendations and requirements of the SAP Notes listed in the SAP HANA Installation and Update Guide.

☐ **C.** Running the hardware configuration check tool with the appropriate configuration template files.

☐ **D.** Hardware configuration checks are only available as part of the SAP GoingLive Check.

10. Which operating systems are supported for the SAP HANA server? (There are two correct answers.)

☐ **A.** Ubuntu Server LTS

☐ **B.** SUSE Linux Enterprise Server (SLES)

☐ **C.** Red Hat Enterprise Linux (RHEL) for SAP solutions

☐ **D.** openSUSE Leap for SAP applications

11. Which network zone is used for SAP HANA system replication?

☐ **A.** Internal

☐ **B.** Storage

☐ **C.** Local

☐ **D.** Client

12. Which file system is recommended by SAP for SAP HANA?

☐ **A.** NTFS

☐ **B.** EXT3

☐ **C.** IBM Spectrum Scale (GPFS)

☐ **D.** XFS

Practice Question Answers and Explanations

1. Correct answers: **A, B, C**
    For new SAP software implementations (greenfield) on SAP HANA, SAP recommends using the Quick Sizer tool. For migrations of SAP NetWeaver-based applications, there are specific sizing reports (SAP Notes) depending on whether you're interested in SAP BW on SAP HANA, SAP Business Suite on SAP

HANA, SAP BW/4HANA, SAP S/4HANA, or other applications. Any system that is large or complex requires sizing from an SAP sizing expert.

Answers D and E: these are standard brownfield sizing scenarios addressed in the respective SAP Notes.

2. Correct answer: **A**

   The SAP-certified SAP HANA hardware directory is shown in Figure 3.4.

   Answer B is incorrect because the PAM contains a link to the hardware directory but doesn't provide information about certified and supported appliances. Answer C is incorrect because the SAP ONE Support Launchpad contains information about SAP software but not about SAP-certified hardware. Answer D is incorrect because you might find information about SAP-certified appliances listed on the websites of SAP hardware partners, but this isn't a centrally listed directory.

3. Correct answers: **C, D**

   There are three different versions of the Quick Sizer tool. The version for SAP HANA only contains templates for SAP applications running on SAP HANA, including both the "powered by HANA" releases and the "/4HANA," but not cloud-based editions or for generic (AnyDB) sizing for products such as SAP NetWeaver.

   Answer A is incorrect because the Quick Sizer tool for SAP HANA can't be used to size SAP S/4HANA Cloud. For this, use the SAP S/4HANA Cloud Quick Sizer. Answer B is incorrect because there is no sizing tool for SAP NetWeaver (product family) or SAP NetWeaver AS for ABAP (application server), but there are Quick Sizers for SAP NetWeaver-based applications such as SAP Business Suite both when powered by SAP HANA or when running on AnyDB.

4. Correct answer: **B**

   SAP HANA appliances are standardized offerings and can't be mapped to business requirements in an iterative approach. However, even with appliances, sizing is needed to select the right appliance for the workload.

   Answer A is incorrect because the hardware partner doesn't perform sizing for the appliance as the business requirements aren't known. Answer C is incorrect because the appliance is preconfigure but does need to be sized for the workload. Answer D is incorrect because you can use the Quick Sizer tool for both appliance and TDI configurations. The Quick Sizer tool is typically used in new implementations (greenfield), whereas for SAP application migration projects (brownfield), different SAP Notes with specific SQL scripts attached are used.

5. Correct answers: **B, D**

   Brownfield implementations refer to migration projects of existing SAP applications from AnyDB to SAP HANA. For standard scenarios, such as migrating SAP BW to SAP BW/4HANA, there are specific SAP Notes that detail the actions to perform. Additional information can be found in the sizing guides listed on the SAP Help Portal under "SAP In-Memory Computing Sizing Guidelines."

For new installations, also known as greenfield projects, you use the Quick Sizer tool for SAP HANA.

Complex migration projects typically require expert sizing, but this isn't a requirement per se for brownfield implementations.

The SAP HANA sizing decision tree shows the different sizing approaches for greenfield and migration sizings with guidance on which SAP Note to use.

6. Correct answer: **A**

   This formula is documented in the SAP HANA In-Memory Database Sizing Guideline (PDF) document attached to SAP Note 1514966 Sizing SAP In-Memory Database.

   Answers B and C are incorrect because there is no sizing report for generic applications, and there is no Quick Sizer tool for AnyDB.

7. Correct answer: **A**

   Recommendation from SAP Note 1514966 (see the "Greenfield, Brownfield, and Expert Sizing" section).

   Answer B is incorrect because, in practice, storage throughput in IOPS may provide a more important storage requirement than the actual disk space. However, the question asked about disk space requirements. Answer C is incorrect because the rule of thumb of three times RAM provides a rough calculation for the space requirements of an SAP HANA appliance as this also allows for backups and memory dumps (exports) on the same volume. For production systems, only database data files should be stored on the data volume.

> **Exam Tip**
>
> Formulas provide great material for exam questions. SAP Note 1514966 dates from 2013 when the TDI program was launched and may no longer be used all that much for actual sizing projects.

8. Correct answer: **C**

   Although all listed technologies impact memory sizing indirectly by reducing the amount of memory required to store the tables, only persistent memory (PMEM) does so directly as reflected in a dedicated note. As mentioned in SAP Note 2786237 – Sizing SAP HANA with Persistent Memory, expert sizing is strongly recommended when implementing PMEM.

   SAP HANA smart data access (SDA) uses linked databases, virtual tables, and query federation to access remote data as if it's stored locally, without data copy (only metadata is stored). SDA was introduced with SAP HANA 1.0 SPS 06.

   SAP HANA dynamic tiering is an optional component that extends the in-memory database with a disk-based columnar store. In the temperature analogy, hot data is stored in memory while less frequently accessed warm data is placed in the extensive store. SAP HANA dynamic tiering is an add-on component, separately licensed, with its own documentation set and listing on the PAM. It uses SAP IQ technology for the extended store and supports native SAP HANA applications but not SAP BW or enterprise resource planning (ERP) applications (SAP S/4HANA). SAP HANA dynamic tiering was introduced with SAP HANA 1.0 SPS 10.

SAP HANA extension nodes enable you to allocate a node (host) of a multiple-host, scale-out (distributed) system as warm data memory store. Extension nodes were introduced with SAP HANA 1.0 specific to SAP BW but are currently also supporting native applications. Other warm and cold data aging solutions specific to SAP BW are nearline storage and the "nonactive data" concept.

> **Exam Tip**
> For this topic area, you're not expected to be intimately familiar with all these data tiering solutions, but you should have a general understanding of what they are and how they are used. We return to these technologies in Chapter 9.

9. Correct answer: **C**

   To perform a comprehensive hardware configuration check, you must run the hardware configuration check tool with the appropriate configuration template files.

   Answer A is incorrect because the SAP HANA installer calls the Python script HanaHwCheck.py and exits in case of noncompliance. However, this script only verifies the software prerequisites required for the installation and doesn't perform a comprehensive check of hardware, network, and storage configurations. Answer B is incorrect because running the hardware configuration check tool isn't required, and you could opt to perform all the recommendations and requirement check manually, although this isn't the recommended approach. Answer D is incorrect because SAP strongly recommends using the hardware configuration check as part of an SAP GoingLive Check for SAP HANA, but the tool is freely available for download for every SAP HANA customer and documented in SAP Notes. To use the hardware configuration check tool, the SAP GoingLive Check service isn't required.

10. Correct answers: **B, C**

   SLES and RHEL for SAP solutions are the operating systems supported for the SAP HANA server.

   Answer A is incorrect because, although you may find blogs on the SAP Community about how to install SAP HANA, express edition, on Ubuntu, this Linux distribution is only supported for the SAP HANA client. Answer D is incorrect because openSUSE is the open source project for SUSE Linux and Leap at regular release, but there is no "for SAP solutions" edition as this only exists for SLES.

11. Correct answer: **A**

    An internal network zone is used for system replication.

    Answer B is incorrect because the storage network zone is only used to communicate between the system and storage subsystems (NAS or SAN) for persistence, log, and backups. Answer C is incorrect because local, global, and internal are valid configurations for the listen interface, but local isn't a network zone.

12. Correct answer: **D**

    XFS is the recommended file system by SAP.

    Answer A is incorrect because the Microsoft Windows NT File System (NTFS) isn't supported for SAP HANA as SAP HANA is only supported on Linux. Answer B is incorrect because the EXT4 file system isn't supported. Answer C is incorrect because IBM Spectrum Scale (GPFS) is a clustered file system supported for SAP HANA.

Takeaway

After reading this chapter, you should be familiar with SAP HANA installation preparations from a business perspective and understand the SAP HANA sizing decision tree for greenfield, brownfield, and expert sizing. You also understand what technical preparations are required for systems, networks, and storage and know how and when to use tools such as the Product Availability Matrix (PAM), the SAP-certified SAP HANA hardware directory, and the hardware configuration check tool. Although the technical implementation details are beyond the scope of the exam, you should understand the concepts and where the technical implementation details are documented.

Summary

In this chapter, you learned about the installation preparations for SAP HANA, and we covered the topics of sizing and operating system preparations. These are both specialized activities typically performed by sizing experts and system engineers as this requires intimate knowledge of business processes and hardware technologies. For this reason, the SAP HANA documentation only summarizes this topic and references a long list of SAP Notes for the specifics. For the exam, you're not expected to have memorized the content of these notes, but you should have a general understanding of how sizing for SAP HANA works, including the different scenarios and approaches. You should be familiar with the TDI program and how it differs from SAP HANA as an appliance, and you should have a general appreciation of the tasks involved in preparing the operating system for SAP HANA installations. If you can answer the questions of this chapter successfully, albeit on second attempt, and understand the reasoning, you're ready to proceed to the next chapter, where we'll discuss installing, upgrading, and performing the post-installation tasks of the SAP HANA database.

Chapter 4
Installations and Updates

Techniques You'll Master

- Working with the SAP HANA platform lifecycle management tool in command-line, graphical, and web interface modes

- Working with the SAP HANA platform lifecycle management in interactive, batch, and advanced interactive mode

- Installing SAP HANA

- Updating SAP HANA

- Downloading SAP HANA software

- Automating installations

- Performing a multiple-host installation

- Working with the "resident" installation tool to perform post-installation and system maintenance tasks

- Understanding the architecture of the installation tool and how to troubleshoot issues

In this second chapter about SAP HANA installation, we'll cover the actual installation and the tools used. We'll look at both the database server installation and at the installation of additional components, such as the SAP HANA client. Post-installation activities, such as adding a license, are also included in this chapter. Finally, we also briefly mention the SAP HANA demo tool SAP HANA Interactive Education (SHINE). Although more of a development topic, the tool needs to be installed as well, which we'll also briefly cover.

Real-World Scenario

For an upcoming project, you've been asked to install the latest version of the SAP HANA database. There is already an older version running used for training, but this can be discarded. How would you proceed? Where would you download the software? Would you perform an interactive one-off installation, or would you prepare an installation parameter file and run the installation in batch mode? Should anything go wrong, where would you start with troubleshooting?

In this second chapter about SAP HANA installation, we're going to roll up our sleeves and get hands-on.

Exam Tip

You don't need a system with a 32-core processor and 24 TB RAM to get some practice with the installation topic. An SAP HANA, express edition will do. Just get the latest express edition from SAP Developer Center as a virtual machine, and uninstall the software using the resident version of the installer as explained in the chapter. Then perform an installation with the binary download. This makes for great practice and will help you become familiar with the different options of the installation tool.

Topic and Objectives

In this chapter, we'll cover the topic area SAP HANA database installation and update with post-installation activities. The certification exam expects you to have a good understanding of the following topics:

- SAP HANA lifecycle management tools
- Interactive installation
- Installation automation
- Multiple-host installation
- Updates
- Post-installation activities
- SAP HANA Interactive Education (SHINE)
- SAP HANA release and maintenance strategy

SAP HANA 2.0 SPS 05: What's New?

As of SPS 05, SAP HANA database lifecycle manager (HDBLCM) includes the prompt to enable data and log volume encryption. Not new but now supported for production environments is the local secure store (LSS). We cover the installation of the LSS in a separate section of this chapter.

This is a big chapter. Let's dive in.

Note

This topic area was listed with medium weight (8%–12%) for most editions of the exam but gained some weight since the SPS 04 version due to the split into a topic area on installation preparations and on the actual installation, which is a split we've also used for this book. With 80 questions in total, you can expect about 8 questions each. As mentioned before, keep in mind that the exam guide states this can change at any time, so always check online for any updates.

Learn More

Most of the material for this topic area is documented in the SAP HANA Server Installation and Update Guide at *http://s-prs.co/v507828*.

For post-installation PLM activities, see the SAP HANA Administration Guide for the SAP HANA platform at *http://s-prs.co/v507829*.

Key Concepts Refresher

In this section, we'll highlight the most important installation and updating concepts that you need to know for this exam.

Application Lifecycle Management

As the SAP HANA platform is both a database and a platform to develop and run applications, we need to distinguish platform lifecycle management (PLM) and application lifecycle management (ALM). PLM is concerned with the installation and update of the platform itself, and ALM regards the lifecycle of applications "powered by SAP HANA." For this topic area, our focus is mainly on PLM, but we'll start by briefly covering ALM to help you keep them apart.

ALM concerns the whole lifecycle of an application from development to production with the requirements for transportation, installation, configuration, and deployment. As SAP HANA contains two different application server architectures (covered in Chapter 2), there are also two different approaches to lifecycle management.

To perform lifecycle management activities for SAP HANA extended application services (SAP HANA XS), classic model applications, you can use the following tools:

- `hdbalm` command line
- SAP HANA ALM web application

Figure 4.1 shows the web interface. SAP HANA ALM, which can be integrated with the SAP software logistics tool Change and Transport System (CTS), bundled with ABAP objects using the SAP HANA transport container (HTC) or with SAP HANA Transport for ABAP, depending on the SAP NetWeaver release. We'll return briefly to the topic of ALM tools in the "SAP HANA Interactive Education" section.

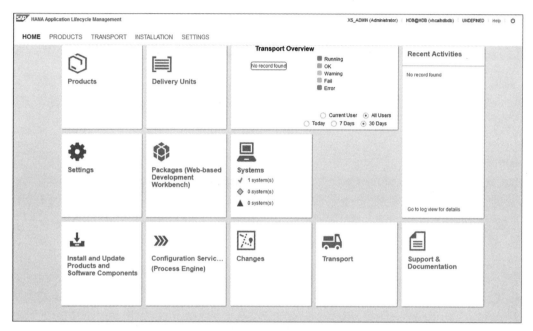

Figure 4.1 SAP HANA Application Lifecycle Management SAP HANA XS (Classic)

> **Exam Tip**
>
> SAP NetWeaver ALM concepts and tools such as CTS and even SAP HANA-related ABAP object management with HTC and SAP HANA Transport for ABAP are beyond the scope of the exam. However, you may find a reference to the terminology in one of the questions. As mentioned in Chapter 1, SAP HANA XS, classic model, the repository, and the SAP HANA studio tool for system administration and development have been deprecated with the SAP HANA 2.0 SPS 02 release, and this includes this part of the SAP HANA ALM architecture. The SAP HANA ALM tool itself is an SAP HANA XS, classic model application. We've included this material to help you identify both SAP HANA XS architectures and the associated tools.

To perform lifecycle management activities for SAP HANA extended application services, advanced model (SAP HANA XSA) applications, you can use the following tools:

- `xs` command line
- SAP HANA XSA ALM web application

The web interface to manage products and software components is shown in Figure 4.2. Unlike the SAP HANA XS, classic model tools, the xs command-line tool and the web application are tightly integrated. The web interface only provides a graphical environment. Behind the screens, the same xs commands are executed. The command-line tool provides more complete control of the installation process.

Figure 4.2 SAP HANA XSA Application Lifecycle Management

Exam Tip

The exam doesn't cover SAP HANA XSA and the related Cloud Foundry architecture and concepts. Installing the SAP HANA XSA runtime (PLM) or updating SAP HANA XSA software components (ALM) is out of scope.

Learn More

For more extensive coverage of this topic, beyond the scope of this exam, see the SAP HANA Application Lifecycle Management Guide for both SAP HANA XS, classic model and SAP HANA XSA model applications at *http://s-prs.co/v507830*.

Platform Lifecycle Management

SAP HANA provides a single tool to install and update components on the SAP HANA platform, including the database server, and to perform post-installation and configuration tasks. Together, these tasks are called lifecycle management tasks. There is a program or executable for each task, but these commands aren't intended to be called directly. Instead, you use what is called a wrapper tool. In the documentation, the wrapper tool is called the SAP HANA database lifecycle manager (HDBLCM), which corresponds to the name of the tool on the command line: hdblcm (lowercase).

There are three different user interfaces for HDBLCM that display a slightly different name but provide (almost) identical functionality:

- **SAP HANA Lifecycle Management**
  - Command line: hdblcm
  - X Window application: hdblcmgui
- **SAP HANA PLM**
  - Web UI

HDBLCM is included with the installation media (the full download of the support package stack [SPS]). When you install SAP HANA, HDBLCM is installed as well, and this is the version of the tool you'll use to perform most post-installation activities. The installed version is called the resident HDBLCM.

We'll take a closer look at each version of the tool in the following sections.

Command Line

The command-line version of the HDBLCM tool provides the most convenient interface to perform lifecycle management tasks. All you need to run this tool is a Secure Shell (SSH) terminal session to the Linux server. You can run the tool in either interactive or batch mode. In interactive mode, we're prompted for input, although for most parameters the default value is provided. This mode is useful for one-off installations but won't be very practical when you need to perform a large number of installations, for example, as a hardware partner working with appliances, or when you want to standardize the installation process.

For installation automation, you run HDBLCM in *batch mode* with a configuration file and an optional password file. While the tool in interactive mode only prompts for the most common settings, with a configuration file, you can specify additional installation parameters, for example, to enable and configure persistent memory or to configure the tenant database isolation mode.

In command-line mode, you can also pass installation parameters on the command line. This is called the advanced interactive mode and can be combined with a parameter file. A simple example would be to pass a unique system identifier (SID) as a command-line parameter with a common set of parameters in a configuration file:

```
hdblcm --batch --sid=DB1 --configfile=HANA_configfile
```

Note that parameters specified in the command line always override parameters specified in the configuration file.

We'll describe installation automation in more detail in the "Installation Automation" section.

X Window Graphical User Interface

You can use the graphical user interface (GUI) of HDBLCM in the same way as the command-line tool: interactively, in batch mode with a parameter file, and in advanced interactive mode with both command-line parameters and a parameter file. In other words, the GUI can be used for both one-off installations and installation automation. The command to start the tool is hdblcmgui.

The graphical version of HDBLCM is an X Window application, which requires both the X Window System (X11) to be installed on the Linux server and a client or monitor to display. Unlike desktop or laptop computers, production servers usually come headless, that is, without a monitor directly attached, and also "hardened" or with all nonessential software removed for security reasons. For this reason, an X Window System environment isn't all that common on SAP HANA production systems.

For training environments, you can add a graphical environment to the server and run the graphical version of the installer directly either on the GNOME or KDE desktop. To display X Window applications remotely on other operating systems, such as Microsoft Windows client computers, additional configuration and software is required. The terminal program PuTTY and Xming for X Window emulation are common examples. Figure 4.3 shows a Windows client computer with Xming emulating an X Window graphical display and PuTTY providing the X11 forwarding through an SSH tunnel.

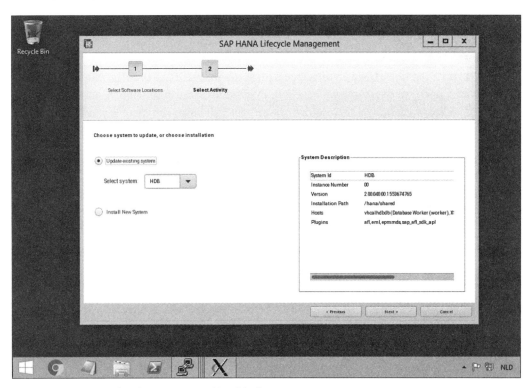

Figure 4.3 SAP HANA Lifecycle Management (Graphical)

Exam Tip

The X Window System has been around for decades and is common to all UNIX-like operating systems, but for those used to the graphical environments of macOS and Microsoft Windows, it might come with a learning curve. X uses a client/server model and doesn't require a local display. Although you can use X to display an entire desktop (similar to Microsoft Remote Desktop), you also can use it to only display single applications. This requires a proper configuration of X11 forwarding, the DISPLAY environment variable, and the xhost command for authorization: all three common sources of errors.

For this topic area, you're not expected to be intimately familiar with how to configure the X Window System, but you should have a general understanding of the technology.

Learn More

For a more extensive coverage of this topic, beyond the scope of this exam, take a look at the following KBAs:

- KBA 2082466 – Known Issues in SAP HANA Platform Lifecycle Management (HDBLCM)
- KBA 2358582 – How-To: Configure Graphical User Interface for SAP HANA Platform Lifecycle Management Tools via PuTTY

Web User Interface

Unlike ALM, SAP HANA XS doesn't host the PLM web interface. Instead, the SAP HANA PLM web UI is hosted by the SAP Host Agent. This agent is installed with the SAP HANA server, so you can't use the web interface for new system installations but only for updates. Nor is there a batch or advanced interactive mode for the web interface.

Figure 4.4 shows the web interface with URL */lmsl/HDBLCM/<SID>/index.html*. The *lmsl* in the path refers to lifecycle management software logistics, which, like the SAP Host Agent, is a technology shared with the SAP NetWeaver product family. We'll get back to software logistics and SAP NetWeaver in Chapter 14.

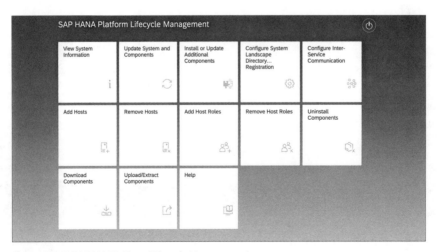

Figure 4.4 SAP HANA Platform Lifecycle Management

The SAP Host Agent uses TCP ports 1128 and 1129 for HTTP/S. These are officially registered ports with Internet Assigned Numbers Authority (IANA) and aren't configurable.

You also can access the tool from the SAP HANA cockpit **Database Overview** screen, in the **Platform Lifecycle Management** section, as shown in Figure 4.5. The external web page icon after each of the links indicates we're leaving the SAP HANA cockpit environment, and each of the links corresponds to a tile on the SAP HANA PLM web page.

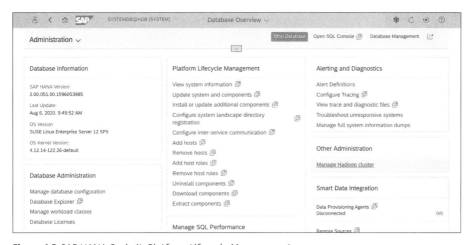

Figure 4.5 SAP HANA Cockpit: Platform Lifecycle Management

Although convenient, connectivity may be an issue with the web interface as proxy servers and firewalls need to allow traffic between the browser on your client computer and the ports of the SAP Host Agent on the SAP HANA host in the data center. This seems to have been anticipated because while the web interface loads, a message is displayed pointing to the SAP Note for troubleshooting. While this is attentive, it also may provide an indication that the web interface might not always work out of the box.

As you need to enter operating system passwords to authenticate, using secure HTTPS is strongly recommended. To enable this functionality, the SAP HANA host comes with a self-signed certificate for Transport Layer Security/Secure Sockets Layer (TLS/SSL), but this is flagged by most browsers as **Not secure** and may prevent you from accessing the URL. Figure 4.4 earlier shows what this looks like in a Chrome browser with **Not secure** in red (in the address bar). Other browsers will present this with a slightly different message. Although not specifically mentioned in the documentation, updating the SAP Host Agent with a properly signed certificate is a recommended post-installation task.

Exam Tip
You're not expected to debug HDBLCM graphical and web UI issues, but you should understand the general architecture of the tool.

Learn More

For a more extensive coverage of this topic, beyond the scope of this exam, see KBA 2078425 – Troubleshooting Note for SAP HANA Platform Lifecycle Management Tool HDBLCM.

Software Downloads

Before you can start the installation, you first need to download the software. For this, SAP provides a single location: the SAP ONE Support Launchpad. Finding the right downloads can be challenging at times as **Software Downloads** provides access to all SAP software (300,000+ entries). For this reason, using the links to **Software Downloads** from the Product Availability Matrix (PAM) or the **Product Support** page on the launchpad can be helpful. We covered these tools in Chapter 3.

As shown in Figure 4.6, you can descend the hierarchy by alphabetical index or by category if you know the exact term; otherwise, just use search and enter "SAP HANA platform edition 2.0" (searching just "HANA" returns 20,000 results).

Figure 4.6 Software Downloads

There are two main areas:

- **INSTALLATIONS & UPGRADES** for the SPS releases
- **SUPPORT PACKAGES & PATCHES (MAINTENANCE)** for the revisions

Software Downloads provides access to all SAP software, and the generic labels used here differ from the SAP HANA terminology. The SPS release comes as a ZIP file with a selection of components included. Figure 4.7 shows the list of the latest supported SPS releases, one for each architecture (x86_64 and Power). Included is the latest SAP HANA XSA collection (runtime with applications).

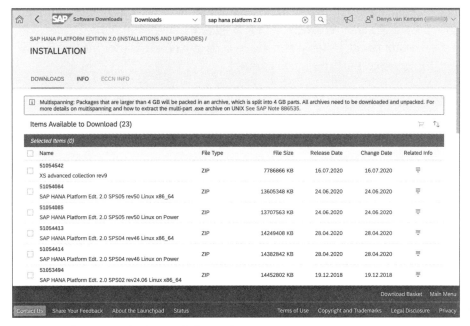

Figure 4.7 Software Downloads: Installation Product

SUPPORT PACKAGES & PATCHES lists each of the SAP HANA, platform edition, components separately, as shown in Figure 4.8. Note that this doesn't include options such as SAP HANA dynamic tiering, SAP HANA smart data integration (SDI), or SAP HANA data warehousing foundation. These have their own entries.

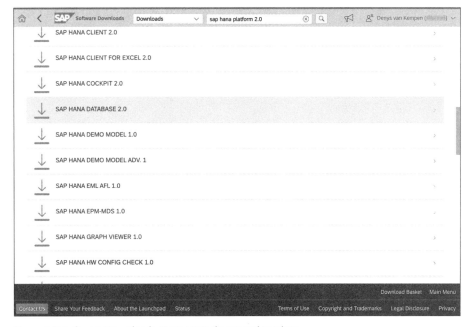

Figure 4.8 Software Downloads: Support Packages and Patches

When selected, the latest revisions for these components will be listed, as shown in Figure 4.9. For the architecture, you now need to use a selector in the header. For the server component, this still remains x86_64 and Power but for the SAP HANA client, for example, the list is much longer.

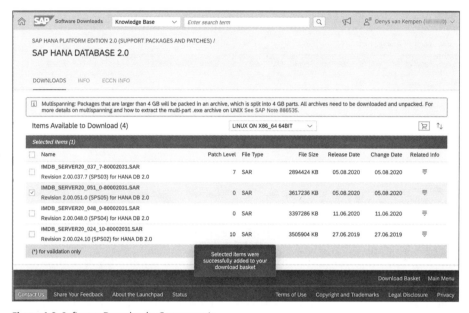

Figure 4.9 Software Downloads: Components

To download, either select the file directly (click the link) or add the component to the download basket and use the SAP Download Manager (Java) application to download the contents of the basket when and where required.

The web interface of HDBLCM also enables you to download software (components) directly from **Software Downloads**, as shown in Figure 4.10. You can select to either download the components to the SAP HANA host, should there be direct connectivity, or to the browser host.

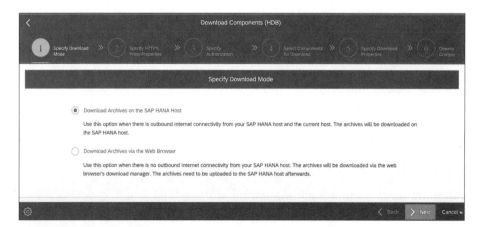

Figure 4.10 Download Components

Figure 4.11 shows the contents of the complete SPS release as an extracted ZIP file. The *HDB_SERVER_LINUX_X86_64* directory contains the HDBLCM installers. When launched, it will return a list of detected components with version number and path. Using the **Browse** button of the GUI and web interface versions of the tool, you can point to alternative or additional component locations. For the command-line tool, the component_medium or component_dirs installation parameter can be defined.

With HDBLCM, you can also install the SAP HANA platform add-on products such as SAP HANA dynamic tiering. Although these add-on products are listed separately on the PAM and have separate release notes, documentation sets, and download locations, you use the same HDBLCM tool for installation. This provides, as the marketer would say, an "integrated experience." Each add-on product may also contain multiple components.

```
hana-vm1:/install/DATA_UNITS # ls
HANASPARK_CTRL_20          HCO_HANA_HADOOP_CONTROLLER   HDB_CLIENT_LINUX_X86_64    LABELIDX.ASC              XSAC_ERTT_20          XS_MIGRATION_1
HANA_LSS_24_LINUX_X86_64   HCO_HANA_SHINE               HDB_EML_AFL_10_LINUX_X86_64 SAP_HANA_EPM-MDS_10      XSAC_SAP_WEB_IDE_20
HANA_SPATIAL_MAP_CLIENT_10 HCO_INA_FILELOAD_10          HDB_LCM_LINUX_X86_64       SAP_HANA_HWCCT_LINUX_X86_64 XSA_CLIENT_10
HANA_TEST_TOOLS            HCO_SAP_HANA_GRAPH_VIEWER_1.0 HDB_MODELCOMPARE_20        SAP_HANA_RSA             XSA_CONTENT_10
HCO_HANA_APPLICATION_LOG_1 HDB_AFL_LINUX_X86_64         HDB_SERVER_LINUX_X86_64    SAP_HANA_SDA_20_LINUX_X86_64 XSA_RT_10_LINUX_X86_64
hana-vm1:/install/DATA_UNITS # ls HDB_SERVER_LINUX_X86_64
HDBCOCKPIT.SMF  adapters.d                  filelist.hdblcm_remote_check filelist.update hdblcmgui  hdbuninst   operations.d
LABEL.ASC       descriptors.d               filelist.install           hdbinst         hdblcmweb  hdbupd      resources
SIGNATURE.SMF   filelist.hdbinst_remote_check filelist.resident        hdblcm          hdbsetup   instruntime server
hana-vm1:/install/DATA_UNITS # ./HDB_SERVER_LINUX_X86_64/hdblcm


SAP HANA Lifecycle Management - SAP HANA Database 2.00.050.00.1592305219
********************************************************************************

Scanning software locations...
Detected components:
    SAP HANA AFL (incl.PAL,BFL,OFL) (2.00.050.0000.1592327743) in /install/DATA_UNITS/HDB_AFL_LINUX_X86_64/packages
    SAP HANA Database (2.00.050.00.1592305219) in /install/DATA_UNITS/HDB_SERVER_LINUX_X86_64/server
    SAP HANA Database Client (2.5.86.1591211272) in /install/DATA_UNITS/HDB_CLIENT_LINUX_X86_64/client
    SAP HANA Smart Data Access (2.00.5.000.0) in /install/DATA_UNITS/SAP_HANA_SDA_20_LINUX_X86_64/packages
    SAP HANA Local Secure Store (2.4.23.0) in /install/DATA_UNITS/HANA_LSS_24_LINUX_X86_64/packages
    SAP HANA XS Advanced Runtime (1.0.127.426) in /install/DATA_UNITS/XSA_RT_10_LINUX_X86_64/packages
    SAP HANA EML AFL (2.00.050.0000.1592327743) in /install/DATA_UNITS/HDB_EML_AFL_10_LINUX_X86_64/packages
    SAP HANA EPM-MDS (2.00.050.0000.1592327743) in /install/DATA_UNITS/SAP_HANA_EPM-MDS_10/packages
    GUI for HALM for XSA (including product installer) Version 1 (1.014.1) in /install/DATA_UNITS/XSA_CONTENT_10/XSACALMPIUI14_1.zip
    XSAC FILEPROCESSOR 1.0 (1.000.76) in /install/DATA_UNITS/XSA_CONTENT_10/XSACFILEPROC00_76.zip
    SAP HANA tools for accessing catalog content, data preview, SQL console, etc. (2.012.20221) in /install/DATA_UNITS/XSAC_HRTT_20/XSACHRTT12_20221.zip
    XS Messaging Service 1 (1.004.8) in /install/DATA_UNITS/XSA_CONTENT_10/XSACMESSSRV04_8.zip
    Develop and run portal services for customer apps on XSA (1.005.0) in /install/DATA_UNITS/XSA_CONTENT_10/XSACPORTALSERV05_0.zip
    SAP Web IDE Web Client (4.005.0) in /install/DATA_UNITS/XSAC_SAP_WEB_IDE_20/XSACSAPWEBIDE05_0.zip
    XS JOB SCHEDULER 1.0 (1.007.12) in /install/DATA_UNITS/XSA_CONTENT_10/XSACSERVICES07_12.zip
    SAPUI5 FESV6 XSA 1 - SAPUI5 1.71 (1.071.8) in /install/DATA_UNITS/XSA_CONTENT_10/XSACUI5FESV671_8.zip
    SAPUI5 SERVICE BROKER XSA 1 - SAPUI5 Service Broker 1.0 (1.000.3) in /install/DATA_UNITS/XSA_CONTENT_10/XSACUI5SB00_3.zip
    XSA Cockpit 1 (1.001.15) in /install/DATA_UNITS/XSA_CONTENT_10/XSACXSACOCKPIT01_15.zip


Choose an action

  Index | Action            | Description
  --------------------------------------------------------------------------
  1     | HDB (update)      | Update SAP HANA Database version 2.00.051.00.1596053985
        |                   | hana-vm1 (Database Worker (worker))
  2     | install           | Install new system
  3     | extract_components | Extract components
  4     | Exit (do nothing) |
```

Figure 4.11 Detected Components

Installation

Figure 4.12 shows the installation prompts from the command-line tool for an interactive installation. This corresponds roughly to the input requested by the graphical installer, which also indicates where you are in the process in the header (look ahead to Figure 4.14).

```
Choose an action

 Index | Action           | Description
 ----------------------------------------------------------------------------------------
 1     | HDB (update)     | Update SAP HANA Database version 2.00.051.00.1596053985
       |                  | hana-vm1 (Database Worker (worker))
 2     | install          | Install new system
 3     | extract_components | Extract components
 4     | Exit (do nothing) |

Enter selected action index [4]: 2


SAP HANA Database version '2.00.050.00.1592305219' will be installed.

Select additional components for installation:

 Index | Components | Description
 ----------------------------------------------------------------------------------------
 1     | all        | All components
 2     | server     | No additional components
 3     | client     | Install SAP HANA Database Client version 2.5.86.1591211272
 4     | lss        | Install SAP HANA Local Secure Store version 2.4.23.0
 5     | smartda    | Install SAP HANA Smart Data Access version 2.00.5.000.0
 6     | xs         | Install SAP HANA XS Advanced Runtime version 1.0.127.426
 7     | afl        | Install SAP HANA AFL (incl.PAL,BFL,OFL) version 2.00.050.0000.1592327743
 8     | eml        | Install SAP HANA EML AFL version 2.00.050.0000.1592327743
 9     | epmmds     | Install SAP HANA EPM-MDS version 2.00.050.0000.1592327743

Enter comma-separated list of the selected indices [3]: 2
Enter Installation Path [/hana/shared]:
Enter Local Host Name [hana-vm1]:
Do you want to add hosts to the system? (y/n) [n]:
Enter SAP HANA System ID: A01
Enter Instance Number [01]:
Enter Local Host Worker Group [default]:

 Index | System Usage | Description
 ----------------------------------------------------------------------------------------
 1     | production   | System is used in a production environment
 2     | test         | System is used for testing, not production
 3     | development  | System is used for development, not production
 4     | custom       | System usage is neither production, test nor development

Select System Usage / Enter Index [4]:
Do you want to enable data and log volume encryption? [n]:
Enter Location of Data Volumes [/hana/data/A01]:
Enter Location of Log Volumes [/hana/log/A01]:
Restrict maximum memory allocation? [n]:
Enter Certificate Host Name For Host 'hana-vm1' [hana-vm1]:
Enter System Administrator (a01adm) Password:
Confirm System Administrator (a01adm) Password:
Enter System Administrator Home Directory [/usr/sap/A01/home]:
Enter System Administrator Login Shell [/bin/sh]:
Enter System Administrator User ID [1001]:
Enter System Database User (SYSTEM) Password:
Confirm System Database User (SYSTEM) Password:
Restart system after machine reboot? [n]:

Summary before execution:
============================
```

Figure 4.12 Installation Prompts

Following is the sequence of steps:

1. Select the action (install or update).

2. Select additional components for installation. The server is automatically selected; you can add the client, Application Function Library (AFL), and so on.

3. Enter the installation path, also referenced as <sapmnt>, with default value /hana/ shared.

4. Enter the local host name (as detected).

5. Add hosts to the system, which triggers a multiple-host installation.

6. Enter a system ID.

7. Enter an instance number, which defaults to the next available starting with 00.

8. Enter a local host worker group (default).

9. Enter system usage, which can be production, test, development, or custom (custom).

10. Enable data and log volume encryption (n).

11. Enter location data volumes (/hana/data/<SID>).

12. Enter location log volumes (/hana/data/<SID>).

13. Set a global allocation limit, which defines the system memory limit.

14. Enter a certificate host name for the host. This addresses the scenario when the internal host name differs from the public host name.

15. Enter a system administration password.

16. Enter a system administrator home directory, which uses the SAP-specific /usr/sap/<SID>/home path and not /home/username.

17. Enter the system administrator login shell (shell sh as default).

18. Enter the system administrator user ID. This should be the next available, starting with 1001; this is relevant for multiple-host installations as the ID of the <sid>adm user needs to be identical on all hosts.

19. Enter a system database user (SYSTEM) password.

20. Configure an automatic system start (n). This configures the auto start parameter in the profile, as explained in Chapter 3 when we described the start-up sequence.

After all input is provided, the installer displays a screen where you can review your choices before proceeding with the installation with the **Are you sure? [y|n]** prompt. Depending on the available resources, an SAP HANA server installation takes about five minutes. For each additional host, add one minute. When the SAP HANA XSA runtime component with applications is included, this extends the installation time by 30 minutes or more.

The system parameter global.ini/[memorymanager]/global_allocation_limit controls the amount of memory each SAP HANA instance can allocate. The default value is 0, which results in 90% of the first 64 GB plus 97% of the remainder. Although HDBLCM detects the presence of other SAP HANA systems, it doesn't adjust this parameter. This parameter needs to be adjusted for multiple components, one system (MCOS) deployments; otherwise, the instance may not start, which causes the installation to fail.

SAP HANA 2.0 SPS 05: What's New?
The prompt to enable data and log volume encryption is new as of SPS 05. The equivalent installation parameter is volume_encryption.

Local Secure Store

The local secure store (LSS) provides an alternative location to store encryption keys and other sensitive data otherwise stored in the secure stores in the file system (SSFS). As we describe LSS in more detail in Chapter 10, we'll cover only the installation aspects here.

To activate LSS during the installation or update, use the command:

```
hdblcm --secure_store=localsecurestore
```

Next, you need to select LSS as an additional component to install because it comes as a separate installation package. During the installation, you then receive the following additional prompts:

1. Enter installation path for local secure store [/lss/shared].
2. Enter local secure store user (a01crypt) password.
3. Enter local secure store user (a01crypt) ID [1002].
4. Enter local secure store user group ID [80]:.
5. Enter local secure store user home directory [/usr/sap/<SID>/lss/home].
6. Enter local secure store user login shell [/bin/sh].
7. Enter local secure store auto backup password.

> **Learn More**
> LSS is documented in the SAP HANA Administration Guide.

Multiple-Host Installation

To perform a multiple-host installation, you use the same software and the same HDBLCM tool. As discussed in Chapter 3 when we described file system recommendations, the built-in support for scale-out configurations is by design. The executables (i.e., binaries or program files, to use some alternative terms) are installed on a shared storage location just like the database data and redo log files. The local SAP HANA host installation only involves creating the pointers (symbolic link files in UNIX terminology) and the directory structure for the home directory and trace files. You see this illustrated in Figure 4.13. The local /usr/sap location mainly contains pointers to the shared /hana/shared location. This makes adding hosts very simple and quick.

For this reason, installing a multiple-host system is nearly identical to installing a single-host system. The only exception is the dialog screen illustrated in Figure 4.14, showing the GUI. In command-line mode, the dialog is similar.

```
hdbadm@hana-vm1:/usr/sap/HDB> ls -l
total 12
lrwxrwxrwx 1 hdbadm sapsys   22 Jun 26 15:19 HDB00 -> /hana/shared/HDB/HDB00
drwxr-x--- 3 hdbadm sapsys 4096 Jun 26 15:23 hdblcm_uploads
drwxr-xr-x 8 hdbadm sapsys 4096 Aug  6 09:04 home
drwxr-x--- 3 hdbadm sapsys 4096 Jun 26 15:16 SYS
hdbadm@hana-vm1:/usr/sap/HDB> ls -l SYS
total 4
drwxr-x--- 2 hdbadm sapsys 4096 Jun 26 15:16 exe
lrwxrwxrwx 1 hdbadm sapsys   23 Jun 26 15:16 global -> /hana/shared/HDB/global
lrwxrwxrwx 1 hdbadm sapsys   24 Jun 26 15:16 profile -> /hana/shared/HDB/profile
hdbadm@hana-vm1:/usr/sap/HDB> ls -l SYS/exe
total 0
lrwxrwxrwx 1 hdbadm sapsys 36 Jun 26 15:16 hdb -> /hana/shared/HDB/exe/linuxx86_64/hdb
hdbadm@hana-vm1:/usr/sap/HDB>
```

Figure 4.13 File System

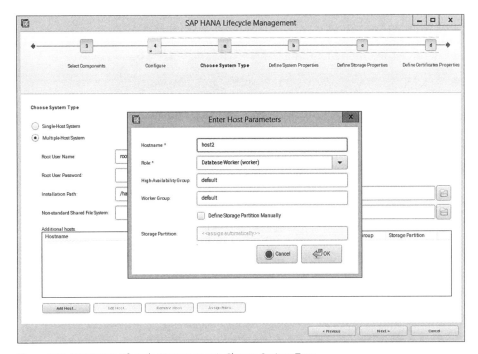

Figure 4.14 SAP HANA Lifecycle Management: Choose System Type

When you select **Multiple-Host System**, you need to provide the **Root User Name** and **Root User Password**. For security reasons, the root user may have been disabled, in which case, you need to enter the user with equivalent superuser privileges. Clicking the **Add Host** button returns the **Enter Host Parameters** dialog. Here you need to provide **Host Name** and **Role** (required). The **High Availability Group**, **Worker Group**, and **Storage Partition** are optional.

The selected default value of the role is **Database Worker**. The alternative for the database is **Database Standby**. Other host roles listed in the dialog are for SAP HANA XSA and for the add-on products SAP HANA dynamic tiering, SAP HANA streaming analytics, and the SAP HANA accelerator for SAP ASE.

High availability (HA) groups are relevant for multiple-host systems with standby hosts or with systems with dedicated hosts for SAP HANA XSA and/or add-ons products. An SAP HANA XSA or dynamic tiering host might have different machine resources compared to an SAP HANA database worker host. With a HA group, you can group these hosts in the right group for failover.

The **Worker Group** parameter is typically set to default. The only exception is when you want to configure SAP HANA extension nodes, in which case, the value **worker_dt** should be used. An extension node is technically the same as a host in an SAP HANA multiple-host system but with a relaxed core/memory ratio and support for different processor types and number of cores. We'll return to this topic in Chapter 9.

Installation Automation

You can run HDBLCM in unattended mode with the `--batch` option or with `-b`:

```
hdblcm -b --sid=TST --password=*** --system_user_password=***
```

At a minimum, you need to provide the SID and a password for the operating system administration account and for the SYSTEM user. In interactive mode, we're prompted for this input. For a number of other parameters, a default value is proposed. There are, however, many more parameters available for configuration than displayed in interactive mode. To set these parameters, you need to either use the advanced interactive mode and pass them on the command line or use the batch mode with parameter file (or a combination of both).

To automate an installation, first instruct HDBLCM to generate a template file via the following command:

```
hdblcm --action=install --dump_configfile_template=/tmp/myfile
```

The command generates a configuration file template and a password file template. This is an editable text file, as illustrated in Figure 4.15.

To perform the actual installation, you need to provide the name of the configuration file: `hdblcm --configfile=/tmp/myfile -b`.

Some parameters in the configuration file use variables that are automatically substituted with the provided input, for example, `datapath=/hana/data/${sid}`.

With the installation parameter `custom_cfg`, you can specify the location of custom system parameter (*.ini*) files. These will be copied to the corresponding location for the system, host, or tenant database. This enables you to set the global allocation limit, for example.

To avoid storing passwords in the configuration files, you can pass these either when prompted in interactive mode or use a separate file in XML format. This file can be distributed and updated separately. The password template file is illustrated in Figure 4.16.

```
hana-vm1:/install/DATA_UNITS/HDB_SERVER_LINUX_X86_64 # ./hdblcm --action=install --dump_configfile_template=/tmp/myfile

SAP HANA Lifecycle Management - SAP HANA Database 2.00.050.00.1592305219
************************************************************

Scanning software locations...
Detected components:
    SAP HANA AFL (incl.PAL,BFL,OFL) (2.00.050.0000.1592327743) in /install/DATA_UNITS/HDB_AFL_LINUX_X86_64/packages
    SAP HANA Database (2.00.050.00.1592305219) in /install/DATA_UNITS/HDB_SERVER_LINUX_X86_64/server
    SAP HANA Database Client (2.5.86.1591211272) in /install/DATA_UNITS/HDB_CLIENT_LINUX_X86_64/client
    SAP HANA Smart Data Access (2.00.5.000.0) in /install/DATA_UNITS/SAP_HANA_SDA_20_LINUX_X86_64/packages
    SAP HANA Local Secure Store (2.4.23.0) in /install/DATA_UNITS/HANA_LSS_24_LINUX_X86_64/packages
    SAP HANA XS Advanced Runtime (1.0.127.426) in /install/DATA_UNITS/XSA_RT_10_LINUX_X86_64/packages
    SAP HANA EML AFL (2.00.050.0000.1592327743) in /install/DATA_UNITS/HDB_EML_AFL_10_LINUX_X86_64/packages
    SAP HANA EPM-MDS (2.00.050.0000.1592327743) in /install/DATA_UNITS/SAP_HANA_EPM-MDS_10/packages
    GUI for HALM for XSA (including product installer) Version 1 (1.014.1) in /install/DATA_UNITS/XSA_CONTENT_10/XSACALMPIUI14_1.zip
    XSAC FILEPROCESSOR 1.0 (1.000.76) in /install/DATA_UNITS/XSA_CONTENT_10/XSACFILEPROC00_76.zip
    SAP HANA tools for accessing catalog content, data preview, SQL console, etc. (2.012.20221) in /install/DATA_UNITS/XSAC_HRTT_20/XSACHRTT12_20221.zip
    XS Messaging Service 1 (1.004.8) in /install/DATA_UNITS/XSACMESSSRV04_8.zip
    Develop and run portal services for customer apps on XSA (1.005.0) in /install/DATA_UNITS/XSA_CONTENT_10/XSACPORTALSERV05_0.zip
    SAP Web IDE Web Client (4.005.0) in /install/DATA_UNITS/XSAC_SAP_WEB_IDE_20/XSACSAPWEBIDE05_0.zip
    XS JOB SCHEDULER 1.0 (1.007.12) in /install/DATA_UNITS/XSA_CONTENT_10/XSACSERVICES07_12.zip
    SAPUI5 FESV6 XSA 1 - SAPUI5 1.71 (1.071.8) in /install/DATA_UNITS/XSA_CONTENT_10/XSACUI5FESV671_8.zip
    SAPUI5 SERVICE BROKER XSA 1 - SAPUI5 Service Broker 1.0 (1.000.3) in /install/DATA_UNITS/XSA_CONTENT_10/XSACUI5SB00_3.zip
    XSA Cockpit 1 (1.001.15) in /install/DATA_UNITS/XSA_CONTENT_10/XSACXSACOCKPIT01_15.zip
Config file template '/tmp/myfile' written
Password file template '/tmp/myfile.xml' written
Configuration file template created
hana-vm1:/install/DATA_UNITS/HDB_SERVER_LINUX_X86_64 # cat /tmp/myfile

[General]

# Location of Installation Medium
component_medium=

# Comma separated list of component directories
component_dirs=

# Use single master password for all users, created during installation ( Default: n )
use_master_password=n

# Directory root to search for components
component_root=
```

Figure 4.15 Installation Automation

Using a pipe, you pass the output of the cat command to HDBLCM with a parameter to instruct the installer to read the password (file) from standard input as follows:

```
cat ~/passwords.xml | ./hdblcm --sid=A01 --configfile=/tmp/myfile
--read_password_from_stdin=xml -b
```

```
hana-vm1:~ # cat /tmp/myfile.xml
<?xml version="1.0" encoding="UTF-8"?>
<!-- Replace the 3 asterisks with the password -->
<Passwords>
    <root_password><![CDATA[***]]></root_password>
    <sapadm_password><![CDATA[***]]></sapadm_password>
    <master_password><![CDATA[***]]></master_password>
    <sapadm_password><![CDATA[***]]></sapadm_password>
    <password><![CDATA[***]]></password>
    <system_user_password><![CDATA[***]]></system_user_password>
    <lss_user_password><![CDATA[***]]></lss_user_password>
    <lss_backup_password><![CDATA[***]]></lss_backup_password>
    <streaming_cluster_manager_password><![CDATA[***]]></streaming_cluster_manager_password>
    <ase_user_password><![CDATA[***]]></ase_user_password>
    <org_manager_password><![CDATA[***]]></org_manager_password>
</Passwords>
hana-vm1:~ #
```

Figure 4.16 Password Template File

Exam Tip

You're not expected to be familiar with all the installation parameters, but we recommend browsing the **Parameter Reference** section of the installation guide and take a look at the **Tutorials** section.

If you prefer, take a look at the video tutorials from the SAP HANA Academy at *http://s-prs.co/v507831*.

Resident HDBLCM

A local version of the HDBLCM tool is automatically added when you install the SAP HANA server with HDBLCM. This is called the resident version of the HDBLCM tool and provides a release-compatible PLM tool to perform post-installation and administrations tasks. For new installations, you always use HDBLCM on the software media. To add or update additional components, you use the resident version. This way, the installer and installed components are of the same release. For the same reason, you use the resident HDBLCM version to perform post-installation configuration activities. This avoids installing software or making configuration changes that aren't supported for the current release. Both the installation media and resident versions of the tool are shown as command-line tools in Figure 4.17. The GUI and web interface versions of the resident HDBLCM tool provide similar menu options (refer to Figure 4.4).

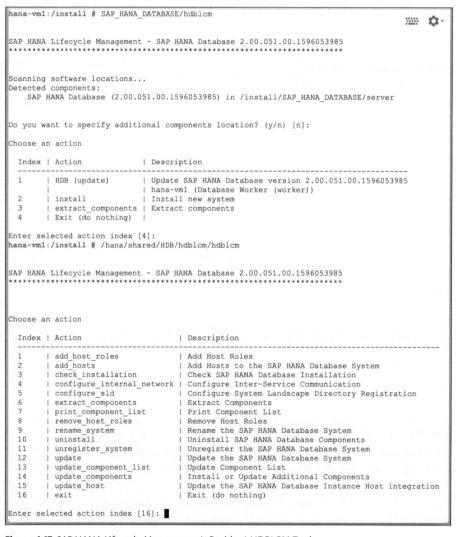

```
hana-vm1:/install # SAP_HANA_DATABASE/hdblcm                              ⌨  ☼·


SAP HANA Lifecycle Management - SAP HANA Database 2.00.051.00.1596053985
*************************************************************************


Scanning software locations...
Detected components:
    SAP HANA Database (2.00.051.00.1596053985) in /install/SAP_HANA_DATABASE/server


Do you want to specify additional components location? (y/n) [n]:

Choose an action

  Index | Action              | Description
  ---------------------------------------------------------------------------------
    1     | HDB (update)        | Update SAP HANA Database version 2.00.051.00.1596053985
          |                     | hana-vm1 (Database Worker (worker))
    2     | install             | Install new system
    3     | extract_components  | Extract components
    4     | Exit (do nothing)   |

Enter selected action index [4]:
hana-vm1:/install # /hana/shared/HDB/hdblcm/hdblcm


SAP HANA Lifecycle Management - SAP HANA Database 2.00.051.00.1596053985
*************************************************************************



Choose an action

  Index | Action                    | Description
  ---------------------------------------------------------------------------------
    1     | add_host_roles            | Add Host Roles
    2     | add_hosts                 | Add Hosts to the SAP HANA Database System
    3     | check_installation        | Check SAP HANA Database Installation
    4     | configure_internal_network | Configure Inter-Service Communication
    5     | configure_sld             | Configure System Landscape Directory Registration
    6     | extract_components        | Extract Components
    7     | print_component_list      | Print Component List
    8     | remove_host_roles         | Remove Host Roles
    9     | rename_system             | Rename the SAP HANA Database System
    10    | uninstall                 | Uninstall SAP HANA Database Components
    11    | unregister_system         | Unregister the SAP HANA Database System
    12    | update                    | Update the SAP HANA Database System
    13    | update_component_list     | Update Component List
    14    | update_components         | Install or Update Additional Components
    15    | update_host               | Update the SAP HANA Database Instance Host integration
    16    | exit                      | Exit (do nothing)

Enter selected action index [16]: █
```

Figure 4.17 SAP HANA Lifecycle Management: Resident HDBLCM Tool

HDBLCM is included as a standalone tool in the installation media, and you use the installer to install the resident version of the tool.

With the resident HDBLCM tool, you can perform several post-installation and system reconfiguration tasks. You can get the tool to print a list of all components installed, for example, which is called **View System Information** in the web interface. You can also check the database server installation, although this requires the command-line version of the tool.

Should any component be missing, you can use resident HDBLCM to add components, for example, to include the AFL. Similarly, you can use resident HDBLCM to uninstall components or the system as a whole.

For SAP landscapes managed by SAP Solution Manager, you can register the SAP HANA system with the System Landscape Directory (SLD). For this, you need to provide the SLD host name port and account with user name and password.

With **Add Host Roles** and **Remove Host Roles**, you can make changes to the roles, for example, by adding the SAP HANA XS worker role to a host with the database standby role. This applies to multiple-host systems. With the **Add Host** and **Remove Host** options, you can create or extend a multiple-host system or reduce the number of hosts. Before you can change a single-host system to a multiple-host system, however, you first need to modify the inter-service communication configuration. For a single-host system, this will be set to **Local** and needs to be changed to either **Internal** or **Global**. We configure these topics in more detail in Chapter 9.

To relocate an SAP HANA single-host instance or even an entire system, you use the unregister option of the resident HDBLCM. This action is performed if there is a hardware failure on a single host, for example, and you need to replace the server. Another example is when you want to move your multiple-host SAP HANA system to more powerful hardware: scale-up of a scale-out configuration—yes, that is possible too. We cover HA in Chapter 12.

Changing the SID, instance number, or host name is complex as these values are recorded in multiple files and are also used in the directory hierarchy. With **Rename System**, you can change these values properly. This requires root privileges, just like a full uninstall and unregister, as shown in Figure 4.18. For most resident HDBLCM actions, however, the operating system administration account <sid>adm suffices.

If the system is an SAP HANA 1.0 system running in single database mode, an additional menu option will be available, and you can use HDBLCM to convert the system to a tenant database system.

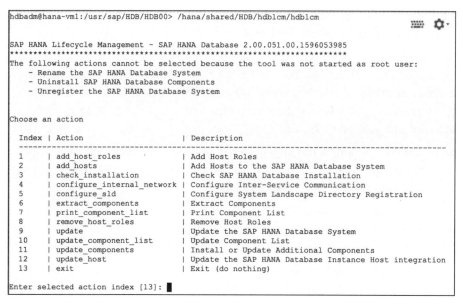

```
hdbadm@hana-vm1:/usr/sap/HDB/HDB00> /hana/shared/HDB/hdblcm/hdblcm

SAP HANA Lifecycle Management - SAP HANA Database 2.00.051.00.1596053985
*************************************************************************
The following actions cannot be selected because the tool was not started as root user:
    - Rename the SAP HANA Database System
    - Uninstall SAP HANA Database Components
    - Unregister the SAP HANA Database System


Choose an action

  Index | Action                      | Description
  ---------------------------------------------------------------------------------------------
   1    | add_host_roles              | Add Host Roles
   2    | add_hosts                   | Add Hosts to the SAP HANA Database System
   3    | check_installation          | Check SAP HANA Database Installation
   4    | configure_internal_network  | Configure Inter-Service Communication
   5    | configure_sld               | Configure System Landscape Directory Registration
   6    | extract_components          | Extract Components
   7    | print_component_list        | Print Component List
   8    | remove_host_roles           | Remove Host Roles
   9    | update                      | Update the SAP HANA Database System
  10    | update_component_list       | Update Component List
  11    | update_components           | Install or Update Additional Components
  12    | update_host                 | Update the SAP HANA Database Instance Host integration
  13    | exit                        | Exit (do nothing)

Enter selected action index [13]: 
```

Figure 4.18 SAP HANA Lifecycle Management: Not Root

Updates

To update an SAP HANA system, you can either use resident HDBLCM or the version from the installation media. The difference is minimal because when using the resident version, we're prompted first to provide the path to the location of the installation media (installation kit in the web interface) after which control is passed to the update tool, as shown in Figure 4.19. The dialog is the same for the command-line and graphical interfaces.

Update System and Components (HDB)

Specify location, containing the new version of the SAP HANA Database Server component. You will be able to add additional component locations afterwards.

SAP HANA Database Installation Kit Location: /install/SAP_HANA_DATABASE

Verify Authenticity of the Installation Kit: ✓

>>> Proceed with Update

Figure 4.19 Update System and Components

Note that you can request the tool to verify the authenticity of the installation kit and do a validation of the checksums to make sure that the software download (copy) is identical to the source files and hasn't been tampered with during transportation.

Next, we're prompted to add software locations, select the components to update, provide passwords, and confirm your selections, as shown in Figure 4.20. Depending on the choices made, additional dialogs might be presented.

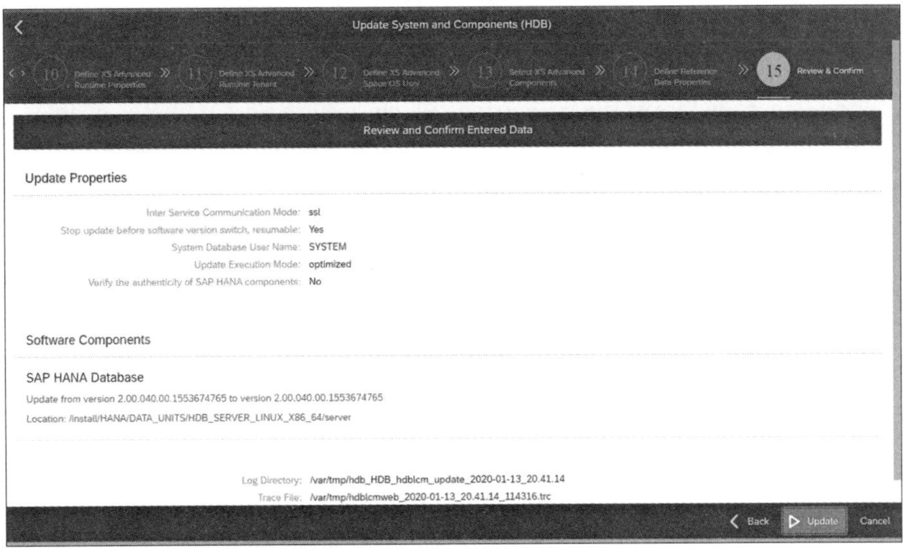

Figure 4.20 Update System: Review and Confirm

Specific to the web interface of the SAP HANA PLM tool is the **Advanced Parameters Configuration** dialog in which to configure general parameters and component-specific parameters. For **SAP HANA Database Update Parameters**, for example, as shown in Figure 4.21, you can specify whether to change the initial SSFS key, the communication mode for the services, whether to use a single database user password for the system database user, and other options.

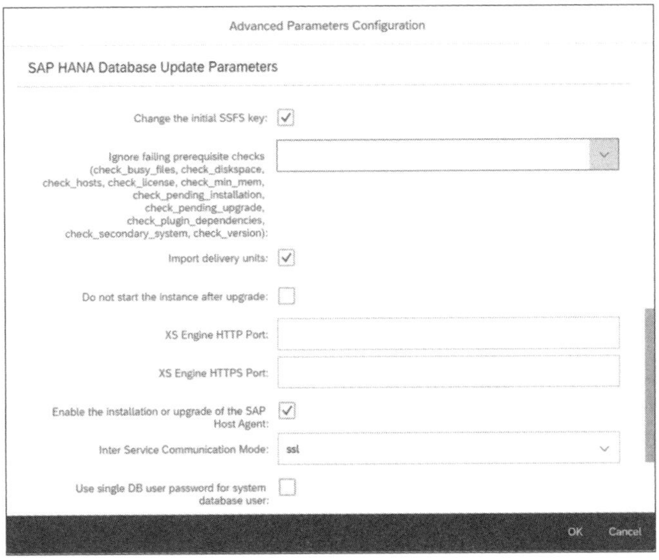

Figure 4.21 Advanced Parameters Configuration: Database Update

Under **General Parameters**, you can configure the update execution mode as either **standard** or **optimized**, as shown in Figure 4.22. Standard updates the components in sequence; optimized updates the components in one go, minimizing system restarts. This setting is relevant if add-on components such as SAP HANA dynamic tiering are updated together with the database. With this setting, multiple system restarts are avoided.

The **Stop update before software version switch, resumable** parameter enables what in the documentation is called a phased system update. This separates the update into an online phase where all the prerequisites are performed and a downtime phase when system access is closed, and the update is executed. With a phased system update, all the preliminary work is performed when the system is still up and running. This includes extracting components and verifying dependencies. Any issues detected can be investigated and corrected before any downtime is required. The command-line equivalent is `hdblcm --action=update --prepare_update`.

For the actual update, run HDBLCM again (any UI), and this time just click the **Update** button. In unattended mode, this is passed as a parameter.

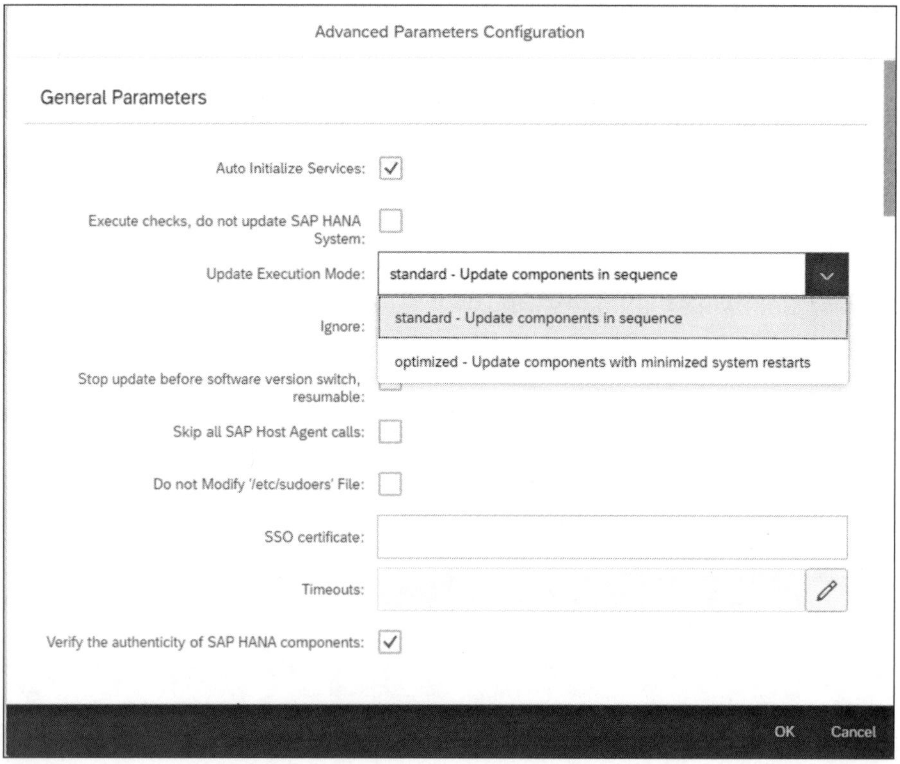

Figure 4.22 Advanced Parameters Configuration

HDB Tools

Regardless of which interface you use and whether you call HDBLCM from the installation media or the resident version, the tool itself only provides a UI to prepare a specific task. Technically, HDBLCM is a wrapper tool that calls other executables to perform the actual platform lifecycle management actions. Figure 4.23 shows the contents of the HDB_SERVER_LINUX_X86_64 directory with the hdblcm, hdblcmgui, and hdblcmweb commands (the latter only prints the URL of the web UI). In addition, hdbinst, hdbsetup, hdbuninst, and hdbupd are listed. These are the actual HDB tools that perform the installation, update, and uninstall with hdbsetup representing the graphical version.

The resident HDBLCM is installed to <sapmnt>/<SID>/hdblcm, but the resident HDB tools are located, or rather hidden, elsewhere on the file system because manual execution of the HDB tools isn't supported. HDBLCM maintains platform lifecycle metadata about the installation for dependencies and updates, but this information isn't recorded when you launch the HDB tools directly.

```
hdbadm@hana-vm1:/usr/sap/HDB/HDB00> ls -l /install/DATA_UNITS/HDB_SERVER_LINUX_X86_64/hdb*
-r-xr-xr-x 1 root root 14360 Jun 16 13:03 /install/DATA_UNITS/HDB_SERVER_LINUX_X86_64/hdbinst
-r-xr-xr-x 1 root root 14360 Jun 16 13:03 /install/DATA_UNITS/HDB_SERVER_LINUX_X86_64/hdblcm
-r-xr-xr-x 1 root root 14360 Jun 16 13:03 /install/DATA_UNITS/HDB_SERVER_LINUX_X86_64/hdblcmgui
-r-xr-xr-x 1 root root 14360 Jun 16 13:03 /install/DATA_UNITS/HDB_SERVER_LINUX_X86_64/hdblcmweb
-r-xr-xr-x 1 root root 14360 Jun 16 13:03 /install/DATA_UNITS/HDB_SERVER_LINUX_X86_64/hdbsetup
-r-xr-xr-x 1 root root 14360 Jun 16 13:03 /install/DATA_UNITS/HDB_SERVER_LINUX_X86_64/hdbuninst
-r-xr-xr-x 1 root root 14360 Jun 16 13:03 /install/DATA_UNITS/HDB_SERVER_LINUX_X86_64/hdbupd
hdbadm@hana-vm1:/usr/sap/HDB/HDB00>
hdbadm@hana-vm1:/usr/sap/HDB/HDB00> ls -l /hana/shared/HDB/hdblcm/hdb*
-rwxr-xr-x 1 root root 14360 Jul 29 22:48 /hana/shared/HDB/hdblcm/hdblcm
-rwxr-xr-x 1 root root 14360 Jul 29 22:48 /hana/shared/HDB/hdblcm/hdblcmgui
-rwxr-xr-x 1 root root 14360 Jul 29 22:48 /hana/shared/HDB/hdblcm/hdblcmweb
hdbadm@hana-vm1:/usr/sap/HDB/HDB00>
hdbadm@hana-vm1:/usr/sap/HDB/HDB00> ls -l /hana/shared/HDB/global/hdb/install/bin/hdb*
-r-xr-xr-x 1 root root 14360 Jul  3 15:43 /hana/shared/HDB/global/hdb/install/bin/hdbaddhost
-r-xr-xr-x 1 root root 14360 Jul  3 15:43 /hana/shared/HDB/global/hdb/install/bin/hdbcheck
-r-xr-xr-x 1 root root 14360 Jul  3 15:43 /hana/shared/HDB/global/hdb/install/bin/hdbhostctrl
-r-xr-xr-x 1 root root 14360 Jul  3 15:43 /hana/shared/HDB/global/hdb/install/bin/hdbinst
-r-xr-xr-x 1 root root 14360 Jul  3 15:43 /hana/shared/HDB/global/hdb/install/bin/hdbmodify
-r-xr-xr-x 1 root root 14360 Jul  3 15:43 /hana/shared/HDB/global/hdb/install/bin/hdbreg
-r-xr-xr-x 1 root root 14360 Jul  3 15:43 /hana/shared/HDB/global/hdb/install/bin/hdbremovehost
-r-xr-xr-x 1 root root 14360 Jul  3 15:43 /hana/shared/HDB/global/hdb/install/bin/hdbrename
-r-xr-xr-x 1 root root 14360 Jul  3 15:43 /hana/shared/HDB/global/hdb/install/bin/hdbuninst
-r-xr-xr-x 1 root root 14360 Jul  3 15:43 /hana/shared/HDB/global/hdb/install/bin/hdbupdrep
hdbadm@hana-vm1:/usr/sap/HDB/HDB00> ▋
```

Figure 4.23 HDB Tools

For client installations, for example, on the Windows platform, the HDBLCM wrapper tool isn't included as there is no PLM data to maintain. Here you only find the HDB tools themselves—hdbinst|hdbuninst (command line) and hdbsetup (graphical)—as illustrated in Figure 4.24. Direct execution in this case is fully supported; it's the only way.

Exam Tip

You're not expected to be familiar with the location and names of the different HDB tools, but you should understand the architecture of the HDBLCM tool with its installation and resident versions.

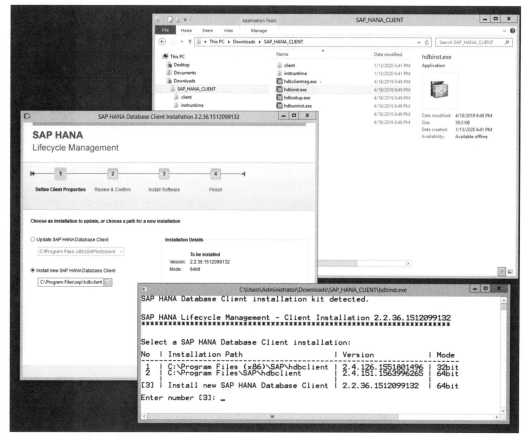

Figure 4.24 SAP HANA Lifecycle Management (Client)

Troubleshooting

For troubleshooting, it may be necessary to access the HDB tools directly. To access the help function of these tools, use the following command:

```
--action=[install|update] --pass_through_help –help
```

Both HDBLCM (hdblcm) and the HDB tool performing the action (e.g., hdbinst) generate log files. These files have the format hdb_<SID>_<action>_<timestamp> and are stored in the directory /var/tmp. Possible actions are install, update, add host, and so on. To activate the trace function, set the environment variable HDB_INSTALLER_TRACE_FILE.

If there is a failed update, the recommendation is to use HDBLCM to uninstall the software, recover the system from backup, reinstall the system, and perform the update again. Similarly, if there are installation issues, first run the component uninstaller (hdbuninst). Should the issue persist, we're advised to contact SAP Support.

Users Created during Installation

During installation, several user accounts are created. At the operating system level, this concerns the software owner or administration account <sid>adm and the account for the SAP Host Agent sapadm. When the LSS is installed, the <sid>crypt will be added. SAP HANA options such as dynamic tiering add additional operating system users.

Inside the database, several uses are created, for example, the system view object owner SYS, as well as a number of internal database accounts starting with _SYS; however, none of these accounts can be used to log on. The one exception is the database superuser account SYSTEM, created inside both the system database and the initial tenant database. This user is granted all system permissions (USER ADMIN, BACKUP ADMIN, etc.), and you should this user to create your own system administration account after which SYSTEM can be disabled.

For Lightweight Directory Access Protocol (LDAP) environments with a central user management system, the operating system accounts can be created prior to installation as HDBLCM won't modify the properties of existing users. The following rules apply:

- UID greater than 999
- User account name, including <sid> in all lowercase
- Primary group name sapsys (default GID 79)
- For multiple-host systems, identical UID and GID

Post-Installation Activities

SAP recommends the following post-installation activities:

- Perform an initial backup.
- Deactivate the SYSTEM user for production systems. Use dedicated task-oriented accounts instead (user admin, backup admin, etc.).
- Update SSFS master and encryption root keys, and, optionally, enable data-at-rest encryption and update passwords in case you received SAP HANA as an appliance or the installation was performed by a third party.
- Install a license.

After installation, the system parameter log_mode is set to overwrite for both the system and tenant database This causes the system to reuse the redo log segments without backup and avoids the situation where the file system is completely filled up with log file backups. After the first backup, the log mode is automatically switched to the default normal mode with automatic log backups enabled, which enables point-in-time recovery. We return to this topic in Chapter 11.

The certificates and public key infrastructure (PKI) to encrypt secure communications (network) and data at rest (persistence) are generated during the installation.

When the SAP HANA installation is performed by a third party, received as an appliance, or cloned (as is common for cloud-based environments), you need to update the encryption root keys and the SSFS master keys. We return to this topic in Chapter 10, where we also address the security implications of the SYSTEM user.

License

When you install SAP HANA, a temporary license key is automatically installed. This key is valid for 90 days, but SAP recommends applying for a permanent license key after installation as soon as possible. As illustrated in Figure 4.25, you can request and install a new license conveniently from the SAP HANA cockpit. Alternatively, you can request a new key from the SAP ONE Support Launchpad under **License Keys**. When you apply for a license, you need to provide the hardware key and SID of the system, specify the quantity of main memory (GB), and enter the desired expiration date. You can install a license key for the system database when it will be valid for all tenants (global) or install one for a single tenant database (local).

There are two types of permanent license keys: unenforced and enforced. When memory consumption exceeds the amount defined in the enforced license (plus some tolerance), the system is locked down and needs to be restarted, or a new license key needs to be installed that covers a higher limit. When both type of keys are present, the unenforced has priority.

When a permanent license key expires, a new temporary key is automatically installed but is only valid for 28 days.

In lockdown mode, access is restricted to users with the LICENSE ADMIN privilege and license-related queries, such as the one to install a new license SET SYSTEM LICENSE <key>. This implies that you can't back up a database in lockdown mode.

When you recover a database on an identical system (ID and hardware key), the license is included. If the license has expired, the same behavior applies, and the database will be locked.

For certain applications (components) and options, additional licenses may be required.

Learn More

For more extensive coverage of this topic, beyond the scope of this exam, see the SAP HANA platform documentation and the KBAs on the SAP ONE Support Launchpad:

- Managing SAP HANA Licenses – SAP HANA Administration Guide for SAP HANA Platform (2.0 SPS 04) at *http://s-prs.co/v507832*
- KBA 2213293 – How to Request SAP HANA Platform or Enterprise Edition License Keys
- KBA 2645528 – How to Install License for Tenant Database

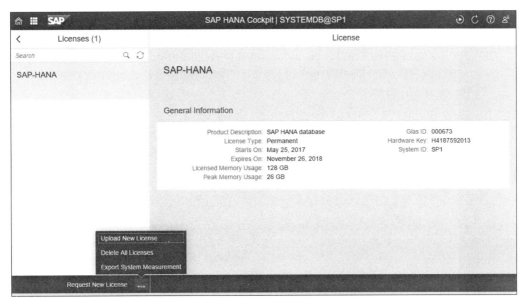

Figure 4.25 SAP HANA Cockpit: License

Release and Maintenance Strategy

In the release and maintenance of SAP HANA, you need to distinguish the following:

- Standard revision
- Maintenance revision
- Support package stack (SPS)
- Support package (SP)

New capabilities are released as a SPS. For SAP HANA 1.0, this used to be twice a year at regular intervals around May and November. For SAP HANA 2.0, the release cycle is a bit less consistent. As of SAP HANA 2.0 SPS 03, the release cycle is no longer twice but once a year. SAP HANA 2.0 SPS 03 and SPS 04 were released in April, but SPS 05 was released in June.

The release-to-customer (RTC) contains the initial revision where SPS 00 corresponds to revision 000, SPS 01 to revision 010, SPS 02 to revision 020, and so on. With each SPS, the revision counter is updated to the next decade (e.g., from 46 to 50).

SAP provides standard revisions until the next SPS RTC. They stay on the decade, so you can align revision 033 with SPS 03 and 042 with SPS 04. Standard revisions only contain incremental fixes.

SAP provides maintenance revisions after the last standard revision until end of maintenance (EOM) of the SPS. They only contain major bug fixes and are numbered as a point release, for example, 2.00.024.10 or 2.00.037.4 (i.e., SAP HANA 2.0 SPS 03 maintenance revision 037.4).

Maintenance (bug fixes and security patches) is provided for two years after SPS RTC. For SPS 04 (RTC April 2019), EOM will be April 2021, as shown in Figure 4.26.

For the last SPS of a major release, EOM is five years after RTC. For SAP HANA 1.0 SPS 12 (RTC 2016), EOM will be in May 2021. These dates are communicated in SAP Notes and in the PAM.

For SAP HANA 2.0 SPS 05, an exception was made as it isn't the last SPS of major release SAP HANA 2.0, yet it does come with five years of maintenance support. This was done to provide a stable upgrade path from SAP 1.0 SPS 12 to SAP HANA 2.0 SPS 05, both with five years of maintenance.

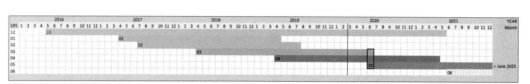

Figure 4.26 Release Cycles and Maintenance

SAP HANA cockpit is released independently as a SP, which contains both corrections and new functionality. SAP HANA cockpit 2.0 SP releases are aligned with SAP HANA 2.0 SPS releases. For SAP HANA platform 2.0 SPS 05, this was SAP HANA cockpit 2.0 SP 12. Other add-on components, such as SAP HANA dynamic tiering or SAP HANA streaming analytics, also have their own SP release cycle aligned with the platform.

SAP HANA 2.0 is upward compatible, and you can update the system without the need to migrate. When changing from version n to $n+1$, existing functions continue to be supported, data can be transformed without major changes, and application programming interfaces (APIs) of version n remain unchanged. Only deprecated features (n-1) may have been removed (n+1 or later).

You can update SAP HANA 1.0 SPS 10 directly to the latest SAP HANA 2.0 SPS release. For older releases, SAP recommends updating the system to SAP HANA 1.0 SPS 12 first. Not every update path is supported, which is documented in an SAP Note.

The Capture and Replay tool in SAP HANA can be used to capture real system workloads in the production environment for replay in the new target environment. This reduces manual effort for testing changes and helps ensure that landscape updates don't degrade system performance. This tool is integrated with SAP HANA cockpit and doesn't require a license or additional third-party software.

> **Learn More**
>
> For more extensive coverage of this topic, beyond the scope of this exam, see SAP Note 2378962 – SAP HANA 2.0 Revision and Maintenance Strategy.

SAP HANA Interactive Education

SAP HANA Interactive Education (SHINE) contains training content to help developers learn how to develop and deploy applications built for the in-memory platform. SHINE started as an SAP HANA native development workshop training based on the SAP HANA XS architecture for SAP HANA 1.0. The content leveraged the SAP NetWeaver enterprise procurement model (EPM) familiar already to many SAP developers. EPM is based on a real enterprise use case and includes a sample sales order dashboard and purchase order worklist application with a complete data model (tables, views, procedures, etc.) and sample data generator. Figure 4.27 shows the SHINE dashboard.

SHINE isn't installed by default, but you can download the content from the SAP ONE Support Launchpad or GitHub and install the app. There is a version for both SAP HANA XS, classic model and SAP HANA XSA, and there is a guide that documents how you can migrate SHINE content, showcasing a real-life scenario.

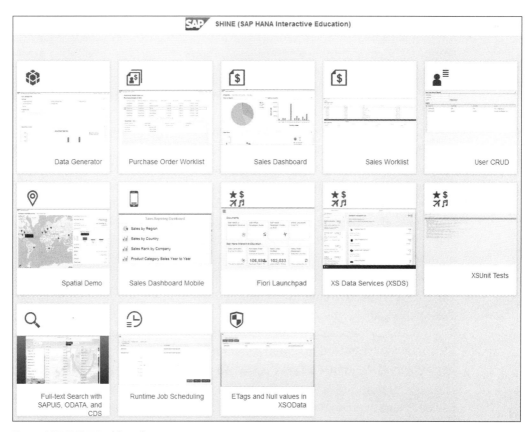

Figure 4.27 SHINE Dashboard

Learn More

For more information, see the openSAP course: SHINE Reference for Native SAP HANA Application Development (2016) at *https://open.sap.com/courses/hssh1*.

Important Terminology

For this exam objective, you're expected to understand the following terms:

- **Capture and Replay tool**
  This SAP HANA cockpit tool enables you to capture a particular workload on system A for replay on system B. This can be useful for system performance testing in migration projects.

- **Local secure store (LSS)**
  LSS provides an alternative location to store encryption keys and other sensitive data otherwise in secure stores in the file system (SSFS).

- **Maintenance revision**
  A maintenance revision provides corrections for components when standard revisions ends and until end of maintenance (EOM) of the support package stack (SPS) release. Maintenance revisions are identified with point releases, for example, 037.4.

- **Multiple-host system**
  A multiple-host system, also called a distributed or scale-out system, is a single SAP HANA system running on multiple computers or hosts.

- **SAP HANA application lifecycle management (ALM)**
  This general term refers to the installation and update of applications running on SAP HANA. The SAP HANA XS, classic model and SAP HANA XSA environments have different ALM command-line tools and web interfaces.

- **SAP HANA database lifecycle manager (HDBLCM)**
  HDBLCM is the platform lifecycle management (PLM) tool for SAP HANA. It's a wrapper tool that calls other commands to perform HDBLCM tasks. The tool has command-line, graphical, and web interfaces and can be used in interactive, batch, and advanced interactive mode using a combination of command-line and configuration file parameters. HDBLCM is included with the installation media but also installed with the system for post-installation system configuration tasks. This is called the resident HDBLCM version.

- **SAP HANA Interactive Education (SHINE)**
  This training and demo application helps developers learn how to build and deploy native applications for SAP HANA. There is a version for the SAP HANA XS, classic model and SAP HANA XSA architectures.

- **SAP HANA platform lifecycle management (PLM)**
  This general term refers to installation and update of the SAP HANA platform itself. It's also the name of the tool on the interface, although the documentation uses SAP HANA database lifecycle manager (HDBLCM).

- **SAP Host Agent**
  SAP Host Agent performs PLM tasks for SAP NetWeaver and SAP HANA platforms. You use the agent for monitoring and system instance management, but it also provides the web interface for HDBLCM.

- **SAR**
  SAR files are compressed archive files similar but not compatible with ZIP files. You use the SAPCAR command-line tool to create and uncompress the archive.

- **Software component**
  A software component is an independently installable unit. For the SAP HANA platform, this includes components such as the SAP HANA (database) server, SAP HANA client, or Application Function Library (AFL).

- **Software Downloads**
  SAP provides a single location for software downloads, appropriately named **Software Downloads**, on the SAP ONE Support Launchpad. In the past, you would go to the Software Download Center (SWDC) on the SAP Service Market Place (SMP), but this has been retired.

- **Standard revision**
  A standard revision provides incremental corrections (bug fixes and security updates) for components until the release-to-customer (RTC) of the next SPS. They are made available for download per component (database, client, etc.) and not for the entire release as with the SPS. Standard revisions continue the decade of the SPS, for example, 041, 042, and so on.

- **Support package (SP)**
  SPs are new releases of SAP HANA add-on products, such as SAP HANA cockpit or SAP HANA dynamic tiering, and they may contain both new capabilities and corrections.

- **Support package stack (SPS)**
  An SPS is the initial release of a new SAP HANA version. The last release of SAP HANA 1.0 is SPS 12 (2016). The latest release of SAP HANA 2.0 is SPS 05 (2020). It's made available for download as a single media set and contains all core components (server, client, etc.). Only an SPS contains new features (capabilities). The revision number of the initial SPS release is a decade (040, 050, etc.).

- **System Landscape Directory (SLD)**
  SLD is the central source of information on systems in your IT landscape used with SAP Solution Manager.

- **X Window System**
  The X Window System (X11) provides a graphical environment for UNIX/Linux operating systems. On hardened production systems, the X Window System is typically not installed. As a consequence, the graphical (X Window) version of HDBLCM is mainly used in training and development environments.

Practice Questions

These practice questions will help you evaluate your understanding of the topics covered in this chapter. The questions shown are similar in nature to those found on the certification examination. Although none of these questions will be found on the exam itself, they will allow you to review your knowledge of the subject. Select the correct answers, and then check the completeness of your answers in the "Practice Question Answers and Explanations" section. Remember that on the exam, you must select all correct answers, and only correct answers, to receive credit for the question.

1. Which command-line tool can you use to install SAP HANA XSA applications?

☐ **A.** hdbalm

☐ **B.** xs

☐ **C.** hdblcm

☐ **D.** cf

2. Which are considerations to use a parameter file with HDBLCM? (There are three correct answers.)

☐ **A.** The SAP HANA server doesn't include a graphical environment.

☐ **B.** You need to perform more complex installations.

☐ **C.** You need to install a large number of SAP HANA systems.

☐ **D.** You want to standardize installations using a parameter file.

☐ **E.** The SAP HANA server doesn't allow any incoming HTTPS traffic.

3. You execute the command hdblcmgui on the SAP HANA server to start the graphical version of the SAP HANA database lifecycle manager (HDBLCM). The tool doesn't display, but an error is returned. What might cause this issue? (There are two correct answers.)

☐ **A.** The SAP HANA server doesn't contain a graphical environment.

☐ **B.** The graphical version of the SAP HANA database lifecycle manager is no longer supported for release 2.0 SPS 05.

☐ **C.** The X Windows DISPLAY environment variable isn't correctly set.

☐ **D.** You used the wrong command. The correct command is hdblcm --gui.

☐ **E.** You can only run the hdblcmgui command from the installation media, not directly on the SAP HANA server.

4. You execute the hdbinst command in a terminal session from the installation media to install the SAP HANA database. What is the result?

☐ **A.** An error is returned because you can't install the SAP HANA database using the hdbinst command. You need to use hdblcm.

☐ **B.** An error is returned because the hdbinst lifecycle management platform tool requires a graphical interface.

☐ **C.** A command not found error is returned because the `hdbinst` command only exists in the resident SAP HANA database lifecycle manager (HDBLCM) tool.

☐ **D.** The SAP HANA Lifecycle Management tool starts and prompts you to provide the local host name.

5. You execute the `hdblcm` command in a terminal session from the installation media to add a host to the system but can only chose between performing a new installation or updating the system. How do you add a host?

☐ **A.** To add a host, first select to update the system. You'll be provided with the **Add Host** dialog at a later stage.

☐ **B.** To add a host, you need to run the HDBLCM tool from its resident location on the file system and not from the installation media.

☐ **C.** To add a host, you need to run the `hdbaddhost` command, not `hdblcm`.

☐ **D.** To add a host, you need to run the command `hdblcm --addhost`.

☐ **E.** You can't add a host to an existing system. You can only add a host when performing a new installation.

6. You need to update your SAP HANA system and connect to the web UI of SAP HANA PLM. How do you proceed?

☐ **A.** This isn't possible. To update an SAP HANA system, you need to run HDBLCM from the installation media.

☐ **B.** This isn't possible. To update an SAP HANA system, you need to run HDBLCM in command-line mode.

☐ **C.** This isn't possible. To update an SAP HANA system, you need to run the `hdbupd` command.

☐ **D.** You select the **Update System and Components** tile and point to the location of the SAP HANA database installation kit.

7. You want to rename the SAP HANA database system and start the SAP HANA Lifecycle Management tool in resident mode but don't see this action listed. What do you need to do?

☐ **A.** You need to start the tool as the root user.

☐ **B.** To rename an SAP HANA database system, you need to run HDBLCM from the installation media.

☐ **C.** To rename an SAP HANA database system, you need to run the `hdbrename` command.

☐ **D.** To rename an SAP HANA database system, you need to run the SQL command `RENAME DATABASE`.

8. You execute the following command to perform an unattended installation of SAP HANA: `hdblcm -b --action=install --sid=DB1`. What is the output of the command?

    ☐ **A.** This command will execute successfully and installs SAP HANA system DB1.

    ☐ **B.** This command will exit with error: **Mandatory parameter 'password' (Password) is missing or invalid**.

    ☐ **C.** This command will exit with error: **Config file missing is or invalid**.

    ☐ **D.** This command will exit with error: **Password file is missing or invalid**.

9. Which activity is supported by both the resident HDBLCM tool as well as the one provided with the installation media? (There are two correct answers.)

    ☐ **A.** Update SAP HANA and its components.

    ☐ **B.** Add or remove SAP HANA hosts.

    ☐ **C.** Install or update additional components.

    ☐ **D.** Uninstall SAP HANA.

    ☐ **E.** Extract components.

10. You access the SAP HANA database and get the message: **System locked: license is invalid or expired**. Which situations always cause this issue? (There are two correct answers.)

    ☐ **A.** The temporary license automatically installed during installation has expired after 90 days, and no new license was installed.

    ☐ **B.** The permanent license was deleted.

    ☐ **C.** The permanent license has expired, and the automatically activated temporary license also expired after 28 days.

    ☐ **D.** The database was restored, and no new license was installed.

    ☐ **E.** Current memory consumption exceeded the licensed amount plus tolerance, which invalidated the license.

11. Which installation parameters are required at a minimum? (There are two correct answers.)

    ☐ **A.** System identifier (SID)

    ☐ **B.** Installation path

    ☐ **C.** Installation components

    ☐ **D.** System user password

    ☐ **E.** Installation action

12. Which operating system users are defined in the configuration file? (There are three correct answers.)

☐ **A.** `<sid>adm`

☐ **B.** `sapsys`

☐ **C.** `<sid>crypt`

☐ **D.** `sapadm`

☐ **E.** `sapinst`

13. Until when are standard revisions provided?

☐ **A.** SAP provides standard revisions until end-of-maintenance (EOM) of the SPS.

☐ **B.** There is no fixed schedule, as communicated in SAP Notes and in the Product Availability Matrix (PAM).

☐ **C.** SAP provides standard revisions until the next SPS release-to-customer (RTC).

14. Which are recommended post-installation activities? (There are four correct answers.)

☐ **A.** Install a license.

☐ **B.** Update the SSFS master and encryption root keys if you received SAP HANA as an appliance or if the installation was performed by a third party.

☐ **C.** Deactivate the `SYSTEM` user.

☐ **D.** Change the `SYSTEM` user password.

☐ **E.** Perform an initial backup.

15. Where are the installation log files located?

☐ **A.** `/hana/log`

☐ **B.** `/tmp`

☐ **C.** `/var/tmp`

☐ **D.** `/usr/sap/< SID >/HDB<nn>/<hostname>/trace`

☐ **E.** `/var/log`

Practice Question Answers and Explanations

1. Correct answer: **B**

    xs is used to install SAP HANA XSA applications.

    Answer A is incorrect because hdbalm is the command-line tool to install SAP HANA XS, classic model applications. Answer C is incorrect because hdblcm is the command-line tool to install SAP HANA platform components. Answer D is incorrect because cf is the command-line tool to deploy (install) Cloud Foundry applications, for example, on SAP Cloud Platform.

2. Correct answers: **B, C, D**

    Use a parameter file to perform more complex installations not addressed in interactive mode, when you want to run HDBLCM in batch mode to perform a larger number of installations, or to standardize the installation process.

    Answers A and E are incorrect because, when the SAP HANA server doesn't include a graphical environment or doesn't allow any incoming HTTPS traffic for the web interface, you can still run the HDBLCM command-line tool in interactive mode.

3. Correct answers: **A, C**

    There are many reasons why an error could be returned by the HDBLCM tool (see SAP Note 2082466), but the most common ones are the absence of a graphical environment and wrong configuration of the DISPLAY environment variable.

    Answer B is incorrect because the graphical version of HDBLCM is supported for all SAP HANA releases. Answer D is incorrect because the hdblcmgui command is correct. Answer E is incorrect because you can run the graphical command both from the installation media and the resident HDBLCM location.

4. Correct answer: **D**

    HDBLCM is a wrapper tool that calls SAP HANA Lifecycle Management commands. You can use the hdbinst command to perform the SAP HANA installation, although this approach isn't supported for server installations. For SAP HANA client installations, on the other hand, you have to use the hdbinst command-line or hdbsetup graphical installer.

    Answer A is incorrect because no error is returned although the tool will display a message: **Warning: Direct usage of hdbinst is not supported. Use hdblcm instead**. Answer B is incorrect because hdbsetup requires a graphical interface, not hdbinst. Answer C is incorrect because hdbinst is included with both the installation media and the resident version of HDBLCM, as illustrated earlier in Figure 4.23.

5. Correct answer: **B**

   To add a host to an existing system, run the resident HDBLCM tool, not the one from the installation media.

   Answer A is incorrect because if you select to update the system, you're prompted to select the components to update and to provide the name and password of the system database user but not to add hosts. Answer C is incorrect because you can add a host by running the hdbaddhost, as shown in Figure 4.28. However, direct usage of the HDB tools isn't supported. Answer D is incorrect because you can use the parameter --addhosts=<host>[,<host2>] when installing a new system but not to add hosts to an existing system.

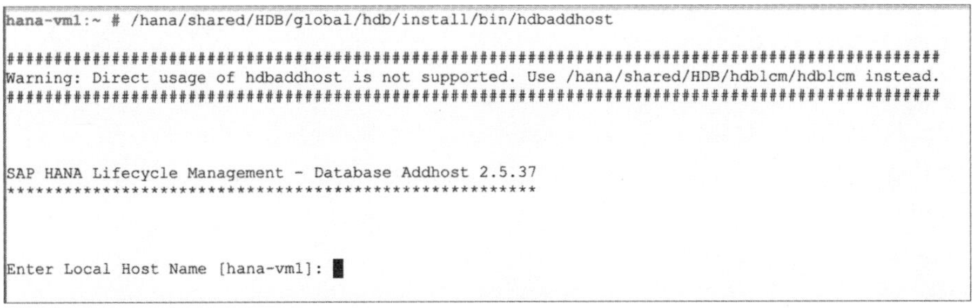

```
hana-vml:~ # /hana/shared/HDB/global/hdb/install/bin/hdbaddhost

############################################################################################
Warning: Direct usage of hdbaddhost is not supported. Use /hana/shared/HDB/hdblcm/hdblcm instead.
############################################################################################


SAP HANA Lifecycle Management - Database Addhost 2.5.37
*********************************************************


Enter Local Host Name [hana-vml]: █
```

Figure 4.28 SAP HANA Lifecycle Management: Database Addhost

6. Correct answer: **D**

   To update a system, HDBLCM needs the software from the installation media. You can use both the resident HDBLCM and the one from the installation media to perform updates.

   Answer A is incorrect because you can update an SAP HANA system using all three interfaces of the HDBLCM tool. Answer B is incorrect because you can update an SAP HANA system using all three modes of the HDBLCM tool (interactive, advanced interactive, batch). Answer C is incorrect because HDBLCM will execute the hdbupd command to perform the update, but running this command directly isn't supported.

7. Correct answer: **A**

   As illustrated previously in Figure 4.18, you need to start HDBLCM as root to rename the SAP HANA database system.

   Answer B is incorrect because you need to use the resident HDBLCM tool to rename a system. Answer C is incorrect because using the hdbrename command directly isn't supported. Answer D is incorrect because you use a SQL command to rename a tenant database but not to rename an SAP HANA system. Note that it isn't possible to rename the system database (SYSTEMDB).

8. Correct answer: **B**

   To perform an unattended installation in batch mode, you need to provide the password either on the command line (advanced interactive), by using a configuration file, or with parameter read_password_from_stdin and password file.

Answers C and D are incorrect because a configuration file or password file isn't required.

9. Correct answer: **A, E**

   The resident HDBLCM tool supports SAP HANA updates and component extraction (refer to Figure 4.17).

   Answers B, C, and D are incorrect because we can only use the resident HDBLCM to add or remove a host from a multiple-host system.

10. Correct answers: **A, B, C**

    You would receive the system locked message if the temporary license that was automatically installed has expired, if the permanent license was deleted, or if both the permanent license and temporary license have expired.

    Answer D is incorrect because when a database is restored, both the SID and hardware key are identical, and the license hasn't expired, the license will be valid (active), and the database won't lock down. Answer E is incorrect because only with an enforced license will the database shut down in case of memory overconsumption.

11. Correct answers: **A, D**

    When you execute the command hdblcm -b, the message is returned: Mandatory parameter 'sid' (SID) is missing or invalid.

    When you execute the command with the SID (hdblcm --sid=ABC -b), the message is returned: Mandatory parameter 'password' (Password) is missing or invalid.

    When you execute the command with the sid and password parameters, the message is returned: Mandatory parameter 'system_user_password' (SQLSys-Passwd) is missing or invalid.

    When you execute the command with parameters sid, password, and system_user_password, the installation proceeds.

    Answer B is incorrect because the installation path defaults to <sapmnt> or /hana/shared. Answer C is incorrect because the installation components default to the component used to launch hdblcm. Answer E is incorrect because the installation action defaults to install.

12. Correct answers: **A, C, D**

    The <sid>adm user is the operating system administration account. The <sid>crypt user is the account used for the local secure store (LSS) as described in Chapter 10, and the sapadm is the account used for SAP Host Agent.

    Answer B is incorrect because sapsys is the name of the operating system group to which <sid>adm belongs. Answer E is incorrect because sapinst is the name of the operating system group used for SAP NetWeaver installations.

13. Correct answer: **C**

    SAP provides standard revisions until the next SPS release-to-customer (RTC). After this date, SAP provides maintenance revisions containing only major bug fixes, until end-of-maintenance (EOM) of the SPS.

    Answer A is incorrect because this statement applies to maintenance revisions. Answer B is incorrect because this statement applies to release and maintenance information in general, which is subject to change and communicated in SAP Notes and in the PAM.

14. Correct answers: **A, B, C, E**

    See the recommended post-installation activities, as documented in the SAP HANA Installation and Update Guide.

    Answer D is incorrect because changing the SYSTEM user password isn't a recommended post-installation activity. The password was provided as installation input. No default passwords are used.

15. Correct answer: **C**

    Both HDBLCM (hdblcm) and the HDB tool performing the action (e.g., hdbinst) generate log files. These files have the format hdb_<SID>_<action>_<timestamp> and are stored in the directory /var/tmp. Possible actions are install, update, add host, and so on.

    Answer A is incorrect because /hana/log is the default location for SAP HANA database (redo) log volume area. Answer B is incorrect because /tmp is the location for Linux temporary files. Answer D is incorrect because /usr/sap/< SID >/ HDB<nn>/<hostname>/trace is the location for log and trace files for a running SAP HANA instance. Answer E is incorrect because /var/log is the location for Linux log files.

Takeaway

After reading this chapter, you should be familiar with the SAP HANA database lifecycle manager tool (HDBLCM), the different interfaces and usage modes, and also how the tool as a wrapper relates to the HDB tools themselves. You should understand the differences between a component revision and the full SPS release and how to download each. Installation automation and an installation with the LSS should be clear regarding when and how to use the resident HDBLCM tool. If the installation returns an error, you should have some ideas about where to find information on the issue and how you might start troubleshooting. We explained some of the post-installation activities, in particular, how to install a new license, and also explained the release and maintenance strategy for SAP HANA and where this is documented.

Summary

Installing and updating SAP HANA systems isn't terribly difficult. However, with three different UIs and three different modes, a wrapper, and individual HDB tools, you do need to understand how the different pieces relate to each other and how to work with them. After this is clear, installing and updating SAP HANA is usually a breeze. Now that the system is up and running, let's proceed with the preparation and tackle the database administration tools.

Chapter 5
Database Administration Tools

Techniques You'll Master

- Understanding the different database administration tools
- Working with the DBA Cockpit
- Working with SAP HANA studio
- Working with SAP HANA cockpit
- Working with the SAP HANA database interactive terminal
- Managing SAP landscapes

SAP HANA was first released a decade ago. Over time, different tools have been made available to perform different tasks or, in some cases, the same tasks but differently. In this chapter, we'll provide an overview of the available tools for system administration and when to use them. Most of the time, the answer will be the same: SAP HANA cockpit. However, there are some situations where using a different tool also works or even provides a better alternative.

Real-World Scenario

Your chief information officer (CIO) has attended an SAP conference and was informed that all SAP applications are now running on SAP HANA. With this in mind, you've been asked to prepare a presentation about the different database administration tools available for SAP HANA. Your colleagues are all seasoned Basis administrators familiar with system administration applications based on SAP NetWeaver Application Server for ABAP (SAP NetWeaver AS for ABAP), and some also have had some experiences with SAP HANA studio. How can you best explain the benefits of the latest SAP HANA tools and get them interested in learning a new tool?

Topic and Objectives

In this chapter, we'll discuss the different database administration tools. For the purposes of this exam, hands-on experience is also expected.

For the exam, you need to have a good understanding of the following topics:

- The different database administration tools available for SAP HANA
- The purposes the different database administration tools serve
- When to use which tool
- How to perform system administration for SAP HANA systems
- How to perform system administration for SAP HANA landscapes

Note

This topic area has a weight of < 8% of the total certification exam score. With 80 questions in total, you can expect about 4 questions on this topic. For those only familiar with SAP HANA studio, we recommend spending some extra time on this chapter as the tools have changed for SAP HANA 2.0. Keep in mind that the exam guide states this can change at any time so always check online for updates.

Learn More

SAP HANA administration tools are documented in the SAP HANA Administration Guide, covering not only SAP HANA cockpit and SAP HANA studio but also the administration tools for the SAP HANA extended application services (SAP HANA XS) application server runtimes and the tools used for installations such as the hardware configuration check tool and SAP HANA database lifecycle manager (HDBLCM) covered in Chapter 3 and Chapter 4, respectively.

See the SAP HANA Administration Guide at *http://s-prs.co/v507833* and the SAP HANA cockpit documentation set at *http://s-prs.co/v507834*.

Key Concepts Refresher

In this section, we'll highlight the most important concepts for the database administration tools topic area.

SAP HANA 1.0 Database Tools

SAP HANA cockpit 2.0 is the quintessential system administration tool for SAP HANA 2.0. The tool evolved through several stages to its current shape and form. In this section, we'll briefly summarize earlier incarnations and related tools, starting with its namesake.

DBA Cockpit

Basis administrators will be familiar with DBA Cockpit, the platform-independent database administration tool for SAP NetWeaver systems in an ABAP environment. Transaction DBACOCKPIT in SAP GUI is all it takes to get started.

You can use DBA Cockpit to do the following:

- Monitor and administer local and remote databases.
- Manage configuration centrally.
- Schedule database backups and other actions with the DBA planning calendar.

The local database is the database that is connected to the SAP NetWeaver AS for ABAP. SAP NetWeaver AS for ABAP runs DBA Cockpit. You can also connect DBA Cockpit to remote databases, either SAP HANA, SAP Adaptive Server Enterprise (SAP ASE), SAP MaxDB, or third-party databases (AnyDB).

In the early days, DBA Cockpit was the only way to schedule backups on the SAP HANA 1.0 release with the DBA planning calendar (excluding Linux cron jobs, which can be tricky to manage).

Another important asset of DBA Cockpit was central configuration management, in particular because the tool is platform-independent. In mixed (heterogeneous) database environments, it's much easier to master a single tool than having to learn a variety of different tools from different vendors. With the latest generation of SAP applications such as SAP S/4HANA and SAP BW/4HANA, the database landscape is becoming homogeneous again, which makes the DBA Cockpit less relevant as an asset.

Figure 5.1 shows a local connection to an SAP HANA database. From the menu in the left pane, you can get an overview and alerts (under **Current Status**), different performance monitoring views, configuration settings (INI files, including change history), jobs, diagnostics, system information, and system landscape views.

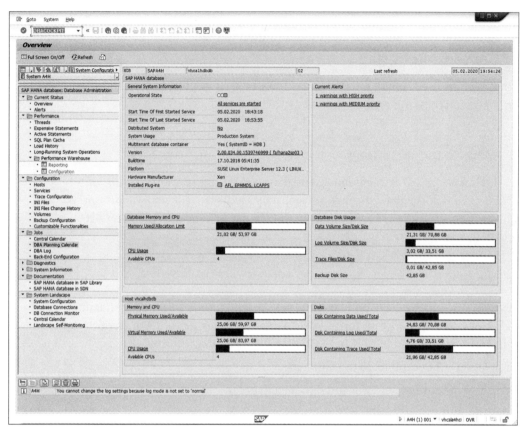

Figure 5.1 DBA Cockpit

For some areas, such as the **Performance Warehouse**, additional configuration is required, in this case, Solution Manager Diagnostics (SMD).

The **SQL Editor** is hidden under the **Diagnostics** folder, as shown in Figure 5.2, and from here, you can enter your SQL statements interactively. You use the same area to browse database objects, such as tables and views, triggers, and procedures. From here, you also access diagnosis files, the backup catalog, the audit log, and database users and privileges.

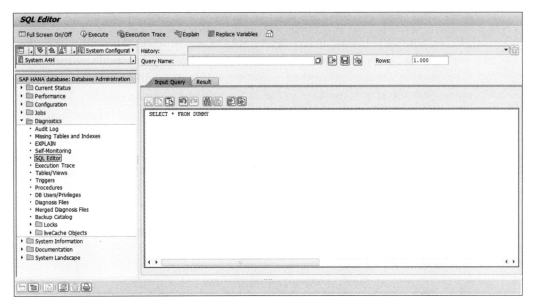

Figure 5.2 DBA Cockpit: SQL Editor

From **System Configuration**, you can add remote databases, as shown in Figure 5.3.

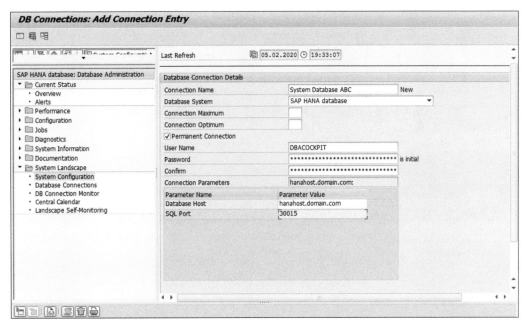

Figure 5.3 SAP DBA Cockpit: Add Connection

Learn More

For a more extensive coverage of this topic, beyond the scope of this exam, see KBA 2222220 – FAQ: SAP HANA DBACOCKPIT.

SAP HANA Database Administration

The HDB command-line script to start and stop local SAP HANA systems includes an admin parameter. When executed (assuming your X Window System environment is properly configured, as covered in Chapter 4), this starts the SAP HANA database administration tool, illustrated in Figure 5.4. One-time administrators of the SAP NetWeaver search and classification tool, text retrieval and information extraction (TREX), or the SAP Business Warehouse Accelerator (SAP BW Accelerator) will instantly recognize the user interface. It's a Python tool, a script language commonly used for miscellaneous tasks on the SAP HANA platform. With its views and tabs, and also the sapcontrol connection to manage the system, the admin tool clearly inspired the development of SAP HANA studio and SAP HANA cockpit.

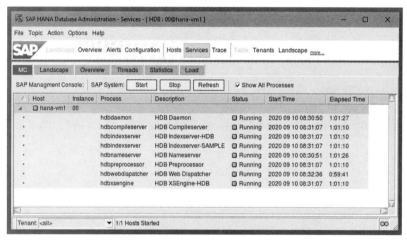

Figure 5.4 SAP HANA Database Administration

Learn More

The SAP HANA database administration tool isn't documented in the SAP HANA platform documentation, and you're not expected to be familiar with its functioning for the exam. However, the tool is referenced in several KBAs and is also covered in the SAP HANA training, so it's good to know that it exists. For more information, beyond the scope of this exam, see KBA 2534881 – Issues While Working with HDBAdmin Tool at *http://s-prs.co/v507835*.

SAP HANA Studio

SAP HANA studio is a plug-in for Eclipse, a popular open-source Java integrated development environment (IDE). Plug-ins make it possible to extend the functionality of Eclipse and change the tool into an IDE for C, PHP, Python, or otherwise as the Eclipse marketplace lists about 2,000 plug-ins. Easy to use, SAP HANA studio quickly turned into a popular tool, and, over time, other SAP products, such as SAP Business Warehouse (SAP BW) and SAP Cloud Platform, also made Eclipse plug-ins available, which further enhanced the adoption. Figure 5.5 lists the available

Eclipse plug-ins on the SAP development tools website at *http://tools.hana.onde-mand.com*.

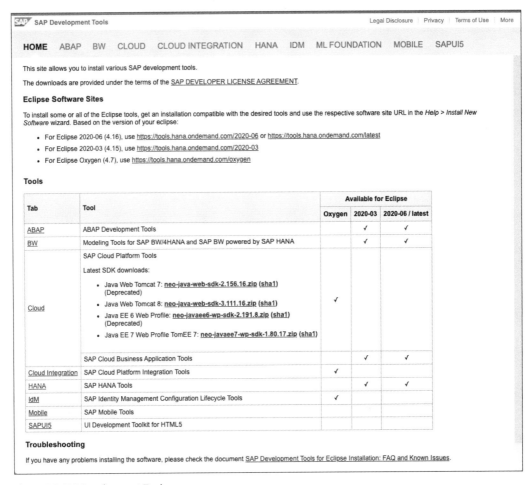

Figure 5.5 SAP Development Tools

To install SAP HANA studio, you can either go to **Software Downloads** on the SAP ONE Support Launchpad and select the component for the installation bundle containing Java runtime, Eclipse, and the SAP HANA studio (hdbstudio) plug-in, or do it yourself and download the latest plug-in from the SAP development tools website for the currently supported Eclipse versions.

Initially, SAP HANA studio came with perspectives for administration and modeling with a development perspective added later. Figure 5.6 shows the SAP HANA administration console perspective. Most of the menus only make sense if you consider that you're working with a Java development tool and not with a database administration tool. The connection to the database is made using Java Database Connectivity (JDBC), and all the tabs, perspectives, and views return the result sets of SQL queries.

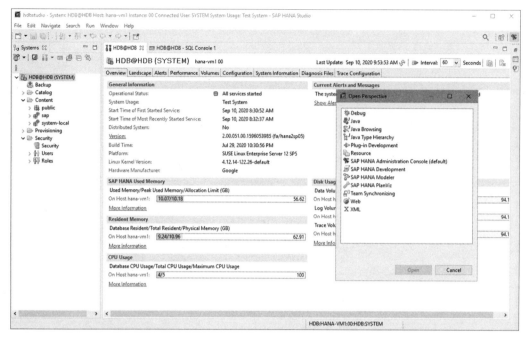

Figure 5.6 SAP HANA Studio

We recognize the DBA Cockpit in the folder structure in the left pane in the systems view. Here, all connected SAP HANA systems are listed with a **Catalog** for the runtime objects (schemas with tables and view) and **Content** for the SAP HANA XS design-time objects (packages). In the main editor area, you find the system overview with additional tabs for landscape, alerts, performance, volumes, configuration, system information, diagnosis files, and other functionality also reminding us of DBA Cockpit and SAP HANA database administration. For backups and security, additional editors (consoles) are included. To execute SQL, you use the SQL console.

Because you can only make JDBC connections with a database that is up and running, a different connection is required to start the system. For this, you can configure the connection properties to enable the SAP start service connection, as illustrated in Figure 5.7. This is the same as the SAP control connection used for SAP HANA cockpit. See Chapter 3 for a reminder about the startup sequence of an SAP HANA system and the components involved.

SAP HANA studio is a client/server tool. When the strategic direction of SAP changed to cloud-first, providing web-based tooling for SAP HANA became a new priority. The developers were first served with the SAP HANA Web-Based Development Workbench, taking inspiration from the ABAP Development Workbench (Transaction SOO1). For the administrators, the web-based equivalent of the DBA Cockpit became the SAP HANA cockpit.

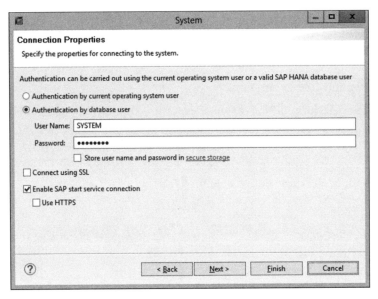

Figure 5.7 System Connection Properties

Although SAP HANA studio will be supported until at least 2025 with SAP HANA 2.0 SPS 05, you need to aware of the following:

- Although new versions are released to provide corrections and security fixes, there is no more development to support any of the new functionality introduced with SAP HANA 2.0. In other words, feature development stopped with SAP HANA 1.0 SPS 12. Lightweight Directory Application Protocol (LDAP), user groups, data masking, log volume encryption, native storage extensions, and so on don't have a corresponding UI, and you'll have to use SQL for configuration and administration of these features.

- As of SAP HANA 2.0 SPS 02, SAP also announced the deprecation of SAP HANA studio together with SAP HANA Repository and the SAP HANA XS, classic model architecture and applications.

- Connections to SAP HANA Cloud and other future SAP HANA editions aren't supported and are no longer available.

> **Learn More**
>
> SAP HANA studio is documented in the SAP HANA Administration Guide and several development guides. For a more extensive coverage of this topic, beyond the scope of this exam, see KBA 2073112 – FAQ: SAP HANA Studio.

SAP HANA Cockpit 1.0

SAP HANA cockpit was introduced with SPS 09. It was developed as an SAP HANA XS, classic model application with an SAP Fiori look and feel. Figure 5.8 shows the system overview page. The focus of the tool was on system administration and monitoring with tiles for **Used Memory**, **CPU Usage**, **Disk Usage**, and **Alerts**. User management required the SAP HANA Web-Based Development Workbench application, which you would also use to execute SQL, browse the catalog for database objects (tables, views), and access trace files.

To start the system and perform offline diagnostics, a third application needed to be launched: *SAP HANA cockpit for offline administration*. This app was hosted by the SAP Host Agent, and, like HDBLCM, both tools received a tile on the SAP HANA cockpit. To manage system landscapes, the *SAP DB Control Center* was added, which web-enabled the SAP/Sybase Control Center (SCC) tool.

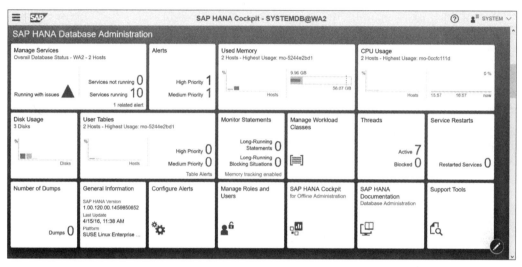

Figure 5.8 SAP HANA Cockpit 1.0

Having four different web applications for system administration called for integration. In addition, the tool needed to be re-architected for tenant databases and SAP HANA extended application services, advanced model (SAP HANA XSA). Whereas the SAP HANA Web-Based Development Workbench continues to be included with the SAP HANA platform 2.0 release, the decision was made to start all over again and only keep the name for the administration tools.

Exam Tip

For the exam, you're not expected to be familiar with the first edition of the SAP HANA cockpit and its associated tools, but knowing how the tools evolved will help reduce the learning curve when moving from SAP HANA studio to SAP HANA cockpit 2.0.

SAP HANA Cockpit 2.0

SAP HANA cockpit 2.0 started as a standalone component (application) with SAP HANA, express edition, embedded and SAP HANA XSA built-in application server runtime included. In addition, performance management tools, such as the Workload Analyzer tool and Capture and Replay (previously available only as a delivery unit for SAP HANA XS, classic model), were now merged with the cockpit.

Figure 5.9 shows the home page. From here, you can connect to the different databases for system management, navigate to the cockpit manager to register new databases and configure metadata, or open the SAP HANA database explorer to browse database objects (catalog with runtime objects) or execute SQL (SQL console). We'll return to SAP HANA cockpit and its architecture, installation, and configuration in Chapter 6.

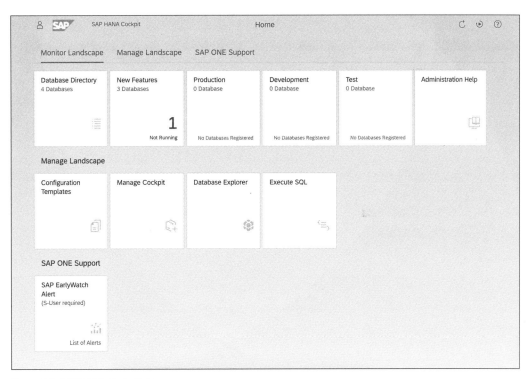

Figure 5.9 SAP HANA Cockpit: Home

SAP HANA Database Explorer

The full client system management tools discussed so far include a SQL prompt, such as the SQL editor for DBA Cockpit and the SQL console for SAP HANA studio. For the first version of the SAP HANA cockpit, however, a SQL interface, database catalog, and trace file explorer were provided as a separate application, known as the SAP HANA Web-Based Development Workbench. For SAP HANA cockpit 2.0, the same approach was used via the SAP HANA database explorer, illustrated in Figure 5.10. The left pane provides access to the runtime objects (**Catalog**) and to the trace files on the server file system. The main pane provides the **SQL Console** tab but also embeds other views such as the SQL Analyzer (displayed), or **Graph Workspace** and **JSON Collections**, which are new SAP HANA 2.0 features.

The SAP HANA database explorer is a far more sophisticated tool compared to its predecessor. Runtime objects are no longer organized by schema but have the schema as a filter, avoiding clutter. On the right pane, you can activate a search tool for more extensive exploration, a debugger, and a console for messages, although this functionality might be more relevant to the developer persona. This menu is included because the SAP HANA database explorer is also embedded in SAP Web IDE, the successor of the SAP HANA Web-Based Development Workbench.

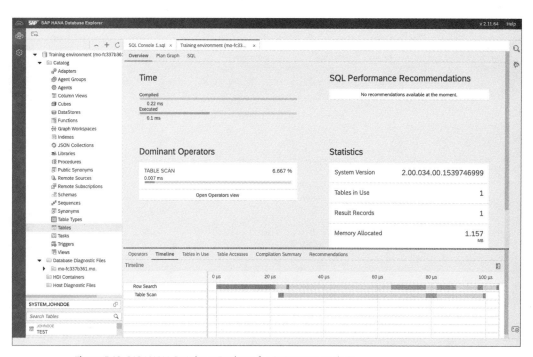

Figure 5.10 SAP HANA Database Explorer for SAP HANA Cockpit

Learn More

The SAP HANA database explorer technical component name is HRTT (HANA Runtime Tool), and it has its own release notes and documentation. For further information beyond the scope of this exam, see "Getting Started with the SAP HANA Database Explorer" at *http://s-prs.co/v507836*.

SQL Analyzer

The SQL Analyzer is another new tool included with the SAP HANA cockpit. Like the database explorer, it's a separate application that also runs embedded. It's accessible from the **Analyze** menu in the SAP HANA database explorer SQL console and also from the **Monitor Statement**, **Plan Trace**, and **Expensive Statement** views in the SAP HANA cockpit. It shows a graphical view of the SQL plan (**Plan Graph**), as illustrated in Figure 5.11, with additional tabs that provide information about the operators, tables, and compilation statistics, with recommendations about how the plan can be improved.

Figure 5.11 SQL Analyzer

SAP HANA Database Interactive Terminal

Every database needs a command-line tool to execute SQL commands and script files. For SAP HANA, this role is taken by a tool called the SAP HANA database interactive terminal. The command to start the tool is hdbsql (the tool is also commonly called by this name). For SAP MaxDB administrators, the learning curve is minimal as HDBSQL is very similar to the SQLCLI command-line tool. This also applies to the secure user store (hdbuserstore), which originates from the SAP MaxDB XUSER tool to securely store connection information.

The HDBSQL tool has a long list of options, including to encrypt connections, set the proxy server, receive input, send output, and format the result set. Running the command with the -h option lists them all, as illustrated in Figure 5.12.

```
hdbadm@hana-vm1:/usr/sap/HDB/HDB00> hdbsql -h
HDBSQL version 2.5.99, the SAP HANA Database interactive terminal

Usage:
  hdbsql [<options>] [<command>]

Options for connecting to the database:
  -i <instance number>     instance number of the database engine
  -n <server>[:<port>]     name of the host on which the database instance is
                           installed (default: localhost:30015)
  -d <database_name>       name of the database to connect
  -u <user_name>           user name to connect
  -p <password>            password to connect
  -U <user_store_key>      use credentials from user store
  -e                       encrypt communication
  -attemptencrypt          attempt encrypt communication, fall back to
                           unencrypted on failure
  -z                       switches autocommit off
  -Z <value>=<property>    sets SQLDBC connect options e.g. -Z SQLMODE=SAPR3
  -r                       suppress usage of prepared statements

Input and output options:
  -I <file_name>           use file <file_name> to input queries
                           (default: stdin)
  -V (<var1>|<var_name1>=<value>),...,(<varN>|<var_nameN>=<value>)
                           specify variable values to use in sql script.
```

Figure 5.12 SAP HANA Database Interactive Terminal: Options List

To connect to tenant database HA0 with the user system, use the following command:

```
hdbsql -i 00 -u system -d HA0
```

You'll be prompted for your user name and password if you don't pass it on the command line. Note that the default connection is to localhost:30015, which is the SQL port of the index server of the initial tenant database, and not to the SQL port of the name server for the system database. As mentioned, for help with the options, use -h. After you're connected, you can also use \? or \h for help with the commands, as shown in Figure 5.13.

```
hdbadm@hana-vm1:/usr/sap/HDB/HDB00> hdbsql

Welcome to the SAP HANA Database interactive terminal.

Type:  \h for help with commands
       \q to quit

hdbsql=> \h

 \? or \h[elp]   show help on internal slash commands
 \q[uit]         quit HDBSQL
 \c[onnect]      -i <instance number>
                 -n <host>[:<port>]
                 -d <database name>
                 -u <user_name>
                 -p <password>
                 -U <user_store_key>
                 connecting to the database
 \di[sconnect]   disconnecting from the database

 \mu[ltiline]    [ON|OFF] toggle the multiline mode on or off
 \a[utocommit]   [ON|OFF] switch autocommit mode on or off
 \m[ode]         [INTERNAL|SAPR3] change SQL mode
 \cl[ientinfo]   [property=value[;...]] send client info
 \ps             [ON|OFF] toggle the usage of prepared statements on or off
 \es             [ON|OFF] toggle the escape output format on or off
 \o[utput]       <filename> send all query results to file, double quotes around filename are allowed
 \i[nput]        <filename> read input from file, double quotes around filename are allowed
 \ie[ncoding]    <encoding> force input encoding, one of "ASCII", "UCS2", "UTF8"
 \hi[story]      <size> number of commands to keep in history buffer (default: 50)

 \p[rint]        print out the current query buffer (only multiline mode)
 \read           <filename> read input from file, double quotes around filename are allowed
 \r[eset]        reset (clear) the query buffer (only multiline mode)
 \e[dit]         <filename> edit the query buffer (or file) with external editor (only multiline mode)
 \g[o]           send query buffer to server and print out the results (only multiline mode)
 ;               send query buffer to server and print out the results (only multiline mode)
```

Figure 5.13 SAP HANA Database Interactive Terminal: Help Menu

To connect (or change connections) to the system database as system user, for example, you would use the following command:

```
hdbsql> \c -n localhost:30013 -u system
```

With all its options and commands, HDBSQL is a powerful tool for automating SQL statement execution.

For unattended connections, you can create a user store key. For the command-line options, just enter the command without any parameters as this will print out the usage information, as shown in Figure 5.14. Note the -i option to enable interactive mode:

```
hdbuserstore -i SET ADMINKEY "hana-vm1:30015@HDB" dbadmin
```

This way, again, you can enter passwords on the command line without leaving a trace (Linux pros will know that starting the command with a space also does this trick).

```
hdbadm@hana-vm1:/usr/sap/HDB/HDB00> hdbuserstore
Usage: hdbuserstore [options] command [arguments]

Options:
  -u <USER>      perform operation for other operating system user
  -v             verbose mode, print operations done
  -i             interactive mode, ask for missing values
  -h             this help message
  -H <HOST>      assume host name <HOST>
Commands (the command name is case insensitive):
  Help
        Print help message.
  Set <KEY> <ENV>[@<DATABASE>] <USERNAME> <PASSWORD>
        Add or update a profile entry.
        <KEY>        entry key name
        <ENV>        database location (host:port)
        <USERNAME>   user name
        <PASSWORD>   password
        <DATABASE>   database name in MDC environment
  AddFromDir <DIR>
        Add entries from a store in <DIR> without overwriting existing keys.
        <DIR>        store directory from which entries to be read
  Delete <KEY>
        Delete entry with key <KEY>.
  List [<KEY> ...]
        List entries of store. The passwords are not shown.
  ListFromDir <DIR>
        List entries from a store in <DIR>.
        <DIR>        store directory from which entries to be read
  ChangeKey
        Generate new encryption key and encrypt passwords again.
hdbadm@hana-vm1:/usr/sap/HDB/HDB00> hdbuserstore -i SET ADMINKEY "hana-vm1:30015@HDB" dbadmin
Password:
hdbadm@hana-vm1:/usr/sap/HDB/HDB00> hdbuserstore list ADMINKEY
KEY ADMINKEY
  ENV : hana-vm1:30015
  USER: dbadmin
  DATABASE: HDB
hdbadm@hana-vm1:/usr/sap/HDB/HDB00> ▮
```

Figure 5.14 Secure User Store

To execute scripts unattended with the HDBSQL, you can use the secure user store key in combination with input and output files, as follows:

```
hdbsql -U ADMINKEY -I /tmp/input.sql -o /tmp/output.log
```

Figure 5.15 shows this command in action.

```
hdbadm@hana-vm1:/usr/sap/HDB/HDB00> echo "SELECT CURRENT_SCHEMA FROM DUMMY" > /tmp/schema.sql
hdbadm@hana-vm1:/usr/sap/HDB/HDB00> hdbsql -U ADMINKEY -I /tmp/schema.sql -o /tmp/schema.log
hdbadm@hana-vm1:/usr/sap/HDB/HDB00> cat /tmp/schema.log
CURRENT_SCHEMA
"DBADMIN"
hdbadm@hana-vm1:/usr/sap/HDB/HDB00> █
```

Figure 5.15 Running Scripts with HDBSQL

HDBSQL and the secure user store (hdbuserstore) are part of the server installation and also included with the SAP HANA client. The secure user store can also be used for ODBC or other types of SAP HANA client connections (JDBC, Python, Go, etc.).

Learn More

HDBSQL is documented in the SAP HANA Administration Guide. For the secure user store, see the SAP HANA Security Guide. The syntax of all the options and commands is beyond the scope of the exam.

SAP HANA XS Runtime Administration

As the architecture of the SAP HANA XS, classic model and SAP HANA XSA models is different, so are the tools. We'll take a quick look at both models in this section.

Exam Tip

You're not expected to be familiar with the different SAP HANA XS, classic model and SAP HANA XSA model tools for runtime administration and application lifecycle management (ALM) for this exam. However, as a SAP HANA system administrator, you should have a general understanding of the concepts of the built-in SAP HANA XS architectures, the tools available, and the purposes they serve.

SAP HANA Extended Application Services, Classic Model

For SAP HANA XS, classic model environment, you use the web client called the SAP HANA XS Admin tool. As illustrated in Figure 5.16, this tool brings together different administration tools for the web application server environment, including **XS Artifact Administration**, **SAML Service Provider**, **Trust Manager**, and **SMTP Configurations**. To access and use each tool, specific roles are required. For example, to access the artifact administration tool, the role sap.hana.xs.admin.roles::Runtime-ConfAdministrator is needed.

Although SAP HANA XS, classic model and its tools are deprecated, there are still valid use cases. For example, to configure cross-origin resource sharing (CORS) and custom headers for the information access (InA) service. This is required (as of the time of writing, fall 2020) to enable SAP Analytics Cloud connections to on-premise SAP HANA systems (live connections), as shown in Figure 5.16.

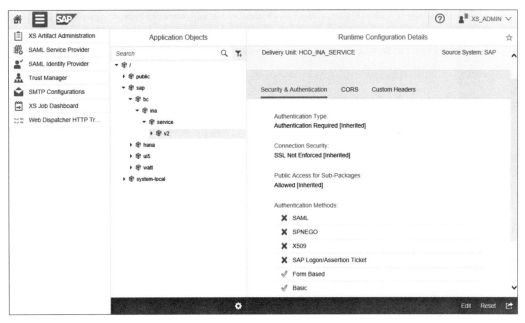

Figure 5.16 SAP HANA XS Admin Tool

SAP HANA Extended Application Services, Advanced Model

To configure the SAP HANA XSA runtime, you use the SAP HANA XS Advanced cockpit, as shown in Figure 5.17.

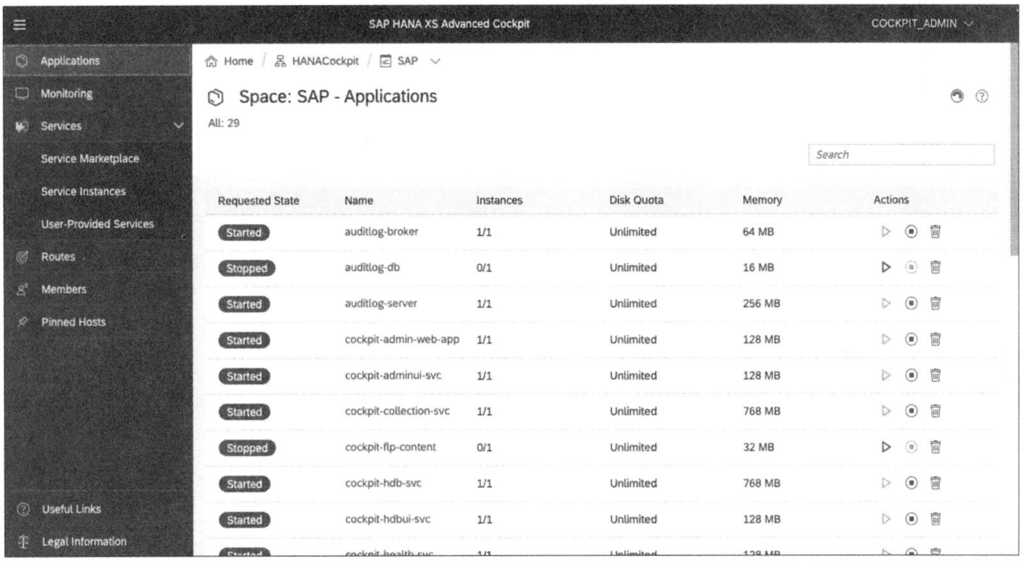

Figure 5.17 SAP HANA XS Advanced Cockpit: Applications

As explained in Chapter 4, these tools bundle the functionality of runtime administration and ALM. The architecture of SAP HANA XSA is an adaptation of Cloud

Foundry, with concepts such as organizations, spaces, services, and marketplaces, which are all beyond the scope of this exam. The command-line tool is the xs client and is similar in usage and options as the Cloud Foundry cf tool.

SAP Tools for SAP HANA Administration

Apart from the already mentioned DBA Cockpit, there are some additional tools available for SAP HANA administration that don't rely on the SAP HANA platform but on SAP NetWeaver either running on top or installed on a different system altogether.

SAP Solution Manager

SAP Solution Manager is a system management platform for SAP applications. It centralizes the ALM and business process lifecycle management for SAP landscapes and supports a range of many management activities, including change control management, IT service management, landscape management, project management, and process management. You can use SAP Solution Manager to manage SAP HANA landscapes. In addition, it can be powered by SAP HANA, but there is no SAP S/4HANA release.

To connect SAP HANA systems to the SAP Solution Manager System Landscape Directory (SLD), you use the resident SAP HANA database lifecycle manager tool, as explained in Chapter 4. You can use SAP Solution Manager for centralized landscape monitoring and include the systems in SAP Early Watch Alerts reporting for system health and growth, alerts, performance, and system parameter configuration monitoring. As SAP Solution Manager collects information from the operating system, database, and applications, it can also provide end-to-end root cause analysis to effectively debug issues. The DBA Cockpit is commonly used from within SAP Solution Manager as are the enhanced Change and Transport System (CTS+) and SAP HANA Transport for ABAP (HTA).

SAP Landscape Management

Although you can use SAP HANA cockpit and SAP Solution Manager for landscape monitoring, the focus of these tools is on system management and ALM, respectively. There is also a tool appropriately called SAP Landscape Management that is dedicated to managing SAP landscapes (see Figure 5.18).

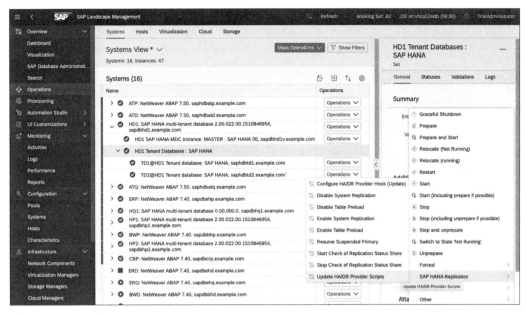

Figure 5.18 SAP Landscape Management

Initially, this product was called SAP NetWeaver Landscape Virtualization Management to indicate that it covered landscape management for SAP systems in both physical and virtualized infrastructures. Virtualization has been dropped from the name since version 3.0 to stress that the orchestration and automation solution works on any infrastructure: on premise, private/public cloud, or hybrid.

Most of the SAP Landscape Management functionality is in the domain of the SAP Basis administrator with post-copy automation (PCA) and Transaction BDLS (Conversion of Logical System Names). Specific to SAP HANA is that you can automate system replication takeovers (and fallbacks) and perform near-zero downtime maintenance. We return to this topic in Chapter 12.

> **Learn More**
> For more information about SAP Landscape Management beyond the scope of this exam, go to the **SAP Landscape Management** topic on the SAP Community at *http://s-prs.co/ v507837*.

Important Terminology

For this exam objective, you're expected to understand the following terms:

- **DBA Cockpit**
  The DBA Cockpit is a platform-independent tool for monitoring and administration of local and remote databases. It appears inside the SAP GUI client and is hosted by SAP NetWeaver AS for ABAP.

- **SAP HANA cockpit**
  SAP HANA cockpit is a web-based tool for monitoring and administration of SAP HANA databases. It comes stand-alone bundled with its own SAP HANA, express edition, database and SAP HANA XSA application server runtime, but it can also be installed on existing SAP HANA systems.

- **SAP HANA database administration tool**
  SAP HANA database administration is a Python tool used primarily by SAP Support services and requires the X Window System environment on the SAP HANA server. The tool is also called HDB Admin, named after the command to start the tool.

- **SAP HANA database explorer**
  SAP HANA database explorer is a web-based tool for runtime database object exploration (catalog) and interactive SQL execution (console). It comes embedded in the SAP Web IDE (for SAP HANA) but also as a separate application to complement the SAP HANA cockpit.

- **SAP HANA database interactive terminal (HDBSQL)**
  HDBSQL can be used to execute SQL commands interactively or to execute scripts. The tool is included with every server installation and is also part of the SAP HANA client package. To run the tool, execute command `hdbsql`.

- **SAP HANA studio**
  SAP HANA studio is a plug-in for the Eclipse IDE with different environments (perspectives) for the administrator, developer, and modeler. Although still supported, development has stopped, and the tool is mainly used in SAP HANA 1.0 environments.

- **SAP HANA XS**
  SAP HANA extended application services (SAP HANA XS) provides native application server functionality to the SAP HANA platform. There is both a classic and advanced model (SAP HANA XSA) that have different architecture and tools.

- **SAP HANA XS Advanced cockpit**
  SAP HANA XS Advanced cockpit is a web-based tool for monitoring and administration of the SAP HANA XSA runtime and its applications. You can think of it as the SAP HANA cockpit for the application server.

- **SAP Landscape Management**
  SAP Landscape Management is the orchestration and automation solution for SAP system landscape management for on-premise, hybrid, and cloud systems. This solution requires SAP NetWeaver AS for ABAP.

- **SAP Solution Manager**
  SAP Solution Manager is the application lifecycle management (ALM) solution for SAP applications. This solution requires SAP NetWeaver AS for ABAP.

- **Secure user store**
  The secure user store utility can be used to store connection information in an encrypted file. The information in this file can be passed to the SAP HANA database interactive terminal (HDBSQL) query tool for unattended use by services or background processes, for example, to perform backups. To run the tool, execute command hdbuserstore.
- **SQL Analyzer**
  SQL Analyzer is a web-based tool to analyze SQL statements. The tool shows relevant SQL statement execution statistics with a graphical illustration of the execution plan.

Practice Questions

These practice questions will help you evaluate your understanding of the topics covered in this chapter. The questions shown are similar in nature to those found on the certification examination. Although none of these questions will be found on the exam itself, they will allow you to review your knowledge of the subject. Select the correct answers, and then check the completeness of your answers in the "Practice Question Answers and Explanations" section. Remember that on the exam, you must select all correct answers, and only correct answers, to receive credit for the question.

1. Which system administration tools are included with the SAP HANA platform? (There are three correct answers.)

    ☐ **A.** SAP HANA cockpit

    ☐ **B.** SAP Solution Manager for SAP HANA

    ☐ **C.** DBA Cockpit

    ☐ **D.** SAP HANA studio

    ☐ **E.** HDBSQL

2. Which system administration tools require SAP NetWeaver? (There are three correct answers.)

    ☐ **A.** SAP HANA cockpit

    ☐ **B.** SAP Solution Manager

    ☐ **C.** DBA Cockpit

    ☐ **D.** SAP HANA studio

    ☐ **E.** SAP Landscape Management

3. Which tool is a database administration command-line tool?

☐ **A.** hdbsql

☐ **B.** hdbstudio

☐ **C.** xs

☐ **D.** hdblcm

4. What do the administration tools SAP Solution Manager, DBA Cockpit, and SAP Landscape Management have in common? (There are three correct answers.)

☐ **A.** They support both SAP HANA and AnyDB databases.

☐ **B.** They provide solutions for central management.

☐ **C.** They are all available as Eclipse plug-ins.

☐ **D.** They are all web-enabled.

☐ **E.** They require SAP NetWeaver.

5. Which tool offers end-to-end application lifecycle management (ALM) to streamline business processes and proactively address improving options, increasing efficiency, and decreasing risk within your existing maintenance agreement?

☐ **A.** SAP HANA cockpit

☐ **B.** SAP Solution Manager

☐ **C.** SAP Landscape Management

☐ **D.** SAP HANA application lifecycle management

6. For which activities can you use the SAP HANA cockpit? (There are three correct answers.)

☐ **A.** Start and stop SAP HANA systems

☐ **B.** Deploy applications

☐ **C.** Monitor landscapes

☐ **D.** Monitor applications

☐ **E.** Perform backups

7. Which tools are integrated with the SAP HANA cockpit? (There are three correct answers.)

☐ **A.** SAP HANA database explorer

☐ **B.** SAP HANA cockpit manager

☐ **C.** SAP Web IDE for SAP HANA

☐ **D.** SQL Analyzer

☐ **E.** SAP HANA XS Advanced cockpit

8. Which tool enables you to execute SQL statements and query information about the database and catalog objects? (There are three correct answers.)

☐ **A.** SAP HANA database explorer

☐ **B.** SQL Analyzer

☐ **C.** SAP HANA studio

☐ **D.** SAP HANA cockpit

☐ **E.** HDBSQL

9. Which tool provides both a system administration and development environment?

☐ **A.** SAP HANA cockpit

☐ **B.** SAP HANA Web-Based Development Workbench

☐ **C.** SAP HANA studio

☐ **D.** DBA Cockpit

10. Why should you use SAP HANA cockpit and not SAP HANA studio? (There are three correct answers.)

☐ **A.** SAP HANA studio doesn't support SAP HANA 2.0.

☐ **B.** SAP HANA cockpit supports the latest SAP HANA 2.0 features.

☐ **C.** SAP HANA studio is deprecated and will be removed from future releases.

☐ **D.** SAP HANA studio is a client/server tool and needs to be installed and updated on every computer used by system administrators.

☐ **E.** With SAP HANA cockpit, you can make secure connections to SAP control to start and stop databases.

Practice Question Answers and Explanations

1. Correct answers: **A, D, E**
    SAP HANA cockpit, SAP HANA studio, and SAP HANA database interactive terminal (HDBSQL) are all included with the SAP HANA platform.

    Answer B is incorrect because there is no product called SAP Solution Manager for SAP HANA, although the product supports SAP HANA as the database. Answer C is incorrect because DBA Cockpit is included with SAP NetWeaver AS for ABAP.

2. Correct answers: **B, C, E**

   SAP Solution Manager, DBA Cockpit, and SAP Landscape Management all require SAP NetWeaver.

   Answer A is incorrect because SAP HANA cockpit is an SAP HANA XS application. Answer D is incorrect because SAP HANA studio is a plug-in for the Eclipse IDE.

3. Correct answer: **A**

   hdbsql is the database administration command-line tool.

   Answer B is incorrect because hdbstudio is the command to start SAP HANA studio on Linux operating systems, and SAP HANA studio is a graphical tool not a command-line tool. Answer C is incorrect because xs is the command-line tool to administer the SAP HANA XSA runtime and applications. It's not a database administration tool. Answer D is incorrect because hdblcm is the command to start the SAP HANA database lifecycle manager tool for platform lifecycle management tasks such as installation and update. It's not a database administration tool.

4. Correct answers: **A, B, E**

   SAP Solution Manager, DBA Cockpit, and SAP Landscape Management all require SAP NetWeaver and support both SAP HANA and other databases. SAP Landscape Management is an SAP NetWeaver/Java add-on. SAP Solution Manager and DBA Cockpit require SAP NetWeaver AS for ABAP. They all provide central management solutions for applications, databases, and landscapes, respectively.

   Answer C is incorrect because these products and tools aren't available as Eclipse plug-ins. Answer D is incorrect because DBA Cockpit isn't web-enabled.

5. Correct answer: **B**

   SAP Solution Manager is an ALM solution for SAP applications. This product description is from the product road map. Other characteristics are as follows:

   – It's a centralized application management and administration solution used to implement, support, operate, and monitor your SAP enterprise solutions. It provides integrated content, tools, methodologies, and access to your solution landscape running on premise, as a hybrid, or in the cloud.

   – It delivers an integrated process flow between project management, process management, requirements management, change and release management, and the test suite, including comprehensive end-to-end traceability, analytics, and reporting.

   Answers A and C are incorrect because the SAP HANA cockpit and SAP Landscape Management don't provide ALM functionality. Answer D is incorrect because SAP HANA application lifecycle management provides ALM features for SAP HANA XS, classic model applications but doesn't for any of the other features of SAP Solution Manager.

6. Correct answers: **A, C, E**

   SAP HANA cockpit provides landscape monitoring capabilities and a database directory with system health indicators. With SAP HANA cockpit 2.0, you can also start and stop SAP HANA systems and perform backups.

   Answers B and D are incorrect because to deploy and monitor applications, you can use the SAP HANA XS Advanced cockpit or the SAP HANA application life-cycle management tool for SAP HANA XS applications.

7. Correct answers: **A, B, D**

   SAP HANA cockpit integrates with SAP HANA database explorer, SAP HANA cockpit manager, and SQL Analyzer, which are all deployed as separate applications with the SAP HANA cockpit.

   Answer C is incorrect because SAP Web IDE for SAP HANA is a development tool that integrates with SAP HANA database explorer for SAP HANA but not with SAP HANA cockpit. Answer E is incorrect because the SAP HANA XS Advanced cockpit is a separate application for management of the SAP HANA XSA runtime and applications. There is a link to the SAP HANA XS Advanced cockpit on the SAP HANA cockpit Database Overview app, but the applications aren't integrated.

8. Correct answers: **A, C, E**

   To execute SQL statements and query information about the database and catalog objects, you can use SAP HANA database explorer, SAP HANA studio, DBA Cockpit, SAP HANA Web-Based Development Workbench, or the command-line tool HDBSQL.

   Answer B is incorrect because you can use the SQL Analyzer to analyze SQL statement but not to execute or query information about the database and catalog objects. Answer D is incorrect because although the SAP HANA cockpit contains a tile named **Execute SQL** (see Figure 5.9), this functionality isn't provided by SAP HANA cockpit but by SAP HANA database explorer.

9. Correct answer: **C**

   SAP HANA studio provides perspectives for **Administration, Modeling**, and **Development**, and it addresses both the administrator and developer personas.

   Answer A is incorrect because SAP HANA cockpit is a system administration tool and complemented with SAP Web IDE for SAP HANA for development. Answer B is incorrect because the SAP HANA Web-Based Development Workbench is a development tool for the SAP HANA XS, classic model architecture. Although it provides functionality to manage security (users, roles, and privileges), database runtime objects (catalog), and trace files, it's not a system administration tool. Answer D is incorrect because the DBA Cockpit is a platform-independent database administration tool and doesn't provide development functionality.

10. Correct answers: **B, C, D**

Although it's easy to update SAP HANA studio when using the update site, this remains a self-service task. Large organizations will need to support many different studio versions.

Answer A is incorrect because SAP HANA studio is only supported for SAP HANA 2.0. Answer E is incorrect because we can make secure connections to SAP control using *both* SAP HANA studio and SAP HANA cockpit.

Takeaway

You should now have a good overview of the different SAP HANA administration tools. In this chapter, we've described the different tools included with the SAP HANA platform. Most relevant for system administration is the SAP HANA cockpit with the SAP HANA database explorer for SQL execution and to browse catalog objects. On the command line, you can use the SAP HANA database interactive terminal command (HDBSQL) and secure user store command (hdbuserstore). To configure the SAP HANA XSA model runtime and applications, you use the SAP HANA XS Advanced cockpit.

For the now deprecated SAP HANA XS, classic model environment, you have SAP HANA Web-Based Development Workbench for development, SAP HANA application lifecycle management for deployment, and the SAP HANA XS Admin tool for application server runtime configuration. Equally deprecated but still popular is the Eclipse plug-in client tool—SAP HANA studio—with perspectives (environments) for administration, modeling, and development.

For central monitoring and administration of SAP applications, you can use SAP Solution Manager, DBA Cockpit, and SAP Landscape Management. They all require SAP NetWeaver, powered by SAP HANA or AnyDB. Their focus is on ALM, database administration, and landscape management, respectively.

Summary

Now that you've finished this chapter, you should be able to confidently answer the questions about the SAP HANA database administration tools topic area.

In the next chapter, we'll make the deep dive for the most important administration tool, the SAP HANA cockpit.

Chapter 6
SAP HANA Cockpit

Techniques You'll Master

- Understanding the SAP HANA cockpit architecture, deployment options, and components

- Understanding the revision and maintenance strategy for SAP HANA cockpit

- Installing and updating SAP HANA cockpit

- Provisioning and configuring SAP HANA cockpit

This chapter is all about SAP HANA cockpit. For the exam, you're expected to be familiar with this tool not only as the pilot but also as the flight engineer. The pilot knows what all the gauges mean and which knobs to turn to make SAP HANA systems fly. It's the responsibility of the flight engineer, however, to know how the cockpit works and support the pilot in doing his job. The pilot role is covered in many chapters of this exam guide: user administration, backup and recovery, monitoring, and other system administration tasks. In this chapter, we're going to focus on the flight engineer role and get under the hood of the SAP HANA cockpit tool itself.

Real-World Scenario

Your company has joined the SAP S/4HANA movement and started a project to migrate its SAP ERP system to SAP S/4HANA. The SAP ERP environment runs on any database (AnyDB), and the DBA Cockpit is used for database administration. Although some Basis administrators prefer to continue using the DBA Cockpit for SAP HANA administration, you've been asked to investigate the accompanying tool for SAP HANA administration: SAP HANA cockpit. How do the two cockpits compare? What are the differences? What effort is required to install and update the software? What is the ease of use? For the next meeting, you need to present your findings followed by a brief email with the main points. Your manager wishes you success and good luck with the challenge.

Topic and Objectives

In this chapter, we'll discuss how to install and configure SAP HANA cockpit. We'll also cover provisioning, which usually refers making systems available for use and could include creating users, enabling firewall access, and so on.

For the exam, you're expected to have a good understanding of the following topics:

- SAP HANA cockpit architecture, including the different components roles they play
- System requirements and the installation process
- Where to find the software and how to run the installation program
- How to update SAP HANA cockpit and understand the maintenance strategy
- How to configure SAP HANA cockpit, and how to define database groups, database users, and cockpit users
- What the technical user is used for and how to create it
- Different cockpit roles and how to assign them

Note

This topic area has a weight of < 8% of the total certification exam score. With 80 questions in total, you can expect about 4 questions on the material of this chapter. It's a minor topic in that sense, however, as almost all other topics areas build on the knowledge acquired in this chapter, we recommend spending sufficient time on this part of the exam.

Learn More

How and when to use SAP HANA cockpit is documented in the SAP HANA Administration Guide. Here you can find, for example, how to make a backup using SAP HANA cockpit and how to make a backup using SAP HANA studio. This is for what we described as the "pilot" role.

For the flight engineer, there is a separate documentation set, including a What's New Guide and the Release Notes, an Installation and Update Guide specific to SAP HANA cockpit, and an extract of the SAP HANA Administration Guide, this time only including the relevant sections (see "SAP HANA Cockpit" on the SAP Help Portal at *http://s-prs.co/v507838*). KBA 2800006 – FAQ: SAP HANA Cockpit is a good place to start, although most of this material is beyond the scope of this exam.

SAP HANA 2.0 SPS 05: What's New?

As explained in Chapter 4, SAP HANA cockpit comes with its own release cycle with more frequent updates. New functionality corresponding with the SAP HANA 2.0 SPS 05 releases was added with SAP HANA cockpit 2.0 SP 11 and SP 12. Listing all new functionality for these releases would take several pages and is, for the most part, beyond the scope of the exam. For more detailed information, see the What's New section in the SAP HANA cockpit 2.0 documentation.

Key Concepts Refresher

In this section, we'll highlight the most important concepts that fall under the SAP HANA cockpit topic, from deployment options and the architecture to installation and provisioning.

Deployment Options

With SAP HANA cockpit 2.0, you can administer not only single SAP HANA 2.0 tenant databases but also entire SAP HANA system landscapes for every supported SAP HANA release. At the time of publication (summer 2020), this covers SAP HANA 2.0 SPS 03 and later but also the previous SAP HANA 1.0 SPS 12 release, in both single database mode and with tenant databases.

One of the mayor differences between SAP HANA cockpit 2.0 and its predecessor is that the cockpit is no longer an integral part of the SAP HANA database but comes with a dedicated system. There are two reasons for this:

- **SAP HANA landscape management**
  The first release of SAP HANA cockpit was included as an SAP HANA XS application with each database, which brought up the question of which one to use to monitor system landscapes. You wouldn't want to add additional load to a production system, but you also wouldn't want to use a developer system that might be shut down unexpectedly. Using a dedicated SAP HANA system would solve both issues but requires an additional license.

- **Offline administration**
  As an application "powered by SAP HANA," with the power off, there is also no SAP HANA cockpit for system administration tasks such as restoring database, troubleshooting unresponsive systems, accessing trace files, and so on.

Initially, SAP HANA cockpit 2.0 came with SAP HANA, express edition, embedded. However, for simple proof of concept (POC) or test/training systems, having two systems to back up may provide too much overhead. Running SAP HANA cockpit inside the SAP HANA system would work just fine for these use cases. To address this, as of SPS 02, you can also install SAP HANA cockpit in a regular SAP HANA tenant database.

Figure 6.1 illustrates the following deployment options:

- Dedicated hardware using embedded SAP HANA, express edition, which was the original plan

- Shared hardware using embedded SAP HANA, express edition

- Shared database using SAP HANA tenant as of SPS 02

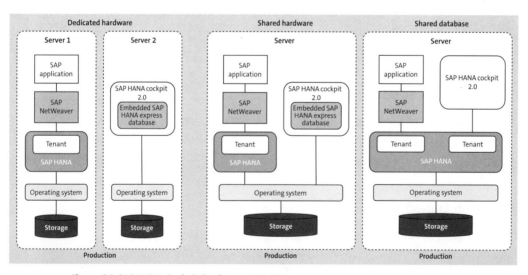

Figure 6.1 SAP HANA Cockpit Deployment Options

The shared hardware and shared database deployment options leverage existing infrastructure and will reduce costs at the expense of agility and (potentially) some resource contention. When sharing, the systems need to be properly sized and global allocation limits adjusted. You may have noticed that option two (shared hardware) corresponds to a multi-SID/MCOS deployment, as discussed in Chapter 3. It's also possible to virtualize the deployment, in which case, a dedicated virtual machine (VM) is preferred.

> **Learn More**
>
> Although out of scope for the exam, we highly recommend you read the following paper that explains how to configure high availability (HA) for SAP HANA cockpit: "How To: High Availability for SAP HANA Cockpit Using SAP HANA System Replication" (*http://s-prs.co/v507839*).

System Architecture

The different components of SAP HANA cockpit are illustrated in Figure 6.2. In SAP HANA cockpit, you encounter cockpit persistence, which refers to the database part—either embedded express or as a regular tenant. Next, the SAP HANA XSA runtime is shown together with two applications: the SAP HANA cockpit manager and the SAP HANA cockpit services. The first is for metadata management, and the second is for landscape and database administration.

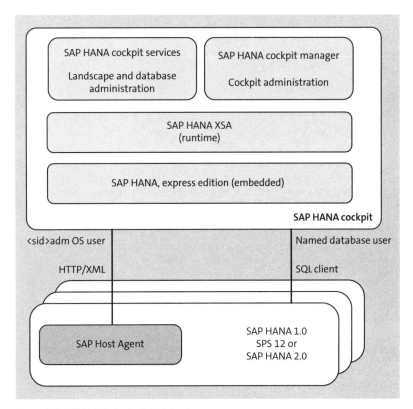

Figure 6.2 SAP HANA Cockpit Architecture

The lower portion shows that SAP HANA cockpit makes an HTTP/XML connection to SAP Host Agent using the `<sid>adm` operating system account and a SQL client connection using a named database user. This is similar to how both SAP HANA studio and the previous cockpit tools made their connections.

We'll take a closer look at the SAP HANA cockpit manager first, before examining the layout of both SAP HANA cockpit and SAP HANA XS Advanced cockpit.

SAP HANA Cockpit Manager

Figure 6.3 shows the interface of the SAP HANA cockpit manager. With this tool, you manage the metadata of an SAP HANA cockpit landscape. This works with databases, database groups, and cockpit users. With groups, you can control database access. By default, only the user who has registered a database can access this database with SAP HANA cockpit. By creating additional users and adding them to groups, this privilege can be extended. How exactly this works will be covered next.

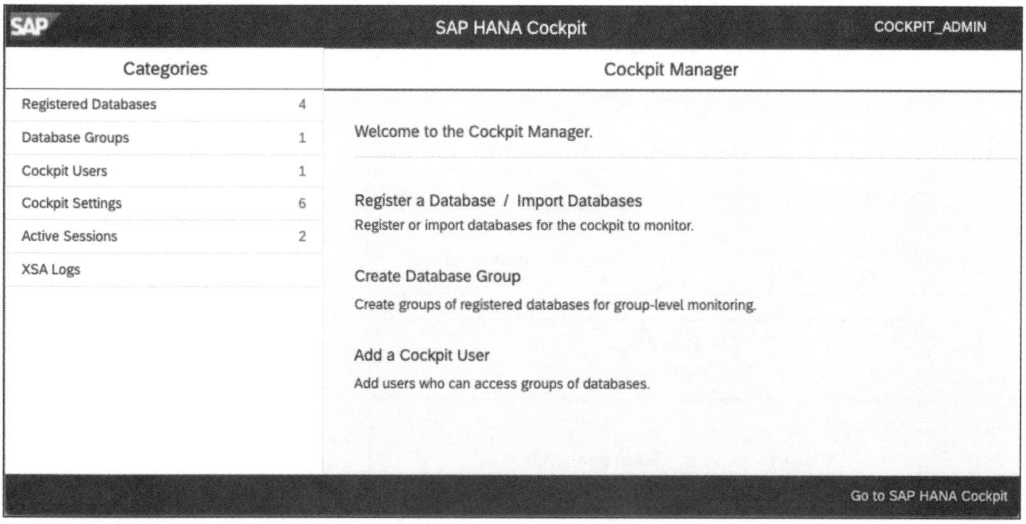

Figure 6.3 SAP HANA Cockpit Manager

> **SAP HANA 2.0 SPS 05: What's New?**
>
> As of SP 12, the more generic term "resource" has been replaced with "database" as in **Register a Database**, **Database Directory**, **Database Overview**, and so on.

SAP HANA Cockpit

The home page of SAP HANA cockpit is also called the **Landscape Overview** page because it provides an overview of the landscape, as shown in Figure 6.4. Seasoned SAP users will recognize the SAP Fiori look with its tiles.

There are three rows: **Monitor Landscape**, **Manage Landscape**, and **SAP ONE Support**. This page is configurable, and you can hide tiles or convert them to links, rename the headers, change the theme, and modify other common SAP Fiori configuration settings.

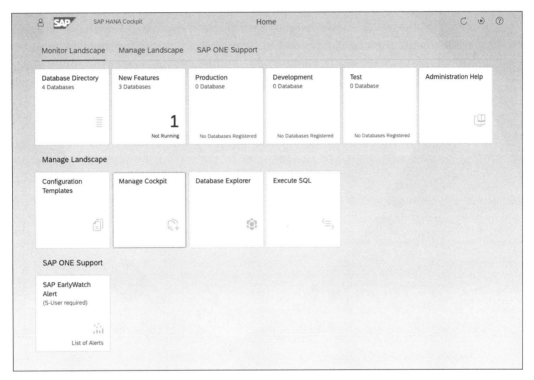

Figure 6.4 SAP HANA Cockpit: Home

With the **Configuration Templates** tile, you can create a collection of system parameter settings, for example, to implement consistent security settings across all registered databases.

Manage Cockpit launches the SAP HANA cockpit manager, and **Database Explorer** or **Execute SQL** opens SAP HANA database explorer in a new tab or window. We cover this tool in Chapter 5.

The **SAP ONE Support** row only displays a single tile: **SAP EarlyWatch Alert**. When configured, this displays the alerts of the SAP EarlyWatch Alert program. The connection is configured in the cockpit manager and can be hidden if not used.

The most important row of **Home** is the **Monitor Landscape** row. Apart from a link to the documentation, here you find the **Database Directory** and a tile for each of the database groups. Three groups have been created for you by default and reflect the three usage types of SAP HANA systems: **Production**, **Development**, and **Test**. Systems configured with any of these usage types are automatically assigned to these groups. For the fourth usage type, *custom*, you can create your own database groups in the SAP HANA cockpit manager. Each of the automatically created database groups can be hidden, and databases can be assigned to multiple databases groups.

The **Database Directory** shows another important aspect of database groups: you can only access databases that are in the same group as your user account. Figure 6.5 shows the two databases assigned to the custom group **New Features**: a system database and a tenant database. Most landscapes will list many more databases, and you can use the search bar and filters to find and organize them. Before you can connect to a database, you need to enter your credentials, which are stored encrypted in the cockpit database. Single sign-on (SSO) is also supported.

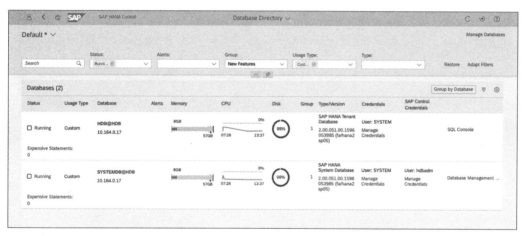

Figure 6.5 Database Directory

The gear icon in the table header of the **Database Directory** screen enables you to list additional information such as the operating system (kernel) version, the SAP HANA XSA version, and any alerts with the key performance area (KPA). From tenant databases, you can directly access the SQL console of SAP HANA database explorer. From the system database, you can access the Database Management app to work with tenant databases and configure restricted features, global allocation limits, audit policies, backup schedules, and other common settings. From here, you can also create new tenants and perform other tenant database management activities, which we'll return to in Chapters 7 and 8.

From the **Database Directory** or from the tiles on the **Home** page, you navigate to **Database Overview** illustrated in Figure 6.6. Some of the tiles display live information, for example, **Services**, **Memory Usage**, and **SQL Statements**. Others contain links to apps such as **Monitor performance**, which opens the Performance Monitor app. **Open SQL Console** in the menu bar opens the SAP HANA database explorer again, the same as when accessed from the **Landscape Overview** page. There are often different ways to access the tools, apps, and views.

When connected to the system database, you can also navigate from **Database Overview** to external applications such as the SAP HANA Platform Lifecycle Management tool or, when installed, add-on web interfaces for products such as SAP HANA dynamic tiering and SAP HANA smart data integration (SDI).

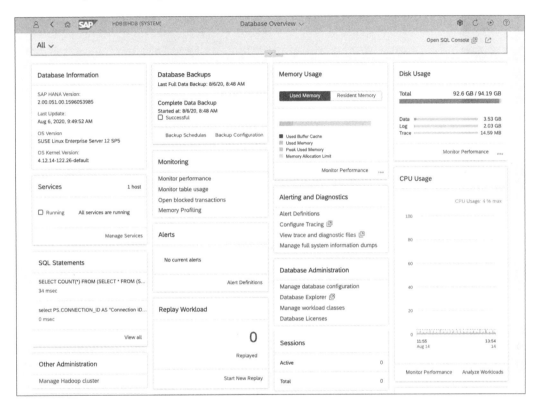

Figure 6.6 Database Overview

SAP HANA XS Advanced Cockpit

SAP HANA cockpit also includes SAP HANA XS Advanced cockpit. This is the same web application you find on the SAP HANA platform system when the SAP HANA XSA runtime is installed. For SAP HANA cockpit systems, the *HANACockpit* organization is created with all applications installed in the SAP space. Spaces and organizations refer to Cloud Foundry/SAP HANA XSA concepts, as discussed in Chapter 2. However, to manage and configure SAP HANA cockpit and the SAP HANA cockpit manager, you'll need to access the underlying SAP HANA XSA environment from time to time using either the xs command-line tool or the SAP HANA XS Advanced cockpit application (and probably both).

Figure 6.7 shows the applications of an SAP HANA XS Advanced cockpit system. The list is filtered on "cockpit" and shows the microservices architecture with multiple web applications (**app**) and services (**svc**).

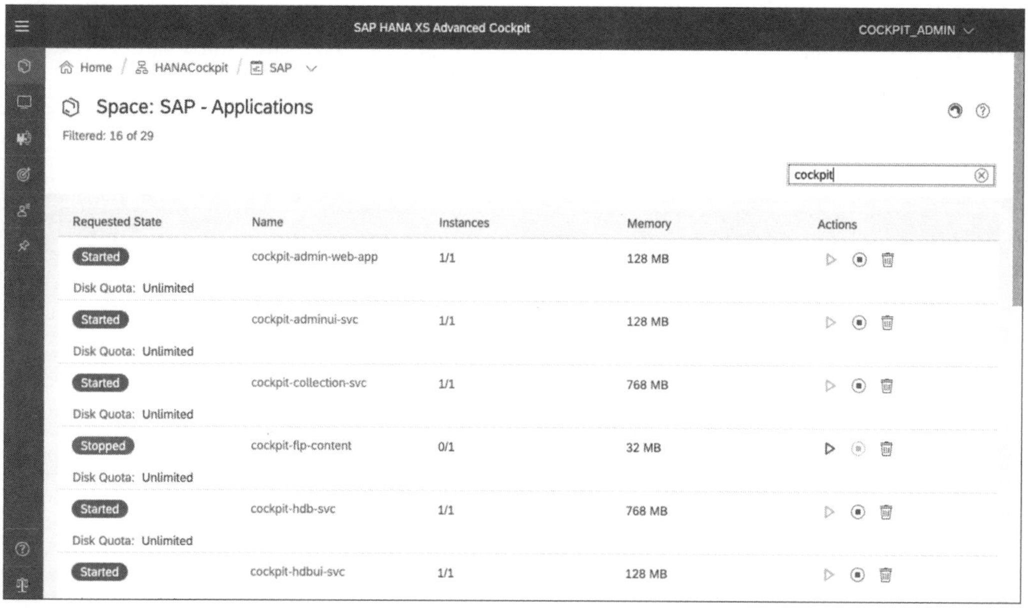

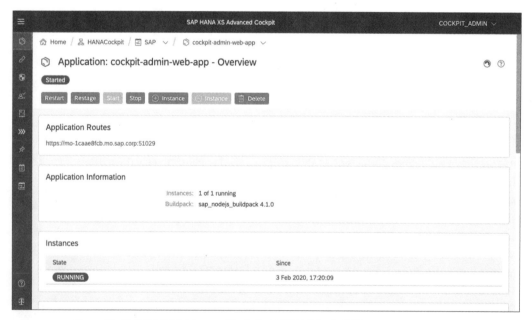

Figure 6.7 SAP HANA XS Advanced Cockpit: Applications

When an application is selected, the application route is listed, which provides the URL to connect to the SAP HANA cockpit manager, as illustrated in Figure 6.8.

Figure 6.8 SAP HANA XS Advanced Cockpit: SAP HANA Cockpit Manager

Release and Maintenance Strategy

In Chapter 4, we described the revision and maintenance strategy of SAP HANA with its support package stacks (SPSs) and release dates, and we mentioned that SAP HANA cockpit has its own release cycle with updates made available as support packs (SPs). Unlike SAP HANA SPSs, SAP HANA cockpit SPs include both new functionality and corrections and security updates. SP releases are synchronized with the release of an SPS of the SAP HANA platform.

SAP HANA cockpit also provides patches for the latest SP release that contain fixes and security updates. Updates are cumulative, and only the latest patch release of all the available SPs is listed (as illustrated in Figure 6.9).

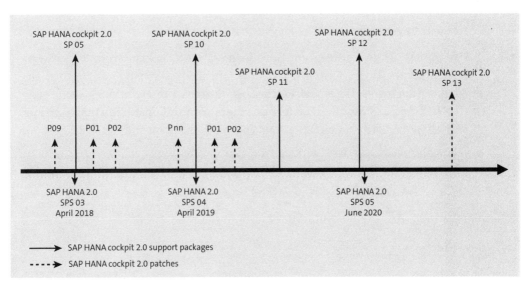

Figure 6.9 SAP HANA Cockpit 2.0: Revision and Maintenance Strategy

---

Note

For a more extensive coverage of this topic, beyond the scope of this exam, see the following SAP Notes:

- SAP Note 2433181 – SAP HANA 2.0 Cockpit Revision and Maintenance Strategy
- SAP Note 2380291 – SAP HANA 2.0 Cockpit Central Release Note

---

Installation

In this section, we'll walk through the installation process for SAP HANA cockpit. Before getting into the steps, we'll cover the requirements and software downloads necessary to begin.

Sizing and System Requirements

SAP HANA cockpit is available, like the SAP HANA platform, on Intel and IBM Power Systems processor architectures and supports both the SUSE Linux Enterprise Server (SLES) and Red Hat Enterprise Linux (RHEL) operating systems (RHEL on IBM Power Systems isn't supported).

We mentioned that SAP HANA cockpit comes with SAP HANA, express edition, embedded. On dedicated hardware, only 16 GB of RAM is required. For disk space, an equally low 16 GB is quoted with the mention that additional disk space is required as data is generated. For the shared database deployment model, a 22 GB RAM allocation is recommended.

Software Download

Like the SAP HANA platform, you download SAP HANA cockpit from the **Software Downloads** area on the SAP ONE Support Launchpad (see Chapter 4). For this, navigate to **Support Packages and Patches**, as illustrated in Figure 6.10, using "SAP HANA Cockpit 2.0" as the search term. As there are no compatibility requirements, SAP recommends updating SAP HANA cockpit to the latest supported release.

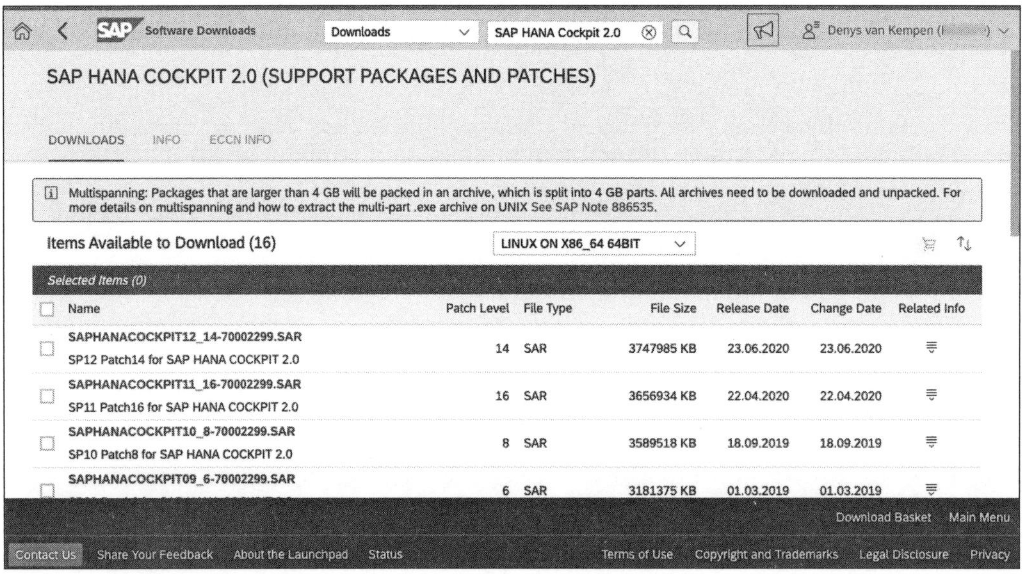

Figure 6.10 Software Downloads

The download is in the SAR file format and requires the SAPCAR utility for extraction, also available from **Software Downloads**. To extract the file, use the following command:

```
SAPCAR -manifest SIGNATURE.SMF -xvf SAPHANACOCKPIT<nn>.SAR
```

The extracted file is illustrated in Figure 6.11.

```
hana-vm1:/install/cockpit # ls
SAPCAR  SAPHANACOCKPIT12_14-70002299.SAR
hana-vm1:/install/cockpit # ./SAPCAR -manifest SIGNATURE.SMF -xvf SAPHANACOCKPIT12_14-70002299.SAR
SAPCAR: processing archive SAPHANACOCKPIT12_14-70002299.SAR (version 2.01)
x COCKPIT2_APP
x COCKPIT2_APP/sap-xsac-cockpit-2.12.14.zip
x hdblcm.sh
x hdblcmgui.sh
x HDB_SERVER_LINUX_X86_64
x HDB_SERVER_LINUX_X86_64/adapters.d
x HDB_SERVER_LINUX_X86_64/adapters.d/HDBLCM.adapter
x HDB_SERVER_LINUX_X86_64/adapters.d/HDBLCM_ext1.adapter
x HDB_SERVER_LINUX_X86_64/configurations
x HDB_SERVER_LINUX_X86_64/configurations/auto_install.cfg
x HDB_SERVER_LINUX_X86_64/configurations/custom
x HDB_SERVER_LINUX_X86_64/configurations/custom/compileserver.ini
x HDB_SERVER_LINUX_X86_64/configurations/custom/daemon.ini
x HDB_SERVER_LINUX_X86_64/configurations/custom/global.ini
x HDB_SERVER_LINUX_X86_64/configurations/custom/indexserver.ini
x HDB_SERVER_LINUX_X86_64/configurations/custom/nameserver.ini
x HDB_SERVER_LINUX_X86_64/configurations/custom/xscontroller.ini
```

Figure 6.11 Extracting Files with SAPCAR

Installation Steps

The installation of SAP HANA cockpit is similar to the installation of the SAP HANA server, but not identical. The same SAP HANA database lifecycle manager (HDBLCM) tool is used, and you can choose between using the command line or the graphical (X Window System) user interface. However, there is a small but important difference. To install (or update) SAP HANA cockpit, you need to start HDBLCM with scripts: hdblcm.sh and hdblcmgui.sh. You see both scripts listed in Figure 6.12.

```
x XSA_RT_20_LINUX_X86_64/packages/manifest
x XSA_RT_20_LINUX_X86_64/packages/NODE_10.TGZ
x XSA_RT_20_LINUX_X86_64/packages/ROUTER.TGZ
x XSA_RT_20_LINUX_X86_64/packages/SAPJVM_8.TGZ
x XSA_RT_20_LINUX_X86_64/packages/XS2_INDEP.TGZ
x SIGNATURE.SMF
SAPCAR: 714 file(s) extracted
hana-vm1:/install/cockpit # ls
COCKPIT2_APP          SAPCAR                              SIGNATURE.SMF  XSA_RT_20_LINUX_X86_64  manifest
HDB_SERVER_LINUX_X86_64  SAPHANACOCKPIT12_14-70002299.SAR  XSAC_HRTT_20   hdblcm.sh
HDB_LCM_LINUX_X86_64     SAP_PORTAL_SERVICES              XSA_COCKPIT    hdblcmgui.sh
hana-vm1:/install/cockpit # cat hdblcm.sh
#!/bin/bash

current_dir=`dirname "$0"`
current_dir=`readlink -f "$current_dir"`
hdblcm_dir=`find "$current_dir" -name "HDB__LCM_*" 2>/dev/null`
if [ ! -f "$hdblcm_dir/hdblcm" ]; then
    echo "$hdblcm_dir/hdblcm not found" >&2
    exit 1
elif [ ! -x "$hdblcm_dir/hdblcm" ]; then
    echo "Cannot execute $hdblcm_dir/hdblcm" >&2
    exit 1
fi
"$hdblcm_dir/hdblcm" --component_root="$current_dir" $*
hana-vm1:/install/cockpit # █
```

Figure 6.12 Installation Script hdblcm.sh

The script files make sure that you use the prepared configuration file for SAP HANA cockpit with default settings depending on whether you select the standalone or shared database installation (auto_install.cfg and auto_install_hdb.cfg, respectively). These setting can be adjusted, although for some configurations, different steps are required, for example, if you want to assign a different port range for the SAP HANA cockpit applications (default 51000–51500).

The first screen prompts you to either install a new system or update the current one when detected, as shown in Figure 6.13.

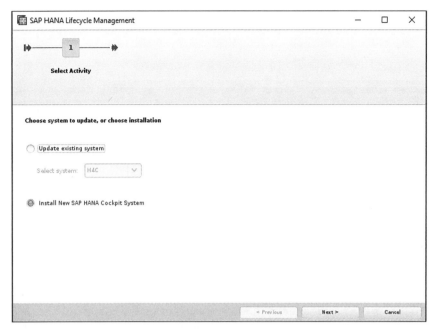

Figure 6.13 SAP HANA Lifecycle Management: Install New System

Even when opting for a new installation, all default values for the system properties are provided, including the SID, unlike with SAP HANA server installations. These values come from the template. You see this illustrated in Figure 6.14. The default value for **SAP HANA System ID** is **H4C** (HANA for Cockpit), and the default for the **Instance Number** is 96 or next available (*n*+1).

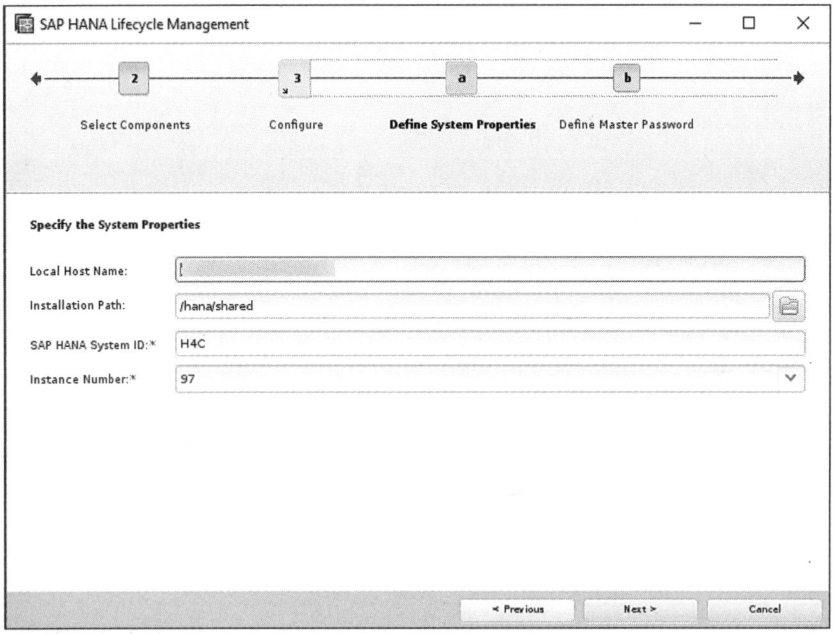

Figure 6.14 SAP HANA Lifecycle Management: Specify System Properties

After clicking **Next**, you're prompted to define the master password, which will be used for the COCKPIT_ADMIN user account for the SAP HANA cockpit and SAP HANA cockpit manager applications. In the last screen, you only need to review your selections and click **Install** to install.

As with the SAP HANA server, you can also run the installation in batch mode with optional command-line parameters to override those defined ign the configuration file. For example, to install SAP HANA cockpit in batch mode and override the default name of the SAP HANA XSA runtime admin user, you can enter the following command:

```
hdblcm.sh --action=install -b --org_manager_user=JDOE
```

For SAP HANA cockpit, the default value for this parameter is COCKPIT_ADMIN. For the SAP HANA platform, the equivalent account is XSA_ADMIN, which corresponds to the SAP HANA XSA administration account. Although this account maps to a database user, it's an application account with the SAP HANA XS user account and authentication (UAA) service managing access control.

Figure 6.15 illustrates the installation in command-line mode and is identical.

```
hana-vm1:/install/cockpit # whoami
root
hana-vm1:/install/cockpit # ls
COCKPIT2_APP             SAPCAR                            SIGNATURE.SMF  XSA_RT_20_LINUX_X86_64  manifest
HDB_SERVER_LINUX_X86_64  SAPHANACOCKPIT12_14-70002299.SAR  XSAC_HRTT_20   hdblcm.sh
HDB__LCM_LINUX_X86_64    SAP_PORTAL_SERVICES               XSA_COCKPIT    hdblcmgui.sh
hana-vm1:/install/cockpit # ./hdblcm.sh


SAP HANA Lifecycle Management - SAP HANA Cockpit 2.0.12.14.0
************************************************************



Choose an action

  Index | Action              | Description
  -----------------------------------------------------------------------------------------------
  1     | HDB (install)       | Install SAP HANA Cockpit on SAP HANA Database version 2.00.051.00.1596053985
  2     | install             | Install new SAP HANA Cockpit system
  3     | Exit (do nothing)   |

Enter selected action index [3]: 2

Enter Installation Path [/hana/shared]:
Enter Local Host Name [hana-vm1]:
Enter SAP HANA System ID [H4C]:
Enter Instance Number [96]:
Enter Master Password:
Confirm Master Password:

Summary before execution:
=========================

SAP HANA Cockpit System Installation
   Installation Parameters
      Remote Execution: ssh
      Use single master password for all users, created during installation: Yes
      Database Isolation: low
      Create initial tenant database: No
      Install Execution Mode: optimized
      Installation Path: /hana/shared
```

Figure 6.15 SAP HANA Cockpit: Install

At the end of the installation, connection information for SAP HANA cockpit and SAP HANA cockpit manager is displayed, but this might be easy to miss (see Figure 6.16). Note the different SAP HANA XSA applications being created and the log file written to /var/temp with SID (H4C), action name (install), and timestamp.

```
Creating application "cockpit-xsa-svc" from MTA module "cockpit-xsa-svc"...
Uploading application "cockpit-xsa-svc"...
Starting application "cockpit-xsa-svc"...
Creating application "cockpit-web-app" from MTA module "cockpit-web-app"...
Uploading application "cockpit-web-app"...
Starting application "cockpit-web-app"...
Creating application "cockpit-adminui-svc" from MTA module "cockpit-adminui-svc"...
Uploading application "cockpit-adminui-svc"...
Starting application "cockpit-adminui-svc"...
Creating application "cockpit-admin-web-app" from MTA module "cockpit-admin-web-app"...
Uploading application "cockpit-admin-web-app"...
Starting application "cockpit-admin-web-app"...
Creating application "cockpit-js-svc" from MTA module "cockpit-js-svc"...
Uploading application "cockpit-js-svc"...
Starting application "cockpit-js-svc"...
Creating configuration change subscription from MTA module "cockpit-health-svc" to MTA resource "cockpit-health-svc-
endpoints"...
    Registering service URL "https://mo-1caae8fcb.mo.sap.corp:51027" named "hana-cockpit"...
    Registering service URL "https://mo-1caae8fcb.mo.sap.corp:51029" named "hana-cockpit-admin"...
    Updating application "hrtt-service" from MTA "com.sap.xsa.hrtt" for subscription "cockpit-persistence-svc"...
    Updating application "hrtt-service" from MTA "com.sap.xsa.hrtt" for subscription "cockpit-landscape-svc"...
    Updating application "hrtt-service" from MTA "com.sap.xsa.hrtt" for subscription "cockpit-hdb-svc"...
    Updating application "sqlanlz-svc" from MTA "com.sap.xsa.hrtt" for subscription "cockpit-hdbui-svc"...
    Updating application "cockpit-health-svc" from MTA "com.sap.hana.cockpit" for subscription "cockpit-health-svc-endpo
ints"
    Stopping application "hrtt-service"...
    Starting application "hrtt-service"...
    Stopping application "sqlanlz-svc"...
    Starting application "sqlanlz-svc"...
    Stopping application "cockpit-health-svc"...
    Starting application "cockpit-health-svc"...
    Installation of archive file '[/install/COCKPIT2_APP/sap-xsac-cockpit-2.11.11.zip]' finished successfully.
SAP HANA Cockpit System installed

Launch SAP HANA cockpit by opening https://mo-1caae8fcb.mo.sap.corp:51027
Launch SAP HANA cockpit manager by opening https://mo-1caae8fcb.mo.sap.corp:51029

Log file written to '/var/tmp/hdb_H4C_hdblcm_install_2020-02-03_15.40.04/hdblcm.log' on host 'mo-1caae8fcb.mo.sap.corp'.
mo-1caae8fcb:/install #
```

Figure 6.16 SAP HANA Cockpit: Installation Finished

If you miss the URL for the cockpit web applications, you can look it up in the **Applications** view of the SAP HANA XS Advanced cockpit (refer to Figure 6.7) or use the equivalent xs apps command to query this information, as illustrated in Figure 6.17.

```
h4cadm@mo-1caae8fcb.mo:/usr/sap/H4C/HDB96> xs login

API_URL: https://mo-1caae8fcb.mo.sap.corp:39630
USERNAME: COCKPIT_ADMIN
PASSWORD>
Authenticating...
ORG: HANACockpit
SPACE: SAP
API endpoint:   https://mo-1caae8fcb.mo.sap.corp:39630 (API version: 1)
User:           COCKPIT_ADMIN
Org:            HANACockpit
Space:          SAP

h4cadm@mo-1caae8fcb.mo:/usr/sap/H4C/HDB96> xs apps | grep web-app
cockpit-admin-web-app        STARTED        1/1        128 MB    <unlimited>        https://mo-1caae8fcb.mo.sap.corp:51029
cockpit-web-app              STARTED        1/1        512 MB    <unlimited>        https://mo-1caae8fcb.mo.sap.corp:51027
h4cadm@mo-1caae8fcb.mo:/usr/sap/H4C/HDB96>
```

Figure 6.17 SAP HANA XS Command-Line Tool

> **Note**
>
> For those less familiar with Linux system administration, the output of the xs apps command (a long list) is sent to the grep tool, which applies a filter on the web-app word:
>
> xs apps | grep web-app

Update

The procedure to update an SAP HANA cockpit system is very similar to the installation except that you select the update action in the SAP HANA Lifecycle Management tool and choose the SID from the list. In the graphical version, you're prompted to select which components you want to update; however, except for support cases, you would normally leave all components selected (database, runtime, applications). Figure 6.18 shows the **Review & Confirm** screen.

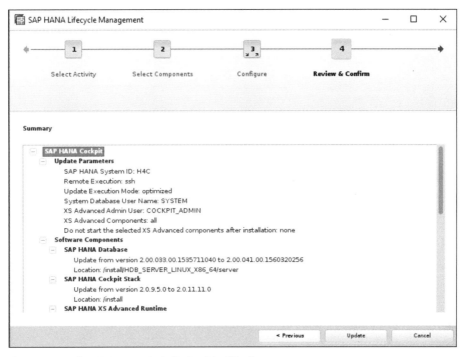

Figure 6.18 Update SAP HANA Cockpit: Graphical Version

Figure 6.19 shows the command-line prompts with default values except for the passwords. As always, it's a common best practice to perform a database backup prior to updating the system. Depending on system resources, a SAP HANA cockpit update takes about 45 minutes.

```
SAP HANA Lifecycle Management - SAP HANA Cockpit 2.0.11.11.0
************************************************************


Choose an action

 Index | Action            | Description
 -----------------------------------------------------------------
  1     | H4C (update)      | Update SAP HANA Cockpit version 2.0.9.5.0
  2     | install           | Install new SAP HANA Cockpit system
  3     | Exit (do nothing) |

Enter selected action index [3]: 1

Enter System Database User Name [SYSTEM]:
Enter System Database User (SYSTEM) Password:
Enter XS Advanced Admin User (COCKPIT_ADMIN) Password:

Summary before execution:
==========================

SAP HANA Cockpit
   Update Parameters
      SAP HANA System ID: H4C
      Remote Execution: ssh
      Update Execution Mode: optimized
      System Database User Name: SYSTEM
      XS Advanced Admin User: COCKPIT_ADMIN
      XS Advanced Components: all
      Do not start the selected XS Advanced components after installation: none
   Software Components
      SAP HANA Database
         Update from version 2.00.033.00.1535711040 to 2.00.041.00.1560320256
         Location: /install/HDB_SERVER_LINUX_X86_64/server
      SAP HANA Cockpit Stack
         Update from version 2.0.9.5.0 to 2.0.11.11.0
         Location: /install
      SAP HANA XS Advanced Runtime
         Update from version 1.0.99.13607 to 1.0.119.14405
         Location: /install/XSA_RT_20_LINUX_X86_64/packages
   XS Advanced Components
      SAP HANA Cockpit
         Update from version 2.9.5 to 2.0011.11
         Location: /install/COCKPIT2_APP/sap-xsac-cockpit-2.11.11.zip
      SAP HANA tools for accessing catalog content, data preview, SQL console, etc.
         Update from version 2.8.33 to 2.011.64
         Location: /install/XSAC_HRTT_20/sap-xsac-hrtt-2.11.64.zip
      Develop and run portal services for customer apps on XSA
         Update from version 1.2.1 to 1.003.2
         Location: /install/SAP_PORTAL_SERVICES/sap-portal-services-assembly-1.14.3.zip
      SAPUI5 FESV5 XSA 1 - SAPUI5 1.60
         Install version 1.060.18
         Location: /install/SAP_UI5_1/sapui5-dist-xsa-1.60.18.zip
      XSA Cockpit 1
         Update from version 1.1.7 to 1.001.15
         Location: /install/XSA_COCKPIT/cockpit-web-xsa-assembly-1.1.15.zip
   Log File Locations
      Log directory: /var/tmp/hdb_H4C_hdblcm_update_2020-02-03_15.31.20
      Trace location: /var/tmp/hdblcm_2020-02-03_15.31.20_25792.trc
```

Figure 6.19 Update SAP HANA Cockpit: Command Line

Uninstall

The procedure to remove SAP HANA cockpit is identical to that for the SAP HANA platform. Note that this time you don't use a script file. Instead, launch the resident HDBLCM, and select the **uninstall** action, as shown in Figure 6.20. You have the option to remove only the runtime or only the SAP HANA cockpit applications, but again, this addresses special cases and would usually only be selected when instructed by SAP Support. Select **All** and confirm your selection.

```
mo-1caae8fcb:/hana/shared/H4C/hdblcm # ls
SIGNATURE.SMF  configurations  filelist.resident  hdblcmgui  instruntime  resources
adapters.d    descriptors.d   hdblcm             hdblcmweb  operations.d
mo-1caae8fcb:/hana/shared/H4C/hdblcm # ./hdblcm


SAP HANA Lifecycle Management - SAP HANA Cockpit 2.0.9.5.0
***********************************************************



Choose an action

  Index | Action               | Description
  ---------------------------------------------------------------------------
  1     | check_installation   | Check SAP HANA Cockpit Installation
  2     | configure_sld        | Configure System Landscape Directory Registration
  3     | extract_components   | Extract Components
  4     | rename_system        | Rename the SAP HANA Cockpit System
  5     | uninstall            | Uninstall SAP HANA Cockpit Components
  6     | unregister_system    | Unregister the SAP HANA Cockpit System
  7     | update_component_list| Update Component List
  8     | update_components    | Install or Update Additional Components
  9     | update_host          | Update the SAP HANA Cockpit Instance Host integration
  10    | update               | Update the SAP HANA Cockpit System
  11    | exit                 | Exit (do nothing)

Enter selected action index [11]: 5


Choose components to be uninstalled for system 'H4C':
  Index | Components | Description
  ---------------------------------------------------------------------------------
  1     | all        | SAP HANA Database version 2.00.033.00.1535711040 and all other components
  2     | xs         | Uninstall SAP HANA XS Advanced Runtime version 1.0.99.13607
  3     | cockpit    | Uninstall SAP HANA Cockpit Stack version 2.0.9.5.0

Enter comma-separated list of the selected indices [1]:

Summary before execution:
=========================

SAP HANA Cockpit System Uninstallation
   Software Components
      SAP HANA XS Advanced Runtime
          Uninstall version 1.0.99.13607
      SAP HANA Cockpit Stack
          Uninstall version 2.0.9.5.0
      SAP HANA Database
          Uninstall version 2.00.033.00.1535711040

Note: All data volumes and all log volumes of SAP HANA Database 'H4C' will be removed!

Do you want to continue? (y/n):
```

Figure 6.20 Uninstall SAP HANA Cockpit

Provisioning and Configuration

Before we can use SAP HANA cockpit in an SAP HANA system landscape, we need to provision and configure the tool. The exact steps required will depend on the situation but usually include the following:

- **Firewall configuration**
  SAP HANA cockpit needs to be able to connect to the different SAP HANA systems using both the SQL port and the TCP port of the SAP start service. In addition, a web connection from the computer of the SAP HANA cockpit administrators and the SAP HANA cockpit system itself needs to be enabled.

  This activity is typically performed by the network administrator and is out of scope for the exam, but you do need to know the relevant HTTP/S ports.

- **Configure single sign-on (SSO) and Transport Layer Security/Secure Sockets Layer (TLS/SSL)**
  Configuring SSO and TLS/SSL isn't required but is certainly recommended. You can enable SSO to connect to SAP HANA cockpit and SAP HANA cockpit manager, so you don't have to enter your user name and password each time. You can also enable SSO from SAP HANA cockpit to a database for the same reason. In addition, it's highly recommended to configure encrypted connections using HTTPS and TLS. Both SSO and TLS can be enforced.

- **Register databases and create database groups and SAP HANA cockpit users**
  By default, only the user who has registered a database can access this database with SAP HANA cockpit. By creating additional users and adding them to groups, this privilege can be extended.

Learn More

For more extensive coverage of how to provision SAP HANA cockpit, which is beyond the scope of this exam, see the "SAP HANA Administration with SAP HANA Cockpit" documentation at *http://s-prs.co/v507840*.

In the following sections, we'll take a closer look into the specific items that must be configured.

Connecting to the SAP HANA Cockpit Manager

Before you can start using SAP HANA cockpit, you first need to register at least a single database. In most cases, you also want to create cockpit users and add database groups so you can map databases to users and control access. Although there is a logic in the sequence of steps, the exact order isn't fixed, and you can always return to the SAP HANA cockpit manager to add or delete users, database groups, and register or deregister databases.

The SAP HANA XSA runtime comes with a self-signed certificate for HTTPS, which most modern browsers no longer accept. Unless you've already performed the steps to update the TLS certificates, you might need to import the certificates on your local computer and set it to trusted. The error page and certificate are displayed in Figure 6.21. We cover this topic in more detail in Chapter 10.

When you proceed and make your first connection to the SAP HANA cockpit manager with the COCKPIT_ADMIN user, you'll receive a **Not Authorized** message, as illustrated in Figure 6.22, which you need to acknowledge.

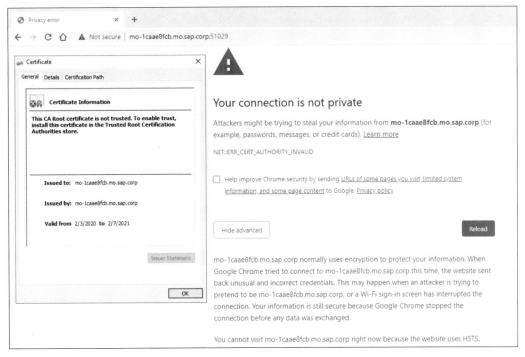

Figure 6.21 Your Connection Is Not Private Error

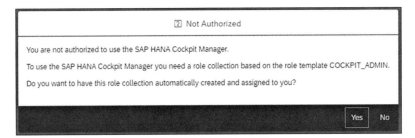

Figure 6.22 Not Authorized

The SAP HANA cockpit manager will appear initially with only a single SAP HANA cockpit user, no registered databases, and no database groups, as shown in Figure 6.23. An alert informs you that you need to register or import databases for SAP HANA cockpit to monitor.

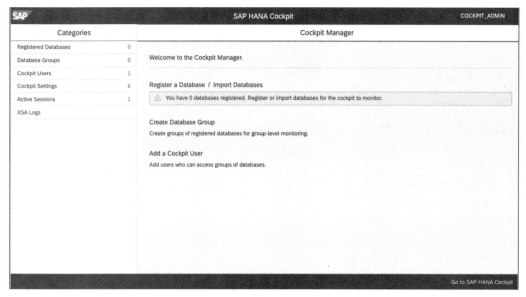

Figure 6.23 SAP HANA Cockpit Manager

SAP HANA Cockpit Users

Selecting **Cockpit Users** enables you to create new users, as shown in Figure 6.24. From the bottom toolbar, you can create new users or edit/delete existing ones. The default COCKPIT_ADMIN user has the five principal roles assigned but no database. A security best practice would be to keep it this way and use the cockpit administrator only for administration. Ideally, for separation of duties, you would even want to create different administrators for the different activities.

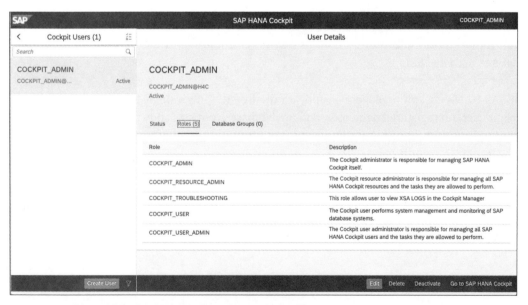

Figure 6.24 SAP HANA Cockpit Manager: User Details

Register Database

Selecting **Register a Database**, as shown earlier in Figure 6.23, and then clicking the **Register** button on the bottom toolbar launches the **Register Database** wizard with five steps:

1. **Database**

   In this step, you need to provide host, identifier, and container information and indicate how you want the database to be listed in SAP HANA cockpit by either using our own format (user-defined) or the system-generated format data-base@system (see Figure 6.25). As an identifier, you can enter either the instance number or the SQL port. This corresponds to how you would connect to the database using HDBSQL (or SAP HANA studio). Single container systems are still supported for SAP HANA 1.0 SPS 12. Otherwise and for SAP HANA 2.0, indicate whether to register the system database or provide the name of the tenant database.

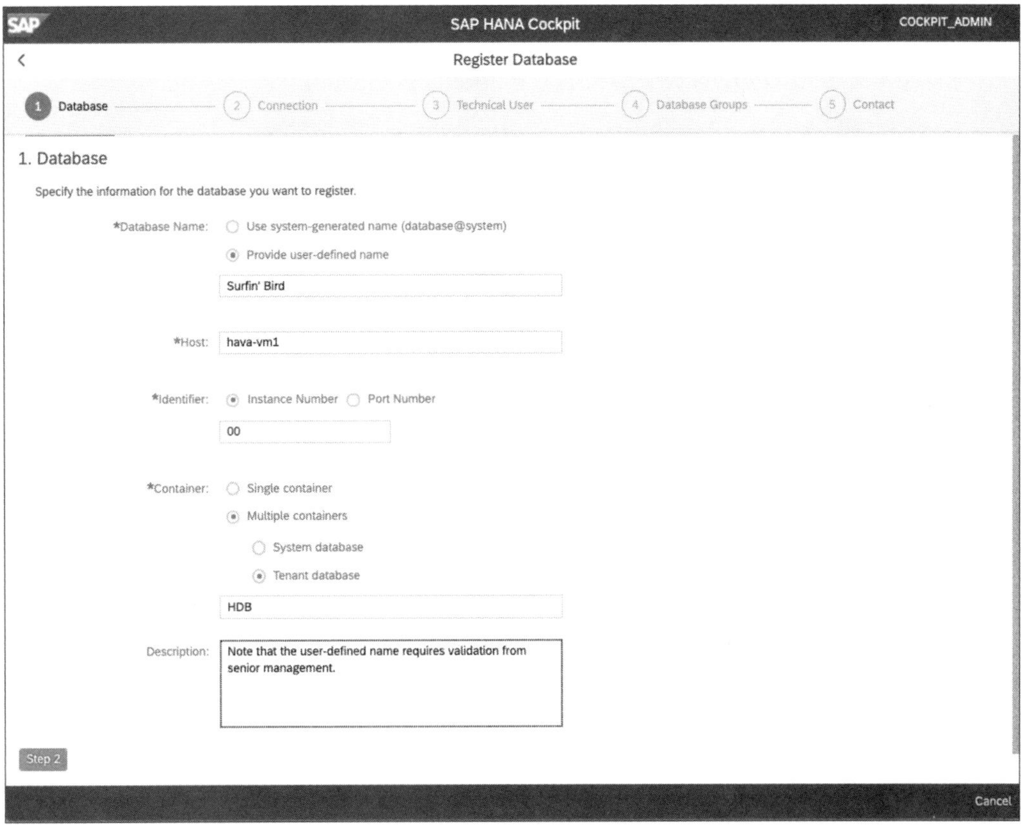

Figure 6.25 Register Database

2. **Connection**

   In this step, you can specify the encryption to use for the database and the sap-control connection. The latter enables you to stop and start the system using the operating system account <sid>adm. Using encryption for this connection is strongly recommended as you're exchanging passwords. Here you can also indicate whether you want to validate the certificate. When selected, you need to import the certificate for the validation to succeed.

3. **Technical User**

   In this step, you need to provide the credentials of a technical database user. This user requires CATALOG READ system privilege and SELECT object privilege on _SYS_STATISTICS schema, and should be not be used for regular connections. The account password should also not expire, and you could consider using a user group and dedicated password policies. We cover this topic in more detail in Chapter 10. In early versions of SAP HANA cockpit, this user first had to be created on the source system, which was cumbersome as this required either SAP HANA studio or the hdbsql command-line utility. Now, a dialog enables you to create this user, as illustrated in Figure 6.26. If applicable, grant the SAP Early-Watch Alert privileges (requires additional privileges).

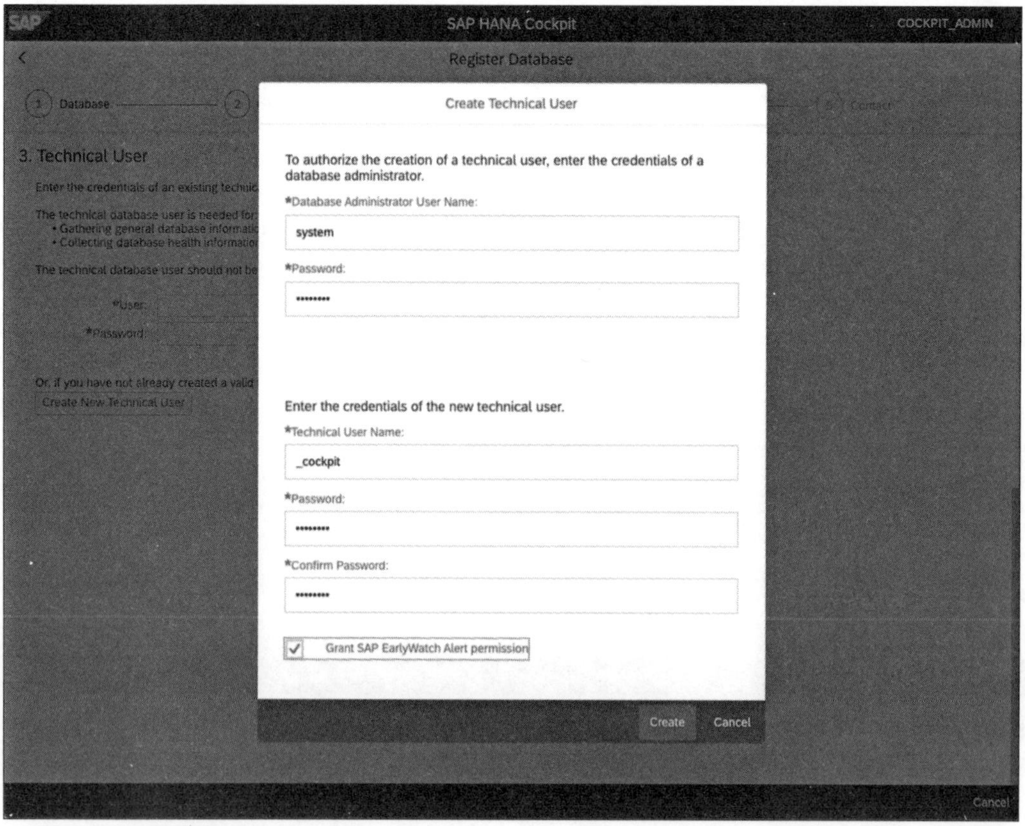

Figure 6.26 Create Technical User

4. **Database Groups**

In this step, you can assign the database to a database group. This step is optional, but as long as the database isn't assigned to a database group, you can't map any users to the database because users are also assigned to database groups but not to the database directly.

5. **Contact**

In this step, you can provide optional contact information and confirm the information in a final review screen.

The result is shown in Figure 6.27. When you edit the registration, you can enable and even enforce SSO. This requires the TRUST ADMIN system privilege on the target database (as indicated).

From the bottom toolbar, you can register additional databases, export the registration details for selected databases, and import database registrations.

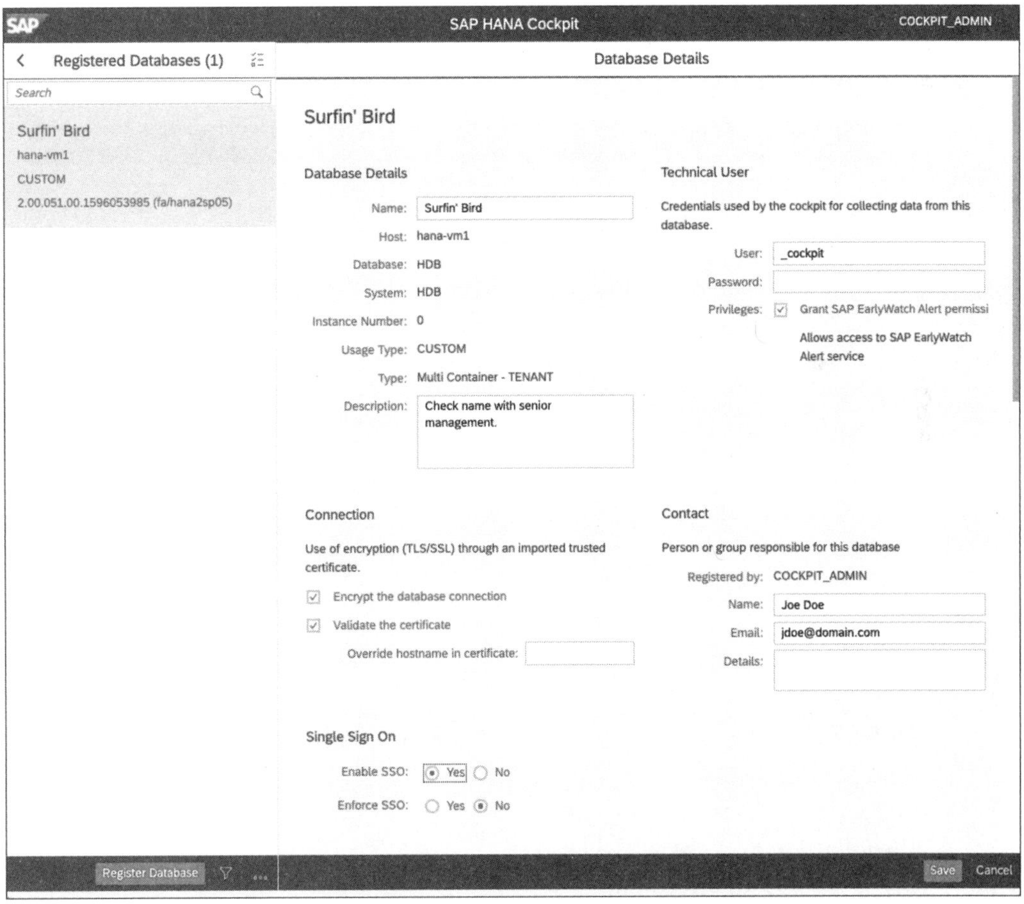

Figure 6.27 Database Details

SAP HANA Cockpit Manager Roles

Clicking the **Cockpit Users** menu option (refer to Figure 6.23) allows you to create users and roles. Creating users is a three-step process:

1. Provide user information.
2. Assign SAP HANA cockpit roles.
3. Assign users to database groups.

A **Create User** wizard helps you complete the procedure:

1. **User Information**
   In this step, you enter user name, password, and email. There is an option to allow existing database users to access the SAP HANA cockpit.
2. **Cockpit Roles**
   In this step, you select the roles for this user, as shown in Figure 6.28. By default, the **Cockpit User Role** is selected.
3. **Database Groups**
   In this step, you can assign any available groups to this user.

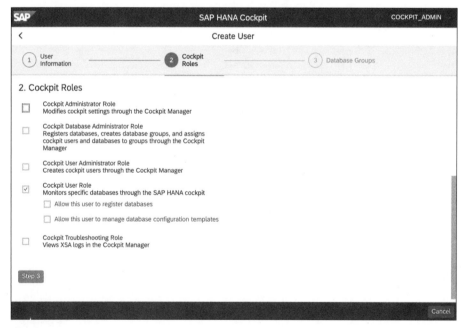

Figure 6.28 Create User

The following roles are available:

- **Cockpit Administrator Role**
  Modifies SAP HANA cockpit manager settings.
- **Cockpit Database Administrator Role**
  Registers databases, creates database groups, and assigns users and databases to groups.

- **Cockpit User Administrator Role**
  Creates SAP HANA cockpit users.

- **Cockpit User Role**
  Monitors specific databases, including the following two options:
  - **Allow this user to register databases**: Select to make a cockpit power user, who can monitor and register databases.
  - **Allow this user to manager database configuration templates**: Select to make a configuration template administrator.

- **Cockpit Troubleshooting Role**
  Views the web application XSA logs.

Users with the cockpit user role can connect only to SAP HANA cockpit and access the databases that are included in the SAP HANA cockpit user database groups, as shown in Figure 6.29.

> **Note**
> Note that there is no master role containing all privileges. The cockpit power user and configuration template administrator are listed in the documentation as roles but aren't displayed as such in the UI.

Figure 6.29 Create Database Group

A similar wizard is available to create database groups in three steps:

1. Enter group name with optional description.
2. Select database to be included in the group.
3. Select SAP HANA cockpit users to be included in the group.

SAP HANA Cockpit Manager Settings

Users with the cockpit administrator role can connect to the SAP HANA cockpit manager **Settings**, as shown in Figure 6.30, to control the following:

- **Data Collection**
  Includes the following collection options:
  - Number of threads for the collection services (**5**)
  - System status and alert counts (**ON**, every minute)
  - Database and feature data (**ON**, every minute)
- **Proxy**
  Includes option to assign a proxy.
- **Connections**
  Includes the following connection options:
  - Database connection timeout (30 seconds)
  - sapcontrol connection timeout (15 seconds)
- **SSO with Kerberos**
  Includes option to enable SSO.
- **Display**
  Includes system-defined groups.
- **SAP Early Watch Alert**
  Includes user, transmission schedule, location, and optional SAP routers.

Note that without additional privileges (roles), a user with only the cockpit manager role can only change SAP HANA cockpit settings, which may be a bit of a disappointment given the title. The system-defined database groups reference the usage types system and installation parameter. Refer to Figure 6.4 for how these database groups are displayed by default on the SAP HANA cockpit home page.

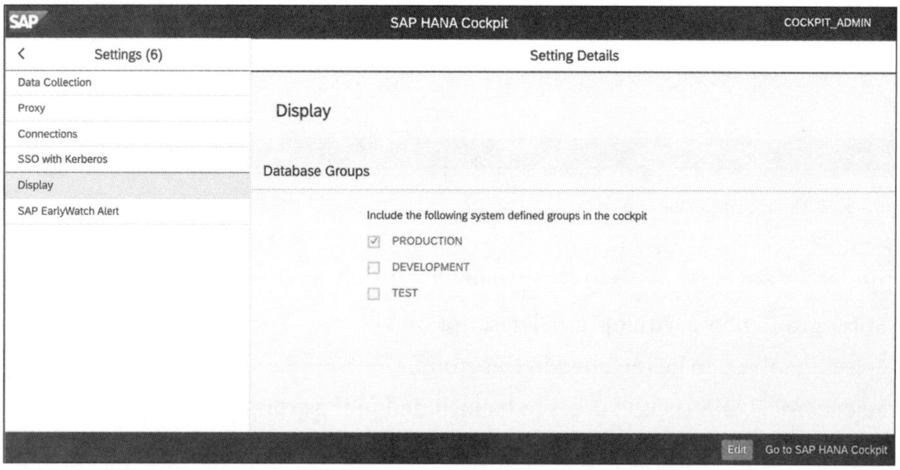

Figure 6.30 Settings

XSA Logs

The cockpit troubleshooting role grants access to the **XSA Logs** section of the SAP HANA cockpit manager but requires an additional privilege, which doesn't yet exist. On the first time access, the following message is displayed: **You need the Space Auditor role in order to view the XSA logs. Ask the cockpit User Administrator to assign this role to you.** If you're the user administrator, you need to know that you have to execute the xs set-space-role command, as illustrated in Figure 6.31.

```
h4cadm@hxehost:/usr/sap/H4C/HDB96> xs l

API_URL: https://hanacockpit.c.sap-hana-academy-174915.internal:39630
USERNAME> cockpit_admin
PASSWORD>
Authenticating...
ORG: HANACockpit
SPACE: SAP
API endpoint:   https://hanacockpit.c.sap-hana-academy-174915.internal:39630 (API version: 1)
User:           cockpit_admin
Org:            HANACockpit
Space:          SAP

h4cadm@hxehost:/usr/sap/H4C/HDB96> xs set-space-role COCKPIT_ADMIN HANACockpit SAP SpaceAuditor

Adding role 'SpaceAuditor' to user COCKPIT_ADMIN in space "SAP" of org "HANACockpit" ...
OK

h4cadm@hxehost:/usr/sap/H4C/HDB96>
```

Figure 6.31 Set Space Auditor Role

With this and the cockpit troubleshooting role, you can then access the different SAP HANA XSA log files, one for each web application and service, as shown in Figure 6.32.

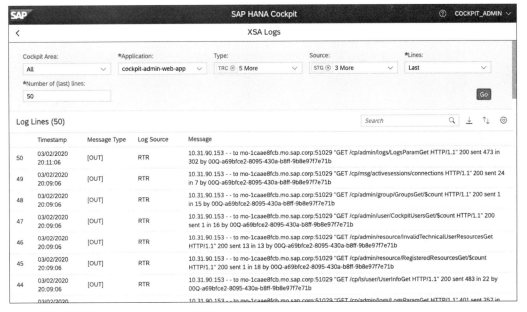

Figure 6.32 SAP HANA Cockpit Manager: XSA Logs

SAP HANA XSA User Administration

Although out of scope of the exam, it's good to realize that the security concept of SAP HANA cockpit maps to the SAP HANA XSA security settings. As illustrated in Figure 6.33, to assign the **Space Auditor** role to your user, you could have also used SAP HANA XS Advanced cockpit.

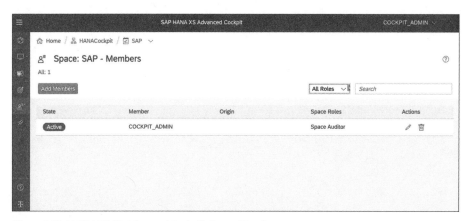

Figure 6.33 SAP HANA XS Advanced Cockpit: Space Members

Although this web application is also called a cockpit, it has nothing to do with your SAP HANA database administration tool. SAP HANA XS Advanced cockpit is the administration tool for the SAP HANA XSA infrastructure and comes with the runtime. SAP HANA cockpit manager provides the UI to abstract any SAP HANA XSA complexities, but it's still an SAP HANA XSA application leveraging the XS UAA service. The user will be created in the system database of the SAP HANA cockpit system or, in case of a shared database installation, in the SAP HANA cockpit database tenant, as shown in Figure 6.34.

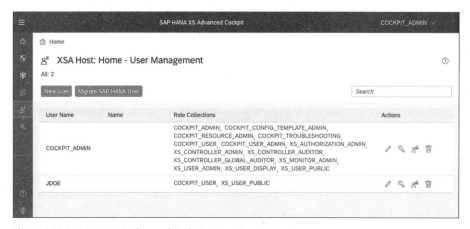

Figure 6.34 SAP HANA XS Advanced Cockpit: User Management

Active Sessions

The **Active Sessions** view in the SAP HANA cockpit manager (refer to Figure 6.23) shows you currently connected cockpit users, with latency and last location. From here you can send a message that displays as five-second popup or, if needed, interrupt with a message that requires acknowledgement, as illustrated in Figure 6.35.

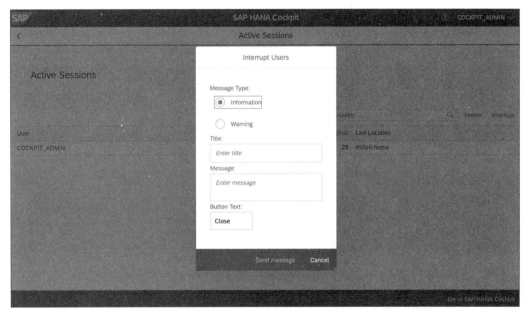

Figure 6.35 SAP HANA Cockpit: Active Sessions

Database Directory

When everything is configured the way you want, you can share the credentials with the SAP HANA cockpit administrators. They can then connect to SAP HANA cockpit, which opens on the **Home** view listing the tiles to monitor and manage the landscape, as illustrated previously in Figure 6.4.

From **Home**, you can either open the **Database Directory** screen or have a filter applied by opening only a specific database group. The **Database Directory** screen lists the databases the currently connected SAP HANA cockpit user has been granted access to (i.e., the database and the SAP HANA cockpit user belong to the same database group). For the **Database Directory** screen, see Figure 6.5.

The default **Database Directory** view shows the following:

- **Status**
  Status of the database (e.g., **Running, Starting, Stopped, Issues)**.
- **Usage type**
  Can be production, development, test, or custom.

- **Database**
  Database name as configured at registration time (system generated, or user defined; refer to Figure 6.25)

- **Alerts**
  Number of alerts, if any.

- **Memory**, **CPU**, and **Disk**
  Graphical indicators.

- **Expensive Statements**
  Number of SQL statements, which consume significant resources.

- **Group**
  Number of groups the database belongs to (click for a list).

- **Availability/Performance/Capacity**
  Aggregated health view for the three key performance areas (KPAs).

- **Type/Version**
  Type and version of the database; system database or tenant with version release number in format 2.00.051.00.*<patch number>*.

- **Credentials**
  Credentials of the database connection.

- **SAP Control Credentials**
  Credentials of the sapcontrol connection.

What is on display is configurable. With enough screen real estate available, you could also select the SID, SAP HANA XSA version, and so on.

The sapcontrol credentials can be only be provided for system databases. With sapcontrol, you stop and start the entire system, and you don't want to delegate this authority to mere tenant database administrators.

Note that even though your SAP HANA cockpit database administrator has made the database available to your user account, you still can't connect because you need to provide your own credentials in the **Database Directory** screen first. If you have no password or have forgotten it, you still can't connect.

If a system database is a registered database, you can also select the **Database Management** link to directly open the app. Alternatively, you can access this app from the header of the **Database Overview** page. We return to this topic when we describe database administration activities in Chapter 7.

Similarly, the **Manage Database** link in the header opens the SAP HANA cockpit manager again, which you could also have accessed from the SAP HANA cockpit **Home** page. There are often multiple ways to access an app.

Important Terminology

For this exam objective, you're expected to understand the following terms:

- **COCKPIT_ADMIN**
  COCKPIT_ADMIN is the initial application administration account that you can use to prepare SAP HANA cockpit for first use. Typically, you would use this account to create other SAP HANA cockpit users and SAP HANA cockpit administrators, after which you can disable the account. The name is configurable, and the password is set during installation.

- **Database Directory**
  The **Database Directory** is a view in SAP HANA cockpit that lists the databases accessible to the SAP HANA cockpit user. The same view also provides an aggregate health view and shows the database status, alerts, and a green checkmark or warning sign for the KPAs of availability, performance, and capacity.

- **Database overview**
  The **Database Overview** page is the default page that SAP HANA cockpit displays when connected to a database. This page is configurable and shows tiles displaying **CPU Usage**, **Memory Usage**, **Disk Usage**, and other performance counters and links.

- **Database (resource)**
  A database is either a system or tenant database and a single container or tenant database system (also known as multitenant database container [MDC] system). You need to register a database with the SAP HANA cockpit manager before you can connect to this database using SAP HANA cockpit. A database is assigned to a group. Prior to SAP HANA Cockpit 2.0 SP 12, the term "resource" was used.

- **Database (resource) group**
  Registered databases are bundled in database groups. Both SAP HANA cockpit users and databases are assigned to a database group.

- **Landscape overview**
  The **Landscape Overview** page is the default page that SAP HANA cockpit displays when you connect. This page is configurable and shows tiles displaying the **Database Directory** screen and database groups assigned to your SAP HANA cockpit user.

- **sapcontrol credentials**
  The sapcontrol credentials are used to connect to the `sapcontrol` command with the operating system credentials of the SAP HANA system, typically with the `<sid>adm` user, the SAP HANA operating system administration account. These credentials are needed to start and stop an SAP HANA system.

- **SAP HANA cockpit manager**
  SAP HANA cockpit contains a number of web applications and services, one of which is the SAP HANA cockpit manager. You use the SAP HANA cockpit manager for the metadata management of your SAP HANA cockpit environment, including users, databases, and database groups.

- **SAP HANA cockpit user**
  SAP HANA cockpit users connect to the SAP HANA cockpit application to administer and monitor databases. Without any of the SAP HANA cockpit manager roles, they can't connect to the SAP HANA cockpit manager, and without the role or privilege to register databases, they can only connect to the databases that are included in the database group the SAP HANA cockpit user belongs to. To connect to a database, the SAP HANA cockpit user will need to enter the database credentials in the **Database Directory** view.

- **SAP HANA, express edition**
  The standard deployment option of SAP HANA cockpit includes the SAP HANA, express edition, database for persistence. The express edition requires no license for configurations up to 32 GB and has been optimized to run on relatively resource-constrained environments such as virtual machines (VMs), run locally on a laptop, or be hosted in the cloud. Although production usage is supported, it's typically used for development and training. For SAP HANA cockpit, the minimum system requirement is 16 GB of RAM.

- **SAP HANA extended application services, advanced model (SAP HANA XSA)**
  SAP HANA cockpit is a collection of SAP HANA XSA web applications and services. An SAP HANA cockpit installation includes the SAP HANA XSA runtime.

- **SAP HANA Lifecycle Management**
  We install SAP HANA cockpit with the SAP HANA database lifecycle manager tool (HDBLCM) with a preconfigured template in limited interactive mode. Instead of the `hdblcm` command, you run the `hdblcm.sh` script.

- **Shared database**
  A shared database is an alternative SAP HANA cockpit deployment option. In this case, you install SAP HANA cockpit in a separate tenant of an existing SAP HANA system.

- **System identifier (SID)**
  The default SID of SAP HANA cockpit is H4C with instance number 96. This is configurable if, for example, you want to install two SAP HANA cockpit systems on a single computer (shared system deployment option).

- **Technical user**
  Registered databases are configured with a technical user, which corresponds to a dedicated database account on that database. This account is used to collect general database information during registration and database health information after registration. The technical user account should not be used to connect to the database for system administration.

- **Usage type**
  There are four predefined usage types for SAP HANA systems: production, test, development, and custom. The usage type of an SAP HANA system is set during installation but is configurable as system parameters. When a database has any of the first three usage types, a database group with a corresponding name is automatically created. These automatically created database groups can be hidden.

Practice Questions

These practice questions will help you evaluate your understanding of the topics covered in this chapter. The questions shown are similar in nature to those found on the certification examination. Although none of these questions will be found on the exam itself, they will allow you to review your knowledge of the subject. Select the correct answers, and then check the completeness of your answers in the "Practice Question Answers and Explanations" section. Remember that on the exam, you must select all correct answers, and only correct answers, to receive credit for the question.

1. Which SAP HANA releases are supported for SAP HANA cockpit? (There are three correct answers.)

   ☐ **A.** SAP HANA 1.0 SPS 12 single database mode

   ☐ **B.** SAP HANA 1.0 SPS 12 multitenant database container (MDC) mode

   ☐ **C.** SAP HANA 2.0 SPS 05

   ☐ **D.** SAP HANA 2.0 SPS 00

   ☐ **E.** SAP HANA 2.0 SPS 02

2. Which platform is NOT supported for SAP HANA cockpit?

   ☐ **A.** SUSE Linux Enterprise Server on Intel x64

   ☐ **B.** SUSE Linux Enterprise Server on IBM Power Systems

   ☐ **C.** Red Hat Enterprise Linux on IBM Power Systems

   ☐ **D.** Red Hat Enterprise Linux on Intel x64

3. How do you install SAP HANA cockpit?

   ☐ **A.** Use hdbinst.

   ☐ **B.** Use HDBLCM and select the SAP HANA cockpit 2.0 component.

   ☐ **C.** Use the `hdblcm.sh` installation script with the configuration file.

   ☐ **D.** SAP HANA cockpit is a web application and doesn't require installation.

4. How do you know the HTTP/S port to access SAP HANA cockpit?

☐ **A.** Although configurable, SAP HANA cockpit uses the default HTTP port 80 and HTTP/S port 443. Only the host name in the URL is required to access the application.

☐ **B.** SAP HANA cockpit uses the HTTP/S ports of SAP Host Agent (1128, 1129).

☐ **C.** The installation summary screen displays the URLs for how to connect to SAP HANA cockpit. If not recorded, you need to do a TCP port scan.

☐ **D.** SAP HANA cockpit is an SAP HANA XSA application. Application URLs are listed in SAP HANA XS Advanced cockpit. On the command line, use xs apps.

5. Which actions can you perform using the SAP HANA cockpit manager? (There are three correct answers.)

☐ **A.** Import users.

☐ **B.** Register a database.

☐ **C.** Access XSA logs.

☐ **D.** Add a SAP HANA cockpit user.

☐ **E.** Assign users to databases.

6. Which SAP HANA cockpit roles can you assign to users? (There are three correct answers.)

☐ **A.** Cockpit power user

☐ **B.** Cockpit troubleshooting

☐ **C.** Cockpit configuration template administrator

☐ **D.** Cockpit pilot

☐ **E.** Cockpit flight engineer

7. Which usage types are automatically assigned to a database group?

☐ **A.** System database

☐ **B.** Cockpit database

☐ **C.** QA (quality assurance)

☐ **D.** Test

8. What aggregated health alerts are displayed in the **Database Directory**? (There are three correct answers.)

☐ **A.** Threads

☐ **B.** Performance

☐ **C.** Availability

☐   **D.** Sessions

☐   **E.** Capacity

9.   Which is the correct order to register databases in SAP HANA cockpit?

☐   **A.** Register database, create user, and create group.

☐   **B.** Create user, create group, and register database.

☐   **C.** Create group, create user, and register database.

☐   **D.** There is no set order.

10.   Which steps are required to grant a SAP HANA cockpit user access to a database? (There are two correct answers.)

☐   **A.** Register database, create user, create group, assign database to group, and assign user to group.

☐   **B.** Register database, create user, and assign to database.

☐   **C.** Create user, register database, and assign to database.

☐   **D.** Create group, create user and assign to group, and register database and assign to group.

11.   Which statements regarding the technical user are true? (There are two correct answers.)

☐   **A.** The technical user account needs to be created before you can register a database with SAP HANA cockpit.

☐   **B.** The technical user requires the CATALOG READ system privilege and the SELECT on the _SYS.STATISTICS schema.

☐   **C.** The SYSTEM user can't be used as technical user.

☐   **D.** The technical user account should only be used by SAP HANA cockpit and not by another person.

12.   Which SSO methods are supported to access SAP HANA cockpit 2.0?

☐   **A.** SAML

☐   **B.** Kerberos

☐   **C.** JWT LDAP

☐   **D.** All three

13.   Which SAP HANA cockpit role is required to assign SAP HANA cockpit users to database groups?

☐   **A.** Cockpit administrator

☐   **B.** Cockpit user administrator

☐   **C.** Cockpit database (resource) administrator

☐   **D.** Cockpit power user

14.   Which user(s) is(are) required to access the Database Management app of SAP HANA cockpit? (There are two correct answers.)

☐   **A.** SAP HANA cockpit user with access to the registered system database

☐   **B.** SAP HANA cockpit technical user

☐   **C.** A database user with `DATABASE ADMIN` system privileges on the system database

☐   **D.** The database administration operating system account `<sid>adm`

15.   Which components are included in SAP HANA cockpit? (There are three correct answers.)

☐   **A.** SAP Web IDE for SAP HANA

☐   **B.** SAP HANA database explorer

☐   **C.** SAP HANA XSA runtime.

☐   **D.** SAP HANA, express edition

Practice Question Answers and Explanations

1.   Correct answers: **A, B, C**
     SAP HANA cockpit supports both SAP HANA 1.0 SPS 12 in single database mode and with tenant databases as in all supported SAP HANA 2.0 releases.

     Answers D and E are incorrect because the SAP HANA 2.0 SPS 00 and SPS 02 releases are no longer supported.

2.   Correct answer: **C**
     SAP HANA cockpit 2.0 doesn't support Red Hat Enterprise Linux (RHEL) on IBM Power Systems. This is a valid statement for the C_HANATEC_16 SAP HANA 2.0 SPS 04 exam. Future hardware requirements may change, so always check the latest SAP Notes. For this reason, questions like these are (or should be) rare on exams.

3.   Correct answer: **C**
     The installation of SAP HANA cockpit is performed using a script file and installation configuration template. You'll be prompted only to provide the host name, installation path, SID, and instance number, for which default values will be given (hostname, */hana/shared*, H4C, 96, respectively).

     Answer A is incorrect because you can use the single component installer `hdbinst` (command line) to install SAP HANA client and SAP HANA studio on client computers but not to install SAP HANA cockpit. Answer B is incorrect

because manual installation with the SAP HANA database lifecycle management tool (HDBLCM) isn't supported. Answer D is incorrect because although
SAP HANA cockpit is web-based, you do need to install the product somewhere!
Typically, this will be a server hosted from the data center most often close to
where the SAP HANA system resides, although this isn't a requirement.

4. Correct answer: **D**

   We can use both the xs apps command on the command line and SAP HANA XS
   Advanced cockpit to query the URLs of the SAP HANA cockpit applications
   (including ports).

   Answer A is incorrect because SAP HANA cockpit ports are configurable and
   could use the default HTTP/S port, but this isn't the default configuration. In
   addition, you would have to choose which application gets the default port:
   SAP HANA cockpit or SAP HANA cockpit manager? Answer B is incorrect
   because SAP Host Agent is used by the resident HDBLCM for its web interface
   and previously also by SAP HANA cockpit 1.0 in offline mode but not by SAP
   HANA cockpit 2.0. Answer C is incorrect because the installation summary
   screen displays the URLs for how to connect to SAP HANA cockpit. However, if
   this hasn't been recorded, you can use the xs apps command on the command
   line or the SAP HANA XS Advanced cockpit to query the URL. A port scan reveals
   open TCP ports but doesn't inform you what ports are being used by SAP HANA
   cockpit.

5. Correct answers: **B, C, D**

   With SAP HANA cockpit, you can register databases, create database groups,
   and add SAP HANA cockpit users. The SAP HANA cockpit manager also provides
   access to the XSA logs.

   Answer A is incorrect because you can import and export databases but not
   users. Answer E is incorrect because users and databases are added to database
   groups, but you can't assign a user to a database group directly.

6. Correct answers: **A, B, C**

   The documentation mentions the following roles:

   - Cockpit administrator
   - Cockpit database administrator
   - Cockpit user administrator
   - Cockpit user
   - Cockpit power user
   - Cockpit configuration template administrator
   - Cockpit troubleshooting

   Although **Cockpit Roles** doesn't list the cockpit power user role, enabling a SAP
   HANA cockpit user to register databases makes this user a power user.

   Answers D and E are incorrect because these roles aren't listed above and don't
   exist.

7. Correct answer: **D**

   For the usage types production, development, and test, database groups are automatically generated, as illustrated earlier in Figure 6.30.

   Answer A is incorrect because system database isn't a usage type, and system databases aren't automatically assigned to a database group. Answer B is incorrect because the database used by SAP HANA cockpit isn't a usage type, and they aren't automatically assigned to a database group. Answer C is incorrect because there is no QA usage type.

8. Correct answers: **B, D, E**

   Aggregated health alerts are displayed for availability, performance, and capacity. Status and alerts are also considered aggregated health alerts.

   Answers A and D are incorrect because used sessions and threads are only displayed on the **Database Overview**.

9. Correct answer: **D**

   The tasks of registering databases, creating groups, and creating SAP HANA cockpit users don't have a set order. This makes answers A, B, and C incorrect.

10. Correct answers: **A, D**

    We can't only assign users and databases to a group. You also can't directly assign a user to a database. This makes answers B and C incorrect.

11. Correct answers: **B, D**

    Technical user accounts need to be created before you can register a database, and also technical user accounts should only be used by SAP HANA cockpit.

    Answer A is incorrect because the technical user can be created while you register the database. In older SAP HANA cockpit releases, this user needed to be created manually. Answer C is incorrect because using SYSTEM as the technical user isn't recommended but can be used.

12. Correct answer: **B**

    We can enable SSO to access SAP HANA cockpit using, **SSO with Kerberos** settings in SAP HANA cockpit manager.

13. Correct answer: **C**

    The database administrator role is required to assign SAP HANA cockpit users to database groups (refer to Figure 6.28).

    Answer A is incorrect because the cockpit administrator role only provides access to the **Settings** menu. Answer B is incorrect because the SAP HANA cockpit user administrator role only allows creating and managing SAP HANA cockpit users. Answer D is incorrect because a SAP HANA cockpit power user has access to the **Registered Database** menu of the SAP HANA cockpit manager and can add (register) databases.

14. Correct answers: **A, C**

    We need, at a minimum, two accounts to access a registered database: a SAP HANA cockpit user and a database (administration) account.

    Answer B is incorrect because a separate SAP HANA cockpit technical user is recommended, but existing database accounts can be used. Answer D is incorrect because the database administration operating system account <sid>adm is required to start and stop the system and some other actions (e.g., restoring a database) but not to access an app in SAP HANA cockpit.

15. Correct answers: **B, C, D**

    The components include SAP HANA database explorer, SAP HANA XSA runtime, and SAP HANA, express edition.

    Answer B is incorrect because the SAP HANA cockpit installation doesn't include the SAP Web IDE for SAP HANA application, although SAP HANA database explorer with SQL console and Catalog Browse with trace file access is included.

Takeaway

You should now have a good overview of SAP HANA cockpit from the point of view of the flight engineer. You know the hardware requirements, deployment options, where to download the software, how to extract, and how to perform installation and updates.

You know how to access SAP HANA cockpit and the SAP HANA cockpit manager: URL and user name/password. You also know which application to use for tasks such as creating database groups or monitoring individual tenant databases.

You're familiar with databases groups and SAP HANA cockpit users and how these are related. You know where to look if your administrator calls you because he can't access a system.

Although beyond the scope of the exam, we also provided a brief description of some of the predecessors of SAP HANA cockpit. The present is often better understood when you know a bit about the past.

Finally, we also listed where you can find more information about particular topics. Again, this will be beyond the scope of the exam.

Summary

In this chapter, we introduced SAP HANA cockpit and described its architecture and deployment options. We looked at how you can install and update SAP HANA cockpit. The revision and maintenance strategy was discussed as this is different from the SAP HANA platform. You learned how to provision SAP HANA cockpit by registering databases, creating technical users, creating database groups, and adding users. We also looked at how you navigate from SAP HANA cockpit manager to SAP HANA cockpit and back, as well as the **Database Directory** and **Database Overview** pages.

In the next chapter, we discuss database administration tasks.

Chapter 7
Database Administration Tasks

Techniques You'll Master

- Starting and stopping SAP HANA
- Performing daily database administration tasks
- Configuring system parameters
- Performing common table administration tasks

In this chapter, we'll cover common daily database administration tasks every SAP HANA system administrator should be familiar with. One such task is how to start and stop the system. As simple as it sounds, there are some gotchas (unexpected behaviors) you should be aware of. Of course, system administrators need to be familiar with how to configure system parameters and know where this is all documented. There are way too many to remember. We'll also look at common table administration tasks, the difference between row and column store tables, and how to load and work with delta merges.

> **Exam Tip**
>
> The exam topic area database administration tasks is a hands-on topic. Get a copy of SAP HANA, express edition, and practice the different activities described in this chapter. This will help you to get familiar with the SAP HANA cockpit interface and also help you better understand the concepts.

Real-World Scenario

A new member just joined your team as a system administrator to support you with common database operations so you can focus on the new migration project. You want to prepare a daily database administration (DBA) checklist to instruct the new recruit on how to perform important activities and key information about the tasks. What would you put on this list? Starting and stopping SAP HANA systems and tenant databases, for sure. Monitoring database health using the SAP HANA cockpit **Database Directory** or **Landscape Overview** page would be good to include. Service Management, Database Management, and System Configuration are important apps your colleague should be familiar with. But you also need to include table management and cover table loads, delta merges, and the peculiarities of row and column store tables. Anything we missed?

Topic and Objectives

In this chapter, we cover how to perform daily administration tasks. When and where appropriate, we'll make sure to showcase SAP HANA cockpit when performing the activities.

For the exam, you need to have a good understanding of the following topics:

- Common system and database administration tasks for the SAP HANA platform
- How to perform database administration tasks in SAP HANA cockpit
- How to configure with system parameters

- Differences between row and column store tables and what administration tasks are associated
- How to perform manual load and unload operations, and how to trigger a delta merge

Note

This topic area has a weight of < 8% of the total certification exam score. With 80 questions in total, you can expect about 4 questions on this topic area. Although classified as a minor topic, daily database tasks should not be overlooked. On the work floor, this knowledge will be taken for granted.

Learn More

As you might have guessed, database administration tasks are documented in the SAP HANA Administration Guide. See the "Database Administration Tasks at a Glance" section of the SAP HANA Administration Guide at *http://s-prs.co/v507841*.

SAP HANA 2.0 SPS 05: What's New

Database administration tasks have not changed much over time. SPS 05 introduced a Python script to set system parameters, `setParameter.py`, which we'll cover in the "Configuring System Parameters" section.

Most changes to database administration come with the database administration tool SAP HANA cockpit. With the SAP HANA cockpit 2.0 SP 12 version released with SAP HANA 2.0 SPS 05, for example, the term "resource" is replaced with "database," and this also applies to the System Overview app, now Database Overview. The number of new features introduced with SP 12 and SP 11 is significant and too extensive to include here. See the SAP HANA cockpit release notes for a summary at *http://s-prs.co/v507842*.

Key Concepts Refresher

In this section, we'll highlight the most important concepts for database administration tasks.

Starting and Stopping SAP HANA

An SAP HANA system is a logical unit that comprises a number of operating system processes, such as the daemon, name server, and index server, which can be hosted on a single or multiple computers (hosts), as described in Chapter 2. A system contains at least a system database and one or more tenant databases (technically, zero tenant databases is also possible, but this serves no functional purpose).

You can start and stop the whole system or any of the tenant databases individually by using client tools such as SAP HANA cockpit, SQL commands, and operating system commands.

As you may recall from Chapter 6, a system database entry in the SAP HANA cockpit **Database Directory** screen required both the credentials of a database administration account and of an operating system administration account, typically the <sid>adm user. The first is used to execute SQL commands, and the second is used to connect to the sapcontrol utility (using HTTPS).

We also explained in Chapter 2 that whether an SAP HANA system starts up automatically with the operating system is defined in the profile of the local instance. This is set during the installation but can be adjusted afterwards by editing the Autostart parameter in the profile file <SID>_HDB<instance_number>_<hostname> in the local directory */usr/sap/<SID>/SYS/profile*. Figure 7.1 shows a partial view of the profile file <SID>_HDB<instance_number>_<hostname>, here HDB_HDB00_hana-vm1 with the **Autostart** parameter set. The value 1 switches on automatic startup of the local instance. The default value for this parameter is 0 (off). The profile is an editable text file. There is no graphical user interface available to configure the profile for SAP HANA.

```
hdbadm@hana-vm1:/usr/sap/HDB/HDB00> cat /usr/sap/HDB/SYS/profile/HDB_HDB00_hana-vm1 | grep -A5 -B5 Autostart
SAP_RETRIEVAL_PATH = $(DIR_INSTANCE)/$(SAPLOCALHOST)
DIR_HOME = $(SAP_RETRIEVAL_PATH)/trace
DIR_PERF = $(SAP_RETRIEVAL_PATH)/trace
DIR_LOGGING = $(SAP_RETRIEVAL_PATH)/log
SECUDIR = $(SAP_RETRIEVAL_PATH)/sec
Autostart=1
SETENV_00 = PATH=$(DIR_INSTANCE)/exe:%(PATH)
SETENV_01 = SAP_RETRIEVAL_PATH=$(SAP_RETRIEVAL_PATH)
SETENV_02 = PYTHONPATH=$(SAP_RETRIEVAL_PATH):$(DIR_EXECUTABLE):$(DIR_INSTALL)/global/hdb/custom/python_support:
SAPSYSTEMNAME = HDB
SAPLOCALHOST = hana-vm1
hdbadm@hana-vm1:/usr/sap/HDB/HDB00> ▊
```

Figure 7.1 Autostart

To manually start or stop an SAP HANA system, you can use either SAP HANA cockpit or command line. Although the user interface is different, technically server-side, the same command is used.

Using SAP HANA Cockpit

A single app, Manage Services, on SAP HANA cockpit can be used to interact (start, stop, restart) both with the individual operating system processes, such as the name server, or with the system as a whole. Figure 7.2 and Figure 7.3 show what is displayed when connected to the system database and to a tenant database.

The exact services listed will depend on the components installed. Note that for the tenant database, the **Stop Service** button is only enabled for the index server and the xsengine service. From the system database, all services can be stopped except for the watchdog (daemon) service. To stop or start services manually using SAP HANA cockpit, the SERVICE ADMIN system privilege is required.

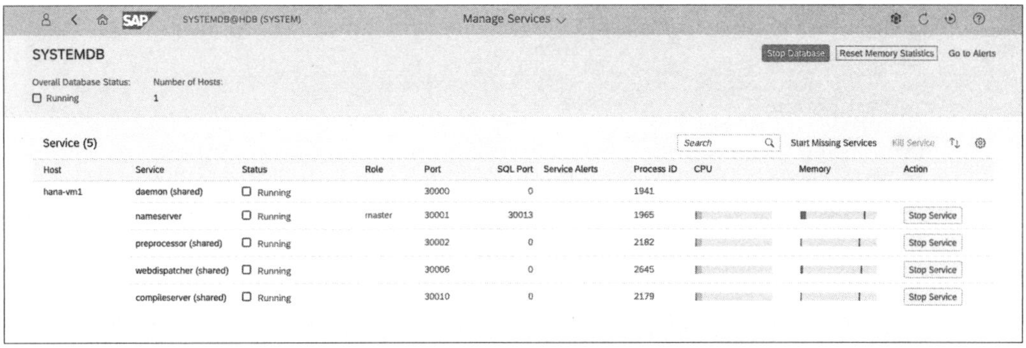

Figure 7.2 Manage Services: SYSTEMDB

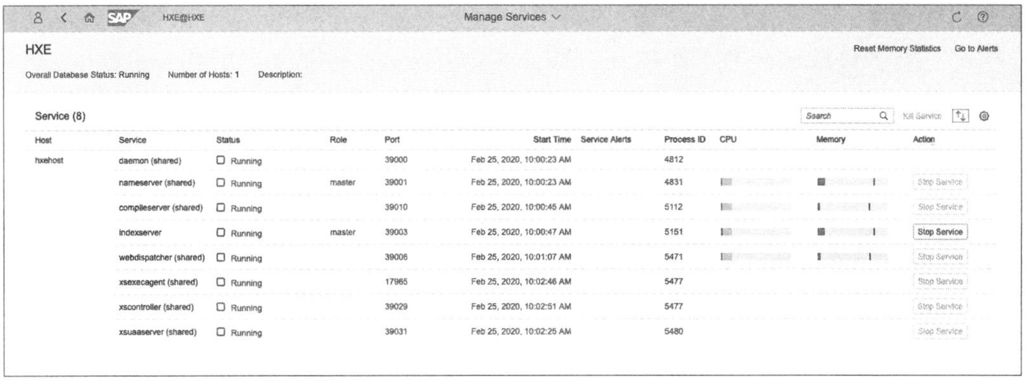

Figure 7.3 Manage Services: Tenant Database

When you select to stop a service, an information dialog will appear with the message that the service might be automatically restarted depending on how the daemon is configured. As you may recall, the watchdog process continuously scans the state of each operating system process and will attempt to start any process not running. Exceptions are made for processes configured not to start automatically, as you'll see when we cover system parameter configuration.

When you're connected to the system database, the **Stop Database** button is displayed and also on the corresponding tile in the **Database Overview** app. When selected, an overlay appears asking whether you want to perform a soft or hard stop, as illustrated in Figure 7.4. A soft stop comes with a configurable time-out of 5, 15, or 30 minutes for transactions to complete. No new connections can be established during this period, but this makes it possible for any work in progress to be completed. After the time-out, the hard (immediate) stop follows.

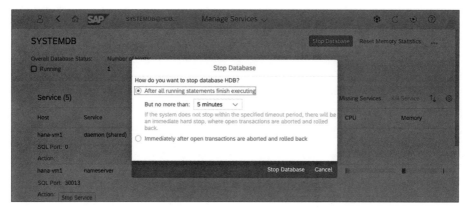

Figure 7.4 Manage Services: Stop Database

As illustrated in Figure 7.5, the **Manage Services** screen shows the overall database status as stopping with a status for each of the services. Only the process ID is displayed, and the formatting of the service names has changed as this information no longer comes from the database but from sapcontrol.

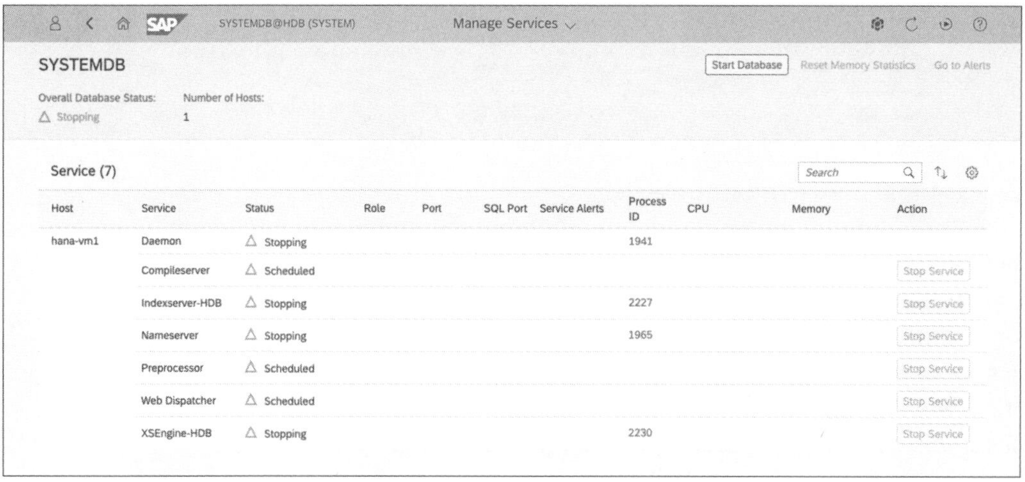

Host	Service	Status	Role	Port	SQL Port	Service Alerts	Process ID	CPU	Memory	Action
hana-vm1	Daemon	△ Stopping					1941			
	Compileserver	△ Scheduled								Stop Service
	Indexserver-HDB	△ Stopping					2227			Stop Service
	Nameserver	△ Stopping					1965			Stop Service
	Preprocessor	△ Scheduled								Stop Service
	Web Dispatcher	△ Scheduled								Stop Service
	XSEngine-HDB	△ Stopping					2230			Stop Service

Figure 7.5 Manage Services: Stopping

When stopped, only the daemon service (process) will be listed (Figure 7.6). The header now displays a **Start Database** button, which enables you to start the system database and, with it, the system.

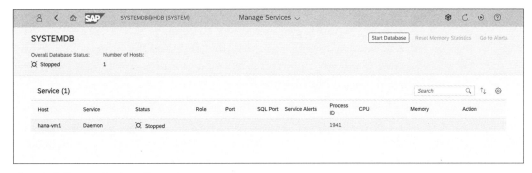

Figure 7.6 Manage Services: Stopped

To stop individual tenant databases, you can use the Database Management app (look ahead to Figure 7.14). This corresponds to the ALTER SYSTEM STOP DATABASE SQL statement.

Using HDB

To start and stop an SAP HANA system on the command line, you can use the HDB utility, illustrated in Figure 7.7.

```
hdbadm@hana-vm1:/usr/sap/HDB/HDB00> head -n 13 /usr/sap/HDB/HDB00/HDB
#!/bin/sh
#set -x
#
# HDB start/stop script
#
# Copyright (c) 2002-2003 by SAP AG
# All rights reserved.
#
if [ $# = 0 ]; then
    COMMAND="usage"
else
    COMMAND="$1"; shift # so, the call of HDBSettings.sh is without parameters. (leeds to problems on bash)
hdbadm@hana-vm1:/usr/sap/HDB/HDB00> HDB
Usage: /usr/sap/HDB/HDB00/HDB { start|stop|reconf|restart|version|info|proc|admin|kill|kill-<sig>|term }
  kill or kill-9 should never be used in productive environment!
hdbadm@hana-vm1:/usr/sap/HDB/HDB00> HDB stop
hdbdaemon will wait maximal 300 seconds for NewDB services finishing.
Stopping instance using: /usr/sap/HDB/SYS/exe/hdb/sapcontrol -prot NI_HTTP -nr 00 -function Stop 400

18.08.2020 09:09:35
Stop
OK
Waiting for stopped instance using: /usr/sap/HDB/SYS/exe/hdb/sapcontrol -prot NI_HTTP -nr 00 -function WaitforStopped 600 2

18.08.2020 09:09:59
WaitforStopped
OK
hdbdaemon is stopped.
hdbadm@hana-vm1:/usr/sap/HDB/HDB00> HDB start

StartService
Impromptu CCC initialization by 'rscpCInit'.
  See SAP note 1266393.
OK
OK
Starting instance using: /usr/sap/HDB/SYS/exe/hdb/sapcontrol -prot NI_HTTP -nr 00 -function StartWait 2700 2

18.08.2020 09:10:35
Start
OK

18.08.2020 09:11:13
StartWait
OK
hdbadm@hana-vm1:/usr/sap/HDB/HDB00> █
```

Figure 7.7 HDB Command (Script)

It's a script file as indicated by the first line of the file with #!/bin/sh. When you enter the command without parameters, as customary, usage information is printed out. You can use the script to start, stop, or restart the system but also to kill processes (with a warning not to do so in production). Other command options show version and process information.

Command HDB stop triggers a soft stop. The actual command executed is sapcontrol with parameters specifying the protocol to use, the instance number, and the (web service) function with time-out. We'll cover these parameters in more detail in this section. To start the system, you use the HDB start command, which makes a similar sapcontrol call.

Using sapcontrol

When you run the sapcontrol command without parameters, the version information, syntax synopsis, and description is returned with an extensive list of options and web methods. The sapcontrol utility is inherited from SAP NetWeaver, and although not all options and web methods apply to SAP HANA, some common web service calls to the SAP start service have been implemented.

As shown previously, the HDB script start parameter calls sapcontrol with StartWait while stop calls sapcontrol with WaitforStopped. These web service calls are valid only for the local instance. For this reason, to start (or stop) a multiple-host system, you need to execute the sapcontrol command directly, as shown in Figure 7.8. With StartSystem, you can start an SAP HANA system (single- or multiple-host).

```
hdbadm@hana-vm1:/usr/sap/HDB/HDB00> sapcontrol -nr 00 -function StartSystem

18.08.2020 09:26:10
StartSystem
OK
hdbadm@hana-vm1:/usr/sap/HDB/HDB00> sapcontrol -nr 00 -function GetSystemInstanceList

18.08.2020 09:26:25
GetSystemInstanceList
OK
hostname, instanceNr, httpPort, httpsPort, startPriority, features, dispstatus
hana-vm1, 0, 50013, 50014, 0.3, HDB|HDB_WORKER, GREEN
hdbadm@hana-vm1:/usr/sap/HDB/HDB00> sapcontrol -nr 00 -function GetProcessList

18.08.2020 09:26:38
GetProcessList
OK
name, description, dispstatus, textstatus, starttime, elapsedtime, pid
hdbdaemon, HDB Daemon, GREEN, Running, 2020 08 18 09:10:36, 0:16:02, 16930
hdbcompileserver, HDB Compileserver, GREEN, Running, 2020 08 18 09:10:44, 0:15:54, 17150
hdbindexserver, HDB Indexserver-HDB, GREEN, Running, 2020 08 18 09:10:44, 0:15:54, 17200
hdbnameserver, HDB Nameserver, GREEN, Running, 2020 08 18 09:10:36, 0:16:02, 16948
hdbpreprocessor, HDB Preprocessor, GREEN, Running, 2020 08 18 09:10:44, 0:15:54, 17153
hdbwebdispatcher, HDB Web Dispatcher, GREEN, Running, 2020 08 18 09:10:59, 0:15:39, 17606
hdbxsengine, HDB XSEngine-HDB, GREEN, Running, 2020 08 18 09:10:44, 0:15:54, 17203
hdbadm@hana-vm1:/usr/sap/HDB/HDB00> sapcontrol -nr 00 -function CheckHostAgent
SAPHostAgent Installed
hdbadm@hana-vm1:/usr/sap/HDB/HDB00> sapcontrol -nr 00 -function ParameterValue Autostart

18.08.2020 09:27:17
ParameterValue
OK

1
hdbadm@hana-vm1:/usr/sap/HDB/HDB00> █
```

Figure 7.8 Executing the sapcontrol Command Directly

There is a long list of web service calls available for the `sapcontrol` command. Useful are `GetSystemInstanceList` to query the hosts and host roles and `GetProcessList` to query the local processes. If the output reminds you of the information displayed in SAP HANA studio, this is because this client tool uses the same web service calls. You can also use `sapcontrol` to check the presence of SAP Host Agent and the values of specific profile parameters, as shown. For the Basis administrator, this will be nothing new as system administration for SAP NetWeaver systems works the same way.

Learn More

Corporate marketing departments rarely descend all the way down to the command line. For this reason, you still find a reference to the internal project name NewDB, going back to the days before SAP HANA was first released. The copyright message in the script mentions 2002–2003, which originates from SAP NetWeaver text retrieval and information extraction (TREX), and the message "impromptu CCC initialization by 'rscpCInit'" returned by sapcontrol has no relation to SAP HANA. For more information about this topic, beyond the scope of the exam, see *http://s-prs.co/v507843*.

Alerts

SAP HANA includes a statistics service with alert checkers that run in the background and monitor for specific events. Alerts are displayed on several SAP HANA cockpit tiles, cards, and views such as the **Database Directory**, **Database Overview**, **Database Management**, and **Manage Services**. Responding to alerts is an important activity for the system administrator and likely to be a daily task. We'll only briefly mention alerts here as we return to the topic in Chapter 13.

Daily Database Administration Tasks

What exactly is considered to be a daily database administration task depends on the organization and situation. The following are some of the most commonly visited apps of SAP HANA cockpit, which we'll discuss in the following sections:

- Database Directory (with aggregated health counters)
- Database Overview
- General Information
- Manage Services
- Database Management
- Table Usage
- Sessions and Threads
- Monitor Statements

We'll return to the topic of monitoring and performance in Chapter 13 and to tenant database management in the next chapter.

Database Directory with Aggregate Health Counters

We already described the Database Directory app in Chapter 6 when we explored the features and functions of SAP HANA cockpit. Here, we'll revisit this app in the context of performing database administration tasks. The **Database Directory** screen lists all databases accessible to you with a search bar to filter on name, status, alerts, groups, usage type, and type. The search bar is editable, and you can save your choices as a view. Figure 7.9 shows the **Default*** view, with the star indicating unsaved changes. You can group and sort the information as well as which columns to display depending on the amount of screen real estate available.

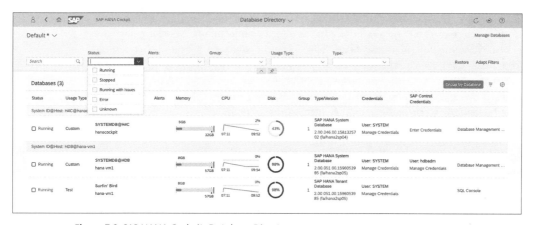

Figure 7.9 SAP HANA Cockpit: Database Directory

By default, the **Database Directory** screen displays the following:

- **Status**
  The values are **Running**, **Stopped**, **Transitioning**, **Running with Issues**, **Error**, **License expired**, **No SQL access**, and **Invalid technical user**, and selecting them opens the Manage Services app.

- **Usage Type**
  The values are **Production**, **Development**, **Test**, and **Custom** for this configurable system parameter that is set during the installation.

- **Database**
  As registered in SAP HANA cockpit manager with a system-generated (database@system) or user-defined name, this opens the Database Overview app when the tile is selected. For system databases, a link to **Database Management** is listed.

- **Description**
  This is the description registered in the SAP HANA cockpit manager.

- **Alerts**
  The values include **High** and **Medium.** Clicking the alerts opens the Alerts app.

- **Group**
  This is as registered in the SAP HANA cockpit manager (see Chapter 6).

- **Availability/Performance/Capacity**
  The three key performance areas (KPAs) show a green checkbox, orange warning triangle, or red circle with exclamation mark. When selected, they open the Alerts app.

- **Type/Version**
  This indicates whether the database is a tenant or system database and shows the SAP HANA version. When selected, it opens the System Information app.

- **Credentials**
  These are the database credentials for the database. When selected, a dialog to provide or delete stored database credentials for the database opens.

- **SAP Control Credentials**
  Operating system credentials opens a dialog to provide or delete stored operating system (sapcontrol logon) credentials for the system when selected. System credentials are only available for system databases. These are used for the sapcontrol web service function calls.

Database Overview

When you select a database in the directory, the **Database Overview** app screen is displayed, as shown in Figure 7.10.

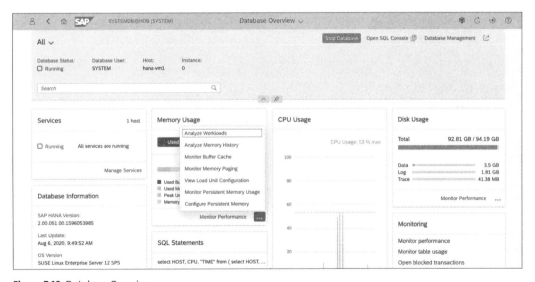

Figure 7.10 Database Overview

This app provides a large number of interactive tiles (cards) that display relevant information about the database. There are tiles that show counters for CPU usage, memory usage, and disk usage with links to other views or to other apps for further investigation.

The **Database Overview** app screen is configurable by selecting the **User** icon in the menu bar to the right. This opens the **Manage Cards** pane. You can save your configuration of the **Database Overview** screen of a database resource as a tile on the SAP HANA cockpit home page (**Landscape Overview**).

From the header, you can switch to other databases listed in the database directory or open the SQL console of SAP HANA database explorer. When connected to a system database, you can also navigate to the Database Management app.

General Information

Release and installation information is displayed in the **General Information** card on the **Database Overview** screen. This card also lists the SAP HANA version, last update, and platform. For more detailed information, you can select the card, which opens the **General Information** app (Figure 7.11). Here you can also view system usage, system start time, a multiple-host indicator, and information about installed plug-ins. The **SAP HANA Version History** tab shows any previous installations. The **Installed Plugins Details** tab provides detailed information about the Application Function Library (AFL), the External Machine Learning Library (EML), and other plug-ins.

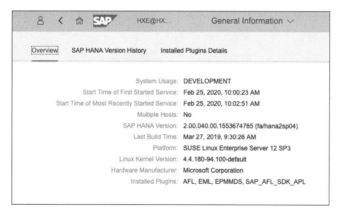

Figure 7.11 General Information

Manage Services

The **Services** card on **Database Overview** displays the status of the services. When selected, the Manage Services app opens. As described, you can use the app to restart individual services and to stop/start an SAP HANA system.

From the header, you can reset memory statistics. A typical use case is to measure the impact of a particular workload. Like the actions of the app, this requires the RESOURCE ADMIN system privilege. The equivalent SQL statement is ALTER SYSTEM RESET MONITORING VIEW M_MEMORY_RECLAIM_STATISTICS_RESET.

When there are issues reported for a service, a link to the trace file is provided in the **Status** column, as illustrated in Figure 7.12. When selected, this will open the

trace file viewer of SAP HANA database explorer as illustrated in Figure 7.13. This
trace file is typically intended for SAP Support.

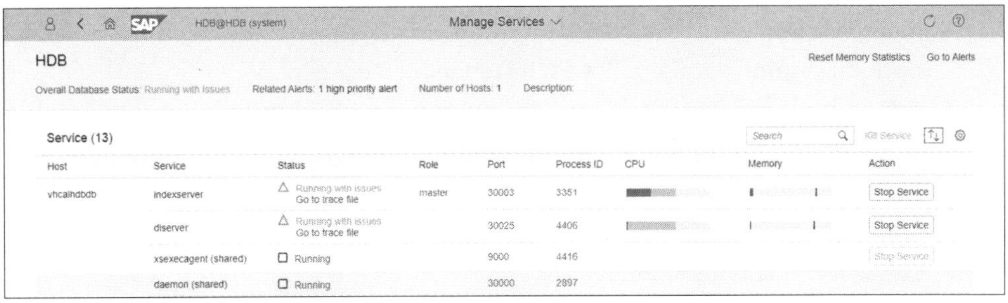

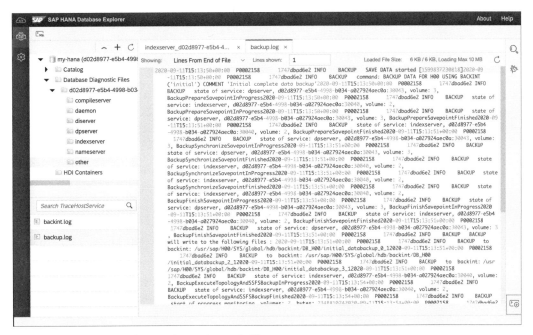

Figure 7.12 Manage Services: Running with Issues

Figure 7.13 SAP HANA Database Explorer: Diagnostic Files

Database Management

You can access the Database Management app from the **Database Directory** screen
or when connected to the system database from the header of the Database Overview app. From the header as illustrated in Figure 7.14, you can access the following:

- **Blacklisted Parameters**
  Restrict tenant database access to particular system parameters.

- **Global Allocation Limits**
  Define the memory and CPU cores allocation limit for each of the databases.

- **Restricted Features**
  Restrict tenant database access to particular features, such as import or export, Lightweight Directory Access Protocol (LDAP), or R integration.

- **Audit Policies**
  Define a common audit policy for all tenant databases.

- **Backup Configuration**
  Configure system-wide backup settings.

- **Backup Schedules**
  Configure database backup schedules.

- **Configure Tenant Replication**
  Launch the tenant database replication wizard.

- **Database Licenses**
  Manage database licenses.

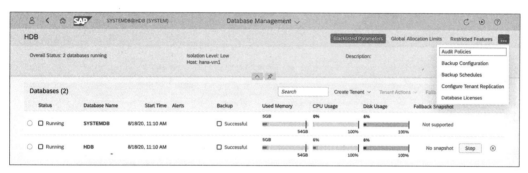

Figure 7.14 Database Management

From the table header, you can select **Create Tenant** to create an empty tenant or create a tenant using replication.

From the table row, you can perform tenant database operations such as stop and starting the selected tenant, backup and recovery, tenant copy, tenant replication, or SYSTEM password reset, as illustrated in Figure 7.15.

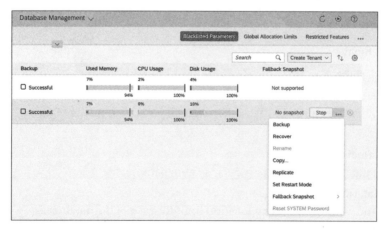

Figure 7.15 Database Management: Row

As in **Manage Services**, when you select a row in the **Used Memory**, **CPU Usage**, or **Disk Usage** columns, the **Performance Monitor** screen opens with the **Memory**, **CPU**, or **Disk** view selected, as illustrated in Figure 7.16.

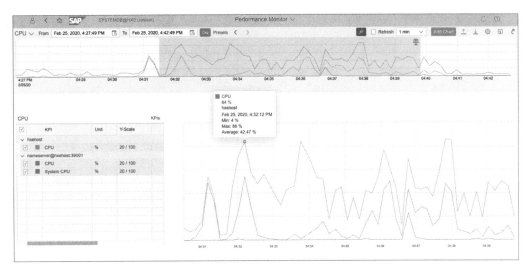

Figure 7.16 Performance Monitor: CPU View

Table Usage

Another interesting app is Table Usage, which is shown in Figure 7.17 and accessible from the **Monitoring** card on the **Database Overview** screen. This app displays column tables by usage and enables you to see instantly which column tables are most active. You can filter the view on access (reads, writes, or both) and size.

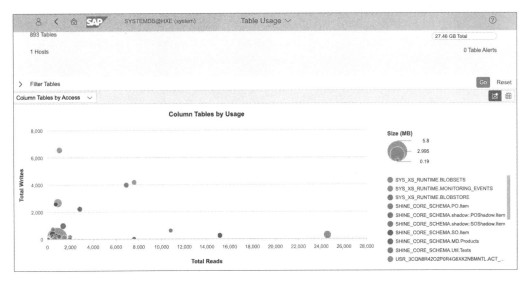

Figure 7.17 Table Usage

Sessions and Threads

Two other important database workload indicators are sessions and threads. A session corresponds to a client database connection, and a thread corresponds to an operation, for example, the execution of a SQL statement. On the **Database Overview** screen, there are cards for both **Sessions** and **Threads**. When selected, the corresponding app opens. You can use them to investigate potential issues for the **Sessions** app (Figure 7.18) and for **Threads (**Figure 7.19). The default view only shows a limited number of columns. With the gear icon, you can change what to display. From the bottom toolbar menu, you can navigate to the threads or blocked transactions view with the same connection identifier; save the view in text, comma-separated values (CSV), or HTML format; or cancel a selected session or operation.

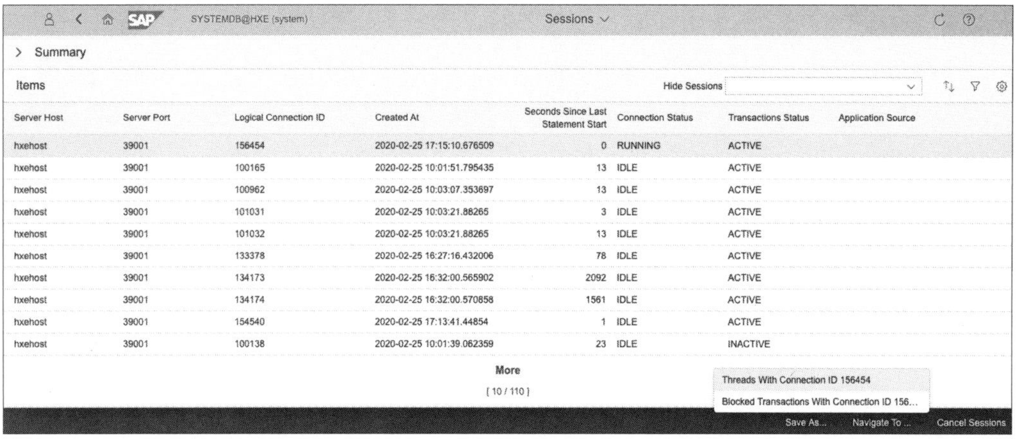

Figure 7.18 Sessions

The **Call Stack** button in the **Threads** screen menu bar displays the active operations with the source (shared object library or *.so* file). As with trace files, interpretation is difficult and usually intended for SAP Support.

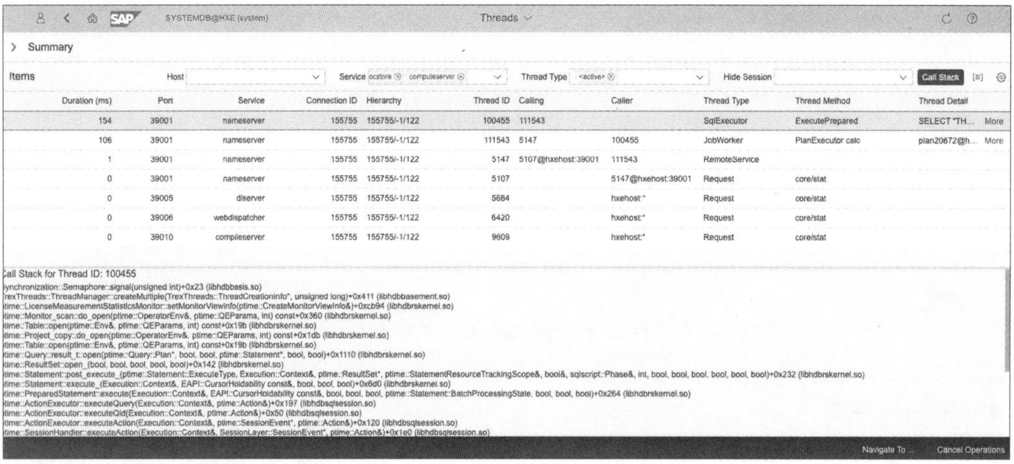

Figure 7.19 Threads

A summary view in the header of the apps displays the top five users and applications (**Sessions**) or total number of threads by status and by type (**Threads**).

Monitor Statements

The SQL Statement app and **SQL Statements** card on the **Database Overview** screen provide information about the most critical statements running inside the database. The app includes a view (tab) for **Active Statements**, **SQL Plan Cache**, and **Expensive Statements** with an analysis of all SQL statements with an execution time above a configurable threshold. The **Overview** tab lists the duration and memory usage of statements with session ID and source (application, application user, or database user) together with the workload class. As with the other views, the gear icon enables you to select other types of information such as lock wait time and additional memory statistics. The same applies to the **Active Statements** view, although for this view, the number of columns available is even larger with minimum, average, maximum, and total counters for most statistics.

SQL Plan Cache, shown in Figure 7.20, provides a menu in the table header bar to save statement and plan information to text, CSV, and HTML files; a button to **Configure** the size of the plan cache; and a button to **Clear all plan cache**. Only 7 of the 90 available columns are displayed by default.

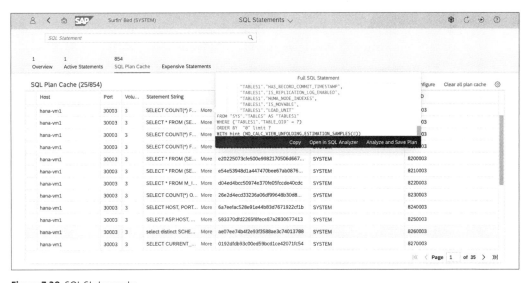

Figure 7.20 SQL Statements

When selecting **More** in the **Statement String** column, a **Full SQL Statement** popup appears with options to open the statement in SQL Analyzer or to analyze and save the plan. The **SQL Analyzer** screen, shown in Figure 7.21, provides a plan graph with more detailed information about the statement in question (discussed in Chapter 13).

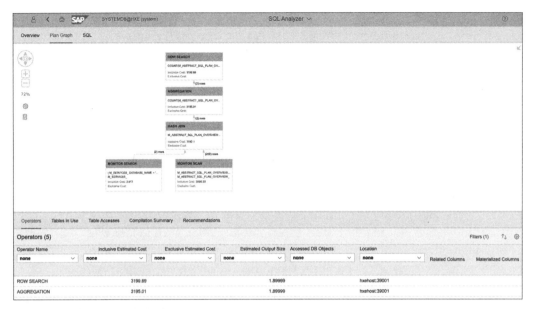

Figure 7.21 SQL Analyzer

Configuring System Parameters

SAP HANA system parameters are persisted in configuration files, also known as system parameter files and as INI files due to their file extension (going all the way back to 16-bit Microsoft Windows and MS-DOS computers). We'll discuss system configuration in SAP HANA cockpit and configuring parameters via the INI files in this section.

System Configuration View

To configure system parameters in SAP HANA cockpit, you can select the **Manage system configuration** link on the **Database Administration** card to open the **System Configuration** app screen, shown in Figure 7.22.

The header of **System Configuration** includes a search bar and filter boxes on **Configuration File**, **Section**, **Host**, and database (not shown). As there are more than 1,600 parameters, you'll find this very useful when working with system parameters. When you connect to a tenant database, the filter on database is implicit and not displayed.

The editor enables you to edit and remove parameters or override default values. Changes are captured and accessible through **View Change History** in the table header bar. From here, you can also add sections, take snapshots, and compare snapshots with other snapshots or databases. Snapshots are listed under the **Snapshots** tab, and the **Compare Snapshots** option opens a new view for comparison.

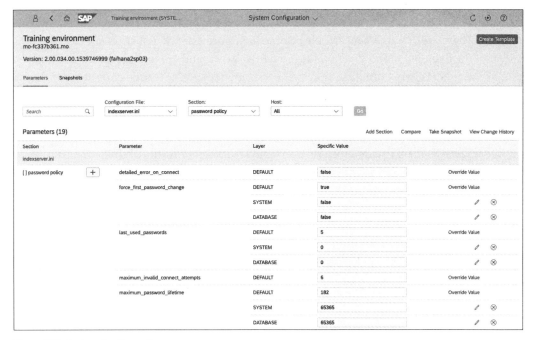

Figure 7.22 System Configuration

The header of **System Configuration** also displays the **Create Template** button. When selected, this will guide you through a three-step wizard to create a system parameter configuration template containing a selection of parameters with desired values. To access any created template, you need to go back to SAP HANA cockpit **Home** and select the **Configuration Template** tile under **Manage Landscape**. When selected, this will open the **Configuration Templates** screen, as shown in Figure 7.23. This view also enables you to create or edit templates but also, more importantly, to apply a template to a database. In particular when working with multiple databases, this allows you to quickly apply a particular password policy, for example, to a range of databases.

Figure 7.23 Configuration Templates

System Parameters

There are 20+ different INI files. Some configure a service, such as *daemon.ini* for the daemon, *nameserver.ini* for the name server, and *indexserver.ini* for the index server. Others configure optional components such as *dpserver.ini* for the data provisioning server used by SAP HANA smart data integration (SDI) or *esserver.ini* for the extended store service used by SAP HANA dynamic tiering. There are also configuration files for internal structures such as *cacheserver.ini* and *executor.ini*.

Each INI file is divided into sections and layers. Sections only bundle the parameters, but the layer defines where the parameter applies. The first layer is the DEFAULT value. The next layer is SYSTEM, which overrules any default value. For some parameters, the HOST layer overrules system (or default) values. Finally, you can also define parameters at the DATABASE layer. To configure SYSTEM or HOST layer parameters, you need to be connected to the system database.

The INI files are stored in different locations as illustrated in Figure 7.24. Files in the local instance directory (default */usr/sap*) contain the installation files (default), overwritten with each update, along with host-specific files (e.g., daemon). Files in the /<sapmnt> path, for example, */hana/shared*, contain the configuration files specific to the entire system or to specific databases (subdirectory under the custom/config path).

```
hdbadm@hana-vm1:/usr/sap/HDB/HDB00> ls exe/config/
attributes.ini      docstore.ini     gbaas.ini        multidb.ini          rsutil.ini            wlreplayer.ini
compileserver.ini   dpserver.ini     global.ini       nameserver.ini       scriptserver.ini      xscontroller.ini
computeserver.ini   esserver.ini     indexserver.ini  preprocessor.ini     statisticsserver.ini  xsengine.ini
daemon.ini          executor.ini     inifiles.ini     property_esp.ini      streamingserver.ini   xsexecagent.ini
diserver.ini        extensions.py    localclient.ini  property_generic.ini  webdispatcher.ini     xsuaaserver.ini
hdbadm@hana-vm1:/usr/sap/HDB/HDB00>
hdbadm@hana-vm1:/usr/sap/HDB/HDB00> ls hana-vm1/*.ini
hana-vm1/daemon.ini  hana-vm1/sapprofile.ini  hana-vm1/webdispatcher.ini
hdbadm@hana-vm1:/usr/sap/HDB/HDB00>
hdbadm@hana-vm1:/usr/sap/HDB/HDB00> ls /hana/shared/HDB/global/hdb/custom/config/
DB_HDB  DB_SAMPLE  diserver.ini  global.ini  indexserver.ini  lexicon  nameserver.ini  webdispatcher.ini  xsengine.ini
hdbadm@hana-vm1:/usr/sap/HDB/HDB00>
hdbadm@hana-vm1:/usr/sap/HDB/HDB00> ls /hana/shared/HDB/global/hdb/custom/config/DB_HDB/
global.ini  indexserver.ini  xsengine.ini
hdbadm@hana-vm1:/usr/sap/HDB/HDB00> 
```

Figure 7.24 INI Files

When you make changes to the system parameter files using the app, server-side ALTER SYSTEM ALTER CONFIGURATION SQL statements are executed. Manual editing of the files is no longer supported. When no SQL interface is available (for example, to make changes to the secondary site in an SAP HANA system replication scenario), use the setParameter.py console tool (see the next section).

Both the app and the ALTER SYSTEM ALTER CONFIGURATION statement requires the INIFILE ADMIN system privilege. The WITH RECONFIGURE clause applies the change to the running instance and the INI file. Without the clause, only the file will be modified. The command syntax and usage are illustrated in Figure 7.25.

Figure 7.25 Alter System Alter Configuration Statement

Exam Tip

You're not expected to be familiar with the exact SQL syntax or the names of all the INI files.

For information about system parameters, you can query the system views CON-FIGURATION_PARAMETER_PROPERTIES and M_CONFIGURATION_PARAMETER_VALUES to find out whether a restart is required, what layer the parameter is active, or if any configuration errors have been made. Alerts 136 and 137 provide support for this as they are triggered when a restart is required due to a parameter change or when an unsupported value has been set.

Before testing your configuration skills on production systems, it may be wise to first consult the SAP HANA Configuration Parameter Reference included in the SAP HANA Administration Guide. Here you can easily search for parameters and find out whether restarts are required, value restrictions, what layer the parameters are active on (if applicable), and where to find more information about the parameter in question, as illustrated in Figure 7.26.

Parameter:	password_lock_time
File name (s):	nameserver.ini,indexserver.ini
Description:	Number of minutes the user is locked after too many invalid connect attempts: After the configured number of invalid connect attempts the user is not able to connect for password_lock_time minutes. If -1 is specified, the user is locked forever.
Data type:	BIGINT
Default:	1440
Restart required?	False
Unit:	Minute
Value Restrictions:	Should be in the range: [-1,525600]
More Information:	'Could Not Save the Connection Data; Invalid User Name or Password'
	SAP IBP / S&OP Password Policy for SAP Managed Systems
	SAP HANA SPS 10 Database Revision 102
	Forgot SYSTEM password
	Security improvement of HANA authentication

Figure 7.26 SAP HANA Configuration Parameter Reference: Detail

Console Tool setParameter.py

If a database or SAP HANA system is offline or doesn't respond to SQL statements, you can use the console tool `setParameter.py`. As indicated by the file extension, this concerns a Python script. Using this approach also enables third-party tools that don't have SQL access to the system to make system parameter changes. The console tool takes care of the synchronization between instances and persistence (the INI files).

A sample command follows:

```
python setParameter.py -set="DATABASE:HDB/indexserver.ini/password policy/
minimal_password_length=10" -comment="Required Policy" -reconfigure
-sapcontrol=1
```

Table Management

So far, we've described system and database administration and how you can use SAP HANA cockpit to perform your activities. For table management, you're more likely to use SAP HANA database explorer, already encountered in the previous chapter.

For the exam, you need to be familiar with the following table management topics:

- Column and row stores
- Creating tables and other runtime catalog objects
- Viewing runtime catalog objects properties
- Import (and export) catalog objects
- Import data
- Load table
- Delta merge table

Column and Row Stores

When we discussed system architecture, we described SAP HANA as a hybrid database with both column-based and row-based data stores that combine read-optimized online analytical processing (OLAP) data access patterns and write-optimized online transactional processing (OLTP) access. SAP HANA is optimized for columnar storage, which is the default table type (although you can switch storage types using the ALTER TABLE ALTER TYPE command). You can join row store tables with column store tables, but better performance is obtained when both tables have the same storage type. This may be a consideration to define even a small metadata table as a column store when it's often joined to large fact tables.

Column-based storage provides the following benefits:

- **Higher data compression rates (especially when sorted)**
  This important when you consider a table with millions of rows and a column containing only countries or gender.

- **Better performance for single-column operations**
  Searches and aggregations are examples of operations that benefit from this performance increase.

- **Reduced need for or elimination of index**
  The column store structure is very similar to an index, reduces memory and disk storage requirements, improves write performance, and simplifies data models and development.

- **Elimination of materialized aggregates**
  Counts, averages, and minimum/maximum values can be calculated and don't require storage (materialization). This simplifies data models and development, reduces locking requirements, and provides more accurate results.

- **Parallel processing simplification for multicore processing**
  This is especially true because column store data is already vertically partitioned.

Good candidates for *column* store tables are as follows:

- When the table is searched or when aggregates (calculations) are executed on a single or a limited number of columns
- When the table has many columns
- When the table has many rows often searched or aggregated
- When most of the columns contain few distinct values and high compression rates can be achieved

Good candidates for *row* store tables are as follows:

- When the table is used for single record processing and selection
- When the table isn't used for search and aggregation
- When the table only has a small number of rows (configuration table)
- When most of the columns have distinct values that provide low compression rates

Create Table

To create database runtime objects, you can use SQL statements such as CREATE TABLE or CREATE TABLE, as shown in Figure 7.27. No special privileges are required to create database objects in your own schema. To create objects elsewhere, you'll need to have this object privilege granted. Manually creating database objects is definitely old-school and not a common activity. Application developers typically create database objects as design-time objects and have the runtime objects created automatically when the application is deployed with all the associated roles, privileges, and interdependencies.

Figure 7.27 SAP HANA Database Explorer: Create Table

Learn More

The syntax of these statements can get quite complicated. See the SAP HANA SQL Reference Guide for SAP HANA Platform at *http://s-prs.co/v507844* for an illustration.

To facilitate working with tables, you can generate CREATE, SELECT, and INSERT statements from the context menu (right-click with the table selected), as shown in Figure 7.28. Note that the syntax might be slightly different as all default parameters are included.

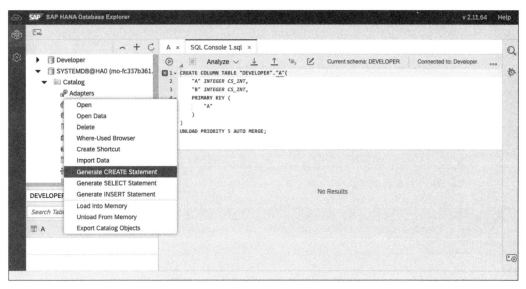

Figure 7.28 SAP HANA Database Explorer: Generate CREATE Statement

View Catalog Object Properties

In the systems view (left pane), all **Catalog** object types are listed. Apart from the common types, such as tables, triggers, views, and synonyms, you also see more exotic types, such as adapters, agents, datastores, and graph workspaces listed. You can select an object type, and the accessible objects of that type will be listed in the bottom area. Here you can filter on **Schema** and search. As there is little space in this area, you can select **Show Tables** or **Show Views** from the context menu (right-click) to have all tables or views displayed in the right pane, as shown in Figure 7.29.

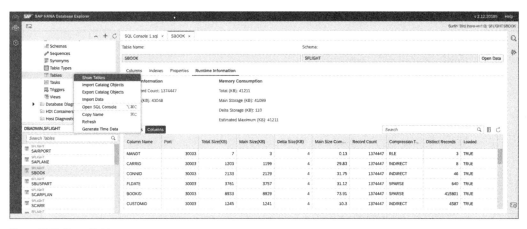

Figure 7.29 Show Tables

Depending on the object you've selected, you get metadata information about the object definition and other relevant data. For tables, this is **Indexes** and **Properties**; for views, the CREATE statement is shown. For columnar tables, runtime information is displayed with statistics about the size of the main and delta storage, distinct records, and whether the column is loaded into memory.

When you click the **Open Data** button in the upper-right corner (or the menu item), the table (or view) is queried, and you choose to view the raw data or do a bit of analysis. Here you can quickly visualize rows and columns by dragging and dropping the columns to the X and Y axes, and by selecting a corresponding graph (bar, line, pie, plot, etc.—there are multiple options), as shown in Figure 7.30.

Figure 7.30 SAP HANA Database Explorer: Analysis

Import Catalog Objects

From the same context menu, you can also choose to **Import Catalog Objects**. You can import objects from your local computer or from the SAP HANA server. The format needs to be a file with *tar.gz* extension (a zipped tar ball, in Linux lingo). You can indicate whether to include dependencies and table data or whether to replace existing objects.

A similar dialog enables you to export catalog objects, as shown in Figure 7.31. Again, you can export to the SAP HANA server or your local computer. The format will still be a zipped tar ball, a format not natively recognized by Microsoft Windows, for example. As the **Column table format**, you can select **CSV** or **Binary**, which is useful for very large tables.

Figure 7.31 Export Catalog Objects

Import Data

You can also select to **Import Data** from the context menu. This will open a simple wizard in the right pane (see Figure 7.32) where you can select the file to import in CSV or XLS(X) format. In addition, you can choose whether to **Create a new table** or **Add the data to an existing table**, perform table mapping, and decide on error handling (**Continue**, **Abort**, **Prompt**).

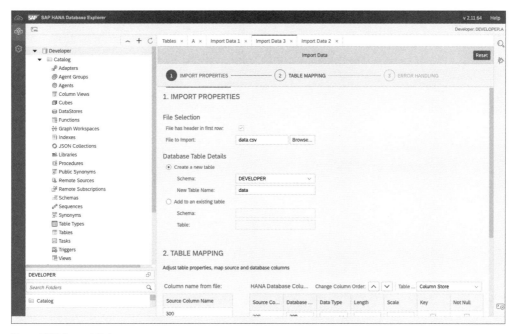

Figure 7.32 Import Data

Load Table

From the same menu, you can also load a table into memory or unload a table, as shown in Figure 7.33. Loading or unloading tables isn't a common operation as normally SAP HANA takes care of this automatically, for example, by unloading the least frequently used objects when running out of free space. However, as developer or administrator, there may be circumstances where you're better informed and can provide a helping hand.

The equivalent statements are as follows:

- `LOAD|UNLOAD <table_name> ALL`
  Load or unload an entire table into or from memory.
- `LOAD|UNLOAD <table_name> (<column_name>)`
  Load or unload specific columns.

Manual load operations require the `TABLE ADMIN` system privilege.

To view which tables are currently loaded into memory, you can query the system monitoring view `M_CS_TABLES`:

`SELECT loaded FROM m_cs_tables WHERE table_name = '<table_name>'`

You can specify an unload priority for column tables, where 6–9 corresponds to early unload, 1–5 to long term, and 0 to nonswappable. The default value is **5**.

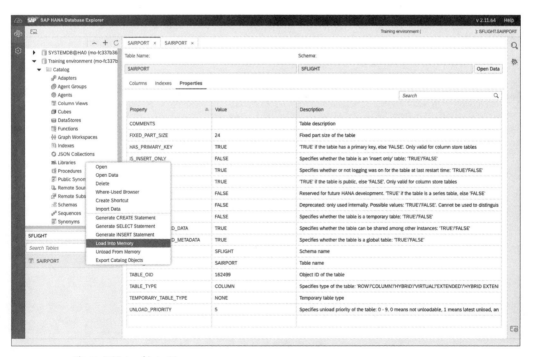

Figure 7.33 Load into Memory

Delta Merge

Column store tables are the standard table format in OLAP systems as they are optimized for read operations. This allows for quick retrieval of large volumes of data needed for aggregations such as SUM, COUNT, AVERAGE, MIN, or MAX. Column store content usually compresses very well and facilitates parallelization. For best compression rates, column stores are presorted. All these characteristics make column store tables not very suitable for updates.

For this reason, SAP HANA column store tables are separated into a MAIN storage area, which resembles a regular OLAP table, and a write-optimized DELTA storage area for the updates. These storage areas are regularly combined in an operation called the delta merge. For the most part, this is an automatic process executed by the merge dog (not to be confused with the watchdog) and configurable with system parameters.

Auto merge by the `mergedog` process is activated by default with system parameter `indexserver.ini/[mergedog]/ACTIVE=TRUE`.

Auto merge can also be configured at the table level with the `AUTO_MERGE` clause of the `CREATE|ALTER TABLE` statement (refer to Figure 7.28).

Manual merges are also supported using the `MERGE DELTA` SQL statement with the following syntax:

```
MERGE DELTA OF <table_name>
```

Like table load, manual delta merge operations require the `TABLE ADMIN` system privilege.

Learn More

Table management is documented in the SAP HANA Administration Guide. For more extensive coverage of this topic, beyond the scope of this exam, see the FAQ articles:

- KBA 1999997 – FAQ: SAP HANA Memory
- KBA 2222277 – FAQ: SAP HANA Column Store and Row Store

Important Terminology

For this exam objective, you're expected to understand the following terms:

- **Catalog objects**
  Catalog objects are schemas, tables, views, triggers, indexes, and other runtime objects. They are listed in the systems view of SAP HANA database explorer under the **Catalog** folder or can be queried from the CONSTRAINTS, FUNCTIONS, INDEXES, OBJECTS, PROCEDURES, SCHEMAS, SEQUENCES, TABLES, TRIGGERS, and VIEWS system views. To access all objects in the catalog, the CATALOG READ system privilege is required.

- **Column store memory management**
  Column store memory management occurs automatically as a background process, but there may be circumstances that require manual intervention, for example, during development or troubleshooting. You can manually load and unload individual columns or complete column tables. For this, you can use SQL statements or SAP HANA database explorer.

- **Delta merge**
  During the delta merge process, the read-optimized MAIN storage area of a columnar table is merged with the write-optimized DELTA storage area. For the most part this, is an automatic process executed by the merge dog and configurable with system parameters. Manual merges are also supported using the MERGE DELTA SQL statement.

- **sapcontrol**
  The SAP start service provides management services for systems, instances, and single server processes. This utility exposes a web service interface with function calls to start and stop systems, processes, and instances executed on the local host by the sapcontrol command. Although there are implementation differences, the service and utility are common to both SAP NetWeaver and SAP HANA systems

- **System parameters**
  System parameters modify the behavior of SAP HANA services and are stored in files with the *.ini* extension, so they are also known as INI files. Although editable, changes to system parameters are normally made using the ALTER SYSTEM ALTER CONFIGURATION statement, which requires the INIFILE ADMIN system privilege. The SAP HANA cockpit **System Configuration** view provides a more user-friendly interface to change system parameters. Alternatively, you can use the console tool setParameter.py.

Practice Questions

These practice questions will help you evaluate your understanding of the topics covered in this chapter. The questions shown are similar in nature to those found on the certification examination. Although none of these questions will be found on the exam itself, they will allow you to review your knowledge of the subject. Select the correct answers, and then check the completeness of your answers in the "Practice Question Answers and Explanations" section. Remember that on the exam, you must select all correct answers, and only correct answers, to receive credit for the question.

1. Which administration tools are available to start and stop SAP HANA systems? (There are three correct answers.)

    ☐ **A.** SAP HANA cockpit Manage Services app
    ☐ **B.** HDB (script) command
    ☐ **C.** SAP HANA database explorer
    ☐ **D.** sapcontrol
    ☐ **E.** SAP HANA database interactive terminal (HDBSQL)

2. Which administration tool is available to start and stop a multiple-host SAP HANA system?

    ☐ **A.** sapcontrol
    ☐ **B.** HDB (script) command
    ☐ **C.** SAP HANA database explorer

3. Which options are available to stop an SAP HANA system? (There are two correct answers.)

    ☐ **A.** Shutdown immediate
    ☐ **B.** Shutdown abort
    ☐ **C.** After running statements finish executing (softly)
    ☐ **D.** Immediately with open transactions aborted and rolled back

4. Which credentials are required to start an SAP HANA system?

    ☐ **A.** SYSTEM database user
    ☐ **B.** Any user with the ALTER SYSTEM system privilege granted
    ☐ **C.** Any user with the DATABASE ADMIN system privilege granted
    ☐ **D.** The <SID>adm operating system account

5. Which web service function call lists the status of the instances associated with a multiple-host system?

    ☐ **A.** GetProcessList
    ☐ **B.** GetSystemInstanceList
    ☐ **C.** GetHostStatus
    ☐ **D.** GetDistributedHostsList

6. Which services can be stopped when connected to a tenant database using the SAP HANA cockpit Manage Services app? (There are two correct answers.)

☐ **A.** nameserver

☐ **B.** daemon

☐ **C.** indexserver

☐ **D.** compileserver (shared)

☐ **E.** xsengine

7. Where can you find detailed information about installed plug-ins? (There are three correct answers.)

☐ **A.** On the **General Information** card, **Installed Plugins Details** tab of a database in SAP HANA cockpit

☐ **B.** In the **General Information** section, **Installed Plug-ins** link of the **Administration Console** perspective of SAP HANA studio

☐ **C.** By executing the SQL statement:
SELECT PLUGIN_NAME, KEY, VALUE
FROM PUBLIC.M_PLUGIN_MANIFESTS
order by PLUGIN_NAME asc, KEY asc

☐ **D.** In the **System Information** view, **Installed Components** tab of the SAP HANA platform lifecycle management web interface

8. Where can you reset memory statistics for a system in SAP HANA cockpit?

☐ **A.** In the header of the Database Management app

☐ **B.** In the header of Manage Services app

☐ **C.** Using the Memory Analysis app

☐ **D.** On the **Memory Usage** card of the **Database Overview** screen (ellipsis menu)

9. How can you access the SQL statements view in SAP HANA cockpit?

☐ **A.** From the **Monitoring** card on **Database Overview**, **Open blocked transactions** link

☐ **B.** From the **Sessions** card on **Database Overview**

☐ **C.** From the **SQL Statements** card on **Database Overview**

☐ **D.** From the **Manage SQL Performance** card on **Database Overview**

10. Where can you enable memory tracking in SAP HANA cockpit?

☐ **A.** From the **Overview** tab of **Monitor Statements**

☐ **B.** On the **Memory Usage** card of **Database Overview** (ellipsis menu)

☐ **C.** From **Memory Analysis**

11. From which locations can you access the **Alerts** view in SAP HANA cockpit? (There are three correct answers.)

    ☐ **A.** From **Manage Services, Go to Alerts** link

    ☐ **B.** From **Database Overview, Alerts** card

    ☐ **C.** From **System Configuration, Alerts** tab

    ☐ **D.** From **Database Directory, Availability/Performance/Capacity** (aggregate health) column

    ☐ **E.** From SAP HANA cockpit home page (**Landscape Overview**).

12. Which layers are included in the configuration framework? (There are three correct answers.)

    ☐ **A.** SYSTEM

    ☐ **B.** NODE

    ☐ **C.** DATABASE

    ☐ **D.** TENANT

    ☐ **E.** HOST

13. You execute the statement shown in Figure 7.34. What will be the result?

```
    ⊚  ◢  ▣    Analyze ∨    ↓    ↑   '≡,  ☑        Current schema: SYSTEM        Connected to: SYSTEMDB@HA0 (mo-fc337b361
  1 ▾ ALTER SYSTEM ALTER CONFIGURATION ('indexserver.ini', 'DATABASE', 'HA0')
  2   SET ('password policy', 'force_first_password_change') = 'FALSE'
  3   WITH RECONFIGURE
  4   COMMENT 'Disable forced password change upon logon';
```

Figure 7.34 ALTER SYSTEM ALTER CONFIGURATION statement

    ☐ **A.** The statement returns an error because you can only change the password policy in SAP HANA cockpit.

    ☐ **B.** The statement returns an error because the password policy isn't defined as a system parameter.

    ☐ **C.** The statement returns an error because the password policy is defined in the *security.ini* file.

    ☐ **D.** The statement executes successfully, and the password policy for the HAO tenant database will have been modified.

14. Which are considerations to create a column table? (There are two correct answers.)

    ☐ **A.** The table stores mainly distinct values.

    ☐ **B.** The table has a large number of columns.

☐   **C.** The table has a large number of rows and is often used for aggregation and search.

☐   **D.** The table is frequently updated.

15.   You can change a row store table to a column store table but not vice versa.

☐   **A.** True.

☐   **B.** False.

16.   You load both tables as individual columns into memory.

☐   **A.** True.

☐   **B.** False.

Practice Question Answers and Explanations

1.   Correct answers: **A, B, D**

To start/stop SAP HANA systems, you can use the SAP HANA cockpit Manage Services app, the HDB (script) command, or the sapcontrol command.

Answer C is incorrect because you can start/stop individual tenant databases using SQL in the SQL console of SAP HANA database explorer but you cannot start/stop the SAP HANA system. Answer E is incorrect because you can start/stop individual tenant databases using SQL with HDBSQL but you cannot start/stop an SAP HANA system.

2.   Correct answer: **A**

To start and stop a distributed SAP HANA system, you need to use the command-line tool sapcontrol.

Answer B is incorrect because, with the HDB (script) command, you can only start/stop the local SAP HANA instance but not a multiple-host system. Answer C is incorrect because you can only use SAP HANA database explorer to start/stop tenant databases (using SQL commands), but you cannot use it to start/stop an SAP HANA system.

3.   Correct answers: **C, D**

This is illustrated earlier in Figure 7.4. The exact text displayed differs slightly with the different SAP HANA cockpit version. Older versions use softly and immediately.

Answers A and B are incorrect because these commands are used to stop Oracle databases.

4.   Correct answer: **D**

SAP HANA systems are started with the sapcontrol utility either automatically by the SAP start service when the Linux operating system starts or manually by running the `sapcontrol` command (directly or by using the `HDB` script command). For this, operating system privileges are required. When you use the `<SID>adm` command, the right environment variables will have been set using the `HDBenv.sh` script at logon. When using root or other operating system accounts, additional configuration may be needed.

Answers A, B, and C are incorrect because the database isn't available when SAP HANA isn't started, which means you can't use the `SYSTEM` user or any other database user, no matter how privileged. System privilege `DATABASE ADMIN` or `DATABASE START` are required to start a tenant database.

5. Correct answer: **B**

   `GetSystemInstanceList` is the command to list the status and roles of the instances associated with the system (shown earlier in Figure 7.8).

   Answer A is incorrect because this function call lists the status of the local processes. Answers C and D aren't valid function calls.

6. Correct answers: **C, E**

   You can stop the `indexserver` and `xsengine` services using the SAP HANA cockpit Manage Services app. Stopping the `indexserver` service has the same effect as stopping the tenant database. Unless configured otherwise, both services will be started automatically again by the `daemon` process.

   Answer A is incorrect because the `nameserver` process hosts the system database and can't be stopped from a tenant database. Answer B is incorrect because the `daemon` process manages the overall system state and can only be stopped using operating system commands (e.g., `sapcontrol`). Answer D is incorrect because the `compileserver` is a shared process and can't be stopped from a tenant database.

7. Correct answers: **A, B, C**

   Information about plug-ins is stored on manifest files and loaded into the database during installation. Both SAP HANA cockpit and SAP HANA studio query monitoring views to display this information, but you can also query the views directly.

   Answer D is incorrect because the web interface of the SAP HANA platform lifecycle management tool provides only version information of installed plug-ins but no detailed information.

Exam Tip

You're not expected to be familiar with SAP HANA studio as it's no longer part of the exam, but there are many similarities between SAP HANA studio and SAP HANA cockpit. The **General Information** section on the **Overview** tab of the **Administration** console of SAP HANA studio is identical to the **General Information** card of SAP HANA cockpit.

You're also not tested on your familiarity with monitoring views. However, it's good to know that all information displayed in SAP HANA cockpit comes from the database and can be queried using SQL. To access this information, you need the system privilege `CATALOG READ`.

8. Correct answer: **B**

   The Manage Services app displays the **Reset Memory Statistics** link in the header (see Figure 7.2).

   Answers A, C, and D are incorrect because these apps don't include a menu or button to reset memory statistics.

9. Correct answer: **C**

   When selected, the **SQL Statements** card on **Database Overview** opens the SQL Statements app.

   Answer B is incorrect because the **Sessions** card opens the Sessions app. From here, you can navigate to the Threads and Blocked Transactions apps but not to the SQL Statements app.

   Answer A is incorrect because the open blocked transactions link of the **Monitoring** card on **Database Overview** opens the Blocked Transactions app. From here, you can navigate to the Sessions and Threads apps but not to the SQL Statements app.

   Answer D is incorrect because the **Manage SQL Performance** card displays the Statement Hints, Plan Stability, Plan Trace, Saved Plans, and Data Cache apps. When selected, each item opens the associated app, but this doesn't include the SQL Statements app.

10. Correct answer: **A**

    Memory tracking can be enabled on the **Overview** tab of the **SQL Statements** app screen. This allows you to monitor the amount of memory used by single statement executions.

11. Correct answers: **A, B, D**

    You can access the **Alerts** view from **Manage Services**, the **Alerts** card on **Database Overview**, and from the **Database Directory**.

    Answer C is incorrect because there is no **Alert** tab on **System Configuration**. Answer E is incorrect because you can't access the **Alerts** view from the **Home** page.

12. Correct answers: **A, C, E**

    The four layers are DEFAULT, SYSTEM, HOST, DATABASE.

    Answer B is incorrect because NODE isn't a layer. The term HOST is used. Answer D is incorrect because TENANT isn't a layer. The term DATABASE is used.

13. Correct answer: **D**

    The statement will be executed correctly, and the password policy will be modified.

    Answer A is incorrect because any configuration change you make in SAP HANA cockpit (or SAP HANA studio) can also be expressed in SQL. Answer B is incorrect because the password policy is defined in the files *nameserver.ini* (for the system database) and *indexserver.ini* (for each tenant database).

    Answer C is incorrect because there is no *security.ini* file.

14. Correct answers: **B, C**

    Column table candidates are mostly accessed for read operations, for example, for search and aggregates. The fewer distinct values, the higher the compression rate, the more data can be stored in memory, and the faster the table can be queried.

    Answers A and D are incorrect because frequent updates and many distinct values are characteristics of row store tables.

15. Correct answer: **B**

    False. With the ALTER TABLE ALTER TYPE statement, you can change from column store table to row store and vice versa.

16. Correct answer: **A**

    True. You can load and unload both entire tables or a selection of columns.

Takeaway

You should now be familiar with how to perform common or daily database management tasks. You should know the different ways to stop and start an SAP HANA system and tenant databases. You should also have an understanding of how the SAP start service and sapcontrol utility relate to SAP HANA and which actions make a SQL call to the database or a web service call to sapcontrol. You should have a good understanding for which SAP HANA cockpit app corresponds to which database administration activity, as well as when to use SAP HANA cockpit and when SAP HANA database explorer would be more appropriate. Although we didn't cover the topic in much detail, you should also have a general understanding of row store versus column store tables and what table management is associated with the second type.

Summary

In this chapter, we covered essential database administration skills, such as stopping and starting an SAP HANA system and an SAP HANA database tenant. We covered the most relevant SAP HANA cockpit apps for database administration with a special focus on system parameters and their configuration. In addition, we covered table management and looked at creating tables and viewing table metadata information, data import, loading and unloading tables, and delta merge operations. Specifically, we looked at how you can perform these tasks using SAP HANA cockpit and SAP HANA database explorer.

In the next chapter, we're going to zoom in on tenant database management.

Chapter 8
Working with Tenant Databases

Techniques You'll Master

- Understanding tenant database architecture
- Creating and configuring tenant databases
- Administrating tenant databases
- Monitoring tenant databases
- Copying and moving tenant databases

In this chapter, we'll focus on tenant databases and cover several administration topics specific to this architecture.

Although tenant databases were introduced with the SAP HANA 1.0 release, this database mode was initially not used all that much, and most systems continued running with a single database container. This changed with SAP HANA 2.0 when the multitenant architecture became the default and only supported database mode. This required significant changes to the operational database management processes.

Real-World Scenario

For the past five years, you've been administrating several SAP HANA 1.0 SPS 12 systems in single-container database mode. Your company is starting to prepare the migration to the latest SAP HANA 2.0 release, and this involves switching to tenant databases. How exactly is this architected, and what are the consequences for database management? What changes do you have to make to the backup procedure, user provisioning, and monitoring? Time to get serious with multitenant database containers (MDCs)!

Topic and Objectives

In this chapter, we discuss how to work with SAP HANA tenant database systems.

For the exam, you need to have a good understanding of the following topics:

- What tenant databases are
- How to create and configure tenant databases
- Tenant database administration activities
- Cross-database access configuration
- Fallback snapshots
- Tenant database monitoring
- How to copy and move tenant databases

Note

This topic area has a weight of < 8% of the total certification exam score. With 80 questions in total, you can expect about 4 questions on the topics covered in this chapter.

The topic area was added to the exam C_HANATEC_12 when the tenant database was still a relatively new and optional feature. As tenant databases is the only supported database mode for SAP HANA 2.0, you might expect, at some time in the future, for this topic area to be merged with database administration covered in Chapter 7.

Exam Tip

You'll encounter tenant database-related topics in almost every chapter of this book, and the same is true for the exam. You might get a question about tenant databases categorized under the Security topic area or under Backup and Recovery. In other words, don't be fooled by the relatively low weight, and make sure to master your tenants!

Learn More

Tenant database topics are documented in several guides, but the SAP HANA Tenant Databases Operations Guide brings all these topics together (*http://s-prs.co/v507845*).

For additional information, beyond the scope of this exam, see KBA 2101244 – FAQ: SAP HANA Multitenant Database Containers (MDC).

SAP HANA 2.0 SPS 05: What's New?

There have been no changes to the tenant database architecture for the SAP HANA 2.0 SPS 05 release, but there are some new features introduced with SAP HANA cockpit 2.0 SP 12. This includes tenant information in the Database License app (covered in this chapter). You can also now configure the retention policy for tenant databases in the Backup Configuration app when connected to the system database.

More significantly, SAP HANA cockpit 2.0 SP 11 removed tenant database administrator access to the operating system level and with it, for example, access to trace files, full system information dumps, and the platform lifecycle management (PLM) tool.

Key Concepts Refresher

In this section, we'll highlight the most important concepts that underlie working with tenant databases.

System Architecture

We'll discuss several key architecture components of tenant databases in the following sections.

Single and Multitenant Container Systems

In the original SAP HANA architecture, all systems were single-container systems, although the term wasn't used at the time. This meant that each SAP HANA system "contained" a single database with a single index server to manage the column and row store engines (on each host, in case of a multiple-host system).

We've already discussed in Chapter 2 the different deployment modes architected to improve resource usage and lower the total cost of ownership (TCO) of SAP

HANA systems with multiple components, one system (MCOS) and multiple components, one database (MCOD). Let's review them here:

- **MCOS**
  Multiple SAP HANA systems are installed on a single operating system. This causes some overhead as you now have as many name servers, preprocessors, and other services as there are systems.

- **MCOD**
  Multiple applications share a single database. This introduces management complexities to keep the applications from interfering with each other. For this reason, not every SAP application could be supported in MCOD deployments.

Tenant databases solve both issues with shared resources and isolated tenant databases.

Learn More

MDC was introduced with SAP HANA 1.0 SPS 09. In SAP HANA 2.0 SPS 01, MDCs became the standard and only supported operation mode. For more extensive coverage of this topic, beyond the scope of this exam, see SAP Note 2096000 – SAP HANA Tenant Databases: Additional Information.

Exam Tip

Although the documentation no longer uses the term "multitenant database container (MDC) system" and uses "tenant databases" instead, the exam still commonly uses MDC. There is no difference between MDC and tenant database systems.

System Architecture of Tenant Database

A tenant database system contains a single system database and one or more tenant databases. The system database is used for system administration. Technically, it's possible to delete all tenant databases so you can have a system with zero tenants, but this wouldn't be very useful as the system database is very limited in scope in the following ways:

- **No support for certain capabilities**
  There is no support for Application Function Libraries (AFL), SAP liveCache, and additional capabilities such as SAP HANA streaming analytics, SAP HANA dynamic tiering, and so on as these features require a tenant database.

- **No support for cross-database access**
  It isn't possible to access actual tenant database content, only metadata.

- **Single host only**
  The system database can't be distributed across multiple hosts and doesn't support copying or moving to another host.

- **Limited SQL support**
  As stated, not all capabilities are supported. Attempting to executed related statements returns a **feature not enabled** message.

Each tenant database contains its own users and roles, catalog, persistence, and log files and traces. Persistence means that each tenant has its own separate backups and, as a result, is also restored independently.

The system database is hosted by the name server process, while the tenant database is hosted by the index server process. On multiple-host systems, there are multiple name and index server process that support one or more tenant databases. There is still only a single system database in a scale-out system, but the other name server services host a read-only replica. We return to this topic in Chapter 9.

In the original single-container database mode, the name server service managed and persisted information about the location of column store tables and table partitions. In tenant database systems, this information is now stored in the tenant catalog. All services that don't persist any data and hence don't require backups are managed by the system database. As a reminder, Figure 8.1 shows the Manage Services app from the SAP HANA cockpit, which we discussed in Chapter 7. You're connected to the system database. Services without persistence are listed as **shared**, that is shared across all tenant databases.

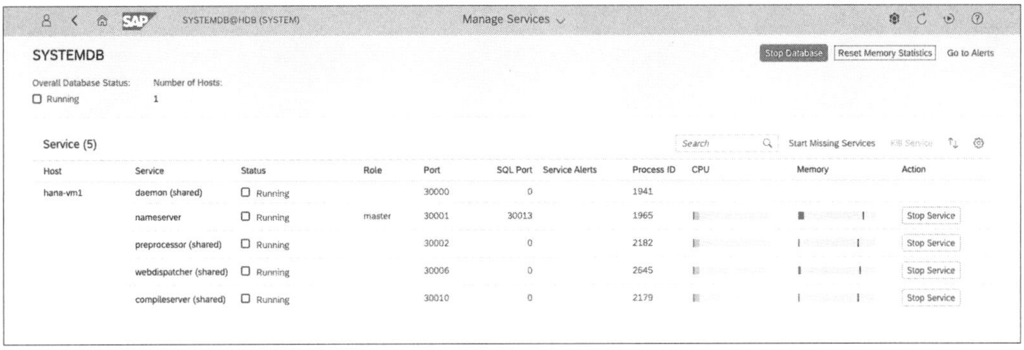

Figure 8.1 Manage Services: System Database

Figure 8.2 shows the tenant database architecture. You see a single name server hosting the system database with a number of index server processes each hosting a tenant database. Services without persistence, such as the script server and the preprocessor, are managed by the name server. SQL clients make a direct connection to the index and name servers, although the latter will be mainly used by administration tools such as SAP HANA cockpit (or SAP HANA studio) and not end-user client applications. Web clients either connect to the platform router (assuming SAP HANA extended application services, advanced model (SAP HANA XSA) where the runtime is installed. SAP HANA extended application services (SAP HANA XS), classic model applications connect directly to the SAP Web Dispatcher associated with the tenant database. The SAP HANA XS engine application server can run as a separate process or embedded, similar to the statistics service server, which now runs embedded by default and is no longer configured as separate operating system process. Figure 8.2 shows a single-host system. We cover multiple-host systems in Chapter 9.

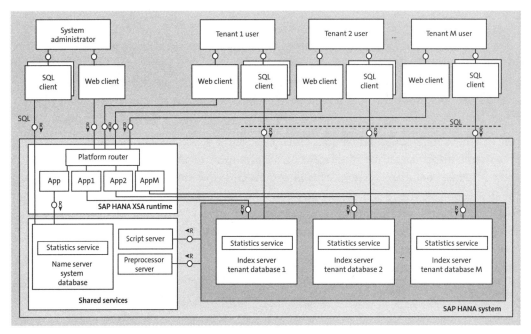

Figure 8.2 System Architecture of Tenant Databases

A standard SAP HANA installation includes a single tenant database with the same name as the system identifier (SID). For SAP HANA, express edition, for example, the SID and tenant database name is HXE.

Client Connections

The system database and tenant databases each have their own dedicated ports for internal connections and for SQL and web client connections. This port starts with 3 followed by the instance number and two final digits. For the system database, the final digits are fixed. For example, for a system with instance number 00, the system database (i.e., the name server process) listens to the following ports:

- 30001: Internal
- 30013: SQL

For the initial tenant database (index server) the ports are as follows:

- 30003: Internal
- 30015: SQL

Note that this initial tenant database uses the same SQL port numbers as the index server in a single container database system. This is by design to facilitate migration. Each service also listens to an HTTP port.

Subsequent tenant databases listen to the next available free port in the range 30040–30099, as follows:

- 30040: Internal
- 30041: SQL
- 30042: HTTP (XS)

Because you need three ports for each database, and the range 40–99 provides 60 ports, you can create up to 20 tenant databases. By changing the system parameter `global.ini/[multidb]/reserved_instance_numbers` from its default value of 0 to 1, the range is updated to 30040–30199 (160 ports).

If you install SAP HANA without tenant database (installation parameter `create_initial_tenant=off`), then the first database starts in the 40–99 range. If you add additional index server processes to a tenant database, the service is automatically assigned the next three available ports. As the port assignment can be confusing, check the Manage Services app in the SAP HANA cockpit (refer to Figure 8.1) or alternatively query the `M_SERVICES` system monitoring view.

Note that you can also connect to the system database and provide the tenant database name as parameter. For ODBC, for example, you could use the following:

`SERVERNODE=hana01:30013;UID=user01;PWD=***;DATABASENAME=Sales`

SAP HANA XS, classic model, connection requests are managed by SAP Web Dispatcher, another component inherited from the SAP NetWeaver architecture. The ports are 80 and 43, plus the instance number for HTTP and HTTPS, respectively, although this is configurable. By default, they are routed to the SAP HANA XS engine process of the system database but only when using the localhost name, not the fully qualified domain name (FQDN) as in `https://myapp.mydomain.com:4300`. Mappings to the tenant databases need to be configured in the tenant database using system parameters `xsengine.ini/[public_urls]/http_url` and `https_url`.

> **Learn More**
>
> For more extensive coverage of how to configure HTTP/S access to tenant databases see the SAP HANA Administration Guide. As with most SAP HANA XS, classic model and SAP HANA XSA topics, this is beyond the scope of the exam.

Updating Single Container Database System

When you update an SAP HANA 1.0 single-container database system to SAP HANA 2.0, the system is updated automatically to a tenant database system with a system database added and the original database converted into a tenant database. As mentioned in the "Client Connections" section, the index server process keeps the original SQL port.

Alternatively, you can also covert a single-container database system for tenant databases using the resident version of the SAP HANA database lifecycle manager (HDBLCM). The menu option will be added automatically when the tool is launched on a single-container system. Alternatively, you can launch the tool with the following action parameter: `hdblcm --action=convert_to_multidb`.

> **Learn More**
>
> For more extensive coverage of this topic, beyond the scope of this exam, see the SAP HANA Tenant Databases Guide.

Managing Tenants from the System Database

To manage system-wide settings for tenant databases, you can use the Database Management app of the SAP HANA cockpit. This app is only accessible from the system database either from the **Database Directory** page or from the Database Overview app of the system database. Most actions require the DATABASE ADMIN system privilege, although additional system privileges may be required, such as BACKUP ADMIN to make tenant database backups.

Figure 8.3 shows the **Database Management** app screen. The header shows the SID and overall status with the number of databases running. The isolation level is also displayed.

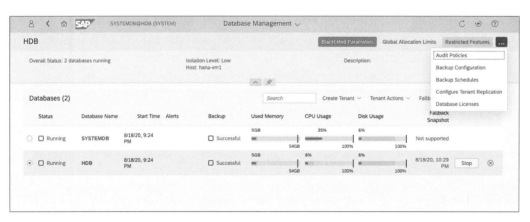

Figure 8.3 Database Management

The following configuration options are available from the **Database Management** screen:

- **Blacklisted Parameters**
- **Global Allocation Limits**
- **Restricted Features**
- **Audit Policies**
- **Backup Configuration**

- Backup Schedules
- Configure Tenant Replication
- Database Licenses

These options are described briefly here, except for tenant replication, which we'll cover in more detail later in this chapter.

Blacklisted Parameters

For security reasons, or to ensure system performance and stability, certain system parameters can be put on a blacklist to prevent modifications by tenant database administrators, as shown in Figure 8.4. A default, noneditable selection of parameters is already included for the system database and available tenants. Blacklisted parameters will display as read-only when viewed from the tenant database.

You can add additional parameters with the **Add Parameter** and **Copy Parameters** links. Note that `multidb/[readonly_parameters]/*` is included. This is where all blacklisted parameters are listed.

Figure 8.4 Blacklisted Parameters

Restricted Features

Similarly, you can restrict certain features for tenant, as shown in Figure 8.5. Examples are AFL, backup operations, R integration, or import and export operations. System monitoring view `M_CUSTOMIZABLE_FUNCTIONALITIES` lists all potential candidates.

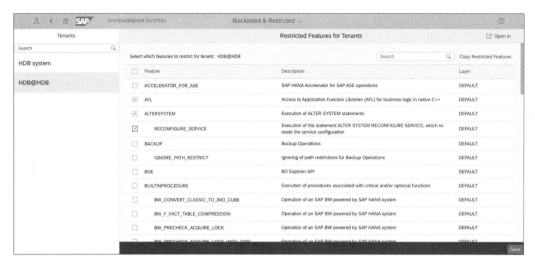

Figure 8.5 Restricted Features

Changes made with this app are persisted as system parameters in `global.ini/[customizable_functionalities]/<feature> = false`.

To make changes to system parameters, you need the `INIFILE ADMIN` system privilege, which applies to both blacklisted parameters and restricted features. No special additional privileges are required, but you need to be connected to the system database.

Global Allocation Limit

With the Global Limits app (Figure 8.6), you can define a maximum memory allocation limit (MB) and set the maximum number of CPU cores as the default value per tenant. This corresponds to the system parameters `global.ini/[memory_manager]/allocationlimit` and `global.ini/[execution]/ max_concurrency`.

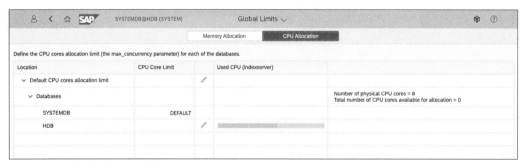

Figure 8.6 Global Limits

Audit Policies

With the Audit Policies app, you can define audit policies that are valid for all databases, as shown in Figure 8.7. We'll return to this topic in Chapter 10.

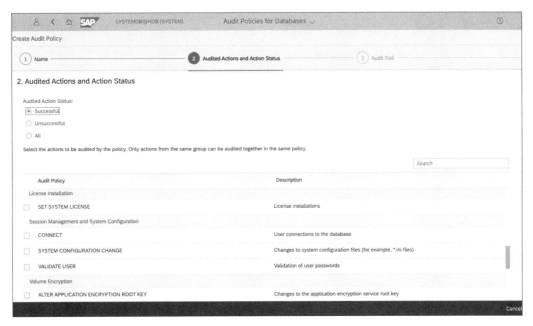

Figure 8.7 Audit Policies for Databases

Database License

With the Database Licenses app, shown in Figure 8.8, you can install SAP HANA license files.

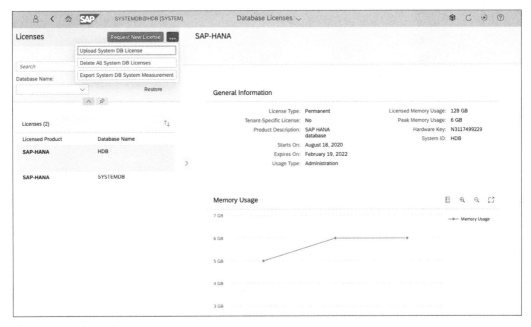

Figure 8.8 Database Licenses

A license can be system-wide or specific to the tenant database. From the app, you can request a new license with SAP Support. The SID and hardware key are required. A graph displays memory usage. This is relevant as the license typically includes a memory allocation limit that can be enforced optionally.

Backup Configuration and Backup Schedule

With the Backup Configuration and Backup Schedule apps, you can configure the backup settings for each tenant database and schedule their occurrence. The Backup Configuration app is illustrated in Figure 8.9. Note that you can enable a per-tenant retention policy. We'll return to the backup and recovery topic in Chapter 11.

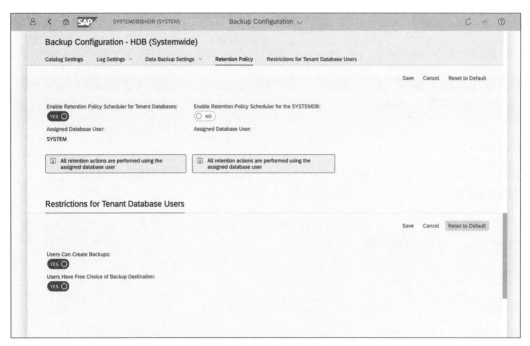

Figure 8.9 Backup Configuration

Creating Tenant Databases

You can create tenant databases either using SAP HANA cockpit or directly using SQL. In SAP HANA cockpit, from the table header, select **Create Tenant** and then either **Create Empty Tenant** or **Create Tenant Using Replication**, which launches a wizard that initiates tenant copy or move (addressed later in this chapter).

Figure 8.10 illustrates the information to create an empty tenant. The required parameters are **Database Name** and the **SYSTEM User Password**. Optionally, you can unselect the option to start the tenant database automatically (as it's selected by default). Under **Advanced Settings**, you can specify the SQL port for the index server (default service). Optionally, you can also add additional services, such as a second **indexserver**, a **scriptserver** for AFLs, **xsengine**, **dpserver** for data provisioning used with SAP HANA smart data integration (SDI), or **diserver** for the SAP HANA deployment infrastructure (HDI). After it's up and running, it would be a good time to make a full data backup.

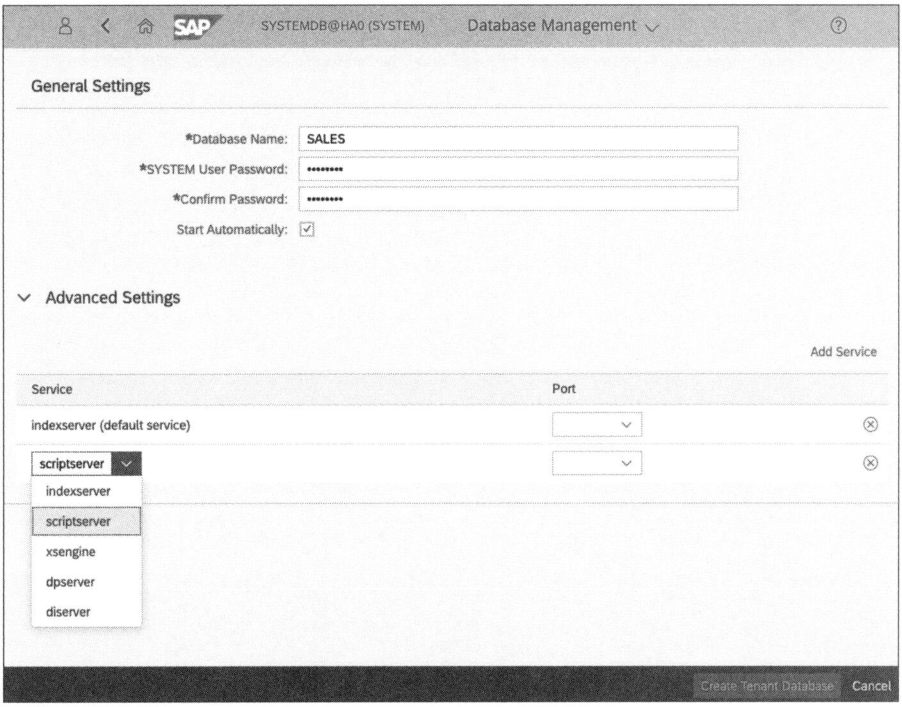

Figure 8.10 Database Management: Create Tenant Database

To create a tenant database using SQL, use the CREATE DATABASE statement. Again, only the tenant **Database Name** and **SYSTEM User Password** are required. You need DATABASE ADMIN system privilege to perform this task, as is the case for most actions described in this section.

Database Isolation

For enhanced security, you can configure tenant databases to run with their own operating system account. By default, as described in Chapter 2, all SAP HANA processes execute with the privileges of the operating system administration account <sid>adm. In high isolation mode, each database will have its own operating system user account.

You can configure high isolation mode during installation, and, afterwards, a little more effort is required. Follow these steps, as shown in Figure 8.11:

1. As root, you need to do the following:
   - Create a dedicated operating system group for each tenant database.
   - Create a dedicated operating system user for each tenant database, and add the user to the `sapsys` group.
   - Add the users to the `<sid>shm` group.
2. As system database administrator, stop the tenant databases.
3. As operating system administration user `<sid>adm`, execute the Python script `convertMDC.py` with options `--change=databaseIsolation --isolation=high`.
4. As system database administrator, configure the tenant databases to run with the operating system users and groups, and subsequently start the tenant databases. The statement is `ALTER DATABASE <name> OS USER <user> OS GROUP <group>`.

The last two steps can also be performed in the Database Management app of the SAP HANA cockpit. The option will have been added to the **Tenant Actions** menu, as shown in Figure 8.12.

```
hana-vm1:~ # groupadd hdb
hana-vm1:~ # useradd -g sapsys hdb
hana-vm1:~ # usermod -G hdbshm,hdb hdb
hana-vm1:~ # su - hdbadm
hdbadm@hana-vm1:/usr/sap/HDB/HDB00> hdbsql -n hana-vm1:30013 -u system "ALTER SYSTEM STOP DATABASE HDB"
Password:
0 rows affected (overall time 10.507851 sec; server time 10.505731 sec)

hdbadm@hana-vm1:/usr/sap/HDB/HDB00> python exe/python_support/convertMDC.py --change=databaseIsolation --isolation=high
Stop System
Execute ['/usr/sap/HDB/HDB00/exe/sapcontrol', '-prot', 'PIPE', '-nr', '0', '-function', 'StopSystem', 'ALL', '600', '600']
Execute ['/usr/sap/HDB/HDB00/exe/sapcontrol', '-prot', 'PIPE', '-nr', '0', '-function', 'WaitforStopped', '600', '2']
Set database Isolation high
Start System
Execute ['/usr/sap/HDB/HDB00/exe/sapcontrol', '-prot', 'PIPE', '-nr', '0', '-function', 'StartSystem', 'ALL']
Execute ['/usr/sap/HDB/HDB00/exe/sapcontrol', '-prot', 'PIPE', '-nr', '0', '-function', 'WaitforStarted', '600', '2']
Database Isolation level change done
Tenants can now be changed and started by execution:
        1. "ALTER DATABASE <tenantName> OS USER '<osuser>' OS GROUP '<osgroup>'"
        2. "ALTER SYSTEM START DATABASE <tenantName>"
hdbadm@hana-vm1:/usr/sap/HDB/HDB00> []
```

Figure 8.11 Change Isolation Mode

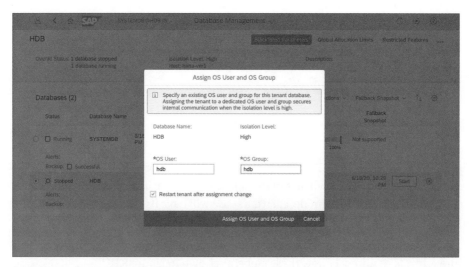

Figure 8.12 Assign OS User and OS Group Popup

Internal database communication is encrypted with certificate-based authentication (TLS).

Learn More

Database isolation is documented in the SAP HANA Security Guide (concepts) and the SAP HANA Administration Guide (configuration).

Exam Tip

Practice configuring the high isolation mode on a training database, such as SAP HANA, express edition, for the exam.

Cross-Tenant Database Access

Each tenant database is an isolated container with its own catalog and security model with users and groups. Read-only queries between tenant databases are possible, but they need to be configured in the system database with system parameter global.ini/[cross_database_access]/enable=true.

In addition, in the same section, you need to define the source and targets for the connection, for example, global.ini/[cross_database_access]/targets_for_db1= db2.

You can add the section and parameters manually in **System Configuration**, as illustrated in Figure 8.13.

Figure 8.13 System Configuration: Cross Database Access

Alternatively, you can execute the corresponding statements in the SQL console of SAP HANA database explorer, as shown in Figure 8.14.

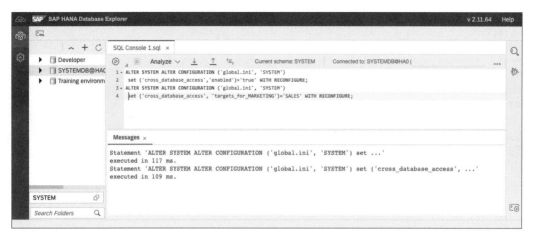

Figure 8.14 ALTER SYSTEM ALTER CONFIGURATION

The final step is to create a user with a remote identity and grant the required priv-ileges. In SQL, this corresponds to CREATE USER <USER> WITH REMOTE IDENTITY <USER2> AT DATABASE DB2 or ALTER USER <USER> ADD REMOTE IDENTITY <USER2> AT DATABASE DB2 fol-lowed by GRANT SELECT ON <SCHEMA>.<TABLE> TO <USER>, just as you would for any other user privilege grant.

There are two restrictions:

- Each user is restricted to one remote identity.
- The association is one-way only (just like for the system parameter).

The system monitoring view REMOTE_USERS displays which users can be used for cross-database access. The **Remote User** column of the **Users** view shows the map-ping.

> **Learn More**
>
> Cross-tenant database access is documented in the SAP HANA Security Guide (concepts) and the SAP HANA Administration Guide (configuration).

> **Exam Tip**
>
> Practice configuring cross-tenant database access on a training database, such as SAP HANA, express edition, for the exam.

Tenant Database Management

To start or stop a tenant database, you can use the same Database Management app. For each tenant database, there is a **Stop/Start** button, as shown in Figure 8.15. For this activity, lesser privileged system privileges are available: DATABASE START and/or DATABASE STOP.

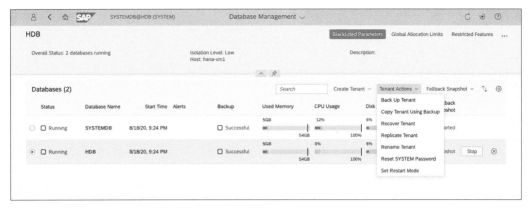

Figure 8.15 Database Management: Tenant Actions

As with the **Stop Database** button from Chapter 7, **Stop Tenant Database** prompts you to select whether you want to stop the database "after running statements finish executing" or "immediately with open transactions aborted and rolled back," corresponding to a soft and hard stop. To start the tenant database, click **Start**, and the database will be started. There is no **Are you sure? Yes/No** dialog.

Alternatively, you can stop a tenant database with the ALTER SYSTEM STOP|START DATABASE <database name> SQL statement, as shown in Figure 8.16. For this, you need to be connected to the system database; otherwise, an error message is returned: **feature not supported: alter system database command on SYSTEMDB only**. This is the case for all ALTER SYSTEM commands.

Figure 8.16 SAP HANA Database Explorer: ALTER SYSTEM

To delete a tenant database, select the entry, and click the encircled cross at the end of the row. You'll be prompted to whether you want to delete the tenant and keep the directories or whether to delete both. The equivalent SQL statement is DROP DATABASE.

For each tenant, from the **Tenant Actions** menu in the header, you can select the following options:

- **Back Up Tenant**
  The **Back Up Tenant** option opens the Backup app.

- **Copy Tenant Using Backup**
  The **Copy Tenant Using Backup** option allows you to copy the tenant.

- **Recover Tenant**
  The **Recover Tenant** option will be discussed further in Chapter 11.

- **Replicate Tenant**
  The **Replicate Tenant** option starts the **Replicate Tenant Database** wizard, the same as when selecting **Create New Tenant · Create Tenant Using Replication** from the header.

- **Rename Tenant**
  A dialog is returned when you select **Rename Tenant**. This also requires a restart of the tenant and hence a selection of a hard or soft stop.

- **Reset SYSTEM Password**
  Resetting the SYSTEM password (when connected to the system database) results in a temporary password that the tenant database administrator will need to change upon first logon. The password is reset when the tenant database is stopped (i.e., the action requires a restart). This is illustrated in Figure 8.18.

- **Set Restart Mode**
  The **Set Restart Mode** action configures the tenant database to either start automatically when the system starts or not. The default is auto-restart.

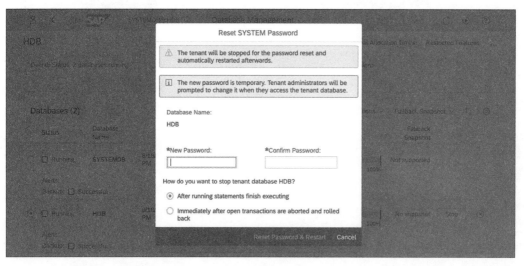

Figure 8.17 Reset Password

Fallback Snapshot

From the header, you can also access the **Fallback Snapshots** menu. Fallback snapshots can be used to quickly revert the state of a tenant database to a specific point in time. A simple use case could be to reset a training or demo database to the original state, but you can also use fallback snapshots as backup for an application upgrade. There are some restrictions, however:

- One per tenant database (and none for the system database)
- No configuration changes (add or remove services)
- Not part of a backup set

You create a fallback snapshot from the context menu: **Fallback Snapshot · Create**. This action completes instantly, and the snapshot timestamp is listed in the **Fallback Snapshot** column. To revert, select **Reset Tenant to Fallback Snapshot**, and to remove the snapshot select **Delete Fallback Snapshot** (see Figure 8.18).

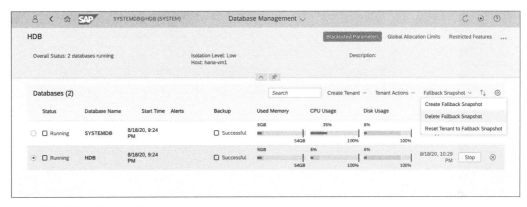

Figure 8.18 Fallback Snapshots

The equivalent statements are as follows:

- ALTER DATABASE <database> CREATE FALLBACK SNAPSHOT
- ALTER SYSTEM START DATABASE <database> FROM FALLBACK SNAPSHOT
- ALTER DATABASE <database> DROP FALLBACK SNAPSHOT

Monitoring and Managing Tenant Databases

Monitoring and managing a tenant database work the same as for system databases in SAP HANA cockpit except that not all functionality and information will be available. To illustrate the workflow, you start with the **Database Directory** screen from the SAP HANA cockpit. This will list all the databases in the database group assigned to your cockpit user account, as shown in Figure 8.19.

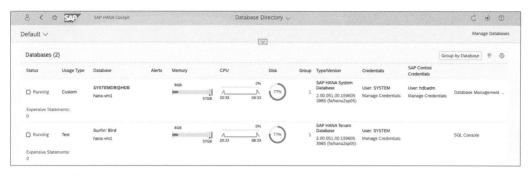

Figure 8.19 Database Directory

From the system database, you can launch the Database Management app, not to be confused with the **Manage Databases** link in the header, which will launch the Cockpit Manager app where you can register databases and assign them to database groups. We've already described the system-wide configurations you can perform with the Database Management app (refer to Figure 8.3, if you need a reminder) and also how you can perform tenant-specific database administration activities, such as create, start, stop, rename, and so on.

To monitor the tenant or to perform additional database management tasks, select the tenant in the database name column. This opens the **Database Overview** app screen, as illustrated in Figure 8.20. From here, you can open, for example, the Services app to restart the indexserver or xsengine service or when you return to **Database Overview**, launch the **Performance Monitor** to investigate CPU, memory, and disk usage.

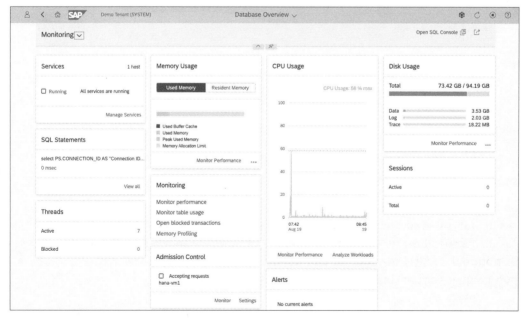

Figure 8.20 Database Overview

As illustrated in Figure 8.21, every database contains a SYS and _SYS_STATISTICS schema, including the system database. For system-wide monitoring, you can query the M_DATABASES system view or any of the views in the SYS_DATABASES schema.

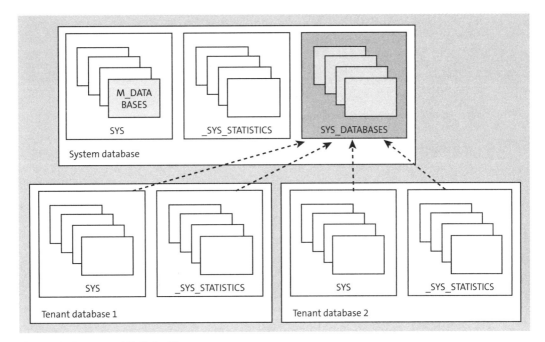

Figure 8.21 System and Statistics Views

The memory required to monitor and manage the system by the system database is restricted with system parameter global.ini | [multidb] | systemdb_reserved_memory. The initial value is 15 GB.

Copying and Moving Tenant Databases

In Chapter 4, when discussing the resident HDBLCM tool, we covered that renaming the SID of an SAP HANA system is a remarkably complex operation. Copying and moving tenant databases from one system to another, fortunately, is remarkably simple. This feature leverages SAP HANA system replication, a topic we'll cover in more detail in Chapter 12.

To kick this off, select **Create Tenant using Replication** from the header of the **Database Management** screen, and follow these steps:

1. Select **Copy** or **Move**.
2. Select the **Source System** (database) and **Source Tenant**, as shown in Figure 8.22. You'll be informed about the latest backup time stamp.
3. Select the **Target System**, as shown in Figure 8.23.
4. Select the **Credentials.**

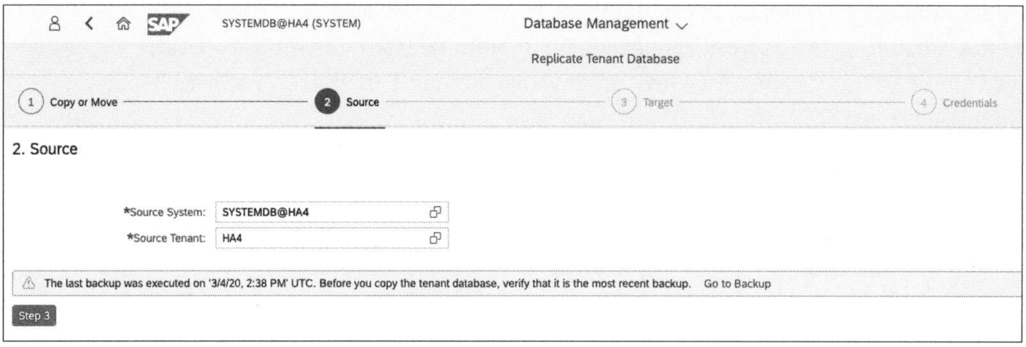

Figure 8.22 Replicate Tenant Database: Source

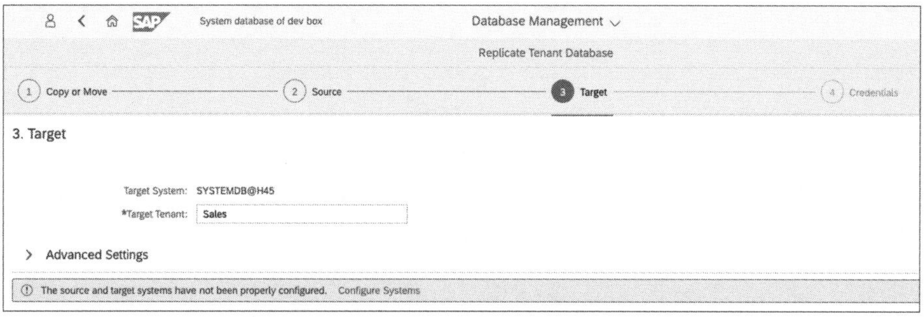

Figure 8.23 Replicate Tenant Database: Target

The first time you replicate a tenant database, you'll be prompted to go to the **Configure Systems for Tenant Replication** screen to set up a secure transfer, as illustrated in Figure 8.24. Here you'll be prompted to provide operating system credentials and to either upload a certificate or use the certificate found on the system (auto detected).

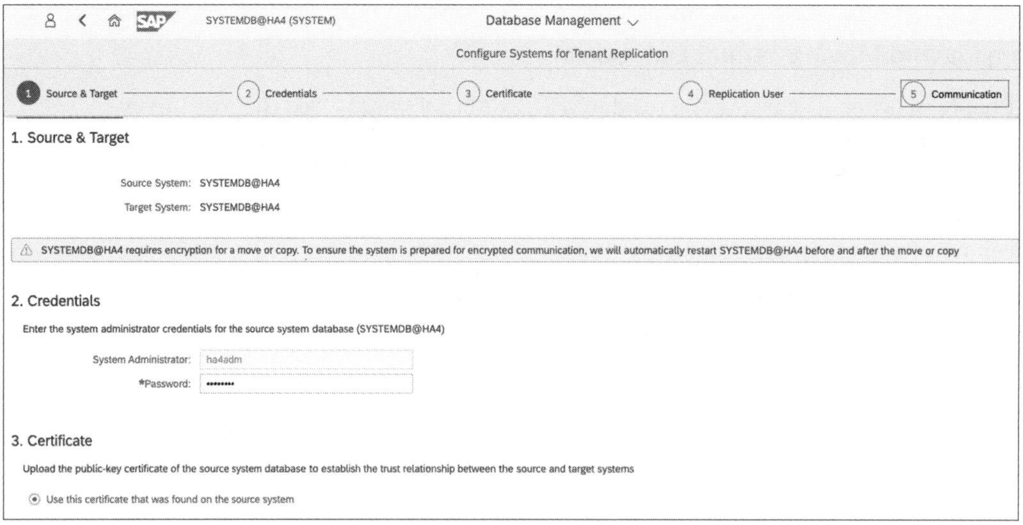

Figure 8.24 Configure System for Tenant Replication

The wizard will verify that secure communication can be established, install the certificate between both systems, and create credentials, as shown in Figure 8.25.

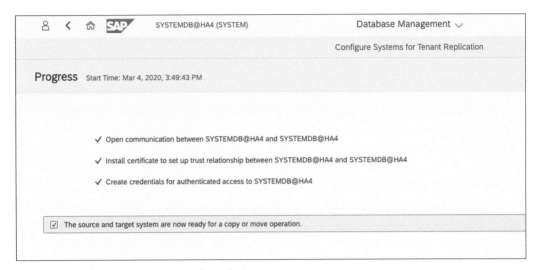

Figure 8.25 Database Management: Configure Systems

You can then initiate the replication process by selecting **Replicate** and optionally indicate to **Run in Background**, as illustrated in Figure 8.26.

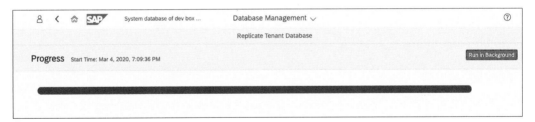

Figure 8.26 Replicate Tenant Database

The **Status** will display **Replicating**, as illustrated in Figure 8.27.

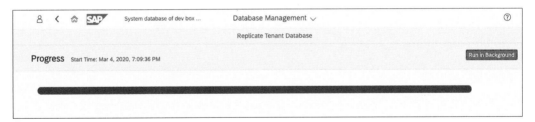

Figure 8.27 Replicating

> **Learn More**
>
> Copying and moving tenant databases is documented in the SAP HANA Tenant Databases Guide.

Important Terminology

For this exam objective, you're expected to understand the following terms:

- **Blacklisted parameters**
  Blacklisted parameters are system parameters not configurable for tenant databases. Typical use cases are parameters related to resource management.

- **Cross-database access**
  Cross-database access allows a tenant database to query data in another database. This feature needs to be enabled, the traffic (A to B, B to A, etc.) needs to be configured, remote identities need to be created for users, and permissions must be granted. The access is read-only. By default, tenant databases are isolated. Cross-database access from the system database to a tenant isn't supported.

- **Database isolation mode**
  A tenant database can operate in low (default) or high isolation mode. A tenant database in high isolation mode runs under its own operating system account, which blocks access at the file system and process level.

- **Multitenant database container (MDC)**
  MDC was the original term used to describe tenant databases. This term is no longer used in the documentation, but you still might find references in blogs, SAP Support KBAs, and training material.

- **Restricted features**
  Restricted features are features not available to tenant databases. Like blacklisted parameters, this is configured using system parameters.

- **Single-container system**
  A single-container system (single database container mode) is the original SAP HANA configuration and still common for SAP HANA 1.0 SPS 12 systems. For SAP HANA 2.0 systems, this mode is no longer available.

- **System database**
  A tenant database system contains a system database and zero, one, or more tenant databases. The system database is managed by the name server. On a multiple-host system, other master name server processes maintain a replica (read-only clone). The system database is used for tenant database management (create, start/stop, etc.) and has access to the metadata of the tenant database. The system database has no access to the content of the tenant.

- **Tenant database**
  A tenant database is an isolated database with its own users, object catalog, repository, dedicated index server (with its log and trace files), and persistence (backups).

Practice Questions

These practice questions will help you evaluate your understanding of the topics covered in this chapter. The questions shown are similar in nature to those found on the certification examination. Although none of these questions will be found on the exam itself, they will allow you to review your knowledge of the subject. Select the correct answers, and then check the completeness of your answers in the "Practice Question Answers and Explanations" section. Remember that on the exam, you must select all correct answers, and only correct answers, to receive credit for the question.

1. How many database modes are supported for SAP HANA 2.0?

    ☐ **A.** One
    ☐ **B.** Two

2. Tenant databases are completely isolated from each other with their own persistence (backups) and can be updated independently for each other. This makes it possible to run an application on different SAP HANA versions.

    ☐ **A.** True
    ☐ **B.** False

3. A tenant database system always contains at least one tenant database.

    ☐ **A.** True
    ☐ **B.** False

4. With the SYSTEM database account of the system database, you can connect to all tenant databases. This user, however, can only access the SYS and _SYS_STA-TISTICS system views, not any user data.

    ☐ **A.** True
    ☐ **B.** False

5. Which isolation modes are supported? (There are two correct answers.)

☐ **A.** Default

☐ **B.** Low

☐ **C.** High

☐ **D.** Complete

6. The system database stores topology information, including information about the location of tables and table partitions of tenant databases.

☐ **A.** True

☐ **B.** False

7. How can you connect a SQL client to a tenant database? (There are two correct answers.)

☐ **A.** By specifying host name, SQL port of the system database (3xx13), and database name in the connect string.

☐ **B.** By specifying host name and SQL port of the tenant database in the connect string. Except for the initial tenant database (3xx15), the SQL port is allocated in the 3xx40–3xx99 range.

☐ **C.** By specifying host name and database name in the connect string.

8. Technically, what limits the creation of tenant databases?

☐ **A.** Available system resources (CPU, RAM)

☐ **B.** The number of available TCP ports

☐ **C.** The number of databases specified in the license

9. Which administration tools are available to start and stop SAP HANA tenant databases? (There are three correct answers).

☐ **A.** Database Management app of SAP HANA cockpit

☐ **B. Systems** view of SAP HANA studio

☐ **C.** SQL console of SAP HANA database explorer

☐ **D.** sapcontrol

☐ **E.** SAP HANA database interactive terminal (HDBSQL)

10. Which command starts a tenant database?

☐ **A.** ALTER SYSTEM START DATABASE <database_name>

☐ **B.** START DATABASE <database_name>

☐ **C.** START TENANT <database_name>

☐ **D.** ALTER SYSTEM <SID> START DATABASE <database_name>

11. Which system privilege is required to configure restricted features?

☐ **A.** DATABASE ADMIN

☐ **B.** FEATURE ADMIN

☐ **C.** INIFILE ADMIN

☐ **D.** INI ADMIN

12. You're connected to the Database Management app with the database administration user and want to stop a tenant database, but you can only view resources. What might have caused this?

☐ **A.** You're not connected to the system database.

☐ **B.** The database administration user doesn't have the DATABASE ADMIN system privilege.

☐ **C.** The indexserver service isn't running. Go to the Manage Services app, and start the indexserver service first.

13. What is the default TCP port for SQL connections for the system database?

☐ **A.** TCP port 3xx13, where xx stands for the instance number.

☐ **B.** TCP port 50013 for HTTP and 50014 for HTTPS.

☐ **C.** TCP port 3xx15, where xx stands for the instance number.

☐ **D.** TCP ports are allocated from the port range 3xx40–3xx99, where xx stands for the instance number, on a first available basis. For the system database, the first three ports are reserved.

Practice Question Answers and Explanations

1. Correct answer: **A**
   For SAP HANA 2.0, tenant databases, or MDC, is the only supported database mode.

   Answer B is incorrect because the single-container database mode and tenant database mode are only supported for SAP HANA 1.0 (SPS 12).

2. Correct answer: **B**
   False. All tenant databases are always on the same release as the system database and the system as a whole.

   Answer A is incorrect because you use the MCOS deployment option to run different SAP HANA versions on a single (operating) system.

3. Correct answer: **B**
   False. You can delete all tenants. Note that when you delete the initial tenant created during installation and create a new tenant, it will allocate its port from

the port range and not the original indexserver ports in single database container mode (i.e., SQL port 3xx15).

4. Correct answer: **B**

   False. Each database is self-contained and has its own SYSTEM user and SYS/_SYS_ STATISTICS schemas. The SYSTEM user of the system database has no access to tenant databases. Cross-tenant database access between the system database and tenant database isn't supported. To access a tenant database from the system database, for example, to use the Database Management app from the SAP HANA cockpit, you need the system privilege DATABASE ADMIN.

5. Correct answers: **B, C**

   You can configure a tenant database in low and high isolation mode.

   Answers A and D are incorrect because default and complete are invalid options for the isolation mode.

6. Correct answer: **B**

   False. In the original single-container database mode, the topology information stored by the name server included information about the location of tables and table partitions. This information is of particular relevance for multiple-host systems, as we'll discuss in the next chapter. With tenant databases, all tenant-specific information is stored in the relevant tenant database catalog.

7. Correct answers: **A, B**

   Answer A is correct because connecting with a SQL client to a tenant database directly through the system database by specifying the database name in the connect string is the recommended approach. Answer B is correct because connecting with a SQL client to a tenant database by specifying the SQL port is a supported alternative. Answer C is incorrect because you can't connect by only specifying the host and database name.

8. Correct answer: **B**

   By default, port range 3xx40–3xx99 is available for tenant databases, which require three ports each (internal, SQL, SAP HANA XS). This is configurable but limits the number of tenant databases that can be created.

   Answer A is incorrect. In practice, system resources will probably provide a more likely limitation to the number of tenant databases that can be supported. This doesn't provide a technical limitation, however. Given enough resources, only the number of available TCP ports will limit this number. Answer C is incorrect because, with the license, a maximum amount of RAM can be enforced but not the number of databases.

9. Correct answers: **A, C, E**

   To start and stop SAP HANA tenant databases, you can use the Database Management app of SAP HANA cockpit, SQL console of SAP HANA database explorer, or the SAP HANA database interactive terminal (HDBSQL).

Answer B is incorrect because SAP HANA studio provides no graphical interface to start and stop tenant databases (although you can use the SQL prompt). Answer D is incorrect because you can't start or stop individual tenant databases using sapcontrol.

Exam Tip

SAP HANA studio is beyond the scope of the exam, but you may find occasional reference to the tool in a question or answer.

---

10. Correct answer: **D**

    The command to start a tenant database is ALTER SYSTEM START DATABASE <database_name>.

    The syntax of the commands in answers A, B, and C is incorrect.

11. Correct answer: **C**

    Restricted features and blacklisted parameters are system parameters configured in the *global.ini* and *multidb.ini* files, respectively. To make changes to system parameters, the system privilege INIFILE ADMIN is required.

    Answer A is incorrect because system privilege DATABASE ADMIN is required to administer tenant databases but doesn't include the privilege to change system parameters (error: insufficient privilege when configuring system properties). Answers B and D are incorrect because these system privileges don't exist.

12. Correct answer: **B**

    The user connected to the database needs DATABASE ADMIN system privileges to manage tenant databases.

    Figure 8.28 shows the view when connected to the database with a user with the CATALOG READ system privilege granted but not DATABASE ADMIN.

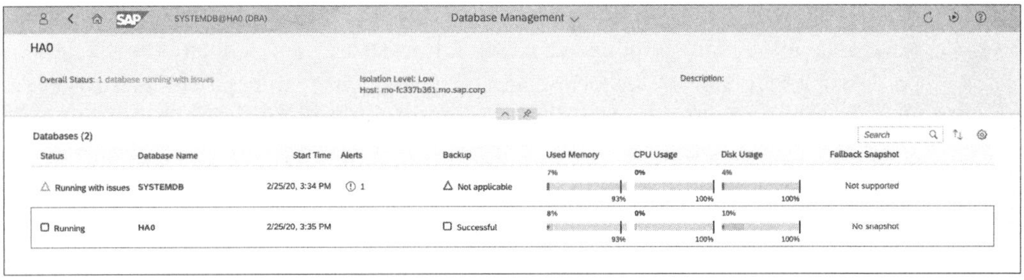

Figure 8.28 Database Management: DBA

Answer A is incorrect because you can only connect to Database Management from system databases. Answer C is incorrect because, if the indexserver service isn't running, the database status would be stopped, but this wouldn't cause view-only access to the Database Management app.

13. Correct answer: **A**

    TCP port 3*xx*13 is the default TCP port for SQL connections.

    Answer B is incorrect because ports 50013|14 are reserved for the SAP start service. Answer C is incorrect because port 3*xx*15 is the default SQL port for the initial tenant database (when created) but not the system database. Answer D is incorrect because tenant databases are created from the port range 3*xx*40–3*xx*99, where *xx* stands for the instance number but not the system database.

Takeaway

You should now be familiar with the architecture of tenant databases and how it differs from the original single-database container mode. You should know how you can create tenant databases using either SAP HANA cockpit or SQL statements directly and also how to connect to the tenant database with a SQL client and what port to use (or know where to find this information). It should be clear what you can (and can't) do as system database administrator to manage and monitor tenant databases and how you can use the Database Management app to configure tenant database licenses, audit policies, backup schedules, and resource allocation limits. Although this may require some practice, you should be able to configure tenant databases in high isolation mode and configure cross-database access. Finally, you should know how you can copy and move tenant databases from one system to another, with the steps and prerequisites involved. The step-by-step wizard of SAP HANA cockpit makes this activity easy.

Summary

In this chapter, we focused on the most important administration tasks related to tenant database management. We covered how to create and delete tenant databases using both SAP HANA cockpit and using SQL commands, as well as use these tools for administration and monitoring.

In the next chapter, we're going to zoom out to scale-out systems, also known as multiple-host systems and distributed systems.

Chapter 9
Scale-Out Systems

Techniques You'll Master

- Preparing an SAP HANA system for scale-out
- Installing an SAP HANA multiple-host system
- Adding or removing hosts from a multiple-host system
- Performing system monitoring on a scale-out system
- Managing tables with partitioning, placement, and replication
- Performing table (re-)distribution

In this chapter, we scale out beyond a single-host SAP HANA system to a multiple-host or scale-out system. Why scale out? To put it simply, because you can no longer scale up. You've reached the limits going vertically, and now you need to go horizontally. More hosts or, if you prefer, more servers or more computers, means more processing power to distribute the load.

Real-World Scenario

Your monthly management reports clearly indicate that if the current growth trends continue, your SAP HANA system will no longer be able to support the load. In the future, there may not be enough resources to support concurrent transaction processing, and some tables may also grow too large. You decide it's time to investigate the SAP HANA multiple-host system feature.

What do you need to know to run SAP HANA on multiple hosts? How do you install such a scale-out system? What are the consequences for your backup procedure? Any changes required? What do you do with the tenant databases? One tenant for each host or distribute the load? Does a multiple-host system provide high availability (HA) out of the box, or do you need special configuration? What do you need to know about data distribution? Clearly, SAP HANA multiple-host, scale-out systems bring many questions to the table. Do you have the answers?

A scale-out system also provides the opportunity to make the system highly available. A hardware or software fault or failure on a single-host system might cause business downtime. With a multiple-host system, single points of failure can be avoided. However, we say "provides the opportunity" and "can be avoided" because high availability (HA) doesn't come out of the box. The built-in automatic failover mechanism only works—or maybe, works best—if the host has someplace to failover to, for example, a standby host (running all hosts at 50% capacity or less would also work, but this is a less common practice).

At first sight, an SAP HANA multiple-host system might resemble the type of database cluster found on the market today with multiple nodes as identical clones and a single shared storage subsystem. However, an SAP HANA multiple-host system is quite different. Each host isn't a cluster node (clone). They all load a different part of the database in memory. To make an SAP HANA multiple-host system highly available requires configuration, which we'll explain in this chapter.

Note

Although the documentation (with some exceptions) references the building blocks of a multiple-host system as hosts, there are few occasions where the term "node" is used as a synonym. Sometimes this is unavoidable, for example, with SAP Business Warehouse

(SAP BW) extension nodes. In SAP BW terminology, it's a node; from the SAP HANA perspective, it's a host.

In SAP Community blog posts, SAP Support knowledge base articles (KBAs), and third-party vendor documentation, the nodes and hosts terms are more commonly used as synonyms, and even occasionally the term "cluster" is used as another word for a multiple-host system. This can be confusing, as cluster can both apply to a configuration with an SAP HANA system replication system and an SAP HANA multiple-host system. In fact, you could configure a multiple-host system without standby hosts (no cluster) and use system replication for HA (cluster).

With each host hosting a unique section of the database, what happens if you need to join table A on host X with table B on host Y? Don't you lose all the benefits of in-memory split-second access times and replace the delays of disk access with the latency of network?

That's a good question, and table partitioning, table groups, table placement, and table replication provide the answer. Proper data distribution greatly reduces the impact of network latency on system performance although the general recommendation remains to scale up before you scale out.

Unfortunately, finding the right way to distribute data can be challenging. What is best also changes over time as the database grows and access patterns change. With a bad data distribution plan, you can actually make performance worse.

Fortunately, SAP HANA comes with built-in data distribution advisors that help you make the right choices. Some applications, such as SAP BW, even take full control of data distribution. In this chapter, we'll also cover the art and science of data distribution.

Exam Tip

Installing a multiple-host system isn't difficult. Most of the complexity lies in system preparation, such as implementing the SAP HANA storage connector application programming interface (API) and configuring the logical unit numbers (LUNs) of the storage area network (SAN). Fortunately, this is beyond the scope of the exam (although we'll explain some of the concepts and terminology).

Data distribution can be tricky. As mentioned, it's both an art and a science. "It depends" is typically the correct answer to the question. Without a distributed system to practice with, it may be more difficult to get a good grip on the concepts. Make sure to understand heterogeneous and multilevel partitioning, as it might come up on the exam.

The free SAP HANA, express edition, is an excellent study companion for most chapters in this book, but it doesn't serve you much here as you can't configure it as a multiple-host system. As this might make it more difficult to practice the different failover scenarios and working with the Table Distribution app of SAP HANA cockpit, we've included a few extra illustrations to help you get the picture. Table partitioning, on the other hand, works just as well on a single-host system as on multiple hosts, as described in this chapter. You could consider doing a little extra hands-on practice to compensate.

Topics and Objectives

The focus of this chapter is on configuring and managing SAP HANA scale-out systems. Apart from the concepts and installation of a multiple-host system, you also need to understand host auto-failover configuration and data distribution (management).

For the exam, you're expected to have a good understanding of the following topics:

- Multiple-host system architecture
- How to install a multiple-host system
- High availability (HA) with multiple-host systems, including host auto-failover
- How to manage multiple-host systems, including adding and removing hosts
- Data distribution on multiple-host systems with partitioning, table placement, and table replication

---

Note

This topic area is listed with a minor weight (< 8%). With 80 questions in total, you can expect about 4 questions on this topic. For the SPS 03 (C_HANATEC_15) exam and earlier, a single High Availability & Disaster Tolerance topic area covered both scale-out systems and system replication. Since SPS 04, these topics have been separated, resulting in a slightly higher weighting than when combined (a couple more questions each).

Keep in mind that the exam guide states this can change at any time, so always check online for the latest updates.

Learn More

The topic is documented in the Availability and Scaling chapter of the SAP HANA Administration Guide. Data distribution topics are documented in the same guide but in the "Managing Tables" section in the System Administration chapter.

Several papers have been published about HA in SAP HANA and related topics over the years. To make sure you read the latest version, an article was even added to the knowledge base (KBA 2407186 – How-To Guides & Whitepapers for SAP HANA High Availability).

These papers make for interesting reading, plus you'll find their content repeated almost verbatim in the documentation and SAP training material. The most relevant papers will be listed in additional Learn More boxes in this chapter.

Key Concepts Refresher

In this section, we'll tackle the key concepts for this part of the exam, namely scale-out, multiple-host, distributed systems. We'll also discuss host auto-failover concepts, multiple-host system architecture and installation, and data distribution, including table partitioning, placement, and replication, as well as working with the SAP HANA cockpit Table Distribution app.

SAP HANA 2.0 SPS 05: What's New?

SAP HANA native storage extension was introduced with SAP HANA 2.0 SPS 04 (2019). With SAP HANA 2.0 SPS 05 (2020), native storage extension is now also supported for scale-out systems.

For this topic area, the latest SAP HANA release introduces no new features. Scale-out has been part of the SAP HANA architecture from the initial release, and you even find similarities in the TREX search engine with failover and master and slaves roles of the TREX-nameserver. The papers written about HA, storage, and networking for the tailored data center integration (TDI) program date from the SAP HANA 1.0 release, and although some were updated for version 2.0, the changes are minimal. For those renewing their certification from an earlier edition, the learning curve will be almost flat. There is no difference in the installation, for example.

Only in the domain of data distribution do you find new features added in some of the releases, but not for SPS 05, although data tiering with native storage extension is related. Most changes are to be found in SAP HANA cockpit of which we'll cover the Table Distribution app and the host auto-failover configuration. Note that although the concepts are the same, the user interface is very different from the tool used with earlier releases, SAP HANA studio, which is no longer part of the exam.

Scale-Out, Multiple-Host, Distributed Systems

When your SAP HANA system no longer has sufficient resources to carry the load, you have two choices: either scale up or scale out. Scaling up, also known as vertical scaling, means adding more processors (or processor cores) and more memory to the computer. Horizontal scaling, or scaling out, means adding more machines, as shown in Figure 9.1. The opposites are scaling down and scaling in.

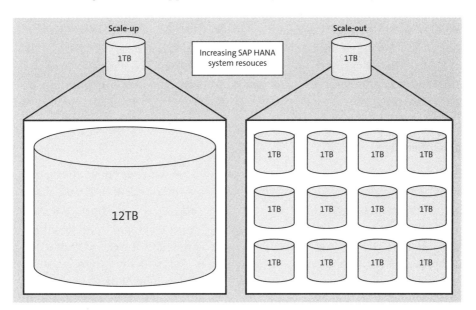

Figure 9.1 Scaling

We'll walk through the key concepts that underlie distributed systems in this section.

Scale Up or Scale Out

In the world of physical machines, scaling up isn't always possible because all the available sockets for CPUs and slots for dynamic RAM (DRAM) dual in-line memory modules (DIMMs) might already be occupied. In the world of virtual machines (VMs), this is no longer an issue because it's usually easy to add more virtual processors and memory (until the limit's reached).

As a rule, SAP recommends to scale up before scaling out for SAP HANA systems that power SAP business applications. This is a consequence of in-memory computing. Being able to access all relevant data directly in memory means you don't have to wait for relatively slow storage devices for data processing. The relevant bits go straight from memory to the processor, if not already cached on the CPU. In a scale-out configuration, there is a risk you might lose this advantage. When the data first needs to be transferred over the network from one host to another, precious time is lost. Although current state-of-the-art networks may deliver data faster than local storage, it's still nowhere near referencing main memory or processor cache.

Why scale out at all? A single server may simply no longer have enough capacity to either support the load, in terms of concurrent requests, or support the volume; database, table, or even a single table partition size may grow beyond the limits of what a single server can support.

As you'll see in the "Multiple-Host Installation" section, it's not difficult to create a multiple-host system to scale out. At installation time or after, simply add a host using the SAP HANA database lifecycle manager (HDLCM) platform lifecycle management tool. On the condition that shared storage and the file system is properly prepared, adding a second host to a single-host system automatically turns the system into a distributed system. No special software, complex configuration, or license is required.

High Availability

Whether an SAP HANA distributed system provides HA depends on the configuration. When you create a system with two hosts, one with the SAP HANA database and the other with the SAP HANA extended application services, advanced model (SAP HANA XSA) server runtime environment, this provides no HA: when either hosts fails, the system as a whole is unavailable. The application server would not automatically become a database or vice versa. However, if you create a system with eight hosts—two of which are standby hosts with all tenant databases shared across all hosts—then any host failure would be mitigated by the SAP HANA host auto-failover HA feature, so with everything properly configured, this would pass unnoticed (transparent) to the client. Distributed systems with and without HA are illustrated in Figure 9.2.

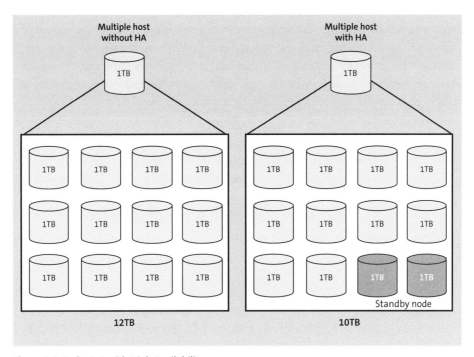

Figure 9.2 Scale-Out with High Availability

> **Note**
> The term "distributed system" is inherited from SAP NetWeaver vocabulary where a single-host installation contains both database and application server instances. To distribute the load, support more users, and improve performance, you can separate the database from the application server instance and add additional application server instances to support the primary application server. However, such a distributed system doesn't provide HA. Each instance is a single point of failure (SPOF). To make an SAP NetWeaver distributed system highly available, third-party cluster solutions need to be implemented for both database and application server tiers. This resembles SAP HANA system replication configurations. The nodes of a cluster are clones that are kept in sync. If one node fails, the other continues. Some configurations support multiple nodes to enhance both system performance and HA.

Data Distribution

Don't confuse an SAP HANA multiple-host system with a database cluster. The hosts of a distributed system aren't clones, but each stores a different part of the database in memory. This allows for efficient data distribution and minimizes any network latency effects. Tables that are often joined can be grouped together on a single host. You can dedicate tenant databases, tables, or table partitions to specific hosts or spread them across. You can group tables together and assign them to specific hosts. You can replicate master data tables to the hosts where fact tables reside, and this is all configurable. To obtain HA, all you need to do is assign worker and standby roles. The built-in host auto-failover feature will take care of the rest.

To reiterate, an SAP HANA distributed, scale-out, or multiple-host system provides scalability in terms of both data volume and user concurrency. Each host provides access to different tables or table partitions of the in-memory database. The hosts aren't compute clones. Data distribution is configurable and efficient. When a multiple-host system includes a standby host, it also provides HA.

For HA of a distributed system without standby hosts, or for even higher availability, you can implement SAP HANA system replication or, alternatively, third-party storage and operating system HA solutions. This type of replication works with both single-host and multiple-host systems, and they complement each other. Note that SAP HANA system replication also supports active/active configurations where both systems are accessible (in the industry this also referenced as a "hot" standby). This is covered in Chapter 12.

Host Auto-Failover

HA support for multiple-host systems is provided with the host auto-failover feature, which we'll explain in this section. Adding one or more standby hosts to a distributed system provides a local fault recovery solution. The services on the standby hosts are running but have no data loaded and don't accept any client requests. There is no "hot" standby concept for distributed systems, but installing additional systems on a standby host, for example, for testing or training, is supported while the host is in this passive role (the multi-SID/MCOS scenario).

Host Roles

To enable host auto-failover, each host in a multiple-host system is assigned to a role and a HA group. A host has either the worker or standby role, and when both are assigned to the same group, host auto-failover is triggered automatically (otherwise, manual intervention is required).

The worker-standby pair is available for the database, SAP HANA XS, and some of the optional components:

- SAP HANA database server: `worker`, `standby`
- SAP HANA XSA: `xs_worker`, `xs_standby`
- SAP HANA dynamic tiering: `extended_storage_worker`, `extended_storage_standby`
- SAP HANA accelerator for SAP ASE: `ets_worker`, `ets_standby`
- SAP HANA streaming analytics: `streaming`

It's possible to assign multiple roles to a single host, that is, `standby` combined with `xs_worker`, but not every combination is supported for production environments.

As you've already seen in Chapter 4, you can use the resident HDBLCM tool to add or remove host roles. However, before removing a host from a distributed system, you first need to redistribute the data, as explained later in this chapter

---

Learn More

Extended storage (ES) and extended transaction server (ETS) are internal code names for SAP HANA dynamic tiering and SAP HANA accelerator for SAP ASE, respectively. The same name is used for the service and configuration file, for example, *esserver.ini* and *esserver.ini*. HA for these optional components is documented separately and beyond the scope of the exam.

Host Groups

Host grouping enables assignment of hosts with the same role to a group with the same (or similar) configuration in terms of system resources, as shown in Figure 9.3. This is configured with the group installation parameter.

When undefined, all hosts belong to the same group default, but you can use names such as HA1 and HA2 to group together hosts with similar resource profiles. Although SAP HANA database hosts typically have identical hardware configuration, hosts dedicated to SAP HANA XSA may not. The same applies for hosts with SAP HANA dynamic tiering or SAP HANA accelerator for SAP ASE installed. These are automatically assigned to a separate (HA) group, with default names extended_ storage and ets, similar to the host role (although any other name can be used).

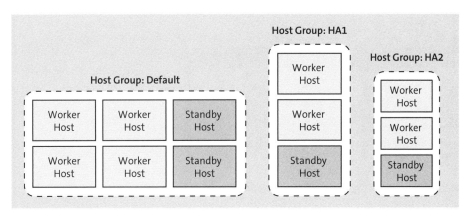

Figure 9.3 Host Groups

Extension Nodes

A special case of the host grouping concept is available for SAP BW/4HANA, SAP BW powered by SAP HANA, and for applications built with SAP HANA XS technology (native applications), as shown in Figure 9.4. An extension node is assigned to an extension group with zero, one, or more standby nodes. To configure a host as extension node, the installation parameter `workergroup=worker_dt` needs to be set. In all other configurations, the value for this parameter will be `default`.

The main objective isn't HA, however, but data tiering (hence, `worker_dt`) where you classify data according to how intensive it's being used, typically using a temperature analogy: hot, warm, and cold. In this configuration, the extension node is dedicated to warm data, that is, data that isn't frequently accessed, mainly for lookups, and only sporadically updated (see Figure 9.5). The illustration also shows the different hardware configurations used for the different groups.

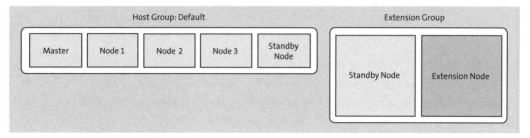

Figure 9.4 Extension Group

The generic hardware sizing guidelines for SAP HANA works with a RAM-to-storage ratio of 2:1. This means that a system with 8 TB physical memory can store up to 4 TB of data in memory. For extension nodes, the ratio is relaxed, and the amount of data loaded can be doubled or even quadrupled ("overloaded" to use a 1:1/1:2 ratio). As SAP BW controls data distribution, it's well suited for this configuration.

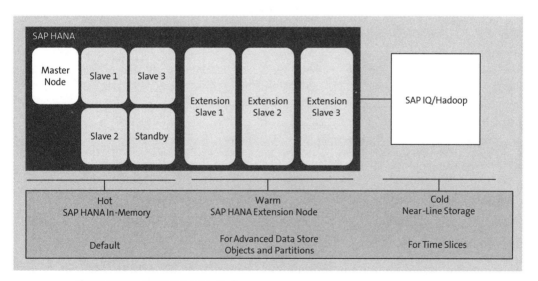

Figure 9.5 SAP HANA Extension Node

Failover

The active master name server process (hdbnameserver) verifies regularly the status of the other name server processes and of the watchdog service (hdbdaemon) In addition to this transmission control protocol (TCP) communication-based heartbeat, the active master name server also performs a storage-based heartbeat validation on the shared storage location and its own data volume storage. The master name servers in the slave role also perform a heartbeat check with the active master.

When both the name server and the watchdog of a host don't respond within defined thresholds, the host is considered inactive, and a failover is triggered, as shown in Figure 9.6. The host with a name server with role master 2 and the index server with the worker role fail. After failover, the index server of the standby host connects to the files of the index server of the failed host. The name server keeps the slave role. The index server switches roles from standby to slave. Exactly what role the name and index servers acquire depends on the configuration and the roles of the failed host.

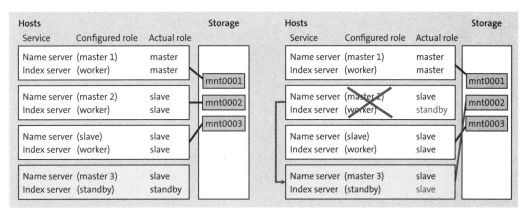

Figure 9.6 Host Auto-Failover

If host auto-failover isn't required, simplified storage configurations are supported as of SAP HANA 2.0 SPS 05 (see "SAP HANA – Storage Alternatives for HANA Scale-Out without Host Auto-Failover" at *http://s-prs.co/v507847*).

Multiple-Host System Architecture

Figure 9.7 illustrates how the system and tenant database hosts relate to SAP HANA hosts. The system database is hosted on a single host by the active master name server. As a reminder, the name server maintains the topology, which lists the hosts connected to the system, the services on each host, tenant databases, associated index servers, and more. You can configure up to three master name servers, but only one name server at a time can have the master role. The other master name servers have the slave role, just as any additional name server present on the system. They store a copy of the topology in memory, which can also be read by the index server processes.

The installer doesn't prompt you to assign a role to the name server. This is configured automatically. The first name server installed is the active master. The second and third host added also get the master role. Any additional host added configures the name server as slave. When a standby host is added to the system, the name server takes over the role of master 3, which we'll discuss later in this section.

Learn More

In tenant database systems, the topology no longer includes information about data distribution, that is, the location of tables and table partitions. This is stored in the catalog of tenant databases.

To view the topology, you can query the M_TOPOLOGY_TREE system view. To make changes, for example, to remove the SAP HANA XS engine service, you execute the ALTER SYSTEM ALTER CONFIGURATION statement against the *topology.ini* file. In SAP HANA, the topology only exists in memory. The file isn't persisted, although you can export the contents with command hdbnsutil -exportTopology.

To learn more, consult SAP Note 2606272 – HANA: How to Read Topology.

Tenant databases are hosted by the index server processes. You could have one tenant database per host (DB1) or a tenant spanning multiple hosts (DB2 and DB3). The index server is configured with the worker or standby role. The actual role is master, slave, or standby.

Figure 9.8 shows the architecture of a scale-out system mapped to persistence. You have the same three hosts but with a standby host added for HA. Only the master name server with master role of host 1 has access to the persistence of the system database, that is, the data and log volumes on shared storage. The name server services on host 2 and host 3 are running but without persistence. Each index server process is connected to its own persistence, even when the tenant database spans multiple hosts.

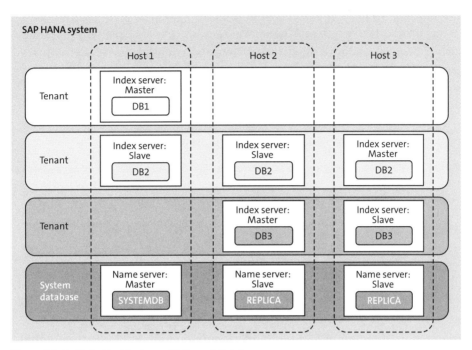

Figure 9.7 Multiple-Host System with Tenant Databases

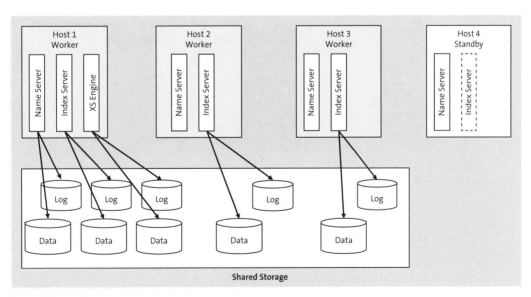

Figure 9.8 Architecture

Let's dig deeper into the key architecture components.

Recommended File System Layout

The multiple-host, scale-out configuration of a SAP HANA distributed system isn't a separately licensed option and doesn't come with complex configuration requirements. It's built in and even a single-host system is already prepared to morph into a scale-out system. What makes this possible is the file system layout, which is identical for both a single-host system and a multiple-host system. This is illustrated in Figure 9.9 with /usr/sap used as the path for the local system instance directory and <sapmnt> used as the path for shared files. Basis system administrators will recognize this pattern: it's similar to the pattern used by SAP NetWeaver. For SAP HANA, the default value of <sapmnt> is /hana/shared. The other "shared" mount points are for data and log volume directories.

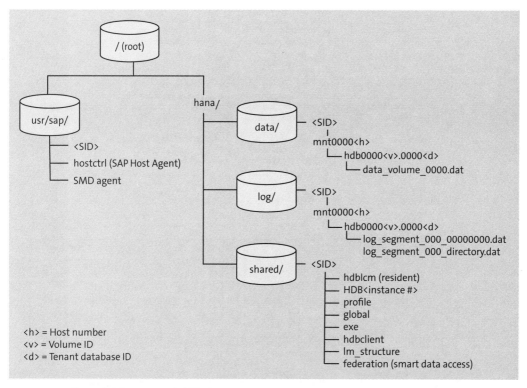

Figure 9.9 Recommended File System Layout

Local Files

The local directory /usr/sap/<SID> only stores files relevant to the local host, mainly log and trace files. You don't find any SAP HANA program files here (also known as executables or binaries) but instead pointers (symbolic links) to /hana/shared/<SID>. As a result, adding a host only involves the creation of the local directory structure. SAP HANA is already "installed" on the shared location.

One level up, so outside the realm of the <SID>, you also find the installation of SAP Host Agent and, when used, the Solution Manager Diagnostics (SMD) agent.

Shared Directories

In the /hana/shared directory (also referenced as the installation path <sapmnt>), the executables (exe), globally shared data, instance profiles, and configuration parameter files (ini) are stored. Here you also find shared components such as the resident HDBLCM and SAP HANA client. The shared directory needs to be accessible to all hosts. On Linux file systems, this is commonly achieved with mount points where the subdirectories /hana/shared, /hana/data, and /hana/shared point to different logical volumes. By default, the shared directory is also used for backups, but this should be updated to point to another location as a post-installation configuration step. The first backup activates automatic log backup, and this can quickly fill up the file system.

Note

The terms "local storage" and "shared storage" go back several decades and shouldn't be taken too literally in the age of cloud computing. Initially, the local path would be stored on direct attached storage (DAS), the magnetic hard disk drives (HDD), or later flash-based solid state drives (SSD) inside the computer/server/blade. As magnetic disks are fragile and DAS difficult to centrally manage, over time, network attached storage (NAS) or storage area networks (SAN) were used even for local storage. A logical "disk" or volume would be created over a large number of physical drives in a redundant array of independent (or inexpensive) disks (RAID) configuration to provide better performance and protection against failure. Only the boot volume and temporary storage were kept on DAS. Both the local and shared storage would be mounted pointing to a central storage area. You see the same concept implemented with virtualization, separating ephemeral storage for the boot disk and shared storage with persistency for user data. Conceptually, however, remember that shared storage is shared among the host of a distributed system, whereas local storage isn't.

Just like you can put the local directory on a shared volume, for a single-host system, you can also put the shared directory on DAS. SAP HANA, express edition, as a VM distribution is installed on a single (virtual) disk and both /usr/sap and /hana/shared and the database directories are "local."

Storage Configuration

Shared storage can be configured differently, and, for this, SAP relies on its hardware partners. Technical implementation details are beyond the scope of the exam, but you should be familiar with the concepts.

The following options are available:

- **NAS with NFS**
  As the /hana/shared directory mainly stores executable and configuration files, this location gets little traffic, mainly read. Storing <sapmnt> on a NAS with Network File System (NFS) is a common choice with dedicated Ethernet, as shown in Figure 9.10. There are no issues with concurrent file access and no stringent performance requirements.

Host auto-failover requires special consideration to avoid data corruptions when both the standby and the failed hosts can access the same files. A "fencing" mechanism is implemented to achieve this.

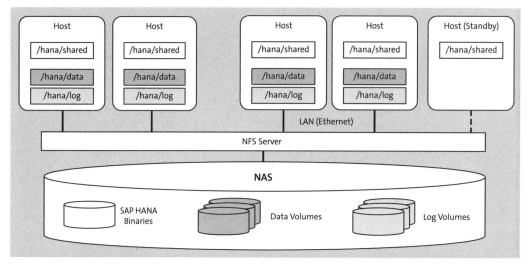

Figure 9.10 NFS

- **SAN**

  NFS implements a client/server protocol, and although all hosts access storage using dedicated Ethernet, this may not match the required performance requirements for the data and log volumes. For this reason, the "database" is often stored on a SAN. Instead of a file system, block storage is used, and the hosts are connected to storage with a fiber channel. This configuration is illustrated in Figure 9.11. Note that the binaries can remain on the file system of the NAS.

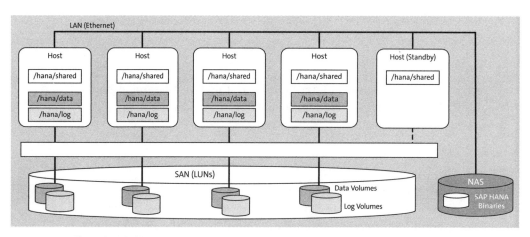

Figure 9.11 SAN

Figure 9.10 and Figure 9.11 show the general concept of NAS and SAN, respectively. How exactly this is implemented depends on the storage vendor. Alternatives exist such as IBM Spectrum Scale (previously General Parallel File System [GPFS]), which implements a clustered file system, as shown in Figure 9.12. The nodes can be SAN-attached, NAS-attached, or a combination, but shared nothing cluster configurations are also possible. IBM Spectrum Scale is sometimes compared to Hadoop Distributed File System (HDFS), although there are many differences.

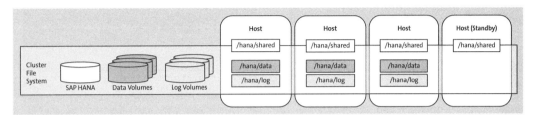

Figure 9.12 Cluster File System

Learn More

For more information, see "SAP HANA TDI – Storage Requirements" (2017) at *http://s-prs.co/v507848*. Implementation details are beyond the scope of the exam.

In addition, each vendor provides additional documentation about how to implement the shared storage for multiple-host systems. All third-party vendor documentation is beyond the scope of the exam.

Storage Connector

For SAN configurations, SAP HANA provides a storage connector API with a fiber channel protocol controlling the mapping of each persistence on the data and log volume areas to a LUN on the SAN. The API supports host auto-failover by updating the LUN-to-host mapping and is typically used in combination with the HA/DR providers.

You use the installation parameter `storage_cfg` to point to location where a *global.ini* file is located. With this configuration, the storage connector enables SAP HANA to use hardware vendor-specific scripts for automated resource allocation and input/output (I/O) fencing during failover. Figure 9.13 shows an implementation example from IBM.

I/O fencing guarantees that only a single host can access the files in the data or log volume areas. This is also implemented through the SAP HANA storage connector API. Although this is vendor-specific, the STONITH call ("shoot the other node in the head") forces a reboot of one of the hosts to avoid parallel reading and writing from different hosts.

Example C-2 A global.ini file to be used at installation time for using the logical volume manager storage connector

```
# cat /hana/shared/global.ini
[storage]
ha_provider = hdb_ha.fcClientLVM
partition_1_data__lvmname = hanadata01-datalv01
partition_1_log__lvmname = hanalog01-loglv01
partition_2_data__lvmname = hanadata02-datalv02
partition_2_log__lvmname = hanalog02-loglv02
partition_3_data__lvmname = hanadata03-datalv03
partition_3_log__lvmname = hanalog03-loglv03

partition_*_*__prtype = 5
partition_*_*__mountoptions = -t xfs
```

Figure 9.13 Storage Configuration

Learn More

Refer to SAP Note 1900823 – SAP HANA Storage Connector API for information specific to the storage connector API, which is beyond the exam's scope.

In addition, each vendor provides additional documentation about the implementation. All third-party vendor documentation is beyond the scope of the exam.

Transparent Client Failover

When host auto-failover is executed, client connections to the failed host are interrupted. There are two approaches to make this transparent to the client, that is, to make the failover pass unnoticed, although they aren't mutually exclusive. One solution is network-based and involves IP or domain name server (DNS) redirection.

With IP redirection, each SAP HANA host will have a virtual IP address assigned, and when the name server triggers a host auto-failover from the failed host to the standby host, it also triggers a virtual IP switch. The mechanism that makes this possible is called the HA/DR provider (see the next section). For DNS redirection, this works the same way. An advantage of network-based solution is its central configuration. You don't need to make client-side changes. A disadvantage is that due to caching and client-side configurations (e.g., TCP keepalive settings), it takes some time before the client connection information is refreshed. IP redirection is typically used in the local area network (LAN or L2), while DNS redirection is more suitable to the wide area network (WAN or L3).

Alternatively, you can configure failover with client libraries. This is supported with industry standard ODBC/JDBC, with SAP proprietary SQL Database Connectivity (SQLDBC) clients, and the SAP HANA client secure user store (hdbuserstore).

Instead of specifying a single host in the connect string, all three hosts with a name server with master role are listed. Should the active master no longer respond, the client will attempt to connect to the next host from the list. When all hosts listed don't respond, only then is an error returned.

Here is a sample connect string for a JDBC connection:

```
jdbc:sap://host1:30015;host2:30015;host3:30015/
```

Host roles and failover groups can be configured for SAP HANA XSA. For the SAP HANA XS, classic model web applications, HTTP load balancing can be configured by adding the master name server list to the SAP Web Dispatcher configuration.

HA/DR Provider

The name server provides a Python-based API that can be called during specific events, for example, host auto-failover (or system replication takeover) to perform additional activities, such as switching a virtual IP address or shutting down a test system on the standby host. The code executed by the name server during these operations contains "hooks" where the HA/DR provider code can be executed.

HA/DR providers, or hooks, if you prefer, are configured by adding a section [ha_dr_provider_<name>] to the *global.ini* configuration file containing the name, path, and execution order Listing 9.1 serves as an example. The path of the provider points to the Python script file for the name server to call.

```
[ha_dr_provider_vIPSwitch]
provider = vIPSwitch
path = /hana/shared/vIPSwitch.py
execution_order = 50
```
Listing 9.1 HA/DR Provider Configuration

These setting are loaded during startup. To update the name server configuration without restart, you can use the following command:

```
hdbnsutil -reloadHADRProviders
```

Learn More

Refer to the SAP HANA Administration Guide, specifically the "Implementing a HA/DR Provider" section, for more information and sample code for vIPMover and mySTONITH hooks.

SAP Landscape Management implements HA/DR providers to automate SAP HANA system replication activities such as takeovers. For additional information, see KBA 2699428 – SAP Landscape Management HA/DR Hook.

Inter-Service Communication

SAP HANA services communicate using IP addresses. For a single-host configuration, the services are bound to the loopback interface, also known as the local host with IP address 127.0.0.1. The inter-service communication is configured with system parameter global.ini/[communication]/listeninterface = .local.

For a distributed system, the listen interface parameter needs to be set to either .internal or .global. The internal setting is recommended and assumes a dedicated network. This requires an additional section in the global parameter file, [internal_hostname_resolution], with the local IP address and (virtual) host name of the hosts as parameters. When the global setting is used, SAP recommends securing communication with TLS (SSL) and a firewall.

Inter-service communication can be configured during installation or as a post-installation activity using the resident HDBLCM (as root), as shown in Figure 9.14.

```
SAP HANA Lifecycle Management - SAP HANA Database 2.00.040.00.1553674765
**************************************************************************

Enter System Administrator Password (mhsadm):

Select Inter-Service Communication

  Index | Inter-Service Communication | Description
  ------------------------------------------------------------------------------------------------
  1     | global                      | The HANA services will listen on all network interfaces
  2     | internal                    | The HANA services will only listen on a specific network interface
  3     | local                       | The HANA services will only listen on loopback interface (127.0.0.1)

The recommended value for single-host system is 'local'
Select Inter-Service Communication / Enter Index [3]: 2

  Index | Internal Network Address
  --------------------------------
  1     | 10.22.112/22

It is recommended to select network address, which is part of an internal network
Select Internal Network Address / Enter Index [1]:

Summary before execution:
=========================

SAP HANA Database
   Installation Parameters
      Remote Execution: ssh
      Execution Scope: system
      Inter-Service Communication: internal
      Internal Network Address: 10.22.112/22
   Log File Locations
      Log directory: /var/tmp/hdb_MHS_hdblcm_configure_internal_network_2020-07-20_11.26.59
      Trace location: /var/tmp/hdblcm_2020-07-20_11.26.59_8957.trc

Note: The SAP HANA Database System will be restarted
Note: The SAP HANA Database System will be restarted

Do you want to continue? (y/n): █
```

Figure 9.14 Inter-Service Communication

With the Monitor Network app in SAP HANA cockpit, you can monitor the network traffic between hosts (**Network Traffic** tab). In addition, the app enables you to measure the network speed and displays the network communication used, as shown in Figure 9.15.

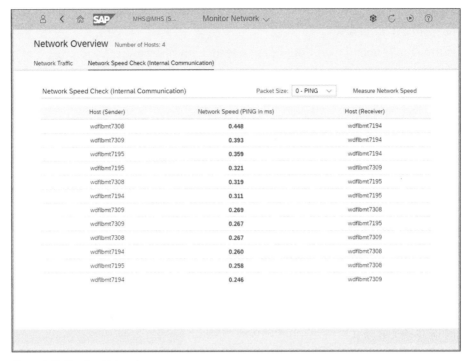

Figure 9.15 Monitor Network

Multiple-Host Installation

We've already covered SAP HANA installation, preparation, and post-installation steps in detail in Chapter 3 and Chapter 4. Apart from the storage and inter-service configuration, there is very little to add for multiple-host installations. There's no special software to download or tools required. You use the same HDBLCM tool for both single-host and multiple-host installations, as you'll see in the following sections.

New Installation

Installing a multiple-host system is almost identical to a single-host installation. Regarding user accounts, the same principles apply. For a multiple-host installation, note the following requirements:

- Although it's a requirement to perform the installation connected as the root user, you can set the root_user parameter if root has been disabled. You can pass installation parameters on the command line (interactive mode) or using the installation parameter file. The password for the root or equivalent user must be identical on all hosts.

- During the installation, the operating system administrator (`<sid>adm`) user and the SAP Host Agent `sapadm` user are created. For the optional components, such as SAP HANA data tiering, additional users will be created. To match corporate user account security requirements, these users can be created prior to the installation. The installer won't modify the user properties in this case.

To start the installation, run the `hdblcm` command from the installation medium, for example, `<install>/DATA_UNITS/HDB_LCM_LINUX_X86_64` (for IBM Power Systems, replace `X86_64` with `PPC64`).

As a reminder, the installation medium also includes a graphical installer for systems with a graphical X Window System environment. This might be available on training environments but typically not on hardened production systems.

You'll be prompted to complete the following steps. The values between square brackets indicate the default values (e.g., [default]):

1. Select the **Install** action.
2. Indicate which additional components to install, such as SAP HANA client.
3. Enter the installation path [`<sapmnt>`].
4. Confirm (or change) the local host name.
5. Indicate if you want to add hosts to the system. With yes, the single-host installation becomes a multiple-host installation.
6. Fill in the following parameters:
   - Enter comma-separated host names to add.
   - Enter root user name "[root]/password".
   - Select roles [worker].
   - Enter host failover group [default].
   - Enter storage partition number (assigns automatically).
   - Enter worker group [default].

The rest of the dialogs are identical, such as system administrator passwords and system properties (SID, instance number, login shell, etc.).

Figure 9.16 shows the multiple-host system type installation dialog. **Hostname** and **Role** are required parameters; **High-Availability Group**, **Worker Group**, and **Storage Partition** are optional.

SAP HANA 2.0 SPS 05: What's New?

As of SAP HANA 2.0 SPS 05, productive use of the local secure store (LSS) is supported. To enable installation of the store, the installation path must be created manually prior to the installation and mounted on all hosts (e.g., `/lss/shared/`).

To activate LSS during installation, run HDBLCM with the parameter `secure_store=localsecurestore`.

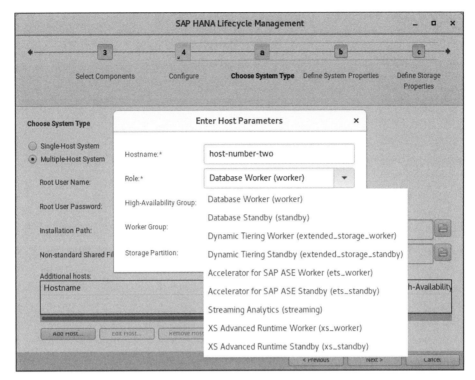

Figure 9.16 SAP HANA Lifecycle Management: Enter Host Parameters

Add/Remove Host

To add or remove a host from a distributed system, use the resident version of SAP HANA HDBLCM located on `<sapmnt>/<SID>/hdblcm`.

To add multiple-hosts in parallel to a system, the host running HDBLCM needs to be "integrated," that is, part of the distributed system. You see this illustrated in Figure 9.17 in the command-line version of the tool. A nonintegrated host can join a distributed system but can't add other hosts in parallel until it has first joined.

Installing a distributed system only takes slightly longer than installing a single-host system. Because hosts are added in parallel, installing a 2-, 5-, or 10-host system makes no significant difference in duration.

The prompts of the tool to add a host are identical to the ones for installation. The values between square brackets indicate the default values (e.g., [default]):

1. Choose an action [add_host].
2. Enter comma-separated host names to add. For each host:
   - Enter root user name [root] with password.
   - Select roles: [worker].

  - Enter host failover group: [default].
  - Enter storage partition number (assigns automatically).
  - Enter worker group: [default].
3. Enter passwords for the `<sid>adm` and SAP Host Agent user.

```
Adding Remote Hosts to the SAP HANA Database System
  Adding 3 additional hosts in parallel
  Adding host 'wdflbmt7195'...
  Adding host 'wdflbmt7309'...
  Adding host 'wdflbmt7308'...
    wdflbmt7308:  Adding host 'wdflbmt7308' to instance '00'...
    wdflbmt7309:  Adding host 'wdflbmt7309' to instance '00'...
    wdflbmt7195:  Adding host 'wdflbmt7195' to instance '00'...
    wdflbmt7309:  Starting SAP HANA Database...
    wdflbmt7308:  Starting SAP HANA Database...
    wdflbmt7195:  Starting SAP HANA Database...
    wdflbmt7309:    Starting 4 processes on host 'wdflbmt7309' (worker):
    wdflbmt7309:      Starting on 'wdflbmt7309' (worker): hdbdaemon, hdbcompileserver, hdbnameserver, hdbpreproc
essor
    wdflbmt7308:    Starting 1 process on host 'wdflbmt7308' (worker):
    wdflbmt7308:      Starting on 'wdflbmt7308' (worker): hdbdaemon
    wdflbmt7195:    Starting 1 process on host 'wdflbmt7195' (worker):
    wdflbmt7195:      Starting on 'wdflbmt7195' (worker): hdbdaemon
    wdflbmt7308:    Starting 4 processes on host 'wdflbmt7308' (worker):
    wdflbmt7308:      Starting on 'wdflbmt7308' (worker): hdbdaemon, hdbcompileserver, hdbnameserver, hdbpreproc
essor
    wdflbmt7195:    Starting 4 processes on host 'wdflbmt7195' (worker):
    wdflbmt7195:      Starting on 'wdflbmt7195' (worker): hdbdaemon, hdbcompileserver, hdbnameserver, hdbpreproc
essor
    wdflbmt7309:    Starting 5 processes on host 'wdflbmt7309' (worker):
    wdflbmt7309:      Starting on 'wdflbmt7309' (worker): hdbdaemon, hdbcompileserver, hdbpreprocessor, hdbwebdi
spatcher, hdbindexserver (MHS)
    wdflbmt7308:    Starting 5 processes on host 'wdflbmt7308' (worker):
    wdflbmt7308:      Starting on 'wdflbmt7308' (worker): hdbdaemon, hdbcompileserver, hdbpreprocessor, hdbwebdi
spatcher, hdbindexserver (MHS)
    wdflbmt7195:    Starting 5 processes on host 'wdflbmt7195' (worker):
    wdflbmt7195:      Starting on 'wdflbmt7195' (worker): hdbdaemon, hdbcompileserver, hdbpreprocessor, hdbwebdi
spatcher, hdbindexserver (MHS)
    wdflbmt7309:      Starting on 'wdflbmt7309' (worker): hdbdaemon, hdbwebdispatcher, hdbindexserver (MHS)
    wdflbmt7308:      Starting on 'wdflbmt7308' (worker): hdbdaemon, hdbwebdispatcher, hdbindexserver (MHS)
    wdflbmt7195:      Starting on 'wdflbmt7195' (worker): hdbdaemon, hdbwebdispatcher, hdbindexserver (MHS)
    wdflbmt7195:      Starting on 'wdflbmt7195' (worker): hdbdaemon, hdbwebdispatcher
    wdflbmt7309:      Starting on 'wdflbmt7309' (worker): hdbdaemon, hdbwebdispatcher
    wdflbmt7308:      Starting on 'wdflbmt7308' (worker): hdbdaemon, hdbwebdispatcher
    wdflbmt7195:      All server processes started on host 'wdflbmt7195' (worker).
```

Figure 9.17 HDBLCM: Add Host

Before you can add a host to a single-host system, you first need to configure the inter-service communication from local to internal or global using the same HDBLCM tool. This isn't performed automatically or integrated in the add host action.

Before you can remove a host, you first need to change the host roles of the services, mark the host as inactive, and redistribute data, as described in this section. When this activity is executed, you can use the resident HDBLCM tool again with its choice of command-line, graphical, or web interface options (Figure 9.18 depicts the web interface option). The dialogs are the same.

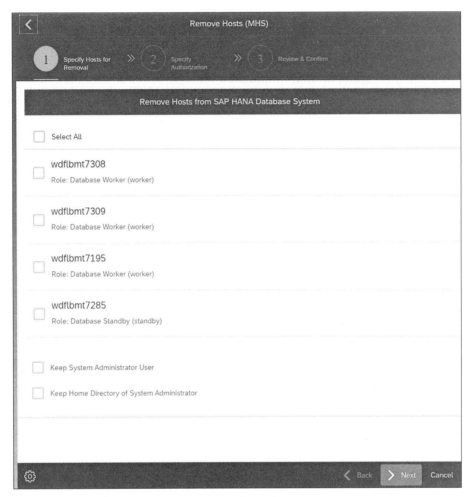

Figure 9.18 SAP HANA Database Management: Web Interface

Configure Host Failover in SAP HANA Cockpit

The initial host role is set during the installation, but this can be changed at any moment either by using the Host Failover app of SAP HANA cockpit or the ALTER SYSTEM ALTER CONFIGURATION statement. Both require the following authorizations:

- RESOURCE ADMIN system privilege
- UPDATE_LANDSCAPE_CONFIGURATION (procedure), EXECUTE privilege

The most common reason to change service roles is to move hosts from the system (also described as "landscape"). The steps are as follows:

1. Change the role of the name server to slave.
2. Change the role of the index servers to standby.
3. Stop the instance (sapcontrol).
4. Remove the host (hdblcm).

In SQL, for example, to change the active master, use the following command:

```
ALTER SYSTEM ALTER CONFIGURATION ( 'nameserver.ini' , 'SYSTEM' )
  SET ('landscape', 'active_master') = '<host>:<port>' WITH RECONFIGURE;
```

Note that the port to use is the internal TCP port, not the SQL port.

The configured and actual role of the services is displayed in SAP HANA cockpit as shown in Figure 9.19. The **Remove Status** column shows the progress of the host removal. Host removal is only possible with the **Reorg finished** status or **Reorg not required** status.

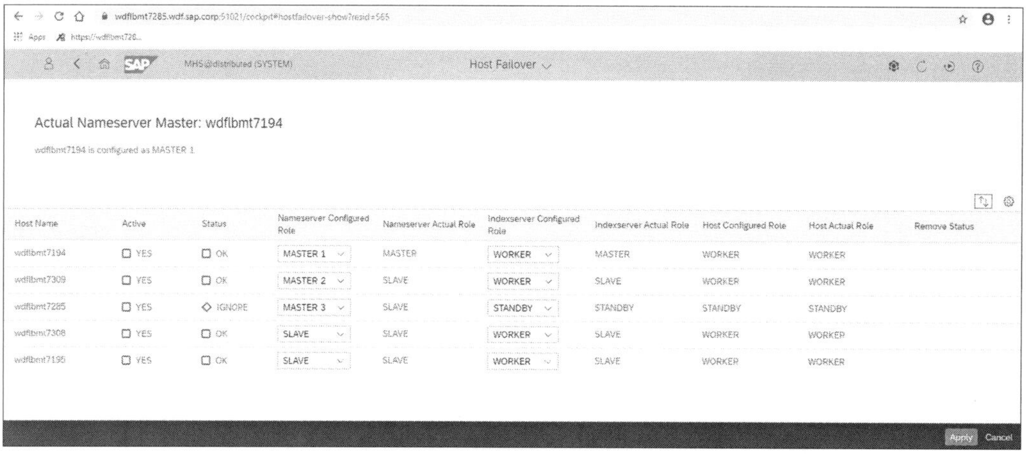

Figure 9.19 SAP HANA Cockpit: Host Failover

Note that the standby host has the name server configured role **MASTER 3**. This configuration is performed automatically when a host is added as first standby.

On the command line, the Python support script `landscapeHostConfiguration.py` provides the same output, as shown in Figure 9.20. The return code can be used for automation. Return code 4 returns OK, but 0, 1, and 2, for example, indicate fatal, error, and warning, respectively, to block any future actions.

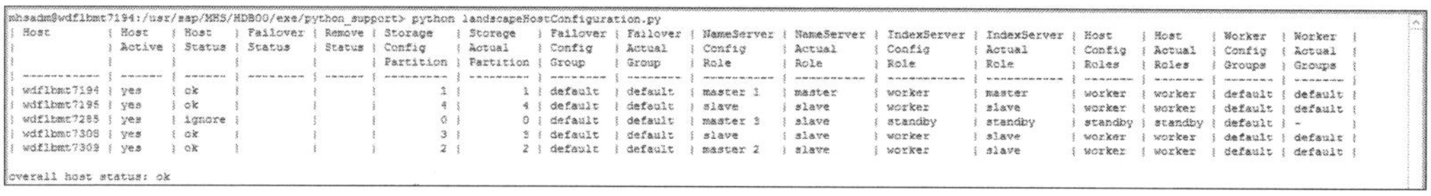

```
mhsadm@wdflbmt7194:/usr/sap/MHS/HDB00/exe/python_support> python landscapeHostConfiguration.py
| Host        | Host   | Host   | Failover | Remove | Storage   | Storage   | Failover | Failover | NameServer | NameServer | IndexServer | IndexServer | Host    | Host    | Worker  | Worker  |
|             | Active | Status | Status   | Status | Config    | Actual    | Config   | Actual   | Config     | Actual     | Config      | Actual      | Config  | Actual  | Config  | Actual  |
|             |        |        |          |        | Partition | Partition | Group    | Group    | Role       | Role       | Role        | Role        | Roles   | Roles   | Groups  | Groups  |
| ----------- | ------ | ------ | -------- | ------ | --------- | --------- | -------- | -------- | ---------- | ---------- | ----------- | ----------- | ------- | ------- | ------- | ------- |
| wdflbmt7194 | yes    | ok     |          |        |         1 |         1 | default  | default  | master 1   | master     | worker      | master      | worker  | worker  | default | default |
| wdflbmt7195 | yes    | ok     |          |        |         4 |         4 | default  | default  | slave      | slave      | worker      | slave       | worker  | worker  | default | default |
| wdflbmt7285 | yes    | ignore |          |        |         0 |         0 | default  | default  | master 3   | slave      | standby     | standby     | standby | standby | default | -       |
| wdflbmt7308 | yes    | ok     |          |        |         3 |         3 | default  | default  | slave      | slave      | worker      | slave       | worker  | worker  | default | default |
| wdflbmt7309 | yes    | ok     |          |        |         2 |         2 | default  | default  | master 2   | slave      | worker      | slave       | worker  | worker  | default | default |

overall host status: ok
```

Figure 9.20 Python Script landscapeHostConfiguration.py

Manage Services in SAP HANA Cockpit

System and database management for multiple-host systems is identical to that of a single host. Table management, of course, is a different story, and we'll cover this in the next section.

Figure 9.21 shows a multiple-host system in the Manage Services app of SAP HANA cockpit. It displays the different services for each host and also shows the services with the active master roles. Note that there is a column for the (internal) TCP **Port** and for the **SQL Port**. Database clients (JDBC/ODBC, SAP HANA studio, SAP HANA cockpit) connect with the SQL port. Inter-service communication uses the (internal) TCP port. This port is relevant for data distribution operations such as moving a table from one host to another.

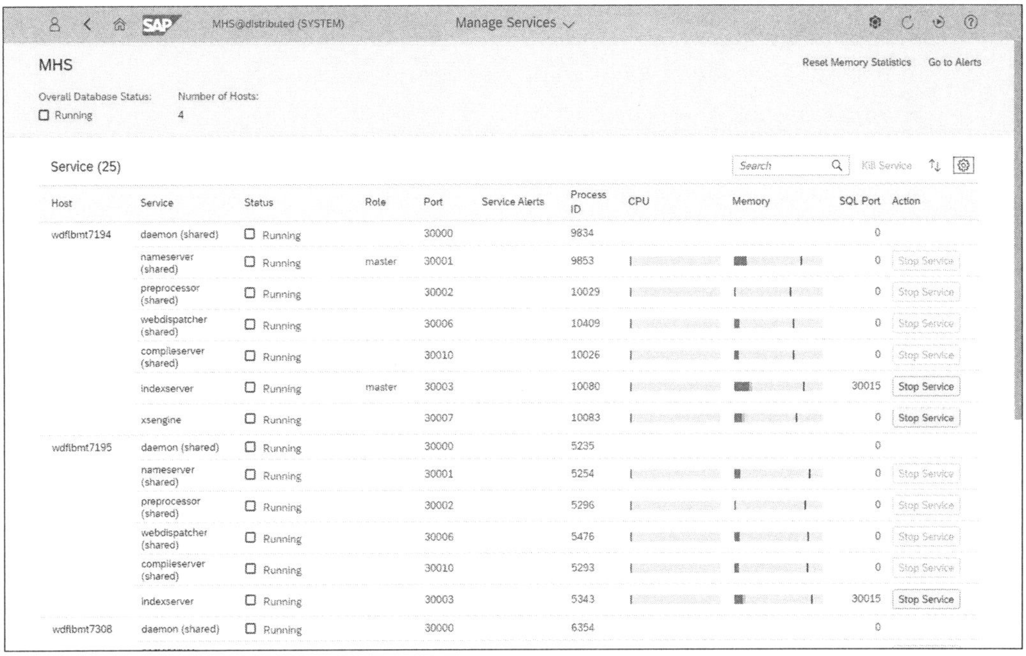

Figure 9.21 Manage Services

Data Distribution

The hosts in a scale-out, multiple-host, distributed system aren't identical clones but store different tables and table partitions. The location of these tables and table partitions may impact query response times, for example, when all involved tables are located on the same or many different hosts. Over time, as the database grows, you may need to add a host and redistribute tables.

The following data distribution options are available:

- **Table partitioning**
  Separate large tables into partitions and divide partitions across hosts.
- **Table placement**
  Assign specific tables to specific hosts.
- **Table replication**
  Replicate small (row) tables containing master data across hosts for joining with large fact tables.

We'll discuss each in the following sections, as well as the Table Distribution app in SAP HANA cockpit and associated SQL commands.

Table Partitioning

To partition is to divide something into parts. Table partitioning enables you to split column-store tables into smaller subtables. Some of the possible motivations are as follows:

- **Load balancing**
  Instead of one server, have multiple servers respond to a request.

- **Parallelization**
  Instead of a single thread, have multiple threads process a query.

- **Overcome size limitation**
  The number of records in a table can't exceed 2^31 (2 billion), but each table supports up to 16,000 partitions, which each again can store 2 billion rows.

- **Partition pruning**
  The WHERE clause evaluation quickly excludes partitions; there's no need to load and scan the whole table first.

- **Delta merge performance improvements**
  Only the main index of changed partitions needs to be merged, not the whole table.

- **Explicit partition handling**
  Applications can leverage partitioning to manage data more effectively.

Note that apart from load-balancing, these advantages also apply to single-host systems. Data distribution with partitioning isn't exclusive to distributed systems.

The following partition operations are supported:

- Split a single table into partitions.
- Merge all partitions into a single table.
- Repartition a table via the following methods:
  - Changing the partitioning specification
  - Changing the partitioning columns
  - Changing the number of partitions

For large tables, these operations are very time-consuming, cause high memory usage, and generate a redo log.

Let's explore some key concepts that fall within table partitioning.

Data Manipulation Language and Data Definition Language

Partitioning is transparent to the client application because the data manipulation language (DML) statements remain unaltered. For those that need an SQL refresher, DML encompasses `SELECT`, `INSERT`, `UPDATE`, and `DELETE` commands in SQL. Only the data definition language (DDL) changes to support the following:

- Create table partition
- Repartition tables
- Merge partitions to one table
- Add/delete partitions
- Move partitions to other hosts
- Delta merge partitions

> **Learn More**
>
> For information about the SQL syntax and all the options, see the SAP HANA SQL Reference Guide.

Single-Level Partitioning

SAP HANA supports three partitioning specifications: single-level, multilevel, and heterogenous. In this section, we'll begin with single-level partitioning.

Following are the single-level partitioning specifications:

- **Round-robin**
  Round-robin partitioning doesn't require a partition column with rows assigned on a rotation basis. A side effect is that this makes partition pruning impossible.

- **Hash**
  Hash partitioning applies a hash function to the specified columns to randomly distribute the rows. Optionally, with the `AT LOCATION` clause, specific partitions can be assigned to specific hosts. An example hash partition is as follows:
  ```
  CREATE COLUMN TABLE T (c1 INT, c2 VARCHAR, PRIMARY KEY (c1))
      PARTITION BY HASH (c1) PARTITIONS 8
  ```

- **Range**
  Range partitioning divides the table according to predefined ranges (date, product, location), which, unlike hash and round-robin, requires detailed knowledge of the contents of the table. As certain date ranges or other range criteria may be more often queried than others, range partitioning is less suited for load balancing, so multilevel partitioning is typically applied. Figure 9.22 shows an `ALTER TABLE` statement converting a column table into a partitioned table.

The partitioning column must be part of the primary key, a requirement shared with hash partitioning. Round-robin partitioning is the opposite, as it doesn't support tables with primary keys.

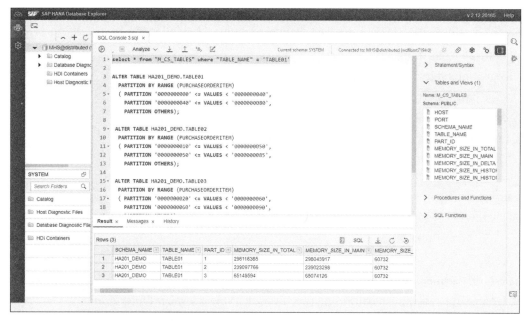

Figure 9.22 Range Partitioning

Multilevel Partitioning

To overcome the primary key requirement limitation, you can implement multi-level partitioning as a primary key inclusion isn't required at the second level.

Supported specifications are as follows:

- Round-robin/range
- Hash/range
- Hash/hash
- Range/range

Hash/range partitioning is the most common type and implements load balancing at the first level and fine-tuned control at the second level, as shown in Figure 9.23.

Time-based partitioning (month or year) with range at the second level is particularly effective to reduce the time required for delta merge operations as old data is typically no longer (or infrequently) changed.

Time-based partitioning is also a classic use case for partition pruning by the Data Distribution Optimizer tool. Static partition pruning is based on the partition definition. Dynamic partition pruning is content-based and takes place at runtime. This requires up-to-date statistics using the CREATE STATISTICS command and the setting indexserver.ini/[query_mediator]/use_dynamic_pruning=true.

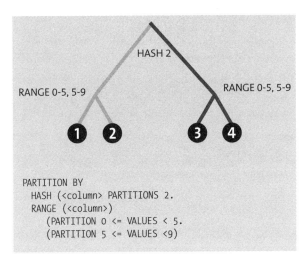

Figure 9.23 Multilevel Partitioning

Heterogeneous Partitioning

For range/range and hash/hash multilevel partitioning specifications, heterogeneous partitioning is supported using the SUBPARTITION BY clause. This allows you to define different second-level ranges for each of the partitions. The default (balanced) partitioning schema uses the same second-level range.

Heterogeneous partitioning makes it possible to define multistore tables that are partly stored in SAP HANA and partly stored in the extended storage of SAP HANA dynamic tiering.

Explicit Partition Handling for Range Partitioning

Range partitions (single or multilevel) allow for explicit handling, that is, partitions can be added and dropped, as follows:

```
ALTER TABLE T ADD PARTITION OTHERS
```

You can even automate explicit partition handling by activating dynamic range partition using the DYNAMIC clause, for example, to avoid the OTHERS partition from getting too large. You can specify a maximum row count as part of the statement as follows:

```
ALTER TABLE T ADD PARTITION OTHERS DYNAMIC THRESHOLD 1000
```

Alternatively, dynamic range partitioning can also be controlled using system parameters dynamic_range_default_threshold and dynamic_range_check_time_interval_sec.

Designing Partitions and Best Practices

What's the best approach to designing partitions? It depends. SAP documents the query performance, DML performance, data lifecycle, partition size, table design, and other considerations for partition design, but you're also informed not to interfere with SAP BW partitioning on SAP HANA as the partition management is done at the application level. For SAP Business Suite, yet other recommendations apply.

Examples include the following (the list is long):

- Use partitioning columns that are used in WHERE clauses.
- Use hash partitioning for the first level, especially in scale-out scenarios, to enable client-side pruning.
- Avoid defining unique constraints on a partitioned table.
- Avoid splitting or merging tables.

In addition, there are a few general best practices to keep in mind:

- Use as few partitioned tables as possible.
- Use as few partitions as possible.
- Use as few partitions key columns as possible.
- When repartitioning, use a factor 2 multiple or divider to enable parallelization.

Partitioning can be complex and requires some consideration before implementation.

Learn More

Table partitioning is documented in the SAP HANA Administration Guide in the Managing Tables chapter.

For a more complete list of partitioning scenarios, see the FAQ within KBA 2044468 – FAQ: SAP HANA Partitioning. This KBA complements the documentation with relevant additional information. Although most of the information will be out of scope of the exam, we recommend taking note.

Table Placement

Normalization goes back to the origins of the relational database. To reduce data redundancy and improve data integrity, you don't store all data in one big table but use separate tables instead with primary and foreign keys defining the relation: one table for books, one for students, and a third to keep track of which student borrowed which book. These tables are often joined together, but the relation is defined in the application code. Table classification makes it possible to "push down" this semantic information to the SAP HANA database by defining table groups. This is relevant for both table partitioning and table placement. For example, for distributed systems, table placement enables you to store tables that belong to the same group together on the same host.

Using SQL, you can define the table group, group type, and subtype with the GROUP NAME, GROUP TYPE, and GROUP SUBTYPE clauses from the CREATE and ALTER TABLE statements. You can also set the group leading table, which defaults to the largest, nonpartitioned, nonreplicated column store table. This information is stored in table TABLE_GROUPS.

The following example is from the SAP BW data store object:

```
ALTER TABLE SAMPLE SET GROUP NAME ZFIGL GROUP TYPE sap.bw.dso
  GROUP SUBTYPE ACTIVE GROUP LEAD;
```

The table classification information (name, type, and subtype) is also recorded in TABLE_PLACEMENTS together with partitioning and location rules:

- MIN_ROWS_FOR_PARTITIONING
  Minimum number of records before a partition is created.
- INITIAL_PARTITIONS
  The number of initial partitions to create.
- REPARTITIONING_THRESHOLDS
  Controls partition splits.
- DYNAMIC_RANGE_THRESHOLDS
  Overrules the default set with the corresponding system parameter.
- SAME_PARTITION_COUNT
  Overrules the corresponding system parameter that controls the number of partitions per table.
- LOCATION
  Master, slave, all (worker group "default").

The M_EFFECTIVE_TABLE_PLACEMENT view shows the result of rules when applied to a table. The table placement rules control partitioning and are applied during redistribution or system migration. As tables grow over time, table redistribution needs to be reconsidered from time to time. Repartitioning is required when the 2 billion row limit comes into view.

SAP HANA table redistribution and the SAP HANA data warehousing foundation Data Distribution Optimizer tool use this information to calculate the most optimal data distribution for a system. This is done in two stages:

1. Generate a distribution plan.
2. Execute the plan.

Learn More

How to partition and configure table distribution for SAP S/4HANA and SAP BW/4HANA (and SAP Business Suite powered by SAP HANA and SAP BW powered by SAP HANA) is documented as scenarios in a corresponding SAP Note with SQL scripts attached. Manual table distribution (DIY) isn't recommended in these scenarios. As an example beyond the scope of the exam, see the notes for SAP Business Suite and SAP BW:

- SAP Note 2334091 – BW/4HANA: Table Placement and Landscape Redistribution
- SAP Note 2408419 – SAP S/4HANA: Multi-Node Support

Table Replication

For those tables that are joined often yet change little, you can use table replication to create a replica for every host or a selection of hosts. This can improve performance on multiple-host systems. There are two approaches: optimistic synchronous table replication (OSTR) and asynchronous table replication (ASR). OSTR was introduced with SAP HANA 2.0 and is the preferred approach because the source and target table are in sync. It's not required to replicate the entire table because subtable replication is also supported.

Although OSTR may present stale table date, this replication mode also has its advantages. It supports, for example, replicating data from row store tables to column store replicas, which may improve join performance for analytics workloads. ASR also supports to replicate only selected partitions of aging tables, which allows you to dynamically only replicate "hot" data and not the entire table.

The REPLICA AT LOCATION 'host' | ALL LOCATIONS clause of the CREATE and ALTER TABLE statement defines table replicas.

When replicating partitioned tables, you can define different partitioning schemes for the source and target tables. Figure 9.24 illustrates this concept with the source table partitioned by range based on the primary key, and the replica partitioned by hash based on the foreign key. This results in both source and replica partitions on the same host. Each server hosts three partitions.

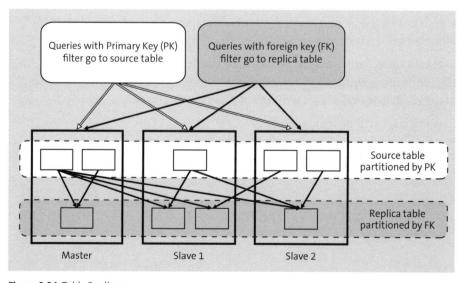

Figure 9.24 Table Replicas

Learn More

Table placement, table replication, and redistributing tables in a distributed SAP HANA system are documented in the SAP HANA Administration Guide, in the Managing Tables chapter.

For additional information on this topic, see the following FAQs. These KBAs complement the documentation with relevant additional information. Although most of the information will be out of scope of the exam, we recommend taking note.

- KBA 2081591 – FAQ: SAP HANA Table Distribution
- KBA 2143736 – FAQ: SAP HANA Table Distribution for BW
- KBA 2340450 – FAQ: SAP HANA Table Replication

Table Distribution in SAP HANA Cockpit

The Table Distribution app in SAP HANA cockpit displays the current table distribution and enables you to generate, store, and execute a table redistribution plan, as shown in Figure 9.25. There are five menu options, which we'll explore in the following sections:

- **View Current Table Distribution**
- **View Redistribution Execution History**
- **Generate Table Redistribution Plan**
- **Edit Table Placement Rules**
- **Table Group Advisor**

To view the card, you need the RESOURCE ADMIN system privilege.

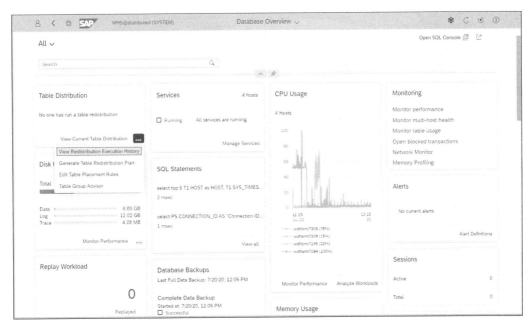

Figure 9.25 Table Distribution Card on the Database Overview Screen

Table Distribution

The **Current Table Distribution** app screen contains an **Analysis** tab displaying a few basic graphs with, for example, number of records, partitions, and table sizes per location (host). More interesting is the **Table Location** tab shown in Figure 9.26.

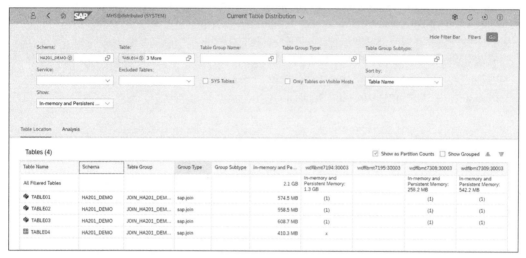

Figure 9.26 Current Table Distribution

From this view, you can filter all tables in the database and get information about the table group, group type, and group subtype. You can also see on which host the table or table partitions are located. An icon displays regular and partitioned tables, and a context menu is available by selecting the table name or partition (see Figure 9.27).

Figure 9.27 Current Table Distribution: Detail

From the context menu, you can view memory usage, content, metadata, runtime data, and access statistics, as well as navigate out to SAP HANA database explorer for the table definition and data preview. In addition, you can perform a number of table management activities, such as delta merge, unload data, rename table, partition table, or create a replica. If you need advice, you can generate a table redistribution plan for the table. Advanced operations include converting a column store table to row store and setting the preload setting for the table after restart of the database, as shown in Figure 9.28.

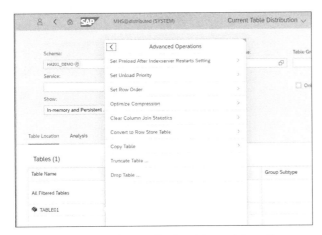

Figure 9.28 Current Table Distribution: Advanced Operations

You can also perform actions of table groups, for example, to load or unload all tables of the group (or load a single table) and move a table or table partition to a selected host.

Table Group Advisor

From the Table Distribution app, you can run the **Table Group Advisor**, shown in Figure 9.29.

Figure 9.29 Table Group Advisor

You can use this tool to find related tables and candidates for a table group. The advisor analyzes the statement cache, existing groups, and dependent objects as standard input, but each analysis is configurable. For the statement cache, this is the Top X statements, execution count, and date range, but there are more advanced options. You can also add another analysis. The **Preview** button shows the result, and you can use this as input for table redistribution.

Table Placement Rules

Table redistribution is configurable and controls grouping, location, and partitioning. The table placement rules are stored in the TABLE_PLACEMENT table, and you can use the Table Placement Rules app to configure your rules, as shown in Figure 9.30. This requires the RESOURCE ADMIN and TABLE ADMIN system privileges.

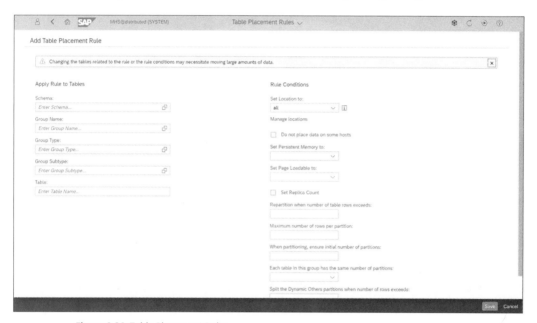

Figure 9.30 Table Placement Rules

You can specify a rule condition for the location, for example, master, slave, or all. You can also set persistent memory, page loadable, replica count, and a number of rules for when to repartition:

- Number of tables rows threshold
- Maximum number of rows per partition
- An initial number of partitions
- Equally divide number of partitions for tables in this group

Table Redistribution Plan Generator

Use the **Table Redistribution Plan Generator** wizard to get advice on how to best perform the data distribution. You can choose from the following five goals, as shown in Figure 9.31:

- Balance table distribution
- Redistribute tables after adding hosts
- Housekeeping
- Check the number of partitions
- Check the correct location of tables and partitions

Figure 9.31 Table Redistribution Plan Generator

When you click the **Step 2** button, you can define the options, for example, which tables to consider and how to balance the outcome, as shown in Figure 9.32.

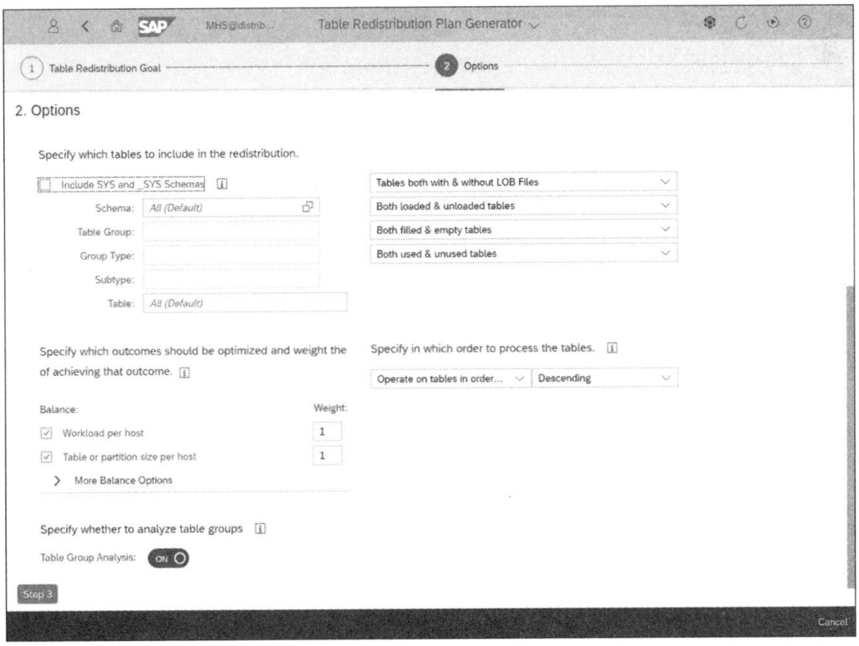

Figure 9.32 Table Redistribution Plan Generator: Options

Step 3 performs the table group analysis, the same as described previously, and, in **Step 4**, you get **Advanced Options**, which influence how the data distribution is to be performed. After a review page, you have the option to generate the table redistribution plan (or to cancel) from the bottom toolbar.

The **Table Redistribution Plan** displays the proposed actions (also accessible from the **Table Distribution** card on the **Database Overview** screen once generated), as shown in Figure 9.33. You can regenerate the plan if you want to make modifications, and an **Analysis** tab shows the effect of the proposed plan. If this corresponds to your intentions, click the **Execute Plan** button.

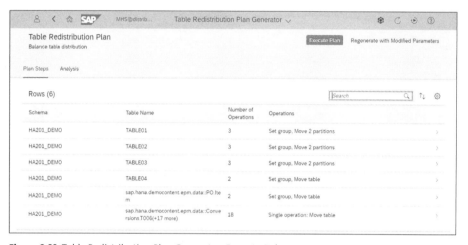

Figure 9.33 Table Redistribution Plan Generator: Execute Rules

Table Redistribution Execution History

The **Table Redistribution Execution History** screen shows execution in progress with the option to stop execution and modify parameters, as depicted in Figure 9.34. You can rerun the plan and select the plan entry for more detailed information about a plan. When selected, you get more information about the current execution with plan steps, failed operations, and defined parameters, with the option to configure parallel execution, as shown in Figure 9.35.

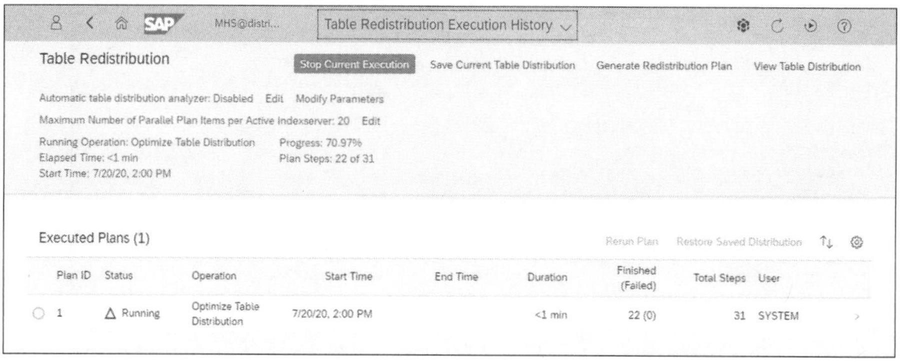

Figure 9.34 Table Redistribution Execution History

Figure 9.35 Table Redistribution Execution History: Detail

SQL Commands

SAP HANA cockpit (and SAP HANA studio previously) is an interactive tool that requires you to respond to its output. For scripted or batch executions, you can also directly use the SQL interface. For data distribution, the procedures are CHECK_TABLE_CONSISTENCY, CALL_REORG_GENERATE, and CALL_REORG_PLAN. We'll discuss each in the following sections.

Check Table Consistency

The CHECK_TABLE_CONSISTENCY procedure can be used to check the consistency of the metadata (structure) and the data of tables. There are about 50 checks in total, and you can call the GET_CHECK_ACTIONS('CHECK_TABLE_CONSISTENCY') procedure to have the system list them all (or read the documentation).

For data distribution, the following checks are relevant:

- CHECK_PARTITIONING
- CHECK_PARTITIONING_DATA
- REPAIR_PARTITIONING_DATA
- CHECK_REPLICATION
- CHECK_REPLICATION_DATA_FULL
- CHECK_REPLICATION_DATA_LIGHTWEIGHT

Each check comes with its own parameters, so you'll need to consult the documentation on how to execute the command exactly. For example, to perform a check on the table replication, enter the following:

```
CALL CHECK_TABLE_CONSISTENCY ('CHECK_REPLICATION', 'MY_SCHEMA', 'MY_TABLE')
```

Depending on the data volume, data checks can be very time consuming.

Reorg Generate and Execute

As with SAP HANA cockpit, table redistribution goes in two steps: first you need to generate the redistribution plan with the REORG_GENERATE procedure, and, second, execute the plan by calling REORG_EXECUTE with the plan ID. This can be queried from the REORG_OVERVIEW system view. As with SAP HANA cockpit, the system privileges RESOURCE ADMIN and CATALOG READ are required to generate the plan (the procedure only considers the tables you can access as catalog objects).

The syntax to generate the plan is CALL REORG_GENERATE(<algorithm>, <optional parameters>):

- Add server (1)
- Clear server (2)
- Save (4)
- Restore (5)
- Balance landscape (6)
- Housekeeping (16)

The algorithm corresponds to the options of the Table Distribution app in SAP HANA cockpit. The number indicates the algorithm to use, for example, CALL REORG_GENERATE(1) generates the add server plan.

With the optional parameters, you can specify the selection (schemas, tables, groups, group types, or subtypes) and scope (LOADED, UNLOADED, FILLED, EMPTY, USED, UNUSED, LOB, NOLOB). This corresponds to **Step 2 (Options)** within the **Table Redistribution Plan Generator**. An example of the syntax is as follows:

```
CALL REORG_GENERATE(6, 'SCOPE=>FILLED,NOLOB').
```

The table redistribution operation is configurable with system parameters (indexserver.ini/[table_redist]). There are many parameters, but some examples are ENABLE_MERGE and MAX_PARTITIONS. In addition, there are number parameters that control the optimization process, for example, balance by number of partitions, balance by memory usage, balance by rows, and more. This corresponds to **Step 4 (Advanced Options)**.

As an example, before you can remove a host from a distributed system, first the tables need to be redistributed. The commands shown in Listing 9.2 are executed.

```
call SYS.UPDATE_LANDSCAPE_CONFIGURATION( 'SET REMOVE','<host>' );
call REORG_GENERATE(2,'');
select * from SYS.REORG_STEPS;
call REORG_EXECUTE(?);
```

Listing 9.2 Remove Host from Landscape

When the reorg status is REORG FINISHED or REORG NOT REQUIRED, the host can be removed from the system using the resident HDBLCM tool.

Learn More

Table consistency checks are documented in the SAP HANA Administration Guide, chapter System Administration, in the "Managing Tables" section. For additional information on this topic, see the following FAQs. These KBAs complement the documentation with relevant additional information. Although most of the information will be out of scope of the exam, we recommend bookmarking these notes.

- KBA 1977584 – Technical Consistency Checks for SAP HANA Databases
- KBA 2116157 – FAQ: SAP HANA Consistency Checks and Corruptions

Monitoring Views

For more information about partitioning, you can query the following tables and monitoring views (M_*):

- `PARTIONED_TABLES`
- `TABLE_PARTITIONS`
- `M_CS_PARTITIONS`
- `M_TABLE_PARTITIONS`
- `M_TABLE_PARTITION_STATISTICS`

For more information about table replication, you can query the monitoring view `M_TABLE_REPLICAS`.

Learn More

Monitoring views are documented in the SAP HANA SQL Reference Guide. For each view, links are listed to the sections in the documentation with additional information. Although most of the information will be out of scope of the exam, we recommend bookmarking SAP HANA SQL Reference Guide for SAP HANA Platform, which can be found at *http://s-prs.co/v507850*.

Important Terminology

For this exam objective, you're expected to understand the following terms:

- **Data distribution**
  For best performance on multiple-host systems, network latency should be minimized with memory access kept local. Proper data distribution to support this is required. A simple example is to assign each tenant database to its own host. More fine-grained data distribution techniques are table grouping and table placement, which enable you to store tables that are often accessed together on the same host. Table replication is another strategy, as is table partitioning, although this also serves other purposes.

- **Distributed system**
  Scale-out, multiple-host, and distributed systems are synonyms in the context

of SAP HANA, and all refer to a single SAP HANA instance with a system database and zero, one, or more tenant databases running on multiple computers, servers, or hosts.

- **Extension node**
  This data tiering solution is specific to SAP BW with additional hosts added to a multiple-host system with less restrictive memory requirements to store less-frequently accessed data (warm data).

- **HA/DR provider**
  HA/DR providers, also known as hooks, are Python methods that can be called by the name server during specific events, such as host auto-failover. Like the backup interface Backint, it's an API. For the implementation, SAP relies on its hardware partners. The SAP HANA Administration Guide provides some code examples.

- **High availability (HA)**
  HA isn't a product feature but a system characteristic, or as described in the documentation, "a set of techniques, engineering practices, and design principles." SAP HANA supports HA with features such as service auto-restart and host auto-failover to address fault recovery, database backups, support for third-party storage replication, and built-in system replication to cover DR requirements.

- **Host auto-failover**
  Host auto-failover is an n + m host fault recovery solution available for distributed SAP HANA systems with one or more standby hosts. It provides a local fault recovery solution.

- **Host grouping**
  With host grouping, you can assign hosts in a distributed system to similarly configured systems in terms of available hardware resources. This enables you to create separate host groups for the SAP HANA database, SAP HANA XS, SAP HANA dynamic tiering, SAP HANA streaming analytics, and so on. If not all hosts of a distributed system are configured with the same system resources, host grouping also makes it possible to group similarly sized machines together.

- **Host types**
  A multiple-host system has two host types: worker and standby. Worker hosts are active SAP HANA server instances processing data. Standby hosts don't have any data loaded and don't respond to any requests, but the services are started.

- **Storage connector**
  The storage connector is both an API and ready-to-use client (implementation) to enable host auto-failover on block-based storage area network (SAN) storage. Unlike the file system-based SAN with Network File System (NFS) configuration, the standby host isn't attached to storage, and this needs to be configured as part of the failover process (logical unit number [LUN]-to-host mapping).

- **Table partitioning**
  Table partitioning splits a table into parts. A simple motivation is that the size of the table exceeds 2 billion rows, but you could also partition a table for data tiering motivations and separate warm and hot partitions, similar to SAP BW extension nodes, or for data distribution and performance reasons, for example, load balancing a hot partition across the different hosts of a multiple-host system. A multiple-host system isn't required for table partitioning.

- **Table placement**
  Table placement and the related table classification enables you to group and store tables that are often joined together on a single host. This pushes semantic knowledge down from the application to the database layer where it can be leveraged to optimize data distribution and query execution.

- **Table replication**
  On multiple-host systems, table replication can improve query performance by storing a copy or replica on all or a selected number of hosts. Replication can be synchronous or asynchronous and involve complete tables (typically row stores) or selected columns of column store tables.

- **Topology**
  The name server process maintains information about the topology: associated hosts, services, tenant databases, and much more. The topology is persisted in the system database and managed by the master name server process with master role. Other name servers keep a copy in memory. In tenant database systems, information about data distribution is stored in the catalog of the respective tenant database and not in the topology as was the case in single database (container) systems.

 Practice Questions

These practice questions will help you evaluate your understanding of the topics covered in this chapter. The questions shown are similar in nature to those found on the certification examination. Although none of these questions will be found on the exam itself, they will allow you to review your knowledge of the subject. Select the correct answers, and then check the completeness of your answers in the "Practice Question Answers and Explanations" section. Remember that on the exam, you must select all correct answers and only correct answers to receive credit for the question.

1. Does an SAP HANA multiple-host system provide high availability (HA)?

☐ **A.** Always—an SAP HANA scale-out system contains multiple hosts. Should one host fail, host auto-failover will cause the standby host to take over its role automatically and transparently.

☐ **B.** Never—an SAP HANA scale-out system contains several single points-of-failure (SPOFs), like a single system database, for example.

☐ **C.** It depends—an SAP HANA scale-out system provides HA features for multiple-host systems (e.g., host auto-failover), but the main reason to scale out is to overcome the hardware limitations of a single physical server.

2. Which are built-in SAP HANA high availability (HA) features? (There are three correct answers.)

☐ **A.** Host auto-failover

☐ **B.** SAP HANA system replication

☐ **C.** Storage replication

☐ **D.** SAP HANA multiple-host systems

☐ **E.** Service auto-restart

3. Why does SAP recommend to scale-up over scale-out? (There are two correct answers.)

☐ **A.** Memory size is a factor for SAP HANA licensing.

☐ **B.** Scale-up doesn't require data distribution.

☐ **C.** SAP recommends scale-out over scale-up!

☐ **D.** Single-host systems can directly access all data in memory. Multiple-host systems may need to join data residing on different hosts, which results in slower response times.

4. What is required for installation of an SAP HANA scale-out system? (There are two correct answers to this question.)

☐ **A.** Shared storage

☐ **B.** A distributed license

☐ **C.** SAP HANA scale-out edition (software)

☐ **D.** Network

5. Does SAP HANA support scale-in from a multiple-host system to a single-host system?

☐ **A.** Yes.

☐ **B.** No.

☐ **C.** It depends.

6.   How can you configure the standby host of an SAP HANA multiple-host system as "hot" standby, accepting query request?

☐   **A.** Add a license to the standby host, after which the feature is activated automatically.

☐   **B.** When you start the SAP HANA instance on a standby host, it takes on the hot standby role automatically.

☐   **C.** Configure the system parameter `indexserver.ini/[active_active]/read_enabled=true`.

☐   **D.** Standby hosts of a multiple-host SAP HANA system don't accept query requests. This isn't configurable.

7.   Which roles are valid (configured, actual)? (There are three correct answers.)

☐   **A.** Name server `MASTER 1, SLAVE`

☐   **B.** Index server `STANDBY, WORKER`

☐   **C.** Name server `MASTER 2, MASTER`

☐   **D.** Index server `MASTER, WORKER`

☐   **E.** Index server `WORKER, SLAVE`

8.   What triggers auto-host failover?

☐   **A.** Failure to automatically restart the index server process `hdbindexserver` with the worker role by the local instance watchdog process `hdbdaemon`

☐   **B.** Failure to automatically restart the name server process `hdbnameserver` with the master role by the local instance watchdog process `hdbdaemon`

☐   **C.** When neither the name server process `hdbnameserver` nor `hdbdaemon` respond to network requests from the active master nameserver process

9.   On a distributed system with four hosts each with the worker role and a single tenant database, how many backups are created when you create a backup of the system database and the tenant database?

☐   **A.** Two backups, one per database.

☐   **B.** Seven backups, one for each service with persistence: four index server, three master name servers. Hosts with the slave and standby roles don't participate in the backup.

☐   **C.** Eight backups, one for each service with persistence per host: four name server and four index server services.

☐   **D.** Four backups, one for each host.

10. Extension nodes enable you to optimize main memory resource management in SAP HANA to store warm data at a more relaxed storage-to-memory ratio. Why is this feature well suited for SAP BW?

☐ **A.** SAP BW controls data distribution.

☐ **B.** Data in a data warehouse is collected from multiple systems of record. These transactional systems, such as SAP Business Suite or SAP S/4HANA, contain the hot data. Most data in a data warehouse such as SAP BW or SAP BW/4HANA is warm at best, and some is probably already cold.

☐ **C.** Data warehouses are typically very large and require a lot of memory. A more relaxed ratio makes this a more cost-effective solution.

11. What are data distribution features? (There are three correct answers.)

☐ **A.** System replication

☐ **B.** Table placement

☐ **C.** Table partitioning

☐ **D.** Distributed system

☐ **E.** Table replication

12. Which table replication advantage only applies to multiple-host systems?

☐ **A.** Partition pruning

☐ **B.** Explicit partition handling

☐ **C.** Delta merge performance improvements

☐ **D.** Parallelization

☐ **E.** Load balancing

13. Which multilevel partitioning schemes are supported? (There are four correct answers.)

☐ **A.** Round-robin/round-robin

☐ **B.** Hash/hash

☐ **C.** Range/range

☐ **D.** Range/hash

☐ **E.** Hash/range

14. Which are partitioning best practices? (There are three correct answers.)

☐ **A.** Don't partition at all.

☐ **B.** Use as few partitions as possible.

☐ **C.** Partition as much as possible.

☐   **D.** Use as few partitions key columns as possible.

☐   **E.** Use as few partitioned tables as possible.

15.   What is the purpose of fencing?

☐   **A.** The fencing mechanism avoids data corruptions by ensuring that column tables can only be loaded into memory by one host at a time in a multiple-host system.

☐   **B.** Fencing is required to avoid a failed host reconnecting to the data and log volumes now attached to the standby host after failover.

16.   How can you configure the role of a name server (master, slave)?

☐   **A.** Using the SAP HANA cockpit Manage Services app

☐   **B.** Using the SAP HANA cockpit Host Failover app

☐   **C.** Using the Python support script `servicecontrol.py`

☐   **D.** Using the SQL procedure `UPDATE_LANDSCAPE_CONFIGURATION`

17.   Which parameters are required to install a multiple-host system? (There are two correct answers.)

☐   **A.** The role (e.g., worker, standby)

☐   **B.** The root user password

☐   **C.** The role (e.g., master, slave)

☐   **D.** The worker group

☐   **E.** The host name

18.   Which actions are required before you can remove a host from a multiple-host system? (There are two correct answers.)

☐   **A.** Run the resident HDBLCM tool with the remove host option.

☐   **B.** Update the topology and set the host for removal.

☐   **C.** Call the SAP HANA Storage API to detach the host from the shared storage subsystem.

☐   **D.** Execute the `REORG_GENERATE` and `REORG_EXECUTE` procedures to redistribute the data.

19.   Can you use the `landscapeHostConfiguration.py` script to change the role of a service?

☐   **A.** Yes

☐   **B.** No

Practice Question Answers and Explanations

1. Correct answer: **C**

   It depends is correct.

   Answer A is incorrect because a distributed system with only two hosts and no standby host may not provide any HA. Answer B is incorrect because, when configured with standby hosts, the presence of a single system database won't be a SPOF as the host auto-failover feature provides a local fault recovery solution.

Exam Tip

Always? Never? It probably depends. Watch out for bold statements in the available answers as the right answer might be more nuanced.

---

2. Correct answers: **A, B, E**

   Host auto-failover, system replication, and service auto-restart are built-in HA features in SAP HANA.

   Answer C is incorrect because storage replication is a third-party HA feature and not built in. Answer D is incorrect because a multiple-host system doesn't automatically provide HA but can be configured as such.

3. Correct answers: **B, D**

   SAP recommends scaling up because this avoids data distribution, and single-host systems can directly access all data in memory.

   Answer A is incorrect because memory size is a factor for SAP HANA licensing, but this has nothing to do with scaling recommendations. Scale-out systems typically use larger memory configuration as they need to support very large systems. Answer C is a wrong answer; the question was right.

4. Correct answers: **A, D**

   Requirements include shared storage and a network.

   Answer B is incorrect because the distributed system feature is built in and doesn't require a special SAP HANA license. Answer C is incorrect because to install an SAP HANA multiple-host system, the same SAP HANA, platform edition, software is used as for a single-host system.

5. Correct answer: **A**

   SAP HANA does support scale-in.

   Answer B is incorrect because removing host number two from a multiple-host system turns it into a single-host system. When removing hosts, you need to distribute the data first. Answer C is incorrect because it doesn't depend. It's supported by SAP HANA. However, it may depend on whether enough system resources are available on a single-host system to carry the load previously supported by two hosts. But that wasn't the question.

6. Correct answer: **D**

   This configuration isn't possible.

   Answer A is incorrect because licenses apply to a system or tenant database but not to a host. Answer B is incorrect because the standby host on an SAP HANA distributed system is already started. Because of the standby role, it does not accept any request. Answer C is incorrect because active/active (read enabled) system replication enables you to use the secondary system in a role similar to a hot standby by accepting read-only SQL queries. This is configured with the replication mode, not by a system parameter, and doesn't apply to a distributed system.

7. Correct answers: **A, C, E**

   The name server can have the master or slave role (both configured and actual). The index server can have the worker or standby role. The actual roles are master, slave, or standby.

   Answers B and D are incorrect because there is no actual worker role.

8. Correct answer: **C**

   The active master name server process uses TCP communication-based heartbeats (ping) to the other master name server processes and the daemon together with storage-based heartbeats. How this works is described in "SAP HANA – Host Auto-Failover" at *http://s-prs.co/v507846*.

   Answer A and B are incorrect because the failure of a single service doesn't trigger host auto-failover. The local instance watchdog process hdbdaemon will attempt to restart any service not in the running state (service auto-restart HA feature), but failure to do so doesn't result in an escalation to host auto-failover.

9. Correct answer: **A**

   There is a backup for each database. The system database has two parts, the backup of the active master name server and the backup catalog. You can see this illustrated in Figure 9.36 and Figure 9.37.

   The tenant database has one part for each of the hosts where an index server service for this tenant database is running, plus one part for the backup catalog. This backup may also include persistence of the xsengine.

   Answers B and C are incorrect because the system database isn't distributed and is hosted by the active master name server. The other name servers host a read-only replica. Answer D is incorrect because the service with persistence is the backup unit, not the host.

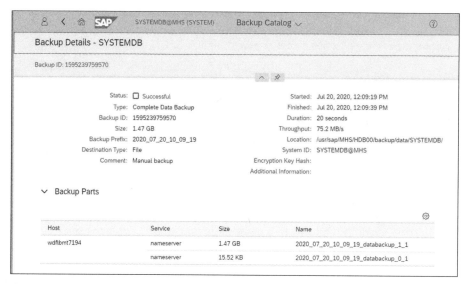

Figure 9.36 System Database Backup Multiple-Host System

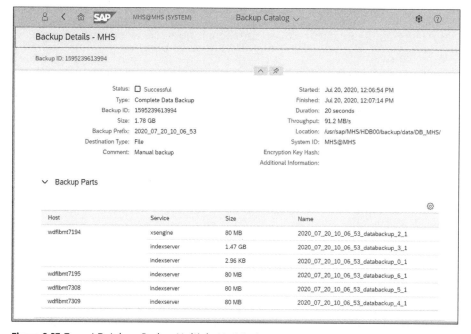

Figure 9.37 Tenant Database Backup Multiple-Host System

Exam Tip

As we didn't discuss backup in this chapter, this may have been a challenging question. What is important to remember is that there is a single system database hosted by the active master server. The tenant databases, on the contrary, are distributed over the available hosts with each of their associated index server services processing a separate section of the database and, as a result, generating a separate part of the backup.

10. Correct answer: **A**

    This feature is well suited for SAP BW because SAP BW controls data distribution.

    Answer B is incorrect because SAP HANA enables hybrid transactional/analytical processing (HTAP), combining transactional processing (OLTP) with analytics (OLAP) for real-time data insights. An SAP BW or SAP BW/4HANA data warehouses doesn't mainly store warm and cold data. Answer C is incorrect because, although data warehouses may well be very large, the benefit of using extension nodes comes with warm data. Storing frequently accessed (hot) data in an extension node with relaxed memory requirements would result in suboptimal performance.

> **Exam Tip**
>
> Elimination is a good strategy. Some questions include answers with statements that are either too specific, such as "most data in a data warehouse is warm," or too general, such as "data warehouses require a lot of memory."

11. Correct answers: **B, C, E**

    Data distribution features include table placement, table partitioning, and table replication.

    Answer A is incorrect because system replication is a HA feature not related to data distribution. Answer D is incorrect because a distributed system distributed the load, but unless data distribution features such as table partitioning, placement, or replication are used, it doesn't automatically provide data distribution.

12. Correct answer: **E**

    Only load balancing requires a multiple-host system. The other advantages listed could also apply to a single-host system. Note that table partitioning is documented under system administration and managing tables, not under availability and scalability.

13. Correct answers: **B, C, D, E**

    Range partitioning enables explicit partition handling but requires the partition column to include the primary key at the first level and doesn't provide load balancing. This restriction and limitation makes range partitioning particularly suitable for level two partitioning (hash/range, round-robin/range, and even range/range). Hash/range is the most common partitioning scheme, but hash/hash is also available. As of SAP HANA 2.0 SPS 05, range/hash is also supported.

    Answer A is incorrect because round-robin is supported at the first level but not the second.

14. Correct answers: **B, D, E**

    While the documentation only lists more general considerations, the SAP HANA Partitioning FAQ KBA lists several partitioning best practices.

    Answer A is incorrect because, in some cases, this might actually be good advice as a bad partitioning scheme can cause more damage than not using partitioning. It's not listed as a best practice, however. Answer C is incorrect because you should carefully consider and evaluate the effect of implementing partitioning. Only uses it where a measurable performance gain is obtained.

15. Correct answer: **B**

    Fencing is required to avoid a failed host reconnecting to the data and log volumes now attached to the standby host after failover.

    Answer A is incorrect because fencing is not related to table distribution.

16. Correct answer: **B**

    To change the role of a service, for example, from master to slave for the name server, you can use the SAP HANA cockpit Host Failover app.

    Answer A is incorrect because the SAP HANA cockpit Manage Services app shows the role of a service, but you can't use the app to make changes to the role. Answer C is incorrect. Although you can manage services with the Python support script `servicecontrol.py`, for example, to remove a service from a topology, you can't use the script to change roles. Answer D is incorrect because the SQL procedure `UPDATE_LANDSCAPE_CONFIGURATION` is used internally to change roles. You need the execute privilege on this procedure when using the Host Failover app, but you can't change the role of a service using this procedure directly.

17. Correct answers: **B, E**

    To add a host during installation or with the resident HDBLCM tool after installation, you are prompted to provide the host name and the root user password without default suggestion. You are also prompted to provide the name of the root user with `[root]` as default.

    Answer A is incorrect because the role parameter has `[worker]` as the default value and isn't required. Answer C is incorrect because the active role of the server, like master or slave, is not configured during installation. Answer D is incorrect because the worker group parameter has `[default]` as the default value and isn't required.

18. Correct answers: **B, D**

    Before you can remove a host from a multiple-host system, you first need to update the topology and set the host for removal. This can be done with the SAP HANA cockpit Host Failover app or by executing the `UPDATE_LANDSCAPE_CONFIG-URATION ('SET REMOVE', '<host>')` procedure. Next, you need to redistribute the data, for example, by using the SAP HANA cockpit Table Distribution app or by executing the `REORG_GENERATE` and `REORG_EXECUTE` procedures.

Answer A is incorrect because you can run the resident HDBLCM tool with the remove host option after both actions have been completed but not before. Answer C is incorrect because you don't have to call the SAP HANA Storage API to detach the host from the shared storage subsystem.

19. Correct answer: **B**

No. You can use the `landscapeHostConfiguration.py` script to get information about the configured and actual role of the name server and index server, the host role, and the storage partition, among others, similar to the output of the SAP HANA cockpit Host Failover app, but you can't use the script to make any landscape changes.

Takeaway

After reading this chapter, you should have a good understanding of the concepts of SAP HANA multiple-host systems, why you might consider scaling out, and what you need to do to make such a system highly available. Installing a multiple-host system is simple. Preparing the LUNs of the SAN or NAS with NFS is a little less simple, but this activity is typically performed by the hardware partner (and we thank them for that).

It should be clear why you need to redistribute tables and table partitions after you add a host to the system, but when you remove a host, you need to perform the redistribution first. Partitioning tables can both solve and create problems. You should understand how to achieve the first and avoid the latter. To get the best performance with a distributed system, you need to properly group tables, work with table placement, and leverage table replication when and where appropriate. The SAP HANA cockpit Table Distribution app supports this activity. To tune table (re-)distribution operations, you can also leverage the SQL interface.

Summary

In this chapter, we've described SAP HANA scale-out systems and how this relates to HA. We covered the architecture of multiple-host systems, storage requirements, and recommended file system architectures. We showed how to install a multiple-host system and how to add or remove a host. The mechanism behind the host auto-failover HA feature with host roles and host groups was explained along with the purpose of HA/DR providers, also known as hooks. The key to great performance with SAP HANA multiple-host systems is getting the data distribution right. We showed how you can use the SAP HANA cockpit Table Distribution app for this task and explained how table partitioning, table replication, table groups, and table placement works.

In the next chapter, we'll move on to database security.

Chapter 10
Security

Techniques You'll Master

- Configuring user authentication
- Working with user groups
- Managing roles and privileges
- Troubleshooting issues with authorization
- Defining a password policy
- Encrypting data at rest and in motion
- Configuring auditing

In this chapter, we explore the security features of SAP HANA and start off with user authentication and authorization. If you need a reminder: *authentication* verifies credentials, and *authorization* checks permissions. The first provides you access, and the second tells you what you can do. Authentication concerns topics such as password policies, single sign-on (SSO), Security Assertion Markup Language (SAML), JSON Web Token (JWT), Lightweight Directory Access Protocol (LDAP), and others. Authorization is about roles and permissions, system privileges, and object privileges. User groups belong to the first category, and we'll explain how this works.

Security isn't limited to user and role management, of course. The topic is much broader, but fortunately for this exam, we can narrow it down to four key areas. Besides authorization and authentication, we describe auditing and data encryption, including both data at rest and in transit (in motion/in flight).

Auditing won't make your system any more secure, but it will enable you to find out about the who, what, and when: actor, object, and time. Auditing alerts you to security vulnerabilities and security breach attempts, and it supports compliance with security standards and regulations.

> **Real-World Scenario**
>
> The chief security officer (CSO) drops by your desk to say, "Hi," and asks about your fishing trip. A little later, the conversation switches to SAP HANA security features, and the CSO wants to know how the corporate data actually is protected in the SAP HANA in-memory database. How exactly do the data access mechanisms work? Using industry standards or home brew? What options are available to enhance security? The CSO is particularly interested in the auditing options. Who did what and when? Could you briefly explain SAP HANA security, encryption, and auditing functions?

The SAP HANA platform comes with a comprehensive security framework for secure data access and applications, with functions for authentication and user management, authorization, masking, anonymization, encryption, and auditing.

Topic and Objectives

We'll focus on SAP HANA security topics in this chapter. The certification exam expects you to have a good understanding of the following topics:

- SAP HANA security functions
- User management and roles
- Authentication and single sign-on (SSO)
- Authorization and privileges

- Encryption techniques
- Auditing techniques

Note

This topic area is listed with medium weight (8%–12%) since the SPS 03 version of the exam. Prior, the topic area was split into a Security topic and Users and Authorization topic, each with medium weight; in relative terms, this topic area has been downsized a bit. With 80 questions in total, you can expect about 8 questions on this topic. Regardless of the weight, security remains a critical topic, and we highly recommend that you master the concepts and activities.

Keep in mind that the exam guide states this can change at any time, so always check online for the latest updates.

Learn More

The Security Guide on the SAP Help Portal is the entry point for all security-related information. This guide also contains the security information map explaining by guide and by topic where to find the right information.

For product information with solution briefs, webinars, white papers, and more, visit *http://sap.com/hanasecurity*.

The product managers responsible for SAP HANA security have published a technical whitepaper that introduces all relevant security-related topics for the IT security expert at *http://s-prs.co/v507851*.

In addition, KBA 2159014 – FAQ: SAP HANA Security is a great place to start, although a lot of material will be beyond the scope of the exam.

Key Concepts Refresher

In this section, we'll address the key concepts that fall under security in SAP HANA, including user management, authentication and SSO, authorization, encryption, and auditing.

SAP HANA 2.0 SPS 05: What's New?

On the server side, there are no new security features introduced with the SAP HANA 2.0 SPS 05 release with the exception of support for using the local secure store (LSS) in production environments.

On the client side with the contemporary SAP HANA cockpit 2.0 SP 12 release, several new features were introduced in the domain of user management and security administration, including a new wizard for user group management and a new wizard for audit policies. For the details of these features, see the release notes for SAP HANA cockpit and SAP HANA database explorer. Note that tools have their own release cycle independent from the SAP HANA platform.

For more information, refer to "SAP HANA Cockpit" on the SAP Help Portal at *http://s-prs.co/v507852*.

Security and User Management in SAP HANA Cockpit

Figure 10.1 displays the SAP HANA cockpit Database Overview app with the **Security and User Management** view. By the end of the chapter, you'll be familiar with all these cards, apps, and security-related links.

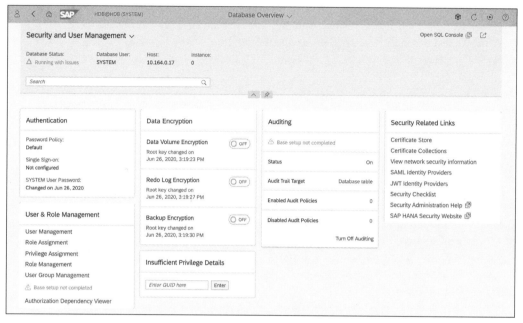

Figure 10.1 Security and User Management

The key sections are as follows:

- **Authentication**
  In the **Authentication** section, we'll cover password policy, password blacklist, SSO with SAML, and JWT identity providers (IdPs). We'll also discuss the role of the database superuser SYSTEM.

- **User & Role Management**
  The principal of the **User & Role Management** section are the users. We'll cover the different user types, that is, standard, technical, and restricted users, as well as explain user groups, how users relate to roles, how to assign privileges to users and roles, and how to troubleshoot authorization issues with the Authorization Dependency Viewer and the Insufficient Privilege Details apps.

- **Data Encryption**
  The **Data Encryption** section protects data in storage, for example, on the data volume of the SAP HANA database or captured in a backup. Encryption also protects data in transit over the network, also sometimes referenced as data in flight. By encrypting data, you can make sure that your authentication and authorization mechanisms aren't circumvented by network snooping or other hacking attempts.

- **Auditing**
  With the **Auditing** section, you can monitor what goes on in the database, but, as the saying goes, to focus on everything is to focus on nothing. You'll need to design an audit policy that is concise and comprehensible. What you want to avoid is firefighting, and SAP HANA cockpit will warn you when you've made too broad a selection.

Security Functions

When discussing SAP HANA security, you first need to distinguish between the system as a whole and the individual database tenants. As a reminder, SAP HANA tenant databases are isolated entities with their own users, catalog, repository, log files, and so on.

At the tenant database level, security comprises the following:

- User and role management
- Authentication using user name/password, LDAP, Kerberos, SAML, and JWT with some restrictions regarding tenant database isolation
- Authorization with optional cross-tenant database access for read-only queries
- Network communication encryption with separate trust and key stores for ODBC/JDBC and HTTP clients
- Data at rest encryption for data volume, redo logs, and backups
- Auditing

To enhance the security of the system as a whole, SAP HANA also provides the following functions:

- High-isolation mode for tenant databases with dedicated operating system accounts and groups to prevent cross-tenant operating system access
- A configuration change blacklist maintained at the system-level containing critical properties, for example, related to resource management, to ensure system-wide stability and performance
- Restricted features list to disable certain functionality, such as application functions, at the tenant database level

Implementation Scenarios

Security configuration and user management is directly related to the implementation scenario. We already described three-tier architecture, native applications, and data mart in Chapter 2. In the following sections, we'll only describe the security-related consequences.

Classic Three-Tier Architecture

In a classic three-tier architecture, illustrated in Figure 10.2, security and user management are enforced at the application server layer. The connection between the application server and the database is made with a "technical" user (the difference between a regular database user and a technical user is conceptual; there is no technical database user account). Application users either have no access to the database at all or connect with a restricted user. These different user account types are addressed in more detail later in this chapter.

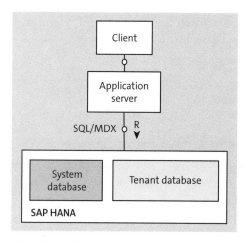

Figure 10.2 SAP HANA in Three-Tier Architecture

Native Application Architecture

When you implement SAP HANA extended application services (SAP HANA XS) for native application development, security and user management are also managed at the application server layer. This resembles the classic three-tier architecture with an external application server but this time, the application server is integrated, and the user and roles will also exist inside the database (see Figure 10.3). Although the SAP HANA XS, classic model and SAP HANA extended application services, advanced (SAP HANA XSA) models share the same name, the architecture is very distinct. SAP HANA XS, classic model is tightly integrated into the SAP HANA system. You can disable the service (xsengine process) but not remove it. The SAP HANA XSA runtime environment, on the other hand, is more like an add-on. You need to install SAP HANA XSA, and the runtime can be hosted on separate servers. SAP HANA XSA can work with an external IdP.

Learn More

Security-related topics for SAP HANA XSA are documented in the SAP HANA Security Guide and the SAP HANA Administration Guide together with the database. There is also a separate developer guide that includes security-related information. To learn more, the FAQ is a great place to start, although most material will be beyond the scope of the exam: SAP Note 2596466 – FAQ: SAP HANA XSA.

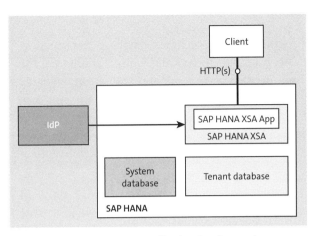

Figure 10.3 SAP HANA Native Application Development

Data Mart

More complex configurations are illustrated in Figure 10.4. Here you have clients connecting directly using ODBC/JDBC, Python, Go, and other client languages and environments combined with client/server connections from platforms such as SAP BusinessObjects Business Intelligence suite. This requires different types of database accounts with authentication and authorization configured either inside the database or mapped to the platform for SSO. The data mart will be populated using replication from a source system with technologies, such as SAP HANA smart data access (SDA) and SAP HANA smart data integration (SDI). These connections require their own security configuration.

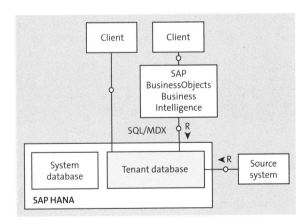

Figure 10.4 SAP HANA as a Data Mart

User Management

User management topics for SAP HANA include user types, user groups, and predefined users. We'll cover each in the following sections, in addition to common user administration activities.

User Types

For user management, you distinguish between technical database users and regular accounts. The difference is conceptual. Technically, both accounts are the same. Technical users can be built-in users such as SYS and SYSTEM, can be highly privileged, and can require special consideration. You can also create your own technical users, for example, the user created for database monitoring using SAP HANA cockpit. These users are identical to regular database users but typically assigned to a different user group with more stringent password policy requirements.

Regular database users come in two flavors: standard and restricted. A standard user can create objects in its own schema and view data in system views. Restricted users don't have these privileges and typically only connect to the database using web clients (HTTP/S). To create a restricted user, you can use the CREATE RESTRICTED USER statement. When you grant the PUBLIC ROLE to the restricted user to enable access to system views, add the privilege GRANT CREATE ANY ON OWN SCHEMA, and execute an ALTER USER <user> ENABLE CLIENT CONNECT, you've converted your restricted user into a regular user. Revoking these privileges from a regular user does the same trick. There is no special sauce. To create users, you need the USER ADMIN system privilege.

User Groups

With user groups, you can manage related users together and optionally assign a dedicated or even exclusive group administrator. User groups don't control data access but enable you to assign different password policies, for, example to a user group with only technical users. To create users in a user group, the object privilege USERGROUP OPERATOR on the group suffices; USER ADMIN privilege isn't required.

Predefined Users

Apart from the <sid>adm operating system user, the following database users are created during installation:

- SYS
  Object owner of system tables and monitoring views.
- SYSTEM
  Default system administration account with irrevocable system privileges.
- _SYS_AFL
  Object owner of Application Function Libraries (AFL).
- _SYS_DI*
  Technical users of SAP HANA deployment infrastructure (HDI).
- _SYS_STATISTICS
  Technical database user for internal monitoring.

- **_SYS_REPO**

  Object owner of SAP HANA repository used with SAP HANA XS, classic model (deprecated).

- **_SYS_DATA_ANONYMIZATION**

  Object owner of data anonymization objects.

Apart from the SYSTEM user, you can't log on with these predefined technical users.

SAP recommends disabling the SYSTEM user for production environments. You should use this account only to create dedicated users (roles) for specific tasks, such as user administration, backups, security administration, and so on. Disable SYSTEM with SQL command ALTER USER SYSTEM DEACTIVATE USER NOW. As SYSTEM can be activated again, SAP recommends creating an audit policy to monitor ALTER USER statements. The SYSTEM user isn't required to update SAP HANA systems with the exception of updates using the Software Update Manager (SUM) and Software Provisioning Manager (SWPM). Both tools are used with SAP application software logistics.

The **Authentication** card on **Database Overview** shows the last time the SYSTEM user password was changed (refer to Figure 10.1).

The **Security Checklist** that you can access under the **Security-Related Links** flags whether the system user is deactivated. We'll discuss this further in the "Security Checklist" section.

Learn More

For the complete list of predefined users and information about deactivating the SYSTEM user, see the SAP HANA Security Guide. Additional information, beyond the scope of the exam, can be found in KBA: 2535951 - FAQ: SAP HANA Users and Schemas.

User Administration

The recommended approach to user administration is to do the following:

1. Assign privileges to roles.
2. Assign roles to users.
3. Assign users to user groups.

To create roles at design-time, you can use SAP Web IDE for SAP HANA (SAP HANA studio or the SAP HANA Web-Based Developer Workbench for SAP HANA XS, classic model applications). Design-time roles are deployed using HDI. Design-time roles are transportable between systems (from development to production) and not directly associated with the creator. Runtime roles, on the other hand, are database objects owned by a user, and if this user is dropped, the roles are also deleted. To grant access to a database object, you need to have access yourself. For these reasons, design-time roles are recommended.

SAP HANA XSA has its own authorization concept with application roles and role collections, independent from database application roles.

Learn More

For more information on this topic, beyond the scope of the exam, see the SAP HANA Developer Guide for SAP HANA XSA and the SAP HANA Deployment Infrastructure (HDI) reference.

Differences between role development for the SAP HANA XS, classic model and SAP HANA XSA environments is highlighted in "Best Practices and Recommendations for Developing Roles in SAP HANA" at *http://s-prs.co/v507853*.

User and Role Management in SAP HANA Cockpit

The **User & Role Management** card on **Database Overview** provides access to the interfaces where you can manage users and roles and assign privileges and roles. You can also manage groups and, in case you're getting authorization errors on your calculation views, access the **Authorization Dependency Viewer**. Like **Insufficient Privilege Details**, this is a troubleshooting tool that supports debugging authorization issues. We'll cover both tools briefly, but let's first start with the basics: users and roles.

User Management

The User Management app is divided into two panes, as shown in Figure 10.5. On the left side pane, all database users are listed. On the right side, the details pane contains the **General Information**, **Authorization Mode**, **Authentication**, and **Custom User Properties** sections for the selected user.

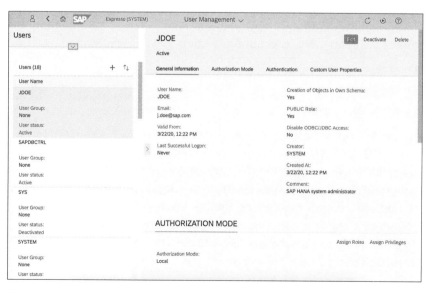

Figure 10.5 User Management

General Information

When you select a user in **User Management**, the creator, creation time stamp, and last successful logon are shown.

To add new users, click the **+** icon in the **Users** header of the list pane. To edit the selected user, click the **Edit** button in the right pane header. This is also where you can deactivate or delete a user.

When you click **+**, you can choose between **Create User** and **Create Restricted User**. As described, restricted users are intended for the classic three-tier or native development implementation scenarios. They can only access the database through another database client (typically via an application server) and don't have direct SQL access (e.g., SAP HANA database explorer). Technically, a restricted user is a regular user minus the following:

- Create object privilege (own schema)
- PUBLIC role
- ODBC/JDBC access

You can enable ODBC/JDBC access for the user (data mart scenario), but granting either the PUBLIC role or the CREATE OBJECT privilege will turn the restricted user into a normal user (or vice versa). A message will display to inform you of this effect, as illustrated in Figure 10.6.

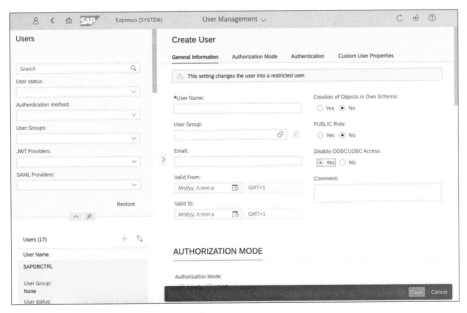

Figure 10.6 User Changed into a Restricted User

Authorization Mode

SAP HANA supports two authorization modes: local and LDAP. When changing the **Authorization Mode** for existing users from local to LDAP, a warning is given: **all**

granted roles and privileges will be revoked. This corresponds to the statement `CRE-ATE USER <user> PASSWORD <password> AUTHORIZATION LDAP`.

LDAP is commonly used in enterprise environments to centralize user management. LDAP is an open, vendor-neutral, industry standard for both authentication and authorization. There are different implementations, of which Microsoft Active Directory (AD) may be the most common one. For AD, SAP HANA supports both LDAP authentication and authorization using LDAP groups, and you also can use LDAP to automatically provision (create) database users. This will be convenient for you as administrator if you need to connect to a tenant database where you don't have an account to perform monitoring or troubleshooting. There is one-way synchronization between the LDAP directory and the SAP HANA user store. As a result, when the user is deleted from the directory, it still will be present in the database.

When using LDAP, encrypting traffic between the database and the LDAP server is highly recommended to prevent password snooping. This is configured with system parameters in `global.ini/[ldap]`.

To establish a connection with an LDAP server, you need to create an LDAP provider in the database. This requires the `LDAP ADMIN` system privilege and uses the `CREATE LDAP PROVIDER` statement. Subsequently, you need to import the LDAP certificates in the SAP HANA certificate store and create a certificate collection with purpose `LDAP`. You can validate the connectivity with the `VALIDATE LDAP PROVIDER <name> CHECK USER <user> PASSWORD` statement.

Authentication

When you create a user, the only required properties are a user name and a password. Password authorization is the default authorization mode, and in SAP HANA cockpit, this is referenced as **Local**. Local passwords are typically used when SSO isn't a requirement. A password policy and a password blacklist provide additional security for local authorization. However, local authorization isn't the only mode. These are your options, as illustrated in Figure 10.7:

- JWT IdPs
- Kerberos
- Passwords (**Local** or **LDAP**)
- SAML identify providers
- SAP Assertion Ticket
- SAP Logon ticket
- X.509 certificates

The Kerberos protocol was designed for client/server authentication on insecure networks going back to the 1980s. It's the default authentication method used by Microsoft Windows, which makes this a good candidate if you want to integrate the SAP HANA database in a Windows environment, for example, to connect SAP

HANA studio (JDBC) or SAP BusinessObjects applications (ODBC) on a Windows client computer. For SAP HANA XSA (and SAP HANA XS, classic model) web clients, Kerberos authentication is enabled using Simple and Protected GSSAPI Negotiation Mechanism (SPNEGO) with GSSAPI unfolding as Generic Security Services Application Program Interface. No surprise, everyone just uses SPNEGO. For SSO, SAP HANA supports both Kerberos based on Microsoft AD and Kerberos authentication servers. Kerberos authentication is also supported for remote source SSO for SDA.

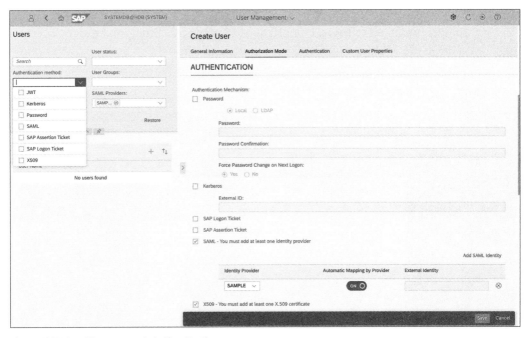

Figure 10.7 User Management: Authentication

> **Learn More**
>
> For more information on this topic, beyond the scope of the exam, see the SAP HANA Security Guide and the SAP HANA Administration Guide. Kerberos SSO can be complex. There is a dedicated note that explains the how to: SAP Note 1837331 – How to configure Kerberos SSO to SAP HANA DB Using Microsoft Windows Active Directory.

For SSO integration into SAP landscapes, you can use SAP Logon and assertion tickets. These are generated, for example, by SAP NetWeaver application servers. The tickets are validated against certificates stored in an SAP HANA certificate collection inside the database for this purpose or on the file system in the *saplogon.pse* file. How this works is explained in more detail in the "Certificate Collections" section.

For web applications, SAP HANA supports X.509 certificates, SAML, and JWT. X.509 is the standard for public key certificates used in TLS (SSL) for HTTPS. SAML is widely used for enterprise SSO. It's an older technology based on XML. JWT uses similar technologies but is more recent and based on JavaScript Object Notation (JSON). JWT is often used in combination with social media integration. Although SAML, like LDAP, supports both authorization and authentication, only authentication is supported for SAP HANA.

Before you can use SAML authentication, you first need to create a SAML provider. For this, you can use the SAML Identity Provider app accessed via the **Security Related Links** (refer to Figure 10.1), as illustrated in Figure 10.8. To add a provider, enter a name, entity ID and certificate from the certificate store.

For JWT, the app is called JWT Identity Provider, but this time, you need to provide name, issuer URL, and identity claim (but no certificate). For both providers, you can indicate whether the user mapping between the assertion user and the SAP HANA database user is case-sensitive.

Figure 10.8 SAML Identity Provider

You can add multiple authentication mechanisms and multiple X.509 certificates, SAML, and JWT IdPs.

By default, all supported authentication mechanism are enabled, but SAP recommends to only enable those in use. System parameter `global.ini/[authentication]/authentication_methods` contains the list:

`pbkdf2,password,kerberos,spnego,saml,saplogon,x509xs,jwt, sessioncookie,ldap`

Exam Tip

Although you should have a basic understanding of the concepts, LDAP, SAML, and JWT are beyond the scope of the exam.

Custom User Properties

When you create a user, you can provide the following additional metadata:

- E-mail
- Validation period
- User group
- Comment

You can also specify additional parameters in the **Custom User Properties** tab:

- Client and locale (for use in SAP HANA information models)
- Time zone
- Priority (0–9, default 5, 9 is highest)
- Statement memory and thread limit

This corresponds to the CREATE USER <user> SET PARAMETER statement.

SAP HANA Extended Application Services, Advanced Model

User management and group management for the SAP HANA XSA environment are managed separately using SAP HANA XS Advanced cockpit, as shown in Figure 10.9. SAP HANA XSA users and roles correspond to database users and roles.

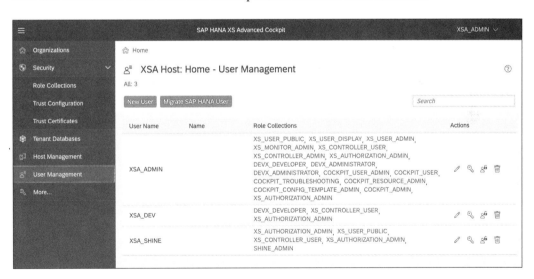

Figure 10.9 SAP HANA XSA User Management

Exam Tip

SAP HANA XSA user management is beyond the scope of the exam.

Authentication

The **Authentication** card on **Database Overview** of SAP HANA cockpit shows the password policy and active SSO implementations together with the last time the SYSTEM user was changed. When selected, the Authentication app opens, which enables you to edit the password policy and password blacklist.

Password Policy

A password policy enables you to define password length and composition, password lifetime, user lock settings, password blacklist, and some miscellaneous settings. This policy is relevant for local authentication mode with user name and password stored inside the database. In the **Password Policy** tab shown in Figure 10.10, you can assign different password policies to different user groups, which enables you to also apply different rules for interactive and technical database users. The latter won't mind using a string of 30 random alphanumeric and special characters as a password. Requirements such as a password change required upon first logon, however, aren't appropriate, and you may also want to consider implementing a different user lock policy for the technical user.

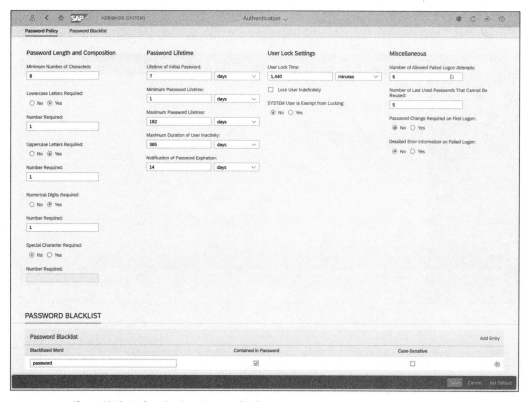

Figure 10.10 Authentication: Password Policy

Configuration changes are persisted as system parameters, for example: `index-server.ini/[password_policy]/minimal_password_length = '8'` (*nameserver.ini* for the system database).

While on the SQL console, to query the password policy in effect for a particular user, use the following statement:

```
SELECT * from M_EFFECTIVE_PASSWORD_POLICY" where USER_NAME = 'JDOE';
```

Password Blacklist

Besides a policy, you can also create a password blacklist to exclude commonly used passwords such as "Password1" in the **Password Blacklist** tab. The values are stored in table `_SYS_PASSWORD_BLACKLIST` in the `_SYS_SECURITY` schema. To make changes, object privileges on this table are required.

Although the app is easier to use, to insert a list of 1,000 blacklisted words, the SQL interface as follows might be more convenient:

```
INSERT INTO _SYS_SECURITY._SYS_PASSWORD_
BLACKLIST VALUES ('password', 'TRUE', 'FALSE');
```

Role Assignment and Privilege Assignment

From the header of the **Authorization Mode** section, you can select **Assign Roles** and **Assign Privileges**, as illustrated previously in Figure 10.5. Alternatively, these apps are also accessible from the **User & Role Management** card on **Database Overview**. As a rule and best practice, you assign privileges to roles and grant roles to users. There are, however, exceptions to this rule which require you to grant a privilege directly to a user.

Selecting the **Assign Roles** option opens the **Role Assignment** screen, where you can add or remove a user's roles and edit the **Grantable to Others** property, as shown in Figure 10.11. Grantable to others corresponds to the `WITH ADMIN OPTION` of the SQL statement, meaning that not only are you granted the privilege, you can also grant the privilege to others.

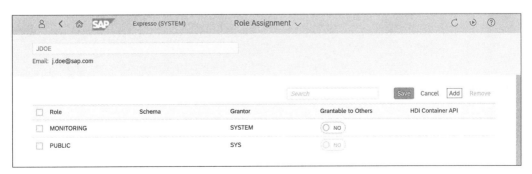

Figure 10.11 Role Assignment

The **Privilege Assignment** screen shown in Figure 10.12 works the same way as role assignment. In this view, you can directly add system, object, analytical, application, and package privileges. System privileges grant system configuration authority to the user, for example, to configure and create backups, import and export data, and perform other system administration tasks.

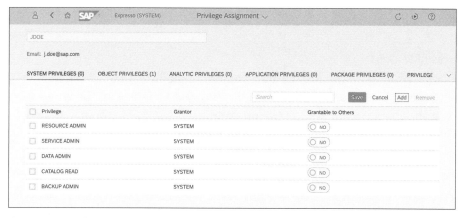

Figure 10.12 Privilege Assignment

Object privileges grant the user the authority to create runtime objects, such as schemas, tables, indexes, or views. Usually, these runtime objects are created when design-time artifacts are deployed, for example, using HDI. Standard database users typically don't need object privileges, but if they do, they usually receive the required privilege through a role and not with a direct grant.

Analytical privileges provide fine-grained, row-level access control. As with object privileges, in SAP HANA XSA environments, these are developed and deployed using HDI and not at runtime manually.

Package and application privileges authorize actions and access to SAP HANA Repository. These authorizations, like SAP HANA Repository and the SAP HANA XS, classic model architecture, are now deprecated.

A rather peculiar privilege is the ATTACH DEBUGGER privilege, which isn't a database object but a user privilege. This privilege is mostly used in development systems but may occasionally be granted in production environments in the context of SAP Support incidents.

System privilege USER ADMIN is required for privilege management. To grant a specific privilege to another user, you must have the privilege and/or role yourself plus have the authorization to grant the role or privilege.

With HDI, roles are granted by the container administrator.

Note that you can't explicitly deny privileges. You're denied all privileges by default and can only perform those activities or access those objects you've been granted access to.

> **Exam Tip**
>
> Although you should have a basic understanding of the concepts, role administration in both the SAP HANA XS, classic model environment with SAP HANA Repository and in the SAP HANA XSA environment with HDI are beyond the scope of the exam.

Data Masking and Anonymization

Data masking provides an additional layer of access control by obfuscating data or making it only partially visible for unprivileged users, for example, by returning a random string for a Social Security number or only the last four digits of a credit card number. Data masking works at the table object level and supports both basic and complex formulas. The data itself isn't changed, and with the `UNMASKED` object privilege on the table, no data masking takes place. Data masking doesn't return `Not authorized` error messages.

You can use the Privilege Assignment app of SAP HANA cockpit to add the object privilege to a user or role, but for the table definition, you should use SAP HANA database explorer or a development tool such as SAP Web IDE.

Data anonymization enables data analysis while protecting the privacy of individuals. There are three anonymization methods supported:

- K-anonymity
- l-diversity
- Differential privacy

Data anonymization can be applied to a SQL or calculation view, as illustrated in Figure 10.13.

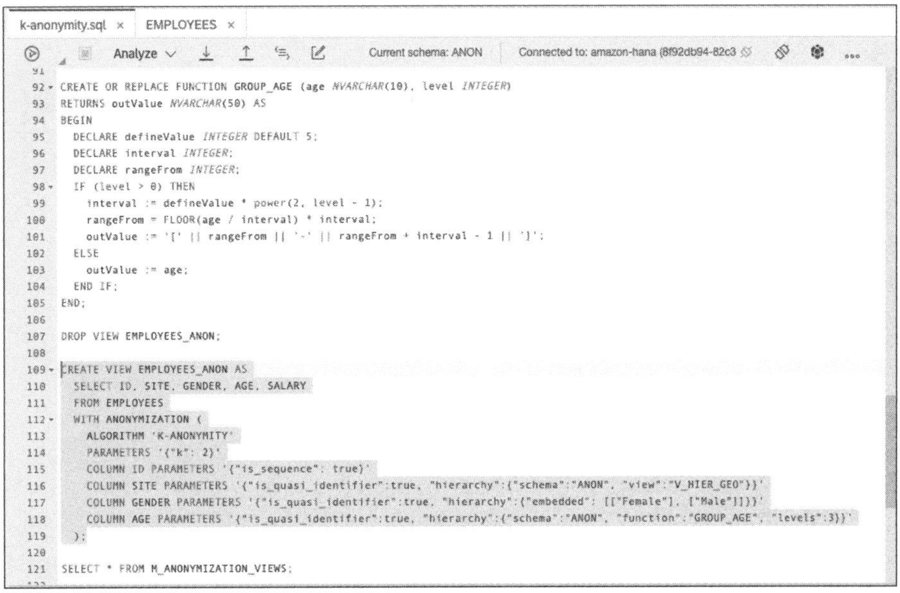

Figure 10.13 Data Anonymization

SAP HANA cockpit provides the Anonymization Report app, as illustrated in Figure 10.14, which returns information about the data anonymization method used with supporting KPIs for the associated SQL view or calculation views. This report can be used for compliance reasons.

Figure 10.14 SAP HANA Cockpit: Anonymization Report

User Group Management

You can assign users to user groups in the following ways to simplify user management:

- Assign a dedicated user group administrator to delegate user management, for example, for temporary workers.
- Configure the user group for exclusive administration, for example, to protect technical users from tampering.
- Set user properties, for example, password policies, at the group level.

System privilege USER ADMIN is required for user group management.

To create and change user groups, you can use the **User Group Management** option under **User & Role Management**, as illustrated in Figure 10.15. You can use the view to create groups, add users to groups, and specify the password policy for the group. You can also create users from the view and, alternatively, assign user groups from **User Management**.

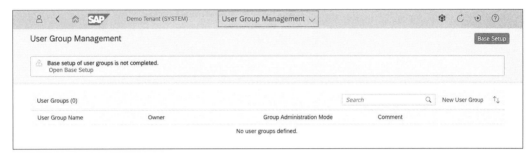

Figure 10.15 User Group Management: Create and Change Groups

As of SAP HANA cockpit 2.0 SP 12, you're prompted to first perform the base setup of user groups, as shown in Figure 10.16. A wizard prompts you to create a user group for administration accounts, technical accounts, and regular users.

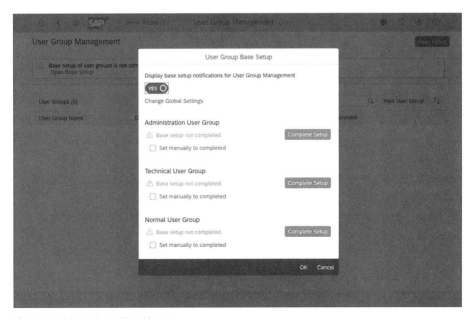

Figure 10.16 User Group Base Setup

This activity is performed in three steps, as displayed in the header in Figure 10.17:

1. **Name**

   Provide the name of the group.

2. **Admin Mode**

   Indicate whether any user with the USER ADMIN system privilege can manage this user group or only group administrators. In addition, indicate whether the group creator (you, in this case) can manage the group.

3. **Password Policy**

   Define the password policy for this user group. The password policy editor is the same as described earlier.

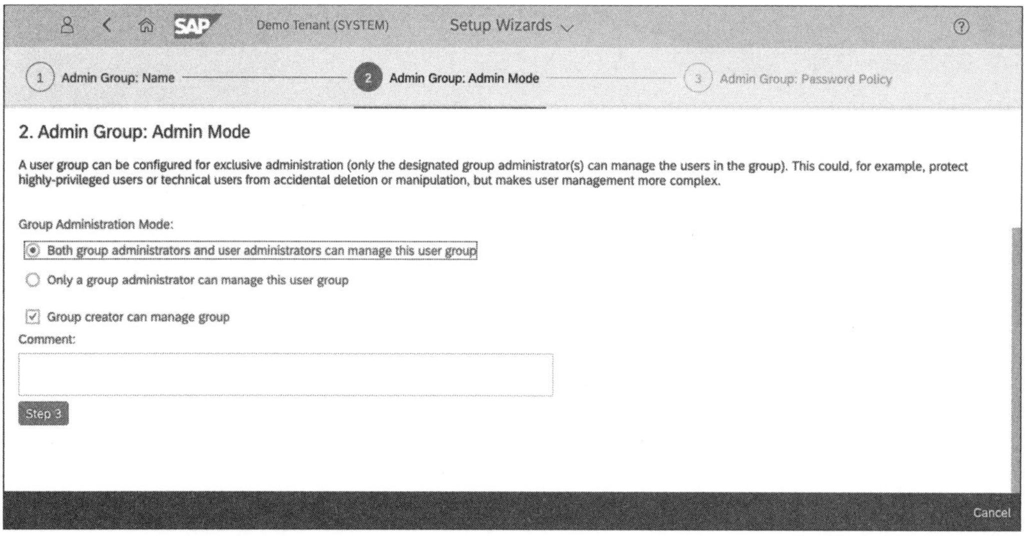

Figure 10.17 Setup Wizard

With SQL statements, use the SET PARAMETER clause of the CREATE USERGROUP statement:

```
CREATE USERGROUP sample SET PARAMETER 'password_layout' = 'A1a!',
  ENABLE PARAMETER SET 'password policy';
```

Role Management

With the **Role Management** option under **User & Role Management**, you can edit existing roles and create new roles, as shown in Figure 10.18. While privileges are used to control access, roles are used to structure access and to model reusable business roles. Roles can be nested, and by granting users roles instead of privileges, you can quickly update user authorizations when their actual business role changes.

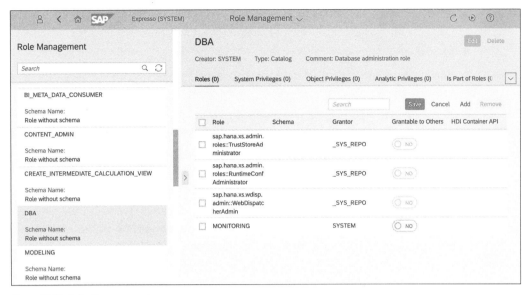

Figure 10.18 Role Management

A number of predefined catalog roles are included by default. These roles are highly privileged and shouldn't be used in production systems. Examples are as follows:

- **CONTENT_ADMIN**
  All privileges to use the information modeler in SAP HANA studio and interact with the repository.

- **MODELING**
  All privileges to use the information modeler in SAP HANA studio, including predefined analytical privilege _SYS_BI_CP_ALL.

- **MONITORING**
  Read-only access to all metadata, system and monitoring views, and data collected by the statistics server.

- **PUBLIC**
  Filtered read-only access to system views on objects to which the user has access rights. This is ranted to every user except restricted users.

- **SAP_INTERNAL_HANA_SUPPORT**
  System and object privileges that allow access to low-level internal system views. To avoid accidental use, this role can't be granted to the SYSTEM user, can't be granted to other roles, and can only be granted to a single user at a time (configurable).

The different role types are as follows:

- **Catalog**
  Runtime role created with the SQL statement CREATE ROLE (or indirectly using SAP HANA cockpit or SAP HANA studio)

- **HDI**
  Design-time role associated with the SAP HANA XSA environment.
- **Repository**
  Design-time role associated with the SAP HANA XS, classic model environment, such as `sap.hana.xs.admin.roles::WebDispatcherAdmin`.

Only catalog and HDI roles can be mapped to LDAP groups as the repository roles are deprecated.

When creating a new role, you need to provide a name, whether to create the role in a specific schema or not (as a consequence, the role will be dropped when you delete the schema) and whether to assign the role to an LDAP group. For the role to serve any purpose, you then will grant the role other roles, system privileges, object privileges, or analytical privileges. Package and application privileges only apply to SAP HANA XS, classic model environments.

To grant roles to users, you use the **Role Assignment** screen that we discussed previously, assuming the authorization mode is local, not LDAP.

System privilege `ROLE ADMIN` is required for role management. The equivalent SQL statement is `CREATE ROLE`.

Authorization Dependency Viewer

Troubleshooting authorization errors can be complex. The **Authorization Dependency Viewer** view (see Figure 10.19) accessed under **User & Role Management** aims to simplify and troubleshoot errors such as the following:

- Not authorized (258)
- Invalidated view (391)
- Invalidated procedure (430)

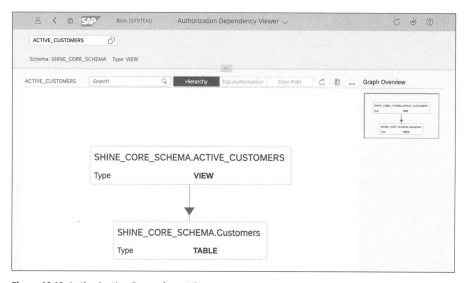

Figure 10.19 Authorization Dependency Viewer

Authorization and invalid objects errors are returned if the object owner doesn't have the required privileges on the underlying objects or lacks the WITH GRANT OPTION on the object.

Encryption

SAP HANA supports encryption of both data in transit (network) and data at rest (storage). The database also includes an internal application encryption service that can be used to encrypt sensitive data for applications. Besides server-side services, SAP HANA also supports client-side encryption.

In the following sections, we'll walk through the available encryption functionalities and how to use them in SAP HANA cockpit.

Cryptographic Service Provider

SAP HANA uses the CommonCryptoLib (CCL) cryptographic library (libsap-crypto.so) to encrypt both network traffic and data at rest. Earlier SAP HANA releases relied on the OpenSSL library included with the SUSE Linux operating system, but this cryptographic library was deprecated with the SAP HANA 1.0 SPS 10 release.

Communication Encryption

For data in transit, you distinguish internal network communications and external access. Both type of communications can be encrypted using the TLS protocol. SAP recommends using encrypted communication channels where possible.

Examples of internal communication are as follows:

- Name server and index server for the system and tenant database on a single-host system
- Name servers on a multiple-host system
- Primary and secondary site with system replication
- SAP HANA server and SAP HANA dynamic tiering extended store

Only for communication between the SAP HANA database and optional server components such as SAP HANA dynamic tiering is TLS automatically enabled. For the communication between SAP HANA services, systems, databases, and hosts, encryption needs to be enabled with system parameter global.ini/[communication]/ssl=systemPKI. The default value is off.

Public key infrastructure (PKI) (systemPKI) references the public and private key pair and public key X.509 certificates created for each host and database for mutual authentication. The certificates are signed by the SAP HANA instance acting as the dedicated trusted certificate authority (CA). The keys are stored in a PIN-protected personal security environment (PSE) file stored in the system PKI secure stores in the file system (SSFS). PSE and SSFS are SAP security concepts also encountered in SAP NetWeaver systems. X.509, PKI, CA, and TLS are industry standards.

Enabling TLS for SAP HANA system replication requires additional configuration steps beyond the scope of this exam. However, even if you don't want to encrypt the communication between sites, you still need to copy the system PKI SSFS store and key file from the primary server to the secondary servers to establish the trust. This requirement is covered in Chapter 12.

Next, let's move on to external access. Examples of external access are as follows:

- HTTP/S web clients for SAP HANA XS, classic model or SAP HANA XSA, such as SAP HANA cockpit
- Client/server SQL connections using ODBC, JDBC, and other types of client libraries, such as SAP HANA studio
- Data provisioning connections such as those made with SDA and SDI
- sapcontrol connections used by SAP HANA cockpit and SAP HANA studio to stop and start the system
- SAP Host Agent used by the web interface of the SAP HANA database lifecycle manager tool (HDBLCM)
- Connections made by SAP Support through an SAP Router (hdbrss, the remote support daemon) or SAP Solution Manager

To secure SQL-based traffic between clients and the SAP HANA database, TLS provides server authentication, data encryption, and even client authentication, if required. Client authentication is common when the only client is the application server. It's possible to enforce the usage of TLS with system parameter global.ini/ [communication]/sslEnforce=true. How exactly TLS needs to be configured differs per client connection protocol: ODBC, JDBC, Python, and so on.

For SQL-based traffic, the PSE (keys and certificates) is typically stored in the database as a certificate collection although file-based configurations are supported.

To configure secure HTTPS for SAP HANA XS, classic model applications, you only need to configure SAP Web Dispatcher. The SAP HANA XSA model uses a completely different architecture, and you have to configure the platform router, the SAP HANA XSA system area, and the JDBC connections from the application server runtimes to the database.

Certificate Collections

Certificate collections enable you to manage certificates in the database instead of the file system. This makes certificate management easier as the certificates are automatically included with database backup and recovery and also clearly separated per database (certificate collections were introduced with the tenant database feature). In addition, you can now create different certificate collections for different purposes, as illustrated in Figure 10.20 and Figure 10.21. The file *sapsrv.pse* stores the keys and certificates for both external access using TLS for authentication, including X.509 certifications and SAML and JWT tokens. With certificate collections, you can clearly separate the different configurations.

Figure 10.20 shows the different purposes of certificate collections: those that are used for authentication (SAML, X.509, SAP Logon, JWT) and those that are used for TLS (TLS, tenant database replication, LDAP, SDA).

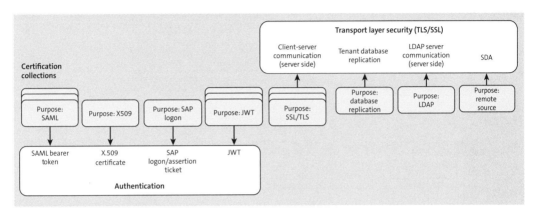

Figure 10.20 Certificate Collections

Alternatively, Figure 10.21 shows the different PSEs stored in the SSFS. This shows that the server PSE (*sapsrv.pse*) is used for both TLS and three types of authentication. In addition, note that for internal communication, three different PSEs are used. This makes file-based PSE more difficult to manage.

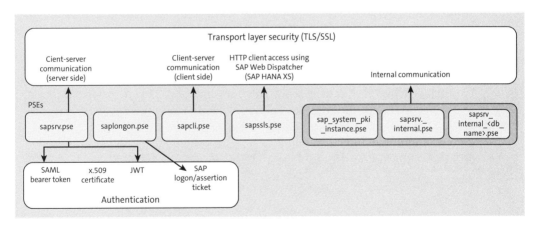

Figure 10.21 Personal Security Environment (PSE)

Server-Side Encryption Services

SAP HANA supports encryption of data at rest stored on the data volume (persistence), log volume, and for backups (data and log), as shown in Figure 10.22. Data is encrypted with a root key stored in a secure store, typically the instance SSFS, and protected by a master key, the same mechanism as used for internal communication.

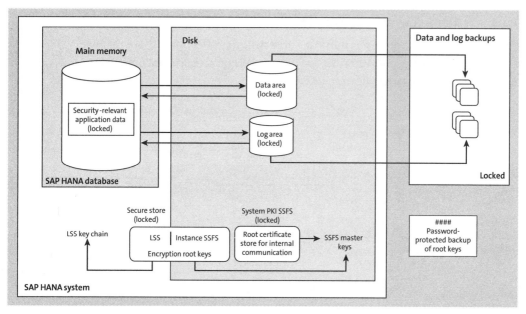

Figure 10.22 Encryption Keys and Services

You see both the instance SSFS for data at rest encryption and the system PKI SSFS for data in transit, each with a master key. The root keys are used to encrypt persistence, redo logs, backups, and for the internal encryption service. This service is used by SAP HANA to store the credentials for SDA to connect to remote data sources, but developers can also leverage this service to encrypt sensitive data used in their applications (e.g., credit cards). Each database has its own unique root keys.

For enhanced security, new root keys are typically generated at intervals. This requires a backup of the current key. This backup is protected by password that is also stored in the secure store. The backup of the root keys together with the password may be required for database recovery.

> **Note**
> Don't confuse the backup root key (the key used to encrypt backups) with the root key backup!

We'll see how server-side encryption works for secure storage and encryption key management in the following sections.

Local Secure Store

SAP HANA 2.0 SPS 04 introduced an alternative for the instance SSFS called the local secure store (LSS), depicted in Figure 10.23. Like the instance SSFS, the LSS stores encryption keys and security-related data, such as the root key backup password and some configuration information. Unlike SSFS, the LSS runs as a separate service (process) and operating system account (<sid>crypt), separating system and security administration.

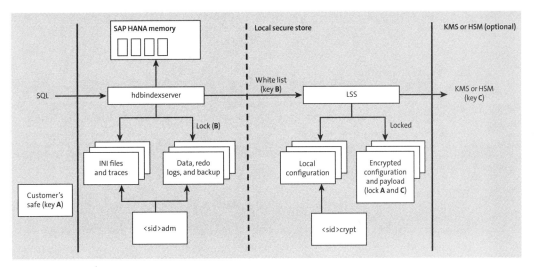

Figure 10.23 Local Secure Store

The SAP HANA operating system administration account <sid>adm can only read configuration and trace files. Data, redo log, and backup files are accessible but encrypted. Only whitelisted processes such as hdbindexserver can decrypt the data using the keys from the LSS. The <sid>crypt user can access the keys but not the user data. Optionally, the LSS can be secured by an external key management service (KMS) or hardware security module (HSM). To configure the LSS, the lsscfg tool is used.

Learn More

LSS is documented in the SAP HANA Security Guide for the concepts and SAP HANA Administration Guide for the activities.

SAP HANA 2.0 SPS 05: What's New?

As of SAP HANA 2.0 SPS 05, LSS is supported for production environments and can be used in combination with an external KMS. For more information on this topic, beyond the scope of the exam, see SAP Note 2917358 – How to Configure an SAP HANA System to Use an External Key Management System.

Encryption Key Management

Certificates and keys, both master and root, are generated during installation. For third-party installations, SAP recommends updating the keys immediately after hand-over. This applies to both appliances and to cloud-based hosting environments where systems are often cloned and not actually installed.

When you start a new instance of SAP HANA, express edition, as a virtual machine (VM) on your local computer or launch as an instance using a template of a cloud provider, the operating system initializes with a script to perform these steps automatically.

Client-Side Encryption

For client-side data security, SAP HANA provides a secure user store where connection information can be stored as a key. This enables client applications, for example, a backup program, to connect to the database without the requirement to enter a password interactively or hard-coded in a script. To create a key, use the hdbuserstore command. The name of the store is SSFS_HDB.DAT.

With client-side data encryption, you can encrypt database table columns using an encryption key stored on the client. Common examples are credit cards or Social Security numbers, and the typical use case is for hosted environments which require a guarantee that only the data owner and not the database administrators can view the data. Client-side encryption works with a column encryption key (CEK) and client key pair (CKP) of which the public key is stored on the server, and the private key is stored on the client in the secure user store. Currently, only ODBC and JDBC clients support client-side data encryption, and the application must use prepared (precompiled) statements to write or read encrypted data. Unlike the server-side encryption for persistence or redo log, client-side data encryption isn't activated with a simple on/off switch.

Learn More

Client-side security-related topics are beyond the scope of the exam. As of SPS 05, there is a dedicated SAP HANA Client-Side Data Encryption Guide for the SAP HANA platform, which can be found at *http://s-prs.co/v507854*.

In addition, as of SPS 05, the SAP HANA client now has its own home on the SAP Help Portal (*http://s-prs.co/v507855*). For more information, see SAP Note 2393013 – FAQ: SAP HANA Clients.

Network Security Information in SAP HANA Cockpit

The Network Security Information app, accessible from the **Security Related Links** card, lists relevant information about data in motion protection (see Figure 10.24). Most of these settings are configurable through system parameters. The cryptographic provider used is the CCL, and the maximum and minimum TLS protocol versions accepted are listed.

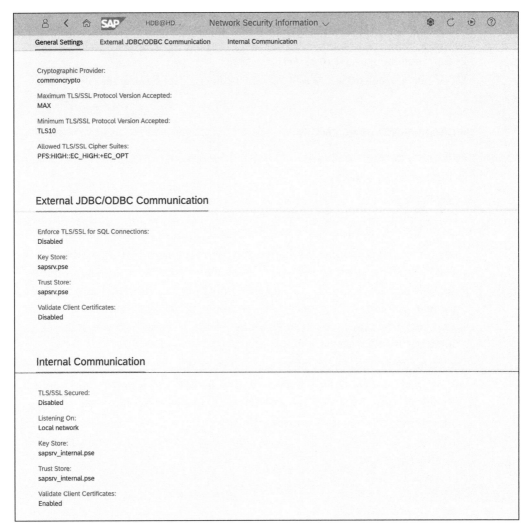

Figure 10.24 Network Security Information

> **Note**
>
> TLS replaced the SSL cryptographic protocol some two decades ago. Although SSL is deprecated, the term is still commonly used. For this reason, SAP HANA cockpit uses TLS/SSL as the description but lists the actual version as TLS 10. To enforce TLS, you set system parameter sslEnforce=true.

The **External JDBC/ODBC Communication** section is relevant for SAP HANA clients. The key store for the public and private keys is the *sapsrv.pse* file. This is also where the certificates are located.

The **Internal Communication** section lists information about the network used (local network for single-host system) and the location of the key and trust store PSE, that is, *sapsrv_internal.pse*. TLS isn't enabled, which is common when the services are bound to the local network (loopback adapter).

> **Learn More**
>
> For more information on this topic, see the "SAP HANA Network and Communication Security" section in the SAP HANA Security Guide.
>
> Secure configuration of the SAP HAN XS environment is out of scope of the exam.

Certificates in SAP HANA Cockpit

The **Security Related Links** card on **Database Overview** also includes the following certificate-related options:

- **Certificate Store**

  The certificate store lists all imported certificates. You can import certificates from a file or by pasting the content of a privacy-enhanced mail (PEM) file. PEM is a common standard to exchange cryptographic keys and certificates. PEM uses Base64 to convert binary data into ASCII text. PEM files are recognizable by the `-----BEGIN <label>-----` header and similar footer. Common file extensions are *.pem*, *.cer*/*.crt*, or *.key*, depending on the contents. A PEM file can contain multiple certificates, for example, to include the certificate chain or combine public certificate with private key.

  Selecting the certificate displays detailed information, as illustrated in Figure 10.25. Click the **Show PEM Representation** button to view the certificate as imported. From the store, you can navigate to **Certificate Collections**.

  Imported certificates correspond to the `CREATE CERTIFICATE FROM <PEM>` SQL statement and require the `TRUST ADMIN` system privilege. The data comes from the `CERTIFICATES` view.

Figure 10.25 Certificate Store

- **Certificate Collections**

  The **Certificate Collections** area (see Figure 10.26) enables you to create collections, assign a purpose, and add certificates. Available purposes are as follows:

  - User authentication (SAML, X.509, JWT, SAP Logon)

- SSL (client/server)
- LDAP
- Database replication (tenant database copy/move)
- Remote source (SDA)

The USER ADMIN system privilege is required when the purpose is user authentication. SSL, LDAP, and DATABASE ADMIN for SSL, LDAP, and replication, respectively, and CREATE REMOTE SOURCE for SDA. This action corresponds to the SET PSE <name> PURPOSE <purpose> SQL statement. The data comes from the PSEs and PSE_CERTIF-ICATES views.

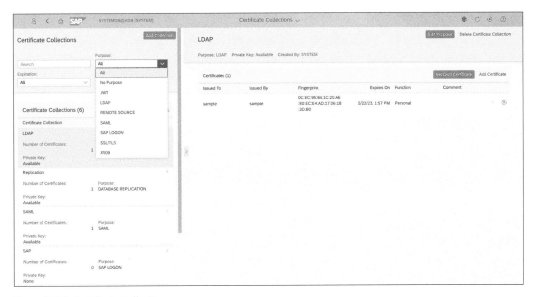

Figure 10.26 Certificate Collections

Data Encryption in SAP HANA Cockpit

The **Data Encryption** card illustrated in Figure 10.27 shows you the status of data volume, redo log, and backup encryption with toggles to switch encryption ON or OFF together with a time stamp of the latest root key change. This information comes from system view M_ENCRYPTION_OVERVIEW. Enabling encryption corresponds to the statement ALTER SYSTEM [PERSISTENCE | LOG | BACKUP] ENCRYPTION <encrypt_option>. Besides ON/OFF, encryption options also include creating or activating new root keys. This statement requires the ENCRYPTION ROOT KEY ADMIN system privilege.

When you select the **Data Encryption** card, the Data Encryption app opens, as illustrated in Figure 10.28. This app provides more detailed information about data at rest encryption. Like the card, it provides the ON/OFF toggle and displays the time stamp of the root key and latest encryption configuration change. Note the SAP recommendation to enable both data volume and redo log encryption for full protection.

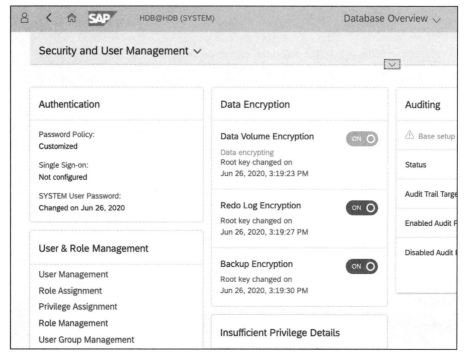

Figure 10.27 Database Overview: Data Encryption

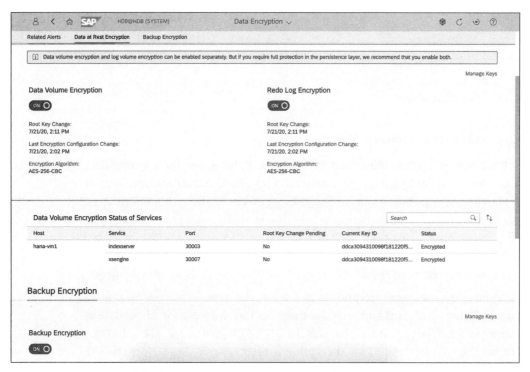

Figure 10.28 Data Encryption

The encryption algorithm used is AES-256-CBC, which stands for the Advanced Encryption Standard with 256 bits key length (largest) with cipher block chaining. This is an industry standard and also used by governments, for example, to encrypt sensitive data. The data volume is encrypted per service. The **Data Volume Encryption Status of Services** table lists the current key ID. This corresponds to system view M_PERSISTENCE_ENCRYPTION_STATUS.

From the Data Encryption app, you can navigate to **Manage Keys**, as shown in Figure 10.29. Here you can find information about the file location of the master key and SSFS used for data encryption (at rest). **System Public Key Infrastructure (PKI)** shows the same information for internal communication (in transit). The **Manage Keys** screen also provides the active key ID and last changed time stamp for data volume, redo log, and backup encryption root keys. The **See All Keys** link displays a popup frame that also shows earlier and now deactivated keys. The same information can be found in the ENCRYPTION_ROOT_KEYS system view.

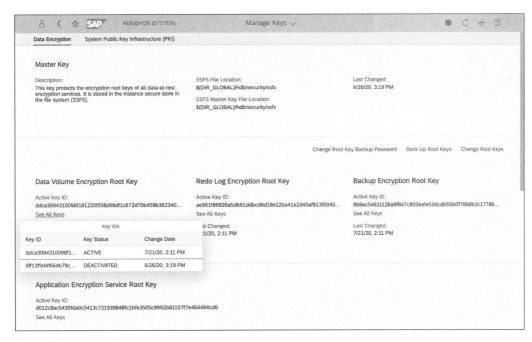

Figure 10.29 Manage Keys

From the root key section, you can select **Change Root Key Backup Password**, **Back Up Root Keys**, and **Change Root Keys**.

Change Root Key Backup Password displays a layover to change the password with a warning message that this password protects the root key backup files and that losing it may result in the database being unrecoverable.

This action corresponds with the ALTER SYSTEM SET ENCRYPTION ROOT KEYS BACKUP PASSWORD <passphrase> statement. This password is set and stored in the instance (data encryption) SSFS, and you'll be prompted to provide this password to import root keys from backup into the database. You can use command `hdbnsutil -validate-RootKeysBackup <filename> [--password=<passphrase>]` to verify whether a backup file can be recovered with the current root key backup password or whether you may have to use an older one.

The **Change Root Keys** link opens a wizard where you're first prompted to select the root keys you want to change in step **1** (**Keys to Be Changed**), as illustrated in Figure 10.30:

- **Data volume encryption root key** (persistence)
- **Redo log encryption root key**
- **Backup log encryption root key**
- **Application log encryption root key**

This will execute the same `ALTER SYSTEM [PERSISTENCE | LOG | BACKUP | APPLICATION ] ENCRYPTION <encrypt_option>` statement, but instead of `ON | OFF`, the encryption option is now `CREATE NEW KEY`.

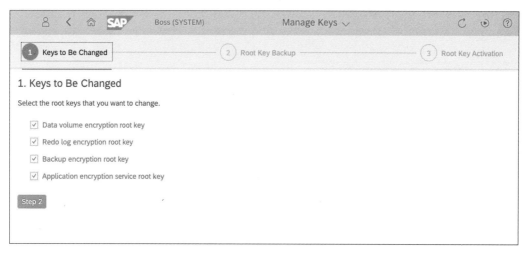

Figure 10.30 Manage Keys: Keys to Be Changed

In step **2** (**Root Key Backup**), you're given a warning that you must make a backup of the root keys and store to an external location as the keys will be required for recovery. There is a button to download the root keys to your local computer, which you need to select to activate step **3**. This downloads the same *rootKey-Backup-<database@instance>.rkb* file from **Manage Keys** shown earlier in Figure 10.29.

In step **3** (**Root Key Activation**), you're prompted to confirm that you've backed up the root keys, after which the **Activate Root Keys** button is activated. This executes the previously mentioned statement with encryption option `ACTIVATE NEW ROOT KEY`.

The best time to encrypt a database is just after creation. When encryption is applied at a later point in time, it takes some time for all pages to be encrypted, and a backup and recovery cycle is recommended. The page encryption key used to encrypt data can be changed, and SAP recommends doing so from time to time. Before recovery, you need to import root keys used for encryption via the hdbn-sutil tool.

By default, encryption is controlled at the tenant database level and requires the system privilege ENCRYPTION ROOT KEY ADMIN. Alternatively, the tenant database administrator can hand over control using statement ALTER SYSTEM ENCRYPTION CONFIGURATION CONTROLLED BY SYSTEM DATABASE (no user interface yet), in which case, the DATABASE ADMIN system privilege is required to configure tenant database encryption. This is configurable per database. Should you want to continue with encryption configuration using SQL, the respective commands are ALTER SYSTEM [PERSISTENCE | LOG | BACKUP] ENCRYPTION ON or ALTER DATABASE <database> [PERSISTENCE | LOG | BACKUP] ENCRYPTION ON.

> **Exam Tip**
>
> All encryption operations are documented in the SAP HANA Administration Guide, but the exact syntax is beyond the scope of the exam.

Auditing

Auditing allows you to monitor and record selected actions performed in the SAP HANA database. While logging records everything, auditing only records selected actions as defined in an audit policy. Good candidates for auditing are the following:

- **System parameters**
  Is anyone attempting to modify the auditing configuration?
- **User authentication**
  Who changed the password of technical users?
- **User authorization**
  Is anyone getting superuser grants?
- **Database objects**
  Are tables created or deleted where it's not expected?

Auditing records what happened. It doesn't interfere with the action nor does it trigger any alerts. As such, auditing doesn't make the database any more secure. However, it does enable you to comply with security standards and identify potential security vulnerabilities.

We'll walk through the auditing functionality in the following sections, as well as how to use auditing in SAP HANA cockpit.

Audit Policy

The audit policy defines which actions are audited. The auditable actions are divided into several audit policy groups, for example, backup and recovery, data definition, data query and manipulation, granting and revoking of authorization, and operations on tenant databases. Only actions from the same group can be audited together in the same policy. The base setup, which we'll discuss later in this section, provides SAP's recommended settings with policies for the following:

- Authorization, including GRANT and REVOKE ANY.
- Configuration changes, including changes to the system parameter files using the ALTER SYSTEM ALTER CONFIGURATION statement.
- Design-time privileges (SAP HANA Repository).
- License deletion; without a license, the database is no longer accessible.
- Recover database.
- User administration (ALTER | CREATE | DROP user).

Most actions correspond to a single SQL statement, although some, such as GRANT and REVOKE ANY, combine several GRANT and REVOKE statements.

Apart from the action, you can also define the users included and choose **All** (users), **All Except Selected**, or **Only Selected**. Auditing all actions performed by a particular user is called a firefighter policy. As these policies generate a lot of entries and may even impact system performance, they should be avoided. A warning will display when a firefighter type policy is created.

Audit Trail

You can define different audit trail targets for the audit occurrences. The default is an internal database table. This has the following advantages:

- Easily accessible for reporting and analysis using SQL-based tools
- Secure storage and database-managed access
- Configurable retention period
- Table management to prune or clear the log and alerting when size thresholds are exceeded

Another audit trail target is the Linux operating system syslog file. This facilitates consolidation of auditable events at the database and operating system level for entire landscapes. We need to stress that SAP HANA auditing is configured at the tenant database level. Changes made to the system parameter configuration files (INI) when the database is stopped using an operating system editor aren't tracked. This also applies to the SYSTEM user reset password procedure in emergency mode and activities performed with the HDBLCM tool. To capture these events, SAP recommends enabling auditing at the operating system. HDBLCM actions are auditable through SAP Host Agent auditing, when enabled, and are also recorded in the syslog.

Other audit trail targets are kernel trace files and comma-separated values (CSV) text files. Trace files can be converted into CSV file using the hdbltracediag command. Using CSV files for a production system isn't recommended as access control is problematic.

You can assign an audit level to each policy that ranges from info and warning to alert, emergency, and critical. For the last three levels, you can assign multiple targets and write to tables, syslogs, and trace files simultaneously.

Although not recommended, it's possible to modify the audit trail target for individual tenant databases by removing the system parameter global.ini/[auditing configuration]/*_audit_trail_type from the blacklist and configuring it to the desired trail type for the tenant database in question.

Default Audit Policy

When auditing is enabled, the internal audit policy MandatoryAuditPolicy is activated and includes the following SQL statements:

- AUDIT POLICY (ALTER | CREATE | DELETE)
- ALTER SYSTEM CLEAR AUDIT LOG
- ALTER DATABASE <database name> SYSTEM USER PASSWORD

Changes to several auditing system parameters using the ALTER SYSTEM ALTER CONFIGURATION statement on global.ini/[auditing configuration] are also audited by default. This covers enabling and disabling auditing, as well as changing the audit trail target, which includes changing the location if the target is a CSV file.

Best Practices

Besides the base setup, the following best practices are encouraged (refer to the SAP HANA Security Guide for more details):

- Create as few audit policies as possible.
- Combine related audit actions, such as the base setup SAP authorizations policy for GRANT | REVOKE ANY privileges.
- Avoid audit policies for DML (SELECT, INSERT, UPDATE, DELETE).
- Avoid firefighter policies.
- Don't audit actions included in the default audit policy.
- Don't audit database-internal tables.

Auditing in SAP HANA Cockpit

The Auditing app in SAP HANA cockpit provides a convenient and easy-to-use interface to configure auditing, create audit policies, and view the audit trail when the database table is configured as target. The alternative is to use the SQL interface directly.

The **Auditing** card on **Database Overview** shows the status (on/off), the audit trail target, and the number of enabled and disabled audit policies (refer to Figure 10.1). When selected, the Auditing app opens. Like the card, the Auditing app shows the number of enabled and disable policies in the header. You can also enable/disable auditing, (re-)run the setup wizard (**Base Setup**) or go to the **Alerts** view. The Auditing app has three views or tabs: **Audit Policies**, **Configuration**, and **Audit Trail**. Before we walk through each in the following sections, we'll start with the base setup.

Base Setup

Select the **Base Setup** link to configure auditing for the database with SAP's recommended settings, illustrated with Figure 10.31. The setup wizard includes the following steps:

1. **Auditing Status**
   Switch auditing on (recommended).
2. **Audit Trail Targets**
   These targets are configurable for the system database, which presets the target for tenant databases with the database table as default.
3. **Audit Policies**
   Six audit polices are recommended here.

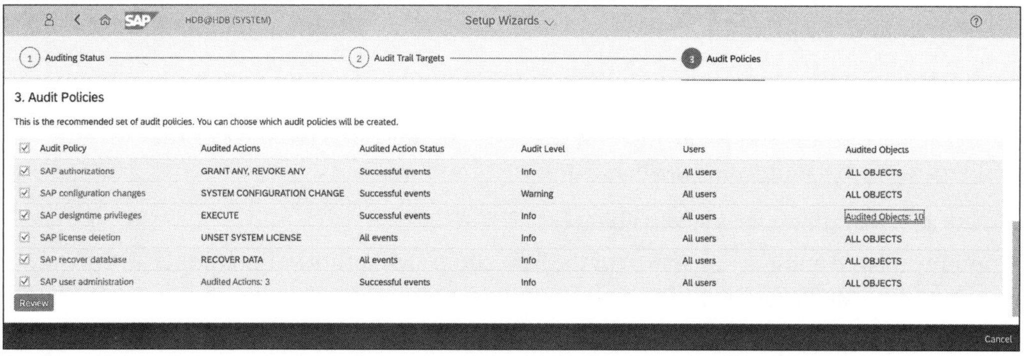

Audit Policy	Audited Actions	Audited Action Status	Audit Level	Users	Audited Objects
☑ SAP authorizations	GRANT ANY, REVOKE ANY	Successful events	Info	All users	ALL OBJECTS
☑ SAP configuration changes	SYSTEM CONFIGURATION CHANGE	Successful events	Warning	All users	ALL OBJECTS
☑ SAP designtime privileges	EXECUTE	Successful events	Info	All users	Audited Objects: 10
☑ SAP license deletion	UNSET SYSTEM LICENSE	All events	Info	All users	ALL OBJECTS
☑ SAP recover database	RECOVER DATA	All events	Info	All users	ALL OBJECTS
☑ SAP user administration	Audited Actions: 3	Successful events	Info	All users	ALL OBJECTS

Figure 10.31 Auditing Setup Wizard

Audit Policy

With the base setup completed, you can add new audit policies from the table header or disable/enable existing policies in the **Audit Policies** view shown in Figure 10.32. **Show SQL Statements** enables you to capture the SQL, for example, to apply the same configuration to other tenant databases.

When selected, the audit policy opens in a detailed view with functionality to edit or delete the policy (and show the SQL), as shown in Figure 10.33.

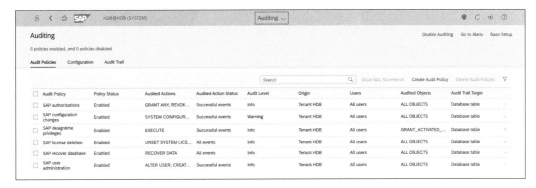

Figure 10.32 Auditing: Audit Policies

Figure 10.33 Auditing: Audit Policy Details

From the audit policy detail view, you can edit the following:

- **Policy Status**
  Enable or disable the particular policy.

- **Audited Action Status**
  Set as **Successful**, **Unsuccessful**, or **All** to indicate whether you want the policy just to capture success execution of the event, failed execution, or both. As an example, for privileged database users, you may want to audit both successful and unsuccessful password changes, whereas for regular users, only unsuccessful attempts are recorded.

- **Audit Level**

  Set as **Info**, **Warning**, **Alert**, **Emergency**, or **Critical**.

- **Audit Trail Target**

  Can be set as **Default target (Database table)** or **Database Table with Retention**. To configure the retention period, you need to explicitly assign the audit trail to a database table. You can either specify a number of **days** to trigger the log entry deletion or **one week**, **one month**, **six months**, or **year**.

- **Audited Actions**

  Select the action you want to audit.

- **Users Included in Policy**

  Select the users you want to include in this policy.

To create a new audit policy, the same input is requested using a configuration wizard with the following steps:

1. **Policy Name**

2. **Audited Actions and Status**

3. **Audited Users**

4. **Audit Trail Level and Audit Trail Target**

5. **Retention Period**

6. **Policy Status**

Configuration

The audit trail target is only configurable from the system database, as illustrated in the **Configuration** view shown in Figure 10.34.

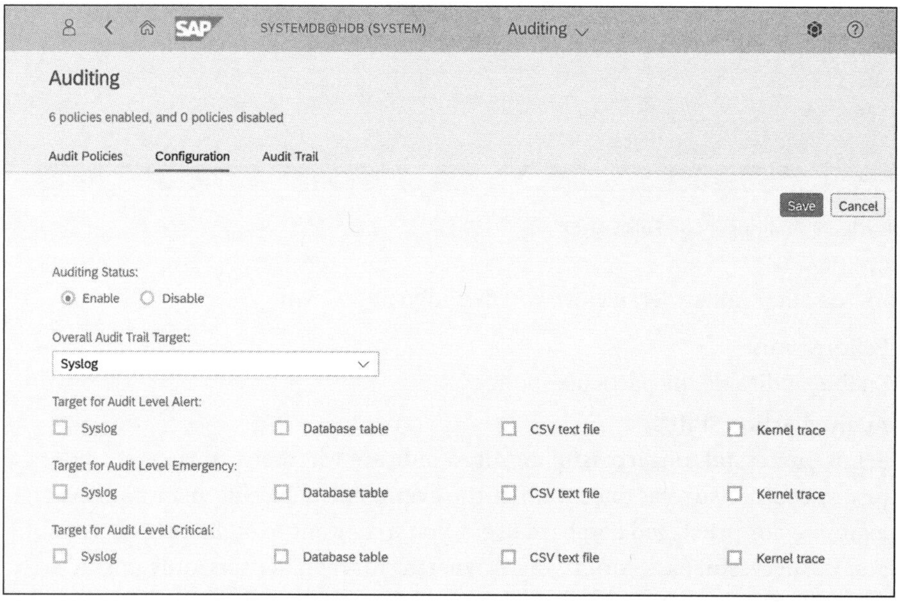

Figure 10.34 Auditing: Configuration

You can set the overall audit trail target to **Syslog**, **Database table**, **CSV text file**, or **Kernel trace**. For the alert, emergency, and critical levels, you can specify multiple targets.

Audit Trail

Figure 10.35 shows the audit entries from the internal database table. It also displays log entries from the audit logs of the SAP HANA XSA runtime environment, when configured. Clicking on **Delete Audit Entries** in the header prompts you to provide a number of days, specific date, or delete all entries.

Figure 10.35 Auditing: Audit Trail

The **Audit Trail** tab in the **Auditing** screen queries the AUDIT_LOG system view because the internal database table isn't directly accessible. To query the view, you need the AUDIT READ, AUDIT OPERATOR, or AUDIT ADMIN system privileges.

AUDIT OPERATOR enables you to delete entries from the audit table using either SAP HANA cockpit or SQL command ALTER SYSTEM CLEAR AUDIT LOG ALL.

AUDIT ADMIN is required to create an audit policy. To modify auditing settings, you need both AUDIT ADMIN and INIFILE ADMIN. To change auditing settings for tenant databases from the system database, you need system privilege DATABASE AUDIT ADMIN.

Database Management

When connected to the system database using the Database Management app, you can create audit policies for tenant databases with a limited list of auditable groups and actions, as shown in Figure 10.36. The policy can be applied to multiple tenant databases on the condition that the database is up and running.

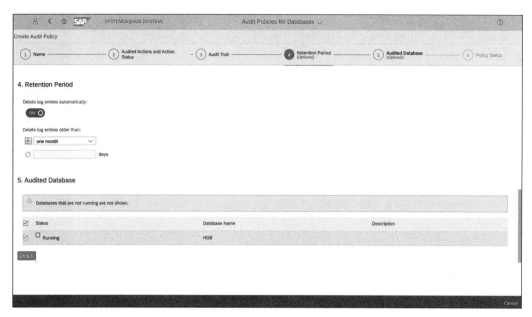

Figure 10.36 Audit Policies for Databases

> **Learn More**
>
> Auditing is documented in the SAP HANA Security Guide for the concepts and the SAP HANA Administration Guide for the tasks.
>
> You can audit activities for the SAP HANA XSA runtime as well—it's even integrated with the database—but this is out of scope for this topic area.

System Views

To get information about an SAP HANA system, you can use SQL commands to query views. For this, you can use the SQL console of SAP HANA database explorer.

There are three types of views, which require the system privilege CATALOG READ:

- **System views**
  System views provide information about the system, such as users, roles, tables, privileges, hints, certificates, AFL functions, and so on—the list is long.

- **Monitoring views**
  Monitoring views provide statistical information mainly for monitoring and performance troubleshooting purposes. These views all start with M_, such as M_CONNECTIONS, M_BACKUP_CATALOG, and M_EXPENSIVE_STATEMENTS.

- **Statistics service views**
  Statistics service views provide access to the _SYS_STATISTICS schema, containing both tables and views, and are populated by the statistics service and the

internal monitoring infrastructure. Here you find information about status, performance, and resource usage, such as HOST_DELTA_MERGE_STATISTICS and HOST_DISK_USAGE.

Figure 10.37 shows an example of how you can query system monitoring views in SAP HANA database explorer. In the system view (top-left pane), select **Tables**, and then apply a filter on the _SYS_STATISTICS schema to display the list of all available views.

In the SQL console, you query the EFFECTIVE_ROLES system view, which returns all roles granted to a user (here, PUBLIC and MONITORING). The view GRANTED_ROLES only displays roles directly granted to the user.

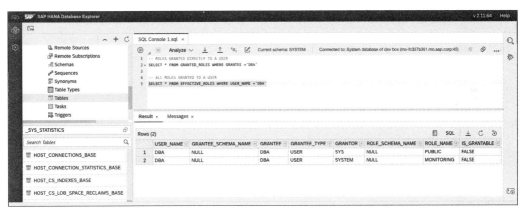

Figure 10.37 Querying System Views

Learn More

For the complete list of all system and system monitoring views, see the SAP HANA SQL Reference Guide. This is beyond the scope of the exam.

Security Checklist

SAP HANA cockpit includes a security checklist to assist you in securing your SAP HANA system and tenant databases. The checklist is illustrated in Figure 10.38 and documented in the SAP HANA Administration Guide. The list isn't exhaustive and only provides recommendations, which may or may not apply to your environment.

The **Deviations** tab shows noncompliant configurations. The checklist includes auditing, encryption, network, file system, traces, authentication, and authorization checks.

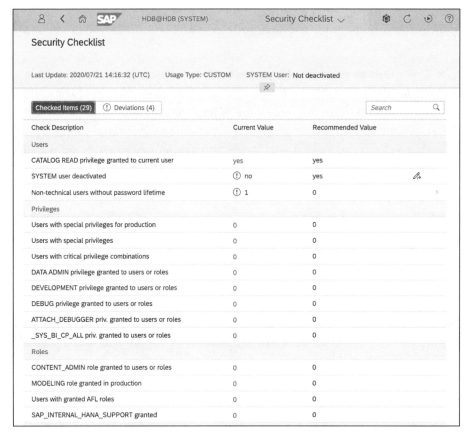

Figure 10.38 Security Checklist

Important Terminology

For this exam objective, you're expected to understand the following terms:

- **Auditing**
  Auditing allows you to monitor and record selected actions performed in the SAP HANA database. The audit policy defines which actions to audit. When the action occurs, an audit entry is written to the audit trail, which can be an internal database table, syslog, kernel trace, or CSV file. Typical auditable actions are changes to user authorization and system configuration.

- **Authentication**
  Authentication is the process used to verify identities. The most common method uses an internal mechanism with passwords (basic authentication), but SAP HANA also supports external authentication using a corporate identity provider (IdP) (LDAP) or single sign-on (SSO) through Security Assertion Markup Language (SAML) and JSON Web Token (JWT).

- **Authorization**
  Authorization is the process to verify the actions an authenticated user can perform. This covers system privileges, such as making backups or exporting data; object privileges, such as creating tables in a schema; or analytical privileges, such as viewing sales figures for specific regions or company codes. Users are granted authorizations either directly or through roles. When granted with admin privileges, the user can pass the authorization to other users or roles.

- **Certificate collection**
  A certificate collection is a personal security environment (PSE) in the database to store public and private keys together with certificates. Certificate collections are included in database backups, separated by purpose for user authentication type and server communication, and are database specific.

- **JSON Web Tokens (JWT)**
  JWT is a standard to exchange data in text in attribute-value pairs. Although the name suggests otherwise, it can be used in any programming language. JWTs are encoded credentials in JSON format.

- **Lightweight Directory Access Protocol (LDAP)**
  LDAP is an open, vendor-neutral industry standard for authentication and authorization commonly used for enterprise environments. With SAP HANA, you can use LDAP for both authentication and authorization via LDAP groups, as well as leverage LDAP to automatically provision (create) database users.

- **Local secure store (LSS)**
  LSS, introduced with SAP HANA 2.0 SPS 04, provides an alternative to the instance secure stores in the file system (SSFS) to secure root keys and root key backup passwords. LSS runs under an isolated operating system account and only provides encryption root key access to whitelisted processes (hdbindex-server). LSS can be configured to use an external key management service (KMS).

- **Personal security environment (PSE)**
  A PSE is a secure location where public and private key pairs are stored with the corresponding certificate chain. There are different PSE types. The PSE can be stored in secure stores in the file system (SSFS) or inside the database as a certificate collection.

- **Secure stores in the file system (SSFS)**
  SSFS is a conceptual safe that stores passwords, root keys, and encryption-related information. The store (DAT file) is protected by a master key (KEY file). SAP HANA includes an SSFS for internal communication called system PKI and an SSFS for data at rest encryption called instance SSFS. This SSFS stores the root keys used to encrypt the data volume (persistence), redo logs, backups, and internal application server encryption service.

- **Security Assertion Markup Language (SAML)**
  SAML is an open standard to exchange authentication and authorization data, typically between an identity provider (IdP) and a service provider, such as the SAP HANA database. SAML is based on XML. SAP HANA supports SAML for authentication only and can be used for SSO.

- **Single-sign on (SSO)**
  SSO enables you to log on once and connect to related but independent systems. You can configure SSO, for example, for SAP HANA cockpit to enable uninterrupted navigation to all registered databases after the initial logon.

- **Transport Layer Security (TLS)/Secure Sockets Layer (SSL)**
  TLS is a cryptographic protocol used to secure data in transit. The first version was introduced in 1999 as successor of the SSL protocol. Although SSL is deprecated, the name is still commonly used for network traffic encryption; for example, SAP HANA cockpit describes the protocol as TLS/SSL.

Practice Questions

These practice questions will help you evaluate your understanding of the topics covered in this chapter. The questions shown are similar in nature to those found on the certification examination. Although none of these questions will be found on the exam itself, they will allow you to review your knowledge of the subject. Select the correct answers, and then check the completeness of your answers in the "Practice Question Answers and Explanations" section. Remember that on the exam, you must select all correct answers, and only correct answers, to receive credit for the question.

1. Which type of users can you create using SAP HANA cockpit? (There are two correct answers.)

    ☐ **A.** Restricted users

    ☐ **B.** Database users

    ☐ **C.** Technical database users

    ☐ **D.** Predefined users

2. Why should you model roles as design-time objects? (There are two correct answers.)

    ☐ **A.** Catalog roles aren't transportable.

    ☐ **B.** Catalog roles can't be nested (role hierarchy).

    ☐ **C.** Deleting a user revokes all catalog roles.

    ☐ **D.** You can create design-time roles in a development environment.

3. Which SAP HANA authorization modes support single sign-on (SSO)? (There are three correct answers.)

☐ **A.** JSON Web Token (JWT)

☐ **B.** Kerberos

☐ **C.** LDAP

☐ **D.** SAML

☐ **E.** OAuth

4. For which authentication method do you need to create a provider?

☐ **A.** SAML

☐ **B.** LDAP

☐ **C.** JWT

☐ **D.** Kerberos

☐ **E.** SAP NetWeaver Logon and Assertion tickets

5. How can you change a restricted user into a regular user? (There are two correct answers.)

☐ **A.** Enable ODBC/JDBC access

☐ **B.** Grant creation of objects in own schema

☐ **C.** Execute ALTER USER <user> SET PARAMETER RESTRICT='FALSE'

☐ **D.** Grant public role

6. SAP HANA doesn't support direct user privilege grants. You need to first assign a privilege to a role and next grant the role to the user.

☐ **A.** True

☐ **B.** False

7. Both successful and unsuccessful events are auditable.

☐ **A.** True

☐ **B.** False

8. A retention period can only be specified for audit policies that explicitly have database table as the audit trail target.

☐ **A.** True

☐ **B.** False

9. Which events aren't auditable? (There are three correct answers.)

☐ **A.** Resetting the `SYSTEM` user password of `SYSTEMDB` using command `hdbnameserver -resetUserSystem`

☐ **B.** Changes made to the LDAP configuration using SAP HANA cockpit

☐ **C.** Changes made to the system parameter files (INI) when the database is stopped.

☐ **D.** SAP HANA system upgrades

☐ **E.** SAP HANA tenant database recovery

10. Which events are captured by the internal audit policy `MandatoryAuditPolicy`? (There are three correct answers.)

☐ **A.** Selecting **Delete Audit Entries** from the **Audit Trail** view of the Auditing app in SAP HANA cockpit

☐ **B.** Using SQL command `TRUNCATE TABLE AUDIT_LOG`

☐ **C.** Enabling auditing

☐ **D.** Making changes to system parameters using the `ALTER SYSTEM ALTER CONFIGURATION` statement

☐ **E.** Changing a tenant database `SYSTEM` user password using the SAP HANA cockpit Database Management app.

11. Client connections using the SQL interface can be forced to use SSL.

☐ **A.** True

☐ **B.** False

12. SAP HANA supports both LDAP authentication and authorization.

☐ **A.** True

☐ **B.** False

13. SAP HANA supports both SAML authentication and authorization.

☐ **A.** True

☐ **B.** False

14. SAP HANA internal communication is encrypted by default.

☐ **A.** True

☐ **B.** False

15. Which purposes are supported for certificate collections? (There are three correct answers.)

☐ **A.** Remote source

☐ **B.** ODBC/JDBC

☐ **C.** LDAP

☐ **D.** System replication

☐ **E.** Database replication

16. For which security functions can you use SAP HANA cockpit? (There are three correct answers.)

☐ **A.** Authentication

☐ **B.** Auditing

☐ **C.** Authorization

☐ **D.** Encryption

☐ **E.** Anonymization and data masking

17. When data (persistence), log, and backup encryption is enabled, all data at rest is encrypted.

☐ **A.** True

☐ **B.** False

18. You can only use the CommonCryptoLib (CCL) encryption library to connect to the SAP HANA database.

☐ **A.** True

☐ **B.** False

Practice Question Answers and Explanations

1. Correct answers: **A, B**
   You can create restricted users and database users with SAP HANA cockpit.

   Answer C is incorrect because technical database users only exist conceptually. These user accounts don't correspond to a real-life person but are used for connections between the database and an application server, for example. You can assign technical database users to a separate user group and assign different password policies. Answer D is incorrect because predefined users are database users, such as SYSTEM and SYS. These can't be created at runtime using SAP HANA cockpit.

2. Correct answers: **A, C**

   Catalog roles cause duplication of effort. Design-time roles are created once and can be deployed to one or more environments. Changes are made at the source, which allows for version control, and they can be easily be redeployed. Keeping track of role changes with catalog roles, in particular for complex role hierarchies, can be very challenging.

   Another important aspect is that catalog roles are database objects owned by database users. When you delete the user, this also deletes the role. To grant the role to other users, the grantor needs to have all privileges assigned to the role.

   Answer B is incorrect because both catalog and design-time roles can be nested. Answer D is incorrect because both catalog and design-time roles can be created in a development environment. The major difference is between how roles are transported to the production environment.

3. Correct answers: **A, B, D**

   JSON Web Token (JWT), Kerberos, and LDAP authorization modes support SSO.

   Answer C is incorrect because the SAP HANA LDAP implementation doesn't use SSO. Answer E is incorrect because OAuth is used for SAP HANA XSA authentication and supports SSO, but it's not a supported database authentication mechanism.

4. Correct answers: **A, C**

   SAP HANA web clients support SAML, JWT, Kerberos, and X.509 authentication. For SAML and JWT, you need to create an authentication provider.

   Answer B is not correct because LDAP is only supported by SQL-based clients using JDBC/ODBC and other database client protocols but not for HTTP/S web clients. Answer D is not correct. Although Kerberos is supported for both SQL-based and web-based clients (using SPNEGO), it doesn't require a provider. Answer E is incorrect because SAP NetWeaver Logon and Assertion tickets aren't supported for web-based clients.

5. Correct answers: **B, D**

   You can change a restricted user into a regular user by granting the creation of objects in your own schema or granting a public role.

   Answer A is incorrect because although ODBC/JDBC access is one of the three differences between regular and restricted users, granting this privilege doesn't change the user type (refer to Figure 10.6). Answer C is incorrect because examples of user parameters are CLIENT, LOCAL, and TIME ZONE, but not RESTRICTED.

6. Correct answer: **B**

   False. Although it's a best practice to assign privileges to roles and roles to user, SAP HANA doesn't enforce this.

7. Correct answer: **A**

   True. For each auditable event you can select **Successful**, **Unsuccessful**, or **All** (refer to Figure 10.33).

8. Correct answer: **A**

   True. Retention periods are per policy and require a database table as an explicit audit trail target (refer to Figure 10.33).

9. Correct answers: **A**, **C**, **D**

   SAP HANA auditing monitors selected events in the database, including changing the SYSTEM user password using SQL statements but not using the emergency procedure. When the database is stopped, auditing isn't active.

   Answer B is incorrect because all configuration changes made with ALTER SYSTEM ALTER CONFIGURATION statements, including LDAP configuration using SAP HANA cockpit, are auditable. Answer E is incorrect because tenant database recovery is included in the auditing base setup. System database recovery isn't an auditable event.

10. Correct answers: **A**, **C**, **E**

    Delete Audit Entries executes the ALTER SYSTEM CLEAR AUDIT LOG statement, which is included in the internal audit policy. This also applies to answers C and E.

    Answer B is incorrect because AUDIT_LOG is a view and executing the TRUNCATE TABLE statement on a view returns an error. The internal table isn't directly accessible and can't be modified. Answer D is incorrect because only specific system parameters related to auditing are included in the internal audit policy.

11. Correct answer: **A**

    True. With the global.ini/[communication]/sslEnforce=true setting, you can force all clients who communicate with the SAP HANA database through the SQL interface to use secured connections. Connections not using TLS/SSL are refused.

12. Correct answer: **A**

    True. For Microsoft Active Directory (AD), SAP HANA supports both LDAP authentication and authorization using LDAP groups, and you also can use LDAP to automatically provision (create) database users.

13. Correct answer: **B**

    False. Although SAML supports both authentication and authorization, SAP HANA only support this protocol for authentication purposes.

14. Correct answer: **B**

    False. TLS is automatically enabled only for communication between the SAP HANA database and optional server components, such as SAP HANA dynamic tiering. For communication between SAP HANA services, systems, databases, and hosts, encryption needs to be enabled with system parameter global.ini/ [communication]/ssl=systemPKI. The default value is off.

15. Correct answers: **A, C, E**

    Valid purposes are as follows:

    – User authentication using SAML, X.509, JWT, or SAP Logon

    – SSL (client/server)

    – LDAP

    – Database replication for tenant database copy/move

    – Remote source for SDA

    Answer B is incorrect because ODBC/JDBC isn't a valid purpose for certificate collections. Answer D is incorrect because system replication isn't a valid purpose for certificate collections.

16. Correct answers: **A, B, C, D**

    The security functions authentication, authorization, auditing, and encryption have been covered in this chapter.

    Answer E is incorrect because to work with anonymization and data masking, you can use a SQL interface such as SAP HANA database explorer or a development tool such as SAP HANA Web IDE.

    SAP HANA cockpit does provide the Anonymization Report app to view what data anonymization method is used with supporting KPIs for the associated calculation views, as illustrated previously in Figure 10.14.

17. Correct answer: **B**

    False. Log, trace, and configuration files aren't encrypted. For security reasons, SAP recommends only to use short-term analysis and not to keep the trace files after the analysis has completed.

18. Correct answer: **B**

    False. OpenSSL is supported to encrypt JDBC/ODBC client connections to the SAP HANA database. On the server side, however, SAP HANA only uses the CommonCryptoLib (CCL) encryption library.

Takeaway

After reading this chapter, you should be familiar with a lot of acronyms, such as SSO, LSS, SAML, JWT, TLS, SSFS, and LDAP and what they stand for, even though you're not expected to be a master in all these subjects. You should now be familiar with who can configure user authentication and authorization and how to create user groups and configure password policies. You clicked through the **Manage Keys** and **Audit Policy** wizards and understand the items on the security checklist.

Summary

In this chapter, we've described the SAP HANA security functions for authentication, authorization, encryption, and auditing, and how you can use SAP HANA cockpit to configure and monitor security settings. After a brief description of the security impact of the different implementation scenarios, we covered the different authentication options and described using SAML and JWT as IdPs for SSO. We covered how users, roles, and privileges related to each other and how these can be assigned and configured. We looked at data encryption at rest and in transit, auditing, and the security checklist to validate that your SAP HANA system is safe and sound.

In the next chapter, we'll switch gears to backup and recovery processes.

Chapter 11
Backup and Recovery

Techniques You'll Master

- Understanding the concepts of database backup and recovery with SAP HANA

- Creating file-based database backups

- Scheduling database backups

- Using SAP HANA cockpit to create backups and perform recovery

- Recovering a system database and a tenant database

- Using backup and recovery for database copy

- Working with tenant database fallback snapshots

Making backups and, most importantly, being able to recover SAP HANA databases, are essential database administration tasks. Unexpected events may happen, and you need to protect your system against faults and failures. Creating backups at regular intervals and storing these backups in a safe location safeguards the system from such events. A sound backup strategy requires careful thought and planning. Understanding the concepts of SAP HANA database backup and recovery is a prerequisite.

Real-World Scenario

The senior database administrator of your company is moving on to another position. You're the lucky database administrator replacement. Over the years, the database administrator has crafted a backup strategy that has kept the business up and running. You request a test system to practice tenant database and full system recovery and point-in-time recovery (PITR), and experiment with how to recover the database in case the data area volume is lost or when the redo log files on the file system are deleted. You prepare an operations handbook containing the steps to take because you know that database recovery is a rare event, likely to happen at unexpected times, potentially costing the company a lot of money, and hence typically involving special attention from senior management. Mastering backup and recovery is a skill acquired with a lot of practice and, where possible, automation.

Topic and Objectives

In this chapter, we'll discuss how to perform an SAP HANA backup and recovery. For the exam, you need to have a good understanding of the following topics:

- Backup and recovery concepts
- Performing a data backup
- Configuring log backups
- Recovering a database
- Creating a fallback snapshot
- Using backup and recovery for database copy

Note

Database backup and recovery is a "classic" exam topic and has been on the list since the beginning with a medium weight of 8%–12% of the total certification exam score. With 80 questions in total, you can expect about 8 questions about backup and recovery. This makes this topic area one of the more important ones.

Keep in mind that the exam guide states this can change at any time, so always check online for the latest updates.

SAP HANA 2.0 SPS 05: What's New

SPS 05 introduced two new features for database backup and recovery. With the Python tool `hdbrecovercheck.py`, you can check whether point-in-time recovery (PITR) is possible for the indicated time stamp and whether the corresponding backups are consistent. The tool works for both file-based backups and backups created with third-party backup tools. In addition, the SAP HANA Backint agent now also supports Amazon S3 storage for both backup and recovery.

SAP HANA cockpit 2.0 SP 12 adds support to specify a threshold size for multistreamed backups using the Backup Configuration app. SP 11 already introduced a new **Backup** card (**Recover Database** card if the database is offline), and you can now configure the tenant database retention period from the system database (see Chapter 9).

Learn More

For this topic area, we only cover SAP HANA database backup and recovery and exclude the backup requirements of SAP HANA extended application services, advanced model (SAP HANA XSA) and optional components, such as SAP HANA dynamic tiering, as this is beyond the scope of the exam. For more information on these topics, see the following SAP Notes:

- SAP Note 2300937 – Backup and Restore for SAP HANA Extended Application Services, Advanced Model
- SAP Note 2375865 – SAP HANA Dynamic Tiering 2.0: Backup and Recovery Functional Restrictions

Key Concepts Refresher

In this section, we'll touch on the key concepts that fall under the backup and recovery topic, including features, backup strategies and concepts, authorizations, backup types, configuration, third-party tools, creating backups, recovery scenarios, database copies, and alerts.

Learn More

Database backup and recovery is documented in the SAP HANA Administration Guide. For some recommended reading for additional information beyond the scope of this exam, see the following FAQ KBAs:

- KBA 1642148 – FAQ: SAP HANA Database Backup & Recovery
- KBA 2444090 – FAQ: SAP HANA Backup Encryption

Features and Strategy

In a nutshell, SAP HANA supports both manual and scheduled backups. You can perform complete and delta data backups. You can use SQL commands or use the backup tools from SAP HANA cockpit and SAP HANA studio. For enterprise backup solutions, SAP HANA integrates with third-party backup tools. Backup and recovery is configurable, supports backup lifecycle management (also known as housekeeping), and there are dedicated tools to perform integrity checks on backups. PITR is available, and you can also use backup and recovery to perform database copies.

Murphy's law that, "anything that can go wrong, will go wrong," could apply to your backups when there is no thought-through backup strategy in place. You need to consider the different scenarios for disaster and fault recovery, regularly check the integrity of your backups, and perform dry-run recoveries. Here are SAP's recommendations:

- Create a data backup after initial load, before upgrades, and after configuration changes that cause log write interruptions (e.g., changing the log mode).
- Create a data backup at regular intervals to reduce recovery time. A backup scenario could include daily data snapshots and a weekly complete data backup to file or a third-party backup tool.
- Remotely store a backup set with data and log backups to a secure location.
- Regularly delete backup sets (generations) no longer needed for recovery.

Architecture

Like any other database, SAP HANA uses persistent storage to save changes. This allows the system to recover from faults and failures, which can range from small and local issues with hardware or software (bugs) to more widespread incidents with the network or data center, either man-made or caused by natural disasters.

To persist data, SAP HANA uses two volumes: one for data and one for the redo logs as illustrated in Figure 11.1.

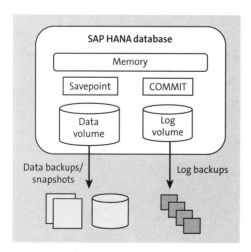

Figure 11.1 Architecture

Changed data is saved from memory every five minutes (default setting) during an event called a savepoint. This is a quick and nondisruptive operation during which transaction processing proceeds as normal. Shouldn't you save your data more often? No, because each transaction records its data changes in the redo log buffer, which is saved from memory either when the transaction commits or when the buffer is full.

If there is a power loss, for example, and the database needs to restart, SAP HANA uses the last savepoint (time stamp) as a baseline and applies the changes recorded in the redo log to reconstruct the in-memory area exactly like it was at the time of failure. Without savepoints, you would need to traverse all the redo logs ever made since the database was created. The savepoint and commit mechanism is shown in Figure 11.2.

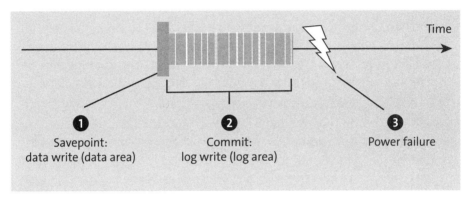

Figure 11.2 Savepoint

During a savepoint, SAP HANA saves all changed data from memory to persistence. This provides a consistent image of the state in memory. Each service (name server, index server, etc.) has its own savepoint image, but the savepoint event itself is coordinated to ensure transaction consistency. System parameter savepoint_interval_s controls the savepoint event occurrence with a default value of 300, that is, every 5 minutes. In addition, a savepoint is also executed when you execute the backup command, make a snapshot, request a delta merge, or perform a normal shutdown. With the ALTER SYSTEM SAVEPOINT command, you can manually trigger a savepoint event, for example, before a system load.

Learn More

For more extensive coverage of this topic beyond the scope of this exam, see the following KBA FAQs:

- KBA 2100009 – FAQ: SAP HANA Savepoints
- KBA 2400005 – FAQ: SAP HANA Persistence

Why make backups? Unfortunately, persistent storage can also fail. Issues with hardware or software may cause corruptions, or a fire may destroy the device. For this reason, you need to make a copy of your data and redo log files and save it someplace else. If a fault or failure requires the database to restart with loss of persistent storage (or parts of it), you can restore a backup of the files to the original location after the persistent storage device is back online. This will enable the database to start and return to a consistent state.

Have you lost any data? It depends. If the last backup you have is seven days old, and the persistent storage device with both data and redo log volume was completely lost, then yes—one week of data, to be precise. However, if the redo log volume is still accessible, and all the redo log files are still online, the database can recover from the restored data file up to the last transaction with no data loss. For this reason, data and redo log files are typically stored on different physical devices to avoid a single issue causing the loss of both the data and log volume (there are performance considerations as well).

You can't always blame hardware or software when things go wrong. Sometimes we cause the trouble ourselves. Data may have been deleted that should have been kept. To address these types of issues, you can perform a PITR by restoring the necessary data and redo log files and then recover the database to the desired time.

Data backups can also be used to make a database copy. Besides backup to file, SAP HANA also supports third-party backup tools. You can make a backup of the entire database, called full data backups, or make a partial one, called delta backups for which there are differential and incremental varieties. In addition, you can make a savepoint copy, called a data snapshot, and use it for database recovery. All these topics will be covered in more detail later in this chapter, together with backup lifecycle management and backup integrity checks.

Before a database backup starts, a global savepoint across all services and hosts is written. All data marked in the savepoint is read from the data volumes (not memory) and written to the backup location. These I/O operations are done in parallel and asynchronously, as shown in Figure 11.3.

Figure 11.3 also illustrates that database backups are made at the service layer, which means that each service with persistence creates its own backup. For the system database, this concerns the name server service, and for a tenant database, it concerns the index server service. Other services, such as the compile server or script server, don't have persistence, so they aren't included. On more recent SAP HANA systems, the built-in SAP HANA XS, classic model application server process (xsengine) usually runs embedded in the name server or the index server process, although this is configurable. On older systems, the xsengine service typically runs as a separate service with its own persistence and backups.

For multiple-host systems, the backup is written in parallel from the different hosts to the single shared backup location, as shown in Figure 11.4.

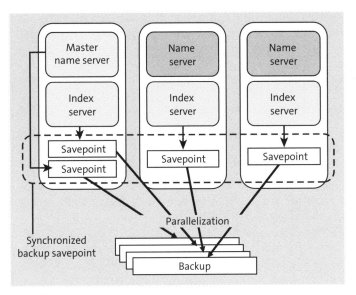

Figure 11.3 Backup Architecture

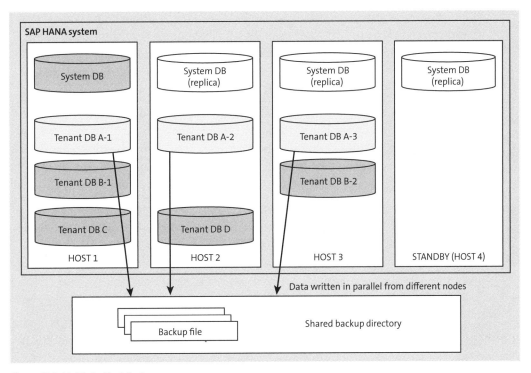

Figure 11.4 Multiple-Host Systems

Backups are physical operations at the file level and not logical operations at the database level. This means that you can't back up or restore individual database objects, such as tables from a backup. You can only restore a complete backup set. For logical backups, you need to export the database objects or use the SAP HANA system replication secondary time travel feature, for example. This enables you to return to a specific point in time on the secondary (backup) system and export the data.

Authorizations

To perform backup and recovery, specific authorizations are required. The two main system privileges are BACKUP ADMIN and BACKUP OPERATOR. The administrator can perform all backup activities, including configuration, backup scheduling, backup retention, and housekeeping tasks, such as deleting backups. The operator is intended for technical accounts, for example, those used by backup tools, and is restricted to catalog view operations and the create database backup task.

This applies to both system and tenant databases. Backup activities from tenant databases can be disabled by marking backups as restricted feature, as covered in Chapter 8. To perform and manage backups for tenant databases from the system database, the system privileges DATABASE ADMIN or DATABASE BACKUP ADMIN (OPERATOR) are also required.

To recover the system database, the database needs to be stopped, and you need to run commands as the <sid>adm user. This is also required to copy a database. To recover a tenant database, the system database administrator needs the DATABASE ADMIN or DATABASE RECOVERY OPERATOR system privilege. You can't restore a tenant database from the tenant database itself.

For backup scheduling and to specify a retention policy, you also need object privileges: select and delete authorization for the tables JOB_SCHEDULES and JOBS on schema _SYS_XS. Without these authorizations the Backup Schedules app won't display, and the **Backup Retention** section of **Backup Configuration** will return an insufficient privileges message (as discussed later in the chapter).

The scheduler is enabled with system parameter xsengine.ini/[scheduler]/enable=true. The backup schedule job can then be enabled from the Backup Schedule app.

Backup Types

There are data backups and log backups. A data backup only includes actual data, sometimes referenced as the payload, not empty space. As described, the backup is made per service. For multiple-host systems, this service-specific backup includes the data of all hosts.

After you've created a full database backup, you can also make a delta backup that only contains the data that has changed (see Figure 11.5). This is faster to make, obviously, and helps to recover more quickly as delta backups are processed quicker and with fewer resources when compared to log backups. However, log backups are required for recovery using delta backups. If the log volume area isn't accessible, you can only recover using a full data backup.

Another point to note is that changed data means the physical state. A minor update may trigger a delta merge of a large table, which means a lot of data is changed physically and hence a large backup size. Partitioning the table and limiting the number of partitions with data changes can significantly reduce the size of the delta backup.

A differential backup contains the data changed since the last full data backup. This backup type increases in size each time, and with each new differential backup, the previous one is obsolete. Incremental backups only contain the data that has changed since the last full data or delta backup.

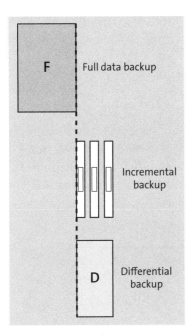

Figure 11.5 Delta Backups

The log area stores all the log volumes, one per service with persistence. A log volume contains log segments that store the individual redo log entries.

If a log segment is full, it's closed, and a backup is made. This happens automatically, and there is no log backup SQL command. A log backup is also created when the service-specific time-out has been reached.

SAP HANA supports the following two log modes:

- Normal
- Overwrite

Initially, after installation, the database is configured in the overwrite log mode. In this mode, no log backups are created, and log segments are freed immediately after each savepoint. This setting avoids log backups filling up the log volume before a proper backup strategy is in place. Test systems are typical candidates for the log mode. Both log modes are illustrated in Figure 11.6.

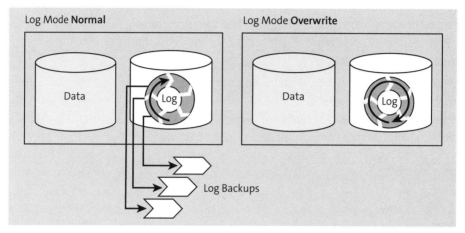

Figure 11.6 Log Modes

After you perform a first data backup, SAP HANA automatically switches to the normal log mode. In this mode, log segments are backed up automatically (assuming automatic log backup is enabled, which is the default setting). After a backup of the segment is made, it's closed and after the next savepoint, it becomes available again for writing. Reuse of the log segments avoids the log area from filling up the entire file system.

> **Note**
> Deleting log segments at the operating level makes the log area unusable, may cause the database to crash, and prevents it from starting up. Always do your housekeeping through the SQL interface (ALTER SYSTEM RECLAIM LOG) or the Backup Catalog app in SAP HANA cockpit.

Backup Destinations

As the backup destination for data and log backups, you either use a file (default) or Backint, which refers to the backup application programming interface (API) to integrate third-party backup tools, as shown in Figure 11.7. You can use SAP HANA cockpit to create a backup, but behind the screen, SQL commands will be executed. You could run the same commands in the SAP HANA database interactive terminal (HDBSQL) or any other tool with an SQL prompt. To execute SQL, of course, the database needs to be up and running, and this also applies to making backups. You can't make a backup if the database is stopped.

Ideally, file backups are located on an external backup storage device using Network File System (NFS), network attached storage (NAS), or storage area network

(SAN). Storing the backups on the same physical host and storage volumes as the data and log areas isn't without risk.

Alternatively, Backint uses named pipes, which is a common inter-process communication (IPC) mechanism on UNIX and Linux that, although it appears as a file, takes up no space in the file system. The implementation of the API that uses the Backint for the SAP HANA interface must be certified by SAP, and you need to have a support contract with the tool vendor. Although implementations differ, Backint works with a locally installed backup agent that communicates with the backup server. You can continue to use SAP HANA cockpit for backup and recovery tasks, although the third-party tool may also have its own tools.

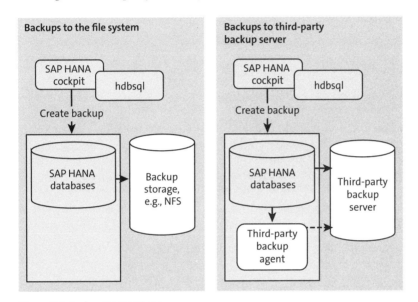

Figure 11.7 Backup Destinations

To improve I/O throughput to third-party backup tools, multiple channels can be configured. This is called multistreaming and allows backup data to be written in parallel to multiple devices (Figure 11.8). You enable multistreaming by changing the system parameter `global.ini/[backup]/parallel_data_backup_backint_chan-nels` from its default value of 1 to a value between 2 and 32. Each service has its own stream, but the backup size needs to be bigger than 128 GB for the stream to become operational. Each stream also requires more memory (I/O buffer) so this needs to be configured correctly.

Learn More

For more information about third-party backup tools beyond the scope of this exam, besides the often extensive documentation of the vendors, see also the following KBA and take a look at the directory:

- KBA 1730932 – Using Backup Tools with Backint for HANA
- SAP Certified Solutions Directory (HANA-BRINT) at *http://s-prs.co/v507861*

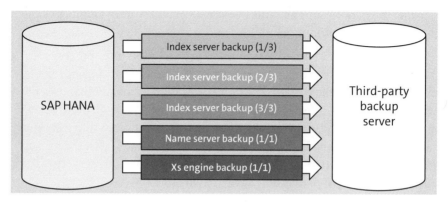

Figure 11.8 Multistreaming

Backup Encryption

SAP HANA supports native backup encryption; that is, the system can encrypt its own backups. Backup encryption with third-party tools is also supported. When you enable backup encryption, both the data and log backups are encrypted, but not the catalog. They use the same encryption root key. You can't encrypt on a per-backup basis.

The size of an encrypted backup is the same as a regular backup. However, it can take up to three times as much memory to create encrypted backups due to additional I/O buffers.

To encrypt a data snapshot, you need to enable both data volume and backup encryption.

When encryption is enabled for the system database, all subsequently created tenant databases are encrypted as well but this is configurable. Each tenant has its own backup encryption root key.

Backup Catalog

The backup catalog stores information about backups and includes the backup ID, with external backup ID (EBID) in case of Backint, the backup type, time stamps, statuses, log positions, and other relevant information. The Backup Catalog app of SAP HANA cockpit displays this information as illustrated in Figure 11.9. Alternatively, you can query M_BACKUP_CATALOG, M_BACKUP_CATALOG_FILES, and M_BACKUP_PROGRESS. There is a catalog for each database.

SAP HANA uses the catalog to decide which backups are needed for a recovery (and which ones are obsolete). To make sure the catalog always contains the latest information, a catalog backup is made after each backup. Without a catalog, you can only recover the database to the data backup provided but you can no longer perform PITR. If the catalog isn't available, you can use `hdbbackupdiag` to rebuild from the present data and log backups. This tool can also be used to determine the backups needed for recovery and whether they are available and accessible.

The backup catalog location is stored, by default, in the same place as the log backup area: `$(DIR_INSTANCE)/backup/log` with the variable `DIR_INSTANCE` pointing to `/usr/sap/<SID>/HDB<nr>`, which links to `/hana/shared/<SID>/HDB<nr>`, the shared storage location common to all hosts in a multiple-host system.

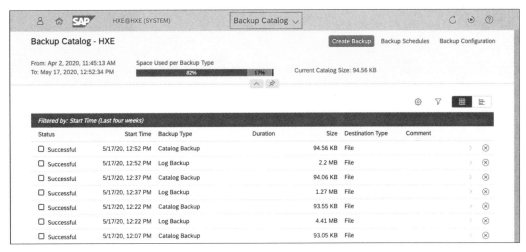

Figure 11.9 Backup Catalog

Creating Backups

Behind the screens, backups are always created by executing the SQL statement `BACKUP DATA`, but you can use SAP HANA cockpit, SAP HANA studio, or a third-party tool to run the statement. This is not only easier, it also performs backup size estimation. Otherwise, you would have to query `M_BACKUP_SIZE_ESTIMATIONS` to know how much space is needed and run the SQL command `BACKUP CHECK` to be informed how much space there is. With SAP HANA cockpit, you create backups from the Backup Catalog app, as illustrated in Figure 11.10. While running, the interface displays a progress bar and you also have data about the last successful backup with information about size and throughput. You don't have to wait for the backup to complete to continue or work because you can click the **Run in Background** button; alternatively, when you've changed your mind, you can select **Cancel Backup**.

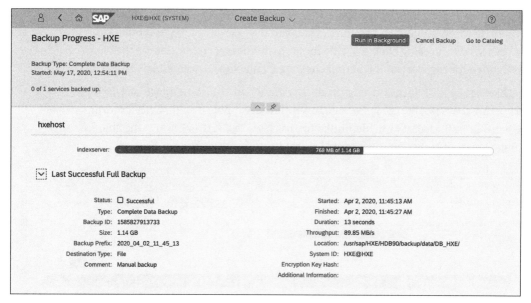

Figure 11.10 SAP HANA Cockpit: Create Backup

Configuration

In this section, we'll walk through configuration topics related to backups. This includes the Backup Configuration app, backup retention, naming conventions, and system parameters.

Backup Configuration App

The Backup Configuration app in SAP HANA cockpit shows tabs for **Catalog Settings**, **Log Settings**, **Data Backup Settings**, **Retention Policy**, and **Restrictions for Tenant Database Users**, as illustrated in Figure 11.11.

When connected to the system database and launched from **Database Management** with DATABASE ADMIN privileges, you can perform the following:

- Select the location for the ca]talog, log, and data backups.
- Choose the log mode (normal, overwrite).
- Enable automatic log backups.
- Enable consolidated log backups.
- Set the log backup time limit.
- Set the data backup file size limit.
- Enable data backup scheduler for system and tenant databases.
- Enable the retention policy scheduler for system and tenant databases (and configure parameters).
- Disable tenant database backups.

Figure 11.11 Backup Configuration

Backup Retention

With the retention policy scheduler, you can automatically delete backup generations, which corresponds to a full backup plus any subsequent delta and log backups, including the catalog. The retention policy scheduler enables you to retain
backup generations younger than a specified number of days and the minimum
number of generations to keep. You also indicate whether to delete just the catalog
entry or also the files themselves. Keeping more backup generations is prudent in
case there is an issue with the latest one.

Naming Conventions

Backups are identified by file name and not by internal identifier. For this reason,
backup file names should not be changed using operating system tools. The full
data backup file name contains the path on the file system, a prefix, and a suffix.

The default **Backup Prefix** is **[date]_[time]**, as illustrated in Figure 11.12. Time
stamps have the advantage of being unique because when neither prefix nor suffix provides a unique identifier, files are overwritten with the next backup.

The **Backup Destination** from the configuration is provided but can also be user
defined. This is usually not recommended but may be useful if the default location
isn't available, and an emergency backup needs to be made.

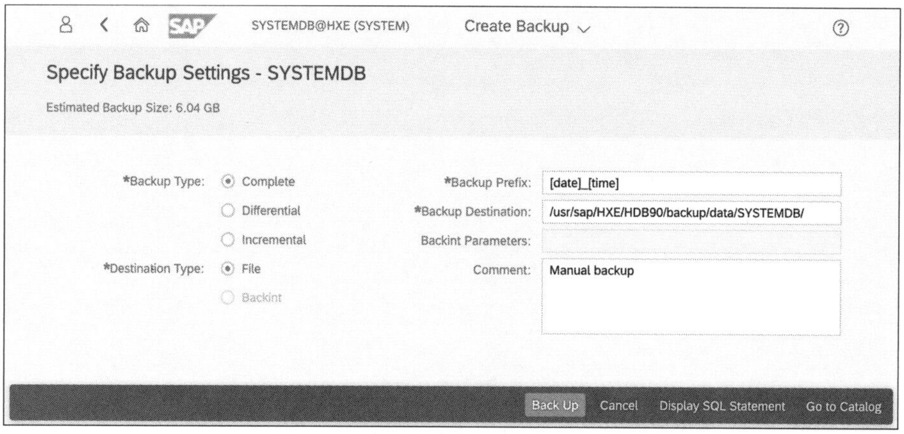

Figure 11.12 Create Backup: Naming Convention

When using SQL, path and prefix are provided as part of the `USING FILE` clause, as follows:

```
BACKUP DATA USING FILE ('/usr/sap/HXE/HDB90/backup/data/DB_HXE/FULL',
'FULL' ).
```

Note that the backup command doesn't create the directory path, so make sure it exists before you start your backups.

The suffix file name convention for data backups is `_databackup_<volume ID>_< partition ID>`.

The suffix file name convention for delta backups is `_databackup_[differential|incremental]_<backup_ID>_<delta_backup_ID>_<volume ID>_< partition ID>`.

The file name convention for log backup is `log_backup_<volume ID>_<log partition ID>_<first position>_<last position>.<backup_ID>` and `log_backup_0_0_0_0.<backup_ID>` for the backup catalog.

Data backups automatically have the volume and partition ID appended. Log backups have the backup ID. When using Backint, the backup ID isn't appended.

System Parameters

A backup doesn't include any changes made to system parameters and persisted to the INI configuration files. You can manually make a file copy backup or alternatively execute the SQL script documented in the SAP HANA Administration Guide, which queries the `M_INIFILE_CONTENTS` monitoring view and generates the required `ALTER SYSTEM ALTER CONFIGURATION` statements to update the settings.

Learn More

For the script, see "Back Up Customer-Specific Configuration Settings" in the SAP HANA Administration Guide at *http://s-prs.co/v507862*.

Data Snapshot

Data snapshots can be used to complement data backups or as an alternative for them. A snapshot provides a consistent state of the system database and all tenant databases. Unlike data backups, data snapshots are at the system level. You can't make a tenant data snapshot.

Snapshots are quick to create and are made at the storage level, which means that the impact on regular database operations is minimal. Recovery is also faster, but there are some disadvantages as well, as follows:

- During recovery, you need to recover the system database first and then each tenant database separately.
- There is no corresponding user interface in SAP HANA cockpit. You can only make data snapshots using SQL.
- You can't schedule data snapshots.
- Whereas a backup includes integrity checks made at the block level, there is no such check with data snapshots.
- Snapshots are system wide and cover the entire data area, whereas a data backup only contains the payload. However, as empty space compresses very well, this is usually not an issue.

To create a data snapshot, execute the following statement:

```
BACKUP DATA FOR FULL SYSTEM CREATE SNAPSHOT
```

This creates an internal database snapshot, as shown in Figure 11.13.

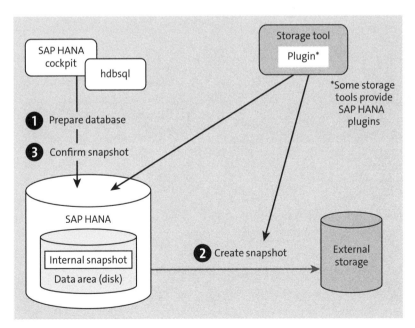

Figure 11.13 Data Snapshot

Next, you need to copy all the files and directories from the data area to a separate storage location. The third step is to inform the system about the status and to update the catalog. This requires the backup identifier, which you can obtain by querying view M_BACKUP_CATALOG. With the ID, you can then close the snapshot using the following statement:

```
BACKUP DATA FOR FULL SYSTEM CLOSE SNAPSHOT BACKUP_ID <id> SUCCESSFUL
```

Until you close the snapshot, you can't make any new backups or snapshots. In addition, data changes are written for the time being to a separate area, causing the data volume to grow. It's important to close the snapshot ASAP.

After service restart, the internal database snapshot is lost and needs to be retaken.

Fallback Snapshots

With fallback snapshots, you can reset a tenant database to a previous point in time. This could be useful to reset the training database to its initial state or quickly return a database to a consistent state before an application update.

You create and manage fallback snapshots using **Database Management**, which requires the DATABASE ADMIN system privilege but not any of the specific backup privileges. As illustrated in Figure 11.14, from the **Fallback Snapshot** menu, choose either **Create Fallback Snapshot**, **Delete Fallback Snapshot**, or **Reset Tenant to Fallback Snapshot**.

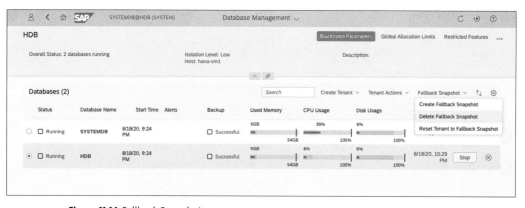

Figure 11.14 Fallback Snapshot

The following points are key to note:

- You can only create one fallback snapshot per tenant database.
- Services can't be removed or added as long as a fallback snapshot is present.
- Fallback snapshots aren't included in database backups and hence don't replace the backup.

You create and delete a fallback snapshots with an ALTER DATABASE statement, as follows:

```
ALTER DATABASE <database name> [CREATE|DROP] FALLBACK SNAPSHOT;
```

To reset the database, you use ALTER SYSTEM:

```
ALTER SYSTEM START DATABASE <database name> FROM FALLBACK SNAPSHOT;
```

The monitoring view with information about fallback snapshots is M_SNAPSHOTS.

Backup Scheduling

You can schedule backups using the app Backup Schedules app in SAP HANA cockpit, as shown in Figure 11.15. For this to work, the xsengine process needs to be running on the connected database, and the scheduler needs to be enabled. This is controlled by system parameters and their values default to true and false, respectively. You also need to enable the scheduling job, but you can do this from the Backup Schedules app or from the **Backup Configuration** screen. With the Backup Schedules app, you also design the schedule and indicate when full and delta backups should be executed. The account used to activate the schedule is also the account used to execute the backup. Schedules can be paused.

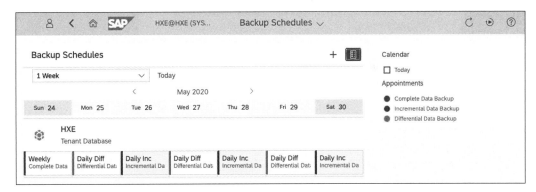

Figure 11.15 Backup Schedules

You can click the **+** icon to create backup schedules, as shown in Figure 11.16.

The schedule is stored and triggered on the connected database, not on the SAP HANA cockpit system. When the database isn't running, the job isn't triggered. It also isn't triggered if the database is started after the scheduled time; it's skipped instead.

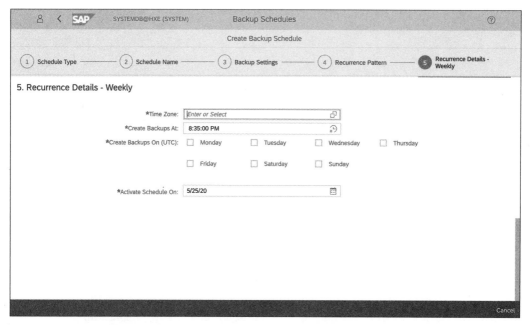

Figure 11.16 Create Backup Schedules

> **Note**
> Although SAP HANA cockpit 2.0 supports database management for SAP HANA 1.0 systems, backup scheduling isn't supported. Schedules created with the previous SAP HANA cockpit version aren't compatible and need to be deleted first for migrations.

Recovery

You may need to recover the database if the data or log area (or both) can no longer be used. There may also be a logical issue with the data—machine-made or man-made—and you need to return to a previous point in time. In addition, you can use database recovery to make a copy of the database.

There are three standard recovery scenarios:

- **Unusable data area**
  If the data area is unusable, after the defect has been repaired, you need to first restore the latest data backup or data snapshot. As the log area wasn't impacted, a complete recovery is possible by replaying the log backups and current logs. No committed data is lost.

- **Unusable log area**
  If the log area is unusable, you can no longer recover the database to the most recent time stamp. Any changes made after the last log backup are lost. After the defect has been repaired, you need to restore the log backups with the most

recent data backup and replay the log backup. After recovery, the log area must be initialized to clean the redo logs.

After the defect has been repaired, you need to first restore the latest data backup or data snapshot. As the log area wasn't impacted, a complete recovery is possible by replaying the log backups and current logs. No committed data is lost.

- **Logical error**
  Fault recovery from logical error also assumes data loss as you need to restore backups and recover the database until a specific point in time prior to the logical error (corruption or accidental deletion). To avoid data loss, other solutions should be considered, such as system replication secondary time travel.

Figure 11.17 illustrates the different recovery options. At a minimum, you need a full data backup ❶. Recovery starts with restoring the data files. When available, you can then apply the latest differential backup ❷ and after all subsequent incremental backups ❸. After the data recovery phase, you then proceed with the log replay, first from the log backups ❹ and finally from the log segments still present in the log area.

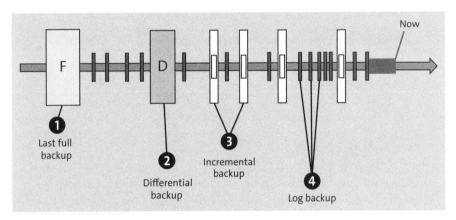

Figure 11.17 Recovery Options

Figure 11.18 shows this sequence as recovery phases: data recovery, log replay, and restart.

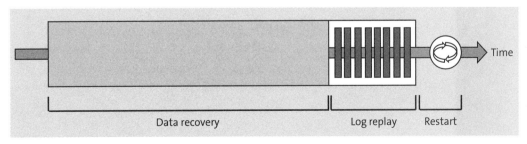

Figure 11.18 Recovery Phases

It can take considerable time to recover large databases. If, for whatever reason, the backup media become temporarily unavailable, you can resume recovery. After successful recovery of the data backup and replay of the redo log, fallback points are set, which can serve as departing points for a subsequent recovery. Fallback points are recorded in the *backup.log* file.

Candidates for resumed recovery are listed in the Recovery Database app in step 3: **Backups to Be Used** (look ahead to Figure 11.20).

To perform the recovery of the system database, the entire system needs to be stopped, and you need the credentials of the operating system administration account <sid>adm. When using SAP HANA cockpit, these are stored in the **Database Directory**. For a tenant database, this isn't necessary because you recover tenants from the system database, as illustrated in Figure 11.19.

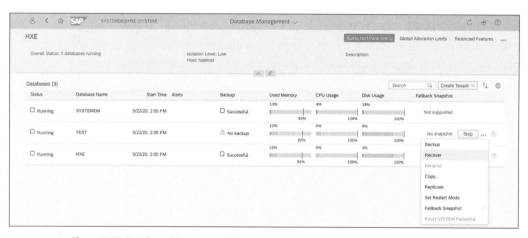

Figure 11.19 Database Management: Recover

To recover the entire system, you use the Recover Database app, as illustrated in Figure 11.20. The recovery process prompts for the following information:

- Recovery target (most recent or point in time)
- Location of the latest backup catalog (default file system location, Backint [when configured], or alternative location)
- Backup to be used and whether to use any delta backup; (a data snapshot can also be selected as the source)
- Alternative location for data and log backups (not specified in the catalog)
- Whether to perform a backup availability check
- Whether to initialize the log area (required when the log area is unusable or when you're recovering to a different system)

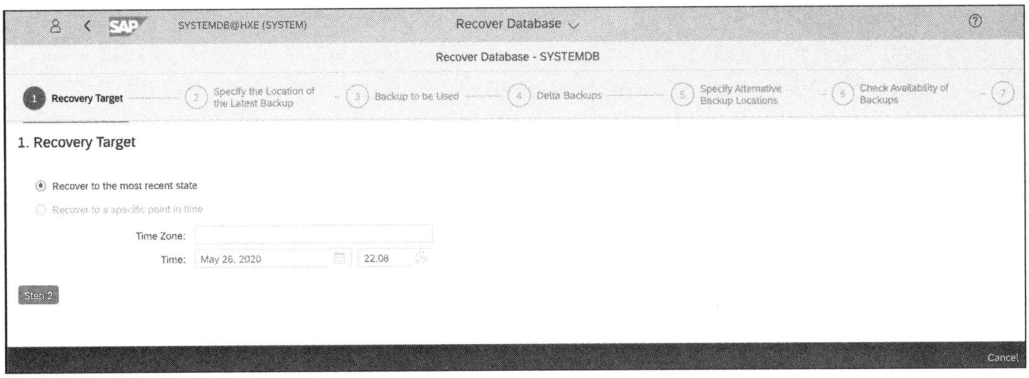

Figure 11.20 Recover Database

Recovering SAP HANA to a specific data backup corresponds to the following SQL statement:

```
RECOVER DATA USING FILE ('/backup/WEEK20') CLEAR LOG
```

With the CLEAR LOG clause, you initialize the redo logs because the data they contain can no longer be used. To recover a tenant database, add the FOR <database_name> clause.

Recovering SAP HANA to a specific point in time or log position corresponds to the following SQL statement:

```
RECOVER DATABASE FOR HXE UNTIL TIMESTAMP '2021-05-26 09:14:44' USING CATALOG
PATH('/usr/sap/HXE/HDB90/backup/log/DB_HXE') USING BACKUP_ID 1589720051366
CHECK ACCESS USING FILE
```

> **Learn More**
>
> For more information about database recovery and the use of the hdbbackupdiag tool, which is beyond the scope of this exam, see KBA 1821207 – Determining Required Recovery Files.

Database Copy

You can use data backups to create a cloned database for training, test, or development purposes. Both full data backup and data snapshot can be used and, if needed, delta and log backups applied to recover to a more recent time stamp. The log area of the source database can't be used, so you can't recover to the current time stamp.

Tenant databases can be copied to the same target system or to a different one, but you can't copy a system database to the same system. You can, however, use a database copy to clone a single container SAP HANA 1.0 system (SPS 10 or later) into a tenant database.

Some restrictions apply:

- The target database needs to be same version or higher.
- A valid license key must be available.
- Backups must be either from a file or Backint (catalog, data, and log).
- When using snapshots, only single-tenant systems are supported, and you need to recover both system and tenant database. The system needs to be stopped. The number of hosts and type of services assigned to each host must be identical, as well as the mountpoint IDs (e.g., /hana/shared).

Database copy supports different hardware configurations (CPU and memory). Figure 11.21 illustrates the database copy process. First, you make a backup of the tenant database to storage. This backup set is then copied or moved to the storage attached to the target database system. These files are then used to perform database recovery. This works the same for data snapshots.

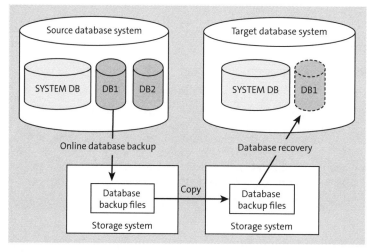

Figure 11.21 Database Backup

The target system can have any number of hosts when using data backups (but not when using data snapshots), as shown in Figure 11.22. With fewer hosts, you need to manually remove any superfluous index server processes. With more hosts, you need to manually distribute the data to the additional hosts.

Making a backup after the database copy is recommended but not required, and recovery is still possible from backups of the source system.

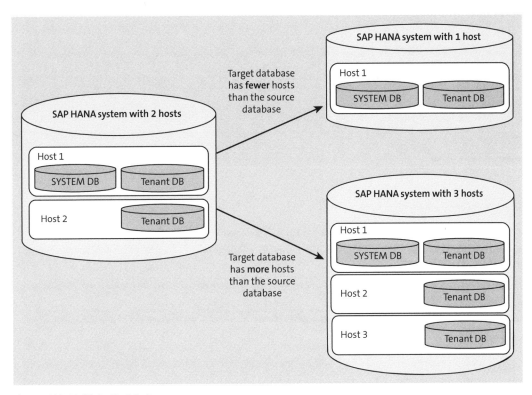

Figure 11.22 Multiple-Host Systems

To perform a database copy using SAP HANA cockpit, connect to the system database and open **Database Management**, as shown in Figure 11.23. Then, follow these steps:

1. Select the target database, and choose **Copy** from the context menu. If the database is still running, you'll be prompted to stop it.
2. In the **Copy Database** wizard, first select the copy type: **Full data backup only** or **Data and log backups**.
3. Indicate whether you want to select the backup from the catalog.
4. Enter the location of the backup catalog on the file system (e.g., tenant database HXE of SAP HANA, express edition: /usr/sap/HXE/HDB90/backup/HXE_DB).
5. Select the backup to be used.
6. Choose the location of the full data backup (otherwise, the catalog will be used).
7. In the last review step, you're informed of your choices and can take note of the corresponding SQL statement:

```
RECOVER DATA FOR HXE USING BACKUP_ID 1589720051366 USING CATALOG
PATH('/usr/sap/HXE/HDB90/backup/log/DB_HXE') CLEAR LOG
```

As an alternative, you can use system replication to copy and move tenant databases between systems. We'll cover this topic in Chapter 12.

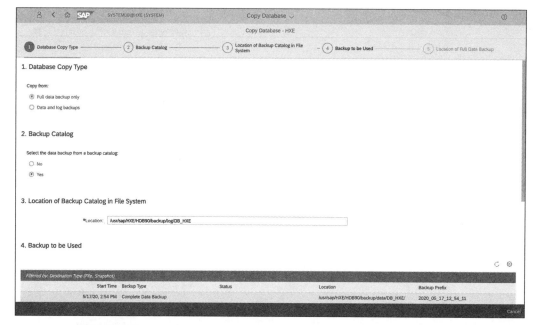

Figure 11.23 Copy Database

Diagnosis Files for Backup and Recovery

The *backup.log* file records information about both backups (data, log, and catalog) and recovery activity, for example, the SQL statement used. If third-party tools are used, this file will be *backint.log*. You can view the contents of the file using SAP HANA database explorer, as illustrated in Figure 11.24.

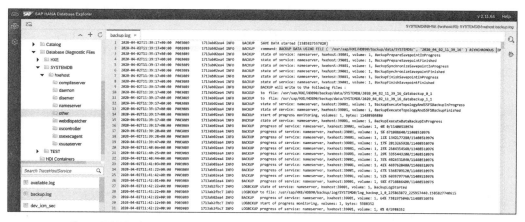

Figure 11.24 Backup Log

To keep this file from getting too large, you can enable file rotation with system parameters global.ini/[backup]/max_trace_file_size and max_trace_files. The default file size is -1, which disables rotation. The default number of trace files is 2.

To truncate the log file, you can use statement: `ALTER SYSTEM CLEAR TRACES` (`'BACKUP'`). To only compress the file, add `WITH BACKUP`. Alternatively, the SAP HANACleaner tool can be used. Deleting the files at the operating system level isn't supported.

Important Terminology

For this exam objective, you're expected to understand the following terms:

- **Backint**
  SAP HANA provides an interface for backups called Backint to enable the use of third-party backup tools. This requires certification and installation of a backup agent on the SAP HANA system.

- **Backup catalog**
  The backup catalog stores information about data, delta, and log backups and is used to determine whether a recovery is possible, which files to use, and which files can be deleted. By default, the backup catalog is located in the log area, and a backup is made automatically after each backup operation.

- **Database copy**
  This is the procedure to quickly clone SAP HANA databases using backups. Database copy is valid for both system and tenant databases, although you can't copy the system database on the same system.

- **Data snapshot**
  Data snapshots complement or provide an alternative for full data backups. Unlike backups, data snapshots aren't made at the database level but at the system level. You can't make tenant data snapshots.

- **Delta backups**
  Backup of data changes taken after a full data backup. Differential backups store all the data changed since the last full data backup. Incremental backups stores the data changed since the last backup (full, differential, or incremental). Delta backups help reduce recovery time by reducing the redo log replay, which requires significant resources. Delta backups require log backups during recovery.

- **Fallback snapshot**
  Fallback snapshots enable you to reset the state of a tenant database to a specific point in time. Snapshots aren't included in a backup set and don't replace backups as they aren't stored externally to the system. Note that you can only store a single snapshot at a time.

- **Multistreaming**
  To improve I/O throughput to third-party backup tools, multiple channels can be configured, which is called multistreaming. It allows backup data to be written in parallel to multiple devices.

- **Payload**

  In the context of backup and recovery, payload refers to the actual data. A backup contains only the payload. A data snapshot mirrors the physical state of the data area and payload, plus empty pages.

- **Persistence**

  Persistence is a general term for storage devices. In the past, this would have been a synonym for the hard disk drive (HDD), but today with non-volatile memory (NVM) growing in popularity, this also includes solid-state drive (SSD) and other flash memory type storage.

- **Point-in-time recovery (PITR)**

  PITR enables you to recover the database to a specified point in time in the past.

- **Savepoints**

  During a savepoint, SAP HANA saves all changed data from memory to persistence. This provides a consistent image of the state in memory. A savepoint is also executed when you choose the **Backup** command, make a snapshot (see the term earlier in this list), request a delta merge, or perform a normal shutdown.

- **Scheduler**

  To schedule database backups, the backup scheduler needs to be activated, which requires the xsengine process to be enabled. Using the Backup Schedules app of SAP HANA cockpit, you can configure schedules for complete, differential, and incremental backups, as well as indicate the recurrence pattern (weekly, monthly, bi-monthly, quarterly, semi-annually, and annually).

  The DBA Planning Calendar from the DBA Cockpit provides similar functionality.

Practice Questions

These practice questions will help you evaluate your understanding of the topics covered in this chapter. The questions shown are similar in nature to those found on the certification examination. Although none of these questions will be found on the exam itself, they will allow you to review your knowledge of the subject. Select the correct answers, and then check the completeness of your answers in the "Practice Question Answers and Explanations" section. Remember that on the exam, you must select all correct answers, and only correct answers, to receive credit for the question.

1. Which of the following statements is correct? (There are three correct answers.)

   ☐ **A.** To make a database backup, the SAP HANA system needs to be started.

   ☐ **B.** To recover the system database, the SAP HANA system needs to be stopped.

☐   **C.** To recover a tenant database, the SAP HANA system needs to be started, but the tenant database needs to be stopped.

☐   **D.** To make a database backup, the SAP HANA system needs to be stopped.

☐   **E.** To recover a tenant database, the SAP HANA system needs to be stopped.

2.   At what level is a database backup made? (There are two correct answers.)

☐   **A.** Service level

☐   **B.** Database level

☐   **C.** System level

☐   **D.** Host level

3.   System parameters configuration is included in the database backup.

☐   **A.** True

☐   **B.** False

4.   The location of the file-based database backups is configured using system parameters. Which configuration file stores these settings?

☐   **A.** File *backup.ini*, section `basepath`

☐   **B.** File *persistence.ini*, section `backup`

☐   **C.** File *global.ini*, section `persistence`

☐   **D.** File *indexeserver.ini*, section `backup`

5.   The database administrator has accidentally deleted a table. How can you recover from this mishap?

☐   **A.** Open Time Machine, and select the table from a backup set to restore.

☐   **B.** Shut down the database and recover from a backup or data snapshot to perform a point-in-time recovery (PITR).

☐   **C.** Execute the `RECOVER TABLE` command, which restores the objects from the `_SYS_BIN` schema.

6.   You're a system database administrator. Which authorizations do you need to view and create tenant database backups? (There are two correct answers.)

☐   **A.** `BACKUP ADMIN`

☐   **B.** `DATABASE BACKUP OPERATOR`

☐   **C.** `DATABASE ADMIN`

7.   When should you make a backup of the backup catalog?

☐   **A.** Never. A backup of the backup catalog is made automatically after each backup action.

☐   **B.** At regular intervals but at least once a month.

☐   **C.** Only when using file-based backups. Backups using a third-party backup tool maintain their own catalogs.

8.   Which system privileges do you need to recover or copy a tenant database? (There are two correct answers.)

☐   **A.** RECOVERY ADMIN

☐   **B.** DATABASE RECOVERY OPERATOR

☐   **C.** DATABASE ADMIN

☐   **D.** Operating system user <sid>adm

9.   To make it easier to locate the correct SAP HANA database backups on external storage media, you've updated scheduled backups to include the tenant database in the file name as a prefix. How can you rename previously made backups to also include this prefix?

☐   **A.** This isn't possible. The backup catalog keeps track of any previously used prefix.

☐   **B.** Use the SQL statement ALTER DATABASE RENAME FILE.

☐   **C.** Use the SAP HANA cockpit Backup Catalog app.

☐   **D.** Use operating system utilities.

10.   A tenant database is used for test purposes and doesn't require a backup. How can you avoid log files taking up space on the file system?

☐   **A.** Take no action. As long as no backup is made, the redo log mode is configured in log mode overwrite. When savepoints are written, log segments are freed and can be reused, and no log backups are made.

☐   **B.** Every database requires at least one backup to stop any alerts being triggered. If backups aren't required, it can be deleted from the backup catalog. Configure log backups in log mode overwrite.

☐   **C.** Disable automatic log backups using the SAP HANA cockpit Backup Configuration app (**Log Settings**, **Create Log Backups: No**)

☐   **D.** Set system parameter global.ini/[persistence]/enable_auto_log_backup= false.

11. Which of the following are benefits of using data snapshots? (There are two correct answers.)

   ☐ **A.** Integrity checks at the block level
   ☐ **B.** Faster recovery compared to data backups
   ☐ **C.** Backup contains payload only
   ☐ **D.** Minimal impact on database performance

12. Which of the following are disadvantages of using data snapshots? (There are two correct answers.)

   ☐ **A.** You can't use delta backups and log backups.
   ☐ **B.** You need to recover the system database and tenant database separately.
   ☐ **C.** You can't selectively recover tenant databases. You need to recover the system database and all the tenant databases.
   ☐ **D.** Data snapshots aren't recorded in the backup catalog.

13. Which of the following are disadvantages of using fallback snapshots? (There are three correct answers.)

   ☐ **A.** You can only create fallback snapshot using SQL.
   ☐ **B.** You can't use delta backups and log backups.
   ☐ **C.** Fall snapshots aren't included in a database backup.
   ☐ **D.** You can only create one fallback snapshot per tenant database.

14. Can you use an SAP HANA 1.0 SPS 11 (single-container system) database data backup to recover a tenant database using database copy?

   ☐ **A.** Yes
   ☐ **B.** No

15. Which command-line tools are available to support SAP HANA database backup and recovery? (There are three correct answers.)

   ☐ **A.** hdbbackup
   ☐ **B.** hdbbackupcheck
   ☐ **C.** recoverSys.py
   ☐ **D.** hdbbackupdiag
   ☐ **E.** hdbrecoverycheck

16. Which authorizations are required for tenant database copy using backup and recovery?

☐   **A.** The user needs the DATABASE ADMIN system privilege on the system database.

☐   **B.** The user needs the BACKUP ADMIN system privilege on the tenant database.

☐   **C.** The user needs the operating system user <sid>adm credentials.

17. Can you perform a point-in-time recovery (PITR) to the current time stamp with database copy?

☐   **A.** Yes

☐   **B.** No

18. Does the target database require a valid license with database copy using backup and recovery?

☐   **A.** Yes

☐   **B.** No

19. To recover a database, you can use a combination of backups from a third-party system and from the file system.

☐   **A.** True

☐   **B.** False

20. When you want to clone a database using data snapshots, the system can only contain a single tenant, and you need to recover both the system and the tenant database.

☐   **A.** True

☐   **B.** False

Practice Question Answers and Explanations

1. Correct answers: **A, B, C**

   To make a database backup, the database needs to be started. To recover a database, the database needs to be stopped. This applies to both the system and the tenant database. Tenant databases can be stopped individually. To stop the system database, you need to stop the SAP HANA system.

   Answer D is incorrect because when the SAP HANA system is stopped, file system backups can be made. However, with the different mount points used for local (/usr/sap), shared (/hana), data area, and log area volumes, this would be complicated enough for a single-host system. Multiple-host systems would add even more complexity. For this reason, the only supported way to make a backup of an SAP HANA system is with database backups, which requires the database to be started.

2. Correct answers: **A**, **B**

   A database backup is made at the service level and at the database level. In many cases, this will be the same as the `nameserver` service that corresponds to the system database and an `indexserver` service that corresponds to a tenant database. However, the SAP HANA XS, classic model service (`xsengine`) can be configured to run as a separate process, in which case, it has its own persistence that would need to be included in a backup.

   Answer C is incorrect because database backups aren't made at the system level but at the database level by a service. Several services, such as the `compileserver` don't have persistence (saved data) and don't require backup. Answer D is incorrect because database backups aren't made at the host level. For a multiple-host system, a single data backup includes the persistence of each host.

3. Correct answer: **B**

   False. Although you can view and edit system parameters through the SQL interface, for example, using SAP HANA cockpit, the settings are persisted in configuration files with an *.ini* extension and not in a database table. Configuration files aren't included in the database backup. If you want to back up customized parameter settings, you need to do this manually.

4. Correct answer: **C**

   The location of the file-based database backups is stored in the *global.ini* configuration file, section `persistence`, with parameters starting with `basepath`. The default locations are `$(DIR_INSTANCE)/backup/data` and `$(DIR_INSTANCE)/backup/log`. Although a backup is made at the service level, all files need to be written to the same location, preferably on an external backup location. On multiple-host systems, each host needs to be able to access this shared backup storage.

   Answers A and B are incorrect because there is no *backup.ini* or *persistence.ini* file to store system parameters related to backup. Answer D is incorrect because, while the file *indexserver.ini* exists, it doesn't contain a `backup` section. Backup configuration settings are system-wide and stored in the *global.ini* file.

5. Correct answer: **B**

   To restore even a single database object, you need to recover the entire database from a backup or data snapshot. This concerns a PITR as you're effectively turning back the clock. This also means that any transactions committed after this time stamp aren't included. For this reason, restoring a single database object using a full database backup isn't a common operation.

   Answer A is incorrect because Apple macOS includes a Time Machine solution that enables you to restore individual files but not the SAP HANA database. Answer C is incorrect because there is no `RECOVER TABLE` command nor a `_SYS_BIN` schema that stores deleted database objects.

6. Correct answers: **B, C**

   To view and create a database backup for a tenant database, when connected to the system database, you need the DATABASE BACKUP OPERATOR, DATABASE BACKUP, or DATABASE ADMIN system privilege in order from most to least restrictive.

   Answer A is incorrect because the BACKUP ADMIN and BACKUP OPERATOR system privilege enable you to make a backup of the connected database—in this scenario that would be the system database—but not any of the tenant databases.

7. Correct answer: **A**

   After each backup action, a backup of the backup catalog is made.

   Answer B is incorrect because you can't manually make backup catalog backups. You can use the hdbbackupdiag tool to regenerate the backup catalog. Answer C is incorrect because backups made by third-party backup tools include the backup catalog.

8. Correct answers: **B, C**

   You recover a tenant database from the system database using the Database Management app from SAP HANA cockpit or SQL. This requires the DATABASE ADMIN or the more restricted BACKUP RECOVERY OPERATOR system privilege. Figure 11.25 shows the context menu options for a tenant database when connected to the system database with a user with only the DATABASE RECOVERY OPERATOR system privilege granted. Note that this user doesn't need any privileges on the tenant database.

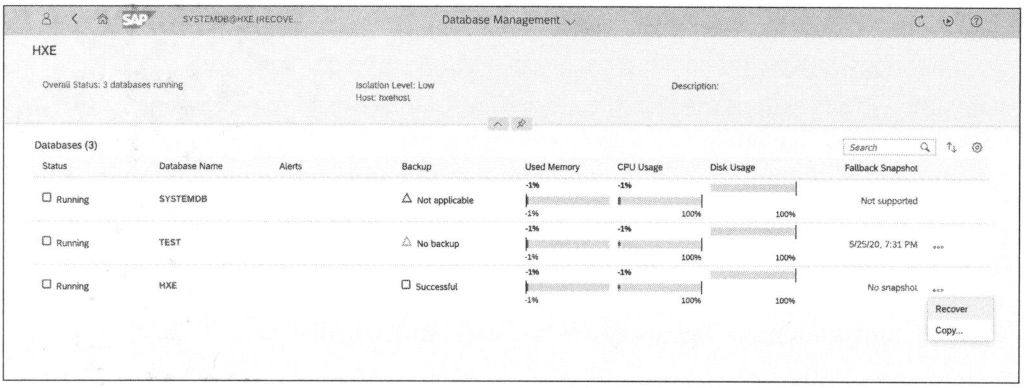

Figure 11.25 Database Management: Database Recovery Operator

   Answer A is incorrect because the RECOVERY ADMIN system doesn't exist. Answer D is incorrect because you need the operating system user <sid>adm user to recover the system database but not to recover tenant databases.

9. Correct answer: **A**

   It's not possible to change the prefix of a backup after it has been created. The prefix is part of the file name and recorded in the backup catalog.

   Answer B is incorrect because ALTER DATABASE RENAME FILE doesn't exist.

Answer C is incorrect because you can't use the backup catalog to rename backup files. Answer D is incorrect because changing the file name on the file system means that the file can no longer be identified and used for recovery.

10. Correct answer: **A**

As long as no backup is made, the redo log mode is configured in log mode overwrite. After the first backup, the log mode automatically switches to normal and automatic log backup is activated (defaults to true). To disable log backups, change the log mode back again to overwrite. You only need to change the automatic log backup setting in case the destination isn't available temporarily.

Answer B is incorrect because backups aren't required. If you delete the last backup from the backup catalog, the alert will be triggered again. To stop receiving the alert, disable alert 35 (check whether a data backup exists). Answer C is incorrect because disabling automatic log backups using the SAP HANA cockpit Backup Configuration app doesn't impact the log mode. As long as the database runs in log mode normal, the system will continue to create new log segments that eventually take up all the space on the file system. Answer D is incorrect because configuring system parameter global.ini/[persistence/enable_auto_log_backup=false is the equivalent of disabling automatic log backups using the SAP HANA cockpit Backup Configuration app.

11. Correct answers: **B, D**

Data snapshots are very quick to recover, depending on the storage tool, and they have minimal impact on the database when created, again, as executed on the storage layer.

Disadvantages are that unlike regular data backups, no integrity checks are executed at the block level, and the data snapshot equals the size of the data area. This makes answers A and C incorrect. Note that empty space compresses very well so size isn't the biggest issue.

12. Correct answers: **B, C**

When you recover SAP HANA from a data snapshot, you need to recover the system database first and then each tenant separately. Tenant databases can't be recovered in a single operation. All tenants must be recovered.

Answer A is incorrect because you can use delta backups and log backups to recover the database to its most recent state or opt for a point in time. Answer D is incorrect because snapshots are recorded in the backup catalog.

Another disadvantage is the absence of graphical interface support (SAP HANA cockpit or SAP HANA studio) to create data snapshots. You need to use SQL commands plus an external storage tool to copy the data snapshot. Note that SAP HANA cockpit can be used for recovery using data snapshots.

13. Correct answers: **B, C, D**

Fallback snapshots enable you to quickly restore a previous state of a tenant database. You can't use delta backups and log backups because you can't recover (to a point in time or most recent state) a tenant database using fallback snapshots. You can only reset (restore) a tenant database. It's also correct that you can only make a single fallback snapshot of a tenant databases, and you can't make a fallback snapshot of the system database. Fallback snapshots aren't included and don't replace database backups.

Answer A is incorrect because you can create fallback snapshots using both SQL and the SAP HANA cockpit Database Management app.

14. Correct answer: **A**

Yes. An SAP HANA backup created with SAP HANA 1.0 SPS 10 (single container system) or newer can be used to recover a tenant database using database copy.

15. Correct answers: **B, C, D**

The `hdbbackupcheck` command-line tool checks the metadata for correctness, consistency, and whether the contents have changed. The `hdbackupdiag` tool determines which backups are required for recovery and whether they are available and accessible. The `recoverySys.py` python script (tool) can be used to recover the system database to a point in time. With the SAP HANA cockpit Recover Database app, you can only recover to the most recent state, as shown in Figure 11.26.

Answers A and E are incorrect because these tools don't exist.

Figure 11.26 Recover Database: SYSTEMDB

16. Correct answer: **A**

The user needs the DATABASE ADMIN or DATABASE RECOVER OPERATOR system privilege on the system database.

Answer B is incorrect because to create, view, and delete backups, and to configure and schedule backups, you need the BACKUP ADMIN system privilege. This privilege doesn't enable you to recover tenant databases. Answer C is incorrect because you need operating system user credentials to recover or clone a system database but not to recover a tenant database. For system database recovery, the entire system, including all tenant databases, needs to be stopped, and recovery is performed using operating system commands.

17. Correct answer: **A**

    Yes. The log area of the source database can't be used for database copy. Only the data, including delta, and log backups can be used.

18. Correct answer: **A**

    Yes. Database copy using backup and recovery requires a valid license in the target host. Regardless of whether the same host (tenant) or different hosts (system and tenants) are used, the license isn't included. Different hosts will have a different hardware ID and require a new license key. Note that you need to create the target database first before you can copy or clone a source database.

19. Correct answer: **A**

    True. This doesn't apply to database copy using backup and recovery when you can't mix backups from different sources.

20. Correct answer: **A**

    True. Restrictions apply when using data snapshots for database copy using backup and recovery. Using a data snapshot for a system with multiple tenants may make the data area on the target system unusable for all tenants.

> **Exam Tip**
> To better understand the concepts and familiarize yourself with the different backup tools, it's highly recommended to practice backup and recovery on a test or training system, for example, using SAP HANA, express edition.

Takeaway

After reading this chapter, you should now be comfortable with how the machinery works: log entries for committed transactions and savepoints to persist changed data. You make a backup of your data area volumes in case of faults and failures using a combination of full data backups, data snapshots, and delta backups, both differential and incremental. The system automatically makes a backup copy of the log segments. It's up to you to protect this and store it safely as well. Although the backup interface uses SQL, SAP HANA cockpit provides a comprehensive and easy-to-use interface to configure, schedule, and create backups, as well as perform recovery for both the system database and tenant databases. The built-in or native backup destination is file-based, but through the Backint interface, you can integrate SAP HANA with third-party backup tools. Should anything go wrong, you need to restore the data and log backup, and perform a recovery.

There are different recovery scenarios. In most cases, you would want to recover until the most recent time stamp to avoid any data loss. For logical faults, you may need to recover to a specific point in time. A nice bonus is that you can use the backup and recovery mechanism to copy or clone databases.

Summary

In this chapter, we covered the backup and recovery topic area. We looked at redo logs and savepoints, some of the concepts and architecture, the different backup types, data snapshots and fallback snapshots, authorizations, Backint, and the third-party backup tools. In addition, we covered how to configure backups using SAP HANA cockpit, how to schedule backups, and how to define a retention policy. Finally, we discussed your recovery options, how to perform a recovery, copying a database using backup and recovery, diagnosing files, and copying tenants.

In the next chapter, we're going to uncover a related availability topic: system replication.

Chapter 12
System Replication

Techniques You'll Master

- Understanding high availability and system replication
- Enabling, disabling, and configuring system replication setup
- Performing takeover and failback of system replication operations
- Understanding active/active read-enabled system replication, secondary time travel, and multitier and multitarget systems
- Monitoring system replication
- Creating a tenant database in a replication scenario

SAP HANA system replication is a high availability (HA) topic. Although the name includes replication and may remind you of SAP Landscape Transformation Replication Server or SAP Replication Server, it's quite distinct, and system replication doesn't concern data integration. With system replication, you maintain identical copies of a production system on two different sites. The source is called the primary system, tier 1, and the target is called the secondary system, tier 2. If anything happens with number 1, then number 2 can take over. If number 1 comes back online, you can decide to failback (or continue running number 2 as the new number 1).

System replication isn't a cheap solution: you pay twice for the hardware and software licenses. However, losing data during major outages or having to wait for database recovery while production is down usually doesn't come cheap either. To improve the total cost of ownership (TCO) and return on investment (ROI) of this type of solution, you can configure the secondary system to host a development or test environment. Instead of a hot standby, the secondary site will run without the column store data loaded, which comes with a longer ramp-up time. SAP HANA 2.0 introduced active/active read-enabled system replication. This enables you to use the secondary system for read operations and can greatly enhance overall system performance. In fact, you now have two systems for read operations and one system for write operations.

Another new SAP HANA 2.0 feature is secondary time travel, which enables you to start the secondary system at some time in the past, for example, to export data no longer present on the primary system. This could be considered a logical backup mechanism on the object level. On top of that, you can also use the system replication mechanism to perform near-zero downtime maintenance (nZDM). In other words, system replication addresses both planned and unplanned scenarios.

Real-World Scenario

SAP announced a new release of SAP HANA, platform edition, containing many new features that may be of interest to the business but also many fixes and security patches that address IT operations. You propose to implement system replication and perform nZDM. System replication provides both HA and disaster recovery (DR) capabilities. The features protect you against hardware failures, data center outages, corruptions, and human errors. However, this does require some configuration. If you want protection against accidental deletion of data, you need to build in a time delay to keep errors from being replicated immediately. If you want protection against hardware or site failure, you need to make sure that the time delay is near zero (or even zero) to avoid any data loss. Is this possible? Yes, read on to find out how you can have your cake and eat it too.

> **Exam Tip**
>
> To master system replication concepts, it's best to get hands-on and try it out for your-self. Why not use SAP HANA, express edition, to try this out for yourself? You may also enjoy watching the system replication tutorial videos on the SAP HANA Academy at *http://youtube.com/saphanaacademy*.

Topic and Objectives

In this chapter, we cover SAP HANA system replication, including configuration, operations, and monitoring.

For the exam, you need to have a good understanding of the following topics:

- Disaster recovery and storage/system replication concepts
- System replication configuration, including the active/active read-only and secondary time travel features
- How to perform a takeover on the secondary system and return to the primary with a failback
- Near-zero downtime maintenance
- Multitier and multitarget system replication
- How to create a tenant database in a system replication scenario

> **Note**
>
> Until the SPS 04 edition of the exam (C_HANATEC_16), the system replication topic was covered under High Availability and Disaster Recovery together with multiple-host sys-tems and with medium weight of 8%–12% of the total certification exam score (8 ques-tions). These topic areas have been split with each assigned a minor weight of < 8% (4 questions).
>
> As system replication and multiple-host systems are indeed very distinct topics, we've followed this separation by covering each in a separate chapter.
>
> Keep in mind that the exam guide states this can change at any time, so always check online for the latest updates.

> **SAP HANA 2.0 SPS 05: What's New?**
>
> SAP HANA cockpit 2.0 SP 11 introduced *takeover with handshake*. This suspends transac-tions on the primary system and executes the takeover after the redo log is available on the secondary system, avoiding any data loss. The old primary system is now also stopped automatically. The same release also introduced *secondary time travel*. This feature enables you to access data no longer available on the primary system.
>
> With SAP HANA cockpit 2.0 SP 12, both features have been enhanced, in particular in the domain of system replication monitoring. In addition, there is now a parameter setting to enable *invisible takeover*. We cover these topics in more detail in this chapter.

On the server side, SAP HANA 2.0 SPS 05 introduced no new features for system replication. For the complete list, see the What's New Guide for the SAP HANA platform at *http://s-prs.co/v507863*.

Learn More

The SAP HANA platform documentation set includes a dedicated guide about SAP HANA System Replication at *http://s-prs.co/v507864*. This guide brings together the relevant sections from the SAP HANA Administration Guide, SAP HANA Security Guide, SAP HANA Performance and Troubleshooting Guide, and the SQL and System View Reference.

Recommend reading, although mostly beyond the scope of this exam, is provided by the following KBAs:

- KBA 1999880 – FAQ: SAP HANA System Replication
- KBA 2057595 – FAQ: SAP HANA High Availability

Key Concepts Refresher

In this section, we'll touch on the key concepts for system replication, including HA, replication and operation modes, configuration, operations such as takeover and failback, near-zero downtime upgrades, and tenant database management.

High Availability

HA isn't a product feature; rather, it's a set of techniques, engineering practices, and design principles that support the goal of business continuity. Availability means that a system is operational, which is expressed in "nines." Three nines, for example, corresponds to 99.9% availability.

The opposite of availability is downtime. The remaining 0.1% as downtime might sound small, but on an annual basis, this amounts to 9 hours of system unavailability. Note that this could be 1.5 seconds each day and pass unnoticed or be concentrated during a full working day, for example, on Black Friday (the busiest shopping day of the year in the United States and increasingly in other parts of the world).

You might have downtime because of planned system upgrades or unplanned system crashes. Unplanned downtime is typically caused by faults, which could be hardware malfunctioning, software or network failures, or disasters (e.g., power loss, fires, earthquakes, etc.). In the descriptions and terminology, DR is often combined with HA as HA/DR.

To make a system highly available, you need to remove the single points of failure (SPOFs). This makes the system fault tolerant and also designs the system to

resume operations, preferably without data loss, after outages attest to fault resilience. Two key performance indicators (KPIs) often used in this context are recovery period objective (RPO) and recovery time objective (RTO), as shown in Figure
12.1. Note that these indicators don't capture the whole story, as performance
ramp-up for systems with terabytes of RAM can take a considerable amount of
time. The RTO stated in the service-level agreement (SLA) may have been met, but
returning to business-as-usual might take longer.

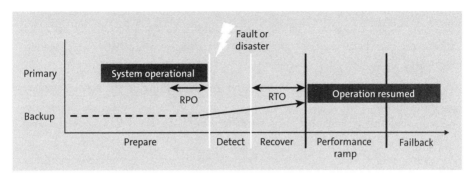

Figure 12.1 Recovery Period Objective and Recovery Time Objective

Table 12.1 provides an overview of your options. Service auto-restart and host auto-
failover are examples of engineered HA features. You learned about service auto-
restart in Chapter 2 and how it concerns the fault resilience of SAP HANA services
as operating system processes being constantly monitored by the watchdog or
daemon service and restarted when not running. But who watches the watchdog?

Recovery	Capability | Solution	TCO	RPO	RTO
Fault	Service auto-restart	0	0	Low/medium
Fault	Host auto-failover	$$	0	Medium
Disaster	Database backup	$	> 0	High
Disaster	Third-party storage replication	$$	~0	Medium
Disaster	SAP HANA system replication	$$$	0	Low
Disaster	Active/active read-enabled system replication	$	0	Low

Table 12.1 High Availability: TCO, RPO, and RTO Compared

On a single-host SAP HANA system, the daemon is a SPOF. To improve system
availability, you can implement a scale-out or multiple-host system. Now, you
have 2, 3, 5, 10, or more daemon processes, one on each host, watching the health
of each instance. When a host with the master role fails, host auto-failover is triggered automatically. To activate host auto-failover for worker hosts as well, you
can add one or more standby hosts to the multiple-host system. A standby host, as
indicated by the name, doesn't accept any client requests and has no data loaded.

When neither the daemon nor name server process responds to requests, the host is marked as inactive, and the standby takes over, as described in Chapter 9.

Host auto-failover automatically causes the remaining hosts to take over the load of the failed host. Whereas service auto-restart is a capability without associated cost, you need to spend some money for host auto-failover because you need to acquire the hardware to run multiple SAP HANA instances and, typically, adjust the license to account for a higher RAM capacity assigned to your system. The RPO of both capabilities is 0 as no data recovery is needed. No committed transactions are lost, but transactions in progress might need to be restarted. In case of host auto-failover, clients can be configured to automatically connect to the next available instance.

The RTO of service auto-restart is low to medium depending on the type of service impacted and whether, for the index server, the fast restart option or persistent memory are enabled. (Recall that the name server hosts the system database and the index servers host the tenant databases, but a compileserver crash will have little to no impact.) Restarting a tenant database in the upper gigabyte or terabyte range without fast restart can take considerable time. This also applies to a host auto-failover event: data redistribution takes time.

When you look at your DR options, you can see that database backup comes relatively cheap in cost but requires patience and potentially involves data loss, for example, in case of a system crash combined with the loss of the redo log area (test case scenario: data center fire destroying the hardware). As downtime and data loss both express business loss, these also come with associated costs that should be included in the equation.

Third-party storage replication solutions, such as SAP HANA scale-out systems, require additional hardware and software licenses. The RPO typically approaches zero, but it will take some time to be back in business. The SAP HANA system on the other side of the fence will need to be powered up and, as mentioned, this can take some time with large database systems.

Only with SAP HANA system replication can you achieve zero RPO with low RTO. Unfortunately, this requires the expense of two production-sized systems, hardware, and all SAP operating system and possible third-party licenses (e.g., Backint), which may amount to the most expensive HA/DR solution. Active/active read-enabled system replication takes this pain point away by not only enabling active usage of the standby secondary system replication system (no longer idle hardware and unused licenses) but also by providing a performance boost to the system as a whole by taking some of the load of the primary system. The result is relatively low TCO, zero RPO, and low RTO.

Note that SAP HANA system replication also provides fault recovery support. We mentioned that a multiple-host system removes the SPOF element from the watchdog process. The same holds true for a system replication configuration because all processes are now duplicated. Depending on the scenario and the requirements, system replication might provide a more elegant and less costly solution when compared to a scale-out system.

In addition, system replication also enables you to perform near-zero downtime upgrades, increasing system availability for planned downtime.

Storage Replication

Prior to the introduction of system replication in SAP HANA 1.0 SPS 06, storage replication was the only alternative to database backups with the associated costs of a relatively high RTO and potential data loss. Like the third-party solutions working with the Backint interface mentioned in Chapter 11, storage replication solutions also require certification from SAP to be supported for use with SAP HANA.

As illustrated in Figure 12.2, the data and log area volumes are replicated to a secondary location. The SAP HANA instance is stopped (cold standby). The replication can be synchronous if the distance between both sites is short enough (100 km or less); that is, any savepoint or redo log write is written to both storage locations simultaneously, guaranteeing zero data loss. For longer distances, the replication will be asynchronous, which may introduce potential data loss. Storage replication requires a reliable, high-bandwidth, and low-latency connection between both sites.

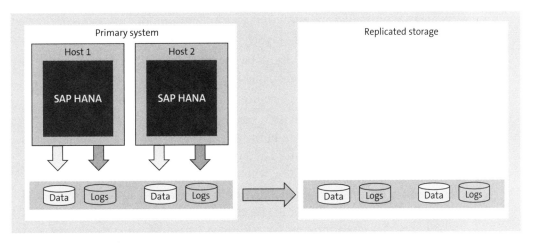

Figure 12.2 Storage Replication

Learn More

For more information about storage replication and the supported solutions, which are beyond the scope of this exam, see SAP Note 1755396 – Released Disaster Tolerance Solutions for SAP HANA with Disk Replication.

The release date for most solutions, some generally available others for pilot implementations, goes back to 2012 or 2013. Vendors listed are Cisco, Dell, Fujitsu, HP, Hitachi, and Lenovo.

Tools and Prerequisites

SAP HANA system replication is a built-in HA and fault recovery solution that requires two or more SAP HANA systems but no third-party solution.

To configure and manage system replication, you can use SAP HANA cockpit and the hdbnsutil command-line utility (hybrid database name server utility). With these tools, you can enable (and disable) system replication, monitor systems, and perform secondary takeover with optional failback to the primary. SAP HANA cockpit calls the hdbnsutil commands behind the screens but provides a more friendly interface. Although not recommended for SAP HANA 2.0 systems, SAP HANA studio is also supported and functions similarly.

The command-line tool has the advantage that after you're familiar with all the options and flags, it allows for scripting and automation.

To manage system replication at the enterprise level, beyond a single SAP HANA system, you can use SAP Landscape Management. System replication is only a minor part of the functionality and capabilities offered by this tool.

> **Learn More**
>
> For more information about SAP Landscape Management, beyond the scope of this exam, see the topic area on the SAP Community at *http://s-prs.co/v507865*.

Before system replication can be enabled, the following conditions must be met:

- SAP HANA is installed and started on both systems.
- The host names of the systems involved must be different.
- The version of the systems must be identical with exception of a system upgrade when a newer version on the secondary system is supported.
- The SAP system ID (<SID>) and instance number must be identical.
- The public key infrastructure (PKI) secure stores in the file system (SSFS) key and store must be identical on both systems (corresponding to the primary), which includes the key and store of SAP HANA extended application services, advanced model (SAP HANA XSA) when installed.
- The number of active hosts, and the name of the host roles, failover groups, and worker groups must be identical. These settings apply to multiple-host systems and imply that if the primary system is configured with a standby host, this should be the same for the secondary system.
- System parameters of the systems involved must be identical.
- The system must be running in the normal log mode setting (not overwrite mode, see Chapter 11).

Considerations

Before getting started with system replication, there are a few considerations that must be kept in mind:

- System replication on the same host isn't supported (doesn't meet the condition that the host name must be different).
- To enable or disable system replication and to perform takeover or failback operations, you'll need to connect with the operating system administration account `<SID>adm` (either on the command line or for the registered database in SAP HANA cockpit).
- A parameter checker is configured by default to check for differences in system parameters and can be configured to automatically replicate changes from the primary to the secondary system. Alternatively, changes made on the primary system must be duplicated manually to the other systems.
- SAP HANA dynamic tiering requires specific configuration and comes with restrictions. Multitarget system replication, for example, isn't supported.

Additionally, the points to consider for system replication with tenant databases are as follows:

- System replication is enabled and operated at the system level with the system database and all tenant databases included. You can't exclude tenant databases from the process, and you can't perform takeover or failback at the database level.
- When a new tenant database is created, a backup must be made to make the database participate in system replication. If a takeover is performed when the

initial data shipping isn't yet completed, the new tenant database will need to be recovered.

- When you stop a tenant database on the primary system, it will be stopped on the secondary system as well.

Log Replication Modes

The following redo log replication modes are supported. They differ in when transactions on the primary system are committed or, more technically, when and where the log write from the log buffer in memory to the log file on persistent storage is performed.

- **Asynchronous**
  Primary commits the transaction (executes the log write) after sending the log buffer. There is no delay in commit.

- **Synchronous in-memory**
  Primary commits the transaction after acknowledgement from the secondary that the log buffer was received. The commit delay is the time required to transmit the data over the network.

- **Synchronous**
  Primary commits the transaction after the acknowledgement from the secondary that the log write was successful on the secondary. Commit delay is the time required to transmit and persist the data.

When using the hdbnsutil command-line tool, the parameters are ASYNC, SYNCMEM, and SYNC, respectively. Performance-wise, ASYNC has the least impact as there is no delay to commit the transaction. In SYNCMEM mode, there is a slight delay as you need to wait for the log buffer to be sent over the network and the secondary to confirm the reception (network I/O). In SYNC mode, this delay again will be bigger as the transaction now also has to wait for the log buffer to be saved to persistent storage (I/O).

The latency, or time it takes for the data to get from primary to secondary and for the acknowledge message to get back again, will play a big part in the decision of how to configure system replication. Typically, you would expect asynchronous to be used for system replication between different regions, distanced by 100 km or more. The SYNCMEM mode can be used for system replication in the same region but different data centers. The SYNC mode will most often be found for system replication within the same data center.

But there is another consideration: potential for data loss. The main scenarios are simultaneous system failure of the primary and the secondary site, or the need to perform takeover without a network connection. With Murphy's Law in mind, "anything that can go wrong, will go wrong," these scenarios can happen simultaneously with multitier system replication (which we'll discuss later in this chapter). Let's consider a few points of concern:

- What is the potential for data loss when both systems fail at the same time? Typically, this will be in SYNCMEM mode when a power loss event or fire impacts an entire data center.

- What is the potential for data loss if the primary site fails, and the network connection is lost? How does this affect the takeover? This scenario needs to be considered in all replication modes but is most likely in the SYNC replication mode, for example, when the dedicated fiber-optic cable between two data centers is damaged by construction work.

In ASYNC mode, the potential for data loss is biggest, as both site and network failures may cause transactions marked as committed on the primary site never to arrive on the secondary site.

In SYNC mode, this isn't possible as the secondary at least will have acknowledged the reception of the log buffer. However, there is a subtle yet important difference between the SYNC and SYNCMEM modes. If both systems fail simultaneously after the moment the primary received the acknowledgement but before performing the actual log write, there is a potential for data loss in SYNCMEM mode. Note that a transaction is marked as committed before being persisted on either the primary or secondary system. Without system replication, this isn't possible because transactions are only marked as committed after a successful log write of the log buffer. With system replication in SYNC mode, this isn't possible either, as the log write will have been performed on the secondary.

Why take the risk? Why not always run in SYNC mode and forget about SYNCMEM? As mentioned, the trade-off is performance. SYNC comes with a delay for network and persistent storage I/O. In SYNC mode, you need to accept a longer delay and wait for every single transaction to be persisted on the secondary system, just to avoid the potential of data loss if both systems fail at the same time. We mention data loss potential and not just data loss. When there are no transactions replicated at the time of the failure, there is no data loss.

> **Note**
> Unlikely events? You can look up the numbers for this year on the Internet, but according to a survey by the Uptime Institute for 2018, almost one-third of the data centers had had an outage. The top three causes were power outages, network failures, and hardware/software errors, roughly equally divided. Then there is also the odd human intervention, of course.

What about when the network connection is lost? During this time, transaction processing continues on the primary system, including the commit to persistence, regardless of any response of the secondary site (log received, log persisted). If you need to perform a takeover in this situation, there is potential for data loss as committed transactions on the primary might have never reached the secondary—this time in both ASYNC and SYNC modes. (See the upcoming "Operation Modes" section about redo log retention.)

Do all replication modes have the potential for data loss even unlikely scenarios? No. To absolutely guarantee no data loss, you can configure system replication in SYNC mode with the full sync option. Transactions are now only committed when the log write (from the log buffer in memory to the log file on persistent storage) is successful on both systems. When the secondary system is disconnected, either because of site failure or network issues, the primary system suspends all transaction processing until the connection with the secondary system is established again. This guarantees full protection against events that might never happen at the cost of any hiccup in the network completely stopping all transaction processing.

Given the impact on transaction processing of the different replication modes versus the potential of data loss due to simultaneous site failure or network loss due to takeover time, what would you choose as default option?

The default system replication mode of SAP HANA is SYNCMEM. Multitier and multitarget system replication provide additional protection against data loss potential, as described later in this chapter.

Operation Modes

You can run system replication in three different modes:

- `delta_datashipping`
  The secondary site receives but doesn't replay redo log entries until takeover.

- `logreplay`
  The secondary site continuously replays redo log entries and is ready for immediate takeover. This is the equivalent of a hot standby database.

- `logreplay_readaccess`
  This is the same as `logreplay` but replication to an active/active read-enabled secondary system is required.

The main difference between delta shipping and log replay is whether the secondary system is completely up to date with committed transactions or whether it still needs to perform recovery during takeover.

When system replication was introduced, delta data shipping was the only available mode, as illustrated in Figure 12.3. After the initial full data shipping required to start the replication, the secondary system continuously receives log buffers supplemented with delta data shipping in the form of snapshots every 10 minutes (default setting 600 seconds).

Buffers and snapshots are persisted on the log and data volume, respectively. The secondary system doesn't process the redo. In memory, the database remains in the initial state of the full data shipping. Only when you perform a takeover will the secondary replay the log. Delta data shipping greatly reduces the time this takes as the system only needs to process the deltas plus the latest log entries. Note that the delta data shipping instances are differential, not incremental.

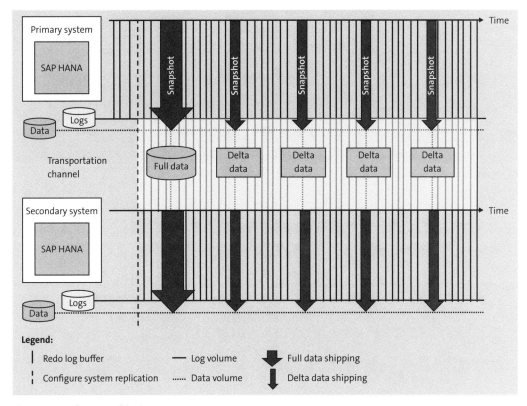

Figure 12.3 Delta Data Shipping

Figure 12.4 illustrates the alternative operation mode introduced with SPS 11, that is, log replay. In this mode, the secondary system constantly applies the redo it receives. This makes the primary and secondary systems logically compatible but no longer physically compatible. The page layout may be different, unlike the delta data shipping mode. As a consequence, you can't mix and match. You can't combine continuous log replay with delta shipping. This is important if the connection is lost between both systems. If the primary system starts to reuse a log segment not yet replayed on the secondary system, the systems are out of sync, and you would have to initiate a full data shipping again to reestablish system replication. For a database in the upper terabyte range, this can take hours.

Fortunately, log retention on the primary system avoids this undesirable situation. It's active by default (system parameter `enable_log_retention=true`) and causes the primary system to retain and not overwrite log segments. When the secondary system gets back online, it receives the backlog and replays, and it gets back in sync.

Of course, if the disconnect lasts too long, at some point, either the log area or the log itself (limited to 10,000 log segments sized 1 GB each) will fill up completely causing the system to freeze, which isn't a desirable situation in a HA setup. System parameter `logshipping_max_retention_size` can be configured to avoid this situation.

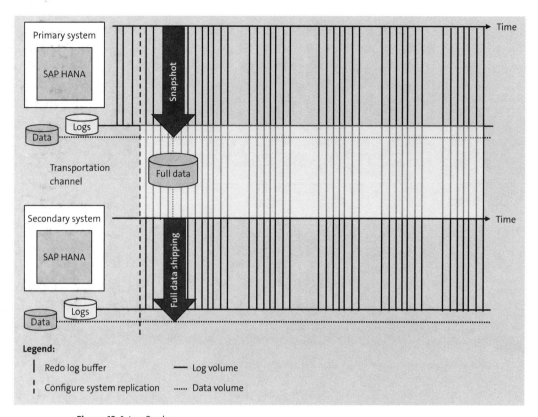

Figure 12.4 Log Replay

Figure 12.5 illustrates the difference in network load for both operation modes. Both receive a constant stream of log buffers, but in delta data shipping mode, you also get regular spikes that may stress the network and require additional throughput. As mentioned, log replay is a more recent configuration and default setting.

To reduce network load, you can enable compression for both log buffers and data pages. The relevant system parameters are `enable_log_compression` and `enable_data_compression`. The default value for both parameters is false, but compression should be considered for replication over larger distances (typically in `ASYNC` mode). For shorter distances, for example, replication within the same data center, compression and decompression would add too much overhead and could potentially slow down takeover times.

Log buffers are 4 KB in size and typically contain a "filler" entry to fill up the empty space at the end. This filler entry is removed before shipping and added again on the secondary site. This is called log buffer tail compression and is enabled automatically.

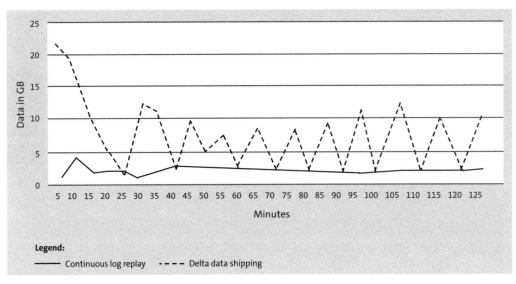

Figure 12.5 Log Shipping Network Statistics

Enable System Replication

The easiest way to enable system replication is to use SAP HANA cockpit. This tool provides a graphical user interface to enable (or disable), system replication, configure settings, and perform takeovers.

The procedure for the two tiers (primary and secondary systems) is as follows:

- On tier 1, the site with the primary system:
  - Start the system, and create a full data backup for all databases, including the system database. Alternatively, create a storage snapshot.
  - Enable system replication.
- On tier 2, the site with the secondary system:
  - Stop the system.
  - Copy the system PKI SSFS key and store files from the primary system.
  - Register the system with the primary system.
  - Start the system.

We'll walk through enablement in both SAP HANA cockpit and the command line in the following sections.

SAP HANA Cockpit

The **System Replication** card on the **Database Overview** page provides replication status information once configured and up and running. Before that, only a message is displayed: **System replication hasn't been configured.** If there is no data backup, a warning is shown with a convenient link to the Backup tool, as illustrated in Figure 12.6.

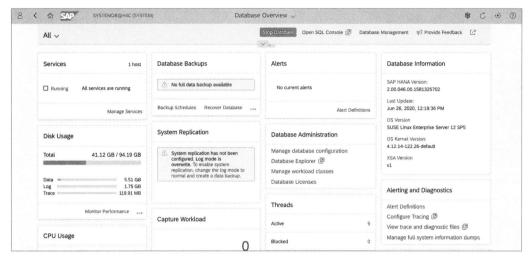

Figure 12.6 SAP HANA Cockpit: Database Overview

After a data backup is available for all the databases on the system, system replication can be enabled. When selected, the card opens the System Replication app, illustrated in Figure 12.7. From the header, you can select **Configure System Replication** or **Enable This System as Primary**. The first option configures both primary and secondary system in one go. The other option only configures the primary system, and you would have to configure the secondary system at a later stage.

Figure 12.7 SAP HANA Cockpit: System Replication

No matter which item you select, **Enable This System as Primary** is displayed first, as illustrated in Figure 12.8. All you need to enter here is the **Site Name** for tier 1.

Figure 12.8 Enable This System as Primary: Tier 1

In the next step, you need to provide the registration information for tier 2, the remote site, as illustrated in Figure 12.9. You need to provide input for the required parameters **Site Name** and **Secondary System Host**. For the replication and operation modes, the default values are listed (**Synchronous in Memory** and **Log Replay**, respectively). You can also indicate whether you want to initiate data shipping and check the box to stop the secondary system before the registration and start it up after. Optionally, you can add a tier 3 system.

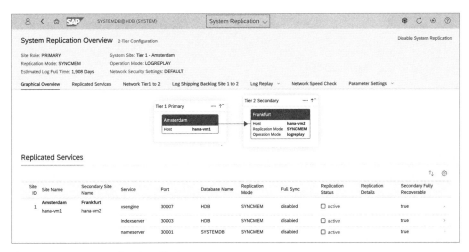

Figure 12.9 Configure System Replication

After the system replication is enabled, data shipping and log shipping will start, and the **Replication Status** is marked as **active** for each of the replicated services, as illustrated in Figure 12.10 In the header, the replication between both sites is illustrated with green boxes, the replication flow, and the log replication mode, plus some additional statistics.

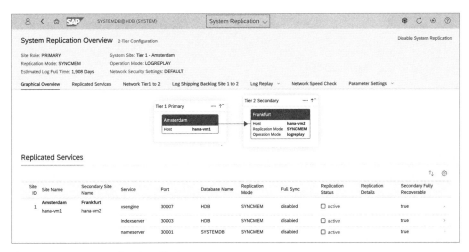

Figure 12.10 System Replication: Tier 1

Command Line

To automate system replication configuration and operations, you can use the command-line tool hdbnsutil. SAP HANA cockpit makes the same hdbnsutil calls behind the screens (and queries system views for the detailed information), but this time you're not guided and need to make sure you use the correct parameters and sequence of steps. The command is located, like all other executables, in the local directory: /usr/sap/<SID>/HDB<instance_nr>/exe.

To enable system replication, enter the following command (corresponds to Figure 12.8 shown earlier):

```
hdbnsutil -sr_enable --name=WDF
```

To register the secondary, enter the following command (corresponds to Figure 12.9 shown earlier):

```
hdbnsutil -sr_register --name=ROT --remoteHost=hanahost-xyz
--remoteInstance=00 --replicationMode=[sync|syncmem|async]
--operationMode=[delta_datashipping|logreplay|logreplay_readaccess]
```

To check the status, enter the command:

```
hdbnsutil -sr_state
```

Alternatively, you can check the replication status with the Python tools system-ReplicationStatus.py or landscapeHostConfiguration.py.

You can also query the M_SERVICE_REPLICATION system monitoring view for current status information.

Learn More

For all the commands and options, see the command-line reference included in the SAP HANA System Replication guide. The details are beyond the scope of the exam.

Disable System Replication

The disable system replication, you follow the reverse order: first unregister, and then disable.

For disablement, the following procedure applies:

- On tier 2, the site with the secondary system:
  - Stop the system.
  - Unregister the secondary system.
- On tier 1, the site with the primary system:
  - Disable system replication.

Let's first look at disabling system replication in SAP HANA cockpit. On a running system replication environment, the **Disable System Replication** command is available from the header on the primary system (refer to Figure 12.10). As with enabling, the secondary system will be configured from the primary system.

On the command line, there are two steps. On tier 2, enter the following command for the site with the secondary system:

```
hdbnsutil -sr_unregister --name=ROT
```

On tier 1, enter the following command for the site with the primary system:

```
hdbnsutil -sr_disable
```

Monitoring

To monitor system replication, you can use SAP HANA cockpit or the command line. Alerts and the configuration parameter checker provide additional support. We'll walk through each in the following sections.

SAP HANA Cockpit

SAP HANA cockpit makes system replication monitoring comprehensive and easily accessible. The **System Replication** tile on the Database Overview app displays a tile showing the status—**All services are active and in sync**—illustrated by two green systems with the site name and the replication flow with information about the replication and operation mode and which site you're connected to (see Figure 12.11).

Valid status messages are as follows:

- **Not configured**
- **All services are active and in sync**
- **All services are active but not yet in sync**
- **Errors in replication**

The following replication statuses can be displayed:

- **Unknown**
  The secondary system hasn't connected (yet) to the primary system since the last restart of the primary.
- **Initializing**
  Initial data transfer is running. The secondary system isn't available yet for takeover.
- **Syncing**
  The secondary system is syncing again (e.g., after a temporary connection loss or restart of the secondary).

- **Active**

  Initialization or sync with the primary system is complete, and the secondary system is continuously replicating. If a crash occurs, no data loss occurs in SYNC replication mode.

- **Error**

  Replication can't take place because the secondary system isn't accessible (details displayed in **Replication Details**).

When selected, the System Replication app opens listing more detailed information about the system replication at the system and network level with tabs about replicated services, network tiers, log shipping, log replay, and network performance and security settings (see Figure 12.12). Possible actions are listed in the header; for example, when replication is enabled, you can disable it (and vice versa), and when you're connected to the secondary system, you can initiate a takeover.

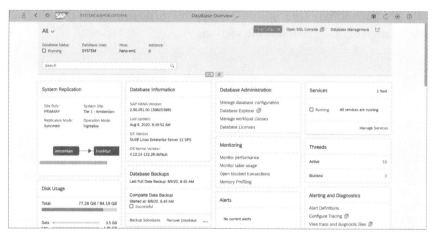

Figure 12.11 SAP HANA Cockpit: Database Overview

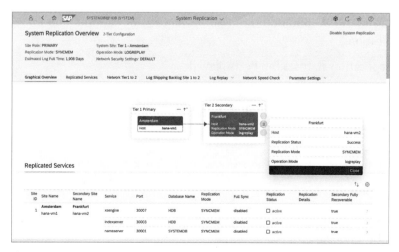

Figure 12.12 SAP HANA Cockpit: System Replication

To get even more detailed information, you can select each of the replicated services to get the statistics about log positions, savepoints, data replicas, and the backlog (see Figure 12.13).

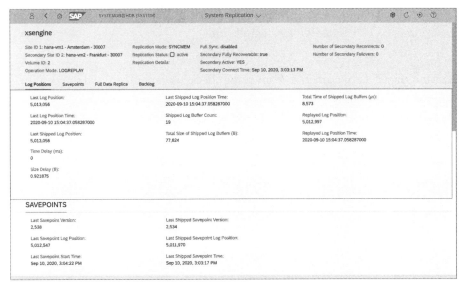

Figure 12.13 SAP HANA Cockpit: Log Position

Command Line

For command-line monitoring of system replication, use the `hdbnsutil -sr_state` command.

The relevant system monitoring views for system replication are as follows:

- `M_SYSTEM_REPLICATION` (overview)
- `M_SERVICE_REPLICATION` (details)

The information provided by these views corresponds to what is presented by the System Replication app overview and replicated service detail pages.

Alerts

As you can't stare at the cockpit screen indefinitely, monitoring is also enhanced with a number of alerts:

- 78: Connection closed
- 79: Parameter mismatch
- 94: Logreplay backlog increasing (causing longer takeover time)
- 104: Logshipping backlog
- 106: ASYNC replication in-memory buffer overflow
- 107: Inconsistent failback snapshot

We'll discuss alerts further in Chapter 13.

INI File Checker

To avoid system parameter mismatch, a configuration parameter checker is enabled by default on the primary site. Optionally, you can automatically replicate parameter changes. The relevant parameters are as follows:

- `[inifile_checker]/enable = true` (default true)
- `[inifile_checker]/replicate = true` (default false)

To exclude particular parameters from being checked or modified, add the system parameter to the section. The formula is `exclusion_[inifile name|*][/<LAYER>] = [section][/parameter]`, for example, `exclusion_global.ini/SYSTEM=memorymanager/global_allocation_limit`.

Configuration

Let's move on to system replication configuration. First, to change the log replication mode, enter the command:

```
hdbnsutil -sr_changemode --mode=[sync|syncmem|async]
```

Full sync isn't a log replication mode but an option. Before you enable the option, the recommendation is to first configure the system in the `sync` replication mode and verify that the replication status is active for all services.

When all flags are green, execute the command:

```
hdbnsutil -sr_fullsync --enable|disable
```

This command configures the system parameter `global.ini/[system_replication]/enable_full_sync=true|false`.

To change the operation mode, you need to stop the secondary system first and then re-register the primary system, changing the operation mode as required. You don't have to unregister the secondary system.

When switching from `logreplay` to `delta_datashipping`, full data shipping is required. For very large databases, data shipping takes a long time and might saturate the network. To avoid this situation, you can also use a storage copy of the primary system. This concerns a regular file system backup of the data area with the SAP HANA system stopped. The `force_full_replica` parameter informs the system not to initiate a full data shipping. Execute the following command:

```
hdbnsutil -sr_register […] --force_full_replica
```

Takeover

The takeover process switches the active system from the primary to secondary system. You can perform a takeover for planned downtime, for example, for near-zero downtime upgrades, or for unplanned downtime (e.g., because the data center has just caught fire). When the primary system isn't available, the takeover will be a failover. In this case, you need to make sure that the primary system doesn't reconnect to the network to claim it's role. It first needs to be stopped and registered as secondary. If everything is back online again and working as expected, you can return to the original situation by repeating the takeover, now called failback. The steps required for takeover, failover, and failback are all the same; only the situation is different and whether the primary system is available or not.

A very basic decision tree to help you decide whether a takeover is advisable starts with the question: Will it solve the issue? If so, will it reduce downtime? If so, can you guarantee no data will be lost? When all answers are yes, you can perform the takeover. In real life, the decision will probably be a little bit more complicated.

The Python script `getTakeoverRecommendation.py` supports the decision-making process. It calls two other scripts: `landscapeHostConfiguration.py` and `systemReplicationStatus.py`. Depending on the outcome, it returns the following results:

- **Required**
  The primary system has errors.
- **Cannot decide**
  The system replication status is unknown.
- **Possible**
  All flags are green with the primary system up and running and with system replication in sync.

> **Learn More**
> For the guideline, which is beyond the scope of the exam, see SAP Note 2063657 – SAP HANA System Replication Takeover Decision Guideline.

The procedure for the two tiers (primary and secondary systems) is as follows:

- On tier 2, the site with the secondary system:
  - Perform a takeover. This configures the secondary system as the primary system.
- On tier 1, the site with the primary system:
  - Stop the system.
  - When the issue causing the downtime is fixed, and the system is available again, register it with site B as the secondary system. The roles are now reversed.
  - Start the system.

Now, let's see how this looks in SAP HANA cockpit and on the command line.

SAP HANA Cockpit

When connected to the tier 2 system, or secondary, both options are available from the header of the System Replication app. When the primary system isn't available, perform a failover, and select **Enable This System as Primary** (see Figure 12.14). You'll need to stop the primary system, reestablish the network connection, and register the system as secondary.

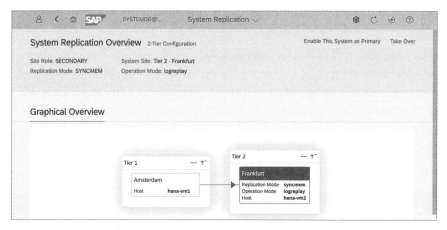

Figure 12.14 System Replication: Tier 2

When you select **Take Over** from the header menu, a popup window appears with the question: **Verify that the secondary is fully synchronized?** (see Figure 12.15). Selecting yes corresponds to what is called *takeover with handshake*. During the takeover, writing new transactions on the primary is suspended until all redo logs are available on the secondary. For this operation to succeed, the primary system must be accessible and the replication services must be in sync. This avoids a "split-brain" situation with multiple active primary systems. It also guarantees that there will be no data loss.

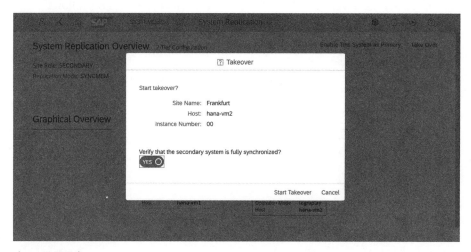

Figure 12.15 Takeover

After the takeover is running, the secondary system takes over the role of the primary system, and the System Replication app changes accordingly. Note the **Configure System Replication** and **Disable System Replication** links in the header, as illustrated in Figure 12.16.

Figure 12.16 Takeover Running

Command Line

Alternatively, to perform a takeover on the command line, execute the following command:

```
hdbnsutil -sr_takeover [--comment="Some text"]
```

The secondary system must be fully initialized (system view M_SERVICE_REPLICA-TION) and all services active. Optionally, you can add a comment that will be persisted in the system view M_SERVICE_REPLICATION_TAKEOVER_HISTORY.

To perform a takeover with handshake, execute the following command (corresponding with Figure 12.14):

```
hdbnsutil -sr_takeover –suspendPrimary
```

HA/DR Providers

To route the client to the new primary system after takeover, you can use either Internet Protocol (IP) or domain name server (DNS) redirection. IP redirection only works on L2 or local area networks (LANs). For L3 or wide area networks (WANs), DNS redirection is required. Both approaches require several steps and include the flushing of caches of the clients, routers, and other network equipment to consistently establish the correct client connections to the new primary system. This can be automated using HA/DR providers (also known as "hooks"), which you can register with the SAP HANA system to be called automatically at particular events.

HA/DR providers are Python scripts, provided by the customer or third party, stored on the SAP HANA server, and registered in the *global.ini* system parameter configuration file referencing the location of the script and execution priority.

With the `hdbnsutil` tool, the providers are loaded into the name server process so they can be executed during takeover or other name server operations:

`hdbnsutil -reloadHADRProviders`

HA/DR providers aren't specific to system replication and can also be used to handle host auto-failover operations gracefully.

Learn More

How to implement HA/DR providers for SAP HANA is documented in the SAP HANA Administration Guide, including several examples. The implementation details are beyond the scope of the exam.

Invisible Takeover

On the client side, the SQL Database Connectivity (SQLDBC) library supports transparent session recovery, which provides automatic recovery of the client session after takeover. This is configured with system parameter `enable_session_recovery`, which defaults to true and triggers the connection manager to recover the session variables from the primary system and to restore the client connections to the secondary system (illustrated in Figure 12.17). This feature is also called *invisible takeover*.

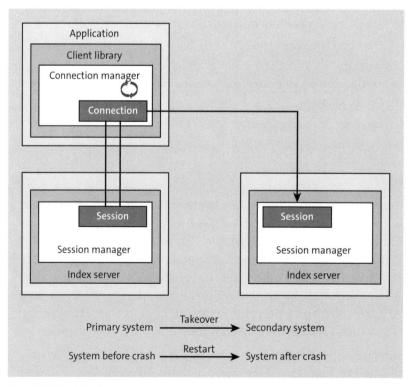

Figure 12.17 Invisible Takeover

Secondary Time Travel

Secondary time travel is a system replication feature that enables you to query data on the secondary system at a time in the past. In our discussion of HA so far, we've mentioned faults, failures, and disasters. However, we've not yet mentioned another common source of issues: the human factor. Sometimes data simply gets deleted because the power user mistook the production system for the test environment. Time travel allows you to query the database just before the accident and repair the issue using data export or other approaches without the downtime for database restore and recovery.

Technically, time travel is made possible with snapshots and retained logs and only supports the `logreplay` operation mode. System parameter `global.ini/[system_replication]/timetravel_max_retention_time` defines in minutes how far back in time you can travel (0 turns it off).

The procedure to start time travel is as follows:

- Stop the secondary system.
- Execute command `hdbnsutil -sr_timetravel --startTime=<timestamp>`.
- Start the secondary system.

Optionally, you can define HA/DR providers (see the previous section) by using the `hdbnsutil` flag `[--callTakeoverHooks=on|off]` or the system parameter `timetravel_call_takeover_hooks`.

As with takeovers, you can also enter a comment `[--comment="Your Comment"]` to be persisted in system view `M_SERVICE_REPLICATION_TAKEOVER_HISTORY`.

Log replay can be started automatically with system parameter `timetravel_logreplay_mode` or by using command `hdbnsutil -sr_recoveruntil {--endTime=<timestamp|max}`.

Multitier and Multitarget System Replication

Multitier system replication enables you to establish replication over longer distances (also called geo-clustering). This is configured by adding a third replication site with tier 2 as the replication source. The operation modes must be the same (although `logreplay_readaccess` and `logreplay` can be combined). `Logreplay` modes `SYNC` and `SYNCMEM` on tier 1 can be combined with all three modes on tier 2. Only if tier 1 is configured in `ASYNC` mode does tier 2 need to run in this mode as well, which if you think about it logically makes sense.

Multitarget system replication, on the other hand, enables you to replicate to two or more secondary systems, as shown in Figure 12.18. Here you have system replication running in two data centers with the primary replicating to a secondary in the same data center and to a secondary in a remote data center simultaneously.

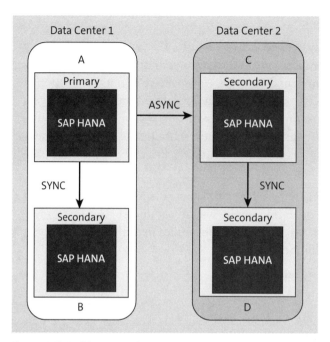

Figure 12.18 Multitarget Replication

Active/Active Read-Enabled

Active/active read-enabled is a licensed system replication feature that enables read access to the secondary system. Active/active read-enabled improves system performance by offloading read-intensive operations from the primary system to the secondary. The secondary system now handles the heavy lifting for long-running or complex queries in a dedicated fashion, improving the response times for those requests. In addition, performance for the remaining operations on the primary system now also improves because the system no longer has to deal with the heavy hitters. It's a win-win. The overall architecture is illustrated in Figure 12.19.

Technically, it's enabled with the `logreplay_readaccess` operation mode. To access the secondary system, the database client can either make an explicit direct connection (no session sharing), or you can use `HINT` clauses in `SELECT` statements. In the second case, the statement is initially parsed on the primary system but redirected to the secondary. An example statement is as follows:

```
SELECT column FROM table WHERE column = x WITH HINT(RESULT_LAG('hana_sr'))
```

> **Learn More**
>
> For information about more advanced options that are beyond the scope of this exam, see the documentation "Client Support for Active/Active Read-Enabled, SAP HANA Client Interface Programming Reference for SAP HANA Platform" at *http://s-prs.co/v507866*.

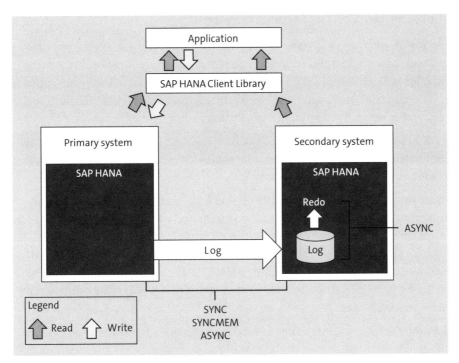

Figure 12.19 Active/Active Read-Enabled

Active/active read-enabled system replication is more demanding in terms of system requirements, as follows:

- Primary and secondary system need to run on the same processor architecture (either Intel or IBM Power, but no mixture).
- Active/active read-enabled requires the same SAP HANA version on both systems. For this reason, you need to disable the feature during rolling upgrades.

There are also a number of caveats and limitations to consider:

- Not really a limitation but a logical consequence of the configuration is that in case of a takeover, instead of two systems supporting the workload you're again back at a single system. To maintain acceptable performance levels, you may need to temporarily reduce or even stop the read-intensive operations until both systems are operational again.
- In multitier system replication, active/active read-enabled is only supported on tier 2. This is consistent with the `logreplay_readaccess` operation mode not being supported for tier 3 registration.
- Log replay on the secondary system is an asynchronous process. This may introduce a delay.
- Workload classes aren't supported (see the next chapter).
- Binary table export aren't supported, only comma-separated values (CSV).
- Hint-based session routing is supported for SQLDBC for ODBC/JDBC, ADO.NET, and Node.js.

Additional Systems on the Secondary System

As mentioned, with active/active read-enabled system replication in the previous section, you can significantly reduce overall TCO of system replication. Prior to the introduction of this feature with SAP HANA 2.0, alternative use-case scenarios were also architected and supported, the most common being to install additional systems on the secondary system for quality assurance (QA) or development.

This requires different system identifiers and system numbers as well as highly recommended, separate, and isolated persistent storage for the data and log area of the additional systems.

To reduce the memory footprint of the secondary system, you need to adjust the amount of memory made available to the system and probably also disable loading of column tables (system parameters `global_allocation_limit` and `preload_column_tables`). As a consequence, the takeover time and performance ramp-up will be slower as the secondary is running as the "cold" standby. If needed, the allocation limit can be adjusted with the `hdbnsutil - reconfig` command, as the SQL interface isn't available.

In the event a takeover needs to be executed, you first need to stop the additional systems and update the system parameter of the secondary.

Near-Zero Downtime Upgrades

One very convenient consequence of system replication is that you can perform near-zero downtime upgrades. This is supported out of the box, as no particular configuration or setup is required. All you need to remember is to update the secondary system first, followed by a takeover, after which you can update the primary, followed by a failback.

> **Note**
>
> Semantically, an update is a new software version. If it makes it better, it's an upgrade. If it makes it worse, it's a downgrade (at least from the user point of view). The documentation uses both terms, which might be confusing, but they should be considered as synonyms.

There is always a little downtime during takeover, hence the near-zero and not zero downtime upgrade. Systems will automatically reconnect after a system restart. No manual intervention is required. However, depending on the time it takes for the update and the system to restart, you might need to adjust the log retention size parameter.

For the repository content to be replicated correctly, you need to create a key named SRTAKEOVER in the local user store of both the primary and secondary system with connection to the system database.

To perform a near-zero downtime upgrade, execute the following steps:

1. Update the system on site B (secondary). Verify that system replication is active again and all systems are in sync before proceeding.
2. Stop the system on site A (primary).
3. Perform a takeover on site B (secondary becomes primary).
4. Update the system on site A (original primary), including the flag not to restart (`hdblcm --action=update --hdbupd_server_nostart`).
5. Register the system on site A (original primary becomes secondary).
6. Start the system on site A (secondary).
7. Optionally, perform a failback to return to the original situation.

To minimize system downtime during update, consider using the prepare update flag (`hdblcm --action=update --prepare_update`) and include only the server component. When done, run the update again to perform the actual update involving system restart. When replication is active again, and all systems are in sync, proceed with updating all other components.

Alternatively, if downtime isn't an issue, perform the update with both systems running and without takeover (but do maintain the secondary first and primary second sequence).

> **Learn More**
>
> For information about more advanced options beyond the scope of this exam, see the following SAP Notes:
>
> - SAP Note 1984882 – Using HANA System Replication for Hardware Exchange with Minimum/Zero Downtime
> - SAP Note 2386973 – Near Zero Downtime Upgrades for HANA Database 3-Tier System Replication

Copying and Moving Tenant Databases

You can leverage system replication technology to copy or move tenant databases between SAP HANA systems. This is similar to using backup and recovery to copy/move a database except there is no downtime in this case.

Typical use cases for tenant database copy/move are as follows:

- **Template**
  Copy a tenant with default configuration for development projects.
- **Load balancing**
  Move a tenant database with high resource usage to a system with low load.
- **Deployment**
  Move a tenant database from test to production.
- **Release update**
  Move a tenant to a system with a new release.

As system replication technology is used, data and redo log files are copied but not trace and regular log files in text format, configuration files, and backups. Note that database-specific root keys used for backup and log encryption are included with the move but not with the copy; otherwise, security could be compromised. You can copy databases simultaneously with support for different isolation levels on source and target.

To perform the operation, the following system privileges are required on the target database: DATABASE ADMIN, CREDENTIAL ADMIN, and CATALOG READ. If you want to encrypt the copy, you also need INIFILE ADMIN on the source database and CERTIFI-CATE ADMIN and TRUST ADMIN on the target.

The process is the same for a tenant database copy as for a tenant database. The only difference with move is that the source database is dropped after a successful copy.

As a prerequisite, you need to verify that the Transport Layer Security (TLS)/Secure Sockets Layer (SSL) communication channels are configured correctly for system parameters:

```
global.ini/[communication]/ssl=systempki
global.ini/[system_replication_communication]/enable_ssl=true
```

You also need to open the communication from the target to the source system by changing the listen interface from the default local setting for single-host systems to global using either the resident SAP HANA database lifecycle manager (HDBLCM) tool and selecting the **Configure Inter-Service Communication** option, a topic we covered in Chapter 4, or executing the equivalent SQL statement:

```
ALTER SYSTEM ALTER CONFIGURATION ('global.ini', 'SYSTEM') SET (
'communication', 'listeninterface') = '.global' WITH RECONFIGURE
```

Next, you need to create a credential in the system database of the target system to enable authenticated access to the source system for the DATABASE_REPLICATION purpose, a topic we covered in Chapter 10.

```
CREATE CREDENTIAL FOR COMPONENT 'DATABASE_REPLICATION' PURPOSE 'host:30001'
TYPE 'PASSWORD' USING 'user="SYSTEM";password="***"';
```

With the security in place, you can proceed with the tenant database copy.

While connected to the system database of the target system, execute the SQL command:

```
CREATE DATABASE <target> AS REPLICA OF <source> AT 'host:30001'
```

In the AT clause, specify the host name and port number for internal communication of the system database (name server) of the source system.

Query the M_DATABASE_REPLICAS system monitoring view for the replication progress. As with system replication, the REPLICATION_STATUS column lists the current status, that is, **Initializing**, **Synching**, **Active**, or **Error**.

When the status is **Active**, the operation can be completed with the following statement:

```
ALTER DATABASE <new_database_name> FINALIZE REPLICA
```

This will start the new tenant, update the root key (and re-encrypt data, when enabled), and delete any remote identity in case cross-tenant database access was configured. If the objective is to move the tenant database, append DROP SOURCE DATABASE to the ALTER DATABASE statement.

As with system replication, there are some limitations. SAP HANA dynamic tiering or the R server aren't supported. See the documentation for the fine print.

Learn More

Copying and moving tenant databases is documented in the SAP HANA Administration Guide under Tenant Database Management.

You might have expected this feature to be documented under HA like all other system replication topics, but this isn't the case and an important point to note. For tenant database copy (and move), you're making use of HA technology for the purpose of database management. In fact, you would not use this feature to copy a tenant database from the primary system to the secondary. There's no need to: just making a backup of a new tenant database is enough to get it cloned on the secondary. Trying to move a tenant database from the primary system to the secondary isn't even possible.

Important Terminology

For this exam objective, you're expected to understand the following terms:

- **Active-active read-enabled**
  Active/active read-enabled is a licensed system replication feature that enables read access to the secondary system. Active/active read-enabled improves system performance by offloading read-intensive operations from the primary system to the secondary.

- **Delta data shipping mode**
  The original system replication operation mode sends savepoints as delta data shipping to the secondary site. Like differential backups, this reduces the time required for takeover. In this mode, the secondary system persists received log buffers but doesn't replay the redo until takeover.

- **Failback**
  A failback references a takeover to the original site. After the first takeover (failover, if the primary is offline), the secondary is now the new primary. If both

systems are online again, and system replication is established, you can perform a takeover on the new secondary to make it the primary system again and return to the original situation.

- **Failover**
  A failover is a takeover with the primary system offline.

- **High availability/disaster recovery (HA/DR) provider**
  An HA/DR provider, also known as a "hook," is a Python script provided by the customer or third party to automate additional tasks external to the SAP HANA system such as IP redirection. HA/DR providers can also be used in case of host auto-failover.

- **High availability (HA)**
  HA isn't a product feature but a system characteristic, or as described in the documentation: a set of techniques, engineering practices, and design principles. SAP HANA supports HA with features such as service auto-restart and host auto-failover to address fault recovery and with database backups, support for third-party storage replication, and built-in system replication to cover disaster recovery (DR) requirements.

- **Host auto-failover**
  This fault recovery solution requires a multiple-host system and one or more standby hosts. When an active (worker) host fails, the standby host takes over. As the term indicates, the failover is triggered automatically.

- **Invisible takeover**
  The SQLDBC client library enables session variables on the primary system to be recovered and restored on the secondary system during takeovers. This makes the takeover "invisible" or transparent to the client. Session state recovery and restore also works in case of a system crash.

- **Log replay mode**
  This system replication operation mode configures the secondary system to continuously replay received log buffers. This minimizes the time required for takeover and reduces the overall network load.

- **Log replication mode**
  There are three log replication modes that control when and where committed transactions are persisted first: asynchronous, synchronous, and synchronous in-memory. When both sites fail simultaneously or when takeover needs to be performed with loss of the network, the vulnerability to data loss is largest in asynchronous mode. No data loss can be guaranteed in synchronous mode with the full sync option enabled.

- **Log retention**
  In the log replay operation mode, log segments are continuously transferred to the secondary system. To avoid the need to initiate full data shipping in case the connection between the systems is temporarily lost, log retention can be

enabled (default setting true). This causes the primary system to store and not overwrite log segments.

- **Multitier system replication**
  With multitier system replication you can chain system replication sites, for example, to combine SYNCMEM system replication between site A and B in the same data center with ASYNC system replication to remote site C, also known as geo-clustering. Note that for site C, site B is the replication source.

- **Near-zero downtime upgrades**
  Downtime for system updates can be minimized using system replication. You need to follow a specific sequence (first number two, then number one), but this requires no particular setup and works out of the box. The update can be performed as-is or combined with takeover to further reduce the downtime required.

- **Primary and secondary system**
  System replication requires at least two systems: a primary and secondary, also known as tier 1 and tier 2. Additional tiers can be added using multitarget and/or multitier configuration. During takeover, the systems switch roles: secondary becomes primary, and primary, when accessible, becomes the secondary. A takeover can be planned or unplanned. To switch roles again to the original configuration is called failback.

- **Replication**
  When you copy a database, you duplicate; when you continuously copy data, you replicate. This can be used for data integration scenarios, for example, when you replicate data from SAP ERP to an SAP HANA system, known as a sidecar scenario, where SAP HANA acts as an accelerator for reporting and analysis. You can also replicate data to achieve HA, for example, using storage or system replication.

- **Secondary time travel**
  Secondary time travel is a system replication feature that enables you to query data on the secondary system at a time in the past.

- **Storage replication**
  This third-party solution operates at the storage subsystem level outside control of SAP HANA, also known as remote storage mirroring.

- **System replication**
  This is a built-in (or native) SAP HANA HA solution providing both fault and DR support.

- **Takeover**
  During takeover, the primary and secondary system switch roles. This is also known as failover. When you go full circle and return to the initial situation and configure the primary system to be the primary system again, this is called failback.

✔ Practice Questions

These practice questions will help you evaluate your understanding of the topics covered in this chapter. The questions shown are similar in nature to those found on the certification examination. Although none of these questions will be found on the exam itself, they will allow you to review your knowledge of the subject. Select the correct answers, and then check the completeness of your answers in the "Practice Question Answers and Explanations" section. Remember that on the exam, you must select all correct answers, and only correct answers, to receive credit for the question.

1. Which high availability (HA) solution provides the shortest recovery time objective (RTO)?

    ☐   **A.** SAP HANA system replication

    ☐   **B.** Third-party storage replication

    ☐   **C.** SAP Landscape Transformation Replication Server

    ☐   **D.** SAP Replication Server

2. Which tools can you use to configure SAP HANA system replication? (There are three correct answers.)

    ☐   **A.** SAP Solution Manager

    ☐   **B.** SAP HANA cockpit

    ☐   **C.** SAP Landscape Management

    ☐   **D.** The HSR command-line tool

    ☐   **E.** The hdbnsutil command-line tool

3. Which log replication modes are available for SAP HANA system replication? (There are three correct answers.)

    ☐   **A.** Full sync (FULL_SYNC)

    ☐   **B.** Asynchronous (ASYNC)

    ☐   **C.** Synchronous (SYNC)

    ☐   **D.** Synchronous in-memory (SYNCMEM)

    ☐   **E.** Synchronous on disk (SYNCDISK)

4. Which log replication mode has the least impact on transaction processing?

    ☐   **A.** Asynchronous (ASYNC)

    ☐   **B.** Synchronous (SYNC)

    ☐   **C.** Synchronous in-memory (SYNCMEM)

    ☐   **D.** Synchronous (SYNC) with full sync option

5. Which log replication mode is most vulnerable to data loss?

☐ **A.** Asynchronous (ASYNC)

☐ **B.** Synchronous (SYNC)

☐ **C.** Synchronous in-memory (SYNCMEM)

☐ **D.** Synchronous (SYNC) with full sync option

6. What are two advantages of continuous log replay? (There are two correct answers.)

☐ **A.** The secondary system is always in synch with the primary system.

☐ **B.** Compared to the original delta data shipping mode, there is less impact on overall network throughput and less data needs to be transferred.

☐ **C.** It's supported on all SAP HANA versions.

☐ **D.** The secondary system is ready for immediate takeover.

7. How can you check the status of system replication? (There are three correct answers.)

☐ **A.** Run command HSR info.

☐ **B.** Run command hdbnsutil -sr_state.

☐ **C.** Run command python systemReplicationStatus.py.

☐ **D.** Query the M_SERVICE_REPLICATION system monitoring view.

☐ **E.** Query the M_REPLICATION_STATUS system monitoring view.

8. What are three differences between system replication in SAP HANA 1.0 and 2.0? (There are three correct answers.)

☐ **A.** Operation mode logreplay_readaccess

☐ **B.** Support for SAP HANA studio

☐ **C.** Support for active/active read-enabled system replication

☐ **D.** The full sync option of the SYNC log replication mode

☐ **E.** Requirement to copy the system PKI SSFS store and key files from the primary system to the secondary system

9. How can you enable the full sync option?

☐ **A.** Using command hdbnsutil -sr_register --replicationMode=fullsync

☐ **B.** Using command hdbnsutil -sr_fullsync --enable

☐ **C.** Using command hdbnsutil --replicationMode=sync –fullsync=enable

10. The operation mode log replay provides a more continues network flow while delta data shipping causes spikes in the network load. What is the default interval for delta data shipping?

☐ **A.** 6 seconds

☐ **B.** 60 seconds.

☐ **C.** 600 seconds.

11. Which prerequisites need to be fulfilled to use the secondary site in multiple components, one system (MCOS) scenarios, for example, for development or QA systems? (There are three correct answers.)

☐ **A.** Table preloading needs to switched off.

☐ **B.** The secondary system needs to be stopped.

☐ **C.** The instance number +1 of the primary system must not be used on the secondary site.

☐ **D.** The secondary system needs to have the standby role.

☐ **E.** The global allocation limit for each system needs to be configured accordingly.

12. Compression is enabled by default.

☐ **A.** True.

☐ **B.** False.

13. Which are valid replication status states? (There are two correct answers.)

☐ **A.** STOPPED

☐ **B.** STARTING

☐ **C.** SYNCHRONIZING

☐ **D.** SYNCHING

☐ **E.** INITIALIZING

14. Which are restrictions for active/active read-enabled system replication? (There are two correct answers.)

☐ **A.** Multitier system replication isn't supported.

☐ **B.** The same SAP HANA version is required on both systems.

☐ **C.** Multitarget system replication isn't supported.

☐ **D.** The same processor architecture is required on both systems.

15. You've created a new tenant database, but the database isn't available on the secondary site. What may cause this issue?

☐ **A.** You also need to create the database on the secondary site.

☐ **B.** You need to make a backup of the tenant database.

☐ **C.** You need to register the database for system replication using SAP HANA cockpit or the `hdbnsutil` command-line tool.

Practice Question Answers and Explanations

1. Correct answer: **A**

   SAP HANA system replication is built-in, or native, replication technology that can provide a RTO of zero. When configured in synchronous (persistent storage or "on disk") replication mode with full sync option enabled, immediate consistency is guaranteed with no data loss.

   Answer B is incorrect because third-party storage replication can provide acceptable recovery times and might be a preferred solution for data center replication of both SAP and non-SAP multivendor systems. However, as the technology has no knowledge of the savepoint and redo log status of an SAP HANA database, some recovery time and data loss is inevitable. Answers C and D are incorrect because the SAP Landscape Transformation Replication Server and SAP Replication Server are data integration solutions and not HA solutions. They can be used, for example, in SAP HANA as sidecar implementations to copy source data, often from an SAP system, into SAP HANA for real-time analysis. Together with SAP Data Services for extract, transform, and load (ETL)-based replication, these products propose solutions to data integration challenges. These three different technologies, each with their own use cases, shouldn't be confused with the kind of replication of this chapter.

2. Correct answers: **B, C, E**

   The command-line tool `hdbnsutil` is included with every SAP HANA system, whereas SAP HANA cockpit and SAP Landscape Management require installation and configuration, and typically run on separate systems.

   Answer A is incorrect because SAP Solution Manager is an application lifecycle management (ALM) tool for SAP business applications, in particular and can't be used for SAP HANA system replication. Answer D is incorrect because there is no HSR tool.

3. Correct answers: **B, C, D**

   Asynchronous, synchronous, and synchronous in-memory replication modes are available.

   Answer A is incorrect because you can enable the full sync option for the synchronous ("on disk") log replication mode, but it's not a mode as such. Answer E is incorrect because the synchronous log replication with the secondary site persisting the log buffers to the redo log before the transaction is committed is called SYNC not SYNCDISK.

4. Correct answer: **A**

In asynchronous mode, the transaction is committed after sending the log buffer but without waiting for a response.

Answer B is incorrect because SYNC delays the response with both network and persistent storage I/O for the log buffer to be persisted on the secondary site. Answer C is incorrect because SYNCMEM delays the response with network I/O for the log buffer to be received in-memory on the secondary site. Answer D is incorrect because synchronous (SYNC) with full sync option has the biggest impact because besides the delays of SYNC, transaction processing will now also be suspended whenever the network connection to the secondary is lost.

5. Correct answer: **A**

In asynchronous mode, the transaction is committed after sending the log buffer but without waiting for a response. Transactions may be committed on the primary site without the secondary site having received the redo log buffers.

Answer B is incorrect because, in the SYNC log replication mode, the log buffers are persisted on the secondary site before the transaction is committed on the primary site. This can be further enhanced with the full synch option (FULL_SYNC=YES [Answer D]). Answer C is incorrect because SYNCMEM provides some protection against data loss potential by acknowledgement of the reception of the log buffer. When both sites fail simultaneously, data loss can occur.

6. Correct answers: **B, D**

In both the delta_datashipping and logreplay operation mode, redo log buffers are transmitted over the network. In delta_datashipping mode, at regular time intervals, savepoints (data snapshots) are also transmitted. This greatly increases the overall network load. In addition, delta data shipping demands much higher throughput capacity for the network to correctly process the regular data shipping bursts. In the log replay operation mode, redo log buffers are continuously processed, and the secondary system is ready for takeover.

Answer A is incorrect because, when configured for asynchronous system replication, the secondary system may lag behind the primary system a little and not always be in sync. Answer C is incorrect because log replay was introduced with SAP HANA 1.0 SPS 11 in 2015 and could not be used for near-zero downtime upgrades of SPS 10 systems or older. Today, with SPS 12 as the oldest supported system (until May 2021), this may no longer appear to be relevant knowledge but as it's still documented it may be good to be aware of this.

7. Correct answers: **B, C, D**

You can use the hdbnsutil command-line tool or the systemReplicationStatus.py Python script. Alternatively, you can query the M_SERVICE_REPLICATION system monitoring view. The system replication data displayed in SAP HANA cockpit and SAP HANA studio is also sourced from this view.

Answer A is incorrect because there is no HSR command. Answer E is incorrect because M_REPLICATION_STATUS is the system monitoring view.

8. Correct answers: **A, C, E**

SAP HANA 2.0 introduces active/active read-enabled system replication, which technically is implemented with the logreplay_readaccess operation mode. As of SAP HANA 2.0, the data and log shipping are secured, which requires copying the PKI SSFS store and key files from the primary system to the secondary system before system replication can be enabled.

Answer B is incorrect because SAP HANA studio supports configuration and monitoring of both major SAP HANA releases, although using SAP HANA cockpit is recommended. Answer D, the full sync option of the SYNC log replication mode, is available in both major releases.

9. Correct answer: **B**

When system replication runs in operation mode SYNC, you can enable (or disable) the full synch option. Running in full sync requires careful consideration as this option can potentially stop processing on the primary system. The command hdbnsutil -sr_fullsync --enable configures the system parameter enable_full_sync=true.

Answer A is incorrect because the syntax of the command is invalid. Full sync isn't a system replication operation mode but an option. Answer C is incorrect because this syntax of the command is invalid.

10. Correct answer: **C**

The default interval for the delta data shipping mode is every 10 minutes (600 seconds).

Answers A and B are incorrect.

11. Correct answers: **A, C, E**

As explained in Chapter 3, the MCOS scenario supports multiple SAP HANA installations on a single (operating) system. This is also known as multi-SID environments. To reduce the TCO of system replication, MCOS is supported. A common requirement of such an environment is that the global allocation limit needs to be adjusted. Specific to system replication is that preloading of column tables needs to be disabled, and the instance number +1 of the primary system can't be used on the secondary site because the associated ports are used for system replication.

The corresponding system parameters are global.ini/[system_replication]-> preload_column_tables=false and global.ini/[memorymanager]-> global_allocation_limit.

Answer B is incorrect because the secondary system needs to be running to process incoming redo logs. Answer D is incorrect because worker and standby roles are relevant for multiple-host systems but not for system replication. SAP HANA system replication in active/active read-enabled mode resembles the "hot" standby mode of other database vendor solutions, but this term isn't used with SAP HANA.

> **Exam Tip**
> Tough question? Correct. We didn't cover the instance number + 1 small print requirement. However, with elimination you might have been able to rule out answers B and D and are left with the correct answer. Eliminating the wrong answers can be a good exam question strategy.

12. Correct answer: **B**

    To reduce network load, you can enable compression for both log buffers and data pages. By default, compression is disabled but should be considered for replication over larger distances (typically in ASYNC mode). For shorter distances, for example, replication within the same data center, compression, and decompression would add too much overhead and could potentially slow down takeover times.

13. Correct answers: **D, E**

    Valid status states are **Unknown, Initializing, Synching, Active,** and **Error**.

14. Correct answers: **B, D**

    System replication is only supported on systems with the same processor architecture and the same SAP HANA version.

    Answer A is incorrect because multitier system replication is supported, but active/active is only available for the secondary system. Answer C is incorrect because multitarget system replication is supported but active/active is only available for the secondary system.

15. Correct answer: **B**

    You need to make a backup before newly created tenant databases can participate in system replication.

    Answer A is incorrect because you can't connect with the SQL interface to the secondary system except for active/active read-enabled configurations, in which case, the connection is read-only. Answer C is incorrect because system replication operates at the system level and not at the database level.

Takeaway

The objective of this chapter was to familiarize you with system replication. We discussed how this feature relates to other replication technologies and what role it plays to enable HA/DR. We covered the different log replication modes (synchronous, synchronous in-memory, asynchronous) and operation modes (delta shipping, log replay, log replay read access). You used SAP HANA cockpit to enable system replication, change configurations, and perform a takeover with the command-line equivalents using the hdbnsutil tool. We also showed how you can use

SAP HANA cockpit for system replication monitoring. We also introduced some more advanced system replication topics such as invisible takeover, secondary time travel, active/active read-enabled, multitier and multitarget replication, and how you can use system replication for near-zero downtime upgrades.

Summary

In this chapter we covered the system replication topic area. We looked at HA and system replication concepts. We described how to enable (and disable) system replication, how to perform system administration in a system replication scenario and addressed takeovers and failbacks. We also covered how to create tenant databases leveraging system replication and how to perform near-zero downtime upgrades.

In the next chapter, we're going to dig into monitoring and troubleshooting.

Chapter 13
Troubleshooting and Performance Analysis

Techniques You'll Master

- Monitoring SAP HANA databases
- Working with alerts
- Troubleshooting
- Collecting diagnostic information
- Recognizing common issues related to memory, CPU, SQL statements, and disk

In this chapter, we cover troubleshooting and performance analysis; in other words, how do you solve issues and find out what might cause them. In addition, we also address working with alerts, which support the system administrator with monitoring and can help you stay out of trouble in the first place. Workload management serves to maximize overall system performance by keeping transactional (online transactional processing [OLTP]) and analytics (online analytical processing [OLAP]) workload types and resource usage in balance. Capture and Replay enables you to capture the workload of a source system for replay on a target system, for example, after a change in hardware or software update.

In this chapter, a distinction is made between the following:

- **Emergency analysis and troubleshooting**
  This is panic mode; something goes wrong and you need to know how to fix this *now*.

- **Root cause analysis of structural issues**
  Performance is degrading over time, and you need to zoom in on what might be the cause: memory, CPU, disk, expensive SQL statement, a combination, or something else.

- **Proactive monitoring and safeguarding performance**
  This covers your efforts to avoid having to troubleshoot in the first place and includes a good understanding of the SAP HANA alerting framework and features such as workload management and Capture and Replay with their use cases.

Real-World Scenario

Panic! It's the weekend and you're enjoying your time off, but your manager calls with an exceptional request. The SAP HANA system of an important customer no longer responds, and could you please dial in remotely and troubleshoot the situation? Being the hero that you are, you help out the customer and get some bonus points with your manager. Come Monday, you meet with the customer for a more thorough root cause analysis. Turns out that the alerts were switched off as it generated too many emails on irrelevant issues. Together with the customer, you properly configure alerts and also take advantage of the opportunity to implement workload management for the database. This type of proactive thinking will keep the system running smoothly and avoid having to troubleshoot during the weekend. The company's SAP HANA implementation is a success, and it has many more users working on the system than initially sized. The customer agrees to a system update, and you explain how you can use Capture and Replay to avoid any surprises. Needless to say, the customer (and your manager) are extremely pleased with your professionalism.

Happy about your achievements, you go home Friday in anticipation of the weekend. Your manager calls. Panic! It's the same issue but with another customer. Good thing you like your job.

Topic and Objectives

In this chapter, we cover troubleshooting and performance analysis topics. For the exam, you need to have a good understanding of the following topics:

- System monitoring with SAP HANA cockpit
- The alerting mechanism and how to configure alerts
- How to collect diagnostic information and work with trace files
- Troubleshooting of common symptoms and slow system-wide performance
- How to identify and solve memory-related issues, root causes of high CPU consumption, disk and input/output (I/O) issues, and application performance (expensive SQL statements)

Note

Earlier editions of the exam included one topic area for Monitoring and one for Troubleshooting. Later, these were combined into a single Monitoring and Troubleshooting topic area with a new one added for Performance and System Tuning. More recently, this became the Proactive Monitoring topic area and the Troubleshooting and Analyzing System Performance Root cause Analysis topic area. Both topic areas are minor topics with a weight of < 8% of the total certification exam score. With 80 questions in total, you can expect about 4 questions for each topic area. Combined of course, this gets a medium weight (8 questions), and this is how we recommend approaching the topic area. As the topics are closely related, we've combined them in a single chapter.

Keep in mind that the exam guide states this can change at any time, so always check online for the latest updates.

Learn More

In this chapter, we focus on what you need to know to pass the exam. However, the monitoring, troubleshooting, and performance analysis topic is much broader, and there are many aspects we haven't covered. If not for the exam, then at least for the job, you should be familiar with the documentation, and we recommend checking out the documentation on this topic in your spare time.

Monitoring, which includes alerts and diagnostics, workload management, and Capture and Replay are system administration topics and documented in the SAP HANA Administration Guide. Analyzing generic symptoms, root causes and solutions, tools and tracing, and the alerts reference is documented in the SAP HANA Troubleshooting and Performance Analysis Guide. For information about how to develop responsive applications and what you need to know about SQL query performance and SQLScript performance guidelines, consult the SAP HANA Performance Guide for Developers.

Key Concepts Refresher

In this section, we'll touch upon the key concepts that are included in troubleshooting and performance analysis, including monitoring, alerts, unresponsive systems, diagnosis files, generic symptoms, and root cause analysis.

SAP HANA 2.0 SPS 05: What's New?

As of SAP HANA 2.0 SPS 05, you can now enable the kernel profiler with a SQL statement. We'll cover this topic in this chapter.

On the frontend, with SAP HANA cockpit 2.0 SP 12 (and SP 11), minor changes have been added to the Expensive Statement app, Plan Trace, and SQL Plan Stability. SP 11 introduced the Memory Profiler app.

For the complete list of new features, see the What's New Guide on the SAP Help Portal for the SAP HANA platform at *http://s-prs.co/v507867*.

Monitoring

In Chapter 6, we already made a grand tour around most of the cards, tiles, and apps of SAP HANA cockpit. Before we dive into troubleshooting and analysis, let's first quickly review how this tool supports system monitoring and, together with alerts, can help you prevent getting into serious trouble.

Directly after you've connected to SAP HANA cockpit and arrive on the **Home** page, you're informed about the health of your landscape. Database group cards display when databases aren't running or are **Running with Issues**, as illustrated in Figure 13.1.

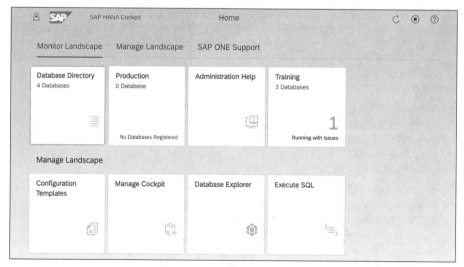

Figure 13.1 SAP HANA Cockpit Home

When you open the **Database Directory**, you get some more information about any alerts that were raised and about the status of the three key performance area (KPA) groups: **Availability**, **Performance**, and **Capacity**, as illustrated in Figure 13.2.

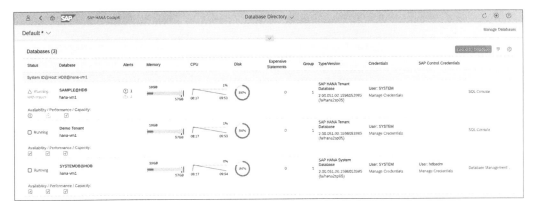

Figure 13.2 Database Directory

Selecting the KPA or alert indicators will open the Alerts app for the corresponding database. Selecting **Status** will open the Manage Services app.

When you click the database link, you're directed to the Database Overview app. Figure 13.3 shows the app with the **Monitoring** view selected.

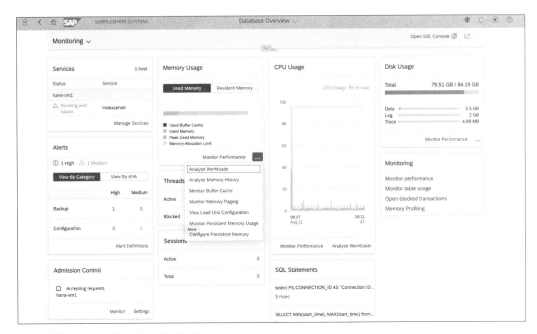

Figure 13.3 Database Overview Monitoring

This shows the **Memory Usage**, **CPU Usage**, and **Disk Usage** cards with interactive graphs that give access to the **Performance Monitor** and other monitoring and analysis tools. The cards for **Alerts** and **Services** (previously Overall Database Status) are displayed with access to the corresponding apps. In addition, you'll see the cards for **Sessions**, **Threads**, and **SQL Statements**, which we'll cover in this chapter. The **Monitoring** card adds some more links to the app with no real estate on the view yet, such as **Table Usage**, **Blocked Transactions**, and the new **Memory Profiling**.

The Admission Control app falls under workload management and enables you to control access when the system is reaching full capacity. The app shows current status with access to the apps for configuration and the monitoring.

When you select **Services**, the Manage Services app opens, and you've now arrived at the service level, as illustrated in Figure 13.4. We've already covered this app when we discussed SAP HANA cockpit, so we won't repeat all the links and buttons, but just point out the **Reset Memory Statistics** link in the header. A typical use case is to compare two load jobs so you can start each job with a clean slate.

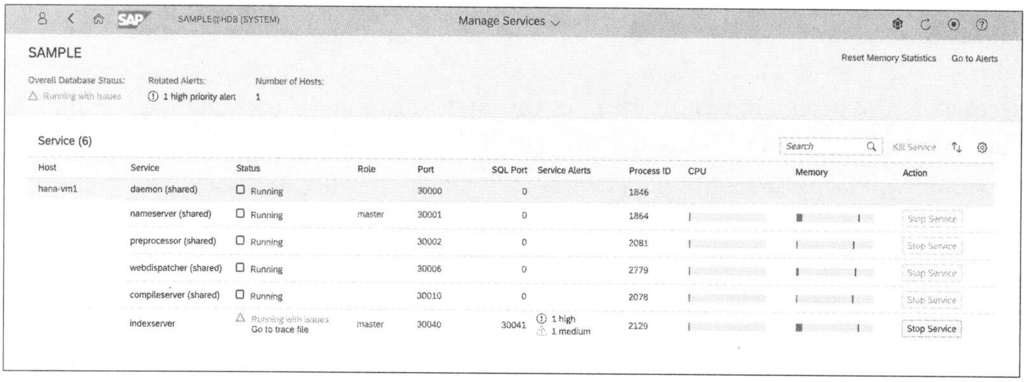

Figure 13.4 Manage Services

Alert information is displayed in the header of **Manage Services** screen, and when selecting the alert (or the **Go to Alerts** link), you can navigate to the Alert app once again. However, for the most detailed level of information, you can now select the **Go to trace file** link, which will open SAP HANA database explorer with the corresponding trace file, as illustrated in Figure 13.5.

Although typically difficult to read, trace files may provide the necessary clues when troubleshooting. Here the message is clear: you need a backup to ensure recoverability of the database.

The journey we just covered from system landscape to database to service to traces illustrates a typical monitoring flow where you start at a high level and descend into detail with every step. The objective of this chapter is to make you familiar with these troubleshooting flows, as there are many, and help you know which tools to use in which circumstances.

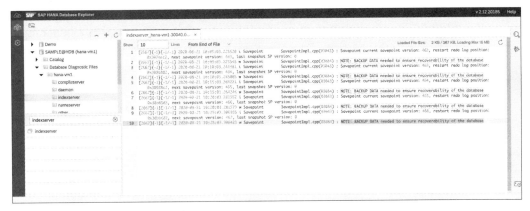

Figure 13.5 Database Explorer Trace File

Learn More

Apart from the well-documented SAP HANA Troubleshooting and Performance Analysis Guide, there are also a number of KBAs that provide for recommended reading:

- KBA 2000000 – FAQ: SAP HANA Performance Optimization
- KBA 2400024 – How-To: SAP HANA Administration and Monitoring

---

Alerts

When you're monitoring an SAP HANA system, you're not alone. The statistics server is continuously collection information, performing checks, and raising alerts. We'll walk through the statistics server, as well as alert monitoring and configuration, in the following sections.

Statistics Server

The statistics server is the engine of SAP HANA's internal monitoring infrastructure and contains two components:

- Data collectors
- Alert checkers

Technically, the statistics server relies on a set of SQLScript procedures with corresponding tables. The data collector runs embedded in the index server of every tenant database. The statistics scheduler runs as a thread in the master name server and regularly, as configured, invokes the procedures. The data collectors query different system views and tables and then store this information in the measurement tables. The alert checkers also query the original source tables but this time to compare current values with defined thresholds and check whether a condition is met to write the result to table STATISTICS_ALERTS.

The data is persisted in the _SYS_STATISTICS schema. You can query this data using SQL yourself or have SAP HANA cockpit do this for you, for example, by opening the Database Overview app. This app, together with the cards and apps for **Alerts**, **CPU Usage**, and many others, some illustrated previously, are populated with data collected by the statistics server.

To manage the volume of data collected, you can configure the following:

- Data retention period
- Maximum number of alerts

Most data collectors have a default retention period of 42 days. Older data is deleted automatically. The default maximum number of alerts is one million, but this also is configurable using the SQL interface. There is no corresponding user interface in SAP HANA cockpit. In addition, you can control alerts and collect behavior with profiles (S, M, L, HXE). The profile for SAP HANA, express edition, disables most alerts.

> **Learn More**
>
> The statistics server is documented in the SAP HANA Administration Guide. This information is complemented by KBA 2147247 – FAQ: SAP HANA Statistics Server.

Alert Monitoring

As you've already seen, SAP HANA cockpit displays alerts in several locations. There is a dedicated **Alerts** card and Alerts app, but alerts are also displayed in **Database Directory**, **Database Overview**, **Manage Databases**, and **Manage Services** and associated **Services** card. To view alerts, you need the following privileges:

- CATALOG READ system privilege
- SELECT object privilege on schema _SYS_STATISTICS

Alerts are categorized in three key performance areas (KPAs; refer to Figure 13.2 and Figure 13.3):

- Availability: Availability, backup, diagnosis files, security
- Performance: CPU, disk, memory
- Capacity: Configuration, sessions/transactions

Alerts have the following priorities:

- **Information**
  Action is recommended to improve system performance or stability.
- **Low**
  Medium-term action is required to mitigate risk of downtime.
- **Medium**
  Short-term action is required (hours, days).

- **High**

  Immediate action is required to mitigate risk of downtime, data loss, or data corruption.

- **Error**

  Immediate action is required to fix the issue (see trace files).

From the **Alerts** cards on **Database Overview**, you can navigate to the Alerts app and the Alerts Definition app.

The Alerts app is illustrated in Figure 13.6. The app lists all alerts in a table view, which, like for many other apps, is customizable. You can add columns, group, and sort, and you can adjust and save the filter.

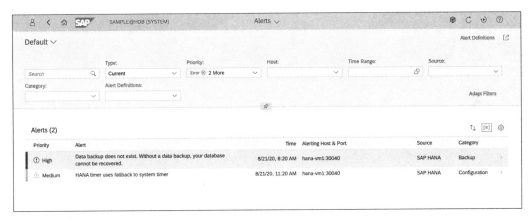

Figure 13.6 Alerts

When you select the alert, the detailed view opens, as illustrated in Figure 13.7. This provides more detailed information and also a proposed solution with a graph showing the number of recent occurrences. For the **Data backup does not exist** alert, the proposed solution by SAP is to perform a data backup as soon as possible; to expedite the process, a link to the Backup app is included. For the other alert shown in Figure 13.7, there is a reference to an SAP Note.

When the issue is fixed, you can click the **Check Now** button, which will trigger the alert checker to run and will display a message within a few seconds with the results: issue solved or not.

When an alert fails to run, for example, because not enough system resources are available, the alert is marked as failed. Failed alerts can be manually re-enabled, but the system will also attempt to activate failed alerts after one hour. This is controlled by two configurable values in table STATISTICS_SCHEDULE: INTERVALLENGHT and SKIP_INTERVAL_ON_DISABLE.

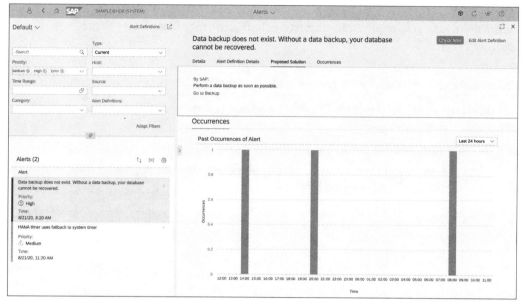

Figure 13.7 Alerts Detail

Alert Definition

Click **Edit Alert Definition** to enable or disable the alert, configure the interval of the alert check, and add email recipients, as shown in Figure 13.8.

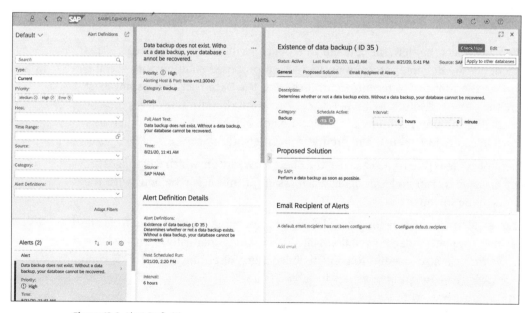

Figure 13.8 Alert Definition

When email recipients are configured for a specific alert, the default recipients aren't notified. Email alerts are only sent on the first occurrence and not each and every time. When the alert no longer triggers, a final email is sent to inform the recipients. Note that you can apply any changes made to other databases.

The Alert Definitions app shown in Figure 13.9 lists all available alerts categorized according to the KPA.

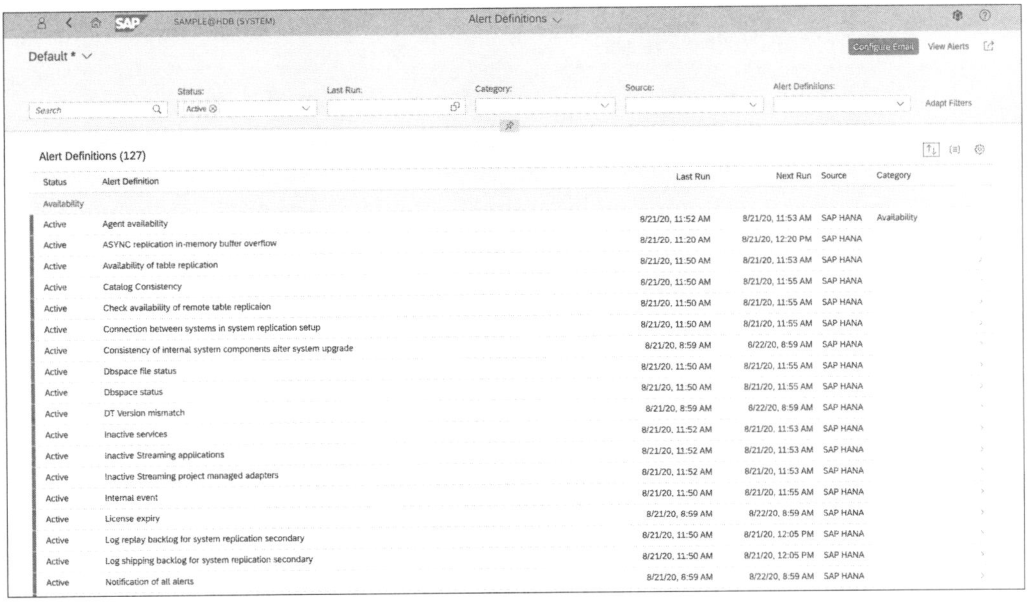

Figure 13.9 Alert Definitions

Click the **Configure Email** button in the header of the app, and click **Sender** to configure the settings for outgoing mail: email sender (email), SMTP server, and SMTP port. Select **Default Recipient** to add the email addresses of the default recipients, for example, a help desk account that is monitored 24/7.

The default threshold values are defined per alert. Some alerts only check a condition (alert 4 Restarted Services).

Because you're making changes in the Alert Definitions app, besides the previously mentioned privileges, this also requires INSERT, DELETE, and UPDATE privileges on the _SYS_STATISTICS schema.

Learn More

What to do (user action) and where to find more information (SAP Note) is documented in the Alerts Reference of the SAP HANA Troubleshooting and Performance Analysis Guide. As with any reference, you're not expected to know all 150 alerts by heart. However, you might want to inspect the reference at least once, so you know what kind of information it provides. Besides the database alerts, there are also some alerts available for some of the optional components: SAP HANA dynamic tiering (500), SAP HANA streaming analytics (600), and SAP HANA smart data integration (SDI) (700).

See also KBA 2445867 – How-To: Interpreting and Resolving SAP HANA Alerts.

> **SPS 05: What's New?**
> When changing the configuration of an alert, you can now apply the change to multiple databases.

System Monitoring Views

For environments without access to SAP HANA cockpit, or if you want or get an overall picture and run a health check on one or more databases maybe for the purpose of monthly reporting, you can query system monitoring views for live data or the _SYS_STATISTICS schema for historic data. Figure 13.10 shows the contents of table HOST_SAVEPOINTS_BASE in the _SYS_STATISTICS schema.

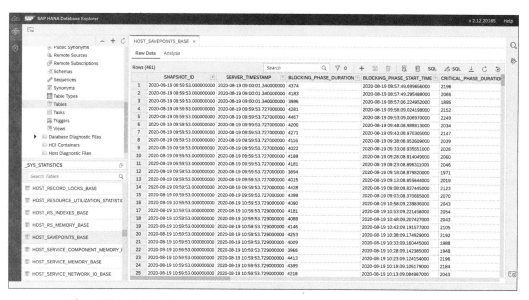

Figure 13.10 _SYS_STATISTICS

Working with the system monitoring views and SYS_STATISTICS tables directly can be challenging. To make this easier to work with, SAP HANA database explorer includes a **Statement Library**, as illustrated in Figure 13.11. In this library, you find a number of preformatted SQL statements and scripts that query the system monitoring views and statistics server. From here, you can execute the scripts directly or have them displayed in the SQL console for editing. You can export the script or add your own statements, for example, from the collection of SAP HANA mini checks.

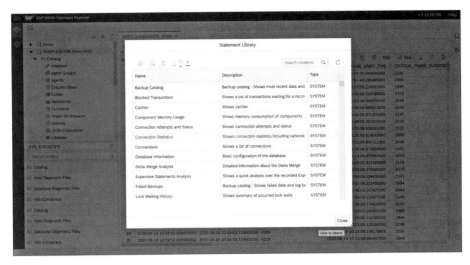

Figure 13.11 Statement Library

Mini Checks

SAP HANA mini checks are a collection of SQL scripts provided by SAP Support. As the checks aren't documented in any of the SAP HANA guides, the mini checks aren't very well known. However, SAP HANA system administrators are well advised to check them out. The script collection is attached to a KBA (and explained in another) that was created by the now defunct technical performance optimization (TPO) service for SAP HANA. The scripts perform a large number of checks and report potential issues. Figure 13.12 shows the output, with the **C** column indicating detected issues with an X pointing to relevant SAP Notes for more information. This can be quite helpful to quickly identify issues.

	CHID	DESCRIPTION	HOST	VALUE	EXPECTED_VALUE	C	SAP_NOTE
1	****	SAP HANA MINI CHECKS					1999993
2							
3	M0009	Mini check version		2.00.010+ / 2.1.63 (2019/10/05)			
4	M0010	Analysis date		2019/11/25 15:56:21 (UTC)			
5	M0011	Database name		M22			
6	M0012	Revision level		24.08	>= 0.00		2378962
7	M0013	Version		2.0			2378962
8	M0110	Everything started		yes	yes		2177064
9	M0111	Host startup time variation (s)		0	<= 600		2177064
10	M0115	Service startup time variation (s)	mo-...	163086	<= 600	X	2177064
11							
12	****	OPERATING SYSTEM					
13							
14	M0207	Recommended bigmem kernel flavor not used		no	no		2240716
15	M0208	Supported operating system	mo-...	yes	yes		2235581
16	M0209	Recommended operating system kernel version	mo-...	no (3.12.62-60.64.8-default instead of >= 60.64.40)	yes	X	2235581
17	M0211	Hosts with varying CPU rates		no	no		2235581
18	M0215	Hosts with outdated CPU type		1	0	X	2399995
19	M0222	Time since CPU utilization > 95 % (h)		never	>= 12.00		2100040
20	M0227	External CPU utilization (%, last hour)	mo-...	4	<= 10		2100040
21	M0228	Erroneous system CPU calculation	mo-...	no	no		2222110
22	M0232	Hyperthreading active in critical context		no	no		2711650

Figure 13.12 SAP HANA Mini Checks

> **Learn More**
>
> For more detailed information about mini checks, beyond the scope of this exam, see the following KBAs:
>
> - KBA 1969700 – SQL Statement Collection for SAP HANA
> - KBA 1999993 – How-To: Interpreting SAP HANA Mini Check Results

System Parameters

Mini check scripts aren't the only SQL scripts included in the SQL statement collection. There are also scripts that verify system parameter settings. According to the FAQ KBA on the topic, incorrect configurations can cause the following:

- High memory usage, including out-of-memory issues
- High CPU usage
- Slow performance
- System crashes, corruptions, and more

There are many system parameters documented (and even more not documented), and the right setting for a particular environment may very well be a wrong setting for another. Stick to the defaults unless it's very clear why a different setting should be used. As of SPS 03, you can add comments when you make configuration changes and query the monitoring view M_INIFILE_CONTENT_HISTORY for past changes.

> **SPS 05: What's New?**
>
> As of SPS 05, you can use the Python script setParameter.py to configure system parameters. You may recall that system parameters are persisted in text files with the *.ini* extension but modified through the SQL interface with the ALTER SYSTEM ALTER CONFIGURATION statement. When the system is stopped, you can manually make changes to the configuration files, but this is an error-prone activity. With console tool setParameter.py, you can automate the parameter configuration also when the database is up and running, for example, if you're using a third-party system management tools without access to the database.

> **Learn More**
>
> System parameters are documented in the SAP HANA Configuration Parameter Reference. For more detailed information about system parameters, beyond the scope of this exam, see the following KBAs:
>
> - KBA 2186744 – FAQ: SAP HANA Parameters
> - KBA 2600030 – Parameter Recommendations in SAP HANA Environments

Troubleshooting

Troubleshooting, such as performance tuning, is often called as much art as science. Usually, the more experienced you are, the better you can perform this activity. It requires extensive knowledge of the SAP HANA architecture, the different components, and how they relate. You also need to know where to look for information and make sense of it. A special case is when you can no longer access the system at all.

In the following sections, we'll walk through key troubleshooting topics in SAP HANA.

System Appears to Hang

Some situations cause the system to appear to hang; for example, no response and no new connections possible are common enough and easy to reproduce. Just let the system fill up the log volume, for example. There isn't much you can do to solve this issue on the database side. You need to fix this at the operating system level by allocating more storage.

It's also possible that specific Linux operating system settings cause trouble. When Transparent Huge Pages (THP) are enabled, the system can behave erratically. This is documented in the SAP HANA Installation and Update Guide and normally caught by the hardware configuration check tool, but the issue was common enough for a mention in the SAP HANA Troubleshooting and Performance Guide and a KBA on the SAP ONE Support Launchpad.

When you need to troubleshoot a system that appears to hang, you typically spend most your time on the Linux operating system, and it helps to be familiar with commands such as `top` and `sar`, as well as know where to find operating system messages, for example. You'll find this documented in the SUSE Linux Enterprise Server (SLES) or Red Hat Enterprise Linux (RHEL) documentation for SAP HANA. For some suggestions and to help you get started, SAP Support has compiled several KBAs (even on the usage of `sar`).

Learn More

Common symptoms and troubleshooting for systems that appear to hang are documented in the SAP HANA Troubleshooting and Performance Guide. Even though you're not expected to be familiar with operating system commands for the exam, for the job as system administrator, you're well advised to do your homework and read the guide and articles. You might also want to have an emergency suitcase ready. You never know.

The following KBAs provide further detail, beyond the scope of this exam:

- KBA 1999020 – How-To: SAP HANA Troubleshooting When Database Is No Longer Accessible
- KBA 202699939 – SAP HANA Emergency Suitcase

Unresponsive System

To troubleshoot an unresponsive system, go to SAP HANA cockpit, access the Database Overview app, select the **Alerts and Diagnostics** card, and select **Troubleshoot Unresponsive System**. When connected to the system database, you notice a slight delay while the message displays **Collecting emergency information...**. When the app opens, information about connections, transactions, blocked transactions, and threads is displayed on separate tabs, as illustrated in Figure 13.13.

HOST	PORT	LOGICAL_CONNECTION...	START_TIME	CONNECTION_STATUS	AUTO_COMMIT
hxehost	39040	209159	Jun 15, 2020 02:06:04.61...	IDLE	FALSE
hxehost	39040	200218	Jun 14, 2020 09:06:06.31...	IDLE	FALSE
hxehost	39040	200219	Jun 14, 2020 09:06:06.32...	IDLE	FALSE
hxehost	39040	200190	Jun 14, 2020 09:06:11.87...	IDLE	TRUE
hxehost	39040	200194	Jun 14, 2020 09:06:04.53...	IDLE	FALSE
hxehost	39040	200106	Jun 14, 2020 09:06:15.00...	IDLE	FALSE
hxehost	39040	200107	Jun 14, 2020 09:06:15.00...	IDLE	FALSE
hxehost	39040	200073	Jun 14, 2020 09:06:06.30...	IDLE	TRUE

Figure 13.13 Troubleshoot Unresponsive System

Note that you're connected to the system database and that the app is about troubleshooting an unresponsive system, not an unresponsive database. In fact, you're making use here of the sapcontrol connection defined in the **Database Directory** with the credentials of the operating system administration user account <sid>adm. The sapcontrol connection executes operating system commands on your behalf, and, in this case, it's calling hdbcons commands.

The hdbcons console is mentioned in the SAP HANA documentation as the SAP HANA database server management console (hdbcons) but with a cautionary remark: technical expertise is required to use the command-line tool and it's only to be used with the guidance of development support.

For this reason, you're not expected to be familiar with the tool; just note that with the Troubleshoot Unresponsive System app, you can execute operating system commands, and this enables you to cancel connections and transactions even without a SQL interface. Figure 13.14 illustrates the help function of hdbcons (here, **SAP HANA DB management client console**).

Learn More

How to work with the Troubleshoot Unresponsive System app is documented in the SAP HANA Administration Guide (System Administration chapter, "Getting Support" section). This is also the location where hdbcons is mentioned.

> For more information about hdbcons, consult SAP Note 2222218 – FAQ: SAP HANA Database Server Management Console (hdbcons). Here again, you'll find the cautionary message that improper usage can have severe consequences and should only be used under guidance. The command options of the tool are beyond the scope of this exam.

```
hxeadm@hxehost:/usr/sap/HXE/HDB90> hdbcons
SAP HANA DB Management Client Console (type '\?' to get help for client commands)
Try to open connection to server process 'hdbindexserver' on system 'HXE', instance
SAP HANA DB Management Server Console (type 'help' to get help for server commands)
Executable: hdbindexserver (PID: 2607)
[OK]
--
> help
## Start command at: 2020-06-15 14:50:59.787
Synopsis:

help [<command name>]: Print command help
   - <command name> - Command name for which to display help



Available commands:
ae_tableload - Handle loading of column store tables and columns
all - Print help and other info for all hdbcons commands
authentication - Authentication management.
binarysemaphore - BinarySemaphore management
bye - Exit console client
cd - ContainerDirectory management
cfgreg - Basis Configurator
checktopic - CheckTopic management
cnd - ContainerNameDirectory management
conditionalvariable - ConditionalVariable management
connection - Connection management
context - Execution context management (i.e., threads)
converter - Converter management
cpuresctrl - Manage cpu resources such as last-level cache allocation
crash - Crash management
crypto - Cryptography management (SSL/SAML/X509/Encryption).
csaccessor - Display diagnostics related to the CSAccessor library
```

Figure 13.14 SAP HANA DB Management Client Console

Collecting Diagnosis Information

When you get into serious trouble with your SAP HANA system, SAP Support may request that you collect diagnosis information. Like the emergency suitcase mentioned previously, it's a good idea to familiarize yourself with this task well before any issues arise, so you know what to do when they come. The easiest way to perform this task is to use SAP HANA cockpit. Alternatively, you can use the command line and run the same commands the tools would use.

In the following sections, we'll walk through different types of diagnosis information to collect.

Diagnosis Files

From the same **Alerting and Diagnostics** card where you launched the Troubleshoot unresponsive System app, you can also select the **Manage Full System Information Dumps** link. The app lists any previously made collection of diagnosis files. You can download the collection as a ZIP file from the app and optionally delete the collection. When the system is running, you need to have the privilege to execute the SYS.FULL_SYSTEM_INFO_DUMP_CREATE procedure (plus the ones to retrieve and optionally delete the info dumps), together with access to the FULL_SYSTEM_INFO_DUMPS view for the system database and the relevant tenants. When the system is stopped, you can still collect information, but this time, you need the sapcontrol credentials.

You can use the app to collect information by selecting **Collect Diagnostics** and making a choice (illustrated in Figure 13.15):

- **Collect from Existing Files**
- **Create from Runtime Environment**

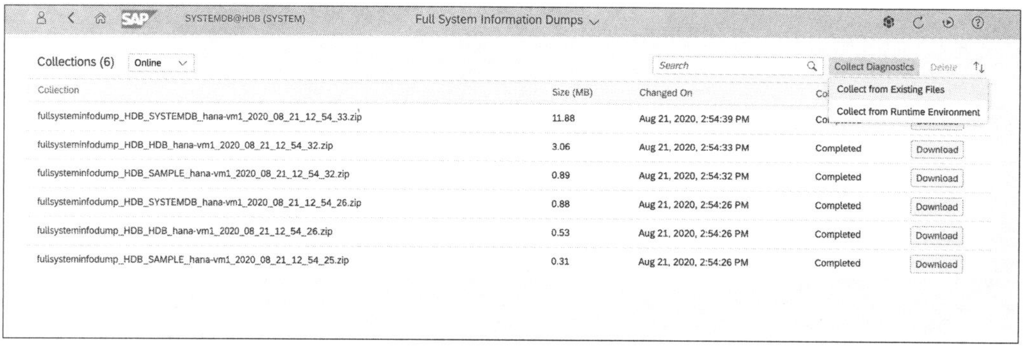

Figure 13.15 Full System Information Dumps

We'll discuss the first option in this section. In the first case, further illustrated in Figure 13.16, you get to select a **Date Range** (default 7 days) and the files to include. To start with, all file types are selected except for the performance traces. As mentioned on the dialog, it can be time consuming to collect all files due to large file sizes, so you might want to make choices. you can also opt, not shown in the illustration, to include system views and/or exported system tables and views. Of course, this requires a SQL connection and a database that is up and running. This isn't required if you only want to collect files as this is done with the help of sapcontrol and a Python script.

The collection is a compressed file called *fullsysteminfodump_<SID>_SYSTEMDB_ host.domain_<timestamp>.zip*, which you can download to your computer. Depending on your selection, the ZIP contains the trace, log, text, and comma-separated values (CSV) files, as well as some additional information about secure stores in the file system (SSFS), the topology, the network configuration (/etc/hosts), and the operating system diagnostics (/var/log) you didn't ask for. You see the log output from a minimal diagnosis selection (only **ini files**) listed in Figure 13.17. The command-line options are logged (--fileTypes --fromData --toDate -tenant) and listed, so you can use this information if you need to execute the command again, this time from the command line if no SAP HANA cockpit connection is available.

Figure 13.16 Collect Diagnosis Information

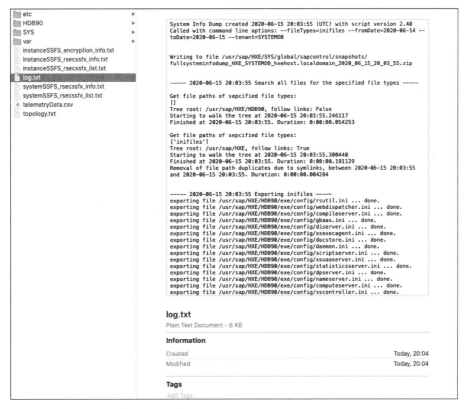

Figure 13.17 fullsysteminfodump ZIP File

Runtime Dumps

The second option is to collect runtime environment (RTE) diagnosis information. This time you need to select the number of collection points (1–5) and the interval (1, 5, 10, 15, 30), as shown in Figure 13.18. For each host, you can select the services and for each service the section, as shown in Figure 13.18. When the system is online, you can also use the SQL interface to create a runtime dump with the `ALTER SYSTEM CREATE RUNTIMEDUMP` command. This requires the `RESOURCE ADMIN` system privilege.

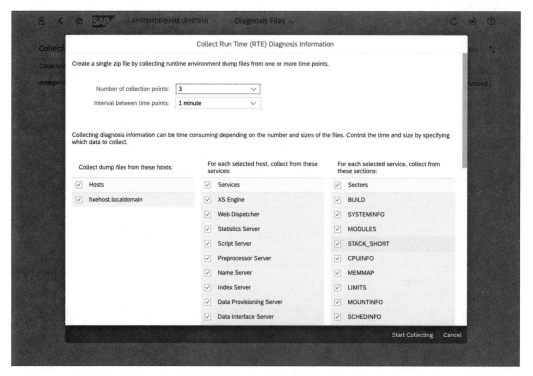

Figure 13.18 Collect Run Time (RTE) Diagnosis Information Screen

There is also a guided answer available on the topic that informs you about the steps to take. There are different ways to go about this, but one of your options is the command line and using the Python script `fullSystemInfoDump.py`, as illustrated in Figure 13.19. you can specify the number of collections, interval, and any of the other options listed previously because, as mentioned, SAP HANA cockpit will run exactly the same python script for you behind the screens.

> **Learn More**
>
> How to collect diagnosis information for SAP Support is documented in the SAP HANA Administration Guide (System Administration chapter, "Getting Support" section). For more detailed information, beyond the scope of this exam, see KBA 2400007 – FAQ: SAP HANA Runtime Dumps.

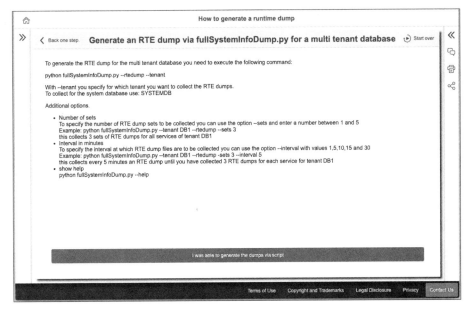

Figure 13.19 Guided Answer Runtime Dump

Trace and Diagnostics Files

Trace files are another important source of information when troubleshooting systems. To access files and configuration, select the **View trace and diagnostic files** link on the **Alerting and Diagnostics** card to open SAP HANA database explorer. From the context (right-click) menu of the database connection, you can open the **Trace Configuration** menu, as illustrated in Figure 13.20.

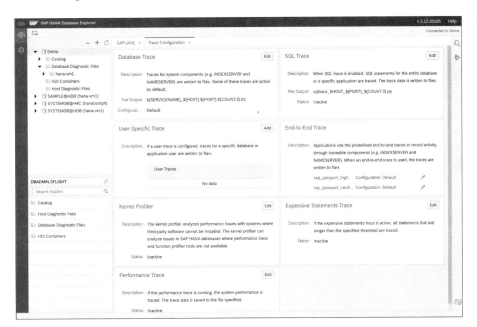

Figure 13.20 Trace Configuration

From the **Trace Configuration** menu, you can enable the following:

- **Database Trace**
  Traces system components such as the index server and name server. Some are enabled by default.

- **User-Specific Trace**
  Adds user-specific context to a database component trace.

- **Kernel Profiler**
  Analyzes performance issues with systems where third-party software can't be installed.

- **SQL Trace**
  When enabled, traces SQL statements for a specific database user.

- **Performance Trace**
  Captures system performance, optionally filtered by user or application and may include execution plans.

- **End-to-End Trace**
  Predefined end-to-end traces are used by SAP applications to record activity through components.

- **Expensive Statements Trace**
  When enabled, traces SQL statements exceeding predefined CPU, memory, or execution duration thresholds

Figure 13.21 shows the **Database Trace Configuration** screen for component join_ eval. Available trace levels are as follows:

- **NONE**   - **INFO**
- **FATAL**   - **DEBUG**
- **WARNING**

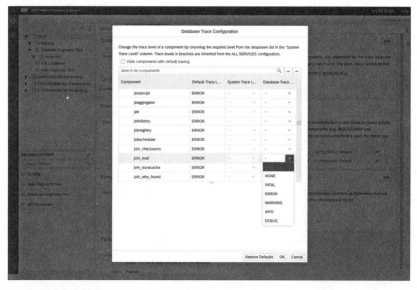

Figure 13.21 Database Trace Configuration

Figure 13.22 shows the **SQL Trace Configuration** menu. The output of trace files is typically overwhelming, and you can use the system parameters global.ini/[trace]/maxfiles and maxfilesize to control the volume and avoid massive trace files filling up the file system.

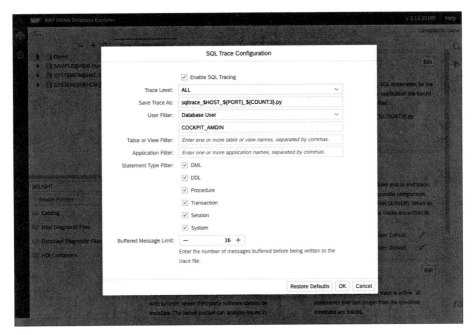

Figure 13.22 SQL Trace

SAP Support Tools

Most advice found in the guides and articles is reactive. However, there is also a proactive action you can undertake: implement HANASitter. Like the SAP HANA mini checks, HANASitter originates from SAP Support and isn't included with the official software distribution. For this reason, it's also not officially documented (although a reference was recently added to the SAP HANA Administration Guide). HANASitter is a Python script documented in a SAP Note. To download the tool, you're directed to a private GitHub repository (as of the time of writing, summer 2020). It should be clear that this isn't officially supported software, delivered as-is, of the use-at-your-own-risk type. However, after the testing has been done and everything works as expected, you can use HANASitter to "babysit" SAP HANA and automate trace creation or runtime dumps when certain conditions are met.

> **Exam Tip**
>
> Although not documented nor supported by SAP, HANASitter is covered in the SAP HANA training material and hence might be referenced on the exam. There is also a tool from the same source that can help you keep your system clean from trace files, backup catalog entries, and many other items no longer relevant. For more information, beyond the scope of the exam, see the following:

- KBA 2399979 – How-To: Configuring Automatic SAP HANA Data Collection with SAP HANASitter

- KBA 2399996 – How-To: Configuring Automatic SAP HANA Cleanup with SAP HANA-Cleaner

Memory

It should come as no surprise that memory is a common source of issues for an in-memory database. In fact, leaving aside alert 0 for internal issues, alert numbering starts with number 1 on host physical memory usage. If there's no memory, there's no performance. When investigating memory issues, you can ask ourselves questions such as the following:

- Is the issue consistent, recurrent, or intermittent?

- Is it getting worse?

- Is it present in certain areas, for example, row store, column store, elsewhere?

- Is the issue related to technical tables or user data? Logging or auditing information may be stored in tables that can easily be pruned or truncated (unlike last month's sales figures).

- Is the issue related to large objects (LOBs)?

- Are there long-running or blocked transactions?

- Is the row store suffering from fragmentation?

Memory management and memory troubleshooting is a huge and complex topic, but fortunately the technical details are mostly beyond the scope of the exam. In the following sections, we'll discuss the most important topics: system-wide (global) memory allocation limit and how to monitor and analyze memory issues with SAP HANA cockpit.

Global Allocation Limit

The system parameter `global.ini/[memorymanager]/global_allocation_limit` controls the amount of memory assigned to the system. In Chapter 4, you've seen that the allocation limit is one of the installation parameters. We also discussed that memory is the only "option" actually recorded in the license, although the limit isn't enforced by default. You may need to configure a global allocation limit in multi-SID (also knowns as multiple components, one system [MCOS]) environments, for example, when you want to use a standby host in a scale-out system or a secondary site in a system replication scenario to also host a test or development system. Another scenario is to limit the memory allocation to the licensed amount.

The default value of the parameter is 0, which corresponds to no limit. In this case, SAP HANA makes the following calculation:

- 10 GB (or less): total physical memory minus 1 GB.
- Between 10 and 64 GB: 90% of the physical memory
- 64 GB or larger: 57.6 GB (90% of 64) + 97% of remaining memory

Memory Analysis

As you've already seen in Figure 13.2 and Figure 13.3, SAP HANA cockpit provides ample graphical insights about **Memory Usage**. SAP HANA cockpit provides several apps to support you with memory analysis.

From the **Database Overview** card, you can select to view **Resident Memory** from an operating system perspective with total physical memory, total resident memory, and database resident memory. Alternatively, you can select **Used Memory** and see the allocation limit and how much is occupied by used memory and buffer cache, as well as the peak used memory.

When selected, the **Performance Monitor** screen opens with the **Memory** view selected (the **CPU Usage** and **Disk Usage** cards on **Database Overview** open the respective **CPU** and **Disk** views), as shown in Figure 13.23. For the host and the index server service—you're connected here to a tenant database—the several memory-related KPIs are selected. However, as also indicated in the figure, you can select many more to support your troubleshooting efforts.

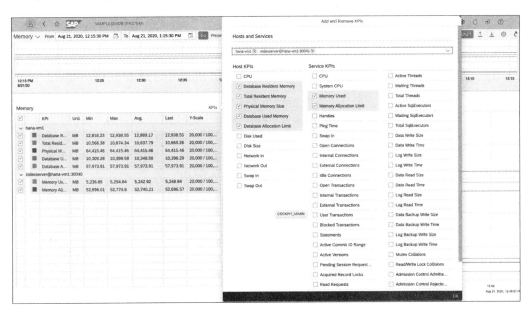

Figure 13.23 Performance Monitor

From the **Memory Usage** card, you can also launch the Workload Analysis app, illustrated in Figure 13.24.

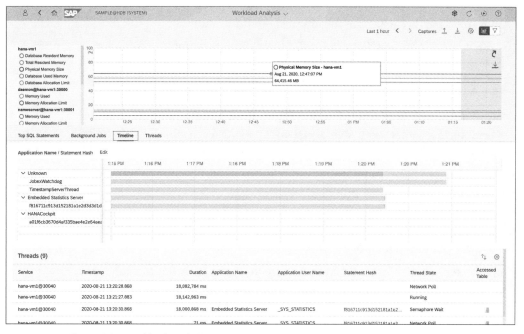

Figure 13.24 Workload Analysis

Like the Performance Monitor app, this app is common to the **Memory Usage**, **CPU Usage**, and **Disk Usage** cards and will open with a preselected view. The top pane shows a timeline with a selector for the last 5, 15, or 30 minutes; last 1, 3, 6, 12, 24 hours; last 2 or 7 days, and so on. The bottom pane shows information on the **Top SQL Statements**, **Background Jobs**, (another) **Timeline**, and more detailed information for **Threads**.

The Memory Analysis app, also accessible from the **Memory Usage** card, takes a different point of view, as shown in Figure 13.25. The top pane shows the timeline with the same indicators as on the card with host and service allocation limit and total used memory. For the details, you can now zoom into **Components**, which references row store tables, column store tables, stack size, code size, caches, monitoring data, and working memory. Or take a look at the **Allocators**, which now concerns the row engine, SQLScript, malloc, metadata, and the persistence manager, to name but a few. The view also shows tabs for **Top Consumers**, **Tables**, and **Out of Memory Events** and **Out of Buffer Events** for the native storage extension (NSE) buffer cache.

This NSE buffer cache was introduced with SAP HANA 2.0 SPS 04, and you can use the Buffer Cache Monitor app for its monitoring and configuration, as illustrated in Figure 13.26. The buffer cache is enabled by default and sized to 10% of the available memory.

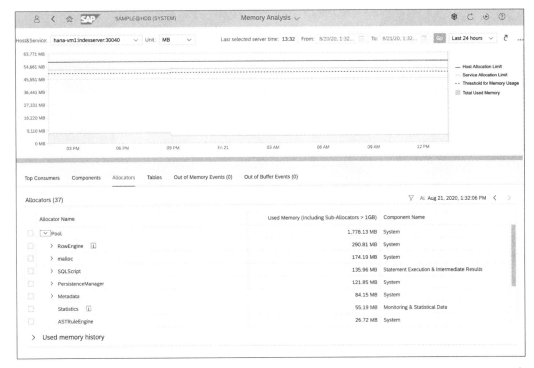

Figure 13.25 Memory Analysis

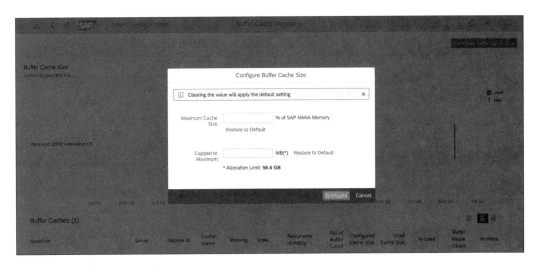

Figure 13.26 Buffer Cache Monitor

Learn More

For more information about this topic, beyond the scope of the exam, see Getting Started with NSE in the SAP HANA Administration Guide. Another good source is the SAP Support KBA 2799997 – FAQ: SAP HANA Native Storage Extension (NSE).

The **Memory Paging Monitor** screen, illustrated in Figure 13.27, and also accessible from the **Memory Usage** card on **Database Overview**, shows the amount of data loaded, unloaded, and in the buffer cache per table and column. The **View Load Units Configuration** button opens the corresponding app (also accessible from the **Memory Usage** card) where you can configure per table the load unit setting for each column (default, page, or column).

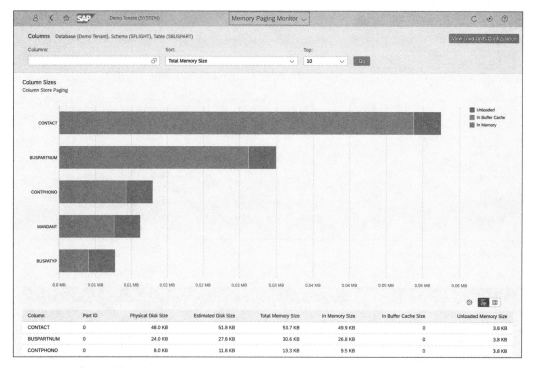

Figure 13.27 Memory Paging Monitor

The **Persistent Memory Monitor** provides a similar interface as the Memory Paging Monitor. With the Persistent Memory Configuration app, you can specify the file system path for persistent memory, otherwise configurable at installation time, as covered in Chapter 4.

Not accessible from the **Memory Usage** card but from the **Monitoring** card on **Database Overview** is the Memory Profiling app. With the app, you can start (or upload) a recording, selecting host and services, sampling interval, and duration for one or more of the allocators and optionally including the call stack. You can then analyze this recording, which is illustrated in Figure 13.28.

> **Learn More**
>
> The different types of memory problems that may arise, typical root causes, and the corresponding KBAs are extensively documented in the SAP HANA Troubleshooting and Performance Analysis Guide. If you want to get a clearer picture of how memory allocation works, there is also a paper on the topic titled "SAP HANA Memory Usage Explained" at *http://s-prs.co/v507868*.

The list of KBAs is too long to mention here but the FAQ is always a good place to start, as is the Guided Answer:

- KBA 1999997 – FAQ: SAP HANA Memory
- How to Troubleshoot HANA High Memory Consumption

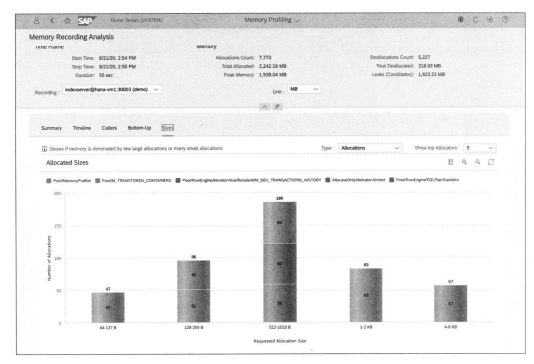

Figure 13.28 Memory Profiling

CPU Usage

High processor usage as such isn't necessarily a bad thing. Processors are expensive, so it's a good thing that they aren't sitting idle. However, when CPU usage is consistently in the high 90s, response times may suffer, in particular when the processing load isn't distributed properly over adjacent processor cores. Alert 5, **Host CPU Usage**, is raised when the defined thresholds are surpassed. This will be visible on the **Alerts** card on **Database Overview** and on the different apps with an alert indicator.

Learn More

For more detailed information about this topic, beyond the scope of this exam, see KBA 2100040 – FAQ: SAP HANA CPU.

We'll take a closer look at CPU issues in the following sections.

Threads

We've already encountered the **CPU Usage** card and the associated Performance Monitor and Workload Analyzer apps to support you investigating CPU issues. For more extensive analysis, you need to go down to the thread level via the **Threads** card and the Threads app, as illustrated in Figure 13.29.

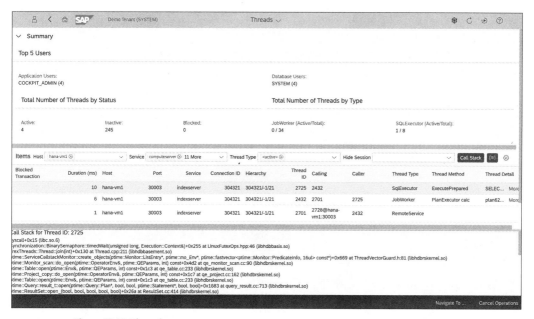

Figure 13.29 Threads

In Chapter 2, we described the different processes, such as the name server and the index server. When these processes are at work, they execute threads. There are threads for client connections, such as the SqlExecutor, and there are threads for background processes such as the JobWorker, MergedogMerger, or Queue. The list of threads is long; take a look at the threads in the Threads app to get an idea. Each thread can call different methods, and the list of methods is even longer. A thread can be running, sleeping, inactive, or in an I/O wait, mutex wait, semaphore wait, or some other state. For information, you can query the monitoring view M_SER-VICE_THREADS; for insights into past activities, query M_SERVICE_THREAD_SAMPLES. These are the views SAP HANA cockpit queries for the **Threads** card and Threads app. When there are many threads in the waiting or pending to run state, this could point to issues with locks, expensive statements, or excessive CPU consumption.

From the app you can select **Cancel Operations** to stop the execution of a thread that is causing high CPU load. However, as this will make any further analysis impossible, it might be necessary to make a full system info dump first (see the "Collecting Diagnosis Information" section).

For each thread, you can request the call stack with the **Call Stack** button, although this is unlikely to return much insight for anyone outside of SAP development (see Figure 13.29).

You may need to configure the system parameters global.ini/[resource_tracking]/enable_tracking and cpu_time_measurement_mode for the **CPU Time** column in the app to return data.

> **Learn More**
>
> You don't need to be a thread expert for the exam, but to get an idea what kind of information is available for threads, see KBA 2114710 – FAQ: SAP HANA Threads and Thread Samples.

Kernel Profiler

The kernel profiler is a built-in tool that records CPU consumption and CPU wait times for SAP HANA's internal processes. You can enable it, for example, to collect additional information about a certain operation or SQL statement. The trace volume generated is considerable, and the kernel profiler may impact system performance, so you typically only activate the kernel profiler for short durations in the context of an SAP Support case.

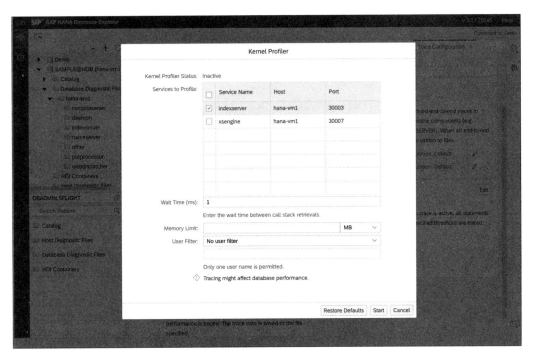

Figure 13.30 Kernel Profiler

Figure 13.30 illustrates how you can enable the kernel profiler for a particular service, with the wait time between stack retrievals, an optional memory limit, and user filter. Note the warning: **Tracing might affect database performance.** The kernel profiler is accessible from the same **Database Trace Configuration** menu as the database and other performance traces (refer to Figure 13.20). To start the profiler, SAP HANA database explorer will make an operating system call to hdbcons using the sapcontrol connection. When you stop the trace, you're prompted to store the file in either .dot or.kcachegrind format. Sounds familiar? Probably not. Kernel profiler output is primarily intended for SAP development.

SPS 05: What's New?

Previously, the profiler could only be activated with hdbcons (as just mentioned), but as of SAP HANA 2.0 SPS 05, you can now run and manage the kernel profiler using SQL: ALTER SYSTEM START KERNEL PROFILER.

There are commands to start, stop, save, and clear the profiler with options to run the profile for a specific user or service. The output files have the *.dot* extension. The view M_ KERNEL_PROFILER provides information about the profiler and, like the command, requires the RESOURCE ADMIN and TRACE ADMIN system privileges.

Expensive Statements

Not surprising for a database, but SQL execution and in particular expensive statements are a common cause for high CPU usage. The subject itself merits a book. Here we'll only scratch the surface and mention a few topics of interest.

SAP HANA 2.0 SPS 02 introduced two new processing engines:

- Extended SQL Executor (ESX)
- SAP HANA Execution Engine (HEX)

Both are enabled by default and are expected to replace the older structures in the long run. Currently, all engines work in close cooperation, and it's up to the SQL optimizer to decide which engine will be used. HEX combines the functionality of the join and OLAP engines, original SAP HANA structures. The OLAP engine processes aggregate operations such as COUNT (although not exclusively, as they may be executed in the calculation engine as well). This engine specializes in working with large data sets of the fact-dimension type (hence, the name). The ESX engine takes over the role of the row engine and works together with lower-level engines. Figure 13.31 illustrates the relation between the different engines. The functioning of these engines is controlled by system parameters, and you can direct queries to a particular engine using hints.

Expensive SQL statements can consume considerable processor time and cause the memory to spill over, that is, trigger column table unloads or out-of-memory errors. In other words, bad SQL can cause system-wide performance issues and needs to be fixed.

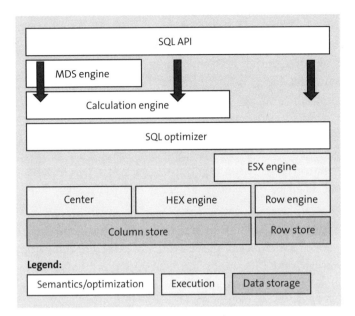

Figure 13.31 SAP HANA Engines

For real-time monitoring, SAP HANA cockpit provides the **SQL Statements** card and SQL Statements app. In addition, alert 39, **Long Running Statements**, also keeps an eye on the SQL. Statements are stored in table HOST_LONG_RUNNING_STATEMENTS of _SYS_STATISTICS for future analysis.

You can also look for expensive statements in the SQL plan cache. From both apps, you can select individual statements and open them in SQL Analyzer. This tool, similar to the Explain Plan tool in SAP HANA studio and Explain Plan in DBACOCK-PIT, provides a graphical illustration of the execution plan with operation details, such as join, union, aggregation, the execution engine involved, the tables, and the estimated cost. Minor modifications of the query or the usage of hints can have a dramatic impact and convert a 10-minute query run into a subsecond execution plan.

Learn More

For more information about the different SAP HANA engines, see the SAP HANA Performance Guide for Developers. This guide also contains extensive information about SQL query performance with tuning guidelines. SQL statement optimization and analysis is documented from a different perspective in the SAP HANA Troubleshooting and Performance Analysis Guide. In addition, see the following KBAs:

- KBA 2000002 – FAQ: SAP HANA SQL Optimization
- KBA 2180165 – FAQ: SAP HANA Expensive Statements Trace

Disk and Input/Output

Even though SAP HANA is an in-memory database, you shouldn't ignore disk (or more generally storage) and input/output (I/O) addressing either out-of-space or out-of-time issues. Improving database startup times may be the most important aspect of troubleshooting this area.

Out of Space

The most common disk-related issue is running out of space. It's alert 2: **Disk usage**. The alert monitors disk space for the data area, log area, and backup volume.

The **Alerts** card on **Database Overview** will inform you of this situation as will the **Disk Usage** card. As with memory and CPU usage, you can navigate from this card to the **Performance Monitor** with the **Disk** view selected to zoom in on disk- and I/O-related KPIs or open the **Workload Analyzer** for disk. Refer back to Figure 13.23 and Figure 13.24 for these apps.

Specific to disk is the Disk Volume Monitor app, illustrated in Figure 13.32 and Figure 13.33, which shows the details.

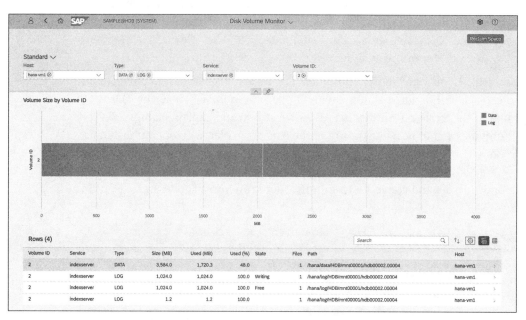

Figure 13.32 Disk Volume Monitor

The monitor shows both usage and volume I/O statistics and provides information about the configuration.

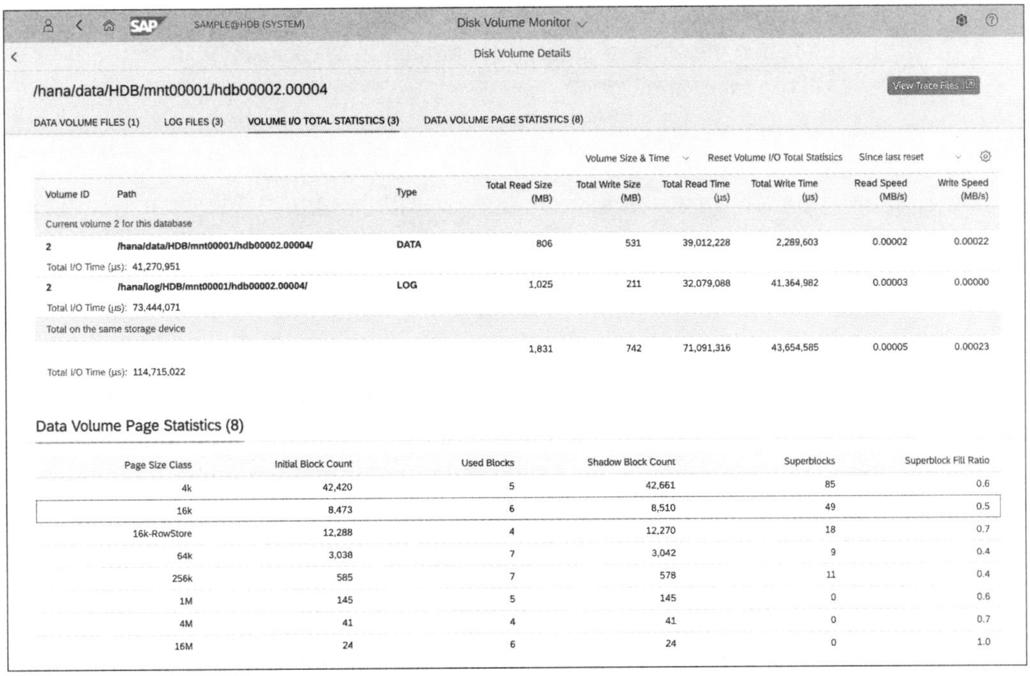

Figure 13.33 Disk Volume Monitor Details

When the data volume is full, and this isn't because of the size of the column store tables, you might need to investigate other areas, such as the following:

- **LOBs**
  LOBs are large objects, which, depending on their size, may be stored either in memory or on disk. There are different types such as binary large objects (BLOBs) for pictures, character large objects (CLOBs) for plain text data, and more. You can configure LOBs only to be loaded into memory if their size doesn't exceed a certain value (hybrid LOBs). They may impact startup times, memory, and disk requirements due to the way they are allocated, although you can also store LOBs together (packed LOBs). LOBs can get orphaned, that is, still present on storage but no longer in memory, and there are several system parameters that control how the system manages LOBs.

- **Multi-version concurrency control (MVCC)**
  The MVCC mechanism, as implied by the name, maintains several versions of a record to enable concurrent access during data changes. As long as transactions only read data, you don't need any copies, but as soon as a transaction wants to make a change, MVCC copies are created. This enables concurrent access. Otherwise, all read requests would have to wait until the write request was done. After a transaction has committed, this triggers the garbage collection (GC) to remove any obsolete copies. In addition, as defined by the gc_interval system parameter (by default, after an hour), the MVCCGarbageCollector wakes up to clean up any remaining stale records. If transactions are blocking GC and too many

active versions are created, this might eventually lead to out-of-memory errors. The solution typically is to cancel the transaction or connection or, in the worst case, kill the client application.

- **Database snapshots**

  Database snapshots are taken just before a backup. If there have been many failed backups, for example, because the backup volume is full, you may also fill up the data volume with old database snapshots. These are automatically deleted during database restart but may require manual intervention prior. The earlier mentioned HANASitter may help with this activity.

The **Disk Volume Monitor** includes a **Reclaim Space** button. When selected, you have the option to reclaim log segments and/or the data volume, as illustrated in Figure 13.34. This corresponds to the statements ALTER SYSTEM RECLAIM DATAVOLUME and ALTER SYSTEM RECLAIM LOG. The expected gains are listed. Using SQL, you can also run the ALTER SYSTEM RECLAIM statements with the ROW DATA SPACE, VERSION SPACE, and [ROW|COLUMN] LOB SPACE clauses for more fine-grained control.

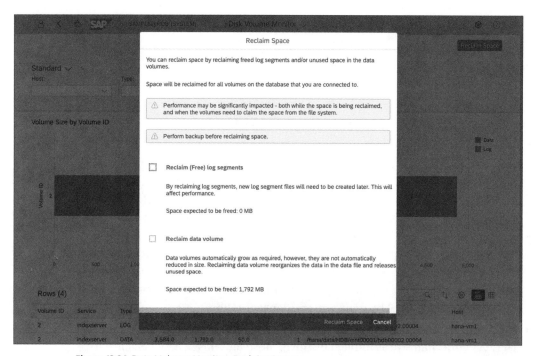

Figure 13.34 Data Volume Monitor: Reclaim Space

For more thorough investigation, the **Disk Volume Monitor** also includes a **View Trace Files** link, which opens the relevant trace file in SAP HANA database explorer.

Learn More

For more detailed information about this topic, beyond the scope of this exam, see the following KBAs:

- KBA 2083715 – Analyzing Log Volume Full Situations
- KBA 2220627 – FAQ: SAP HANA LOBs
- KBA 2169283 – FAQ: SAP HANA Garbage Collection

Out of Time

I/O references data access and can be logical (memory), physical (disk), or network related (and possible some others). All three can cause the system to slow down, but here, you're mainly concerned with physical I/O. As often explained in the context of SAP HANA and in-memory technology, disk access is a magnitude slower when compared to memory access, regardless of whether the disk here is a mechanical hard disk drive (HDD) or flash-based solid-state drive (SSD). Although SAP HANA is an in-memory database, there are many scenarios that involve I/O, and slow transfer rates can impact the system in several ways. Note that although most I/O is asynchronous and doesn't cause a wait, data structure may get locked and hence still be affected by slow I/O.

Learn More

For more detailed information about this topic, beyond the scope of this exam, see KBA 1999930 – FAQ: SAP HANA I/O Analysis.

This KBA describes the different disk I/O scenarios such as row store load, system replication data shipping, data backups, commits, and more. It also lists the alerts defined for I/O-related issues and the available SAP HANA mini checks. A check list is included for check disk performance, check duration of critical savepoint phases, I/O-related parameters, and more.

Database Startup

Database startup provides a special case where slow I/O has a significant impact as several data structures need to be read and loaded into memory. The steps are as follows:

1. **Open volumes**
   Services with persistence, usually the `nameserver` and indexservers, but when not embedded, this could also include the `xsengine` and other services, need to access and open their volumes and files.

2. **Load and initialize persistence structures**
   The anchor and restart page are loaded together with LOBs. Undo files are searched for uncommitted transactions (read data volume).

3. **Row store is loaded (read data volume)**
   This can take a significant amount of time depending on I/O throughput and the size of the row store as typically about 10–20 GB can be loaded per minute. It's possible to keep the row store in memory during a software shutdown (and

start) and, as of SPS 04, also in case of a crash or hard shutdown, under certain conditions.

4. **Clean up**

The garbage collector cleans up any remaining MVCC versions for the column store (read data volume).

5. **Redo logs**

The redo logs are replayed, committed transactions are rolled forward, and uncommitted are rolled back. The first column store tables are loaded into memory as well, starting with those involved in transactions. This step involves both the read log volume and the read and write data volume, and the time required depends on the transaction volume (number and changes).

6. **Consistency check**

All services perform a transactional consistency check, and a restart savepoint is written. A row store consistency check is performed, and the SQL port is opened. Transaction processing can start, but it may take some time before all column store tables are loaded.

Which column store tables are loaded depends on whether they are marked for preload, were being used just prior to shutdown or, as mentioned, were involved in a transaction. Several system parameters control this behavior.

> **Learn More**
>
> For more detailed information about this topic, beyond the scope of this exam, see the following KBAs:
>
> - KBA 2222217 – How-To: Troubleshooting SAP HANA Startup Times
> - KBA 2159435 – How-To: Keeping SAP HANA Row Store in Memory When Restarting

Workload Management

The objective of SAP HANA workload management is to maximize overall system performance and balance the resource requirements of the different types of workloads. To reach this goal, workload management uses workload classes, which restrict, for example, the amount of resources (CPU, memory, threads) a batch job can consume. Alternatively, a workload class may prioritize particular database or application users.

Workload management is an iterative process with the following steps:

- Monitor and analyze system performance and resource usage.
- Understand the workload, including the business requirements, technical users, interactive versus batch, and workload conflicts.
- Map workloads to system resources with workload classes, and set priority and resource limits.

Workloads can be managed at the operating system level, system (global) and database level with system parameters, and session level with workload classes. Workload management at the operating system, from the SAP HANA perspective, is static and with coarse granularity; there is little control and understanding of the workload.

Examples are configuring CPU affinity for specific SAP HANA processes, for example, by assigning a number of logical cores to the indexserver service for a particular tenant database. You can also configure non-uniform memory access (NUMA) and assign a certain amount of memory to each processor, which in some cases could provide better performance. With the Linux lscpu command, you can get information about the number of available NUMA nodes. With this information, you can configure the system parameters that control the watchdog process, for example, with command ALTER SYSTEM ALTER CONFIGURATION ('daemon.ini', 'SYSTEM') SET ('nameserver', 'affinity') = '0-7'. You can even use the NUMA NODE clause of the CREATE and ALTER TABLE statements to apply NUMA node location preferences to tables, columns, or partitions. The system monitoring views M_NUMA_RESOURCES, N_NUMA_NODES, and the hdbcons console utility can help you with this configuration.

> **Learn More**
>
> NUMA configuration is documented in the SAP HANA Administration Guide. See also the FAQ KBA: KBA 2470289 – FAQ: SAP HANA Non-Uniform Memory Access (NUMA).

Workload management, on the other hand, works at the session level and is dynamic and fine-grained, enabling you to configure the workload in line with business requirements. When you focus too much on abstract statistics such as I/O throughput, CPU usage, and so on, you might be hard at work optimizing workloads that don't provide much value to the business. As management consultant Peter Drucker said, "there is nothing so useless as doing efficiently that which should not be done at all."

The SAP HANA cockpit app to configure workload management is called Workload Classes, as shown in Figure 13.35.

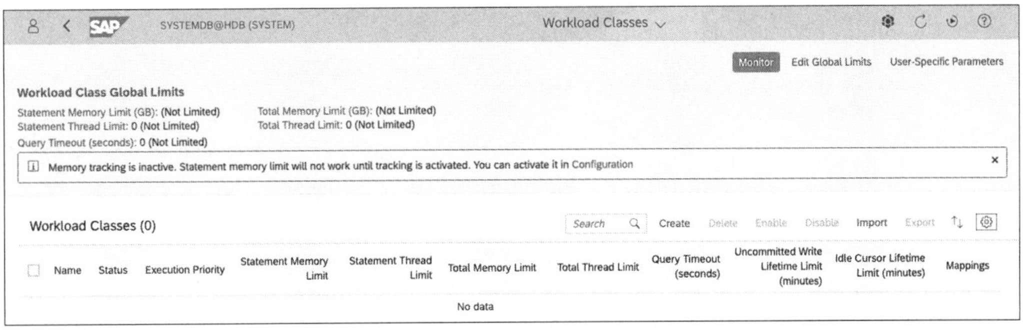

Figure 13.35 Workload Classes

When you first launch the app, a message displays informing you that memory tracking needs to be enabled, which you can do by clicking the **Configuration** link and confirming the request. This configures the system parameter settings `global.ini/[resource_tracking]/enable_tracking=on` and `memory_tracking=on`.

In the header, you can select **Edit Global Limits**, which enables you to configure both individual statement limits and total aggregated statement limits, as well as set a statement memory limit (GB), statement thread limit, and query time-out in seconds. This corresponds to the system parameters `global.ini/[memory_man-ager]/statement_memory_limit` and `total_statement_memory_limit` for the statement limits, for example. For thread limit and query time-out, corresponding parameters are used. You also define user-specific parameters with this app by clicking the **User-Specific Parameters** button in the header. This will return a configuration screen where you first need to select a database user. For this user, configure the execution priority (0 lowest, 9 highest) with a statement memory and statement thread limit.

Besides these system-wide (global) and user-specific settings, you can also create workload classes, as shown in Figure 13.36. At a minimum, you need to give the class a name, for example, "Batch Load Jobs", with an execution priority (default = 5). As with the global and user-specific settings, for the workload class, you can also configure a statement memory and statement thread limit. In addition, you can specify a query time-out (in seconds) and an uncommitted write and idle cursor lifetime limit (in minutes). This make sure the connections in this workload class remain busy. The mapping details are optional. Here you can map the workload class to a specific schema (e.g., an application technical user) or even specific object (load table). Alternatively, you can map the class to an application user, client, application name, database user, or even database user group, which shows another use case of the SAP HANA user group feature (discussed in Chapter 10). After the class is created, you can export it as a ZIP file, which contains both the classes and the mappings, and then use this to import a finely tuned configuration into another database.

The Workload Classes app includes a **Workload Class Monitor** screen that provides statistics about the number of statements, connections, user memory per statement, number of threads, and so on.

> **Learn More**
>
> Workload management is documented in the SAP HANA Administration Guide. See also the FAQ KBA: KBA 2222250 – FAQ: SAP HANA Workload Management.

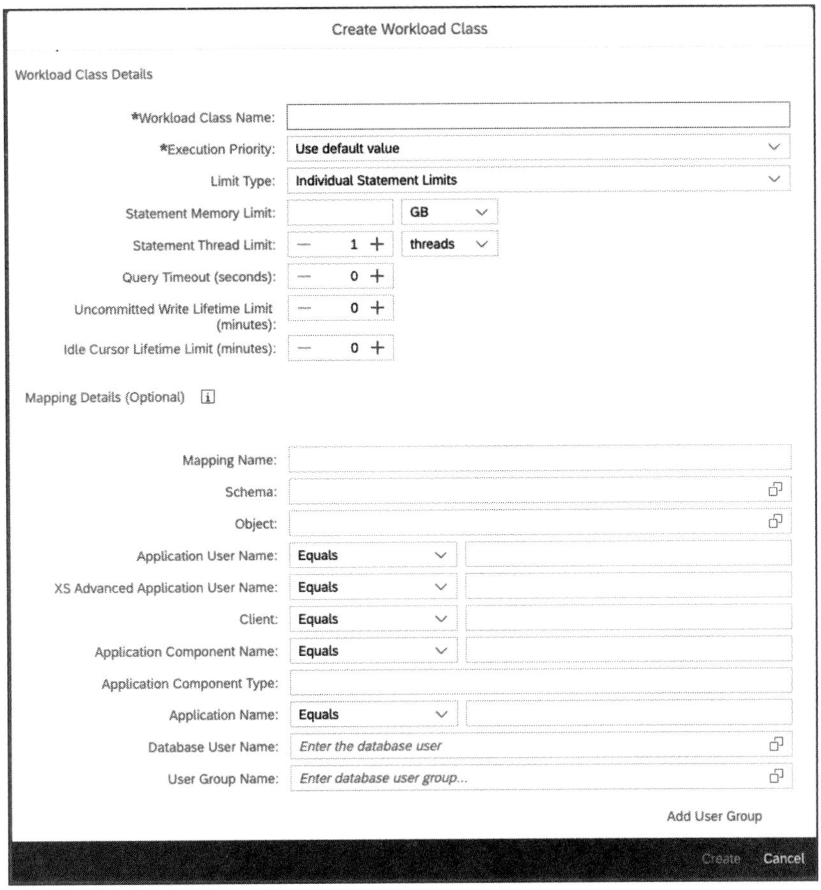

Create Workload Class

Workload Class Details

*Workload Class Name:	
*Execution Priority:	Use default value
Limit Type:	Individual Statement Limits
Statement Memory Limit:	GB
Statement Thread Limit:	— 1 + threads
Query Timeout (seconds):	— 0 +
Uncommitted Write Lifetime Limit (minutes):	— 0 +
Idle Cursor Lifetime Limit (minutes):	— 0 +

Mapping Details (Optional)

Mapping Name:	
Schema:	
Object:	
Application User Name:	Equals
XS Advanced Application User Name:	Equals
Client:	Equals
Application Component Name:	Equals
Application Component Type:	
Application Name:	Equals
Database User Name:	Enter the database user
User Group Name:	Enter database user group...

Add User Group

Create   Cancel

Figure 13.36 Create Workload Class

Admission Control

Admission control (or managing peak loads) is part of workload management, but as the name indicates, it serves a different purpose. SAP HANA cockpit provides both an **Admission Control** card on the **Database Overview** and an Admission Control app. The card only shows whether the database is accepting (green), queuing (orange), or rejecting (red) requests. **Settings** opens the Admission Control Settings app, as shown in Figure 13.37. Here you define the CPU and memory threshold for queuing and for rejecting new requests, with 90% as default value for queuing and 0% as default value for rejecting (i.e., no rejections).

The configuration is recorded as system parameters under global.ini [session_admission_control].

Under **Advanced options**, you can configure maximum queue size, batch size, and parameters related to statistics collection and admission control log management with queue wait time threshold and record limit.

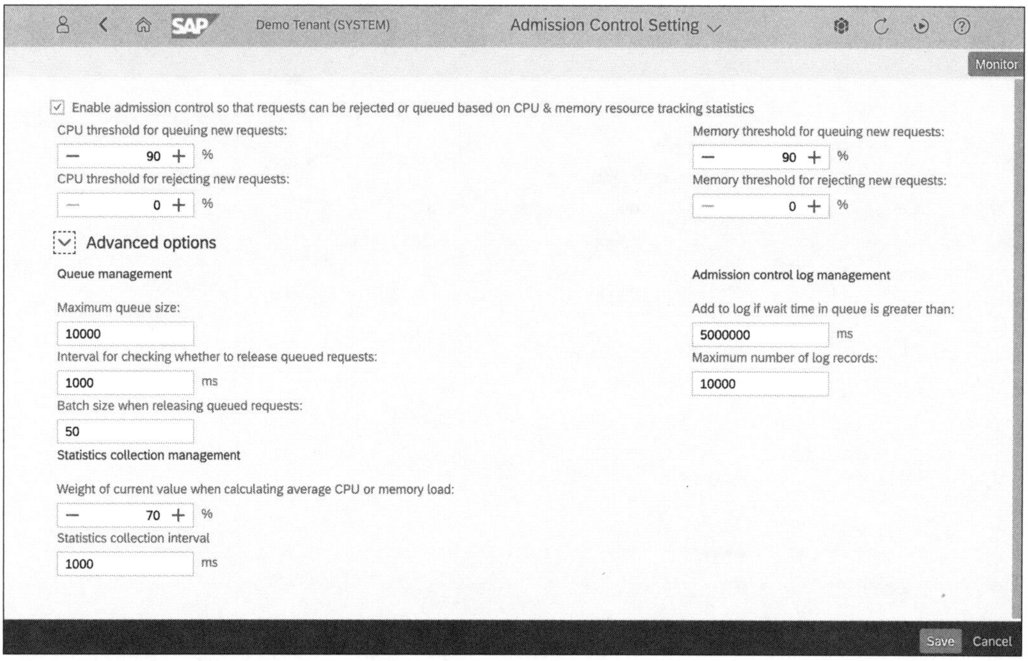

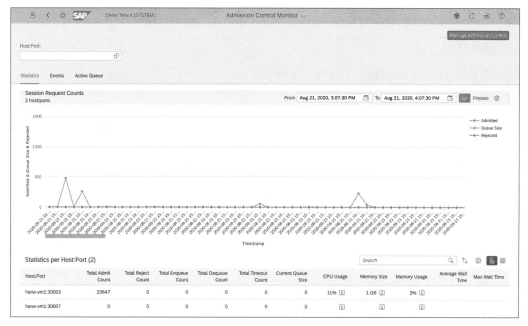

Figure 13.37 Admission Control Settings

When statements are rejected, you can query the system monitoring view M_ADMISSION_CONTROL_EVENTS for the event type and the event reason.

Real-time monitoring is provided by the **Admission Control Monitor** screen displayed in Figure 13.38.

Figure 13.38 Admission Control Monitor

Capture and Replay

With the Capture and Replay tool, you can record the workload information of the database and replay the exact same workload at a later point in time on the same or another SAP HANA system, for example, to evaluate the impact of hardware changes, revision upgrades, changes to system parameters, table partitions, or data distribution changes on multiple-host systems.

Four steps are required for Capture and Replay, as shown in Figure 13.39. The replay is executed on either the target system or, for a three-tier setup, on the control system. When using a control system, for example, SAP HANA cockpit, the replay results aren't lost when the target system is recovered. This also avoids any performance impact of the replay control management, reflecting the captured workload more closely.

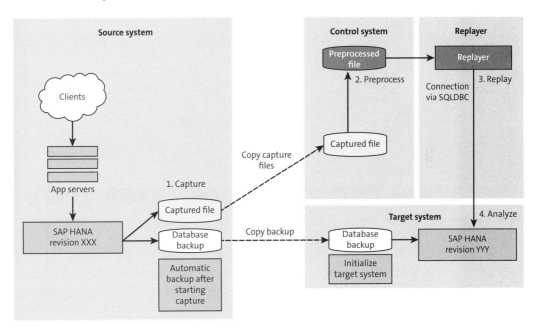

Figure 13.39 Capture and Replay Architecture

First, you need to capture a workload on the source system. For this you can use the Capture Workload app of SAP HANA cockpit. The corresponding **Capture Workload** card on **Database Overview** shows the number of captures. Selecting the card opens **Capture Management**. From here, you can start a new capture that loads the Capture Configuration app shown in Figure 13.40. Here you can define the usage type, give the capture a name, optionally schedule the capture (convenient for those nighttime loads), trigger the automatic creation of a backup (required for the replay, as you can see on the architecture diagram), and perform data collection configuration (e.g., to include SQL Explain Plan and input parameters) with some optional filters. To start a capture requires the WORKLOAD CAPTURE ADMIN system privilege. To start a backup from this app, the BACKUP OPERATOR (or BACKUP ADMIN) system privilege is required.

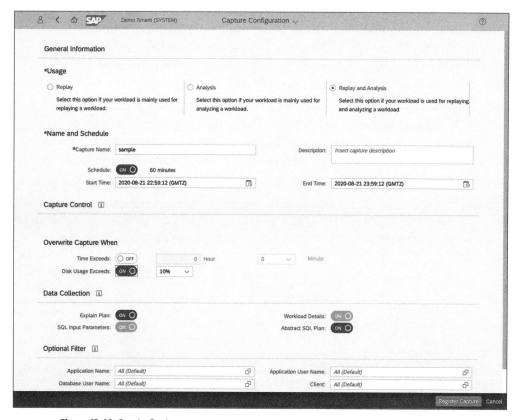

Figure 13.40 Create Capture

The status of the capture is displayed in the Capture Management app as shown in Figure 13.41. When you select a running capture, the Capture Monitor app opens (see Figure 13.42). On the monitor, you can see the number of captured statements, throughput, connections, and related information, but also the remaining disk space, which is relevant because a long-running capture can grow quite large. To make changes to capture destination, click the **Configure Capture** button. The default location is the instance trace directory. To avoid filling up the file system and interfering with I/O throughput, using a separate storage area is recommended. As this concerns a system parameter, you'll need the INIFILE ADMIN system privilege to make changes. The extension of capture files is *.cpt*.

Scheduled captures will stop automatically, but for interactive captures, you can use the **Stop Capture** button on the monitor. This will return you to the Capture Management app again (see Figure 13.41).

Figure 13.41 Capture Management: Capturing

Figure 13.42 Capture Monitor

For a more thorough analysis of the capture, after the capture has stopped, you can select it to open the Workload Analysis app shown in Figure 13.43, resembling the app you could launch from the CPU, memory, and disk usage cards on **Database Overview** (refer to Figure 13.24). The objective here is to make sure you've captured the correct workloads from the source environment before you start the replay. Viewing the report requires the WORKLOAD ANALYZE ADMIN system privilege.

Captures are also listed on the **Replay Candidate** list of the Replay Management app, as shown in Figure 13.44. This is step 2 in the architecture. Here you need to preprocess the capture for replay. Select the **Start** link to start the preprocessing. This requires the WORKLOAD REPLAY ADMIN system privilege. As preprocessing requires significant resources, SAP recommends performing this step on the target or control system. You can export (and delete) the preprocessing candidates from the table header.

Figure 13.43 Workload Analysis

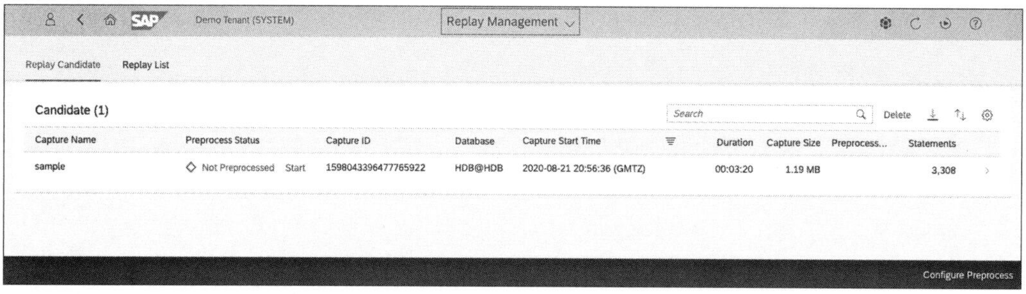

Figure 13.44 Replay Management

After preprocessing has finished, you can start with step 3 in the architecture diagram: replaying.

First, you need to restore the tenant database backup to the target system. Next, either on the control system (recommended) or target system, you need to start a replayer process. For this, you can use the following command (example):

```
hdbwlreplayer -controlhost hana-vm1 -controlinstnum 00 -
controladminkey SYSTEM,REPLAYKEY -port 54321
```

Execute the command as the operating system administration user (<sid>adm). The control host and instance number correspond to the replay host, and the admin key corresponds to the account with the WORKLOAD REPLAY ADMIN system privilege. You need to use a secure user store key for the replayer, which was covered in Chapter 10. Any available port can be used, but you might have to check the firewall configuration if you're using a control system.

You can then select the replay candidate from the list, which will open the Replay Configuration app. Here you can configure how you want to execute the replay by selecting the replayer from the list and providing replayer and user authentication, as shown in Figure 13.45. Select **Start Replay** to execute.

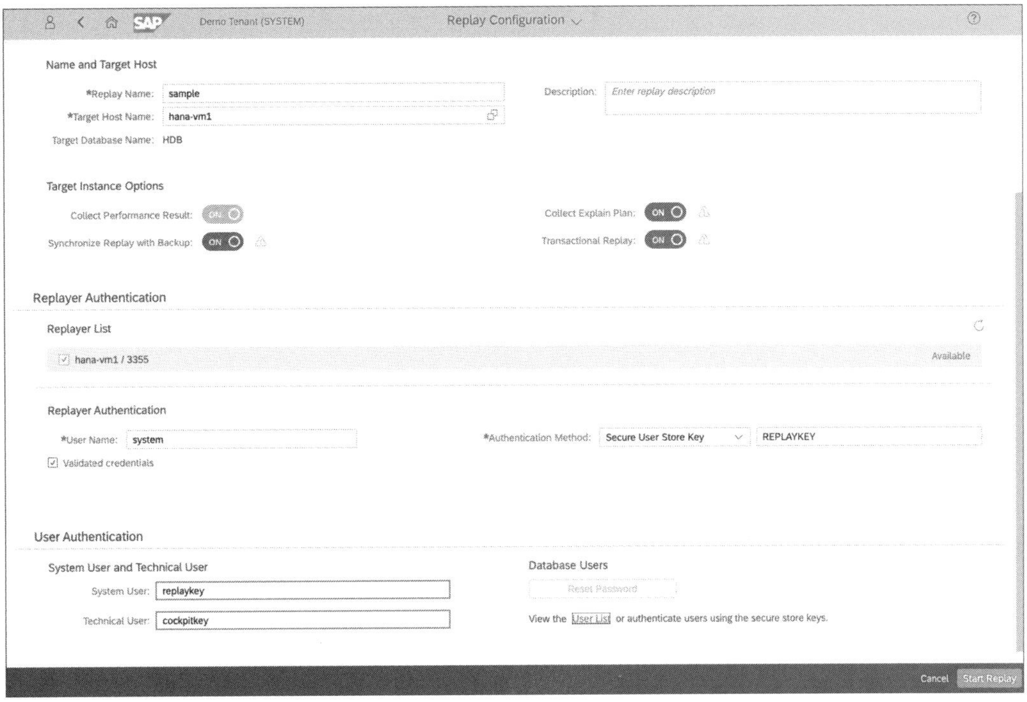

Figure 13.45 Replay Configuration

The Replay Management app shows the status of the replay, this time on the **Replay List** tab (see Figure 13.46).

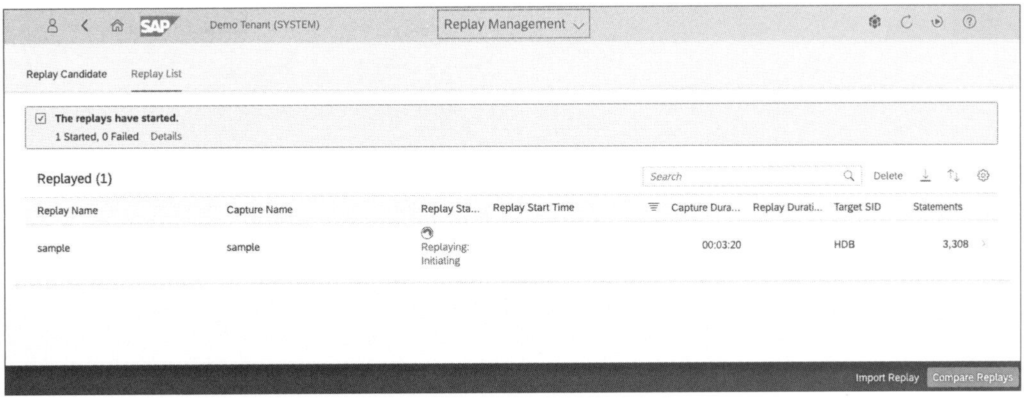

Figure 13.46 Replay List

When selected, the Replay Monitor app opens, as shown in Figure 13.47. This app shows the progress of the replay with replay and capture information.

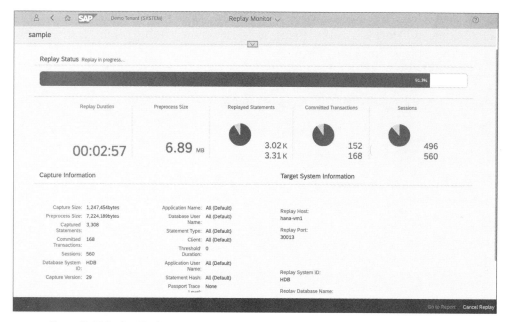

Figure 13.47 Replay Monitor

The final step, number 4 on the architecture diagram, is the analysis. When the replay has finished, you can click the **Go to Report** link at the bottom of Figure 13.47 to see the report illustrated in Figure 13.48.

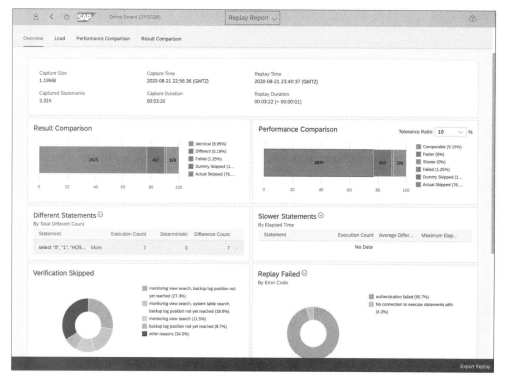

Figure 13.48 Replay Report

The replay report provides very detailed information about how the original capture compares to the replay. On the first page, you find the statement result and performance compared, showing the number of different and slower statements, reasons why the replay failed, and many other graphs. To drill down even deeper at the SQL statement level, you can analyze the numbers on the **Load**, **Performance Comparison**, and **Result Comparison** tabs. This will show data about statement preparation, cursor fetches, and execution counts with graphs showing CPU time, wait time, memory used, network traffic, compile time, and lock wait duration. This requires the WORKLOAD ANALYZE ADMIN system privilege.

You can also compare two replays that return a similar report; this time, the report doesn't compare source and target, but two target runs.

There is a card for **Capture Workload** and **Replay Workload** on the **Database Overview** screen of SAP HANA cockpit displaying the number of captures and available replays, respectively. From here, you can also start and stop captures and/or replays, as illustrated in Figure 13.49.

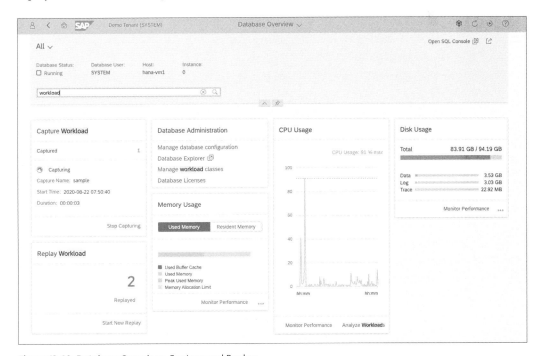

Figure 13.49 Database Overview: Capture and Replay

Learn More

Capture and Replay is documented in the SAP HANA Administration Guide. See also the FAQ KBA on the SAP One Support Launchpad: KBA 2669621 – FAQ: SAP HANA Capture and Replay. This KBA contains the link to the latest version of the SAP HANA Capture and Replay Guide – Best Practices for Setting Up, Capturing, Replaying, and Analyzing. This provides highly recommended reading for anyone interested in working with Capture and Replay.

Important Terminology

For this exam objective, you're expected to understand the following terms:

- **Admission control**

  Admission control is a workload management feature that enables you to configure how SAP HANA should respond to situations where the workload is approaching or exceeding the available system resources. When predefined thresholds are reached, incoming requests can be queued or even rejected.

- **Alerts**

  When predefined and configurable thresholds are surpassed, alerts are triggered. In SAP HANA cockpit, there are several cards and apps that display alerts. The Alerts app provides detailed information about each alert with recommended actions. Using the Alert Checker app, you can enable/disable alerts, configure thresholds, and provide email recipients.

- **Capture and Replay**

  With Capture and Replay, you can record and re-execute SAP HANA database workloads to evaluate the impact on performance or stability after changes in hardware, software, or configuration settings.

- **Kernel profiler**

  The kernel profiler is a built-in tool that records CPU consumption and CPU wait times for SAP HANA's internal processes. It's an advanced troubleshooting tool that may be required in the context of SAP Support incidents. You can enable the profiler using the **Trace Configuration** menu of SAP HANA database explorer or directly using either SQL or SAP HANA database server management console (hdbcons).

- **Multi-version concurrency control (MVCC)**

  The multi-version concurrency control (MVCC) mechanism creates multiple versions of a record to enable concurrent access during data changes. After a transaction has committed, this triggers the garbage collection (GC) to remove obsolete copies. If transactions are blocking GC and too many active versions are created, this might eventually lead to out-of-memory errors.

- **Replayer**

  A replayer is a process that needs to be started on either the control system or the target system to execute a replay. It's not part of the services managed by the daemon and needs to be started and stopped manually with the hdbwlreplayer command.

- **Runtime dump**

  A runtime dump is a plain text file with call stacks, thread information, statistics, and other structures that provides information about the state of the database. Runtime dumps are used to troubleshoot technical issues such as system hangs, high memory consumption, and so on.

- **SAP HANA database server management console (hdbcons)**
  The SAP HANA database server management console (hdbcons) is an advanced troubleshooting tool included with SAP HANA that may be required in the context of SAP Support incidents.

- **SAP HANA mini checks**
  SAP HANA mini checks are a collection of SQL scripts provided by SAP Support (attached to an SAP Note) and can be used to gather information about the SAP HANA system. You can run them ad hoc or add them to the statement library in SAP HANA database explorer.

- **SAP Support tools**
  SAP HANASitter and SAP HANACleaner are two tools provided by SAP Support to facilitate and automate SAP HANA system administration tasks.

- **Statistics server**
  This is the engine of the internal monitoring infrastructure. The statistics server collects data and performs checks, written to the `_SYS_STATISTICS` schema. It runs embedded in the `indexserver` of each tenant database and is configurable through the SQL interface.

- **Threads**
  All activities of SAP HANA processes, such as executing SQL statements by the index server service, are executed as threads. The system takes regular thread samples for monitoring and troubleshooting purposes.

- **Workload**
  A workload is a set of request with common characteristics. Common examples are OLTP workloads with many concurrent users performing small transactions, OLAP workloads with a limited number of statements processing large amounts of data, and extract, transform, and load (ETL) type workloads consisting mainly of batch type processing without any end-user eagerly waiting for the result.

- **Workload management**
  The objective of SAP HANA workload management is to maximize overall system performance and balance the resource requirements of the different types of workloads. To reach this goal, workload management uses workload classes, which restrict, for example, the amount of resources (CPU, memory, threads) a batch job can consume.

 Practice Questions

These practice questions will help you evaluate your understanding of the topics covered in this chapter. The questions shown are similar in nature to those found on the certification examination. Although none of these questions will be found on the exam itself, they will allow you to review your knowledge of the subject.

Select the correct answers, and then check the completeness of your answers in the "Practice Question Answers and Explanations" section. Remember that on the exam, you must select all correct answers, and only correct answers, to receive credit for the question.

1. The database no longer responds to SQL queries. You connect with the Troubleshooting Unresponsive System app to investigate the issue. How is the connection made?

☐ **A.** The app uses sapcontrol to execute the hdbcons operating system command.

☐ **B.** The app uses a dedicated SQL administration channel.

☐ **C.** The app makes a Secure Shell (SSH) connection to the SAP HANA system.

☐ **D.** Troubleshooting Unresponsive System is an SAP HANA cockpit app and depends on the SQL interface. If the database doesn't respond, nor will the app.

2. Which are three key performance areas (KPAs) for alerts? (There are three correct answers.)

☐ **A.** Availability: Availability, backup, diagnosis files, security

☐ **B.** Performance: CPU, disk, memory

☐ **C.** Monitoring: Sessions, threads, statements

☐ **D.** Capacity: Configuration, sessions/transactions

☐ **E.** Performance: CPU, disk, memory, SQL statements

3. After how many days is the data collected deleted from _SYS_STATISTICS tables in the default configuration?

☐ **A.** After 30 days.

☐ **B.** After 42 days for all collectors.

☐ **C.** As configured. By default, this is 42 days for the majority of collectors, but this is configurable and can be changed by the alert and collector profile.

4. How can you change the data retention period?

☐ **A.** Use the SAP HANA cockpit Alert Checker app.

☐ **B.** Use SQL (STATISTICS_SCHEDULE table).

☐ **C.** Use the SAP HANA cockpit Data Collector app.

5. Which information does the replay report provide?

☐ **A.** Statistics about database performance

☐ **B.** Statistics about SQL statement performance and results

☐ **C.** Statistics about hardware, software, and configuration changes

6. Which are examples of proactive system administration in SAP HANA? (There are three correct answers.)

☐ **A.** Alerts

☐ **B.** SAP HANA Capture and Replay

☐ **C.** Runtime dumps

☐ **D.** SAP HANA workload management

☐ **E.** Troubleshoot unresponsive systems

7. Which are motivations for Capture and Replay? (There are three correct answers.)

☐ **A.** Logical backup

☐ **B.** Table partition changes

☐ **C.** Security breaches

☐ **D.** Changes in data distribution (landscape reorganization)

☐ **E.** Implementation of SQL statement hints

8. Which input is required before you can run a replayer? (There are three correct answers.)

☐ **A.** Target host name

☐ **B.** Backup location

☐ **C.** Usage (replay, analysis, replay and analysis)

☐ **D.** Replayer

☐ **E.** Secure store keys of the system and technical user

9. Which system privilege is required for preprocessing a capture?

☐ **A.** `WORKLOAD REPLAY ADMIN`

☐ **B.** `REPLAY ADMIN`

☐ **C.** `CAPTURE ADMIN`

☐ **D.** `WORKLOAD CAPTURE ADMIN`

10. Which database user should you use as replayer?

☐ **A.** SYSTEM.

☐ **B.** _SYS_REPLAYER.

☐ **C.** You need to run the replayer with the operating system credentials of the `<sid>adm` user.

☐ **D.** Any database user with the WORKLOAD REPLAY ADMIN system privilege.

11. Which parameters are required to configure email alerts? (There are three correct answers.)

☐ **A.** SMTP sender (email address)

☐ **B.** Default recipient (email address)

☐ **C.** SMTP port

☐ **D.** SMTP host

☐ **E.** Protocol: SMTP, POP3, or IMAP

12. Which parameters are required to set memory limits for SQL statements? (There are two correct answers.)

☐ **A.** `global.ini/[resource_tracking]/enable_tracking=on`

☐ **B.** `global.ini/[memory_manager]/global_allocation_limit`

☐ **C.** `global.ini/[resource_tracking]/memory_tracking=on`

13. Which are valid admission control settings? (There are two correct answers.)

☐ **A.** Execution priority

☐ **B.** Memory thresholds for rejecting new requests

☐ **C.** CPU thresholds for incoming new requests

☐ **D.** User group

14. Which tool can you use to reclaim space?

☐ **A.** SAP HANA cockpit Disk Volume Monitor app

☐ **B.** `HANACleanSpace.py`

☐ **C.** SAP HANA database explorer SQL console

☐ **D.** hdbcons

15. You have a multiple-host system on four hosts with 512 GB each, but you purchased an SAP HANA license for only 768 GB. Which global allocation limit setting do you need to configure?

    ☐ **A.** Set the `global_allocation_limit` to `786432` (768 × 1024 MB).

    ☐ **B.** Set the `global_allocation_limit` to `196608` (192 × 1024 MB on each host).

16. Which items are configurable in the Alert Definitions app in the SAP HANA cockpit? (There are three correct answers to this question.)

    ☐ **A.** Threshold (high, medium, low).

    ☐ **B.** Email recipient.

    ☐ **C.** Schedule active.

    ☐ **D.** Proposed solution.

    ☐ **E.** Interval.

17. What information is collected by the Troubleshoot Unresponsive System app in the SAP HANA cockpit? (There are three correct answers to this question.)

    ☐ **A.** SQL statements.

    ☐ **B.** Transactions.

    ☐ **C.** Connections.

    ☐ **D.** Alerts.

    ☐ **E.** Threads.

18. How can we create a full system info dump? (There are two correct answers to this question.)

    ☐ **A.** Using the SQL console.

    ☐ **B.** Running the command `python fullSystemInfoDump.py`.

    ☐ **C.** Using the Diagnosis Files app in the SAP HANA cockpit.

    ☐ **D.** Using the SAP HANA database server management console (hdbcons).

19. Where can we find information about out-of-memory (OOM) events? (There are two correct answers to this question.)

    ☐ **A.** Using the Out of Memory Analysis app in the SAP HANA cockpit.

    ☐ **B.** Using the SAP HANA database explorer trace file viewer.

    ☐ **C.** Using the **Out of Memory Events** tab in the Memory Usage app in the SAP HANA cockpit.

    ☐ **D.** Using the M_OOM system monitoring view.

Practice Question Answers and Explanations

1. Correct answer: **A**

   The app uses sapcontrol to execute the hdbcons operating system command.

   Answer B is incorrect because there is only a single SQL port and no dedicated administration channel. Answer C is incorrect because the app calls sapcontrol directly to execute the hdbcons operating system command. It doesn't first establish the SSH on port 22. Answer D is incorrect because troubleshooting unresponsive system, the start and stop system command, and diagnosis files are examples of functionality that doesn't make use of the SQL interface but of sapcontrol.

2. Correct answers: **A, B, D**

   The three KPAs are availability, performance, and capacity.

   Answer C is incorrect because monitoring isn't a KPA. Answer E is incorrect because performance is a KPA but doesn't include SQL statements.

Exam Tip

Silly question? True. You're not likely to be questioned about KPAs on the exam. However, a bulleted list is hard to resist for question makers. When you see one in the text think a moment if it might have inspired a question.

---

3. Correct answer: **C**

   Data is deleted based on your configuration.

   Answer B is incorrect because the majority of data collector data is kept for 42 days but not for all, and the profiles S, L, and HXE modify this number. Answer A is incorrect because the number of days is configurable, and 30 days would be a valid configuration. However, this isn't the default setting.

4. Correct answer: **B**

   You can change the data retention period by using SQL.

   Answer A is incorrect because the Alert Checker app enables you to configure the alerting functionality of the statistics server but not the data collector. Answer C is incorrect because this app doesn't exist.

5. Correct answer: **B**

   The replay report shows statistics about SQL statements for performance comparison (execution times) and results (stability) (see Figure 13.48).

   Answer A is incorrect because the report doesn't provide information about the database level. Answer C is incorrect because the Capture and Replay feature can be used to evaluate the impact of hardware, software, and configuration changes but doesn't provide any direct information about this.

6. Correct answers: **A, B, D**

   There are three approaches to system administration: proactive, reactive (monitoring and responding to issues), and what is often called post-mortem or root cause analysis. The alerting framework, workload management, and Capture and Replay are examples of proactive system administration.

Answer C is incorrect because runtime dumps are used for root cause analysis. Answer E is incorrect because troubleshooting unresponsive systems is reactive system administration.

7. Correct answers: **B, D, E**

   The objective of Capture and Replay is to anticipate issues with performance and stability. Hardware changes, revision updates, changes to system parameters (INI files), data distribution, partitions, SQL hints, and so on are all motivations to use SAP HANA Capture and Replay.

   Answer A is incorrect because a capture doesn't provide a consistent image of a database at a point in time and can't be used as logical backup. For this purpose, the SAP HANA system replication time travel feature is more suitable. Answer C is incorrect because a capture doesn't provide information about security breaches. For this purpose, you can use auditing.

8. Correct answers: **A, D, E**

   Backup location, replayer, and the secure store keys are required before you can run a replayer, as previously illustrated in Figure 13.45.

   Answer B is incorrect because, although a backup is required, the replay configuration doesn't prompt you for the backup location. Answer C is incorrect because you need to select the **Usage on Capture Configuration** screen (replay, analysis, replay and analysis) but not for replay configuration.

9. Correct answer: **A**

   The `WORKLOAD REPLAY ADMIN` privilege is required for capture processing.

   Answer D is incorrect because the `WORKLOAD CAPTURE ADMIN` system privilege is required only for the capture. Answers B and C are incorrect because these system privileges don't exist.

10. Correct answer: **D**

    You should use any database user with the `WORKLOAD CAPTURE ADMIN` privilege for the replayer.

    Answer A is incorrect because the `SYSTEM` user isn't intended for production systems. SAP recommends to only use `SYSTEM` to create lesser privileged users for particular purposes and then deactivate it. Answer B is incorrect because the `_SYS_REPLAYER` user doesn't exist. Answer C is incorrect because you need to run the replayer with the operating system credentials of the `<sid>adm` user, but you also need to configure a database user (hence the question).

11. Correct answers: **A, C, D**

    For email, a sender, SMTP port, and SMTP host are required. Traditionally, port 25 was used for this purpose. Today, for security reasons, port 587 is more common. The configuration interface is illustrated in Figure 13.50.

Answer B is incorrect because you can optionally define a default recipient, but this isn't required. you can configure one or more recipients for each alert, for example, to inform the network administrators about network issues and storage administrators about storage issues. When alert-specific recipients are configured, the default recipient is no longer used. Answer E is incorrect because SMTP is the protocol for outgoing mail. POP3 and IMAP are only used for incoming mail clients such as Microsoft Outlook.

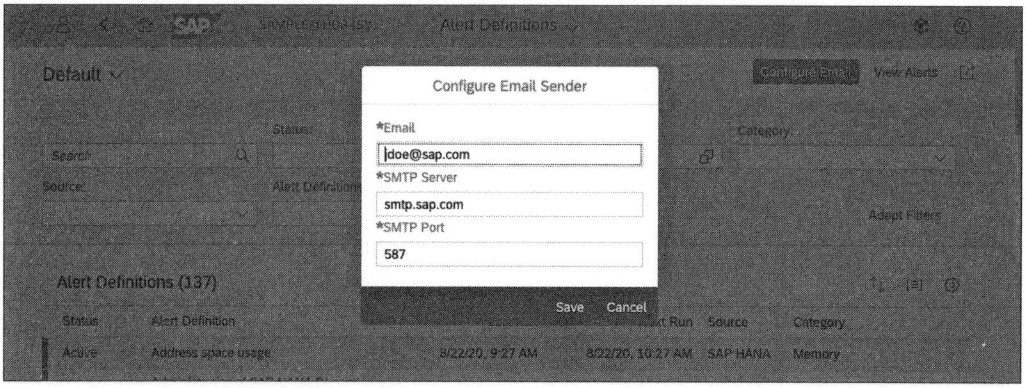

Figure 13.50 Configure Email Sender

12. Correct answers: **A, C**

    The prerequisites to set memory limits for SQL statements are the system parameters `enable_tracking` and `memory_tracking` (refer to Figure 13.35).

    Answer B is incorrect because you need to configure the global allocation limit in multi-SID (also knowns as MCOS) environments or to limit the memory allocation to the licensed amount.

13. Correct answers: **B, C**

    Valid admission control settings define the thresholds for incoming and for rejecting new requests for a CPU and memory threshold (refer to Figure 13.37).

    Answers A and D are incorrect because execution priority and user group are workload class configuration settings.

14. Correct answer: **A**

    You can use the SAP HANA cockpit Disk Volume Monitor app to perform reclaim space operations (refer to Figure 13.34). Alternatively, you can run the corresponding SQL `ALTER SYSTEM RECLAIM` statements.

    Answer B is incorrect because this tool doesn't exist. SAP Support provides an unsupported Python tool (script) called SAP HANACleaner, which can be used for housekeeping and reclaiming space. Answer D is incorrect because hdbcons can't be used to reclaim space.

15. Correct answer: **B**

    Although called a global allocation limit, you need to account for the number of hosts in a multiple-host system and adjust the setting accordingly.

Answer A is incorrect because this setting is larger than the available memory on each system.

16. Correct answers: **A, B, C**

    Thresholds, email recipients, and schedule activation are configurable in the Alert Definitions app.

    Answer D is incorrect because the proposed solutions are provided by SAP. Answer E is incorrect because the alert check interval is not configurable in the Alert Definitions app.

17. Correct answers: **B, C, E**

    The Troubleshoot Unresponsive System app in the SAP HANA cockpit makes an operating system connection using the sapcontrol credentials and collects information about connections, transactions, blocked transactions, and threads. For this, the console tool hdbcons is used.

    Answer A is incorrect because this app does not collect information about SQL statements. Answer D is incorrect because this app does not collect information about alerts.

18. Correct answers: **B, C**

    To create a full system info dump, either run the `fullSystemInfoDump.py` Python script file directly or use the SAP HANA cockpit Diagnosis Files app to do this for you. This results in a ZIP archive file named `fullsysteminfodump_<SID>_<DBNAME>_<HOST>_<timestamp>.zip`. This file contains a wide range of diagnostics information including log files, trace files, and configuration files.

    Answer A is incorrect because we cannot create a full system info dump using the SQL console. Answer D is incorrect because, while we can generate runtime dumps and collect a wide range of internal information with the SAP HANA database server management console (hdbcons), we cannot create a full system info dump.

19. Correct answers: **B, C**

    Alert 46 is triggered when an out-of-memory (OOM) event occurs. A trace file will be generated with format `<processname>_<hostname>.<number>.rtedump.<number>.oom.trc`.

    We can view this trace file in the SAP HANA database explorer trace file viewer and also find information about the event on the **Out of Memory Events** tab in the Memory Usage app in the SAP HANA cockpit.

    Answer A is incorrect because there is no app for OOM events. Answer D is incorrect because there is no system monitoring view for OOM events.

Learn More

For more information about this topic, beyond the scope of the exam, see the SAP Support how-to KBA 1984422 – How-To: Analyzing SAP HANA Out-of-Memory (OOM) Dumps.

Takeaway

The objective of this chapter was to familiarize you with troubleshooting and performance analysis in SAP HANA. You should now understand proactive monitoring concepts with Capture and Replay, workload management, and alerts. You should also understand reactive monitoring and how you can use the different apps in SAP HANA cockpit to perform CPU, memory, and disk performance analysis. This includes troubleshooting an unresponsive system and the tools and activities required to collect diagnostic information. Finally, you should have a good understanding of the post-mortems or root cause analysis, that is, the after-the-fact tools you can use to investigate issues. However, as explained, this often concerns call stacks and runtime dumps that are hard to decipher for those outside the SAP development organization.

Summary

We've covered key troubleshooting and performance analysis topics in this chapter, including monitoring and alerts. We dove into specific troubleshooting issues, explored how memory, CPU usage, and disk usage are involved in performance analysis and troubleshooting, and walked through workload management, admission control, and the Capture and Replay tool.

In the next and final chapter, we'll address system migration from third-party database systems to SAP HANA.

Chapter 14
Database Migration

Techniques You'll Master

- Using Software Update Manager (SUM) with Database Migration Option (DMO) to perform system update with database migration in a single procedure

- Navigating the DMO user interface and using the different menus

- Responding to DMO dialogs

- Monitoring DMO processing

- Resetting DMO

- Benchmarking DMO processing and optimizing DMO runs

Let's get the acronyms out of the way first: Database Migration Option (DMO) and Software Update Manager (SUM). SUM is the tool. DMO is the option. There is no DMO tool, although we'll be using this abbreviation for the sake of readability.

Real-World Scenario

Management has been informed about the performance improvements that can be obtained by migrating some of their SAP business applications to SAP HANA. Business downtime should be minimized. You start to investigate which tools you can use to update SAP NetWeaver-based systems and how to perform database migrations and discover the database migration option of the SUM or DMO, for short, as everybody seems to call it. It provides a simplified migration experience by combining system update with database migration with reduced downtime and even a fast reset option. Sounds interesting and checks the box of reduced downtime. What is this all about?

SUM is part of the Software Logistics (SL) Toolset. This toolset was introduced to simplify software lifecycle management for SAP system landscapes. The systems in these landscapes are primarily SAP NetWeaver-based systems and not necessarily SAP HANA (database) systems. SAP HANA database lifecycle manager (HDBLCM) isn't part of the SL Toolset nor SAP HANA XSA application lifecycle management (ALM) tools. On the other hand, ALM for SAP HANA XS, classic model repository content and SAP HANA Transport for ABAP (HTA) are part of the SL Toolset as they are more closely related to the ABAP world. Lifecycle management tools for products that use other technologies, such as SAP Data Services or SAP IQ, again, aren't included.

SAP NetWeaver is a product family that includes the ABAP and Java application server runtimes but also SAP Enterprise Portal, SAP Process Orchestration, and many other components. In this chapter, we're only concerned with SAP NetWeaver Application Server for ABAP (SAP NetWeaver AS for ABAP).

Exam Tip

System administrators with Basis responsibilities will be very familiar with the SL Toolset. SAP HANA database administrators with a more generic database administration background, familiar with database and data management technologies of other vendors and less with SAP business applications, may want to spend some extra time on this chapter.

The focus of this chapter is on DMO, and the intricacies of SAP NetWeaver, SAP NetWeaver AS for ABAP, SUM, and the SL Toolset are beyond the scope of this exam.

In this final chapter, we'll address a common scenario: moving SAP business applications from *AnyDB* to SAP HANA, where AnyDB stands for any other supported database for SAP NetWeaver AS for ABAP systems. This scenario requires two distinct activities:

- Update SAP NetWeaver AS for ABAP (using SUM).
- Migrate AnyDB to SAP HANA (using DMO).

Using SUM with DMO, you can perform this scenario in a single run, as a one-step migration procedure. The alternative is to first update/upgrade the application server and then migrate the database server. This is considered as the classical approach and involves other steps and tools (more about this later).

For those familiar with SAP HANA but less with SAP NetWeaver, this might be a bit intimidating at first as you read about ABAP stacks, near-zero downtime maintenance (nZDM), Transactions SPAM/SAINT, and a range of other acronyms and abbreviations. Steep learning curve ahead? Not really. For this part of the exam, you don't have to memorize transaction codes or know how to navigate SAP GUI. What we'll cover in this chapter are the ins and outs of DMO, concise yet comprehensive, and what you need to know to pass this part of the exam.

Topic and Objectives

For the exam, you need to have a good understanding of the following objectives:

- DMO concepts
- DMO run preparation
- Tool installation
- Preparation and planning for a DMO run
- The different DMO road map steps and what input can be expected (dialogs)
- How to monitor DMO runs and adjust processing parameters
- DMO reset and cleanup
- How to reduce downtime

> **Note**
>
> Like backup and recovery, database migration using DMO is another classic on the C_ HANATEC exam with a medium weight of 8%–12% of the total certification exam score. With 80 questions in total, you can expect about 8 questions about database migration. As it is for all other exam topic areas, the exam guide states that this can change at any time, so always check online for the latest updates.

> **SAP HANA 2.0 SPS 05: What's New?**
>
> Very few of the DMO dialogs actually reference specific SAP HANA functionality, and no changes were introduced with the SAP HANA 2.0 SPS 05 release.
>
> Regarding new features for the tool itself, see the "What's New" section of the SUM with DMO Guide available from the SAP Help Portal at *http://s-prs.co/v507857*.

> **Learn More**
>
> As mentioned, SUM isn't an SAP HANA tool, and you don't find it documented in the SAP HANA documentation set. For information on this topic, you need go to Software Logistics Toolset page on the SAP Support Portal at *http://support.sap.com/sltoolset*.

Key Concepts Refresher

In this section, we'll touch on the key concepts for data migration, including software logistics, DMO concepts, planning and preparation, installation, performing a DMO run, and benchmarking.

Software Logistics Toolset

For the SAP Business Suite and other SAP business applications, the tools to install, update, upgrade, migrate, and transport content from development to production were initially delivered as part of the product. As a result, you needed to wait for a product update to get an update for the tools. The SL Toolset separates the tooling from the product, which improves software lifecycle management of SAP system landscapes. The SL Toolset is complemented and integrates with other products and services, such as SAP Landscape Management and SAP Solution Manager.

The principle SL Toolset domains are as follows:

- **System maintenance**
  SUM belongs to the system maintenance category together with the support package manager (Transaction SPAM) and the add-on installation tool (Transaction SAINT).

- **System provisioning**
  System-provisioning tools cover installation, system copy, and tools to rename the system identifier (SID), such as the Software Provisioning Manager (SWPM), which are used in what is called the classical approach to system update and migration, that is, to update first and then migrate. As we'll cover in this chapter, DMO with SUM performs this procedure in one step.

- **Change control and transport management**
  Change control and transport management concerns the Change and Transport System (CTS). In this chapter, we briefly touch on change management as DMO supports the inclusion of customer transports in a run. Moving changes from development (and test) into production can involve downtime. By including transports in the DMO run, you only need to stop the system once and reduce (optimize) downtime.

Learn More

For more information about the tools, where to download, and where to find the documentation, visit the Software Logistics Tools – System Maintenance page on the SAP Support Portal at *http://s-prs.co/v507856*.

There are two SUM DMO versions. Version 1.0 targets older SAP NetWeaver-based systems (7.4), which, at the time of writing (summer 2020), are approaching or past end of mainstream maintenance support. Version 2.0 targets Basis 7.50 (released 2015) and higher. Basis is the kernel component of SAP NetWeaver AS for ABAP. Higher versions reference SAP NetWeaver 7.5 and 7.52. There are no plans for any future releases as the technology has evolved into the ABAP Platform, which is integrated into SAP S/4HANA and is no longer delivered as a separate and independent product (family), such as SAP NetWeaver.

In 2020, mainstream support for SAP NetWeaver was aligned with the SAP Business Suite until 2027 with extended maintenance until 2030. For detailed support information, see the Product Availability Matrix (PAM) of SAP NetWeaver 7.5. In short, however, this means that SUM 2.0 will be around for some time to come.

SAP HANA isn't the only target databases for the migration. SUM with DMO for Microsoft SQL Server, IBM DB2, SAP Adaptive Server Enterprise (SAP ASE), and SAP MaxDB are also documented, although, as you'll see, the tool only proposes SAP HANA and SAP ASE as targets. For the AnyDBs, additional preparation of SUM is required.

The SUM with DMO guide is available from the SAP Help Portal at *http://s-prs.co/v507857*. The guide also includes a list of important SAP Notes and other required documentation. When working with SUM, this will be essential reading, but for our purposes, most of the information will be out of scope of the exam. Consider browsing the guide, but don't get sidetracked on the notes.

Exam Tip

A good way to prepare for the material of this chapter (and stay up to date on the topic) is by following the Software Logistics tag on the SAP Community at *http://s-prs.co/v507858*. Sort the blog posts by most liked to get popular content that is also referenced in the documentation and training manuals. Most material goes back to 2013–2015 when the tool was first released.

Getting Started with Database Migration Option

Many businesses run their business applications on SAP. Business downtime needs to be reduced to a minimum, and we already looked at the high availability (HA) options available with SAP HANA to support this objective. To make use of the latest functionality and remain protected with the latest security patches, you need to update your system from time to time but with as little downtime as possible.

In this section, you'll see how the DMO tool achieves this, including prerequisites, architecture, and optimization options.

Business Benefits

With DMO, you can perform an "in-place" migration; that is, you don't need to copy the system and make landscape changes, such as changing the name of the operating system (host name) or the database (SID). This is important because each change, no matter how small, comes with a risk, which you need to keep to an absolute minimum.

A one-step in-place update/migration also means that you only have to test the system once as compared with the classical approach where you would have to test the system after the update and after the database migration. DMO reduces risk by keeping the system landscape stable and allowing for fast reset without the need to perform any database recovery.

Prerequisites

Technology is always evolving. Before you can actually perform an SAP NetWeaver AS for ABAP system update and database migration, in particular on older SAP systems, additional preparations might need to be performed first. Relevant here are Unicode conversion and what is called the "dual-stack" split. You also need to consider the complete picture and include database, operating system, and other parts.

Let's take a closer look at these prerequisites:

- Unicode
  SAP NetWeaver 7.5 only supports Unicode, so any update to this release from older versions often involves Unicode conversion (often, not always as the conversion may have been executed at an earlier stage). SAP HANA only supports Unicode as well, as is common in the industry today.

> **Exam Tip**
> SAP NetWeaver 7.5 only supports Unicode. It doesn't include non-Unicode code pages and hence can't be used for Unicode conversion. Only DMO with SUM 1.0 targeting systems below Basis 7.50 supports Unicode conversion.

- Dual-stack split
  Some SAP applications, such as SAP Process Integration (prior to release 7.5) require a dual-stack system that combines both the ABAP and the Java application server runtimes. Dual-stack isn't supported on SAP HANA, nor on the latest SAP NetWeaver-based product versions, so a dual-stack split needs to performed first.

- Hardware and software requirements
  You can use SAP Logon to verify the currently installed software components versions (SAP_BASIS) and product versions (SAP NetWeaver), illustrated in Figure 14.1. For database release information, you can use DBA Cockpit (Transaction DBACOCKPIT).

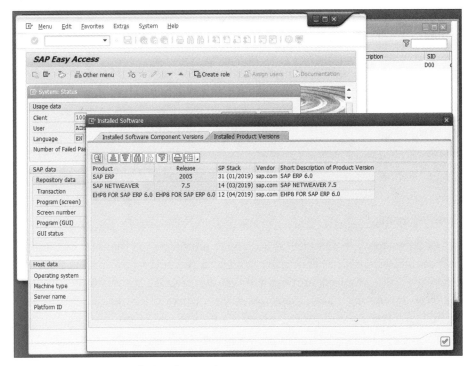

Figure 14.1 SAP Logon: Installed Product Versions

To support SAP HANA as the target database, the SAP NetWeaver AS for ABAP system requires a certain software level. Support for SAP HANA as database for SAP NetWeaver AS for ABAP was introduced in 2012, but each new SAP HANA release also comes with component update requirements.

Before you can update your SAP NetWeaver AS for ABAP system, however, you first might need to update the source database release because you can't run the latest SAP systems on legacy database software.

However, before you can update the database version, you might first need to update the operating system, which, in turn, might require updates to hardware, storage, network components, and so on. System updates and database migration can be complex.

Road Map

DMO works with a road map separated into different steps or phases. This road map gets loaded after some initial choices that dictate what the road map will look like. In this section, we'll describe the most common scenario, but keep in mind that alternative choices exist. You can run DMO without system update, that is, just performing the database migration part. You can also go for DMO with a system move, that is, not opt for the in-place migration. DMO also provides a benchmarking tool and table comparison tool, and each comes with its own road map as well. We'll describe the without system update and with system move scenarios briefly and also cover the benchmarking tool later in this chapter, but not in much detail. In brief, you can do more with DMO than covered in this chapter (and for the exam).

For the most common in-place update plus migration scenario, the road map distinguishes the following steps, as shown in Figure 14.2:

❶ Extraction

❷ Configuration

❸ Checks

❹ Preprocessing

❺ Execution

❻ Postprocessing

The first three steps are relatively short. You're prompted to provide some input, and SUM runs a large number of checks and performs several operations, such as extracting the SAP HANA database client files and creating the database schema. Preprocessing, execution, and postprocessing is where the actual work is done. Depending on the size of the database, configuration, and resources, this can run for days.

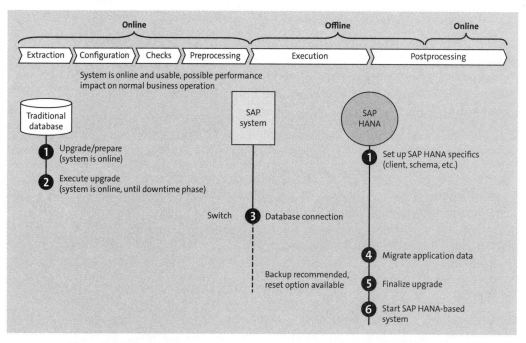

Figure 14.2 DMO Road Map

Architecture

SUM processing takes place on what is called a shadow system, which includes a copy or "shadow" ABAP instance created on the source system and a "shadow" repository created on the target database, as shown in Figure 14.3. Note that the source database isn't modified and remains a fallback database for the reset option during the entire procedure. When the DMO procedure is completed, the source database can no longer be used (although you could revert to the original database in exceptional circumstances, but this requires you to accept data loss for any transactions already executed on the new target database).

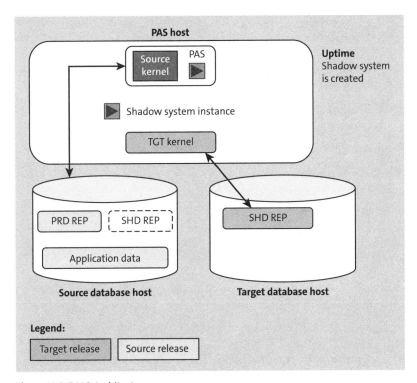

Figure 14.3 DMO Architecture

Exam Tip

Exam questions get refreshed from time to time as old ones start to appear on exam dump websites. What better topic to address in new questions than the latest features?

SUM 2.0 SP 08, for example, introduced the creation of the shadow repository on the target database instead of the source database.

Database Migration Option without System Update

Although the one-step procedure of DMO is a business benefit, this doesn't mean you have to update the system when using DMO. If the SAP system already meets all the requirements for running on the target SAP HANA database, then you can migrate without update by selecting the **DMO without System Update** option.

The small print for this option is that because SUM still needs to create a shadow system, you need to prepare the download directory with the latest kernel archives for both the source and target database but without any archives for software updates. Nor do you need to provide the update stackfile. We cover this topic in more detail in the "Preparation" section.

Database Migration Option with System Move

The in-place update and migration of DMO is a business benefit, but this doesn't mean that you can't use DMO to move the primary application server (PAS) instance of an SAP system.

The small print for this option is that because the source database tables are exported as a dump file, albeit compressed, in the SUM directory, enough space needs to be available on the file system.

Uptime and Downtime Optimizations

In the **Migration Parameters** dialog of the first **Extraction** road map step, you have the option to select the **Migration Repetition** option. When selected, the tool will stop after the downtime migration phase and enable repetition to optimize the procedure by adjusting SUM process parameters (ABAP, SQL, R3Load). You're warned, although this really should go without saying, that you shouldn't use this option for a productive run!

SUM generates data about table migration duration in XML files, such as MIGRATE_DT_DUR.XML, for example (DT = downtime, DUR= duration), and this data can be used to optimize future DMO runs. These migration duration files can also be used for migrations of different (but similar) systems with other SIDs. This way, the actual migration can benefit from a dry run on a production system copy. The same location also contains a text file MIGRATE_*_TAB.TXT that can be used for auditing purposes.

The downtime-optimized DMO scenario strategy makes it possible to migrate large application tables during the uptime phase (EU_CLONE_MIG_OPTDMO_RUN). Any changes to these tables are recorded in the source system, and a delta migration is executed subsequently either during uptime or downtime, depending on the change rate. During business downtime, only the remaining tables need to be migrated (EU_CLONE_MIG_DT_RUN).

SAP recommends to first run a standard DMO procedure, for example, using the duration files. Then, determine the candidate large tables for uptime migration. Next, run a downtime-optimized DMO procedure on a production system copy. Finally, perform the actual update, and use one weekend for the initial data transfer and a second weekend for the downtime.

There is some small print for this scenario. See the documentation for the relevant SAP Notes on prerequisites and restrictions before selecting this choice for productive environments.

Preparation

To avoid any unnecessary downtime, you need to make sure you're well prepared. DMO helps you with that in the preparation road map steps **Extraction**, **Configuration**, and **Checks**. During these phases, the system remains open for transaction processing. Only during the execution phase is the system stopped, and you enter business downtime. SAP recommends starting the preparations as early as possible and also resetting and repeating this step as often as needed. If you can't get the execution phase into an acceptable downtime window, for example, you can consider using downtime-optimized DMO to make it a one-step, but two-weekends run.

Let's walk through key activities that are performed during the preparation phase.

Software Downloads

Every DMO run starts with the **Get Roadmap** phase and a welcome screen, as shown in Figure 14.4. In this first dialog, you need to specify the scenario category, with or without a stack configuration file (**STACKFILE**). The stackfile refers to a file that contains the installation sequence of the required support and enhancement packages (import queue) and is saved as *stack.xml* (default name).

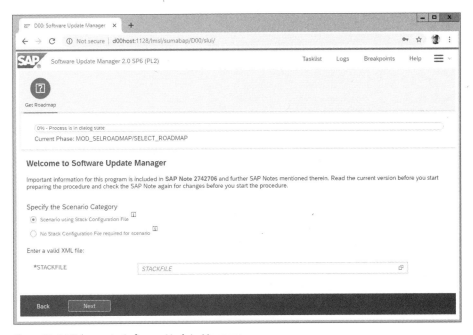

Figure 14.4 Welcome to Software Update Manager

To generate this stack configuration file, you use a tool called the maintenance planner (see Figure 14.5), which is part of SAP Solution Manager and the SL Toolset. In the maintenance planner, you can select the SAP kernels for both source and target databases, the latest version of the SAP Host Agent, SUM, and additional components that you need to include, such as Internet Graphics Server (IGS). You can then download the maintenance files directly using the maintenance planner or push the selection to the download basket of **Software Downloads** from the SAP ONE Support Launchpad (the **Push to Download Basket** button). You need to download the stack and save this to a download location, either on a shared drive or directly on the PAS of your SAP NetWeaver AS for ABAP system.

From the same screen, you also need to download the stack XML file using the **Download Stack XML** button. This file serves as input for the DMO run and needs to be included on the download location.

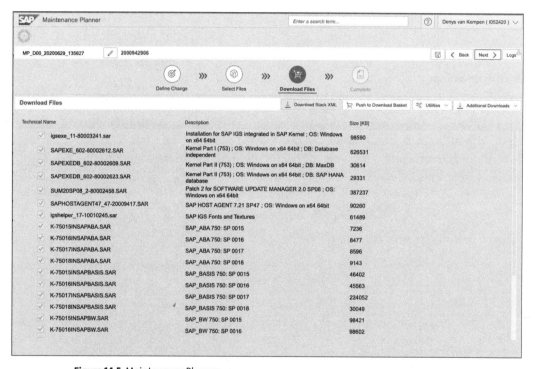

Figure 14.5 Maintenance Planner

Not everything is included in the *Stack.XML*, however, as you also need to include the latest SAP HANA client version. For this, you can visit **Software Downloads** again, and download the file, which comes as a zipped archive (SAR). Because SUM will request the path to the installation executable hdbinst, you'll need to extract the SAP HANA client SAR file using SAPCAR.

Transactions SPAM and SAINT

Although the maintenance planner includes the latest SPAM and SAINT updates, SAP recommends running the transactions again on the source system for the very latest updates. Imagine that you've downloaded the stack on Tuesday and intend to start the DMO run on Saturday; you might have missed important

SPAM/SAINT updates released by SAP on Fridays. So before starting the DMO run, execute Transactions SPAM and SAINT.

> **Exam Tip**
>
> As mentioned, you don't have to master SAP NetWeaver system administration to pass this section of the exam. If you're not familiar with Transactions SPAM and SAINT, no need to sign up for the additional training. How to update an SAP system with the Support Package Manager (SPAM) and the System Add-on Installation Tool (SAINT) is beyond the scope of this exam objective.

SAP Host Agent

SUM won't prompt for the SAP Host Agent installation files. You need to make sure yourself that the latest version is installed on all application server instances. This is important because SUM communicates with the SAP systems via the SAP Host Agent.

To update the SAP Host Agent, execute the following command:

```
saphostexec -upgrade -archive SAPHOSTAGENT.SAR
```

> **Learn More**
>
> For more information about how to install, upgrade, or configure SAP Host Agent, visit the SAP Host Agent page on the SAP Support Portal at *https://help.sap.com/viewer/host_agent*.

License and Migration Keys

When you're prompted to provide the migration parameters in the extraction phase of the DMO procedure, you also need to enter the migration key. This is self-service, and you can get one from the SAP Support Portal using the tool. The source SAP NetWeaver AS for ABAP system requires a permanent SAP license, but the target SAP HANA database doesn't, although you'll have an opportunity to provide a license during the configuration phase.

Preparing Target Database

DMO will prompt you for the name and password of the SYSTEM database user (or the database security account in case SYSTEM is deactivated). You'll also need to know the connection details (host name, SID, instance number).

SAP recommends configuring the log mode to overwrite due to massive amounts of logs generated that may cause issues with log backups. After the migration, change the setting back to normal and immediately make a first data backup.

Checks

During the DMO run, hundreds of checks are executed. Some checks are quite specific, for example, on pool and cluster tables. This is documented in the DMO guide with reference to the corresponding SAP Note. Other checks are specific to specific products, such as SAP Business Warehouse (SAP BW). For SAP BW, there is even an application-specific upgrade toolbox (ASU Toolbox). For financial accounting and controlling, there are also specific consistency checks to be performed, and others if the source database is Oracle (not supported as the target database). Apart from application-specific concerns, you also need to take scenario-specific considerations into account. One example is the DMO with system move scenario. This requires both additional preparations of the source system landscape and the target environment. Application- and scenario-specific migrations are beyond the scope of the exam.

Installation

Before you can start using SUM with DMO, you first need to install the SUM tool. Installation here means extracting the SUM SAR file and registering SUM with SAP Host Agent. We'll walk through the steps in this section.

Download and Extract

You can download the latest SUM version using the maintenance planner or directly from **Software Downloads**. As mentioned, make sure that the SAP Host Agent on the PAS of the SAP system is running the latest version.

Configure SAP Host Agent

With a single command you can configure (register) SUM with SAP Host Agent, as shown in Figure 14.6:

```
SUMSTART confighostagent <SID>
```

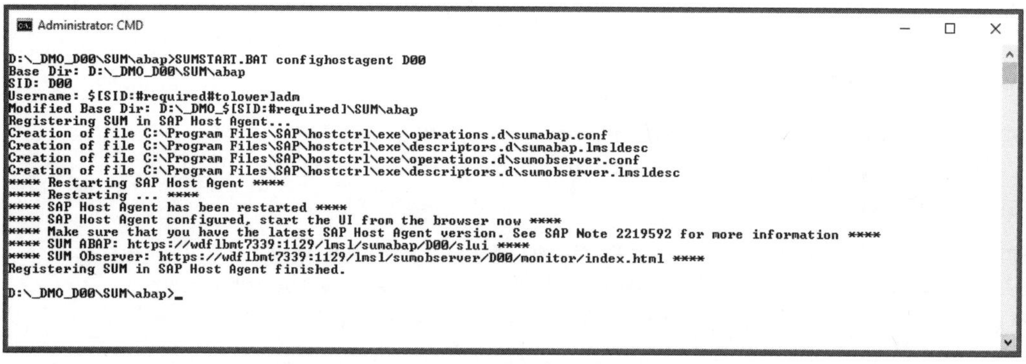

Figure 14.6 SUMSTART

On UNIX/Linux, this is a shell script; on Windows, it's a BAT file. This command will generate the SUMABAP.conf configuration file in the path of the SAP Host Agent installation and provides the agent with the command, user, and work directory, as shown in Figure 14.7.

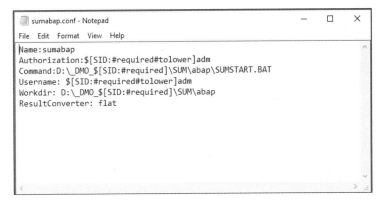

Figure 14.7 SUMABAP.conf

As you saw previously in Figure 14.4, SUM with DMO is a browser-based tool. The "application server" is SAP Host Agent, which uses TCP ports 1128 and 1129 for HTTP/S. As several dialogs prompt for user name passwords, using HTTP/S is highly recommended. The SAP Host Agent ports aren't configurable.

The path of the DMO URL is /lmsl/sumabap/<SID>/slui. As a mnemonic, lmsl is short for lifecycle management software logistics. You're running SUM for ABAP (there is also a Java version), and you need to include the SID and end with software lifecycle user interface (slui). Except for the SID, the path is in lowercase.

> **Note**
> You may recall from Chapter 4 that the web interface of the HDBLCM tool also relies on SAP Host Agent with URL path /lmsl/HDBLCM/<SID>/. This makes sense because you need to restart the SAP HANA system as part of the update, and there would be no web server to host your application.

Before you can start to use DMO, you first need to log in as the <sid>adm user of the PAS. With these credentials, SAP Host Agent starts SAPup, the actual upgrade program for SAP NetWeaver AS for ABAP systems. During the DMO run, SAPup calls additional processes, such as R3Load or tp.

After login, you're presented with the **Welcome to Software Update Manager** screen (refer to Figure 14.4) in the phase MOD_SELROADMAP submodule SELECT_ROADMAP. The road map, phases, and submodules help you keep track of where you are. After a couple of runs, these sometimes-cryptic names will become quite familiar.

Running Software Update Manager with Database Migration Option

Now that you've planned and prepared the procedure, installed the tool, and connected, you're ready for your first SUM run. We'll walk through the steps in this section.

Database Migration Option Menu and Dialogs

The welcome page includes a link to the product release note for SUM (SAP Note 2742706). This note is maintained and kept up to date. This way, SAP can make sure you always have the latest information at your disposal. You can also access the **SUM Note** from the "hamburger" menu in the top-right corner (i.e., the **More** menu in documentation). This menu also provides access to the online **SUM Guide** and the **SAP Help Portal**, as shown in Figure 14.8.

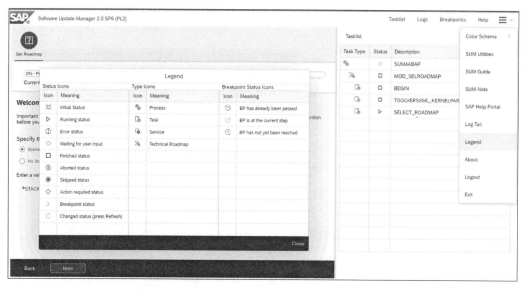

Figure 14.8 SUM: User Interface

> **Learn More**
>
> Although beyond the scope of the exam, take a look at the following SAP Note to see what type of information and references to other notes it contains: SAP Note 2742706 — Central Note: Software Update Manager 2.0.

Next, from the hamburger menu, you can access **SUM Utilities** to configure and analyze the SUM run. From here, you can access the **SUM Parameters** submenu, for example, where you can enter host configuration and passwords. Although DMO prompts you to enter the number of process parameters in the configuration phase of the road map, you can easily adjust these during the run using this menu.

Another utility is the SUM **Phase List**, which provides detailed insights into the different road maps, road map steps, modules, phases, and associated log files.

As an example, Figure 14.9 shows the road map for the migration tool with sub-module **SUBMOD_EVALUATE** expanded. You're here in the phase **EU_CLONE_SIZES** with action **Determine table sizes for optimizing migration** logged to **EUMIGRATE-SIZES.LOG**. This submodule is part of the module **MIGTOOL_POSTPROCESSING**, road map step **Postprocessing**. Using the SUM **Phase List** enables you to discover exactly what activities are performed and in what log file you can find the output.

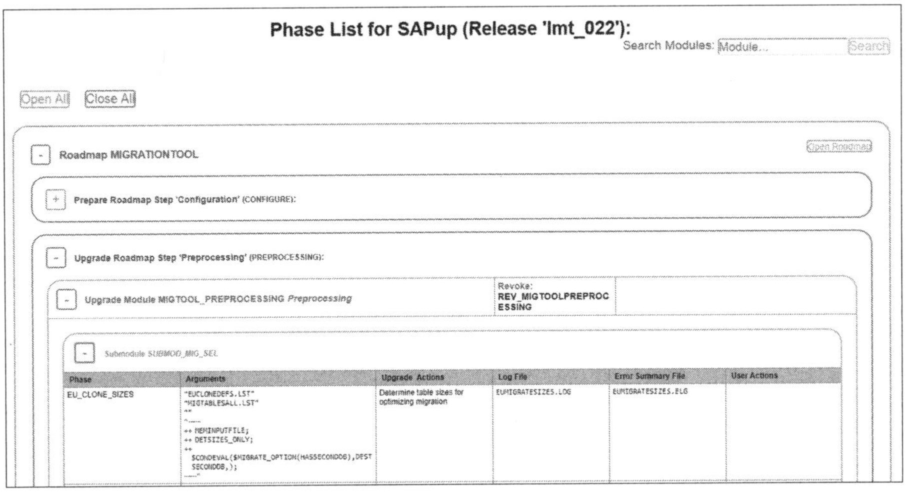

Figure 14.9 SUM Phase List

Another relevant utility is **SUM Analysis**. This displays system, tool, and component version information, configuration, duration of the different road map steps, table sizes, and processing statistics, as recorded in the *UPGANA.xml* file by SUM and illustrated in Figure 14.10.

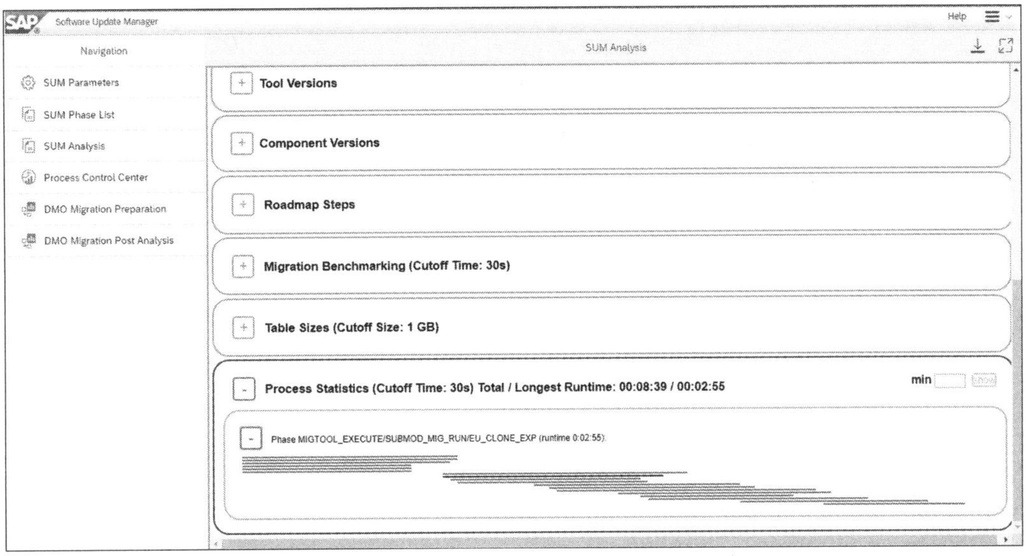

Figure 14.10 SUM Analysis

The **Process Control Center** provides access to the **Charts Control Center**, shown in Figure 14.11, with a **Realtime Process Graph**, adjustable **Process Buckets**, a **Replication Process Monitor**, and a **Background Process Monitor**. Note that from the **Process Buckets** list, you can access the log file for a particular bucket and reschedule the task.

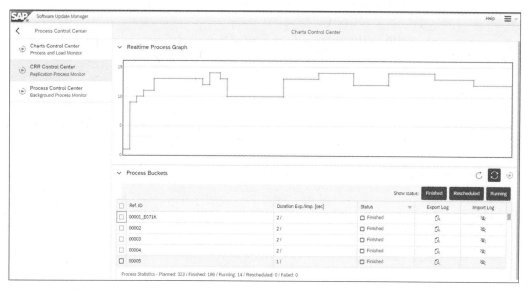

Figure 14.11 Process Control Center

Also part of the utilities menu are **DMO Migration Preparation**, and **DMO Migration Post-Analysis**, which we'll cover in more detail later in this section.

When you go back to the main menu (refer to Figure 14.8), you also have a **Log Tail** selection. Those familiar with UNIX/Linux system administration will recognize the `tail` command, which shows the "tail," or last couple of lines, of a file. This is exactly what this menu option does, and it's a convenient shortcut if you get a warning or an error. To access all the generated logs, select the **Logs** menu in the header bar.

In the same header, you can also select **Breakpoints**. This enables you to set a breakpoint in the execution flow, similar to the way you would do this in code when developing applications and using a debugger. Breakpoints are useful if processing returns issues, and you want to go through the procedure step by step and maybe perform the necessary interventions to allow the process to complete.

The header also displays the **Tasklist**, which displays exactly where you are on the road map, which module and submodule, and what the status is: **Done**, **Skipped**, **Running**, **Warning**, or **Error**. For the meaning of the icons used in the tasklist, select **Legend** from the **More** menu (shown previously in Figure 14.8).

Other **More** menu items are **About** for version information, **Logout**, and **Exit** to properly disconnect and leave the tool. Just closing the browser window isn't always a good idea. Remember, you're working here with a tool that updates an enterprise business application.

After the DMO road map has been loaded, two more entries are added to the **More** menu: **Reset** and **Cleanup**. We discuss this topic in a dedicated "Reset and Cleanup" section later in this chapter.

Learn More

For a more detailed description of the SUM UI and how to plan, prepare, and work with SUM, see "Updating SAP ABAP Systems on UNIX and Linux: SAP HANA DB" at *http://s-prs.co/v507859*. This material is beyond the scope of the exam.

Scenario Selection

On the welcome screen (refer to Figure 14.4), you're prompted to specify the scenario category:

- With stack configuration file
- Without stack configuration file

Without the stack file, you can only run the benchmarking tool, run the table comparison tool, or perform the DMO run without system update.

You need the stack file for update, upgrade, and system conversion. When you select with stack file, SUM checks the source database and you're prompted next to select the target database:

- SAP HANA
- SAP ASE
- No migration (i.e., DMO without database migration)

Although the documentation set includes the SUM with DMO guides for IBM DB2 and Microsoft SQL Server as the target database, the UI doesn't include these targets as selections by default, and you need to use SWPM to first prepare the target database.

Depending on the selection, you can choose the scenario strategy: standard or downtime-optimized. Next, you'll be prompted to provide additional input, such as whether you want to include any customer transport request into the procedure to avoid additional business downtime, whether you want to switch the expert mode on (resulting in more requests for input), and whether you want to perform archive verification (digital signature check to avoid tampering during file transfer). With these choices, SUM has enough information to provide a road map, which is displayed in the header bar. What the road map looks like will depend on your choices.

> **Exam Tip**
>
> The SUM **Phase List** (refer to Figure 14.9) shows that there are different road maps, and how the tool responds and which prompts appear will depend on previous selections. You're not expected to be familiar with SUM in all its facets nor with all of the DMO options. In the remainder of this chapter, we'll cover the road map for an SAP ERP system update with migration from SAP MaxDB to SAP HANA, which showcases the database migration using DMO.

Extraction

The extraction phase is a short phase that takes less than 10 minutes. As shown in Figure 14.12, you're prompted to provide the location of the **Download Directory** with the stack configuration file and all extracted files. During this phase, the files listed on the stack file will be extracted, hence the name.

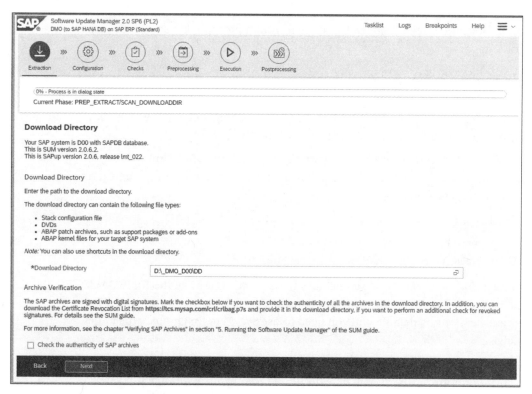

Figure 14.12 Download Directory

Some of the modules executed are PREP_EXTRACT, PREP_PRE_CHECK, PREP_INPUT_CHECK, and PREP_INPUT. These phases are displayed in the progress bar on the main screen and in the **Tasklist** menu, as shown in Figure 14.13.

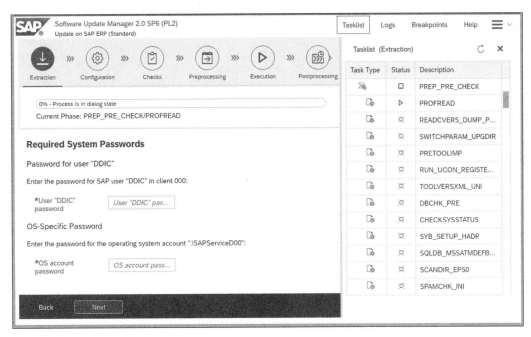

Figure 14.13 Required System Passwords

During the extraction phase, you're prompted to provide the passwords for the Data Dictionary (DDIC) user, which is a user with special authorizations for installation, software logistics, and the ABAP Dictionary, and the only user that is allowed to log on to SAP NetWeaver AS during an upgrade. You also need to provide the password for the `<sid>adm` user (the `SAPService<SID>` account on Windows). SUM performs a large number of validations based on the stackfile and the connection made with DDIC to the SAP system.

Next, you're also prompted to provide migration parameters and indicate how you want to perform the table comparison checks: **Do not compare table contents**, **Compare the content of all tables**, or **Compare only the content of selected tables**, which you then need to provide (see Figure 14.14).

As part of the migration, SUM DMO perform a table row count and compares source and target with a `COUNT(*)`. In addition, you can also request that SUM perform a content check. This is done with a checksum, that is, the cyclic redundancy check (CRC), as any issues are logged as `Error "CRC differences for table 'xxxx'"`. Performing a content verification check will extend the duration of the DMO run and isn't recommended for the final production run.

At this stage, you need to provide the migration key. For more information about how to get this key, a link to an SAP Note is included.

Another migration parameter is the **Migration Repetition Option**. You can select this to perform a dry run with the DMO procedure on a test system and find the optimal settings for the final run on the production system.

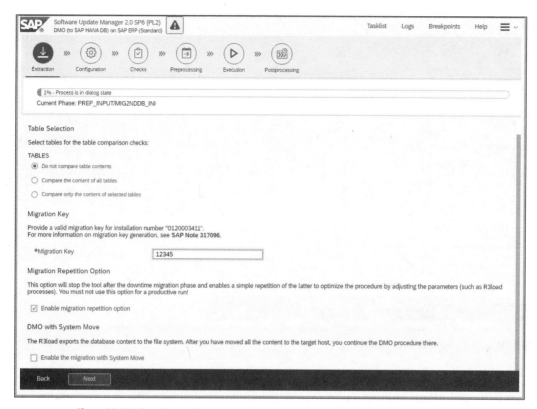

Figure 14.14 Migration Options

From the migration parameter dialog, you can also opt for **DMO with System Move**. When selected, the R3load processes won't directly pump the data into the target database but instead will export the database content to the file system. This option requires additional steps beyond the scope of the exam and also impacts how you need to handle the reset.

The triangle with exclamation mark in the header provides additional information: here you're informed that the product type SAP ERP was detected. This is also displayed in the header: **DMO (to SAP HANA DB) on SAP ERP (Standard)**.

An orange color in the progress bar indicates that input is required. Otherwise, the color is green when the DMO is at work, or red if the DMO has encountered an error it can't solve. The issue will be explained on the main screen, as shown in Figure 14.15.

In the extraction phase, SUM will go through a large number of "prep" modules without any further prompting. At the end of the step, you're prompted to click **Next** and **Continue with road map step "Configuration"**. You're informed that there are manual steps that might need to be executed first, listed in the *CHECKS.TXT* file, as shown in Figure 14.16.

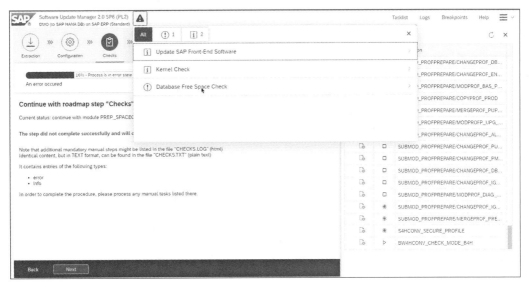

Figure 14.15 SUM Processing Error

Figure 14.16 SUM: Configuration

The **Tasklist** menu not only shows you exactly where you are and reveals what (sub)modules have been executed and which ones were skipped, but it also enables you to re-execute the task if any issues are detected.

Configuration

During the configuration phase, you provide input on processing parameters and SAP HANA as target database. We'll walk through the steps in the following sections.

Key Parameters

At the beginning of the configuration phase, you're prompted for the parameter to configure the procedure. Here you can modify the following for **Update** and **Downtime**:

- Maximum number of ABAP processes
- Maximum number of parallel processes for the execution of SQL commands
- Maximum number of parallel import processes (R3TRANS)
- Maximum number of parallel load or table compression processes (R3Load)

For the **R3load processes**, the number you enter is for a pair because half are used on either side. These processing parameters can be adjusted at any time during the run using the **SUM Parameters** menu from SUM, as illustrated in Figure 14.17.

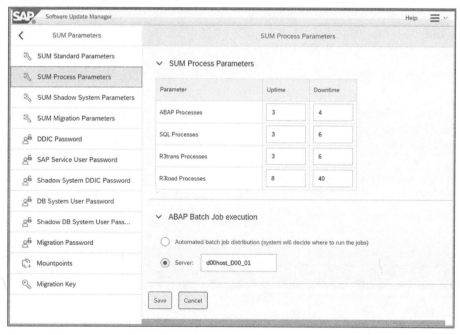

Figure 14.17 SUM Process Parameters

In addition, R3Load processes can also be adjusted with the SAPup command, as shown in Figure 14.18: SAPup set procpar gt=scroll.

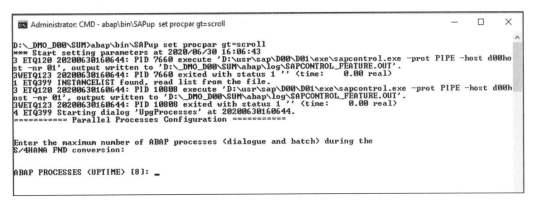

```
▣ Administrator: CMD - abap\bin\SAPup  set procpar gt=scroll                    —  □   ×

D:\_DMO_D00\SUM>abap\bin\SAPup set procpar gt=scroll
*** Start setting parameters at 2020/06/30 16:06:43
3 ETQ120 20200630160644: PID 7660 execute 'D:\usr\sap\D00\D01\exe\sapcontrol.exe -prot PIPE -host d00ho
st -nr 01', output written to 'D:\_DMO_D00\SUM\abap\log\SAPCONTROL_FEATURE.OUT'.
3WETQ123 20200630160644: PID 7660 exited with status 1 '' (time:     0.00 real)
1 ETQ399 INSTANCELIST found, read list from the file.
3 ETQ120 20200630160644: PID 10808 execute 'D:\usr\sap\D00\D01\exe\sapcontrol.exe -prot PIPE -host d00h
ost -nr 01', output written to 'D:\_DMO_D00\SUM\abap\log\SAPCONTROL_FEATURE.OUT'.
3WETQ123 20200630160644: PID 10808 exited with status 1 '' (time:     0.00 real)
4 ETQ399 Starting dialog 'UpgProcesses' at 20200630160644.
=========== Parallel Processes Configuration ===========


Enter the maximum number of ABAP processes (dialogue and batch) during the
S/4HANA FND conversion:

ABAP PROCESSES (UPTIME) [8]: _
```

Figure 14.18 SAPup

Next, you're prompted to indicate where to run the background jobs: PAS or AAS? The PAS of an SAP system also hosts ABAP Central Services (ASCS), message server and enqueue server. Most SAP systems include additional application servers (AAS), and executing the R3Load processes here might improve performance.

You also need to choose an execution strategy for Transaction SGEN (i.e., SAP's load generator), which compiles ABAP repository objects. Transaction SGEN compilation will take some time, and your options are to skip Transaction SGEN during the update, generate the loads on the shadow system during update, start asynchronously in post downtime, or a combination of the last two.

After some checks and calculations, you're then prompted to enter the password for the source database user **SAPD00**. After some more processing, you'll also be prompted for the path to the hdbinst executable for the SAP HANA client installation and the password of the installation account.

Next, you need to provide the connection parameters for the target database: **Target DB hostname**, **Target DB SID**, and **Target DB instance number**, as shown in Figure 14.19.

It's at this stage (**HDB_MIGCONFIG**) that you can point to the location of the system license, but this isn't required.

Next, you're prompted to enter the following:

- Password of the system user
- Target database schema: **SAPABAP1** (default value)
- Password for the target database schema
- Password for the DBACOCKPIT user (this user will be created)

You're also prompted regarding whether you want to enable the load of automatic table placement statements for the SAP HANA database, a topic we discussed in Chapter 9.

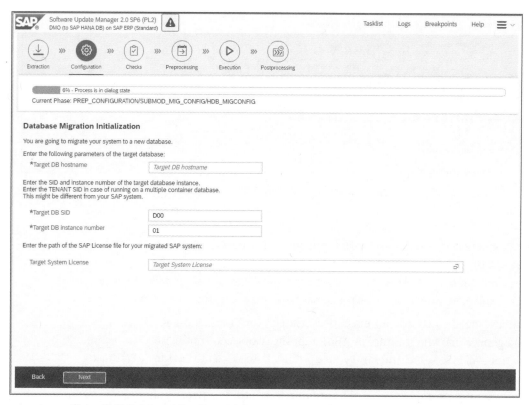

Figure 14.19 Database Migration Initialization

Although you can reset the DMO run at any point, not every task will be rolled back. The installation of the SAP HANA client and the configuration of the SAP HANA target database is a case in point. For example, if you've selected a migration repetition scenario and perform the DMO run for the second time, dialogs will change. The installation of the SAP HANA client will be detected, and the task skipped.

Products, Add-Ons, and Support Packages

Depending on previous selections, additional prompts may appear. For SAP Business Suite, you're also prompted to enable the automatic load of table placement parameters with a reference to an SAP Note for more information. For other products, different dialogs will be presented.

After some more calculations, you're prompted to select the add-ons to change for the target system. For this, you might need some advice from the SAP Basis administrator (if this isn't you). The same applies to the next screen where you need to select the support packages to include.

Transport Requests and Modification Adjustments

At this stage, you're prompted to enter the names of the transport request. Skip the dialog, if not applicable. After some more processing, you can make a modification adjustment and enter the transport request for Transaction SPDD (Support Pack Data Dictionary) and Transaction SPAU (Support Pack Adjustments for Repository Objects). You can even select to double-check the modifications at a later stage.

This concerns standard SUM functionality and isn't specific to DMO. The modification adjustments take place on the shadow system instance, and you're prompted to enter an unused instance number plus the password of the ABAP database user that will be created specifically for this purpose (and deleted at the end of the procedure). If you are doing test migration runs and have already generated the shadow system profile, you can ask SUM to reuse them (location SUM > abap > save).

For an SAP BW system, additional input is requested in this phase for housekeeping, that is, the deletion of unused data (not recoverable by DMO reset). In this phase, you may also be prompted for the ASU Toolbox when performing a release change.

After about 20 minutes—your mileage may vary—you're prompted to close the **Configuration** step and continue with the next. As with the end of the **Extraction** step (refer to Figure 14.16), you're informed that additional mandatory steps are listed in the *CHECKS.TXT* file, accessible from the **Logs** item in the header bar or the green/orange triangle with exclamation mark.

Checks

Like the extraction phase, the checks phase runs for about 10 minutes. This time, however, no more dialogs appear, and SUM performs, no surprise, a large number of checks and calculations (e.g., the file system space required for the shadow system and whether enough space is available in the database). If any issue is detected, for example, as illustrated previously in Figure 14.15 on a database free space check, this can be corrected, after which SUM proceeds. There's no need to restart or reset the procedure when a single (sub-)module returns an error. Just execute the module again. As with the previous road map steps, you're informed that at this stage, additional mandatory manual steps may be required.

Preprocessing

During the preprocessing phase, the real work starts as now the shadow system will be created and the shadow import of tables started. First, after a bit of activity, you're prompted to lock the development environment, as shown in Figure 14.20. This will lock the repository and imports, or transport requests can no longer be executed. This doesn't mean downtime is starting. Production can still continue, but you can't make any more modifications (and this includes transports).

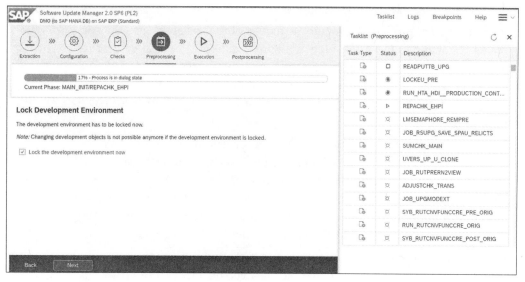

Figure 14.20 Preprocessing: Lock Development Environment

Next, SUM continues with cloning tables from the original to shadow system (DBCLONE). This part of the DMO run no longer takes several minutes but many hours, depending on the size of the source system.

In particular, the migration of the repository tables in task EU_CLONE_MIG_UT_RUN, illustrated in Figure 14.21, is a very time-consuming activity. Note the CRC_RUN task to calculate the checksums. Repository tables are migrated during uptime (UT). You can distinguish the activity's table size determination (_SIZES), table creation on target database (_CREATE), prepare (_PRP), creation of directories (migrate_*) and R3Load control file's structure (STR), task (TSK), and command (CMD), and then RUN when SAPup triggers the migration of tables into the target database.

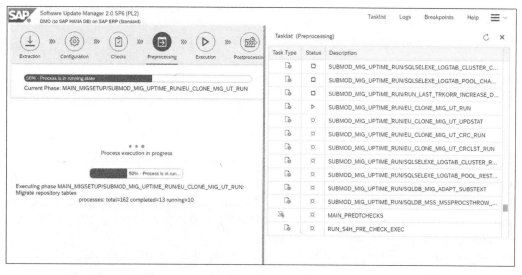

Figure 14.21 Migrate Repository Tables

When the procedure has reached the end of the **Preprocessing** road map step, you're informed you need to carry out the following actions:

- Stop all production activities.
- Ensure scheduled batch jobs can't start anymore, and wait for the regular completion or currently running jobs.
- Ensure all users have logged out.
- Isolate the PAS.

You need to select the **Actions Completed** box before you can click **Next**.

The SAP system is now stopped, and, after some more processing, you're informed the system is ready to enter the downtime. It's time for a backup. To restart from this point, you must be able to restore the source and target databases, and the system and program directories.

You can select **Resume production operation** (after system restore) or **Backup completed**, as shown in Figure 14.22.

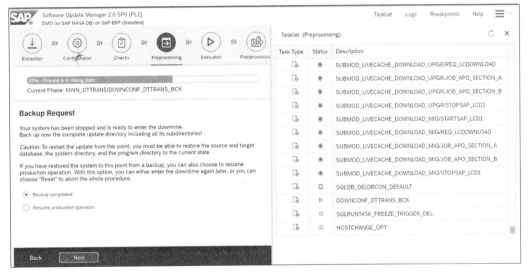

Figure 14.22 Backup Request

After a bit more processing, SUM prompts you to continue with the next road map step.

Execution

The execution phase starts with a task that stops all SAP transactions and then continues into the MAIN_SWITCH module with the migration of application tables (EU_CLONE_MIG_DT_RUN). Like the repository tables, this activity takes considerable time.

The time estimation is written to the *SAPupStat.log* file and migration progress to TSK files in the SUM directory `migrate_dt_run`. If any error occurs during the data migration run, subsequent runs won't have to start all the way from the beginning again but can continue where you left off.

The progress bar shows the percentage completed. In addition, you can view the log (tail) for *SAPupStat.log*, which informs you about total, completed, running, and failed buckets (work page for `R3Load` pair). We'll discuss this further in the "Postprocessing" section. For more detailed information, view the log files for the migration phases buckets, process execution, and migration rates.

SUM Utilities also includes the **Process Buckets** monitor, shown previously in Figure 14.11. This provides a real-time process graph with a process bucket list and the option to select buckets for rescheduling. The `R3Load` processes divide the work up in buckets, which may contain several tables or only part of a table.

For other interested parties, or if you want to continue keeping an eye on the progress offsite, you can launch the **SUM ABAP Observer Monitor** from URL path `/lmsl/sumobserver/<SID>/monitor` to show an **Overall progress** bar, **Current Status**, and **Current Phase** (module, submodule, phase), as shown in Figure 14.23.

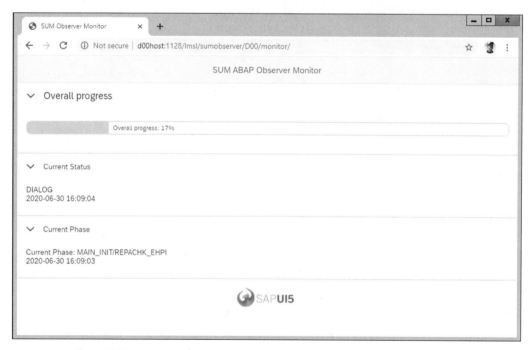

Figure 14.23 SUM ABAP Observer Monitor

After the kernel switch to the target database (`KX_SWITCH` phase), the system is started again, and you're presented with the **End of SUM technical Downtime** action screen, as shown in Figure 14.24. The system is unlocked, and, for a system with multiple application servers, you can start them up and perform the required maintenance. End of the SUM technical downtime doesn't mean that the system is open for processing again.

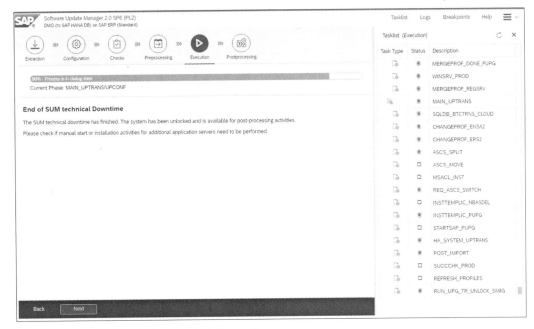

Figure 14.24 Execution: End of SUM Technical Downtime

After a few seconds, you're then prompted to continue with the next road map step.

Postprocessing

After the long preprocessing and execution phases, fortunately, postprocessing again is a short one. During this phase, after further continued processing, you receive two more prompts:

- **Start of Cleanup Processing**
  You're informed SUM is ready for the start of cleanup processing. During this time, you can carry out manual postprocessing activities, such as transport imports, perform additional software installations, or reschedule background jobs.

- **Confirmation Required for Imports**
  The second confirmation screen asks you to confirm all this work has been done: **I confirm that no more imports are running**. This is only possible after the update.

Another five minutes for activities, such as TOOLIMP_DELETE_ABAP and SAVELOGS, and you're done.

You can take a last look at the log files using the **Log Tail Viewer**, as illustrated in Figure 14.25, and finish, as instructed, by selecting **Cleanup** from the **More** menu.

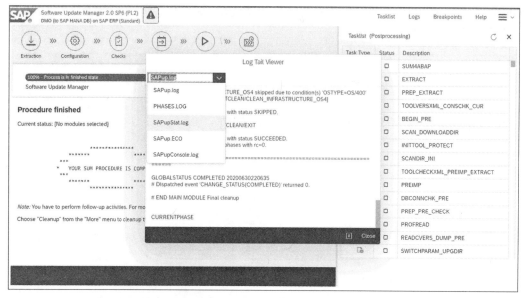

Figure 14.25 Log Tail Viewer

Performance-related data is written to the *UPGANA.XML* file, which can be visualized using the **SUM Analysis** tool from the SUM utilities menu, as shown earlier in Figure 14.10.

Reset and Cleanup

After you've passed beyond the initial dialogs, the **Reset** option is added to the menu. As SUM doesn't modify the source system (small print coming up), reset enables you to quickly return to the initial state and execute the run again, ideally after fixing what caused the need to reset in the first place.

Performing a reset is easy. Click **More • Reset**, select **Yes** to the "do-you-really-really-want" prompt, and click **Next**. SUM will execute REV_PRPPARSETUP and REV_PRPPARINIT. To finalize the reset, you'll also have to select, as instructed, **Cleanup** from the menu. The SUM web UI will exit, and you'll get a message that the SUM ABAP server process (SAPup) has ended and that you can either close the browser or refresh to start again.

The command line equivalent is /SUM/abap/bin/SAPup gt=scroll, which returns a menu from which you can select **Reset**.

Of course, there is some small print:

- SUM can only perform a reset if the AnyDB source database is still available and if the SUM directory hasn't been modified; that is, no files have been deleted to free up some space, for example.

- SUM doesn't undo Transaction SPAM/SAINT changes or those of SAP Notes implementations.

- SUM doesn't undo the changes made to the target environment, for example, the SAP HANA database client installation or the creation of the `DBACOCKPIT` user and related roles.
- SUM doesn't undo application-specific (e.g., SAP BW) housekeeping operations.
- For the DMO with system move procedure, the consequences of a reset are different and require consideration. For this, you'll need to consult the SUM with DMO Guide.

Benchmarking

The main objective of DMO is to shorten the downtime as much as possible. By combining system update with database migration, in-place, in a single step, multiple downtime phases are brought back into a single one. But this isn't where it stops. You can tune DMO downtime and try to reduce or shorten it as much as possible. The benchmarking tool supports this objective.

Let's quickly review your tuning options:

- Preparation:
  - Benchmarking (get insights)
  - Migration repetition option (apply and evaluate)
- Configuration: Downtime-optimized DMO
- Dry run: SUM Analysis tool (visualize *upgana.xml* [duration])
- Execution: Adjusting parallel processing (`R3Load`)

The benchmarking tool, shown in Figure 14.26, migrates a part of the tables to provide insights into the migration rate. The tool is launched when you opt for a SUM with DMO run with stackfile (refer to Figure 14.4).

There are two options: export only or export and import depending on whether you just want to tune the export rate (e.g., for DMO with system move) or both.

In the **Benchmarking Parameters** dialog, indicate whether the benchmark should be performed on the whole database or a selection of tables. When you select all tables, you can provide a sample size plus a limit for the size of the largest table to avoid a single table taking up the whole sample.

As with a regular DMO run, you get to specify the number of parallel processes for SQL and `R3Load` for uptime and downtime phases. There will be no downtime during benchmarking, but this simulates the productive run. Uptime references the preparation road map step when the candidate tables for export are selected, whereas downtime corresponds to the execution step, when the actual table content is exported (and imported, when selected).

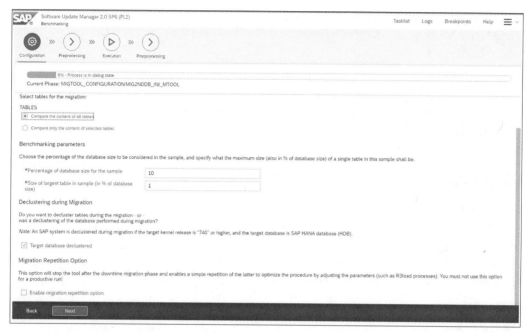

Figure 14.26 Benchmarking

The **Benchmarking** road map has four phases:

- **Configuration**
- **Preprocessing**
- **Execution**
- **Postprocessing**

Just like a regular DMO run, you're prompted before going to the next phase. There are no more dialogs between the steps. After postprocessing, you're instructed to analyze the log files for the results. Export-only data is discarded. Any imported data is deleted.

For analysis, access the **SUM Utilities** menu from **More**, and select **DMO Migration Post Analysis**. **Tail Viewer**, **Bucket Viewer**, and **Duration Viewer** provide insights into migration processing. Figure 14.27 shows the graphical output for time in seconds per bucket with alternative selections available in the header (duration, number of tables, number of rows, memory usage, etc.).

Figure 14.28 shows how percentage completion and parallel R3Load processes correspond.

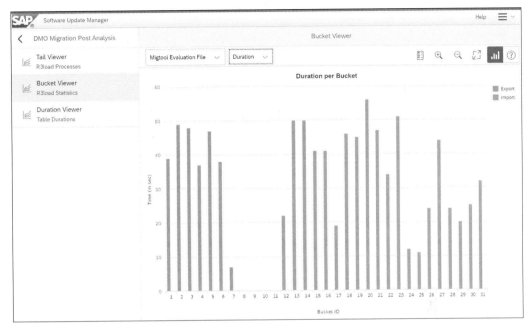

Figure 14.27 DMO Migration Post Analysis: Bucket Viewer

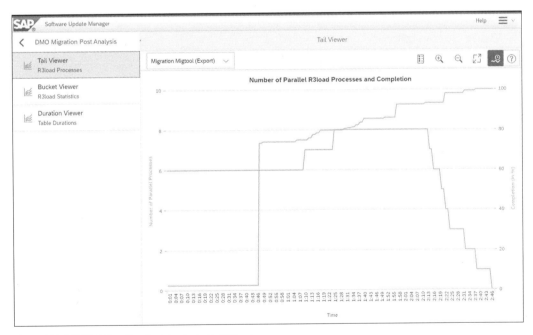

Figure 14.28 DMO Migration Post Analysis: Tail Viewer

Before attempting a second run, first consider the graphs of **DMO Migration Preparation**, also part of the **SUM Utilities**, as shown in Figure 14.29. **Table Sequence** provides insight into the estimated runtime and table sizes. **Table Splits** shows the distribution of splits, one of the approaches for DMO to optimize data transfer.

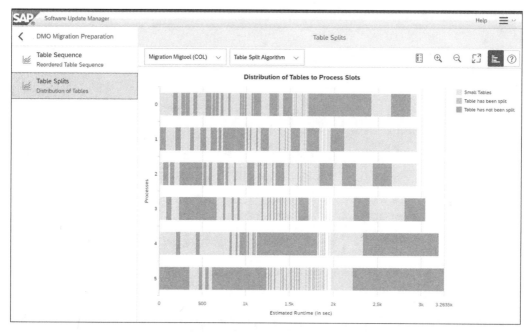

Figure 14.29 DMO Migration Preparation

> **Learn More**
> Benchmarking migration is documented in the DMO guide in the "Migration Tools" chapter at *http://s-prs.co/v507860*.

Important Terminology

For this exam objective, you're expected to understand the following terms:

- **AnyDB**
  The SAP NetWeaver kernel is hardware-, operating system- and database-independent and includes a special layer to provide the communication with specific database implementations, for example, Oracle on Linux, Microsoft SQL Server on Microsoft Windows, and so on. With the SAP HANA-specific product versions of SAP Business Suite and SAP BW applications, such as SAP S/4HANA and SAP BW/4HANA, existing relational databases are grouped together as AnyDB in SAP terminology. This isn't an official term, and the exact interpretation differs; in commercial usage, for example, AnyDB usually references non-SAP databases but not SAP ASE, SAP IQ, or SAP MaxDB.

- **Benchmarking tool**
  SUM includes a benchmarking tool which migrates a part of the tables. This tool enables you to fine-tune process parameter settings. The DMO **Migration preparation and post analysis** submenu on the **DMO Utilities** menu provides visual insights into processing buckets, table splits, and other relevant statistics.

- **Database Migration Option (DMO)**
  DMO is a feature of the Software Update Manager (SUM). DMO combines the update of SAP NetWeaver AS for ABAP systems with the migration to a supported database in a single procedure. The business benefits of DMO are reduced downtime and simplified system migration.

- **Downtime-optimized DMO**
  Downtime-optimized DMO is one of the DMO features that aims to reduce system downtime by migrating part of the application tables during uptime. On the source system, triggers and a delta are maintained, which are applied to the migrated tables after the switch.

- **Dual stack**
  An SAP NetWeaver AS with both ABAP and Java runtimes is called a dual-stack system. DMO only supports SAP NetWeaver AS for ABAP-based systems, and you need to execute a dual-stack split on the source system before you can perform a DMO run. SAP NetWeaver 7.5 no longer supports the dual stack, so this mostly applies to older environments.

- **Maintenance planner**
  Maintenance planner is SAP Solution Manager's cloud-based central tool to plan updates, upgrades, or new installations in SAP landscapes. It's the successor of maintenance optimizer.

- **Migration key**
  The SUM with DMO procedure is considered a heterogeneous system copy (operating system/database migration) and requires a migration key. The SAP ONE Support Portal provides the key request as self-service.

- **Primary application server (PAS)**
  PAS is the primary application server that includes the ABAP Central Services (ASCS) Message Server and Enqueue Server. An SAP system supports a single PAS with zero or more additional application servers (AAS). During the migration switch, you need to isolate the PAS, that is, shut down all AAS instances. One of the migration tuning options is to run the R3Load processes on the AAS and not the PAS.

- **Processing parameters**
  Some of the most important configuration settings are the processing parameters. You define the number of processing parameters for both uptime and downtime for ABAP, SQL, R3Trans, and R3Load. These parameters are set during the configuration phase of the road map but can be adjusted later using the **SUM Utilities** menu or on the command line (SAPup). Using the same **SUM Utilities** menu, you can analyze processing parameter performance. One of the objectives of migration test runs is to fine-tune processing parameters.

- **Road map**
  The first activity of a DMO run is to load a road map. Each DMO scenario has its own road map, which is prominently displayed in the tool with progress indicators. Each road map step contains several modules and submodules that need

to be executed. SUM keeps track of the status and progress of each step and, when interrupted, can resume at the point where processing stopped. To start processing from the start again, you need to perform a reset and cleanup.

- **SAP Host Agent**
  SAP Host Agent is installed on every SAP system to provide lifecycle management tasks such as operating system and database monitoring, system instance control, and provisioning. SUM is hosted by SAP Host Agent.

- **SAP NetWeaver AS for ABAP**
  SAP NetWeaver is the integration and development platform for SAP business applications. AS stands for application server and ABAP for one of its application runtimes.

- **SAPup**
  SAPup is the executable that performs updates for SAP NetWeaver AS for ABAP systems. SUM provides the UI. SAP Host Agent exchanges the messages, and SAPup performs the activities. During a SUM run, a second SAPup process manages the road map, and additional processes, such as R3Load, are called to perform the actual task.

- **Shadow instance**
  During the DMO procedure, a copy of the source system kernel is created on the source system where all processing takes. This leaves the source kernel untouched and facilitates a fast reset, that is a quick return to the original situation in case of issues.

- **Shadow repository**
  During the DMO procedure, a copy of the source repository is created on which all processing takes place. Initially, the shadow repository was created in the source database, which required the source database to support the target release of the SAP HANA system. As of SUM SP 6, the shadow repository is created in the target database. During downtime, SUM switches the PAS from the original source to the updated target repository.

- **Software Logistics (SL) Toolset**
  The Software Logistics (SL) Toolset is a product-independent delivery channel for software logistics tools for all products based on SAP NetWeaver.

- **Software Provisioning Manager (SWPM)**
  SWPM is an SL Toolset tool used to install software, rename systems, perform a dual-stack split, and copy/migrate systems, or, technically, perform a homogeneous or heterogeneous system copy. Homogeneous indicates that the operating system and database remain the same (kind). In a "classical" migration, you use SUM to update the system and SWPM to perform a heterogeneous system copy (i.e., the migration).

- **Software Update Manager (SUM)**
  SUM is a tool to update SAP NetWeaver-based systems and is part of the SL Toolset.

- **Stack file**

  The stack file, or *stack.xml* file, is generated by the maintenance planner, which informs SUM about component updates and sequences. The DMO procedure starts with parsing the stack file after which the road map will be presented.

- **Table comparison check**

  SUM automatically performs a COUNT(*) check on migrated tables to verify that both source and target table contain the same number of rows. In addition, you can configure SUM to also execute a checksum (CRC) check on the table (or section of the table, for very large tables). This guarantees that not only the table will have the same number of rows but also that the content is identical. CRC verification is time consuming and only recommended as part of a DMO run in migration repetition mode and not on productive runs.

- **Transaction SPAM/Transaction SAINT**

  Transaction SPAM and Transaction SAINT are the transactions for the support package manager and the add-on installation tool, which are often used together. Initially, components could be updated independently using these transactions. Because of the many dependencies and other complexities, system updates are now orchestrated through SUM using the stack file generated by the maintenance planner.

- **Unicode**

  Computers use code pages for character encoding, and this goes back to the days of the mainframe. There are thousands of code pages around for different operating systems. When computing evolved from mainframes to networked computers and ultimately to an interconnected World Wide Web, the different code pages became an obstacle. The solution was found in Unicode, a superset of existing character pages, the most common being Unicode Transformation Format-8 (UTF-8).

Practice Questions

These practice questions will help you evaluate your understanding of the topics covered in this chapter. The questions shown are similar in nature to those found on the certification examination. Although none of these questions will be found on the exam itself, they will allow you to review your knowledge of the subject. Select the correct answers, and then check the completeness of your answers in the "Practice Question Answers and Explanations" section. Remember that on the exam, you must select all correct answers, and only correct answers, to receive credit for the question.

1. What are the benefits of DMO? (There are three correct answers.)

   ☐   **A.** Migration steps are simplified.

   ☐   **B.** There's no need for Unicode conversion.

- ☐ **C.** System update and database migration are combined in one tool.
- ☐ **D.** Business downtime is reduced.

2. Which tool would you use to migrate a PL/SQL-based Oracle application to SAP HANA?

- ☐ **A.** DMO
- ☐ **B.** SAP S/4HANA migration cockpit
- ☐ **C.** Oracle SQL Developer
- ☐ **D.** SAP Advanced SQL Migration

3. What target databases are supported for SUM with DMO? (There are two correct answers.)

- ☐ **A.** SAP HANA
- ☐ **B.** SAP ASE
- ☐ **C.** SAP IQ
- ☐ **D.** SAP NetWeaver AS for ABAP

4. Your SAP system requires Unicode conversion, and you want to perform this activity as part of the DMO run. Which release of the SUM with DMO tool should you use, and what target release is supported?

- ☐ **A.** Always use the latest SUM SP release. Any target is supported.
- ☐ **B.** DMO with SUM 2.0. Any target is supported.
- ☐ **C.** DMO with SUM 1.0 targeting systems before SAP Basis 7.50.
- ☐ **D.** DMO with SUM 2.0 targeting systems with SAP Basis 7.50 and later.

5. You want to use SUM with DMO to perform a one-step, in-place update of your SAP system and migrate from SAP HANA 1.0 to the latest SAP HANA 2.0 SPS 05 release. Which restriction applies? (There are two correct answers.)

- ☐ **A.** SAP HANA as both source and target database isn't supported.
- ☐ **B.** SAP HANA 2.0 SPS 05 as target database isn't supported.
- ☐ **C.** SAP HANA 1.0 as source database isn't supported.
- ☐ **D.** There is no restriction.

6. What should you select at a minimum in the maintenance planner to prepare the stack file? (There are two correct answers.)

- ☐ **A.** SAP kernel source database
- ☐ **B.** SAP kernel target database

☐   **C.** SAP Host Agent

☐   **D.** SUM

7.   What software is required for a DMO run with SAP HANA as the target data-
     base? (There are three correct answers.)

☐   **A.** Latest SAP Host Agent (patch) release

☐   **B.** Latest SUM release

☐   **C.** SAP HANA cockpit

☐   **D.** Latest SPAM/SAINT updates

☐   **E.** Latest DMO release

8.   What license and/or keys, if any, are required for a DMO run? (There are two
     correct answers.)

☐   **A.** A permanent SAP license for the system that will be migrated

☐   **B.** A valid SAP HANA license

☐   **C.** A migration key

☐   **D.** A valid operating system license

9.   Which steps needs to be executed before you can access SUM in a browser?
     (There are three correct answers.)

☐   **A.** Install SUM with command `suminst`.

☐   **B.** Register SUM with the SAP Host Agent with command `SUMSTART confighos-
     tagent <SID>`.

☐   **C.** Extract SUM with command `SAPCAR -xf SUM2OSP<version>.SAR`.

☐   **D.** Upgrade the SAP Host Agent to the latest release with command
     `saphostexec -upgrade –archive SAPHOSTAGENT<version>.SAR`.

☐   **E.** Update Google Chrome to the latest release as SUM only supports the latest
     version.

10. How can you access SUM log files? (There are three correct answers.)

☐   **A.** From the **Log Tail** item on the **More** menu

☐   **B.** Using Transaction SM21

☐   **C.** From the command line using the UNIX/Linux `tail` command

☐   **D.** On the PAS server in the `<path> > SUM > abap > log` directory

☐   **E.** From the **Logs** header menu

11. How can you make sure the target tables are identical to the source tables?

☐ **A.** Run the `COUNT(*)` SQL command for all tables on the source and target databases after the migration.

☐ **B.** Select the **Compare the content of all tables** option in the **Migration Parameters** dialog of the Extraction phase.

☐ **C.** Use the table comparison tool.

12. Which processes are paired (half used on either side)?

☐ **A.** ABAP

☐ **B.** SQL

☐ **C.** `R3Trans`

☐ **D.** `R3Load`

13. How can you change process parameters during a run? (There are two correct answers.)

☐ **A.** Use the migration repetition option and repeat the run.

☐ **B.** Use **SUM utilities • SUM Parameters • SUM Process Parameters**.

☐ **C.** From the command line, run command `SAPup set procpar gt=scroll`.

☐ **D.** Use Transaction RZ11.

14. What are the consequences of locking the development environment during the preprocessing phase?

☐ **A.** The repository is locked, and the shadow repository created.

☐ **B.** Business downtime starts.

☐ **C.** Changing development objects is no longer possible, but transport requests can still be executed as these only affect application tables (data).

☐ **D.** No more updates using Transactions SPAM/SAINT, only emergency updates are allowed (Transaction SNOTE).

15. Which actions do you need to perform to prepare for downtime? (There are three correct answers.)

☐ **A.** Isolate the PAS (primary application server).

☐ **B.** Make a backup of the system.

☐ **C.** Ensure all users have logged out.

☐ **D.** Lock the development environment.

☐ **E.** Ensure all jobs have finished and no more new jobs can be scheduled.

16. When is the system available for business transactions again?

☐ **A.** At the end of the execution road map step: **End of SUM Technical Downtime** screen.

☐ **B.** At the end of the postprocessing road map step after cleanup

17. What changes, if any, aren't undone when you perform a DMO reset? (There are three correct answers.)

☐ **A.** SUM performs all processing on a shadow instance and shadow repository, which are discarded during reset. The source system wasn't modified. All changes are undone.

☐ **B.** Transaction SPAM/SAINT updates and Transaction SNOTE implementation on the source system.

☐ **C.** Users and roles created on the target database.

☐ **D.** Modifications to the source database made by application-specific programs.

☐ **E.** Data, log files, and temporary files in the ABAP directory of the SUM tool.

18. For which users do you need to provide a password? (There are three correct answers.)

☐ **A.** DDIC

☐ **B.** SAP Service user

☐ **C.** SAP HANA SYSTEM user

☐ **D.** SAP Host Agent

Practice Question Answers and Explanations

1. Correct answers: **A, C, D**
   All are benefits except for answer B, which is incorrect because SAP HANA only supports Unicode. Unicode conversion can be included in a DMO run but only for target systems that are supported. This concerns SAP Basis components prior to 7.50 and hence only with SUM 1.0.

2. Correct answer: **D**
   You would use SAP Advanced SQL Migration.

   Answer A is incorrect because DMO only applies to the SAP NetWeaver AS for ABAP system, not applications from other database or application vendors. Answer B is incorrect because, with the SAP S/4HANA migration cockpit, you can migrate master and business data from SAP and non-SAP systems to SAP S/4HANA, the latest incarnation of the SAP Business Suite and successor of SAP R/3, SAP ECC, and SAP ERP. It doesn't migrate applications (SAP or not) to the SAP HANA database. Answer C is incorrect because Oracle SQL Developer is Oracle's migration tool to migrate non-Oracle databases to Oracle (and not Oracle to SAP HANA).

> **Exam Tip**
>
> That is a tricky question that you won't find on the exam as you're not expected to be familiar with Oracle PL/SQL, SAP S/4HANA, or the generic topic of SAP HANA database migrations. Just keep in mind that DMO only concerns SAP NetWeaver AS for ABAP systems.

3. Correct answers: **A, B**

    Other database targets, such as Microsoft SQL Server or SAP MaxDB, are available on request.

    Answer C is incorrect because SAP IQ is a columnar database and isn't supported as a target database. Answer D is incorrect because SAP NetWeaver AS for ABAP is the application server, not the database.

> **Learn More**
>
> Restrictions and limitations are usually documented in SAP Notes, and this also applies to support information about source and target databases (see SAP Note 2742706 – Central Note: Software Update Manager 2.0).

4. Correct answer: **C**

    SAP NetWeaver AS for ABAP systems with SAP Basis 7.50 and later only support Unicode and can't be used for Unicode conversion. As a consequence, the target system needs to be an older release (e.g., 7.4), and, for this reason, you need to use SUM 1.0.

    Answer A is incorrect in this case, even though generally, it's a good idea to always use the latest SUM SP release. Should Unicode conversion still need to be performed, consider doing so before the DMO run.

5. Correct answers: **A, C**

    SUM with DMO doesn't support an update migration scenario with both SAP HANA as source and target database. Technically, upgrading SAP HANA 1.0 to the 2.0 release is considered an update, not a migration.

    SAP HANA as source database isn't supported (concerns both 1.0 and 2.0 releases).

    Answer B is incorrect because SUM with DMO supports all SAP HANA versions as target databases (provided the SAP HANA release is still supported).

6. Correct answers: **A, B**

    As a minimum, you need to select the SAP kernel for both source and target database. You may need to select other components, such as SAP IGS.

Answers C and D are incorrect because selecting the SAP Host Agent and SUM is recommended. However, both the agent and SUM can be downloaded and installed separately. The SAR files for these components aren't required for the SUM with DMO procedure.

7. Correct answers: **A, B, D**

   You need to upgrade all systems involved with the latest SAP Host Agent, preferably prior to starting the DMO procedure. You also need to use the latest SUM release. SUM includes DMO. In addition, you need to provide the Transaction SPAM/SAINT updates. The functionality to prepare the source system and create the shadow system is provided with a SPAM/SAINT update and not part of SUM.

   Answer C is incorrect because SUM prompts you for the directory to the installation tool (hdbinst) of the SAP HANA client but not for SAP HANA cockpit. As of SAP HANA client 2.4, only a single client is maintained, and there is no need to match server and client versions. SAP recommends using the latest client release. Answer E is incorrect because DMO is an option. SUM is the tool that includes the option. There is no DMO download.

8. Correct answers: **A, C**

   The source system needs a permanent SAP license. In the extraction phase of the road map, SUM prompts for a migration key. The key is required for R3load processing.

   Answer B is incorrect because SUM doesn't perform a license check on the target database, and you can use a temporary license key. Answer D is incorrect because, while using a valid operating system license key is recommended for many reasons, it is not a requirement for a DMO run.

9. Correct answers: **B, C, D**

   You need to extract the SAR file on the PAS host, update SAP Host Agent, and register SUM with the agent, which generates the sumabap.conf configuration file that includes the command to start SUM.

   Subsequently, when you connect to SAP Host Agent with any supported browser, the agent will start up SUM. The agent will also prompt you to authenticate. After successful completion, the agent will establish an HTTPS session to the registered SAPup process, which handles all further processing.

   Using unencrypted HTTP on port 1128 is also supported but not recommended because passwords are exchanged. For SUM 1.0, the command is STARTUP confighostagent <SID>.

   Answer A is incorrect because there is no SUM installer. Answer D is correct because SUM supports multiple browsers as documented in the SUM guides, not just Google. It's correct that SAP recommends to always use the latest available web browser release.

10. Correct answers: **A**, **D**, **E**

    Selecting **Logs** on the header menu will open the **Log Viewer** screen. From here, you can open every SUM log for viewing or save to your local computer. **Log Tail** from the **More** menu provides convenient access to the last section of the currently generated logs. All logs are stored in the log directory of SUM.

    Answer B is incorrect because Transaction SM21 on the SAP system can be used to view and analyze system logs but not SUM logs. Answer C is incorrect; on UNIX/Linux systems, you could use the `tail` command to view the last number of lines from any log file, but this would require access to the PAS system and would not be relevant for other operating systems.

11. Correct answer: **B**

    To be sure the tables are identical, select the **Compare the content of all tables** option in the Migration Parameters dialog of the extraction phase. Note that, as documented, SAP strongly recommends comparing the content of selected tables only and using table comparison not on the productive system but on a test (production copy) system to avoid long downtimes. The CRC check is only performed on application tables.

    Answer A is incorrect because SUM automatically performs a table row count validation. There is no need to repeat this task. An identical row count doesn't guarantee identical table content. Answer C is incorrect because the table comparison tool is intended for alternative scenarios, such as system copy. It performs the same task as the migration parameter selection. There is no benefit to running this activity separately.

12. Correct answer: **D**

    `R3load` processes run in pairs. Configuring 12 processes means 6 run on the source system and 6 on the target system. Instead of exporting to the file system first and importing the data second, `R3load` processes perform the export and import simultaneously and hence require a process on either side. `R3load` also performs the checksum comparison.

    Answer A is incorrect because ABAP processes perform ABAP-specific processing on the shadow instance predominately, such as repository object activation or Transaction SGEN. Answer B is incorrect because SQL processes are executed by the `tp` process to execute SQL statements on the target database, for example, to create tables. Answer C is incorrect because `R3trans` also performs import but operates at the application server (logical), whereas `R3load` works with physical tables (faster).

13. Correct answers: **B**, **C**

    You can change processing parameters either on the command directly or by using the **SUM Utilities** from the **More** menu. This was illustrated earlier in Figure 14.17.

A third alternative is to use the URL: `/lmsl/sumabap/<SID>/set/procpar`.

Answer A is incorrect because, while you can change processing parameters by repeating the migration, this doesn't change parameters during a run. Answer D is incorrect because with Transaction RZ11, you can change profile parameters. This isn't related to SUM.

14. Correct answer: **A**

    The repository is locked to prepare for the creation of the shadow repository. As a consequence, no more development (e.g., Transaction SE80, ABAP Workbench), transports, and updates.

    Answer B is incorrect because business downtime doesn't start when the development environment is locked. You're still in uptime, and business transaction processing continues (e.g., changing application data [Transaction VA01] and user master records [Transaction SU01]). Answer C is incorrect because with a locked repository, the system can process no more transport requests (Transaction SE09). Answer D is incorrect because with a locked repository, the system can process no more notes implementations using the SAP Note Assistant (Transaction SNOTE).

15. Correct answers: **A, C, E**

    You need to ensure the PAS is the only instance running, and there's no more user activity and no more batch activity.

    Answer B is incorrect because the backup needs to be made after the system is stopped. Answer D is incorrect because the development environment is locked some time before you're prompted to prepare the system for downtime.

16. Correct answer: **B**

    The system isn't available for transaction processing until the DMO procedure has completely finished.

    Answer A is incorrect because the end of SUM technical downtime doesn't mean the system is ready for transaction processing yet. First, the postprocessing step needs to be completed.

17. Correct answers: **B, C, D**

    A DMO reset doesn't undo all changes made to the source and target system. Some changes are irreversible.

    Answer A is incorrect because Transactions SPAM/SAINT and Transaction SNOTE all modify the source repository. These changes aren't undone. The same applies to any application-specific processing (e.g., SAP BW ASU Toolbox). Answer E is incorrect because DMO cleanup deletes the contents of the SUM > abap subdirectories, not DMO reset.

18. Correct answers: **A, B, C**

Figure 14.17 shows the users that require a password, which you can set using the SUM **Process Parameters** menu. You also need to specify a password for the DBACOCKPIT user.

Answer D is incorrect because you're not prompted for the password of SAP Host Agent.

Takeaway

In this chapter, we covered the data migration option of the software update manager (SUM with DMO in short, or DMO, even shorter). We explained the business benefits of using DMO and described the architecture, road map, dialogs. and what happens during the different phases. You should now be familiar with the SUM UI and menus and know how to respond to SUM promptings, what is meant by a stackfile, how to install SUM and get started with DMO, how to benchmark the DMO runs, and how to perform a reset. For those less familiar with the wonderful world of SAP NetWeaver AS for ABAP, you've gained some insights into the activities of SAP NetWeaver system administrators, and you even might have memorized a transaction code or two.

Summary

You're done! If you've managed to understand and digest all the information of this last chapter, got most of the answers right, and understood the explanation for those you got wrong, you're ready to sign up for the exam. If you have some extra time, make sure to at least browse the documentation a bit and the most important SAP Notes or KBAs, and spend some time on the SAP Community reading some blogs and looking at some of the Q&As.

On behalf of the entire team here at SAP PRESS, we wish you success and a bit of good fortune for the exam.

The Author

 **Denys van Kempen** is an SAP business technology expert with a focus on cloud platform and data management technologies. He has worked for SAP for more than 12 years and is currently part of the digital enablement team within SAP's Global Partner Organization. Denys has worked hands-on with the SAP HANA in-memory platform since its first release in 2010 and has created hundreds of tutorial videos for the SAP HANA Academy on YouTube. He is also a frequent contributor to SAP Community, for example, on topics like how to get certified! You can reach Denys via Twitter *@dvankempen* and at *linkedin.com/in/dvankempen*.

Index

- Explore SAP HANA from release 1.0 to 2.0

- Understand how to use SAP HANA as a developer, administrator, data scientist, and more

- Learn about security, data integration, analytics, data center architecture, and other key features

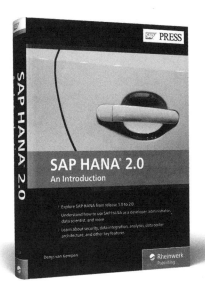

Denys van Kempen

SAP HANA 2.0

An Introduction

Enter the fast-paced world of SAP HANA 2.0 with this introductory guide. Begin with an exploration of the technological backbone of SAP HANA as a database and platform. Then, step into key SAP HANA user roles and discover core capabilities for administration, application development, advanced analytics, security, data integration, and more. No matter how SAP HANA 2.0 fits into your business, this book is your starting point.

438 pages, pub. 09/2019
E-Book: $69.99 | **Print:** $79.95 | **Bundle:** $89.99

www.sap-press.com/4884

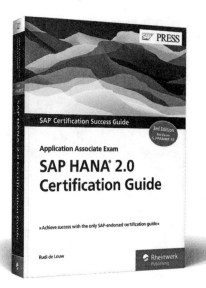

- The comprehensive guide to SAP HANA 2.0 security, from authentication to auditing

- Develop a complete security model using practical examples and case studies

- Identify critical settings necessary to pass an SAP HANA security audit

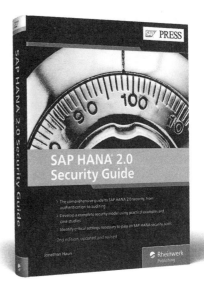

Jonathan Haun

SAP HANA 2.0 Security Guide

Your complete guide to safeguarding your SAP HANA 2.0 platform awaits! Get step-by-step instructions for configuring and maintaining each security element, from the new SAP HANA cockpit to privileges and roles. Learn how to secure database objects and provision and maintain user accounts. Then, dive into managing authentications, certificates, audits, and traces.

608 pages, 2nd edition, pub. 03/2020
E-Book: $79.99 | **Print:** $89.95 | **Bundle:** $99.99

www.sap-press.com/4982

- Learn how to model data in SAP HANA 2.0 with SAP Web IDE

- Build calculation views and table functions, manage models, and more

- Explore advanced concepts like predictive modeling and SAP HANA spatial analysist

Anil Bavaraju

Data Modeling for SAP HANA 2.0

EFind meaning in your business data. Build, manage, and secure calculation views and table functions with the SAP Web IDE for SAP HANA. See how the SAP Web IDE, SAP HANA Live, and SAP S/4HANA embedded analytics all interact to create effective data models. Explore advanced modeling concepts compatible with SAP HANA 2.0, like predictive modeling and geospatial analysis. Begin designing the perfect model today!

432 pages, pub. 07/2019
E-Book: $79.99 | **Print:** $89.95 | **Bundle:** $99.99

www.sap-press.com/4722